AUDITING
PRINCIPLES AND TECHNIQUES

AUDITING
PRINCIPLES AND TECHNIQUES

S. K. Basu
Senior Lecturer
St. Xavier's College,
Kolkata, India

Pearson

Original edition, entitled Auditing Principles and Techniques, by S.K. Basu, published by Pearson Education Ltd., Copyright © 2006.

Indian Subcontinent Reprint

ISBN 9788177581782

First Impression, 2006

Fourteenth Impression, 2024

Fifteenth Impression, 2025

Published by Pearson India Education Services Pvt. Ltd, CIN: U72200TN2005PTC057128.

Head Office: 1st Floor, Berger Tower, Plot No. C-001A/2, Sector 16B, Noida - 201 301, Uttar Pradesh, India.
Registered Office: Featherlite, 'The Address' 5th Floor, Survey No 203/10B, 200 Ft MMRD Road, Zamin Pallavaram, Chennai – 600 044.
Website: in.pearson.com; Email: companysecretary.india@pearson.com

Printed in India at Gopsons Papers Pvt. Ltd., Noida

PREFACE

The development of modern accountancy and the growth of auditing profession in India and, indeed, in the world as a whole must be seen in the context of the enormous expansion of industry, trade and commerce which has taken place in the last decade. The auditing profession is now going beyond the duties prescribed by the Companies Act. It is initiating its own accounting standards, and auditing regulations and guidelines. At present, it has sought to standardise the accounting procedure by issuing mandatory accounting standards and also issuing standardised auditing guidelines for conducting audit work. In addition to that, auditing in its modern form has adopted a multidimensional approach. At present, the scope of auditing is not restricted to only financial audit under the Companies Act but has been extended to cost accounts, managerial policies, operational efficiencies, system applications, social implications of business organisations and environmental aspects too.

In the light of the above changes, *Auditing: Principles and Techniques* has been written in order to describe the modern tools and techniques of auditing. Written in a student-friendly manner, this book is intended for commerce students of all the universities in India as well as for different professional examinations.

This book aims to assist the readers to develop, in a systematic way, a thorough understanding of the concepts and techniques underlying auditing. Simplicity and brevity are the twin characteristics of this book. The contents of the syllabus have been lucidly explained point-wise with charts, examples and illustrations, where necessary, and the subject matter has been summarised at the end of each chapter for quick reference. The book has 20 chapters covering all the important and latest aspects of auditing including bank and insurance audit, audit in a computerised environment, new areas of auditing etc. A separate annexure has been added at the end of the book discussing some important case decisions. Two other annexures include model answers to questions, both subjective and objective.

My endeavour has been to make this book strictly syllabus oriented. I hope my sincere efforts to present the text of the syllabus analytically and methodically is appreciated by students as well as teachers.

I express my deep gratitude to the renowned authors on this subject from whom references have been taken in writing this book. I am also grateful to Pearson Education for publishing this book. If my work is appreciated by the readers, I will consider it as my best reward.

S. K. Basu

CONTENTS

14

Investigation 387

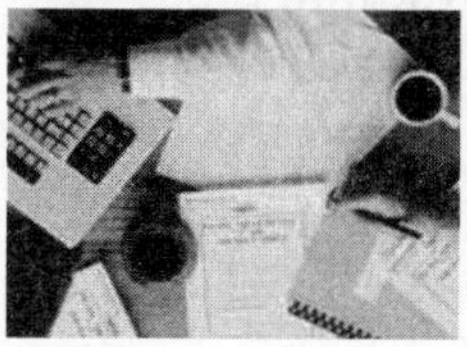

15

New Areas of Auditing 413

16

Professional Ethics and Misconduct 457

17

Special Audit 470

tax cuts

CHAPTER 1

Nature of Auditing

CHAPTER OUTLINE

1.1 INTRODUCTION

The development of modern accountancy and the growth of auditing profession in India, and, indeed, in the world as a whole, must be seen in the context of the enormous expansion of industry and commerce, which has taken place since the Industrial Revolution. While business enterprises were comparatively small, and were managed by their proprietors, there was little need for the development of complex accounting procedures. When the scale of operations increased and capital was invested in joint stock companies by shareholders who took no part in the management of such companies, it became necessary for the managers to present accounts to the shareholders at regular intervals by means of annual accounts. However, the managers (or directors) of unsuccessful companies had an obvious vested interest in hiding the lack of success of their companies from the shareholders; this led to fraudulent accounting and resultant scandals. Governments therefore made provisions for the accounts of companies to be reported by persons other than the directors. In this way auditing was developed. The continuing increase in the size of enterprises and the greater complexity of their accounting procedures, have made increasing demands on the skill of auditors. Hence, it is required that accounts shall only be audited by qualified accountants, who are members of recognised professional bodies.

1.2 ORIGIN OF THE WORD 'AUDIT'

The word 'audit' is derived from the Latin word 'audire', which means 'to hear'. The origin of 'audit' can be traced back to olden times, but auditing as its existing form was established only in the middle of the 19th century.

In olden times, the methods of accounting were so crude and the number of transactions were so small that every individual was in a position to check all the transactions recorded by himself or by his employees. Whenever the owner of the business suspected frauds or misappropriation of funds, he appointed an official to check the accounts. Such a person would meet the concerned employees and hear whatever they had to say in connection with the accounts. The person appointed to examine the accounts came to be known as the 'auditor'.

1.3 EARLY HISTORY OF AUDIT

Historical evidence reveals that soon after the ancient states and empires acquired a coherent organisation, systems of checks were applied to their public accounts as testified by ancient records. The ancient Egyptians, the Greeks and the Romans utilised systems of checks and counter checks among the various financial officials. The duties of the auditor in ancient times were thus limited.

The last decade of the 15th century, witnessed a great impetus in trade and commerce, inspired by the Renaissance in Italy. This led to the evolution of a system of accounts capable of recording completely all kinds of business transactions. The principles of double entry system were published in 1494, in Venice by Luca Pacioli, although the system had already been in existence in the preceding century. The author of the principles also defined and described, for the first time, the duties and responsibilities of 'an auditor' in detail. Since then, the duties and responsibilities of an auditor have increased enormously.

The Industrial Revolution was another landmark in the history of trade and commerce. It resulted in large scale production requiring huge amount of capital investment. Individuals were not in a position to provide adequate capital, because of their limited finances. It was at this time that the company as a form of business organisation came into existence, and this widened greatly, the possibilities of raising capital for industry from the general public by the issue of shares with a limited liability.

In this type of organisation, the shareholders delegated the management of the undertaking to a board of directors and periodically the board submitted the accounts of the company to the shareholders so that the shareholders were in a position to have a true and fair picture of the financial position and the profit and loss of the undertaking.

With the rapid growth in the number of companies, professional accountants came in the picture. In 1880, the Queen of United Kingdom granted a charter, which incorporated the various societies of accountants into a single body, the Institute of Chartered Accountants of England and Wales. By early 1990s, the concept of audit had developed to a stage where professional accountants became prominent as auditors. The objectives of audit were also changed during this time. Apart from detecting frauds and errors, the auditors also started verifying and reporting on the accuracy of the financial records and documents as well as the financial statements. The verification and attestation of financial statements became the primary objective of company audit. Detection of errors and frauds became incidental to the attainment of this objective. The Companies Act of 1948 in UK formalised this position.

Being under the British rule, the developments in the UK had a profound effect on the company legislation in India. The Joint Stock Companies Act of 1857 contained provisions for voluntary annual audit of company accounts. The Companies Act, 1913 made the audit of company accounts compulsory in India. The Act also prescribed, for the first time, the powers and duties of the auditors and the procedures of their appointment. In 1949, the Parliament of India passed the Chartered Accountants Act, under which a body of professional accountants, viz. The Institute of Chartered Accountants of India, was established. The Institute is an autonomous body, which regulates the profession of chartered accountants throughout India. In 1956, a new Companies Act replaced the Act of 1913. The Act now contains elaborate provisions regarding qualifications and disqualifications of auditors, the method of appointment of auditors and their powers and duties.

1.4 AUDITING DEFINED

The word 'Audit' is derived from the Latin word audire, which means "to hear". In olden times, whenever the owners of a business suspected fraud, they appointed certain persons to check the accounts. Such persons sent for the accountant and 'heard' what they had to say in connection with the accounts.

The dictionary meaning of audit is official examination of accounts. Obviously the person who examines the accounts must be a person who knows what to examine, how to examine and to whom his examination report and observations are to be submitted. In brief, it can be said that auditing is the process by which competent independent individuals collect and evaluate evidence to form an opinion and communicate their opinion to the person interested through their audit report.

From the above it is clear that the auditing process involves three components. These are as follows:

- Books of accounts
- Auditor
- Techniques and procedures of audit

Montgomery, a leading American accountant, defines auditing as "a systematic examination of the books and records of a business or other organisations, in order to check or verify and to report upon results thereof".

The ICAI has defined auditing in its Auditing and Assurance Standard –1 (AAS-1) as "the independent examination of financial information of any entity, whether profit oriented or not and irrespective of its size or legal form, when such an examination is conducted with a view to express an opinion thereon".

From the above definitions, it is seen that an auditor has not only to see the arithmetical accuracy of the books of accounts but also has to go further and find out whether the transactions entered in the books of original entry are correct or not. It is possible to perform this function by inspecting, comparing, checking, reviewing, scrutinising the vouchers supporting the transactions in the books of accounts and examining the correspondence, minute books of the shareholders' and directors' meeting, Memorandum of Association and Articles of Associations etc.

1.5 ESSENTIAL FEATURES OF AUDITING

The following are the essential features of auditing:

1. Accounting control

Audit is an instrument of accounting control. The truth and fairness of the accounting information is controlled and checked by auditing activities.

2. Safeguard

Audit acts as a safeguard on behalf of the proprietor/s (whether an individual or a group of persons) against extravagance, carelessness or fraud on the part of the proprietors' agents or servants in the realisation and utilisation of his/their money and other assets.

3. Assurance

Audit assures on the proprietors' behalf that the accounts maintained truly represent facts and expenditure has been incurred with due regularity and propriety.

4. Assessment

Audit assesses the adequacy of the accounting system in order to ascertain its effectiveness in maintaining accounting records of an organisation.

5. Review

Audit carries out a review of the financial statements to know whether the accounting records are in agreement with those statements.

6. Reporting tool

Audit is a tool for reporting on the financial statements as required by the terms of the auditors' appointment and in compliance with the relevant statutory obligations.

7. Practical subject

Auditing is a practical subject. It is something that people do. How it is done today is a result of long history of marginal changes and responses to new commercial and legal developments over the centuries with the most rapid progress in the last few years.

1.6 WHY IS THERE A NEED FOR AN AUDIT?

The problem that has always existed when the managers report to owners is the credibility of the report.

The report may

- contain errors
- not disclose frauds
- be inadvertently misleading
- be deliberately misleading
- fail to disclose relevant information
- fail to conform to regulations

The solution to this problem of credibility in reports and accounts lies in appointing an independent person called an auditor to investigate the report and submit his findings.

A further point is that modern companies can be very large with multi-national activities. The preparation of the accounts of such groups is a very complex operation involving the bringing together and summarising of accounts of subsidiaries with different conventions, legal systems and accounting and control systems. The examination of such accounts by independent experts trained in the assessment of financial information is of benefit to those who control and operate such organisations as well as to owners and outsiders.

Many financial statements must conform to statutory and other requirements. The most notable is that all company accounts have to conform to the requirements of the Companies Act. In addition, all accounts should conform to the requirements of accounting standards. It is essential that an audit should be carried out on financial statements to ensure that they conform to these requirements.

1.7 OBJECTIVE OF AN AUDIT

The original objective of an audit was *principally* to see whether the *personnel* involved in accounting had properly accounted for the receipts and payments of cash. In other words, the objective of audit was to find out whether cash had been embezzled and if so, who embezzled it and what amount was involved. Thus, it was only an audit of cash book. But, at present, the main aim of audit is to find out, after going through the books of accounts, whether the balance sheet and profit and loss account are drawn up accordingly and whether they represent a true and fair view of the state of the affairs of the concern. This is possible when the auditor verifies the accounts and the statements. While performing his duties, the auditor also has to discover errors and frauds.

The ICAI in its "statement on objective and scope of the audit of financial statements"AAS-2 enumerates the following as the objectives of auditing the financial statements:

1. The objective of an audit of financial statements, prepared within a framework of recognised accounting policies and practices and relevant statutory requirements, if any, is to enable an auditor to express an opinion on such financial statements.

2. The auditor's opinion helps determination of the true and fair view of the financial position and operating results of an enterprise.

The auditor should be an independent person who is appointed to investigate the organisation, its records and financial statements prepared from them and thus form an opinion on the accuracy and correctness of the financial statements. The primary aim of an audit is to enable to confirm that the accounts show a true and fair view or, that they do not.

So, the primary aim of an audit is to promote efficiency and accuracy in accounting and to place before the shareholders and management accurate information of the financial condition of the business, which may serve as an aid to overall administration of the business entity. For the fulfillment of the primary objects of an audit, the following subsidiary objects are to be realised:

- Detection of errors
- Detection of frauds
- Prevention of errors
- Prevention of frauds

Again, errors, which arise out of innocence and carelessness, are of three types:

- Clerical errors
- Compensating errors
- Errors of principles

Also, clerical errors may be of two types:

- Errors of omission
- Errors of commission

On the other hand, frauds which arise out of some intention to gain something through some manipulating devices are of three types:

- Misappropriation or embezzlement of cash
- Misappropriation of goods
- Manipulation of accounts

The objectives of auditing can be presented in the following chart:

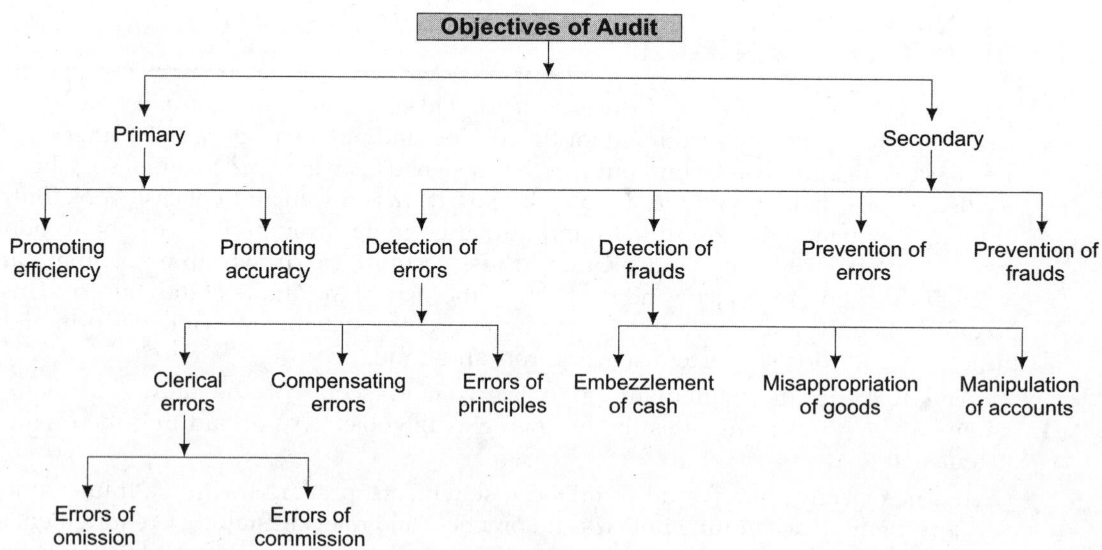

1.8 ERRORS AND FRAUDS IN ACCOUNTING

1.8.1 Errors

Generally errors are the result of carelessness on the part of the person preparing the accounts. During the course of auditing, errors may be detected, though auditing does not ensure detection of all errors. Errors can be described as unintentional mistakes. Errors can occur at any stage in business transaction processing i.e. transaction occurrence, documentation, record of prime entry, double entry record, summarising process or financial statement production. Errors can be of any of a multitude of kinds i.e. mathematical, clerical or in the application of accounting principles.

Accounting errors, which are possible to be detected through auditing, can be of the following types:

1. Errors of omission

When a transaction is omitted completely or partially from the books of accounts, it is known as an error of omission. This type of error is not reflected in the trial balance and hence are more difficult to detect.

Examples

(a) Omission of purchases from purchases day book.

(b) Ignoring depreciation on fixed assets completely.

2. Errors of commission

When entries made in the books of original entry or ledger are either wholly or partially incorrect, they are known as errors of commission. Some of these errors may not affect the trial balance.

Examples

(a) Wrong amount recorded in the books of original entry, e.g. sale of goods of Rs. 15,000 recorded as Rs. 1,500 in sales day book. This error will not affect trial balance.

(b) Posting to the wrong side of an account. In place of debiting, e.g. an amount of Rs. 150 is credited. This error will affect the trial balance.

3. Compensating errors

When an error offsets the effect of another error, it is known as a compensating error. These errors do not affect the agreement of the trial balance, hence cannot be located by it.

Examples

(a) A debit balance is undercast by Rs. 100 and credit balance is undercast by the same amount.

(b) Sales return of Rs. 500 is posted to the Return Inward A/c as Rs. 5,000 and similarly purchase return of Rs. 500 is posted to the Return Outward A/c as Rs. 5,000.

4. Errors of principles

When principles of book-keeping and accountancy are not followed, the error is known as error of principles. Such errors may be committed intentionally to understate asset and to overstate liability and to inflate and deflate profit as and when the circumstance dictates.

Examples

(a) Treatment of capital expenditure as revenue expenditure, e.g. purchase of machinery treated as purchase of goods.

(b) Valuation of stock on the basis of wrong principle.

1.8.2 Fraud

Fraud means false representation or entry made intentionally or without belief in its truth with a view to defraud somebody. Detection of fraud is considered to be one of the important duties of an auditor. The term 'fraud' is used for several sins including the following:

(a) Fraud, which involves the use of deception to obtain an unjust or illegal financial advantage

(b) Intentional mis-statements in, or omissions of, amounts or disclosures from an entity's accounting records or financial statements

(c) Theft, whether or not accompanied by mis-statements of accounting records or financial statements

The following are the main ways in which fraud may be activated:

1. Embezzlement of cash

Defalcation of cash is possible irrespective of the size of the business small or large. The possibility of the misappropriation of cash is small in a small business organisation, where the proprietor has a direct control over the cash receipts and disbursement. The chances are greater in case of large business organisations. There are different methods of misappropriation of cash defalcation, out of which "Teeming and Lading" procedure in usually followed by the employees involved in the misappropriation of cash.

2. Misappropriation of goods

Misappropriation of goods is another type of fraud. It may happen that the valuable goods of an organisation may be stolen by the employees or workers. It may also happen that the storekeeper in collusion with the works manager may sell the goods illegally to some third party. Such frauds are very difficult to locate or identify.

3. Manipulation of accounts

Accounts are manipulated through falsification of accounts. These are fraudulent manipulations through accounts and arise generally through passing of false entries with the motive of misappropriating funds slowly and steadily. Unlike misappropriation of cash and goods, this type of fraud is done by the sophisticated personnel of an organisation.

1.9 ROLE OF AUDITORS IN DETECTING ERRORS AND FRAUDS

There is a difference of perception between the public and the auditing profession in relation to an auditor's duty regarding errors and frauds.

The auditor sees his duty as:

"The independent examination of, and expression of opinion on, the financial statements of an enterprise by an appointed auditor in pursuance of that appointment and in compliance with any relevant statutory obligation."

While certifying the final accounts of the concern, the auditor, has to face a specific problem. He has to certify in his report as to whether the profit and loss account reflects the true profit or loss for the financial year concerned and the balance sheet exhibits a true and fair view of the state of affairs at the end of the financial year. The emphasis is on financial statements. However, the public, including much of the business community, tends to see an auditor's duties in terms of the detection and possibly prevention of error and fraud.

Accordingly, he has a duty to ascertain frauds and errors to justify the correctness of the accounts. This duty of detecting and preventing errors and frauds can be analysed in the following ways:

Detection of errors and frauds

It is desirable that the auditor should exercise reasonable care and skill, so that he may detect errors and frauds. If he carries routine checking and vouching more carefully and checks the books of accounts thoroughly, he may be successful in his duty. Whereas, in doing so, if he is not successful but he himself feels that he has not shown any negligence in his duty, then he cannot be held responsible for any error or fraud which remains undetected in accounts. Hence, an auditor is not an insurer.

Prevention of errors and frauds

The auditor has no authority to introduce remedial measures for the prevention of errors and frauds. All that he can do is to advise his client and suggest the ways and means to prevent them.

1.10 RELATION BETWEEN BOOK-KEEPING, ACCOUNTANCY AND AUDITING

1.10.1 Book-keeping

It is concerned with systematic recording of transactions in the books of original entry and their posting to the concerned ledger accounts. In fact, book-keeping involves the following activities:

- Journalising the transactions
- Posting them into respective ledger accounts
- Casting the total of ledger accounts and
- Finding the balances

1.10.2 Accountancy

Accountancy is concerned with the checking of arithmetical accuracy of ledger accounts as prepared by the book-keeper and preparing the trial balance from the balance available of different ledger accounts. Finally from the balances, profit and loss account and balance sheet are prepared to know the financial result and financial position of the concern. In short, accountancy involves the following activities:

- Preparation of trial balance
- Incorporation of adjustment entries and passing entries for rectification
- Preparation of profit and loss account
- Preparation of balance sheet

1.10.3 Auditing

When the accountancy work is completed, an auditor is invited to check the accounts prepared by the accountants. That is why, it is said that "Auditing begins where accountancy ends". It is the duty of the auditor to critically examine and verify the accounts. In no case, it is the duty of the auditor to prepare accounts. After completing his work, the auditor has to submit a report of the fact whether or not the profit and loss account exhibits a true and fair financial result of the organisation and also whether the balance sheet reflects the true and fair financial picture of the organisation.

1.10.4 Accountancy vs auditing

The differences between accountancy and auditing are outlined in Table 1.1.

1.11 BASIC PRINCIPLES GOVERNING AN AUDIT

AAS-1 describes the basic principles which govern the auditor's responsibilities and which should be complied with whenever an audit is carried out. They are as follows:

1. Integrity, objectivity and independence

The auditor should be straight forward, honest and sincere in his approach to his professional work and should maintain an impartial attitude.

2. Confidentiality

The auditor should respect the confidentiality of information acquired in the course of his audit work.

3. Skills and competence

The audit should be performed and the report should be prepared with due professional care by persons who have adequate training, experience and competence in auditing.

4. Documentation

The auditor should maintain documents which are important in providing evidence that the audit was carried out in accordance with the basic principles.

5. Planning

The auditor should plan his work to enable him to conduct an effective audit in an efficient and timely manner.

TABLE 1.1 Accountancy vs auditing

Points of difference	*Accountancy*	*Auditing*
1. Scope	The scope of accountancy is limited to the preparation of financial statements.	In auditing, the auditor is concerned with the checking of accounts.
2. Objectives	The objective of accountancy is to know the financial result and financial position.	The objective of auditing is to verify the truth and fairness of the accounts.
3. Status	An accountant is an employee of the organisation.	An auditor is an independent outsider.
4. Qualification	Accounting work requires no formal qualification.	To be a company auditor, one should be a qualified chartered accountant.
5. Tenure of service	Accountant is usually a permanent employee of the organisation.	Auditor can be changed from year to year.
6. Knowledge in other subjects	An accountant is not expected to have knowledge in other subjects.	An auditor must have good knowledge not only in accountancy, but also in other related subjects.
7. Ranking of activities	Accountancy is not dependent on auditing work.	Auditing can be started only after the completion of accountancy work.
8. Time period of work	Accounting work is carried out throughout the year.	Auditing is usually carried out at the end of the year.
9. Professional control	There is no professional control over accountancy.	There are professional rules and regulations over the auditing work.
10. Nature of work	The nature of accountancy work is constructive.	Auditing work, on the other hand, is mostly analytical.
11. Submission of report	No report is required to be submitted at the end of the accounting work.	A report on the final accounts are required to be submitted by the auditor at the end of his work.
12. Accountability	The accountant is accountable to the management.	The auditor is accountable to the shareholders.

6. Audit evidence

The auditor should obtain sufficient appropriate audit evidence to enable him to draw reasonable conclusions therefrom on which he can base his opinion on the financial information.

7. Accounting system and internal control

The auditor should reasonably assure himself that the accounting system is adequate and that all the accounting information which should be recorded has been recorded intact.

8. Audit conclusions and reporting

The auditor should review and assess the conclusions drawn from the audit evidence and submit a report that contains a clear written opinion on the financial information of the organisation.

1.12 POSTULATES OF AUDITING

Auditing postulates are matters which are assumed to be true and are taken for granted. It is often considered that it is useful to examine a discipline and to see what, if any, are its postulates. This was done by Mautz and Sharaf in their book *The Philosophy of Auditing* in 1961. Their eight postulates are given below.

1. Financial statements and financial data are verifiable

This is an unspoken assumption by all auditors who otherwise would not attempt to verify the assertions in the accounts they are auditing. Sometimes facts are not strictly verifiable and auditors content themselves with statements of the circumstances, which can be verified.

2. There is no conflict of interest between the auditor and the management of the entity

If this was not so, auditors would not believe the answers given to their questions and, given the complexity of modern businesses, would find conducting an audit impossible. It is this basic assumption which leads auditors to consider whether they should accept a new client where the integrity of the client is suspected.

3. The financial statements are free from collusive and other unusual irregularities

Auditors are expected to uncover material mis-statements in financial statements caused by fraud or other irregularities but collusive fraud is often impossible to discover by auditing procedures. If there were a requirement to uncover such frauds the audit would become impossible or, at the least, require many more detailed and expensive procedures than are currently performed.

4. The existence of a satisfactory system of internal control eliminates the probability of irregularities

Auditors are entitled to rely on satisfactory internal controls as evidence of many assertions. If this postulate was not a fundamental principle of auditing they would not do so. Regardless of the assessed level of risk, auditors should perform some substantive procedures for financial statements assertions of material account balances and transaction classes.

5. Consistent application of generally accepted accounting principles results in fair presentation of the results and positions

Auditors need some criterion for their assessment of the fairness of the view given by financial statements and the GAAPs supply it. Otherwise there would be no standard by which fairness could be judged.

6. In the absence of clear evidence to the contrary, what has held true in the past for the entity will hold true in the future

If this were not so the auditor would be unable to accept the value of debts, the value of fixed assets, the saleability of stock, the effectiveness of internal controls, the integrity of management and many other matters.

7. When examining financial data, the auditor acts exclusively in the capacity of auditor

This is tied up with notions like independence, useful economic function and social responsibility to the public. This postulate is fundamental and yet the necessary independence of mind is still a difficult problem for many auditors.

8. The professional status of an independent auditor imposes commensurate professional obligations

This means that members of the professions have higher duties than economic self-interest. However, it is not always clear to whom professional duties are owed. Are they to the public at large, to the client company or the shareholders? However, it is certain that the professional accounting bodies impose very onerous duties on their members.

1.13 SCOPE AND PROCEDURES OF AUDIT

The scope and procedures of audit for a particular organisation will be determined by the auditor on the basis of the terms of engagement, the requirement of relevant legal formalities and the pronouncement of the Institute. The term of engagement cannot, however, in any way reduce the scope and procedures of audit which are prescribed by the legal provisions or by the pronouncement of the Institute.

To express an opinion on the financial statements of an organisation, the auditor should satisfy himself first whether the information contained in the given accounting records is authentic, reliable and adequate as a basis for the preparation of the financial statements. The audit procedure should be designed in such a manner to cover sufficiently all aspects of the organisation as far as they are relevant to the financial statements. In forming his opinion, the auditor should also decide whether the relevant information is properly disclosed in the financial statements on the basis of its statutory requirements.

The principal areas to be covered in an audit include the following:

1. Accounting and internal control

An examination of the system of accounting and internal control to ascertain whether it is adequate and appropriate for the concerned organisation or not.

2. Arithmetical accuracy

An overall checking of the arithmetical accuracy of the books of accounts by the method of posting, casting and balancing procedures.

3. Authenticity of transactions

A proper verification of the validity and authenticity of the transactions entered into by checking the entries with the supporting documents.

4. Distinction between capital and revenue items

An effective scrutiny over the distinction between the items of capital and of revenue nature of income and expenditure correspond to the accounting period.

5. Verification of assets

A detailed verification of the ownership, existence and value of the assets appearing in the balance sheet.

6. Verification of liabilities

A proper verification of the liabilities of the organisation as stated in the balance sheet.

7. Comparison of the financial statements

A comparison of the balance sheet and profit and loss account or other statements with the available records in order to see that they are in accordance therewith.

8. Truth and fairness of financial statements

An effective checking of the results as shown by the profit and loss account to see that the results shown are true and fair.

9. Statutory requirements

A concrete confirmation about the fulfilment of the statutory requirements and legal formalities in recording the financial transactions and in preparing the financial statements.

10. Appropriate reporting

An appropriate reporting to the concerned persons to explain whether the statements of accounts examined do reveal a true and fair view of the state of affairs and of the profit and loss of the organisation.

1.14 CHANGES IN THE CONCEPT OF AUDITING

The auditing profession has, at present, revised its method of work from the last century. In the early part of the 20th century, the emphasis in auditing was on the detection of error and fraud by massive checking of entries in the books of accounts. The growth in the size of the business entities, and the mechanisation and computerisation of accounting records, have made this approach increasingly realistic. The profession has responded by switching the emphasis of its auditing procedure from massive checking of individual items to establishing whether the organisations have a reliable system. The modern audit has increasingly concerned itself with establishing that the annual accounts have been prepared from a reliable accounting system on which a prudent auditor can reasonably place reliance and then with thoroughly testing and reviewing the final accounts themselves.

Moreover, the profession is now going beyond the duties prescribed on it by the Companies Act in that it is initiating its own accounting standards and auditing regulations and guidelines. At present, it has sought to standardise the accounting procedure by issuing mandatory accounting standards and also issuing standardised auditing guidelines for conducting audit work.

In addition to that, auditing in its modern form has adopted a multidimensional approach. At present, the scope of auditing is not only restricted to financial audit under the Companies Act. The purpose of auditing has been extended to cost accounts, managerial policies, operational efficiencies, system applications, social implications of business organisations and environmental aspects too. Even non-business organisations avail the services of qualified auditors and get their accounts audited. At present, the field of audit also covers the following:

1. Checking cost accounting records and to verify whether costing principles are followed while preparing and presenting costing data.
2. Comprehensive examination and review of managerial policies and operational efficiency.
3. Checking the performance of the organisation and comparing it with the overall performance of the industry in which the organisation belongs.
4. Critical examination and analysis of the contribution of the organisation for the benefit of the society.
5. Evaluation and measurement of efficiency of human resources in the organisation and comparing it with the expected utilisation of the human resources as a whole.

1.15 SOCIAL OBJECTIVES OF AUDIT

An audit is a social science. So, audit has certain social objectives. It should make contributions towards the fulfilment of social purposes. Auditing work to be effectively performed has to function for the following purposes:

1. Protection of shareholders' interest

Auditors are the representatives of the shareholders, naturally it is the duty of an auditor to see whether the interest of the shareholders are protected or not. The shareholders' interest can be protected by ensuring stable solvency, profitability and efficiency position of the company form of organisation.

2. Protection of national interest

Another vital social object of an audit is to see that the national interest is protected. The national interest can be protected only when cases of evasions of taxes are prevented. So, tax evasion should be discouraged for national interest as there is no denying the fact that raising revenue through taxation is a must for the development of the country.

3. Safeguarding capital erosion

Mere examination of the books of accounts will not help to locate those factors which are responsible for capital erosion. In order to stop capital erosion of the business, different system of audit should be introduced. Capital erosion is very dangerous, because it tends to liquidate the business. So, the function of an audit from social point of view is to stress and scrutinise those aspects, which are responsible for capital erosion.

4. Measurement of fair wages

Measurement of fair wages does not come under the purview of general audit. It should be the social objective of an audit to see whether the wages for workers are fair and in conformity with the general price index.

5. Fair prices for consumers

As a part of the society, the business organisation should charge fair prices from the consumers. It not only creates goodwill of the organisation but also ensures its future growth. As an auditor of the organisation, everyone should take care of this social aspect of auditing.

6. Fair return for investors

If the capital of a company is not utilised efficiently, the company will not be able to earn fair profit. On the other hand, the growth of the business may be withheld. Both high and low turnover of capital stand on the way to fair return. This rate of turnover should be compared with turnover rate of other companies belonging to the same industry. Justice to the investors depends on the solvency and profitability position of the business, which becomes favourable through the earning of fair return.

1.16 ADVANTAGES OF AUDITING

The tasks of an auditor are of great importance to all concerned. The auditor must prepare his audit report impartially and effectively based on facts and actual figures. If this is done, the following advantages can be expected from auditing:

From Legal Point of View

1. Filing of income tax return

Income tax authorities generally accept the profit and loss account that has been prepared by a qualified auditor and they do not go into details of the accounts.

2. Borrowing of money from external sources

Money can be borrowed easily on the basis of audited balance sheet from external sources. Most of the financial institutions sanction loan on the basis of audited financial statements.

3. Settlement of insurance claim

In case of fire, flood and the like unexpected happenings the insurance company may settle the claim for loss or damages on the basis of audited accounts of the previous year.

4. Sales tax payments

The audited books of accounts may generally be accepted by the sales tax authorities.

5. Action against bankruptcy

The audited accounts serves as a basis to determine action in bankruptcy and insolvency cases.

From Internal Control Point of View

1. Quick discovery of errors and frauds

Errors and frauds are located at an early date, so that in future no attempt is made to commit such frauds as one is rather careful not to commit an error or a fraud as the accounts are subject to regular audit.

2. Moral check on the employees

The auditing of accounts keeps the accounts clerks regular and vigilant as they know that the auditor would complain against them if the accounts are not prepared upto date or if there is any irregularity.

3. Advice to the management

The management may consult the auditor and seek advice on certain technical points although it is not the duty of the auditor to give advice.

4. Uniformity in accounts

If the accounts have been prepared on a uniform basis, accounts of one year can be compared with other years and if there is any discrepency, the cause may be enquired into.

From External Affairs Point of View

1. Settlement of accounts

The audited accounts would facilitate the settlement of accounts of a deceased partner.

2. Valuation of assets and goodwill

If the business is to be sold as a going concern, there may not be much difficulty regarding the valuation of assets and goodwill as the accounts have already been audited by an independent person.

3. Future trend of the business

The future trend of the business can be assessed with certainty from the audited books of accounts.

1.17 LIMITATIONS OF AUDITING

Truly speaking, an audit should have no limitations of its own. It is designed to protect the interest of all parties who are interested in the affairs of the business. If there be any shortcoming arising therefrom, it may be due to its narrow scope of application in its related field of operation and unextended definition of the concept.

Auditing suffers from the following shortcomings:

1. Want of complete picture

The audit may not give complete picture. If the accounts are prepared with the intention to defraud others, auditor may not be able to detect them.

2. Problems of dependence

Sometimes the auditor has to depend on explanations, clarification and information from staff and the client. He may or may not get correct or complete information.

3. Post-mortem examination

Auditing is a post-mortem examination. There is no use of such examination when events have already been occurred.

4. Existence of errors in the audited accounts

It is not possible for the auditor in all cases, to check each and every transaction of an organisation. As a result, there may be error in the audited accounts even after the checking by the auditor.

5. Lack of expertise

Auditor has to seek opinion of experts on certain matters on which he may not have experts knowledge. The auditor has to depend upon such reports which may not always be correct.

6. Diversified situations

Auditing is considered to be a mechanical work. Auditors may not be in a position to frame audit programme, which can be followed in all situations.

7. Quality of the auditor

Success of audit depends on the sincerity with which the auditor has performed his duties. The same audit work can be done by two different auditors with difference in sincerity.

8. Existence of defective policies

The auditor can only report on the truth and fairness of the financial statements. But other defects, i.e. defects relating to management and control may not be possible to be covered by the auditor.

1.18 QUALITIES OF AN AUDITOR

Only a chartered accountant can be appointed as an auditor of a limited company. Besides the statutory requirement about the qualification of an auditor, he must possess the following qualities:

- An auditor must possess the necessary technical ability and knowledge to audit accounts.
- He must be conversant with the relevant provisions of the companies and other regulations and with both best current accounting practices and current auditing practices.
- He must be objective both in formulating his opinions and in expressing them without bias.
- He must have integrity. Once he has formed his opinion, he must be prepared to express it clearly without fear and favour.
- He must be methodical in his work. An auditor who leaves loose ends will find himself open to allegations of negligence.
- He should have an inquiring mind. An auditor must recognise suspicious circumstances, and once his suspicion has been aroused, he has a duty to probe matters to the bottom.
- He also needs to be tactful and practical in his dealings with his clients.
- An auditor must be independent and must be careful not to compromise his independence.

In the following chart, the qualities needed to become an effective auditor are shown:

Qualities of an Auditor

- Educational
  - Professional
    - (As prescribed by the statute)
  - General
    - Knowledge about accountancy
    - Idea about various techniques of auditing
    - Knowledge about different laws
    - Knowledge about the principles of economics
    - Knowledge about the organisation
    - Knowledge about computerised accounting
    - Knowledge about different common languages
- Other qualities
  - Inherited
    - Honesty and intelligence
    - Patience and reasonableness
    - Sincerity in profession
  - Acquired
    - Caution and vigilance
    - Impartial attitude
    - Man of personality
    - Strategic and conscious approach
    - Common sense

1.19 AUDITING AND OTHER SERVICES

Auditing firms do not describe themselves as auditors. They describe themselves as Chartered Accountants or in some cases just as accountants. Auditing firms are composed of accountants who perform audit for their clients. They also perform other services. The small firms especially may spend more time on other services than on auditing.

Other services may include the following:

- Writing up books
- Balancing books
- Preparing final accounts
- Tax negotiations
- Government form filling
- Management and system advice
- Financial advice
- Liquidation and receivership work
- Investigations
- Risk management
- Corporate governance

Case Study

Arun, Badal and Chavan are partners in a firm of constructions business. Since commencing in business in 15 months ago they have been fairly successful. Arun who has a Diploma in Business Management as well as in building constructions has kept the books and Arun has also prepared the first year's accounts.

Three partners are discussing these accounts, which show a profit in excess of drawings. Badal and Chavan suggest that they could draw out the excess but Arun counsels caution, talking about working capital needs, which confuses the others.

Chavan questions Arun on his interpretation of the partnership agreement, which is a fairly complicated document and suggests that they should pay to have the accounts audited. Arun gets upset and says that it would be a waste of money and he is perfectly capable of maintaining the accounts and will not charge his partners for his work.

Discussion

- What benefits would the partners get from employing an independent auditor?
- Where would they find a suitable auditor?

POINTS TO PONDER

- The word 'audit' is derived from the Latin word audire, which means, "to hear". In olden times, whenever the owners of a business suspected fraud, they appointed persons to check the accounts. Such persons sent for the accountant and 'heard' what they to say in connection with the accounts.
- The dictionary meaning of audit is official examination of accounts. In brief, auditing can be defined as a systematic examination of the books and records of a business or other organisations in order to check or verify and to report upon results thereof.
- The essential features of auditing are accounting control, safeguard, assurance, assessment, review and reporting.
- The primary object of an audit is to promote efficiency and accuracy in accounting. For the fulfilment of the primary objectives of auditing certain subsidiary objectives are to be realised, which include detection of errors and frauds and prevention of errors and frauds.
- Errors are the result of carelessness on the part of the person preparing the accounts. Errors can be of different types—errors of omission, errors of commission, compensating errors and errors of principles.
- Fraud means false representation or entry made intentionally or without belief in its truth with a view to defraud others. Fraud may be activated in different ways—embezzlement of cash, manipulation of accounts and misappropriation of goods.
- It is expected that the auditor should exercise reasonable care and skill, so that he may detect errors and frauds. But the auditor has no authority to introduce remedial measures for the prevention of errors and frauds.
- There exists a close relationship between accountancy and auditing. It is said that 'auditing begins where accountancy ends'.
- AAS-1 describes the basic principles governing an audit. These include integrity, objectivity and independence, confidentiality, skills and competence, documentation, planning, audit evidence, accounting system and internal control, audit conclusions and reporting.

- Auditing postulates are matters, which are assumed to be true and are taken for granted. Mautz and Sharaf have referred eight different postulates of auditing.
- The principal areas to be covered in an audit include accounting and internal control, arithmetical accuracy, authenticity of transactions, distinction between capital and revenue items, verification of assets and liabilities, comparison of the financial statements, truth and fairness of financial statements, statutory requirements and appropriate reporting.
- Auditing in its modern form has adopted a multi-dimensional approach. At present, the scope of auditing is not only restricted to financial audit only, but also covers management audit, cost audit, efficiency audit, social audit and other areas of auditing.
- Audit has certain social objectives. It should function for the protection of shareholder's interest and national interest, for safeguarding capital erosion, for fair wages and prices and fair returns.
- Auditing has a number of advantages, which include filing of income tax return, borrowing of money from external sources, settlement of insurance claim, sales tax payments, action against insolvency, quick discovery of errors and frauds, moral check on the employees, advice to the management, uniformity in accounts, settlement of accounts, valuation of assets and goodwill etc.
- Auditing suffers from a number of shortcomings, which include want of complete picture, problems of dependence, post-mortem examination, existence of error in the audited accounts lack of expertise, diversified situations, quality of the auditor and existence of defective policies.
- The auditor must possess a number of important qualities, which include professional, inherited, acquired and other general qualities.

REVIEW QUESTIONS

Short-answer Questions

1. Offer your comment on the following statements:
   (a) Auditing may be defined as an 'accounting control'.
   (b) Fraud does not necessarily involve misappropriation of cash or goods.
   (c) Auditing is a dynamic social science.
   (d) Accounting is a necessity to business organisation but auditing is a luxury.
   (e) Accountancy begins where book-keeping ends, and where the work of an accountant ends, the work of an auditor begins.
   (f) An auditor is not an insurer.
   (g) The relationship of auditing to accounting is close, yet their natures are different. They are business associates, not parent and child.
   (h) Auditing has its principal roots not in accounting which it reviews, but in logic on which it leans heavily for ideas and methods.

(i) Auditing does not mean ticking or checking totals.

2. Define and explain the term 'auditing'.
3. What are the principles of auditing?
4. Discuss the objectives of auditing.
5. What are the differences between auditing and accountancy?
6. Define and explain the terms 'fraud' and 'error'.

Essay-type Questions

1. Define 'auditing'. Discuss the scope and procedure of audit.
2. What are special and general qualifications that an auditor should possess and why?
3. "Detection and prevention of errors and frauds are the main objectives of auditing". Discuss its scope and explain the duties of the auditor in this regard.
4. Discuss the advantages of audit (a) to the management, (b) to the government, (c) to the shareholders, and (d) to the society.
5. Discuss the different aspects of social object of audit.
6. Discuss various classes of error and state in each case the effect they might have on the trial balance being discovered.
7. "It is nothing to the auditor whether the business is run prudently or imprudently, profitably or unprofitably". Do you agree? Give reasons for your answer.
8. Why are auditors generally required to express an opinion on the truth and fairness of the accounts and why they are not required to certify the accounts?
9. "Audit of the accounts of the sole-proprietor is not compulsory. However, he may get his books of accounts audited for various reasons." Discuss.
10. Write a brief outline of the development of audit profession in India.

CHAPTER 2

Classification of Auditing

CHAPTER OUTLINE

2.1 INTRODUCTION

Auditing is a multidimensional and comprehensive subject. An effective insight into the nature of auditing can be obtained by understanding the various types of audit, which together constitute the auditing discipline. Auditing can be classified from various viewpoints. In this chapter, classification of audit will be discussed in detail.

2.2 CLASSIFICATION OF AUDIT

An audit can be classified under different groups on different bases.

2.2.1 Classification on the Basis of Organisation

Under this category, the audit is classified on the basis of nature of the organisation for which the audit work is undertaken. It includes the following types:

Audit required under law

- Companies governed by the Companies Act, 1956
- Banking companies governed by the Banking Regulation Act, 1949
- Electricity supply companies governed by the Electricity Supply Act, 1948
- Co-operative societies registered under the Co-operative Societies Act, 1912
- Public and charitable trusts registered under various Religious and Endowment Acts
- Corporations set up under an Act of Parliament or State Legislative (e.g. Life Insurance Corporation of India)
- Specified entities under various sections of the Income Tax Act, 1961
- Government departments/Public utilities
- Registered clubs, societies etc. registered under Societies Registration Act, 1960

Audit under voluntary category

- Proprietary concern
- Partnership firm
- Hindu undivided family
- Association of persons
- Non-profit seeking organisations

2.2.2 Classification on the Basis of Function

Under this category, the audit is classified on the basis of functional activities of the auditor. In fact, in this group audit is classified on the basis of the auditor involved in the work of audit. It includes the following types:

(i) External audit/Independent financial audit

(ii) Internal audit

2.2.3 Classification on the Basis of Practical Approach

The classification of audit under this group involves a practical approach to the work. It includes the following types:

- Continuous audit
- Periodical audit
- Interim audit
- Partial audit
- Occasional audit
- Standard audit
- Balance sheet audit
- Complete audit

2.2.4 Classification on the Basis of Audit Dimension

Under this category, the audit is classified on the basis of dimension of audit activities. It includes the following types:

- Management audit
- Cost audit
- Tax audit
- Human resource audit
- System audit
- Propriety audit
- Performance or efficiency audit
- Environment audit
- Social audit
- Cash transactions audit
- Government audit
- Secretarial audit
- Energy audit
- Other types of audit including special purpose audit (e.g. ABC audit, audit of bonus computation etc.).

A detailed classification of audit is presented in the following chart:

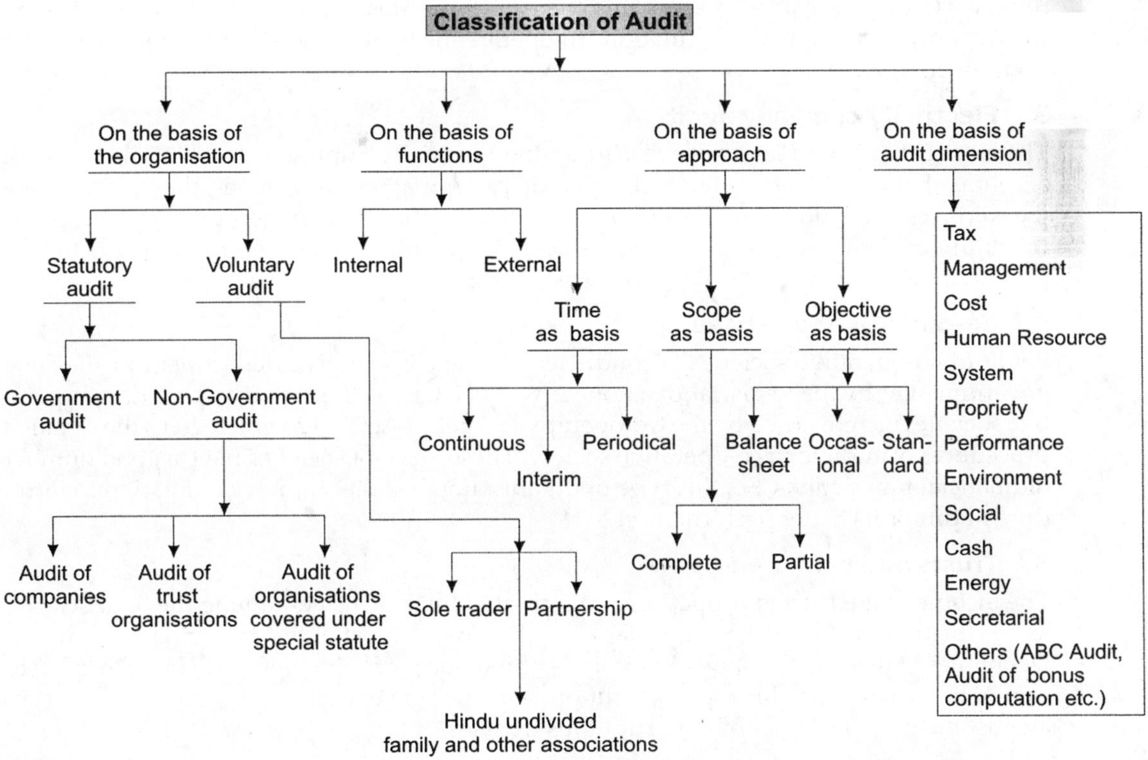

2.3 CLASSIFICATION ON THE BASIS OF ORGANISATION

Audit is not legally obligatory for all types of business organisations. On the basis of organisational structure, audits may be of two broad categories:

2.3.1 Audit Required under Law

This type of audit is also known as statutory audit. The organisations which require audit under law are as follows:

1. Company audit

Audit of accounts of companies registered under the Companies Act is compulsory. As the control of the company is vested with the directors of the company, the need for protection of the interest of the shareholders arises. The introduction of Companies Act, 1956, which outlines the procedure of audit work, the different books of accounts to be maintained, rights, duties and liabilities of the auditor was definitely a right step towards the protection of shareholders' interest over the company.

2. Bank audit

Audit of banking companies is made compulsory under the statute, since it is governed by the Banking Regulation Act, 1949. The objective of bank audit is not only to check the financial result and financial position, so far as its truth and fairness are concerned, but also to review whether the banks are engaging themselves in those businesses which are given in the Act only and follow the regulations to operate the banking business as per the regulations given in the Act.

3. Electricity company audit

The electricity companies are governed by the Electricity Supply Act, 1948. The books of accounts that are to be maintained by electricity companies are given in the provisions of the said Act. The auditor will examine the details of the books of accounts and check the reliability of the internal check system of the organisation. The prescribed forms for the presentation of accounts should be used as per the requirements of the Act.

4. Co-operative society audit

Audit of co-operative societies is conducted by the co-operative department of the state government or by the Registrar of co-operative societies, as the case may be. The co-operative societies are governed by the Co-operative Societies Act, 1912, which gives the detailed procedures of audit for a co-operative society. These types of societies have a good number of financial transactions. So, this type of organisation has the statutory obligation to introduce audit for its better performance.

5. Trusts audit

The income of the trusted properties is distributed by the trustees among the beneficiaries as per the trust deed. As the beneficiaries of the trust in most of the cases do not know the techniques of reading the books of accounts, the chances of being defrauded by the trustees cannot be avoided. So, this type of audit protects the beneficiaries of the trusted properties against the possible losses by unscrupulous trustees.

6. Insurance audit

The insurance companies that are governed by Insurance Act, 1938, include fire, marine and other miscellaneous insurance businesses. The books of accounts that are to be maintained by the insurance companies are governed in accordance with the provisions of the said Act. The auditor will examine the details of the books of accounts and check the reliability of the internal check systems. The audit of insurance companies, in fact, enhances the confidence of the policy holders.

7. Specified entities as per Income Tax Act

According to the various provisions of the Income Tax Act, certain entities are required to get their accounts audited to fulfill the requirement of the income tax regulations. These entities are required to appoint a qualified auditor to conduct audit of their financial statements in order to get exemptions and deduction from the income of the entity.

8. Audit of government departments and government public utilities

Different government departments and public utilities are also subject to independent financial audit. The requirement for such audit is contained in the constitution of India. In addition to that, government departments and public utilities also have the internal audit system of their own.

9. Audit of registered clubs, societies etc.

Though it is not compulsory in all cases, the audit of societies, clubs etc., which are registered under the Societies Registration Act, 1960, conduct audit of their activities to continue registration. In addition to that, different government grants and loans are given to these societies, clubs etc. on the basis of their application along with the audited income and expenditure account and the balance sheet. It is the responsibility of the secretary of the society or club to submit the audited financial statements to the members in the annual meeting of the society or club.

2.3.2 Audit of Other Organisations Not Covered by Any Law

There is no basic legal requirement of audit in respect of certain organisations. These organisations may require audit as a matter of internal rules. Some may be required to get their accounts audited on the directives of government for various purposes like sanction of loan, grants etc. These organisations include:

1. Sole proprietors

The sole proprietors are not required to have their accounts audited under any specific statute. But the sole proprietary businesses, in which the number of transactions are large and a huge amount is involved in the business, get their accounts audited. The proprietor himself takes decision about the scope of audit and the appointment of auditor. In fact, under this type of audit, the auditing work will depend upon the agreement of audit and the specific instructions given by the proprietor.

2. Partnership firm

There is no legal compulsion to get partnership accounts audited. But in partnership, there are possibilities of mistrust and dissatisfactions among the partners. As such, an independent external auditor's view regarding the correctness of accounts is desirable in case of this type of organisation. Usually, the partnership deed includes the provision of audit of their accounts. In conducting partnership business audit, the auditor has to refer to the partnership deed. But in the absence of partnership deed or any aspect which is not included in the deed, the auditor may refer to the Partnership Act, 1932.

3. Hindu undivided family

In respect of accounts of Hindu undivided family, there is no basic legal requirement of audit. But the important motive for getting the accounts of this type of family business audited lies in the inherent advantages that follow from an independent professional audit. If there will be any dispute or mistrust among the members of the Hindu undivided family regarding accounts, that can be settled through the audited accounts.

4. Association of persons

Though it is not legally required to get accounts of such associations audited, some associations of persons, e.g the Bengal Chamber of Commerce, are interested to appoint qualified auditors and get their accounts audited for different reasons. For availing exemption from income tax liability, such associations are required to submit their audited accounts to the income tax authority. In conducting this type of audit, the auditor has to refer the constitution of the association.

5. Non-profit seeking organisations

Certain non-profit seeking organisations, e.g. colleges, libraries, hospitals, clubs charitable institutions etc. get their accounts audited. The basic purpose of audit of these types of organisations is to locate error or fraud committed by the staff members. The governing body of these organisations usually appoints the auditor. These organisations usually depend upon government grants and other aids from different bodies. Audited accounts are helpful in getting grants and aids.

2.4 CLASSIFICATION ON THE BASIS OF FUNCTION

The function of the auditor depends on the role of the auditor, i.e. in which capacity he is conducting the audit work. So, on the basis of function, auditing can be of the following types:

2.4.1 External Audit

External audit is conducted by an independent external auditor. This type of audit is usually conducted to fulfil the requirement of the provisions of law. Qualified chartered accountants who are not connected with the preparation of accounts or management of the organisation can be appointed as external auditors.

The auditor who conducts such an audit is 'independent' of the enterprise under audit, i.e. he is an independent professional who does not have any such relationship with the enterprise as might adversely affect his ability to form an objective judgment about the financial statements. The various matters relating to the procedures of audit, rights, duties and liabilities of the auditor, their appointment procedures and presentation of reports are provided in the concerned statute.

Features of external audit

1. External audit is usually conducted by an independent qualified auditor.
2. In the normal course, this type of audit is conducted periodically.

3. The purpose of external audit is to see whether financial statements give a true and fair view of the financial position and result of the concern.
4. The external auditor can work independently, and enjoys better status.
5. The Indian Companies Act, 1956 and other statutes provide the area of responsibilities and functions of the external auditors.
6. In cases where external audit is being conducted due to legal compulsion the auditor must have a professional qualification.
7. This type of audit is conducted mainly for safeguarding the interest of owners, shareholders and other parties who do not have knowledge of day-to-day operation of the organisations.
8. The Act always provides for the norms regarding the appointment of auditor. The auditor must not be disqualified as per the provision of the law.

Independent financial audit is undoubtedly the most common type of audit. It is generally conducted to ascertain whether the balance sheet and the profit and loss account give a true and fair view of the financial position and financial performance respectively of the enterprise under audit.

2.4.2 Internal Audit

Internal audit is conducted by specially assigned staff within the organisation. It is an audit through which a thorough examination of the accounting transactions as well as the system according to which these transactions have been recorded is conducted. Internal audit is undertaken to verify the accuracy and authenticity of the financial accounting and statistical records presented to the management. As per AAS-7, the scope and objectives of internal audit vary widely and are dependent upon the size and structure of the entity and the requirements of its management.

Features of internal audit

1. The internal audit system is considered to be a part of the management control system and not merely an assistant thereto.
2. Internal audit often differs in its scope and emphasis. It is more managerial than accounting.
3. The nature and extent of checking also depends on the size and type of the business organisation.
4. It embraces not only the operational audit of various operational activities in the organisation but also includes the audit of management itself.
5. The function of internal audit can be considered as an integral part of the internal control system.
6. Internal audit is continuous in nature. The work of internal auditor starts after the transactions are completed.
7. Generally the internal audit is conducted by the permanent staff of the organisation. Sometimes outside agencies may be asked to conduct internal audit.
8. The existence of internal audit is a help to the external auditor.

2.4.3 External Audit and Internal Audit Compared and Contrasted

Internal audit involves an examination and evaluation of various activities of an enterprise. The scope of internal audit in a particular situation is determined by the management in the context of its specific requirements. The internal auditor, thus, engages himself primarily in the task of reviewing the various activities of an enterprise and reporting on the same to its management.

Internal audit is different from independent financial audit in two important aspects. Firstly, independent financial audit is often required under law and the auditors are not usually appointed by the management and the auditors are also not required to report to the management. On the other hand, the internal auditors are appointed by the management and they are required to submit the report to the management. Secondly, the objective of independent financial audit is to ascertain whether the financial statements are reliable, i.e. whether they give a true and fair view of the financial result and financial position of the enterprise.

Similarities between internal and external audit

- An effective system of internal control
- Continuous effective operation of such system
- Adequate management information flow
- Assets safeguarding
- Adequate accounting system
- Ensuring compliance with statutory and regulatory requirements

Areas of differences between internal and external audit

- The extent of work undertaken
- Approach
- Responsibility

Areas of work overlap between internal and external audit

- Examination of the system of internal control
- Examination of the accounting records and supporting documents
- Verification of assets and liabilities
- Observation, enquiry and the ratio measurement

2.4.4 Distinction between External and Internal Audit

The difference between external audit and internal audit can be outlined as shown in Table 2.1.

2.5 CLASSIFICATION ON THE BASIS OF PRACTICAL APPROACH

On the basis of requirements of audit, the approach to auditing may differ. So, on the basis of practical approach for conducting the audit work, the audit can be classified under the following types:

TABLE 2.1 Differences between external audit and internal audit

Area of difference	External audit	Internal audit
1. Nature	It is conducted for reporting on the reliability and fairness of the financial statements.	It is conducted with a view to check adherence to norms and established procedures and protect the assets of the organisation.
2. Qualifications	The auditor must possess specific qualification as prescribed by the respective statute.	No specific qualification is required to be possessed by the internal auditor.
3. Scope of work	This type of audit must be complete in all respects. Its scope can not be curtailed in any way by the management.	The scope of work of the internal audit is determined by the management.
4. Purpose	The object of this type of audit is to protect the interest of the owners and other parties related to the enterprise.	The basic objective of internal audit is to improve performance, efficiency and profitability of the enterprise.
5. Appointment of auditor	The external auditors are usually appointed by the owners and in some cases by the government.	The internal auditor is appointed by the management.
6. Status	The auditor is an outsider and independent person. He is not under any rules and regulations of the organisation.	The internal auditor is an employee of the organisation. He is bound by the rules and regulations of the organisation.
7. Continuity	External audit may be periodical or continuous in nature.	Internal audit is continuous in nature. It is carried out throughout the year.

2.5.1 Continuous Audit

A continuous audit or a detailed audit is an audit which involves a detailed examination of the books of accounts at regular intervals of, say, one month or three months. The auditor visits his clients at regular or irregular intervals of time during the financial year and checks each and every transaction. At the end of the year, he checks the profit and loss account and the balance sheet.

According to R. C. Williams, "A continuous audit is one where the auditor or his staff is constantly engaged in checking the accounts during the whole period or where the auditor or his staff attends at regular or irregular intervals during the period."

Applicability

1. Where it is desired to present the accounts just after the close of the financial year.
2. Where the volume of transactions is very large.
3. Where periodical statements are required to be presented to the management.

Advantages

1. ***Easy and quick discovery of errors*** As the auditor starts checking just after the completion of the transaction, it becomes easier for the auditor to detect fraud and errors quickly.

2. ***Moral check on the client's staff*** As the auditor visits frequently and checks the accounts at regular or irregular intervals, this method of auditing provides moral check on the employees of the organisation.

3. ***Preparation of interim accounts*** Under continuous audit system, interim accounts can be prepared without much delay in time. It will help the Board of Directors to declare interim dividend.

4. ***Up-to-date accounts*** Due to continuous pressure from the auditors, the efficiency of accounts department's staff will increase and their work will be up-to-date and accurate.

5. ***More knowledge of technical details*** Continuous audit will help auditor to understand the technicalities of the business. This will help the auditor to make valuable suggestions for the improvement of the business.

6. ***Audit staff can be kept busy throughout the year*** The auditor can make his audit plan in a systematic manner. He can evenly spread his work to the audit staff throughout the year. It will help the auditor to keep his staff busy throughout the year.

7. ***Quick presentation of accounts*** Audited accounts can be presented just after the end of the financial year as the auditor has already completed most of his routine audit work.

8. ***Efficient audit due to more time*** Since the audit is carried out throughout the year, sufficient time is available for detailed checking. It will result in efficient audit.

Disadvantages

1. ***Expensive system of audit*** As the auditing work is required to be carried out throughout the year, it becomes an expensive system. Small organisations cannot afford to adopt this expensive system of audit.

2. ***Alteration of figures already checked*** After the accounts have been checked, the staff of the client may fraudulently alter the figures.

3. ***Dislocation of client's work*** Frequent visits by the auditor for checking the books of accounts and related documents may dislocate the work flow of the organisation.

4. ***Queries may remain outstanding*** As the work is not completed at a time, the auditor may lose continuity and certain questions and inquiries may remain unanswered.

5. ***Unhealthy relationship*** Frequent visits and disturbances in the daily work may provide scope for unhealthy relationships between the audit staff and the client's staff.

6. ***Reviewing of work already done*** Before starting the audit work, a review of findings of previous audit work should be made to establish link with the past work done.

Ways and means of removing the drawbacks of continuous audit

In a large enterprise, continuous audit is a must for proper and timely completion of audit. So some special measures have to be taken for avoiding the limitations of continuous audit as far as possible. The following measures can be taken to overcome the shortcomings of continuous audit:

1. ***Use of audit note book*** The auditor must record in his notebook the work completed by him and his assistants from time to time, material errors detected and rectified, queries raised by him and his staff and explanations given by the client. Before starting the work each time, the auditor should have a look over the notebook and books of accounts to know the extent of work completed up to last visit or whether any query remains unanswered or whether any alteration is made.

2. ***Use of special ticks in checking*** The auditor may use a different tick for checking the figures altered before the audit. Such variation in tick mark should be slight and unnoticeable. This will enable the auditor to identify whether any unauthorised alteration has been made subsequent to audit.

3. ***No change in audit staff*** The duties of audit staff should not be changed in order to maintain the flow of work undisturbed and to ensure follow up of unresolved points. However, to avoid monotony in work, the nature of duty of the audit staff may be changed after completion of annual audit.

4. ***No change in audited figures*** Clear instructions must be given to the client for not changing any audited figure. If any extra ordinary situation requires such change, it should be done with prior intimation to the auditor and with the help of rectification entry only.

5. ***Casting in ink*** The casting of periodical total of the various books of accounts should be written in ink as and when they are checked.

6. ***Incomplete work*** Checking each part of work, whenever undertaken, should be completed in one visit and should not be left incomplete to be completed for the next visit.

7. ***Sound audit programme*** There should be well-framed audit programme indicating the extent of work to be completed, allocation of work and time schedule of various works. This will make the continuous audit very effective.

2.5.2 Periodical or Final or Complete Audit

Periodical audit is one which is taken up at the close of the financial period, when all the accounts have been balanced and final accounts have already been prepared. It may also commence before the final accounts are prepared and continue till the audit is completed even after the close of financial period.

According to Spicer and Pegler, "A final or complete audit is commonly understood to be an audit which is not commenced until after the end of the financial period and is then carried on until completed."

In case of this type of audit, the auditor visits his client only once a year and goes on checking the accounts until the audit work for the whole of the period is completed.

Applicability

1. Where the volume of transactions of the organisation is small
2. Where there is no urgency to present the audited accounts within a certain period of time
3. Where internal control system is very effective.
4. Where interim statements of accounts are not required by the management for review or for some other purposes

Advantages

1. ***Inexpensive*** It is a less expensive system as compared to continuous audit system. Hence, the method of auditing is suitable for small business organisations.

2. ***Quick completion of audit*** Periodical audit can be finished quickly, within a reasonable time.

3. ***Minimum chances of alteration*** There is minimum chance of alteration of figures after they have been checked as the auditor completes his work on a continuous basis.

4. ***Less disturbance in client's work*** Client's daily office work is not unnecessarily disturbed because auditors visit only once a year.

5. ***Preparation of audit schedule*** The auditor will not face any problem in preparing his audit schedule.

6. ***Requirement of small establishment*** The auditor is not required to maintain a big establishment for this purpose.

Disadvantages

1. ***Delay in presentation of accounts*** This type of audit can be satisfactorily applied in case of small concerns. But in case of large concerns, it takes more time to complete the audit work and hence presentation of accounts to the shareholders is delayed.

2. ***Preparation of interim accounts*** Under periodical auditing system, it is not possible to prepare interim accounts. As a result, no interim dividend can be paid without the availability of audited interim accounts.

3. ***Possibility of undetected errors and frauds*** The auditor may not be able to check and verify all the transactions. As such, there is every chance that some of the errors and frauds may remain undetected.

4. ***Fixation of audit programme*** If the auditor has several clients whose financial year ends on the same date, it may be difficult for the auditor to complete the work of all the clients within the scheduled time.

2.5.3 Interim Audit

Interim audit is an audit, which is conducted in between the two annual audits with a view to find out interim profit of the business to enable it to declare an interim dividend. It is a kind of audit, which is conducted between the two periodical or balance sheet audits.

Advantages

1. This type of audit is helpful to those concerns where the publication of interim accounts is required.
2. The final audit can be completed within the scheduled time, if interim audit has already been conducted by the organisation.
3. Errors and frauds can be found more quickly and detected during the course of the interim audit.
4. There is a moral check on the staff of the client as the accounts are checked after three or six months.

TABLE 2.2 Distinction between continuous audit and periodical audit

Points of difference	*Continuous audit*	*Periodical audit*
Presentation of annual report	It ensures early publication of annual report.	Publication of annual report may be delayed.
Period of audit work	Audit is carried out throughout the year.	Audit is carried out only once at the close of the accounting period.
Work-coverage	Detailed checking of the books of accounts is possible because of the existence of sufficient time at the disposal of the auditor.	Detailed checking is usually not possible. In most of the cases, the checking of the books of accounts is limited to test checking.
Alteration of figures	Alteration of audited figures is possible due to the long gap between the two consecutive visits of the auditor to his client.	Alteration of figures is not possible as there is no break in the process of auditing work.
Cost involvement	It is very expensive to operate this system.	It is economical.
Applicability	It is applicable to large business organisations.	It is applicable in case of small business organisations.
Audit process	The audit staff visits and checks the accounts frequently.	The audit staff visits the client's business only once in a year after the accounts are closed.
Detection of errors and frauds	It is very effective for early detection of errors and frauds.	Errors and frauds are left in the books till audit is conducted at the close of the year.

Disadvantages

1. Figures may be altered in the accounts which have already been audited.
2. It will mean that the audit staff will have to prepare notes when they finish the audit work.
3. This audit implies additional work.
4. In case of interim audit, the interim trial balance has to be prepared and for this purpose, balancing of all existing accounts is required to be made at the middle of the year.

2.5.4 Partial Audit

It is a kind of audit where the work of the auditor is curtailed. The auditor is asked to check a few books. For example, he may be asked to check the payment side of the cash book.

Partial audit is not permitted in case of limited companies (private or public) as, according to the Companies Act, the duties of an auditor of a company cannot be curtailed. Again, in case of a very big proprietary concern, it may not be possible for the proprietor himself to disburse all payments and if he suspects misappropriation of cash, he may appoint an auditor to check only the cash book.

When an auditor is appointed to conduct partial audit, he must make it clear in his report that he has performed partial audit as per the instructions of the client.

Advantages

1. It serves the specific interest of the client.
2. There is much scope to render quick service, as the auditor has to deal with only one or two aspects of business transactions.
3. Critical analysis of the books of account relating to a particular item or group of items is made possible.
4. It may act as a moral check on the part of persons who intend to falsify accounts.

Disadvantages

1. The conduct of this type of audit is strictly restricted under the Companies Act.
2. The audit report does not reflect the financial position of the business as a whole.
3. It cannot be widely used.
4. This type of audit is conducted only for a particular purpose.

2.5.5 Occasional Audit

As the name indicates, this type of audit is conducted once in a while, whenever the need arises and the client desires it to be carried out.

This is possible only in case of proprietary concerns but in case of joint stock companies, banking and insurance companies etc. the audit has to be carried out once or twice a year according to the Companies Act.

Advantages

1. The client can know its actual financial position on the date when the books of accounts are audited.
2. It brings some sort of satisfaction in the mind of the client that the audited accounts are accepted by all.
3. Impartial view can be expressed through the procedure of audit.
4. It can be profitably used in small concerns.

Disadvantages

1. The conduct of this audit brings some confusion about the authenticity of final audit in a big concern.
2. It is expensive to operate.
3. The auditor faces a lot of problems in conducting his audit work, as the client's staff is not accustomed to the procedures of auditing.
4. The books of accounts may not be available according to the requirement of audit procedures.

2.5.6 Standard Audit

Standard audit can be defined as a "complete check and analysis of certain items and contingent upon effective internal check, appropriate test checks on remaining items, the whole of work being in accordance with general auditing standards."

From the above, it is clear that under this type of audit, certain items in the accounts are thoroughly checked and analysed and appropriate test checks are applied to other items, provided there is a good and effective internal check in operation.

Advantages

1. Development of new auditing standards in view of changing socio-economic condition can be made possible through scrutiny of auditing standards so far established.
2. It controls the nature and extent of documents and evidences which are obtained through the procedure of an audit.
3. It influences the audit programme.
4. The destructive criticism often made by the general public that the management, in collusion with auditor, distorts the financial statements may be rooted out through the application of standard audit procedures.

Disadvantages

1. It is very difficult to bring all organisations under the same accounting practices for the uniform application of standard audit.
2. The application of a particular standard procedure to different organisations having different standards may invite chaos instead of development.
3. Standards are always subject to change of circumstances, nature and environment of business.
4. Finally, setting up a standard narrows the development of standard.

2.5.7 Balance Sheet Audit

Balance sheet audit means limited audit in which all the balance sheet accounts are verified and tests imposed only on those profit and loss items which are directly related to the assets and liabilities such as repairs and maintenance, provision for depreciation, bad debts etc. Accounts such as these are analysed, but otherwise no detailed audit is conducted.

Under this type of audit, the audit is commenced from the balance sheet working back to the books of original entry and the related documents etc.

This type of audit is more popular in USA than in England and other European countries. However, this type of audit is more widely used.

Advantages

1. It records the changing events of the period. The change in working capital can be reflected through Balance sheet audit.
2. This type of audit furnishes different information relating to over-capitalisation, under-capitalisation, over-trading and under-trading of the business.
3. It establishes proper relationship between assets and liabilities of the business.
4. It guides different parties interested in the affairs of the business in taking business decisions.

Disadvantages

1. It lacks in disclosing certain material information needed to evaluate different measuring bases.
2. Balance sheet reflects the financial position of the business only at a given point of time. Events occurring after balance sheet date may affect materially the process of decision.

3. Comparison between the two periods may be drawn, but the causes for the change of figures between the two periods are not stated.
4. Information regarding the generation of profit or loss of the business is not stated in the balance sheet. This is required to make the balance sheet more informative and balance sheet audit more dynamic.

2.6 CLASSIFICATION ON THE BASIS OF AUDIT DIMENSION

The scope of an audit varies widely and depends on the purpose of the audit, the dimension of auditing work and the conditions of the audit requirement. On the basis of this dimensional aspect, auditing can be classified under the following types:

2.6.1 Management Audit

Management audit is a comprehensive critical review of all aspects of the management process. In fact, it is a tool of management control. It covers all areas of management like planning, organising, co-ordination, control etc. It assists at all levels of the management in the effective discharge of managerial functions.

A management audit is forward-looking and independent. It is a systematic evaluation of the activities of the management at all levels for the improvement of the organisational profitability and attainment of other objectives of the organisation through improvements in the performance of the management function. In short, management audit is a guide which helps in improving the efficiency of the management.

2.6.2 Cost Audit

Cost audit is an effective means of control in the hands of the management to have an idea about the working of the costing department of the organisation and to suggest ways and means for its smooth running. It is the detailed checking as well as the verification of the correctness of the costing techniques, systems and cost accounts.

Cost audit was introduced in India for the first time in the year 1965 with the introduction of clause (d) to Section 209 and 233B of Section 233 of the Companies Act. The need for such provision in the Act arose as the maintenance and proper use of scientific cost records is essential for those companies, which are engaged in the manufacturing and related activities.

2.6.3 Tax Audit

Tax audit refers to audit of incomes or expenses or specific claims of deductions or exemptions for the purpose of assessment of income tax. Tax audit is required in addition to financial audit, which does not fulfill the specific requirement of the tax authority.

Since the assessment year 1985–86, certain provisions under Section 44AB of the Income Tax Act was inserted to provide that certain persons have to get compulsory tax audit of their accounts. These persons shall get their accounts of the previous year audited by an accountant before the 'specific date' and obtain before that date the report of such audit in the prescribed form duly signed and verified by such accountant.

2.6.4 Human Resource Audit

One of the defects of financial accounting is its failure to show the human resources in the balance sheet. However, it is a fact that external users may wish to know the degree of employee morale, customer satisfaction, product quality and the reputation of an entity. So, disclosure of information regarding human resources in the annual report of the company may help a lot to the investors in framing an opinion whether to invest or not.

The auditor for the purpose of making audit of human resources, if it is included in the annual accounts, should carefully examine the basis of valuation of human resources. His examination should not relate to the tightness of the process of valuation of the human resources but he should see that information upon which the calculations are based are reliable and authentic. So, human resource audit is concerned about the human asset figure that appears in the balance sheet through checking, inspecting and appraising the various facts and figures, which are based on the estimated value of human resources.

2.6.5 System Audit

The purpose of the system audit is to design appropriate system of accounts suitable to the business and to obtain information, through the process of investigation for improving the accounting method. In fact accounting systems are required to be revised in order to ensure that it may provide the information desired by the executives as an aid to management decision.

So, system audit is concerned with that method of checking, which is directed to ascertain whether the accounting practices are up-to-date and economical and whether the existing practices are required to be changed so as to do the work better, quicker and at less cost under the present conditions.

2.6.6 Propriety Audit

Propriety audit is concerned with scrutiny of executive decisions bearing on the financial and profit and loss aspect of the concern with special reference to public interest and commonly accepted customs and standards of conduct. While performing a propriety audit, the auditor would judge whether the standards of propriety have been maintained in making payments, incurring expenditure or entering into transactions.

Propriety audit ensures that the public money has not been utilised for the benefit of a particular person or section of the community and all transactions have been activated for the best interest of the concern itself. Section 227 (1A) and CARO, 2003 issued under section 227(4A) of the Companies Act, 1956 also contain clauses dealing with the examination of transactions from the view point of propriety.

2.6.7 Performance or Efficiency Audit

Efficiency audit provides the means to appraise the performance of the enterprise and to diagnose the weakness of the enterprise. It aims to determine whether the resources of the business flow into remunerative or paying channels. It is concerned with the review of the organisational environment, measuring return on investment, cash flow performance etc. and comparing these with the standard.

The efficiency audit is based on the basic economic principles. The objective of this type of audit is to evaluate and compare the optimum return with the amount of capital invested in the business and to ensure that investment techniques aim at giving optimum results. In short, efficiency audit is introduced to ensure the improvement of organisational efficiency.

2.6.8 Environmental Audit

Environmental audit is an excellent management tool for relating productivity to pollution. Environmental audit is the examination of the correctness of environmental accounts. In broader sense, environmental auditing is the examination of accounts of revenues and costs of environmental and natural resources, their estimate, depreciation and values recorded in the books of accounts.

In India, recognising the importance of environmental audit and its procedure was first notified under the Environment (Protection) Act, 1986 by the Ministry of Environment and Forests. Under this Act, every person running an industry, operation or process requiring consent under Section 25 of the Water (Prevention & Control of Pollution) Act, 1974 or under Section 21 of the Air (Prevention & Control of Pollution) Act, 1981 or both or authorisation under the Hazardous Wastes (Management and Handling) Rule of 1989 issued under the Hazardous (Protection) Act, 1986 is required to submit an environmental audit report.

2.6.9 Social Audit

Business organisations are now regarded as a great social force. They are not expected to be only engaged in profit earning activity and paying dividend to the shareholders. They have an important role to play in the social well being. They have some responsibility to the society.

Social audit is aimed at an assessment of the performance of an entity towards the fulfilment of social obligations. The objective of social audit is to bring to light for public knowledge how far an organisation has discharged its responsibility to the society and to make an assessment of the social performance of an organisation. But audit of social accounts is not yet in practice and the term 'social audit' is still in a conceptual stage in our country.

2.6.10 Cash Transaction Audit

Cash transaction audit is the oldest concept in auditing system. In the olden times, a person was appointed to check cash transactions only, i.e. whether the person responsible for recording cash receipts and payments on behalf of the business owner has done his job properly or not. Hence it was merely a cash audit.

So, when an audit of all items of cash book, is conducted it is known as cash audit. The auditor will check the receipt and payments made by cash with the vouchers and documents. It is useful in an organisation in which most of the transactions are made through cash. It is only a partial audit and at present the concept of this auditing has a wider meaning.

2.6.11 Energy Audit

It is a relatively new branch of auditing. It is emerging as a consequence of heavily depleting physical energy resources in the world. Need for conservation of energy is the most important parameter of modern day world. Energy audit is focussed to see whether right amount of energy, both organic and inorganic, is used by the enterprises and there occurs no avoidable loss or waste of energy due to human indifference. Conducting energy audit inevitably calls for technical input and an audit team with audit professionals and technical personnel is needed for the purpose.

2.6.12 Secretarial Audit

This is also a relatively new concept and is coming to be recognised with growing complexities in the corporate laws. Compliance with the provisions of various corporate laws is as important as to be in the business. Any failure to comply may invite heavy penalty and/or even imprisonment. It is therefore imperative for corporate entities to ensure compliance with the applicable legal requirements, which are numerous. A secretarial audit assures the corporate body that the legal requirements have been duly complied with and in time. If non-compliances are noticed by the audit, management will have time to rectify the situation with much lesser problems and costs.

POINTS TO PONDER

- Auditing is a multidimensional and comprehensive subject. An effective insight into the nature of auditing can be obtained by understanding the various types of audit.
- Auditing can be classified from the following viewpoints: organisation, functions, practical approach and audit dimension.
- Company audit, bank audit, electricity company audit, co-operative society audit, trusts audit, insurance audit etc. are required under law, whereas audit of sole-proprietors, partnership firms, association of persons, non-profit seeking organisations etc. are not required under law.
- On the basis of functions, audit can be of two types: external audit and internal audit. External audit is conducted by an independent external auditor, whereas internal audit is conducted by specially assigned staff within the organisation.
- On the basis of practical approach for conducting audit, the audit can be classified under the following types: continuous audit, periodical audit and interim audit on the basis of time complete and partial audit on the basis of scope and balance sheet; and occasional and standard audit on the basis of objectives.
- On the basis of dimension of audit work, audit can be classified under the following types: management audit, cost audit, human resource audit, system audit, propriety audit, efficiency audit, environment audit, social audit, cash transaction audit, energy audit, secretarial audit etc.

REVIEW QUESTIONS

Short-answer Questions

1. What is management audit?
2. Distinguish between internal audit and statutory audit.
3. Write a short-note on the various classes of audits.
4. 'Continuous audit is a double edged weapon'. Discuss.
5. What is interim audit? Why is it required?
6. Write short notes on:
   (a) Standard audit
   (b) System audit
   (c) Efficiency audit
   (d) Social audit

Essay-type Questions

1. What is statutory audit? Describe the points of differences between statutory audit and non-statutory audit.
2. What is periodical audit? What are the advantages and disadvantages of periodical audit? Distinguish between continuous audit and periodical audit.
3. What is continuous audit? In which case is this audit applicable? State the advantages and disadvantages of continuous audit.
4. Discuss the advantages and disadvantages of balance sheet audit. Also state the auditor's position in relation to balance sheet audit.

CHAPTER 3

Techniques and Procedures of Auditing

CHAPTER OUTLINE

3.1 INTRODUCTION

An auditor must ensure that he fully understands the enterprise with which he is dealing before he determines his basic approach to an audit. He must familiarise himself with its organisation and visit the location at which it operates. He should have a detailed knowledge of its products or services. He must ensure that he has fully grasped any technicalities peculiar to the business. Only then he will be in a position to fully comprehend and identify the transactions which are being recorded in the accounting records, in relation to which the internal controls will be operating.

The auditor should follow the appropriate audit procedure and adopt different techniques of auditing. He should maintain the principles of auditing in conducting audit of an organisation in order to meet the following requirement:

1. Ascertain and record the accounting system and internal controls, assess the adequacy of the accounting system and evaluate the controls on which the auditor wishes to place reliance
2. Test the accounting records and perform compliance tests on the operation of those internal controls on which the auditor wishes to place reliance
3. Compare the financial statements with the accounting records and perform substantive tests to see that they are in agreement
4. Carry out a review of the financial statements
5. Report on the financial statements as required by the terms of auditor's appointment, and in compliance with any relevant statutory obligation.

On the basis of his assessment of the accounting system and evaluation of the internal controls, the auditor will draw up an audit programme specifically designed for that particular audit.

3.2 PREPARATORY STEPS BEFORE COMMENCEMENT OF AUDIT

Effective execution of any audit work requires appropriate planning and a well-designed audit programme. For effective audit planning and for desiging appropriate audit programme, the auditor should prepare himself before the commencement of his audit work. For this purpose, the auditor should take the following steps:

1. Receiving appointment letter

The auditor is usually appointed by the shareholders in the annual general meeting and shall hold office till the conclusion of the next annual general meeting. The auditor should receive the appointment letter before starting his audit work as he has to conduct his audit work on the basis of terms of references as given in the appointment letter. This appointment letter is formally called Audit Engagement Letter. Auditing and Assurance Standard (AAS-26) describes the purposes, applicability and contents of Audit Engagement Letter.

2. Communication with the existing auditor

Before accepting the work of a new audit, in the case of a continuing business, it is established professional etiquette for the proposed auditor to communicate with the previous auditor to see whether he has any objections to raise. This is also an official requirement as per the Institute of Chartered Accountants Act, 1949 and has to be adhered to by the practicing chartered accountants.

3. Acceptance of appointment

If the auditor is satisfied with the reasons for not appointing the previous auditor, he can then accept the appointment. The auditor should confirm his acceptance to the concerned organisation through a letter of acceptance.

4. Ascertaining the scope of audit

After accepting his appointment, he should ascertain the precise nature and scope of his audit work. In case of statutory audit, the scope and the nature of audit work can be ascertained by referring to the statute. In case of other types of audit, the auditor should discuss with the client about his area of auditing work.

5. Knowledge about the organisation

Before the auditor can determine his basic approach to an audit, he must ensure that he fully understands the enterprise. He must comprehend the nature of the business and have a detailed knowledge of its activities. He must familiarise himself with the organisation and visit the location at which it operates. This will enable him to understand the nature of transactions, which are recorded in the books of accounts. AAS-20 describes how the knowledge of business is relevant to the auditors and how the auditors will obtain and use the knowledge of the business in their audit work.

6. Knowledge of the accounting system

The auditor should obtain a list of all books maintained by the organisation for recording its accounting transactions along with the information relating to the existing accounting system. He should also acquire complete information about the internal control system of the organisation. In fact, the extent of his work is greatly influenced by the reliability of internal control system and appropriateness of accounting system adopted.

7. Complete list of principal officers

The auditor should also obtain a list of the principal officers of the organisation. He should also acquire knowledge about the area and extent of authority of each one of them. This will help the auditor to have appropriate clarification from the concerned officer.

8. Knowledge of technical details

The auditor must ensure that he has fully grasped the technicalities peculiar to the business. Only then, he will be in a position to identify the transactions of the accounting records and relate the accounting system with the internal control system adopted.

9. Observation of the previous auditor's report

The auditor should go through the previous auditor's report as well as the final accounts of the previous year. This will help him to understand the nature of accounts, important areas for which detailed checkings are required and the techniques to be used to conduct his audit work effectively.

10. Instructions to the client

After completing the above-mentioned steps, the auditor should issue clear instructions to his client that the accounts should be finalised and kept ready for audit and the necessary schedules required to support the final accounts be prepared and made available to him.

3.3 PREPARATION BY THE AUDITOR

Modern techniques require a new approach to the practical aspects of the auditor's work. Detailed checking and vouching no longer constitute the main aspect of the operations involved; the ascertainment of the internal control system, the investigation of its working and the verification of assets and liabilities in order to ensure the presentation of the true and fair view of the financial statements, now prevail. The attitude that an audit is mainly useful for the discovery or prevention of fraud is no longer accepted. It is now more generally appreciated that an audit not only ensures the true and fair presentation of the affairs of the organisation, but also that it can be of real benefit in bringing about the establishment and maintenance of efficient business methods.

So, in order to conduct the work of audit smoothly and efficiently, at present, the auditor should prepare himself for the following aspects of audit.

3.3.1 Audit Planning

Audit planning is the process of deciding in advance what is to be done, who is to do it, how it is to be done and when it is to be done by the auditor in order to have an effective and efficient completion of audit.

According to AAS-8, "Audit planning refers to planning by the auditor made to enable him to conduct an effective audit in an efficient and timely manner, and includes planning about area, scope, depth of transactions to be audited, time to be devoted, persons to be deployed for audit etc."

Audit planning is necessary for efficient and effective conduct of an audit. It should be continuously followed throughout the course of audit assignment. As per AAS-8, audit planning facilitates the following:

- Appropriate attention devoted to important areas of the audit
- Prompt identification of potential problems
- Timely completion of work
- Proper utilisation of assistants
- Coordination of work done by other auditors and experts

The main objectives of audit planning are to ensure the following:

- That the auditing work is conducted efficiently and profitably
- That high standards of audit works are maintained, so that the risk of litigation against the practice for negligence is minimised

It is important that audit should be carefully planned to ensure that correct number of staff of the appropriate level of seniority are available when they are required. In addition to that, in case of large audits, the work must be planned so that maximum work is done on an interim basis during the year. This has the double advantage of employing staff effectively throughout the year and ensuring that the only audit work that is remaining at the year end is the work that could not be performed earlier. To enable this planning to be carried out efficiently, the auditor will need to liaison with the chief financial officer/accountant of the organisation and ensure that the audit firm is fully aware of the exact proposed timing of the client's own accounting procedures.

In the light of the expected scope of the assignment, the auditor should prepare his audit plan after taking into consideration the following factors:

- Statutory requirement under the assignment
- Terms and conditions of engagement
- Nature and timings of reporting
- Significant audit areas
- Applicable legal provisions
- Reliability of accounting and internal control system
- Existing accounting practices followed
- Areas requiring special attentions

3.3.2 Audit Programme

Before starting an audit, a programme of work is usually drawn up. This is known as the 'audit programme'. It is a detailed plan of work, prepared by the auditor, for carrying out an audit. It comprises a set of techniques and procedures, which the auditor plans to apply to the given audit for forming an opinion about the statement of account of an organisation.

Prof. Meigs defined audit programme as "a detailed plan of the auditing work to be performed, specifying the procedure to be followed in verification of each item in the financial statements and giving the estimated time required."

So, audit programme may be defined as a careful flexibly written layout of the work to be done by the auditor and his staff in the conduct of an audit. The preparation of audit programme involves the following considerations:

- Area or extent of work
- Allocation of work
- Time duration for the completion of the work
- Responsibility of the persons, who have been assigned the work for its' timely completion

The specimen of an audit programme is given here.

Purposes of audit programme

There is no denying the fact that audit programme not only serves as the plan of action to be taken for the completion of assigned audit work efficiently and effectively, but the progress of the audit work may also be ascertained by it. However, different purposes of audit programme are given as follows:

1. Co-ordinating the procedures of audit
2. Ascertaining the progress of audit-work
3. Recording the work done during the process of auditing. Such records can act as an evidence of work done.

4. Assigning responsibilities to the audit staff for the completion of audit work within the time limit.

TABLE 3.1 Specimen of an audit programme
Name of the organisation : M/s *ZYX* Ltd. for the year ended on 31.3.20xx

Particulars of work	*Extent of work to be done*	*Actual work completed*	*Time taken*	*Completed by (signature)*
A. Cash Book:				
1. Posting	One month	June		
2. Casting	Full	Full		
3. Vouching	Three months	July, November and March		
B. Debtors' Ledger:				
1. Posting	One month	April		
2. Casting	One month	March		
3. Vouching	Two months	October and March		
C. Physical Verification:				
1. Cash	as on 31.3.20xx	as on 31.3.20xx		
2. Fixed Assets	as on 31.3.20xx	as on 31.3.20xx		
3. Stock	as on 31.3.20xx	as on 31.3.20xx		

Types of audit programme

An audit programme can be of the following two types:

1. ***Predetermined audit programme*** In this audit programme, all the procedures of audit must be outlined in general, even though all procedures may not be relevant in a particular type of audit. The purpose of this type of audit programme is to offer either procedural guideline or to serve as a 'check off list'. For this reason, this predetermined audit programme is also known as. tailor-made audit programme.

2. ***Progressive audit programme*** The progressive form of audit programme is known as 'skeleton' form of audit programme. It sets forth briefly general scope, character and limitations of audit work. This type of programme is suitable in those cases where the condition of the business changes year after year.

Advantages of audit programme

Whatever may be the nature of audit programme, usually the following benefits are derived from an audit programme:

1. ***Assurance of completion of work*** It ensures that all necessary work has been done and nothing has been omitted.

2. ***Information about work-progress*** The auditor is in a position to know about the progress of the work done by his assistants.

3. ***Uniformity of work*** A uniformity of the work can be attained as the same programme will be followed at subsequent audits.

4. *Simplification of work allocation* It simplifies the allocation of work to various grades of articled and audit clerks.

5. *Guidance to the staff* It is a kind of guidance to the audit clerk for the work he has to perform.

6. *Defence against charge of negligence* The auditor can defend himself in case of a charge of negligence on the basis of the audit programme.

7. *Division of responsibility* Work of the audit can be divided amongst the different juniors who will be held responsible for their work.

8. *Final review of work* An audit programme facilitates the final review of work before the report is signed.

9. *Helpful to the new employees* For a new employee, the audit programme is a guide to his duty.

10. *Basis of future programmes* It is a useful basis for preparing the programme for the subsequent years.

Disadvantages of audit programme

1. *Loss of initiative* An efficient clerk loses his initiative because he has to follow the programme which has been fixed in advance.

2. *Want of flexibility* Even if the audit programme is well drawn up, it may not cover everything that might come up during the course of audit.

3. *Rigidity in programme* Each business may have a separate problem of its own and hence a rigid programme cannot be laid down for each type of business.

4. *Unsuitable for small concerns* Drawing up of an audit programme may be unnecessary for a small concern.

5. *No scope of changes* The audit programme may be followed mechanically year after year though some changes might have been introduced by the client.

6. *Concealment of incapacity of staff* Inefficient audit assistants may also take shelters behind the programme.

Steps to be taken to overcome the disadvantages of written audit programme

Obtaining up-to-date information and encouraging audit assistants to inform the deviations from the standard and the audit programme can avoid the aforesaid shortcomings and accordingly the principal may modify the programme.

In fact the disadvantages of written audit programme arise due to misunderstanding of its purpose. It should be taken as only a guide to audit and should not be treated as rigid and inflexible document. For this purpose, the auditor should take the following steps:

1. *Educating the audit staff* The audit staff should be made known about the purpose of audit programme. They must be clearly stated that they may go beyond the audit programme if the situation so warrants. The opinion of the audit staff may also be taken while drafting the audit programmes.

2. ***Revision of audit programme*** It should be the responsibility of the audit manager to constantly review the existing audit programme and modify it in the light of experience of the previous year's audit and according to the changing circumstances. The audit staff should also be encouraged to give their suggestions in this regard.

3. ***Rotation of work*** The duty of audit staff should be rotated so that no staff does the same job year after year. This will help in reducing the monotony of work.

4. ***Overall supervision*** Proper supervision and review of work is also useful for overcoming the disadvantages of predetermined audit programme.

3.3.2 Audit Notebook

An audit notebook is usually a bound book in which a large variety of matters observed during the course of audit are recorded. It is thus a part of the record of the auditor available for reference later on, if required. The matters may be observed during the course of audit for which no satisfactory answer have been given by the client or those which require to be incorporated in the audit report. It is a kind of permanent record available to the auditor.

The audit notebook may be in two parts:

- For keeping a record of general information as regards the audit as a whole
- For recording special points which have been observed during the course of audit of the accounts of different years

Objectives of audit notebook

The audit notebook is an important document of audit. It serves the following purposes:

1. ***Facilitates future audit*** The audit notebook of current year helps the auditor while he starts audit in the next year. He can easily understand which areas of the organisation should deserve his special attention.

2. ***Documentary evidence*** The audit notebook provides an evidence about the extent of work done and degree of skill and care exercised by the auditor in conducting audit. By producing audit notebook in the court he can defend himself against charge of negligence.

3. ***Helps in preparing audit report*** It is not possible for the auditor to keep in memory all important matters and audit findings that are required to be considered in preparing the audit report. So, maintenance of audit notebook recording all such important matters provides him a lot of assistance in preparation of audit report.

4. ***Settlement of audit queries*** The accounting staff of the client may feel disturbed if the auditor puts audit queries before them every now and then in the course of audit. So, for the sake of convenience of the client's staff, audit queries should be recorded in the notebook as and when they crop up and placed at a time before the staff of the client for their explanations.

5. ***Evaluation of work*** The auditor, by going through the audit notebook, can understand the progress of audit work and the level of efficiency of his staff in audit work.

Value of audit notebook

The audit notebook is of great value to an auditor at the time of preparing the report to be submitted to the shoreholders. In case a charge of negligence is filed against the auditor, a notebook may prove to be a good evidence.

From this notebook, an auditor may know the exact volume of work performed by his assistants. It also helps for future reference and guidance. This can serve as a guide also in framing the audit programme in future, so far as the points recorded in the notebook indicate the weaknesses in the system of the accounting of the client, which requires to be looked into.

Contents of audit note book

Some of the important points which are noted down in an audit notebook are given below:

1. A list of books of accounts maintained by the clients
2. The names of the principal officers, their powers, duties and responsibilities
3. The technical terms used in the business
4. The points which require further explanations
5. The particulars of missing vouchers, the duplicate of which have to be obtained
6. The mistakes and errors discovered
7. Total or balances of certain books of accounts, bank reconciliation statement etc.
8. Notes and queries which might be required at a subsequent audit
9. The points which have to be incorporated in the audit report
10. Any matter which requires discussions with the senior officials or with the auditor
11. Accounting method followed in the business
12. Date of commencement and completion of audit
13. Provisions in the Articles and Memorandum of Association affecting the accounts and audit
14. Abstracts from minutes, contracts etc. having a bearing upon accounts
15. Particulars of accounting and financial policies followed

Advantages of audit notebook

1. From the audit note book, an auditor may know the exact volume of work performed by his assistants.
2. It helps for future reference and guidance. This can serve as a guide in framing the audit programme in future.
3. It facilitates the preparation of the audit report.
4. In case of change of audit assistants, no difficulty is faced by the new assistant in continuing the incomplete work.
5. It ensures that the audit programme has been sincerely followed.
6. It is a reliable evidence in the eye of law, if an auditor has to defend himself.
7. The responsibility of errors undetected can be fixed on the assistant concerned.
8. The important matters relating to the audit work may be easily recalled.

3.3.4 Audit Working Papers

Audit working papers are written records kept by the auditor of the evidence accumulated during the course of the audit, the methods and procedures followed and the conclusions reached. They should include all the information that the auditor considers necessary to adequately conduct his examination and provide support for his audit report.

In short audit working papers are those papers which contain essential facts about accounts that are under audit.

Purpose of working papers

Working papers are actually the compilation of all evidences which are collected by the auditor in the course of his audit. They serve the following purposes:

1. They show the extent of adherence to accounting principles and auditing standards.
2. They are useful as evidence against the charge of negligence.
3. They assist the auditor in co-ordinating and organising the work of audit assistants.
4. They ensure the possibility of quick preparation of audit report.
5. Through the working papers, the auditor can know the distribution and accomplishment of work.
6. Measurement of the efficiency of the assistants can be done with the help of working papers.
7. They can be used as permanent record for future references.
8. They can act as a means to give training to the audit clerk.
9. They provide a means to control the ongoing audit work.
10. Working papers assist the auditor in forming an opinion on the financial statements.

Contents of working papers

Audit working papers should include a summary of all significant matters identified which may require the exercise of judgment, together with the auditor's conclusion thereon. If difficult questions of principle or of judgment arise during the course of the audit, the auditor should record the relevant information received and summarise both the management viewpoints and his conclusions.

AAS-3 issued by the Institute of Chartered Accountants of India makes the following suggestions regarding the form and contents of working papers.

1. The working papers should record the audit plan, the nature, timing and extent of auditing procedures performed and the conclusions drawn from the evidence obtained.
2. The exact form and content of working papers are affected by various matters such as given below:
   (a) The nature of the engagement
   (b) The form of the audit report
   (c) The nature and complexity of client's business
   (d) The nature and conditions of the client's records and degree of reliance on internal controls
   (e) The need in particular circumstances for direction, supervision and review of work performed by assistants

3. Working papers should be designed and properly organised to meet the circumstances of each audit and the auditor's need in respect thereof.
4. Working papers should be sufficiently complete and detailed for an auditor to obtain an overall understanding of the audit.
5. All significant matters which require the judgement, together with the auditor's conclusion thereon, should be included in the auditor's working papers.
6. To improve audit efficiency, the auditor normally obtains and utilises schedules, analysis and other working papers prepared by the client such as analysis of important revenue accounts receivables etc.
7. In case of recurring audits, some working papers may be classified as permanent audit files as distinct from current audit files relating primarily to the audit of a single period.

Responsibility on protection and preservation of working papers

Whosoever is in the possesion of working papers should be responsible for their safe custody. These should in no case be shown to a third party except with the permission of the client. As the working papers are prepared in respect of the client's business, they should be treated as top secret and should be preserved in all circumstances and at all times.

After the audit report has been prepared and delivered to the client, these papers may be filed and preserved for a period of time sufficient to meet the needs of his practice and satisfy any pertinent legal or professional requirements of record retention.

Ownership of working papers

An important and pertinent question arises as to the ownership of these working papers. The claim of the auditor is that it is he who has collected the information for the purpose of discharging his duties. Therefore, he is entitled to the possession of these papers. On the other hand, it is the claim of the client that the auditor is his agent and hence he should surrender these papers to the client.

In fact, this question of ownership in respect to the working papers arose in the case of Sockockingky vs Bright Graham & Co. (1938) in England. The question was whether the auditor had a right to retain the working papers as if it were his own property even after the payment of the audit fees. The court gave judgement in favour of the auditors on the ground that they were independent contractors and not agents of the client.

According to the views of the Institute of Chartered Accountants of India (AAS-3), working papers are the property of the auditor. The auditor may, at his discretion, make portions of or extracts from his working papers available to his clients. Further, according to this standard of auditing practices, an auditor should adopt reasonable procedures for custody and confidentiality of his working papers and should retain them for a period of time sufficient to meet the needs of his practice and satisfy any pertitent legal and professional requirements of record retention.

3.3.5 Audit Files

The file which is used by the auditor for preserving the written statements of necessary matters relating to audit is called the audit file. It maintains different audit documents, viz. audit notes, audit programme, audit working papers etc. The efficient audit filing system strengthens the integrity of the audit work.

The audit file is generally of two types:

- Permanent audit file
- Temporary audit file

Permanent audit file

In the case of recurring audits, some working paper files may be classified as permanent audit files which are updated currently with information of continuing importance to succeeding audit.

A permanent audit file normally includes the following:

1. Information regarding the legal and organisational structure of the organisation. In case of company form of organisation, this includes the Memorandum and Articles of Association
2. Extracts or copies of important legal documents, agreements and minutes relevant to the audit
3. A record of the study and evaluation of the internal controls relating to the accounting system
4. Copies of audited financial statements for previous years
5. Analysis of significant ratios and trends
6. Copies of management letters issued by the auditor, if any
7. Record of communication with the retiring auditor, if any, before acceptence of the appointment as auditor
8. Notes regarding significant accounting policies
9. Significant audit observations of earlier years

Temporary audit file

In the case of single period audit, some working paper files may be classified as temporary audit file, which contain information relating primarily to the audit of a single period.

A temporary audit file usually includes the following:

1. Draft financial statements being audited
2. Schedules supporting the financial statements
3. Extracts from relevant minutes
4. Audit programme and time budget
5. Internal control questionnaire and, where applicable, flow charts and notes on the system of internal control
6. Confirmations obtained from banks and other relevant organisations regarding items in the financial statements
7. Details of queries raised during the audit, and the answers obtained to them
8. Copy of letter of representation

3.3.6 Audit Manual

Audit manual may be defined as a "written internal auditing document". It provides different information regarding detailed auditing procedures, objects of auditing, standard of performance, time recording procedure, preparation of audit report etc. The audit manual is prepared for the general guidance of the auditors with the object of planning the procedure of audit.

Advantages

1. Different information regarding policies of the concern and procedure of audit is available in the manual.
2. Information relating to required steps to be followed for conducting different auditing work can be collected from the manual.
3. Audit manual provides answers to routine questions by the audit staff.
4. Efficient distribution of work among the audit staff can be made possible.
5. Audit manual provides useful information to the new entrants to the profession.

Disadvantages

1. Different audit procedures as contained in the manual become very mechanical.
2. Creative thinking on the part of the audit staff is discouraged.
3. If the manuals are not kept up to date, it may, instead of providing useful guidance, misguide the working staff.
4. It discourages the individual initiative.
5. The procedure of audit as given in the audit manual may sometime fail to co-ordinate the activities of the audit staff during the course of audit.

3.3.7 Audit Memorandum

An audit memorandum is a statement containing all useful information regarding the business of the client. It indicates the method of operation, policies of different aspects of the business as well as all the conditions in respect of audit.

Audit memorandum is very useful in case of first time audit by the concerned auditor in an organisation. While conducting his auditing work, the auditor requires certain information which may be directly related with the method of operation of the business. If the auditor is not informed about the method of operation as well as the operational activities of the organisation, he will not be in a position to conduct his audit effectively. Hence audit memorandum is useful to the auditor while the auditor wants to relate the financial transactions with the business activities, with the condition of the business in which the transactions are being activated.

Contents of audit memorandum

- About the business—its early history and growth
- Nature of ownership of the organisation
- Location of its principal offices and factories
- Sources of factors of production—materials, labour etc
- Details about its manufacturing operations
- Principal products produced by the concern
- Market condition and nature of competition in the market
- Organisational structure and heirarchy
- Method of accounting and nature of books of accounts
- List of persons involved in management

3.4 PRINCIPLES AND TECHNIQUES OF AUDITING

Principles of auditing refer to fundamental consideration that sustain the function of auditing and direct its activities. Auditing has evolved in the satisfaction of a social need to see that the accounting statements on which people rely are reliable. To achieve this broad functional objective, certain techniques and procedures have been developed over the years on the basis of certain concepts and principles that are considered to be the governing forces. AAS-1 on "Basic Principles Governing an Audit" describes the basic principles which govern the auditor's professional responsibilities and which should be complied with whenever an audit is carried out. It also states that compliance with the basic principles requires the application of auditing procedures and reporting practices appropriate to the particular circumstances.

Auditing techniques refer to the methods and means adopted by an auditor for collection and evaluation of audit evidence in different auditing situations. When the audit objective is to see that debtors' balances are correctly stated in the balance sheets, the auditor would introduce confirmation and scrutiny of subsequent years' accounts as the appropriate audit technique. The method of collection of evidence to verify accounts maintained under manual system will be different from that, when accounts are computerised. In the former case, audit trial will be available and usual techniques like posting verification and casting verification would be appropriate. However, in the latter case, because of loss of audit trial and accuracy of the computer, these techniques are replaced by more intensive and extensive examination of the internal control. Also, the technique may vary according to the nature of proposition to be tested.

Thus auditing principles are fundamental in nature which underlie the conduct of the audit. These principles are not liable to change frequently while audit techniques may vary according to the nature of propositions to be tested. For instance, audit technique to test the existence of cash in hand will be different from the method to verify recoverability of sundry debtors. Further, audit techniques may vary from organisation to organisation depending upon the nature of the business but the principles of auditing will remain the same irrespective of the nature of the organisation.

3.4.1 Important Audit Techniques

The techniques or strategies, which are followed in order to collect proper evidence in support of the transactions recorded in the books of accounts, are termed as 'Techniques of Auditing'.

Important techniques usually adopted by the auditors include the following.

- Vouching (of expenses)
- Physical verification (of fixed and current assets)
- Reconciliation (of stock statement)
- Confirmation (of customers or bank balance)
- Re-computation (of depreciation and other calculations)
- Scanning (of legal formalities)
- Scrutiny (of ledger balances)
- Inquiry (of propriety aspect)

3.5 PROCEDURES FOLLOWED IN COURSE OF AUDIT

There is no fixed rule regarding the procedures the auditor would follow in the course of audit. He would fix up the procedures after reviewing the situations on the basis of auditor's own knowledge, intelligence, efficiency and experience. But the generally accepted procedures followed by an auditor include the following:

3.5.1 Audit Evidence

It is the auditor's duty to express a professional opinion on financial statements and it must always be a matter of judgement whether the auditor has sufficient evidence on which to base such an opinion. The auditor can never be absolutely certain that the financial statements show a true and fair view; the question is, whether as an honest and careful auditor, he has adequate evidence on which to base a reasonable opinion?

The term evidence includes "all influences on the mind of an auditor which affect his judgement about the truthfulness of the propositions submitted to him for review."

Types of audit evidence

Professor R. K. Mautz in his work *Fundamentals of Auditing* has rightly observed that "the nature of financial statement assertions leads to the conclusion that the nature of the following kinds of evidences are indicative of the validity of financial statement assertions in varying degrees depending on the circumstances of the examination."

Thus professor Mautz cited nine types of audit evidences, which are as follows.

1. Physical examination by the auditor of the article represented in the accounts
2. Statement by independent third parties:
   (a) oral evidence (b) written evidence
3. Authoritative documents:
   (a) prepared outside the enterprise under examination
   (b) prepared inside the enterprise under examination
4. Statements by officers and employees of the concern under examination:
   (a) formal statement (b) informal statement
5. Calculations performed by the auditors
6. Satisfactory internal control procedures
7. Subsequent actions by the concern under examination and by others
8. Subsidiary or detail records with no significant indications of irregularity
9. Interrelationship within the data examined

Methods of obtaining audit evidence

AAS-5 on "audit evidence" describes the method of obtaining audit evidences. According to this statement, the auditor obtains evidence in performing compliance and substantive procedures by one or more of the following methods:

1. *Inspection* Inspection consists of examining records, documents or tangible assets. Inspection of records and documents provides evidence of varying degree of reliability depending on their nature and source and the effectiveness of internal controls over their processing. Four major categories of documentary evidences, which provide different degrees of reliability to the auditor, are as follows:

(a) Documentary evidence originating from and held by third parties
(b) Documentary evidence originating from third parties and held by the entity
(c) Documentary evidence originating from the entity and held by third parties
(d) Documentary evidence originating from and held by the entity

Inspection of tangible assets is one of the methods to obtain reliable evidence with respect to their existence but not necessarily as to their ownership or value.

2. *Observation* Observation consists of witnessing a process or procedure being performed by others. For example, the auditor may observe the counting of inventories by client personnel or the performance of internal control procedures that leave no audit trial.

3. *Inquiry and confirmation* Inquiry consists of seeking appropriate information from knowledgeable persons inside and outside the entity. Inquiries may range from formal written inquiries addressed to third parties to informal oral inquiries addressed to persons inside the entity. Responses to inquiries may provide the auditor with information which he did not previously possess or may provide him with corroborative evidence.

Confirmation consists of the response to an inquiry to corroborate information contained in the accounting records. For example, the auditor requests confirmation of receivables by direct communication with the debtors.

4. *Re-computation* Re-computation consists of checking the arithmetical accuracy of source documents and accounting records or performing independent calculations.

5. *Analytical review* Analytical review consists of studying significant ratios and trends and investigating unusual fluctuations and items.

3.5.2 Routine Checking

Routine checking is a total process of accounting control, which includes the following:

1. Examination of the totalling and balancing of the books of prime entry
2. Examination of the posting from the primary books to the ledger accounts
3. Examination of totalling and balancing of the ledger accounts and of the trial balance prepared with those balances
4. Overall examination of writing up the transactions properly

In short, the routine checking is concerned with ascertaining the arithmetical accuracy of casting, posting and carry forwards. For the purpose of confirming the arithmetical accuracy and detecting frauds and errors of very simple nature, this method is adopted as basic to all types of audit work. The scope of application of routine checking depends upon the nature and size of the organisation as well as the effectiveness of the internal check and control system.

Objectives

Objectives of routine checking can be described as follows:

1. To ensure the arithmetical accuracy of the books of accounts
2. To form the basis of vouching

3. To prevent alteration of figures
4. To increase reliability of financial statements
5. To detect errors and frauds

Advantages

1. It is the simplest form of audit work.
2. Errors and frauds of simple nature can be detected very easily.
3. The books of accounts can be thoroughly checked.
4. It is the basis of checking the final account as it helps in checking castings and postings.
5. Arithmetical accuracy of all the transactions can be confirmed by this method.
6. It offers an opportunity to train the new entrants to the profession.

Disadvantages

1. It is not generally considered as an important part of audit work where self-balancing system is maintained.
2. As the audit staff are engaged in same type of work the possibility of becoming monotonous may grow in this system.
3. Negligence of work, taking the advantage of internal check system, are frequent.
4. It fails to detect errors and frauds arising from the fraudulent manipulation in accounting principles.

Auditor's duty regarding routine checking

Although routine checking is a monotonous and time consuming process and is not very effective in detecting planned fraud, the auditor cannot skip it. It is an important part of audit. It should deserve equal emphasis from auditor as other techniques of audit. His duties in connection with routine checking are as follows:

1. The auditor will first evaluate the internal control and internal check system existing in the organisation. Based upon his evaluation, he will determine the extent of routine checking to be adopted.
2. In a small firm it is possible for the auditor to undertake thorough routine checking. So, it is advisable that he should undertake thorough routine checking in such cases.
3. In case of audit of large organisations, it is not possible for him to undertake thorough routine checking. So, in such cases, he will apply his judgment, experience and knowledge in determining the extent of routine checking.
4. The auditor should frequently supervise the work of routine checking being done by his subordinates and ensure the adherence to his instructions in this regard.
5. Computerisation of accounting system obviates the necessity of casting carry forward, posting from journal to ledger etc. So, the auditor will determine his duty after examining the degree of computerisation.

3.5.3 Test Checking

The term 'test checking' stands for the method of auditing, where instead of a complete examination of all the transactions recorded in the books of accounts only some of the transactions are selected and verified. The underlying intention is to test some of the transactions to form an opinion for the whole. According to Prof. Meig "test checking means to select and examine a representative sample from a large number of similar items".

The justification of test checking lies on the theory of probability which states in effect that a sample selected from a series of items will tend to show the same characteristics present in the full series of items, which is commonly referred to as "population" or "universe".

Objectives of test checking

Accounts of large organisations usually include an enormous number of transactions. But the auditor is not in a position to check each and every transaction within the limited time and due to the constraint of resources available to him. So, he has to depend on selective verification of the transactions. The selection of transactions will be made in such a way that the auditor will verify a small but representative number of transactions and he can draw conclusions about the transactions as a whole. So, the basic objective of test checking is to draw a valid conclusion by undertaking examination of some transactions from the large number of transactions and thereby save time and cost.

Factors to be considered before resorting to test checking

The auditor should consider the following factors before starting test checking.

1. ***Nature of transactions*** The nature of transactions should be carefully considered for determining the extent of test checking. If the transactions of a particular category are of repetitive nature, the size of sample may be small. However, if the transactions of a particular category are of divergent nature, sample size of test checking should be large.

2. ***Effectiveness of internal control*** The internal control system existing in the organisation should be evaluated. If the internal control system is found to be sound, the auditor may adopt test checking determining the suitable sample size. But if the internal control system is found ineffective, the reliance on test checking should be minimum.

3. ***Materiality of items*** An item becomes material when any mis-statement regarding it is likely to influence the decisions of the users of financial statements. The extent of checking to be adopted should depend upon the materiality of the items.

4. ***Previous experience*** Previous experience should also be considered while determining the extent of test checking. For example, the auditor might have noticed in the last audit that the management had the tendency to inflate the value of work-in-progress, but the cashier had honestly and sincerely recorded all the cash transactions. Based on this experience, the auditor may undertake exhaustive checking of the details of valuation of work-in-progress while restricting his checking to few transactions in the cashbook.

Advantages

1. It is one of the best techniques of auditing through which cost of audit can be reduced.
2. It can ensure the speed of audit work.
3. It can easily locate the deficient areas and thus help to come to the conclusion as to the acceptability of financial records.
4. It is a labour saving device.
5. It acts as a guide to the auditor to arrive at a conclusion regarding the true and fair view of the state of affairs of the business.

Disadvantages

1. It will prove inefficient where internal check and control system are not operating or found ineffective.
2. It is not suitable for small concerns.
3. It will show incorrect results if the samples are not proper representatives of the population.
4. It does not offer any consistency in selecting the percentage of check that will be adopted by all concerns.
5. It is not applicable in case of diversified transactions.

Precautions to be taken before taking test-checking technique

In order to apply test checking technique effectively in the audit work of an organisation, an auditor has to take certain precautionary measures. These measures include the following:

1. The auditor should review the existing internal control in order to ascertain its effectiveness.
2. The transactions to be selected for test checking must be homogenous.
3. The transactions to be test checked must form an adequate sample.
4. As far as possible the transactions to be selected for test checking should be on the basis of random number tables.
5. The results of the test checks themselves should be examined, particularly the nature of errors.

Transactions not suitable for the adoption of test checking

If the number of transactions in any area is sufficiently large, the auditors usually adopt test-check technique. However, as a practical measure, usually the following types of transactions and records are kept outside the purview of test checking :

1. In those industries, where the activities are based on seasonal fluctuations, test checking cannot be adopted on an annual basis.
2. Exceptional transactions or the transactions of a non-recurring nature are also not suitable for adoption of test checking.
3. Some transactions have legal implication, i.e. they have to be recorded on the basis of legal provisions. Such transactions cannot be test checked.
4. Areas involving computation and calculations should not be subjected to test checking.
5. There should not be test checking for opening as well as closing entries.
6. Bank reconciliation statement cannot be checked by adopting this technique.
7. Presentation and disclosure of information in the balance sheet and the profit and loss account should not be subjected to test checking.

Auditor's duty regarding test checking

Test checking is a short-cut method of audit. It curtails costs and time of audit. But it involves risk on the part of the auditor. If some errors or frauds which escaped the notice of the auditor because of sample checking are detected subsequently, the auditor may be held liable for negligence. So, enough care and caution should be taken by the auditor while resorting to test checking. He must evaluate the internal control system existing in the organisation beforehand. He must carefully consider the circumstances for determining the sample size. Materiality of item must not escape his notice while he selects the sample. The items selected should be verified in depth from its origin to the conclusion. Test checking will then be effective. There will be minimum possibility of errors and frauds remaining undetected if the auditor exercises reasonable care according to circumstances in conducting test checking.

He must bear in mind that test checking is just like a double-edged sword. If it is used properly and with reasonable care and caution, it will not hurt the auditor, i.e. the auditor will not be held responsible for any error or fraud left undetected. However, if the tool is applied indiscriminately and negligently, he will not be spared for errors and frauds detected subsequently.

3.5.4 Auditing in Depth

Auditing in depth is a technique, which assists the auditor in conducting test checking and adoption of such a system becomes essential in large organisations, where detailed examination of all the records is not possible. It is a method of auditing under which a few selective transactions are subjected to a thorough scrutiny for arriving at the accuracy of the data.

This technique involves the selection of a sample of transactions from one area of accounting and tracing them from the beginning to the conclusion. This method is undertaken to examine the effectiveness of the internal control and internal check system. In order to conduct the work of auditing in depth of a specific transaction, the auditor has to examine thoroughly the different stages of the transaction.

Practical application of the technique

In respect of goods purchased, the auditing in depth technique will be applied through the following stages.

1. Examining the requisition note from the stores, ensuring that it has been signed by the appropriate official
2. Examining the copy of the order placed by the purchasing department, ensuring that it was properly executed on the official form, complied with all the client's regulations and was authorised by the appropriate official
3. Examining the delivery note from the supplier and comparing it with the copy of the order
4. Examining the goods inward note made out when the goods were received, noting if it has been properly signed, if it indicates that the correct goods have been received and if their quantity and condition have been checked
5. Checking the entries in the store records
6. Checking in the accounts department that the invoice received from the supplier has been matched with the copy of the order and the copy of the goods received note before being processed and that the calculations have been checked
7. Checking the appropriate entries in the accounting records
8. Comparing the cheque with the invoice and supplier's statement, if any

From the above example, it can be seen that the auditor would trace the transaction right through the system. He would not merely satisfy himself that the entries in the records were correct, but would ensure that the appropriate internal controls relating to authorisation of transactions, the checking of one document against another and physical inspection of goods has been properly operated at the appropriate times. He would also ensure that a proper system was in force to claim credits in respect of short deliveries or deliveries of defective goods.

Where the examination of successive stages in the depth test produces satisfactory results, it is an accepted practice that the auditor may progressively reduce the number of items to be examined at subsequent stages. However, if the tests reveal an unacceptable number of errors, it will be necessary for the auditor to increase the number of items examined in order to discover whether the original sample was representative.

Advantages

1. Precision in course of audit work can be achieved.
2. It guards against the fraudulent manipulation of accounts.
3. It does not offer any monotony in work to the auditor. Because the auditor will have to deal all the time with new ideas and techniques.
4. It saves the cost of audit.
5. The experience in auditing in depth can be widely used in preparing audit plan.

Disadvantages

1. As the concept is linked with selective verification, its application may be fruitless if the selection of item is wrong.
2. Instead of saving cost and time, this technique entails loss of time and extra cost because of unskilled handling of audit affairs.
3. Proper selection of transactions for conducting auditing in depth is too much risky. If the items are not properly selected, it will not at all serve the purpose of auditing.
4. This technique can not be applied to small concerns.
5. It has been observed that the auditor relies too heavily upon intuition. Here, he uses no objective method of measuring the adequacy of samples.

3.5.5 Cut-off Examination

Cut-off examinations are the procedures designed to ensure that at the year end trading transactions are entered in the period to which they relate. In other words, the term "cut-off" refers to the procedure adopted to ensure the separation of transactions as at the end of one accounting year from those at the commencement of the next following year, specially for items which may overlap, e.g. sales, purchase, stock etc.

Significance of cut-off in auditing

The cut-off procedure is very significant in auditing to ensure that the revenue and expenditure of one year is not recorded in the following year, as that will distort the true and fair view of the accounts. The auditor must either establish that there are satisfactory internal controls in respect of cut-off and carry out compliance tests to ensure that these controls are functioning properly or carry out appropriate substantive tests. An obvious way in which accounts can be manipulated is for purchase invoices in respect of goods purchased shortly before the year end to be held over and entered in the following accounting period. The goods will be included in stock, but the purchases will not be included in the accounts as either a liability or a charge. Similarly, the profits and assets can be inflated by including goods that have been sold, but not yet despatched, in both stock and sales. Tests should be carried out between the purchase invoices, goods inward records and store records on the one hand, and the sales invoices, goods outward records and store records on the other, to ensure that there is consistency in treatment.

Cut-off manipulation was an important feature in which the auditors of Thomas Gerrard & Son Ltd. (1967) were held to have been negligent. The auditors' negligence arose primarily from their failure to follow up the alterations of the purchase invoices.

3.5.6 Statistical Sampling

Auditors have long considered it sufficient in given circumstances not to check all the items within any section of the work, but to test them to satisfy themselves whether they may consider the whole group as being satisfactory for their purposes. This is based upon the assumption that, subject to special circumstances such as beginning or end of period test, the number of samples tested are sufficiently indicative of the accuracy or otherwise of the whole group.

The use of this method in practice does not require a detailed mathematical or statistical knowledge of the formulae on which the actual tests are based. Sets of tables are available which, on having decided the degree of confidence, the auditor wishes to place in the result and the accuracy he desires he can consult, and the amount of the tests to be carried out is specified.

Procedures for application of statistical sampling

When statistical sampling is to be applied to a certain section of the audit, the procedure to be undertaken is as follows:

1. The nature of the unit and the field of population should be carefully defined, as any indefinite items wrongly included will vitiate the usefulness of the test.
2. The precise nature of the attributes to be tested should be defined, such as errors or authentication signatures, or if the sample is in respect of variables the data must be examined to determine the basic figures to be applied.
3. The population should be broadly examined to ascertain whether any stratification will be necessary.
4. The level of confidence and precision limits should be fixed in accordance with the auditor's judgement.
5. In accordance with the auditor's judgement as mentioned earlier, the sampling tables should be consulted giving the sample size in the case of attributes; where variables are concerned, a preliminary sample may be necessary.
6. Random digit tables should be consulted showing the items to be selected for examination.
7. The test should be evaluated comparing the result obtained with the predetermined acceptance or rejection levels.

8. Where the sample is accepted, the auditor must ensure that the results are properly recorded so that if he is called upon to prove that he has applied due care, skill and diligence to the work, he may be able to show his confidence to have been rightly placed.

3.5.7 Surprise Checking

'Surprise checking' means audit verification on a non-routine and surprise basis. Usually the routine checking plan of the auditor as well as its timing is known to the client. As a result, the client's staff try to cover up incompleteness in the books and records before the visit by the auditor. However, surprise check, as a part of normal audit procedure, significantly enhances the effectiveness of an audit. For carrying out surprise check, the auditor visits the client's office without prior intimation and verifies certain specific matters, the regularity of which is vital for audit. For example, the correctness of cash balance in hand is immensely important because of the nature of this asset. It is the general experience that irregularities and fraud are facilitated when books and records are not maintained systematically and regularly. Many important frauds and errors that are not detected from continuous check may be detected through the process of surprise checking.

Purposes of surprise checking

In any area of audit verification, the process of surprise checking is applicable. However, following are the specific areas, where the process of surprise checking can be effectively applied :

1. For the verification of books of accounts and records, which are maintained in the branch offices
2. For the verification of cash, stock and similar type of assets, which are kept at other places
3. For checking of cash balance on a non-routine basis
4. For checking of investments on a non-routine basis
5. For the verification of the regularity of the maintenance of books of accounts, statutory registers and other important documents
6. For the physical verification of stock and stores on a non-routine basis
7. For verification of the operation of any specific internal control procedures

3.5.8 Audit Flow Chart

A graphical presentation of different stages of a document, flow of goods or cash, with the aid of various symbolic marks, for the purpose of operation and control of audit organisation may be termed as 'audit flow chart'. In other words, it can be described as a map of inter-related operations.

It is arranged specially for indicating the sequence and also the types of operation as a part of total unit. Narrative description is replaced by the use of different symbols. The symbols are standardised in a greater way and the different interconnecting lines indicate the flow direction which is either horizontal or vertical. The reason for the adoption of this chart is due to its advantages of making easy to visualise the relationship between different parts of the integrated system of the organisation. The need for proper study and evaluation of internal control system has long been felt. The efficient preparation and introduction of the flow chart on a wide basis may fulfil the necessity.

Advantages

1. It acts as an effective tool to study internal control system of the organisation. Thus the weaknesses in the internal controls may be revealed by the examination of the flow chart.
2. Identification and location of various responsibility areas of the organisation can be made possible from this chart.
3. It gives a bird's eye view on the happenings of the business operations and areas where more control needs to be emphasised.
4. It can depict a situation relating to accounting and auditing system in a concise and simple way.
5. It is an important tool through which the training of audit staffs can be facilitated.
6. This chart can be introduced by the audit managers as a control device for their audit operation.

Disadvantages

1. It consumes time in preparing this chart.
2. It is not possible to have same pattern of flow chart that will be suitable to all types of organisations.
3. It is not possible to accumulate in a flow chart all the activities or operations of an organisation in all cases.
4. It is very difficult to form a judgement in selecting the level of sub-division that may give proper reflection of actual position.

3.5.9 Internal Control Questionnaires

Internal control questionnaires now form an important part of any efficiently conducted audit. By their use, any system of internal control may be investigated and its weaknesses revealed. It is usual to have sets of standardised questionnaires which may be applied, subject to modification on any type of audit.

The procedure employed is to use the standard questionnaire relevant to the various sections of a concern on the first occasion. These are completed by staff on the job and are thereafter examined by the manager in charge. Points of lesser importance may be dealt with and questions inapplicable to the job eliminated. In conjunction with the questionnaire an audit programme for the job may be prepared. This does not signify that the audit cannot be commenced until the questionnaire has been dealt with or a standard form of programme will have been already in use.

Such questionnaires have already been proved to save much time in audit planning and do much to ensure that no aspect of the work is overlooked from the point of view of the audit. On the first occasion a greater amount of work will be involved than on subsequent audits, as it is necessary to investigate the whole system of control; thereafter checks may be made to ensure that the system is being adhered to. Where changes in the system are deemed necessary, the auditor should request modification, but in any case he should be able to discover any such alterations, and no doubt the questionnaire should be updated from time to time.

3.5.10 Audit Tests

Audit tests are of two types:

- Compliance test
- Substantive test

Compliance test

A compliance test is a test which seeks to provide audit evidence that internal control procedures are being applied as prescribed.

Examples

(a) Checking for authorisation on a credit note. This should confirm that all credit notes are suitably authorised before being issued.

(b) Checking for the casting stamp on a purchase invoice. This should confirm that all invoices are cast before being paid.

Substantive test

A substantive test is a test of a transaction or balance which seeks to provide audit evidence as to the completeness, accuracy and validity of the information contained in the accounting records or financial statements.

Examples

(a) Circularisation of letters to debtors to confirm the accuracy of the balance on the sales ledger.

(b) Matching a purchase invoice with the original order and goods received note to confirm that the purchase is bonafide.

POINTS TO PONDER

- The auditor should follow the appropriate audit procedure and adopt different techniques of auditing. On the basis of his assessment of the accounting system and evaluation of the internal controls, the auditor will draw up an audit programme specially designed for that particular audit.
- For effective audit planning and for designing appropriate audit programme, the auditor should prepare himself before the commencement of his audit work. For this purpose, he should take a number of preparatory steps.
- Audit planning is the process of deciding in advance what is to be done, who should do it, how it should be done and when it should be done by the auditor in order to have effective and efficient completion of audit.
- Audit programme is a detailed plan of work, prepared by the auditor for carrying out an audit. It comprises a set of techniques and procedures, which the auditor plans to apply to the given audit for forming an opinion about the statement of accounts of an organisation. Audit programme can be of two types: predetermined audit programmne and progressive audit programme.
- Audit note book is a bound book in which a large variety of matters observed during the course of audit are recorded. It is of great value to the auditor at the time of preparing the

audit report. In case a charge of negligence is filed against the auditor, a note book may prove to be good evidence.

- Audit working papers kept by the auditor are the written records of the evidence accumulated during the course of audit. As the working papers are prepared in respect of the client's business, they should be treated as top secret and should be preserved carefully.
- Audit file maintains different audit documents. Audit file is generally of two types: permanent audit file and temporary audit file.
- Audit manual is a written internal document, which provides different information regarding detailed auditing procedure. It is prepared for the general guidance of the auditors with the object of planning the procedure of audit.
- An audit memorandum is a statement containing all useful information regarding the business of the client. It indicates the method of operation, policies of different aspects of the business as well as the conditions in respect of audit.
- Principles of auditing refer to fundamental consideration that sustain the function of auditing and direct its activities. On the other hand, auditing techniques refer to the methods and means adopted by an auditor for collection and evaluation of audit evidence in different auditing situations. Audit techniques may vary from organisation to organisation depending upon the nature of the business, but the principles of auditing will remain the same irrespective of the nature of the organisation.
- The techniques, which are followed in order to collect proper evidence in support of the transactions recorded in the books of accounts, are termed as the techniques of auditing.
- Important techniques usually adopted by the auditors include vouching, physical verification, reconciliation, confirmation, re-computation, scanning, scrutiny and inquiry.
- The term 'evidence' includes all influences on the mind of an auditor, which affect his judgement about the truthfulness of the propositions submitted to him for review. Methods of obtaining audit evidence include inspection, observation, inquiry and confirmation, re-computation and analytical review.
- Routine checking is concerned with ascertaining the arithmetical accuracy of casting, posting and carry forwards. It is an important part of audit and deserves equal emphasis from the auditor as do other techniques of audit.
- Test checking is a method of auditing, where instead of examination of all the transactions recorded in the books only some of the transactions are selected and verified. Its basic objective is to draw a valid conclusion by undertaking examination of some transactions from the large number of transactions and thereby save both time and cost.
- Auditing in depth is a technique, which assists the auditor in conducting test checking. In this technique, a few selective transactions are subjected to a thorough scrutiny for arriving at the accuracy of the data.
- Cut-off examination refers to the procedure adopted to ensure the separation of transactions as at the end of one accounting year from those at the commencement of the following year, especially for those items which may overlap.
- Surprise checking means audit verification on a non-routine and surprise basis. Many important frauds and errors that are not detected from continuous check may be detected through the process of surprise checking.

- Audit flow chart can be described as a map of inter-related operations. It makes easier to visualise the relationship between different parts of the integrated system of an organisation.
- Internal control questionnaires form an important part of an efficiently conducted audit. Such questionnaires save much time in audit planning and do much to ensure that no aspect of the work is overlooked from the viewpoint of audit.
- Audit tests are of two types: compliance test and substantive test. A compliance test is a test which seeks to provide audit evidence that internal control procedures are being applied as prescribed. On the other hand, a substantive test is a test of a transaction or balance which seeks to provide audit evidence as to the completeness, accuracy and validity of the information contained in the accounting records or financial statements.

REVIEW QUESTIONS

Short-answer Questions

1. Test checking is based on presumption. What is that presumption?
2. What is audit memorandum?
3. What is audit manual?
4. Discuss the importance of surprise check.
5. Distinguish between principles of auditing and techniques of auditing.

Essay-type Questions

1. What are the considerations to be kept in mind by an auditor before commencement of an audit?
2. What is audit programme? Discuss the advantages and disadvantages of conducting an audit according to a predetermined audit programme. How can these disadvantages be overcome?
3. How is an audit programme prepared? State the objectives of audit programme. What are the steps to be followed in drawing an audit programme?
4. What are audit files? What are the contents of audit files? What are the advantages of audit files?
5. What is an audit note book? What purpose does it serve ? What are the contents of an audit note book?
6. What are audit working papers? What are its objectives? Discuss the essential characteristics of a good working paper. Who can claim the ownership of those papers?
7. What is routine checking? What types of work are included in routine checking? What are the objectives of routine checking? Describe the advantages and disadvantages of routine checking. Discuss the duties of an auditor in this regard.
8. What is test checking? In what circumstances test checking factors are to be considered before resorting to test checking? What are the advantages and disadvantages of test checking? Discuss the duty of an auditor in this regard.

9. What is auditing in depth? Discuss the advantages and disadvantages of this audit technique.
10. Discuss briefly the methods of obtaining audit evidence. In this context, state what do you mean by 'compliance test' and 'substantive test'.
11. What do you mean by techniques of auditing? Discuss the various techniques adopted by an auditor in the course of his audit work.

CHAPTER 4

Internal Control, Internal Check and Internal Audit

CHAPTER OUTLINE

4.1 INTRODUCTION

An auditor must ensure that he fully understands the enterprise with which he is dealing before he determines his basic approach to an audit. He must familiarise himself with its organisation and comprehend the nature of the business. He must also ensure that he has thoroughly grasped any technicalities peculiar to the business. Only then will he be in a position to comprehend and identify the transactions which are being recorded in the accounting records and in relation to which the internal controls will be operating.

Formerly, business systems were usually installed with the object of getting work done by the cheapest and quickest methods available, but whilst these objects have not been lost sight of, it has been realised that establishment of the piecemeal methods of uncoordinated work process is ultimately neither cheap nor efficient. Overall planning is necessary to establish a flow of work through the whole business, enabling it to run smoothly and efficiently and with the added requirement that its assets shall be safeguarded at the same time.

This overall planning and its practical operation is included under the title of internal control which is established by the management. Although the auditor in his role as an auditor has no right to practice any particular method of control to be operated, he is virtually concerned with it, as the efficiency or otherwise of the internal control will greatly influence the auditor's method of working.

4.2 INTERNAL CONTROL

4.2.1 Definition

Internal control refers to the various methods and procedures adopted for the control of production, distribution and the whole system (financial and non-financial) of the enterprise.

In other words, internal control system—the whole system of controls, financial or otherwise, established by the management in order to carry on the business of the enterprise in an orderly and efficient manner— ensures adherence to management policies, safeguards the assets and secures as far as possible the completeness and accuracy of the records.

The special report on internal control of the American Institute of the Certified Public Accountants and its statements on auditing procedures contain the following definition of internal control: "Internal control comprises the plan of organisation and all the coordinated methods and measures adopted within a business to safeguard its assets, check the accuracy and reliability of its accounting data, promote operations efficiency and encourage employees to follow prescribed managerial policies."

In the opinion of W. W. Bigg, "internal control is best regarded as indicating the whole system of controls, financial or otherwise, established by the management in the conduct of a business including internal check, internal audit and other forms of control."

So, on the basis of above definitions, it may be stated that a system of internal control provides a measure for the management to obtain information, protection and control which are quite important for the successful working of a business organisation.

4.2.2 Basic Elements of Internal Control

An effective system of internal control should have the following basic elements:

1. ***Financial and other organisational plans*** This may take the form of a manual suitably classified by flow charts. It should specify the various duties and responsibilities of both management and staff, stating the powers of authorisation that reside with various members. This is important as in the event of staff absence or otherwise the correct flow of work and the internal control system could be vitiated by the wrong implementation of procedures by staff either innocently or willfully.

2. ***Competent personnel*** Personnel are the most important element of any internal control system. If the employees are competent and efficient in their assigned work, internal control system can be operated effectively even if some of the other elements of internal control system are absent.

3. ***Division of work*** This refers to the procedure of division of work properly among the employees of the organisation. Each and every work of the organisation should be divided in different stages and should be allocated to the employees in accordance with quality and skill.

4. ***Separation of operational responsibility from record keeping*** If each department of an organisation is being assigned to prepare its own records and reports, there may be a tendency to manipulate results for showing better performance. So, in order to ensure reliable records and information, record-keeping function is separated from the operational responsibility of the concerned department.

5. ***Separation of the custody of assets from accounting*** To protect against misuse of assets and their misappropriation, it is required that the custody of assets and their accounting should be done by separate persons. When a particular person performs both the functions, there is a chance of utilising the organisation's assets for his personal interest and adjusting the records to relieve himself from the responsibility of the asset.

6. ***Authorisation*** Under the internal control system, all the activities must be authorised by a proper authority. The individual or group which can grant either specific or general authority for transactions should hold a position commensurate with the nature and significance of the transactions and the policy for such authority should be established by top management.

7. ***Managerial supervision and review*** The internal control system should be implemented and maintained in conformity with the environmental changes of the concern. By adapting any specific control system permanently, the extent to which the procedures of flexible controls have been followed in real practice should be observed and re-examined.

4.2.3 Objectives of Internal Control

Internal control is of fundamental importance to the auditor, because before he can plan the tests he intends to carry out in his audit programme, he must decide the extent to which he intends to rely on the system of internal control. But before depending upon the internal control system of the organisation, the auditor should ensure himself that the following objectives of internal control as per AAS-6 is achieved by the organisation:

Proper authorisation Transactions are executed with management's general and specific authorisation.

Prompt recording of transactions All the transactions are promptly recorded in the correct amount in the appropriate accounts and in the accounting period in which they are executed so as to permit preparation of financial information within a framework of recognised accounting policies and to maintain accountability of assets.

Restricted access to assets Access to assets is permitted only in accordance with management's authorisation.

Actions against deviations The recorded accountability for assets is compared with the existing assets at reasonable intervals and appropriate action is taken with regard to any differences.

4.2.4 Types of Internal Control

Internal control can be categorised as follows:

1. Organisational

An enterprise should have a plan of organisation which should (a) define and allocate responsibilities (every function should be in the charge of a specified person who might be called the responsible official) and (b) identify lines of reporting.

In all cases, the delegation of authority and responsibility should be clearly specified. An employee should always know the precise powers delegated to him, the extent of his authority and to whom he should report.

2. By segregation of duties

(a) No one person should be responsible for the recording and processing of a complete transaction.

(b) The involvement of several people reduces the risk of intentional manipulation or accidental error and increases the element of checking of work.

(c) Functions for a given transaction which should be separated include initiation, authorisation, execution, custody and recording.

3. Physical

(a) This concerns physical custody of assets and involves procedures designed to limit access to authorised personnel only.

(b) Access can be direct or indirect.

(c) These controls are especially important in case of valuable, portable, exchangeable or desirable assets.

4. By authorisation and approval

All transactions should require authorisation or approval by an appropriate person. The limits to these authorisations should be specified. For example, all credit sales must be approved by the credit control department or all overtime must be authorised by the works manager.

5. Arithmetical and accounting

(a) These are the controls in the recording function which check that the transactions have been authorised, that they are all included and that they are correctly recorded and accurately processed.

(b) Procedures include checking the arithmetical accuracy of the records, maintenance and checking of totals, reconciliation, control accounts, trial balances, accounting for documents and preview. Preview refers to the procedure in which before an important action involving the company's property is taken, the person concerned should review the documents available to see that all that should have been done has been done.

6. By personnel

(a) Procedures should be designed to ensure that the personnel operating a system are competent and motivated to carry out the tasks assigned to them, as the proper functioning of a system depends upon the competence and integrity of the operating personnel.

(b) Measures include appropriate remuneration, promotion and career development prospects, selection of people with appropriate personal characteristics and training and assignment of tasks to the right level.

7. By supervision

All actions by all levels of staff should be supervised. The responsibility for supervision should be clearly laid down and communicated to the person being supervised.

8. By management

(a) These are controls, exercised by management, which are outside and over and above the day-to-day routine of the system.

(b) They include overall supervisory controls, review of management accounts, comparison with budgets, internal audit and any other special review procedures.

Advantages

The various advantages that may be derived from internal control system are summarised as follows:

1. ***Identification of defects*** Under internal control system, the total activities are segregated in such a way that the work preformed by one employee is automatically checked by another employee. So, if there is any defect in the system, it is easily detected.

2. ***Flexibility*** In this system, year-wise comparative analysis is done. So, if there is any change in the mode of operation, the changes in the system can easily be accommodated. Therefore, the opportunity for flexibility is available.

3. ***Time savings*** If the internal control system is in operation in an organisation, there is no need for the preparation of separate audit programmes for each and every audit engagement. Thus it saves time to a great extent.

4. ***Lesser risk of omission*** Under this system, the total work is sub-divided into a number of activities and each employee is assigned with a particular type of activity. So, there is least chance of oversight or omission of any matter.

5. *Provision for training facility* Due to lack of adequate experience, the auditor may face difficulty in establishing a close relationship between audit programme and the internal control system. This system itself provides training facilities to auditors to overcome this difficulty.

Disadvantages

It is also important to appreciate the following inherent limitations of internal control system:

1. *Chances of human error* The possibility of human error due to carelessness, mistakes of judgment or the misunderstanding of instructions may make the system ineffective.

2. *Cost* Management's usual requirement is that a control procedure should be cost-effective. But in many cases, the cost of internal control procedure will not be proportionate to the potential loss due to fraud and error.

3. *Ignorance of unusual activity* It is a fact that most of the internal control techniques are directed towards anticipated types of transactions and not on unusual transactions.

4. *Collusion* There may be the possibility of circumvention of controls through collusion with parties outside the entity or with employees of the entity.

5. *Abuse of responsibility* It may happen that a person responsible for exercising control abuses his responsibility.

6. *Rigidity* There is the possibility that the system may become inadequate due to changes in the conditions, and compliance with procedures may deteriorate.

4.2.5 Evaluation of Internal Control

Evaluation of internal controls is fundamental to an audit. It is on the basis of this evaluation that the auditor will do the following:

- Determine the nature and extent of his audit procedure, i.e. draw up his audit programme.
- Draft letters of weaknesses, to draw the attention of the management to inform them about the weaknesses of the system.

Because of its importance, evaluation must be clearly distinguished from the process of ascertaining and recording the system.

Before taking up the work of audit in an organisation, the auditor should ascertain the authenticity of the internal control system existing in the organisation. He should evaluate the control system in order to determine whether he would depend on the internal control system or not and if so, to what extent he would depend on it.

The auditor himself should determine the process or procedure applying his own knowledge and judgment in the context of nature and size of the organisation under audit.

The auditor, while evaluating the system of internal control, should consider the following matters.

- Whether the basic principles of internal control, which is prevailing in the organisation have been properly followed.

- Whether the procedures which are stated from theoretical point of view have been properly implemented.
- After definite interval of time, whether any changes are made in the system of internal control in the context of changed circumstances of the organisation.

On the basis of evaluation on the effectiveness of the internal audit system, the external auditor will decide the extent or degree of his reliance on the functioning of the internal audit system.

4.2.6 Internal Control and the Auditor

The Institute of Chartered Accountants of India in its Statement of Standard Auditing Practices (AAS-6) has stated the following.

"The duty of safeguarding the assets of a company is primarily that of the management and the auditor is entitled to rely upon the safeguards and internal controls instituted by the management, although he will of course take into account any deficiencies he may find therein, while drafting his programme."

So far as the auditor is concerned, the examination and evaluation of internal control system is an indispensable part of the overall audit programme. The auditor needs reasonable assurance that the accounting system is adequate and that all the accounting information, which should be recorded, has in fact been recorded. Internal control normally contributes to such assurance. The auditor should gain an understanding of the accounting system and related internal controls and should study and evaluate the operations of these internal controls upon which he wishes to rely in determining the nature, timing and extent of other audit procedures.

He can formulate his entire audit programme only after he has had a satisfactory understanding of the internal control systems and their actual operations. According to the American Institute of Certified Public Accountants, the auditor is required to make a proper review of the existing internal control and on the basis of such a review, the auditor should determine the resultant extent of the tests to which auditing procedures are to be restricted.

A proper understanding of the internal control system in its control and working also enable an auditor to decide upon the appropriate audit procedure to be applied in different areas that are covered in the audit programme. In a situation, where the internal controls are considered weak in some areas, the auditor might choose an audit procedure on test that otherwise might not be required; he might extend certain tests to cover a large number of transactions or other items than he otherwise would examine and at times he may perform additional tests for his satisfaction.

From the above, it can be concluded that the extent and nature of the audit programme is substantially influenced by the internal control system in operation. In deciding upon a plan of selective checking, the existence and operation of internal control system is of great significance.

4.2.7 Internal Control in Specific Areas of Business

This section is divided into the areas of activity usually found in a business. At the beginning of each area are stated the objectives of internal control in the area and some measures which will achieve the objectives then follow.

1. Internal control in general

Objectives To carry on the business in an orderly and efficient manner, to ensure adherence to management policies, safeguard its assets, and secure the accuracy and reliability of the records.

Measures

- An appropriate and integrated system of accounts and records
- Internal controls over those accounts and record
- Financial supervision and control by management, including budgetary control, management accounting reports, and interim accounts
- Safeguarding and, if necessary, duplicating records
- Engaging, training, allocating duties to specific staff who are capable of fulfilling their responsibilities, rotation of duties and cover for absences

2. Cash sales and collections

Objectives

- To ensure that all cash, to which the enterprise is entitled, is received
- To ensure that all such cash is properly accounted for and entered in the records
- To ensure that all such cash is deposited promptly and is intact

Measures

- Prescribing and limiting the number of persons who are authorised to receive cash, e.g., sales assistants, cashiers, etc.
- Establishing a means of evidencing cash receipts, e.g., pre-numbered duplicate receipt forms, cash registers with sealed till rolls; the duplicate receipt books should be securely held and issue controlled
- Ensuring that customers are aware that they must receive a receipt form or ensuring that the amount rung up on the cash register is clearly visible to the customer
- Appointment of officers with responsibility for emptying cash registers at prescribed intervals, and agreeing the amount present with till roll totals or internal registers. Such collections should be evidenced in writing and be initialed by the assistant and the supervisor
- Immediate and intact banking; payments should be made from funds drawn from the bank on an imprest system
- Investigation of shortage and excesses
- Independent comparison of agreed till roll totals with subsequent banking records
- Rotation of duties and cover for holidays (which should be compulsory) and sickness
- Collections by salesmen should be deposited in the bank promptly every day. There should be independent comparison of the amounts deposited with records of the salesmen
- Persons handling cash should not have access to other cash funds or to sales ledger records

3. Payment into bank

Objectives

- To ensure that all cash and cheques received is deposited in the bank promptly
- To ensure that all cash and cheques received are deposited without delay at prescribed intervals, preferably daily
- To ensure that all cash and cheques received are accounted for and recorded accordingly

Measures

- Cash and cheques should be intact
- Cash and cheques should be banked without delay
- The bank paying-in-slip should be prepared by an official with no access to cash collection points or bought or sales ledger
- Banking should be made with security in mind, e.g. for large cash deposits, security guards should be used
- There should be independent comparison of paying-in-slips with collection records, post lists and sales ledger records

4. Cash balances

Objectives

- To prevent misappropriation of cash
- To prevent unauthorised cash payments

Measures

- Establishment of cash floats of specified amounts and locations
- Appointment of officials responsible for each cash transaction
- Arrangement of security measures including use of safes and restriction of access
- Use of imprest system with rules on reimbursement only against authorised vouchers
- Strict rules on the authorising of cash payments
- Independent cash counts on a regular and a surprise basis
- Insurance arrangements, e.g. for cash balances and fidelity guarantee
- Special rules for IOUs. Preferably these should not be permitted

5. Cheque payments

Objective

To prevent unauthorised payments being made from bank accounts

Measures

- Control over custody and issue of unused cheque books. A register should be maintained if necessary
- Appointment of an official to be responsible for the preparation of cheques or traders credits

- Rules should be established for the presentation of supporting documents before cheques can be made. Such supporting documents may include goods receipt notes, orders, and invoices etc.
- All such documents should be stamped 'paid by cheque no..........' with date
- All cheques should be signed by at least two persons, with no person being permitted to sign if he is a payee
- No cheques should be made bearer cheques except for the collection of wages or reimbursement of cash funds
- All cheques should be strictly crossed
- The signing of blank cheques must be prohibited
- Special rules for authorising and checking direct debits and standing orders must be followed
- Separating the duties of custody, recording and initiation of cheque payments

6. Purchases and trade creditors

Objectives

- To ensure that goods and services are ordered only in the required quantity and quality and at the best terms available after appropriate requisition and approval
- To ensure that goods and services received are inspected and only acceptable items are accepted
- To ensure that all invoices are checked against authorised orders and receipts of the subject matter in good condition
- To ensure that all goods and services invoiced are properly recorded in the books

Measures

- There should be procedures for the requisitioning of goods and services only by specified personnel on specified forms with space for acknowledgement of performance.
- Order forms should be pre-numbered and kept in safe custody. Issue of blank order form books should be controlled and recorded.
- All goods received should be recorded on goods receipt notes or in a special book.
- All goods should be inspected for proper condition and agreement with order and counted on receipt. The inspection should be acknowledged.
- A listing of unfulfilled orders should be made and investigated at intervals.
- Invoices should be checked for arithmetical accuracy, pricing, correct treatment of VAT, trade discount and agreement with order.
- Total of entries in the invoice register or day book should be regularly checked.
- Responsibility for purchase ledger entries should be vested in personnel separate from personnel responsible for ordering, receipts of goods and the invoice register.
- The purchase ledger should be subject to frequent reconciliation in total or be checked by an independent senior official.
- Ledger account balances should be regularly compared with the supplier's statements of account.

- Cut-off procedures at the year-end are essential.
- A proper coding system is required for purchase of goods and services so that correct nominal accounts are debited.

7. Sales and debtors

Objectives

- To ensure that all customers' orders are promptly executed
- To ensure that sales on credit are made only to bona fide goods credit risks
- To ensure that all sales on credit are invoiced, that authorised prices are charged and that before issue all invoices are completed and checked as regards price, trade discounts and VAT
- To ensure that all invoices raised are entered in the books
- To ensure that all customers' claims are fully investigated before credit notes are issued
- To ensure that every effort is made to collect all debts

Measures

- Incoming orders should be recorded, and if necessary, acknowledged, on pre-numbered forms. Orders should be matched with invoices and lists of outstanding orders prepared at intervals for management action. Sequence checks should be made regularly by a senior official.
- There should be procedures laid down for verifying the credit worthiness of all persons or enterprises requesting goods on credit. A credit limit should be established.
- Selling prices should be prescribed. Policies should be laid down on credit term, trade and cash discounts and special prices.
- Invoicing should be carried out by a separate department. Invoices should be pre-numbered and the custody and issue of unused invoice books controlled and recorded.
- All invoices should be independently checked for agreement with customer order, with the goods despatched records, for pricing, discounts, VAT and other details. All actions should be acknowledged by signature or initials.
- Accounting for sales and debtors should be segregated by employing separate staff for cash, invoice register, sales ledger entries and statement preparation.
- Sales invoices should be pre-listed before entry into the invoice register or day book and the pre-list total independently compared with the total of the register.
- Customer claims should be recorded and investigated. Similar controls should be applied to credit notes. At the end of the year, all unclear claims should be carefully investigated and assessed.
- A control account should be regularly and independently prepared.
- All balances must be reviewed regularly by an independent official to identify and investigate overdue accounts, debtors paying by instalments, and accounts where payments do not match with the invoices.

- Bad debts should be written off only after due investigation and acknowledged authorisation by senior management.
- At the year end, an analysis of debtors should be prepared to evaluate the need for a doubtful debt provision.

4.2.8 Internal Control Questionnaire

An internal control questionnaire is basically a comprehensive list of questions, covering every aspect of the client's system, the answers to which will enable the auditor to assess the internal controls in operation. To facilitate the assessment, the questions are asked in a form whereby the answer 'yes' is satisfactory, whereas the answer 'no' appears to indicate a weakness.

Basic characteristics of internal control questionnaire

1. The internal control questionnaires will be drafted as far as possible in a form whereby the questions can be answered simply with a "yes/no/not applicable".
2. Though internal control questionnaires are normally in a standardised preprinted form for particular types of enterprises, their application to individual clients in a skilled matter requires the attention of senior staff.
3. The internal control questionnaires will require reviewing and updating at regular intervals and on the basis of changing situations amendments are required to be made to the system.
4. Staff responsible for the completion or review of internal control questionnaires should be required to sign and date them. This fixes both the responsibility and indicates the date the answers to questions were obtained.
5. The answers 'No' will require attention at the subsequent evaluation stage. They will also frequently require cross-reference to systems notes and letter of weaknesses, as well as to the internal control evaluation.

Typical questions to be found in an internal control questionnaire

1. ***In respect to stocks and work-in-progress***
   - (a) Are stocks kept in proper storage accommodation which protects them against the following risks?
     - (i) deterioration
     - (ii) access by unauthorised persons
     - (iii) other risks (e.g. fire)
   - (b) Is there an adequate system in operation in respect of goods received to ensure the following?
     - (i) That the goods are checked for quantity and quality
     - (ii) That the goods are properly mentioned in the records
   - (c) Are all stock issues from stores made only against properly authorised requisitions?
   - (d) By whom can requisitions be authorised?
   - (e) Are bin cards or equivalent records maintained at the stores?
   - (f) Are perpetual inventory records maintained in respect of both quantity and value for the following items?

(i) raw materials (iii) finished goods
(ii) components (iv) consumable stores

(g) Are store records maintained by persons independent of the following?
  (i) the storekeepers
  (ii) the persons responsible for actually checking the physical stocks

(h) Are the physical stock quantities regularly counted and reconciled with the stores records by persons independent of the storekeepers? Do they state approximate frequency of reconciliation?

(i) Are all material discrepancies independently investigated revealed?

(j) Are stores records amended to agree with actual quantities?

(k) Are there proper arrangements in operation for writing down stocks that are (i) defective, (ii) obsolete or (iii) slow-moving?

(l) Is the costing system fully integrated with the financial accounting records?

(m) Is there a sound system in operation for charging direct costs to work-in-progress accounts?

(n) Does the system clearly distinguish between fixed and variable overheads?

(o) Does the treatment of overheads comply with the requirements of generally accepted accounting principles?

(p) Does the system ensure that excess costs are written off and not included in work-in progress?

(q) Has adequate insurance been taken out in respect of the following catastrophe? (i) theft, (ii) fire or (iii) other risks (eg. flood)

2. *In respect of fixed assets*

(a) Are registers of fixed assets maintained, showing adequate details of all material assets?

(b) Are regular physical inspections done to ensure the continued existence and to confirm the condition of assets by responsible officials other than those who (i) maintain registers of fixed assets and (ii) have custody of fixed assets?

(c) Is there a proper system for distinguishing between capital and revenue expenditure?

(d) By whom is capital expenditure authorised? Give details of who may authorise capital expenditure, and the precise limits of their authority.

(e) Is the authorisation of capital expenditure properly evidenced?

(f) By whom is the sale or scrapping of fixed assets authorised? Give details of who may authorise the sale or scrapping of fixed assets and the precise limits of their authority.

(g) Is the authorisation of the sale or scrapping of fixed assets properly evidenced?

(h) When fixed assets are sold or scrapped, are there controls in force to ensure the following?

(i) appropriate entries are made in the accounting records and registers
(ii) receipts for sale are properly accounted for

(i) Are the rates of depreciation for the major classes of fixed assets adequate?

(j) Do the rates of depreciation take due account of obsolescence?

(k) Is the system adequate to ensure the correct calculation of depreciation in respect of individual assets?

(l) Are the balances on the asset register regularly reconciled with the accounting records?

Note: It is difficult to draft a standardised questionnaire of different items of internal control, because there are a number of methods of controlling the business internally. However, the above illustrative questionnaires have been given to give an idea about the internal control questionnaire.

4.3 INTERNAL CHECK

4.3.1 Definition

Internal check is an arrangement of the duties of the staff members of the accounting functions in such a way that the work performed by a person is automatically checked by another.

In the opinion of Spicer and Pegler, "a system of internal check is an arrangement of staff duties, whereby no one person is allowed to carry through and to record every aspect of a transaction, so that without collusion between two or more persons, fraud is activated and at the same time the possibilities of errors are reduced to the minimum."

Internal check has been defined by the Institute of Chartered Accountants of England and Wales as "the checks on day to day transactions which operate continuously as part of the routine system, where the work of one person is proved independently or in complementary to the work of another, the object being the prevention or early detection of errors or frauds."

On the basis of the above definitions, it may be concluded that "internal check is a system where the work is divided amongst the employees in such a manner that no single individual is allowed to carry on the whole function from the beginning to the end and the work of an individual is being automatically checked by another."

4.3.2 General Considerations in Framing a System of Internal Check

Following factors are required to be considered in framing a system of internal check:

1. *Work assignment* No single person should be given the total part of a particular work. All dealings and acts of every employee should, in the ordinary course, come under the review of another.

2. *Rotation of employees* The duties of members of the staff should be changed from time to time without any previous notice, so that the same officer or subordinate does not, without a break, perform the same function for a considerable length of time.

3. ***Compulsory leave*** Every member of the staff should be encouraged to go on leave at least once in a year. Experience has shown that frauds successfully concealed by the employees are often detected when they are on leave.

4. ***Separation of inter-related jobs*** Persons having physical custody of assets must not be permitted to have access to the books of accounts.

5. ***Uses of mechanical devices*** To prevent loss or misappropriation of cash, mechanical devices such as the automatic cash register should be employed.

6. ***Periodical review*** The financial and administrative power should be distributed very judiciously among different officers and in such manners that those which are actually exercised should be reviewed periodically.

7. ***Responsibility*** Responsibility of each individual must be properly defined and fixed. The work of the business should be allocated amongst various staff members in such a manner that their duties and responsibilities are clearly and judiciously divided.

8. ***Safeguards*** For stock taking at the end of the year, trading activities should, if possible, be suspended. The task of stock taking and evaluation should be done by staff belonging to several sections of the organisation. It may prove dangerous to depend exclusively on the stock section staff for these tasks since they may be tempted to under and/or overstate the stock.

9. ***Supervision*** A strict supervision should be exercised to ensure that the prescribed internal checks and procedures are fully operative.

10. ***Reliance*** No staff member of the business should be relied upon too much. The system must provide for an automatic checking of the work of every employee by another employee.

4.3.3 Objectives of Internal Check

The objects of internal check system can be set forth as under.

1. ***Assigning responsibility*** To allocate the duties and responsibilities of every employee in such a manner that they may be identified and held responsible for a particular error or fraud

2. ***Minimising error or fraud*** To minimise the possibility of any error or fraud done by any staff member

3. ***Detecting errors or frauds*** To detect errors or frauds easily due to independent checking of work done by one employee by another employee

4. ***Reducing clerical mistakes*** To minimise the possibility of omission of any transaction from being recorded in the books of accounts

5. ***Enhancing work efficiency*** To enhance the efficiency of the staff, as the management of duties is based on the principle of division of labour

6. *Obtaining confirmation* To obtain confirmation of facts and entries, physical and financial, by the presentation and necessary maintenance of records

7. *Reducing burden of work* To reduce the burden of the work of independent auditor by introducing the internal check system in a scientific way

8. *Exercising moral pressure* To exercise moral pressure on the employees by introducing continuous review process of the total system

9. *Ensuring reliability* To facilitate business control by ensuring the reliability of accounting records and books

10. *Obtaining supervision advantages* To obtain the advantages of supervising the various assets, inflow and outflow of cash and goods of the business

Advantages of internal check

The advantages that can be derived from internal check can be discussed from different points of view as follows:

1. *From business point of view*

The advantages from business point of view are as follows:

(a) Proper allocation of work: Rational allocation of work among the different staff members of the organisation brings precision in work.

(b) Control device: The distribution of work under this system is such that it acts as a control device against unscrupulous employees. The chances of fraudulent manipulation are thus minimised due to the existence of this check.

(c) Speedy work: As the individual staff is engaged in the same type of jobs for a considerable period of time, it results in the efficient performance of the activities and high speed of work.

(d) Increase in efficiency and skill: A good system of internal check increases the efficiency of work among the staff due to its proper planning for assigning the right job to the right person.

(e) Easy preparation of final accounts: Since no individual worker is allowed to handle a job completely and the work is divided among the employees in a proper manner, the books of accounts can be kept up to date; as a result, the final accounts can be prepared easily.

(f) Creation of moral check: Knowledge of subsequent checking of each employee's work by another acts as a great check to commission of errors and frauds.

2. *From the owner's point of view*

(a) Reliability on accounts: If there is a good system of internal check, the owner of the concern may rely upon the genuineness and accuracy of the accounts.

(b) Orientation of accounting: As the responsibility of each staff is clearly defined and fixed, it develops a system of accounting which is known as responsibility accounting.

(c) Economical operation: Although it seems that the introduction of well-integrated system of internal check is costly, in actual practice it is observed that the staff patterns are so arranged that the existing staff be properly filled in different operating areas involving no extra cost.

3. *From the auditor's point of view*

(a) Facilitation of audit work: Sound and efficient internal check system may facilitate to a greater extent, the work of the auditor by relying on 'test check'.

(b) Attention to other important matters: As the auditor gains confidence on the internal check system, he can avoid the basic routine checking work to some extent and can give attention to other important matters.

4.3.4 Shortcomings of Internal Check System

Dependence on each other proves fatal in the quick disposal of the work. If one person is absent, the day-to-day work will be seriously disrupted. This is the main shortcoming of the internal check system.

Following are some more shortcomings of internal check system:

1. ***Monotony*** Involvement in the same kind of work may result in monotonous attitude on the part of the person who is engaged in the same type of job.

2. ***Carelessness*** The possibility of some of the responsible and high level officials being complacent increases, as they believe (though it is not always right) that under a sound system of internal check nothing can go wrong.

3. ***Collusion*** The real purpose of the internal check is bound to fail if collusion among the staff exists in disguise.

4. ***Limited application*** The application of this system is limited only in big organisations. Its application in small organisations may result in loss of time and cause unnecessary expenditure.

5. ***Dependence*** Statutory auditors in almost all cases rely on the internal check system. Accordingly they apply test check and not a thorough check.

6. ***Possibility of disorder*** In the absence of a properly organised system of internal check, there will be chaos and disorder in the working of a business.

4.3.5 Safeguard Against the Shortcomings of Internal Check

The advantages of the internal check system outweigh its disadvantages. Hence the wide acceptability of the system in the conduct of an audit is appreciated. The stated defects of the system, however, may be overcome if the management is careful in its effective implementation. The payment of proper incentives to staff may remove the carelessness of the staff to a great extent. The monotony of a job may be avoided by inter-departmental transfer of the employees. Regarding the collusion, it can be stated that the whole system is bound to fail if the morality of the employees deteriorates. General punishments like fine, termination of service etc. may temporarily check collusion, but without upgrading the morality of the staff, it is not possible to stop collusion permanently.

4.3.6 Internal Check and the Auditor

The basic responsibility of the auditor is to certify the fairness and authenticity of the accounts of the business. For this, the auditor is expected to discharge his duties in such a way as would reveal the actual state of affairs of the business. It is true that an efficient system of internal check can make his work easy and convenient. He may be relieved of detailed checking of the transactions. But to what extent an auditor should depend on the system of internal check is solely a matter of his own discretion. Though the auditor conducts the examination of the accounts independently, he has to depend a lot on the system of the business. Because it becomes practically impossible for the auditor to conduct the examination of accounts thoroughly after the close of the financial accounts.

Where the system of the internal check is not in operation, it is desirable that the auditor should adopt the detailed checking of transactions irrespective of the type of organisation and the volume of transactions. In order to save his time, if he adopts the method of test checking of few transactions and if errors and frauds are detected later on, the auditor will be held responsible. But where the internal check system is in operation and for this where detailed checking is not necessary, in that case to what extent the auditor would depend on internal check system is a matter of consideration.

If through review the auditor thinks that the system of internal check is adequate and free from errors he can depend on the system, and instead of detailed checking he can resort to test checking. But if he observes any weakness in the system, he should not depend on this and conduct his work extensively and in detail.

So, the auditor is expected to apply proper judgement with reasonable care and skill to appraise the system. Thus, he has to determine to what extent he would depend on internal check system. Hence, it is clear that the internal check system does not reduce the liability of the auditor.

4.3.7 General Principles of Internal Check for a Few Transactions

Aspects like cash sales, cash receipts, cash payments, payment of wages, credit purchases, credit sales, stores, and material wastage form important parts in the procedure and conduct of an audit. These matters are important in the sense that fraudulent manipulations or frauds and errors in those areas are bound to prevail unless there exists an efficient system of internal check as regards the above. So, the principles of internal check as regards the stated areas are detailed in the following paragraphs. It should be noted in this context that the application of the principles in actual practice depends upon the nature and size of the organisation as well as in relation to the concept of materiality.

1. Internal check as regards movement of materials

Each and every organisation may have to preserve and maintain the stores of different kinds, viz. finished goods, semi-finished goods and the raw materials, in a proper way. As such, there should be a strict control over these items in order to safeguard against pilferage, theft or misuse. A suitable system of internal check should be devised for stores to ensure correct records, prevent theft and to reduce wastage. The system of internal check to be introduced in this respect may be outlined as follows:

(a) Receipts of goods in stores

(i) Store should be located at a convenient place. It should have an adequate storage facility, so that the goods may not be wasted or misplaced or misused.

(ii) The storekeeper will submit the requisition to the purchase department in order to purchase the necessary goods and store them.

(iii) On receipt of the goods purchased, the storekeeper will prepare a goods received note in triplicate—one for purchase department, one for accounts department and third for the stores department itself.

(iv) The goods received should be recorded in goods inward book by the accounts department and in the Bin card by the stores department.

(v) After the receipt of goods, they should be properly inspected before they are placed in stores.

(b) Delivery of goods from stores

(i) In order to issue different types of stores to the different departments, the proper requisition should be submitted on behalf of the departmental authority.

(ii) For sale of goods, unless the delivery orders are received from the sales department, goods will not be sent to the customers.

(iii) Requisition forms of different colours should be used for different departments.

(iv) The goods, which are to be issued from stores, should be recorded in goods outward book.

(v) If any goods are returned to stores, a goods return note is to be prepared and recorded in that book.

(c) Accounting of store movements

(i) Responsibility for accounting of stores should be assigned to an efficient accountant.

(ii) For each type of goods, separate store ledgers should be maintained.

(iii) For accounting of movement of stores of each item, bin card should be used.

(iv) After a fixed interval of time, the store ledger should be verified with the bin card in order to find out discrepancies, if any.

(d) Counting and maintenance of stores

(i) For each type of stores, a separate list is to be prepared. The list should incorporate the quantity of goods, rate of acquisition and the actual value.

(ii) An employee, who is not in relation with the maintenance of stores, should be entrusted with the counting of stores.

(iii) For counting various types of stores, separate employees are to be engaged.

(iv) The task of recording the rate of valuation of stores and the actual value in the proper column of the stock sheet should be assigned to a responsible employee.

(v) Those who prepare the stock sheets should put their signature on it. The counting and addition of the stock sheet should be verified by a separate employee.

(vi) After verifying thoroughly, the stock sheet should be signed by higher officials.

(e) Preservation of stores

(i) A separate but proper place should be earmarked for each type of stock.

(ii) A separate code number should be used for different classes of stocks.

(iii) The stock should be frequently counted and checked by a responsible official, who should also compare the bin cards with the stores ledger.

(iv) If there is any difference between actual stock and the stock as shown in books, it should be adjusted or written off with the approval of the proper authority.

(v) Stock taking should be conducted at the end of the period or at irregular intervals during the period, if necessary.

(vi) A responsible official should examine whether proper security measures have been adopted for the preservation of stores. If any defect or drawback is found in the system, it should be brought to the notice of the appropriate authority.

2. Internal check as regards to wage payments

The system of internal check for wages should be devised in a careful and planned way, especially in a manufacturing concern. Usually, wages are paid to the workers on the basis of time spent by each worker in the production process. So, correct recording of time is essential for the purpose of determining proper wages. For the purpose of efficient control over the payment of wages, a separate wage department headed by responsible official of the organisation should be there.

For the purpose of recording correct time and to avoid frauds and errors, different time recording devices are used. To implement the effective internal check system for wage payment, it is suggested that the following system be introduced.

(a) Maintenance of wage records

(i) Time work recording: Workers are paid their wages normally on the basis of time. Thus the time spent by each worker should be correctly recorded in the time record-book and for this purpose the following methods are used:

- **Time Recording Clock:** At the time of entering into the factory the worker puts his entry card in the slot of time recording clock, kept at the entry of the gate. The clock records the date and the actual time of his entry in the factory. At the time of leaving the factory, he has to put his card in the slot of the clock again for recording his actual time of departure.
- **Brass Metal Token:** Under this system, each worker is given a brass metal token duly numbered. The workers at the time of entering into the factory put their respective token in the appropriate place of the board. On the basis of this token, the time-keeper records the attendance of the worker in the attendance register.
- **Attendance Card:** Here, the workers are given attendance cards. At the time of entering into the factory, the workers put their attendance cards in the box kept near the gate. The gatekeeper collects the same for the purpose of recording time in the attendance register.

(ii) Piece work recording: When the workers are paid on the basis of work performed, they are provided with cards known as 'job cards' which contain all information relating to workers and their jobs, *viz* the name of the worker, nature of work allotted, the volume of work done and the wage or job rate. This card is checked by the piecework reviewer along with the quality and quantity of goods. This card helps in the preparation of wage sheet.

(iii) Overtime recording: The question of payment for overtime to workers arises only when it is sanctioned by the proper authority. The overtime slip is to be given to each worker, who has been allowed to do the same. This slip contains various information, viz. the name of the workers, details about the job and the rate at which wages are to be paid. The overtime record should be maintained separately and it should be passed either by foreman or by the works manager. After that, the slip should be sent to the accounts department for the preparation of wage sheet.

(iv) Pass-out recording: Normally the workers are not allowed to leave the factory during the hours of work. Sometimes the workers are compelled to leave the factory during the working period on some personal grounds. In that case, pass-out slips are to be issued to the workers. Two copies of the slip are prepared. The original copy is to be handed over to the workers who at the time of leaving the factory hand over the same to the gatekeeper and the other copy is to be sent to the wage department for the preparation of wage sheet.

(b) Preparation of wage sheets

The preparation of wage sheets should be done by a separate department. This work should be assigned to a number of employees of the wage department to minimise the irregularities. Information regarding attendance is available from the attendance registers, job cards, overtime ships, pass-out ships etc. For time workers and piece workers, separate wage sheets should be prepared.

All essential particulars should be entered in the wage sheet, which should have separate columns for

(i) Name of the worker
(ii) Identification number alloted and the department in which he is working
(iii) Total time worked in the production process
(iv) Details of work done
(v) Applicable rate of wages
(vi) Total amount of wages payable
(vii) Bonus entitlement, if applicable
(viii) Overtime wages, if any
(ix) Deductions
(x) Net amount of wages payable

The total process of wage sheet preparation can be divided into different parts to be done by separate staff of the wage department. This process can be implemented in the following ways:

(a) An employee of the department should examine the time and piece wage records, overtime records and other statements relating to wage payment.
(b) One employee should prepare individual worker's statement of wage payment.
(c) Another employee should check the calculations and deductions.
(d) One other employee should check the whole work thoroughly.
(e) All the employees involved in the process should put their initials on the wage sheets and finally the wages sheets should be forwarded to the cash department for payment by some responsible official.

(c) Payment of wages

(i) The employees associated with the preparation of wage sheets must not be given the assignment of making payment of wages to avoid collusion between them.
(ii) On receipt of wage sheets from the wage department, the chief cashier makes necessary arrangements with the bank for the withdrawal of necessary cash for payment.
(iii) Each worker, who is to receive the wages, should be present personally. Thumb impression may be taken as an evidence of wage receipt by the workers.
(iv) The foreman or the concerned officer of each department should be present at the time of payment to identify the worker.
(v) Proper arrangements should be made with regard to unclaimed wages.

(vi) Advances to the workers should be discouraged, and if it becomes unavoidable, they should be given and these should be deducted later on from the wages of the respective workers.

3. Internal check system as regards to purchase

Purchases are of two types—cash purchase and credit purchase. The internal check as regards cash purchase is quite simple in comparison with credit purchase. The internal check as regard cash and credit purchases is elaborated as follows:

(a) Purchase requisition No purchase should be made without purchase requisition slip issued by the stores department. The procedure for issuing purchase requisitions should be specified. The details about the quantity, quality and the time by which the goods must be supplied must be clearly mentioned in the requisition slip.

(b) Enquiry for purchase In order to purchase the required item, the purchase department makes an enquiry about the terms and conditions of purchases from different suppliers. For this purpose, tenders are generally invited and usually tenders having the lowest price are accepted.

(c) Purchase order The purchase manager or any other authorised officer of the organisation should be entrusted with the sole authority to issue purchase order. One original and other three copies of the order should be prepared. The original purchase order is to be sent to the supplier. The first copy should be sent to the stores department; the second copy to the accounts department and the last copy is to be retained by the purchase department for reference.

(d) Receipts of goods All the goods received from the supplier are to be checked as per the copy of the purchase order and the challans of the suppliers. Goods receipt register is to be maintained for the purpose of recording the receipts of the goods after proper inspection regarding their quantity and quality either at the stores department or any centralised godown of the concern. All invoices received from the supplier are to be entered in the purchase day book after proper scrutiny.

(e) Making payment The purchase department should thoroughly check the invoices and send the same to the accounts department for payment. The accounts department should compare the invoice with the purchase order and should also check the calculations. Only responsible officials should draw cheque for the payment of invoice, which are to be marked as 'PAID' after payment. All payments are to be made against "A/c payee cheque."

4. Internal check system as regards to sales

Sales are the most important source of income in a business organisation. In case of most of the business organisations, they are the only source of income. Therefore, the system of internal check to be adopted for sales should be extremely effective.

The system of internal check regarding sales should take care of the following aspects:

(a) Independent sales department There should be a separate and independent sales department, which should function as a composite of several sub-departments. Sales manager or a senior competent officer should be in charge of the department.

(b) Receipts of orders On receipt of an order, it should be numbered and preserved in orders received book with full details of the order. A confirmatory written order should be obtained against verbal orders. The despatch department should be given a copy of the order with necessary particulars.

(c) Packing of goods Packing of the goods should be made by the despatch department as per the copy of the sales order, and accordingly a separate statement showing the goods packed should be prepared by the department.

(d) Preparation of invoices The statement of goods as prepared by the despatch department should be checked with the customers' orders and then the invoice should be prepared in triplicate.

(e) Checking of invoices A responsible official should be assigned to check the invoice, particularly the rates charged and the calculations made. He should also see that the terms and conditions in the order have been duly followed and there is no scope for complaint by the customer. He should then put his initial on the invoice.

(f) Despatching the goods With the help of the copy of invoices, entries should be made in the sales day book. On despatch of the goods, records should be made in the goods outward book. Two copies of the invoice may be sent to the customer who will return one of them after signing it.

5. Internal check system as regards to cash receipts

The risk of misappropriation of cash needs no emphasis. The chances of fraud are numerous in cash transactions. In order to reduce the chances of fraud in cash transactions, the internal check system as regards the cash receipts should be very effective and should take into consideration the following principles of internal check for cash transactions:

(a) Separation of duties The cashier should have no access to the ledgers and other books of original entry except the rough cashbook that is required for spot recording of cash receipts.

(b) Control over receipts book The printed receipts book, serially numbered, should be used as and when cash is collected and the same should be countersigned by the responsible manager. The unused receipt book should be kept in safe custody.

(c) Handling of incoming remittances Incoming correspondences including all remittances should be opened by the cashier in the presence of a responsible officer of the concern. All receipts of cheques should be marked, by means of a rubber stamp as A/c payee only.

(d) Depositing cash into bank All collections, both cash and cheque, should be deposited into bank daily. The counter-foil portion of the paying-in-slip should be filled by the clerk and the portion that is to be retained by the bank should be filled in by the cashier.

(e) Reconciling bank statement Bank reconciliation statement should be prepared at regular intervals by the cashier to know the actual position of bank balances.

(f) Correction of the cash book Any spoiled slip should be marked cancelled and should not be turned out and be removed from the receipt book. For the purpose of altering words or figures, overwriting should be discouraged and fresh writing with proper initial is encouraged.

6. Internal check system as regards cash payments

The principles of internal check as regards payments of cash can be set forth as follows:

(a) Payments through cheques Generally all payments should be made by account payee cheques.

(b) Separation of duties The person in charge of making payments should have no connection with the receipts of cash.

(c) Proper authorisation It should be seen that all cheques have been duly signed by the authorised person and no payments exceeding the amount of Rs. 20,000 should be made without A/c payee cheque. It is according to the provision of Section 40A(3) of the Income Tax Act, 1961 that any sum exceeding Rs. 20,000 is to be paid by a crossed cheque, otherwise the expenses will not be allowed as deductions in computing business income.

(d) Safety measures for unused cheques All the unused cheques should be kept in proper safe custody.

(e) Control over payment vouchers Arrangements should be made to ensure that the vouchers supporting payments are not presented twice for payment. Such vouchers should be stamped as 'paid' before the cheques are signed.

(f) Confirmation with the creditors An official should check the statement received from creditors and verify with the invoices and ledger accounts. Only after proper verification, the cheques should be drawn in favour of the creditors. Confirmation of accounts with the creditors should also be made through direct correspondence.

(g) Cash discount To ensure the availability of cash discounts, monthly or periodic payments should be made on the fixed dates.

(h) Reconciliation of bank balance Bank reconciliation statements should be prepared to reconcile bank and cash balances from time to time by some authorities other than the cashier.

4.4 INTERNAL AUDIT

4.4.1 Definition

Internal audit refers to an independent appraisal of activity within an organisation for the review of accounting, financial and other business practices. It consists of a continuous and critical review of financial and operating activities by a staff of auditors functioning as a part of the management and reporting to it and not to the shareholders.

According to W.B. Meigs, "internal auditing consists of a continuous and critical review of financial and operating activities by a staff of auditors functioning as full time salaried employees."

According to the Institute of Internal Auditors, USA. "Internal auditing is an independent appraisal function established within an organisation to examine and evaluate its activities as a service to the organisation."

As per AAS-7, " internal audit is a separate part of internal control system. The objective of internal audit is to determine whether other internal control systems are well designed and properly operated. Internal auditor is appointed by the management and is part of overall organisation system of internal control".

So, internal audit can be defined as "an independent appraisal function established by the management of an organisation for the review of internal control system as a service to the organisation. It objectively examines, evaluates and reports on the adequacy of internal control as a contribution to the proper, economic, efficient and effective use of resources".

In fact, internal audit is a special type of control. It deals primarily with accounting and financial matters. The work of the internal auditor is more or less same as that of an external auditor. The internal auditor has to make an effort to find out the weaknesses of the internal control system in operation and suggest necessary improvements.

4.4.2 Basic Principles of Establishing Internal Auditing in a Business Concern

Following are the basic principles required to be considered before establishing internal auditing in a business concern.

1. ***Independent Status*** The internal audit department should have an independent status in the organisation. The internal auditor must have sufficiently high status in the organisation. He may be required to report directly to the board of directors.

2. ***Scope of audit*** The scope of internal audit department must be specified in a comprehensive manner to the extent practicable. In fact, the department must have the authority to investigate from a financial angle every phase of organisational activity.

3. ***Clear objectives*** It must have an unambiguous and clear understanding of the objectives on each assignment given to it from time to time.

4. ***Formation of the department*** The management should take care in selecting the staff of the internal audit department. The size and qualification of the staff of the internal audit department should be commensurate with the size of the business organisation.

5. ***Time bound programme*** The programme of the internal auditor should be time bound with the provision for periodic reporting.

6. ***Internal audit report*** The copy of the report of the internal auditor should be made available to the statutory auditor.

7. ***Follow up action*** There must exist a specific procedure to follow up the report submitted by the internal audit department.

8. ***Performance of executive actions*** The internal audit department should not be involved in performance of executive actions.

4.4.3 Scope and Objectives of Internal Audit

The primary objective of internal audit lies in helping the management attain maximum efficiency by providing an important source of review of operations and records for the assistance of all levels of management.

As per AAS-7, following are the objectives of internal audit:

- Review of accounting system and related internal control
- Examination of financial and operating system
- Examination of effectiveness and efficiency of financial control
- Physical examination and verification

Thus, internal audit carries out a thorough examination of the accounting transactions as well as that of the system according to which these have been recorded with a view to reassuring the management that the accounts are being properly maintained. It also ensures that the system contains adequate safeguards to check any leakage of revenue or misappropriation of property and the operations have been carried out in conformity with the plans of the management.

So, the objectives of an internal audit can be stated as follows:

1. *Accuracy in accounts* To verify the accuracy and authenticity of the financial accounting and other records presented to the management.

2. *Adoption of standard accounting practices* To ascertain that the standard accounting practices, as have been decided to be followed by the organisation, are being adhered to.

3. *Proper authority on assets* To establish that there is a proper authority for every acquisition, retirement and disposal of assets.

4. *Confirmation of liabilities* To confirm that liabilities have been incurred only for the legitimate activities of the organisation.

5. *Analysis of internal check system* To analyse and improve the system of internal check to see whether it is working properly and effectively and whether the system is economical.

6. *Prevention and detection of fraud* To implement such techniques in the conduct of the internal audit so that it can detect and prevent frauds in the accounts.

7. *Provision for new ideas* To provide a channel whereby new ideas can be brought to the attention of the management.

8. *Review of the operation of internal control system* To review the operation of the overall internal control system and to bring material departures and non-compliance to the notice of the appropriate level of management.

9. *Special investigation* To provide scope and make avenues for special investigations for the management.

10. *Review of organisational activities* To review the operations carried out in the organisation to assure the management that they are being carried out in compliance with the management objectives, policies and plans.

4.4.4 Functions of Internal Audit

Very large organisations (and some small ones) have found need for internal audit in addition to external audit. Internal auditors are employees of the organisation and work exclusively for the organisation. Their functions partly overlap those of the external auditors and in part are quite different.

The functions of internal auditors can be described as follows:

1. An appraisal function

The internal auditor's job is to appraise the activity of others, not to perform a specific part of data processing. For example, a person who spends his time checking employee expense claims is not performing an internal audit function. But an employee who spends some time reviewing the system of checking employee expense claims may well be performing an internal audit function.

2. As a service to the organisation

The management requires that the auditor ensures the following:

(a) That its policies are fulfilled
(b) That the information it requires to manage effectively is reliable and complete; this information is not only that which is provided by the accounting system.
(c) That the organisation's assets are safeguarded
(d) That the internal control system is well designed
(e) That the internal control system works in practice.

The internal auditor's activities will be directed to ensure that these requirements are met. The internal auditor can be seen as the eye of the board within the enterprise.

3. Other duties

Other duties may include the following matters.

- Being concerned with the implementation of social responsibility policies adopted by top management
- Being concerned with the response of the internal control system to errors and required changes to prevent errors
- Being concerned with the response of the internal control system to external stimuli. The internal control system must continually upgrade itself to deal with change
- Acting as a training officer in internal control matters
- Auditing the information given to management particularly interim accounts and management accounting reports
- Taking a share of the external auditor's responsibility in relation to the figures in the annual accounts and
- Being concerned with compliance with external regulations such as those on the environment, financial services, related parties etc.

4.4.5 Essential Elements of Internal Audit

The essential elements of internal audit are as follows:

1. ***Independence*** Internal auditing is carried out by independent personnel. Internal auditors are employees of the firm and thus independence is not always easy to achieve.

2. ***Staffing*** The internal audit unit should be adequately staffed in terms of numbers, grades and experience.

3. ***Relationships*** Internal auditors should foster constructive working relationships and mutual understanding with management, external auditors, any review agencies and where appropriate with an audit committee. Mutual understanding is the goal.

4. ***Due care*** An internal auditor should behave much as an external auditor in terms of skill, care and judgment. He should be technically up to date and have personal standards of knowledge, honesty, probity and integrity much as an external auditor.

5. ***Specific audit planning*** On the basis of the objectives of the organisation and the objective of the internal audit of the organisation, the internal auditors should prepare the audit programme in order to cover the specified tasks assigned by the management.

6. ***Systems control*** The internal auditor must verify the operations of the system in much the same way as an external auditor, i.e. by investigation, recording, identification of controls and compliance testing of the controls.

7. ***Evidence*** The internal auditor must have similar standards for evidence as an external auditor. He must evaluate audit evidence in terms of sufficiency, relevance and reliability.

8. ***Reporting*** The internal auditor must produce timely, accurate and comprehensive reports to management on a regular basis.

Advantages

Internal audit provides the following advantages.

1. ***Prevention of errors and frauds*** It helps in the prevention of errors and frauds including misappropriation of cash and goods.

2. ***Early detection of errors and frauds*** It makes early detection of errors and frauds possible.

3. ***Continuous review of internal control system*** It undertakes continuous review of the internal control system and, as a result, it is capable of reporting irregularities for enabling corrective action in time.

4. ***Assurance regarding accuracy of books and accounts*** It checks books, records and accounts to ensure correct recording and their maintenance up to date.

5. ***Preparation of interim accounts*** It facilitates the preparation of interim accounts.

6. ***Early completion of annual audit*** It is of great use in early completion of annual statutory audit.

7. ***Periodic physical verification*** It carries out periodic physical verification of assets like cash, stock, investments and items of fixed assets.

8. ***Assistance to the statutory auditor*** It can render direct assistance to the statutory auditor by undertaking detailed checking of the accounting data and leave him free to concentrate on more important issues of principle, presentation and policy on accounting.

Disadvantages

Internal audit suffers from the following limitations.

1. ***Extra cost*** Internal audit system is not possible to be adopted by small organisations because the cost of running an internal audit department is very high.

2. ***Biased opinion*** Internal audit department employees are the paid-staff of the organisation. In most cases, they have to work according to the directions of the management. So it is not expected that they will provide unbiased opinion about the financial statements.

3. ***Possibility of becoming ineffective*** If the employees of the internal audit department are not efficient or if the internal audit is not conducted effectively, it will provide no assistance to the management.

4. ***Possibility of distortion*** If the management is interested to distort financial figures and if it is supported by internal audit department, the users of the financial statements will be totally misguided.

5. ***Inefficient staff members*** As there is no prescribed qualification for the appointment of internal auditors, less qualified persons may get appointment in the department. They will not be able to discharge their duties properly.

4.4.6 Area of Internal Audit

As per AAS-7, the scope and objectives of internal audit vary widely and are dependent upon the size and structure of the entity and the requirements of its management.

Normally, however, internal audit operates in one or more of the following areas:

1. ***Review of accounting system and related internal control*** The establishment of an adequate accounting system and related controls is the responsibility of the management, which demands proper attention on a continuous basis. The internal audit function is often assigned specific responsibility by the management for reviewing the accounting system and related accounting controls, monitoring their operation and suggesting improvements thereto.

2. ***Examination for management of financial and operating information*** This may include review of the means used to identify, measure, classify and report such information and specific inquiry into individual items including detailed testing of transactions, balances and procedures.

3. ***Examination of the effectiveness of operations*** Generally, the external auditor is interested in the results of such audit work only when it has an important bearing on the reliability of the financial records.

4. ***Physical verification*** The internal audit generally includes examination and verification of physical existence and condition of the tangible assets of the entity.

4.4.7 Distinction between Internal Audit and External Audit

On accounting matters, the internal and the external auditors operate mainly in the same field and they have a common interest in ascertaining that there is an effective system of internal control to present or detect errors and frauds and to ensure that it is operating satisfactorily and that an adequate accounting system exists to provide the information necessary for preparing true and fair financial statements. There are, however, some fundamental differences between the work of an internal auditor and that of an external auditor regarding the following:

1. Appointment

The internal auditor is appointed by the management, generally the Directors and is responsible to them.

The external or the statutory auditor is appointed according to the concerned statute. Generally, in case of company form of organisation, the auditors are appointed by the shareholders in the annual general meeting.

2. Scope

The extent of the work undertaken by the internal auditor is determined by the management.

The area of the work to be undertaken by the external auditor arises from the responsibilities placed on him by the governing statute.

3. Approach

The internal auditor's approach is with a view to ensure that the accounting system is efficient, so that the accounting information presented to management throughout the period is accurate and discloses material facts.

The external auditor's approach, however, is governed by his duty to satisfy himself that the accounts to be presented to the shareholders show a true and fair view of the profit or loss for the financial period and of the state of the company's affairs at the end of that period.

4. Responsibility

The internal auditor's responsibility is to the management. It follows that the internal auditor, being a servant of the company, does not have independence of status.

The external auditor is responsible directly to the shareholders. Unlike the internal auditors, he is a representative of the shareholders and has independence of status.

5. Objective

The objective of internal audit is to ensure that the laid down policies, procedures and other internal control functions are functioning as designed, whereas the objective of the external auditor is to express opinion on financial statements whether those statements are showing true and fair view.

6. Independence

External auditor is more independent in reporting than internal auditor.

Notwithstanding these important differences, the work of both the internal auditor and the external auditor, on accounting matters is carried out largely by similar means, such as

- Examination of the system of internal check, for both soundness in principle and effectiveness in operation.
- Examination and checking of accounting records and statements.
- Verification of assets and liabilities.

- Observation, inquiry, making of statistical comparisons and such other measures as may be judged necessary.

The wide experience of the external auditor may be of assistance to the internal auditor; while on the other hand the latter's intimate acquaintance with the business concern may be of help to the external auditor. Co-operation in planning of the respective auditors may save unnecessary work, although the external auditor must always satisfy himself as to the work carried out by the internal auditor.

4.4.8 Relying Upon the Work of An Internal Auditor

The statement on AAS-7 describes the scope of reliance by the external auditor upon the work of an internal auditor. The purpose of this statement is to provide guidance as to the procedures, which should be applied by the external auditor in assessing the work of the internal auditor for the purpose of placing reliance upon that work. This statement states that while the external auditor has the sole responsibility of his report, however much of the work of the internal auditor may be useful to him in his examination of the financial statements. The responsibility of the external auditor is not reduced by any means because of the reliance placed on the work of the internal auditor.

As per AAS-7, the external auditor can use the work of the internal auditor after evaluation of the internal audit function. The external auditor should document his evaluation and conclusion in this respect while evaluating the work of internal audit function to determine the extent to which he can place reliance upon the following aspects considered:

- Whether internal audit is undertaken by an outside agency or by an integral audit department within the entity itself.
- Scope of internal audit and management action and internal audit report.
- Technical compliance of the internal auditors, i.e. whether the internal auditors have the required experience and professional qualification.
- Due professional care by the internal auditor, i.e. whether internal audit work appears to be properly planned, supervised, documented and if there is existence of adequate audit manuals.

This statement suggests the following features.

1. The role of the internal audit function within an entity is determined by management and its prime objective differs from that of the external auditor, who is appointed to report independently on financial information.
2. The external auditor should, as part of his audit, evaluate the internal audit function to the extent he considers that it will be relevant in determining the nature, timing and extent of his compliance and substantive procedures. Depending upon such evaluation, the external auditor may be able to adopt less extensive procedures than would otherwise be required.
3. By its very nature, the internal audit function cannot be expected to have the same degree of independence as is essential when the external auditor expresses his opinion on the financial information. The report of the external auditor is his sole responsibility, and that responsibility is not by any means reduced because of the reliance he places on the internal auditor's work.

Where internal audit is carried out, it is for the external auditor to decide, consistently with his statutory responsibilities, whether and to what extent, he can rely on the work of the internal auditor in order to reduce the extent of his own examination of details.

His decision in this matter will depend upon his judgment on the facts of each case, having regard in particular to the following:

(a) The extent and efficiency of the internal audit; i.e. in order to assess these matters, the external auditor should examine the internal audit programmes, working papers and reports and should make such tests as he thinks fit for the work done by the internal auditor.

(b) The experience and qualifications of the internal auditor and his staff member and the character of their reports and also the action taken by the management on the basis of the report.

(c) The authority vested in the internal auditor and the level of management to which he is directly responsible.

However, the statutory auditor can not in any circumstance divest himself of the responsibilities laid on him by the statute. In other words, if the external auditor has curtailed the extent of his checking, putting reliance on the work of the internal auditor, the responsibility for any deficiency in that financial statements that may remain undetected will be of the statutory auditor, he cannot plead that he has relied on the work done by the internal auditor.

4.5 AUDITOR'S INDEPENDENCE

By the term 'auditor's independence' we mean that the judgment of the auditor is not subordinated to the wishes or directions of any person who might have engaged him or to his own self-interest.

It is not possible to define the term 'independence' in a precise manner. Basically, it is a condition of mind, and personal in character. However, professional conduct of the auditors support auditor's independence. Auditors, by their function of reporting on financial statements, lend creditability to those statements. Parties interested in such statements put implicit faith and trust on those statements based on the opinion of the auditor. So, for the auditors, independence has a special meaning and significance. Unbiased audit can be carried out only when the auditor is able to resist all pulls and pressures. The auditor should not only be independent in fact, but also must appear to be so; otherwise his report would be suspected and would lack creditability.

4.5.1 Advantages of Independent Audit

The principal advantage of an independent audit lies in the society being able to get an informed, objective and unbiased opinion on the financial statements of an organisation which is used in making significant economic decisions by interested segments of the society, i.e. shareholders, creditors, bankers etc. It is to be noted that only the auditor is in a position to examine the accounts and transactions of an organisation with a view to form an opinion. His report is, therefore, the only real safeguard available to the various parties interested in the financial affairs of the organisation.

4.5.2 Provisions for Safeguarding Independent Auditors

Several provisions have been included in the Companies Act with the objective of securing independence of the auditor. In general, these provisions endow the auditor with certain statutory rights, define certain relationships that may entail a compromise in maintaining independence, requiring that normally the auditor would be appointed in the general body meeting by the shareholders and making the removal of auditor difficult by laying down procedures under the Companies Act. The rights of the auditor are statutorily defined in several sections and they cannot be curtailed or limited by the management or even by the shareholders.

The management has no authority to terminate the appointment of any auditor. The auditor when appointed shall be entitled to hold office till the conclusion of the next annual general meeting. Though mid-term removal of the auditor is not ruled out, it can be accomplished only by the shareholders in the general meeting and with previous approval of the central government. It is also worth mentioning that the duties cast on the auditor can not be diluted by any agreement between the organisation and the auditor. There can thus be no temptation for the auditor to do less than what the law requires.

4.6 DISTINCTION BETWEEN INTERNAL CONTROL AND INTERNAL AUDIT

A system of internal control consists of all the measures employed by an organisation for the purposes of

1. safeguarding its resources against waste, fraud and inefficiency,
2. promoting accuracy and reliability in accounting and operational data,
3. encouraging and measuring compliance with the organisational policy, and
4. judging the efficiency of operations in all the divisions of the business.

It is concerned with the plan of the organisation, allocation of duties among the employees and authorising, recording and custody procedures to ensure operation of internal check on the one hand and managerial supervision and review on the other. Managerial supervision and review is accomplished by the sub-system of internal auditing which is a part of the total internal control system.

Though internal audit is a part of the internal control system, it is indeed a significant part as with the introduction of internal audit system, the performance and compliance with management policies and practices are ascertained on a continuous and timely basis and brought to the notice of management. Internal audit also reviews the overall internal control system, its efficiency or redundancy, though it is itself a part of that overall system. In other words, internal auditing, though a part of the total internal control system, is also a significant complement of the system, reviews the system and checks its operations so that the management can be given up-to-date information on the effectiveness of control and the underlying operations.

4.7 DISTINCTION BETWEEN INTERNAL CHECK, INTERNAL AUDIT AND INTERNAL CONTROL

Internal check has been defined by the Institute of Chartered Accountants in England and Wales, as the "checks on day-to-day transactions which operate continuously as part of the routine system whereby the work of one person is proved independently or complementary to the work of another, the object being the prevention or earlier detection of error or fraud." The internal check in accounting system implies the organisation of the system of book-keeping and arrangement of staff duties in such a manner that no one person can completely carry through a transaction, and record every aspect thereof.

Internal audit has been defined by the Institute of Internal Auditors, USA recently of as an "independent, objective assurance and consulting activity designed to add value and improve an organisations, operations. It helps an organisation accomplish its objectives by bringing a systematic disciplined approach to evaluate and improve the effectiveness of risk management, control and governance process." Traditionally internal auditing was considered to be restricted to the examination of the books of accounts of the organisation with a view to ascertaining whether they correctly record the transaction. In fact, a good internal control system should have internal audit as an integral part. The modern concept of internal auditing as given in the aforesaid definition shows that internal auditing has moved significantly ahead by shouldering greater responsibilities to become one of the important management control devices.

It can be seen from the above definitions of both internal check and internal audit that they are parts of overall control system. Internal check operates as a built-in device as far as staff organisation and job allocation aspects of the control system are concerned. On the other hand, the adequacy and operations of internal control on a regular basis is to be reviewed by the management through internal audit system to ensure that all significant controls are operating effectively. Thus, internal check is merely an arrangement of book-keeping and clerical duties, but internal audit involves evaluating the quality and operation of the various controls.

Inter-relationship between internal control, internal check and internal audit can be described with the help of the following diagram:

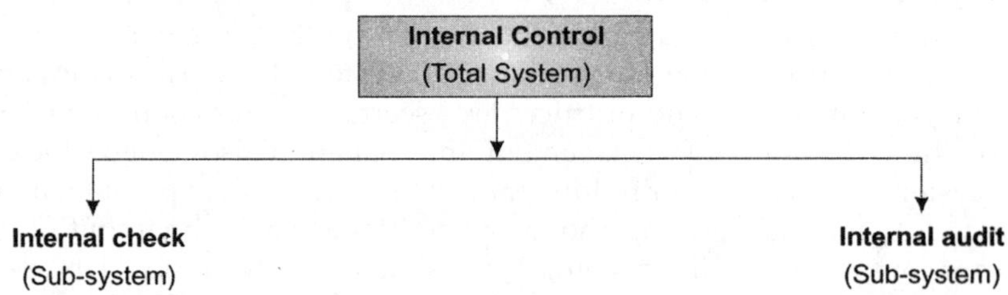

Case Study 1

Fast Move Ltd. is a listed company in the food processing industry. They have 10 factory sites and 2,500 workers. They have grown very rapidly in recent years under the direction of Sidharth, who is a very dynamic character. He tries to operate on the lowest possible costs and sees internal control as himself and his factory managers. The company has recently moved into the production of mass produced South-Indian foods and gambled that they will grab a large market share. They have an audit committee (not liked by Sidharth) but no internal audit department.

Discussion

(a) What advantages might accrue to the company if they set up an internal audit department?

(b) How might the auditors approach the audit?

(c) What are the specific duties imposed on the auditor regarding internal control and internal audit?

Case Study 2

Skylark Real Estate Ltd. is a company offering estate agency services to the public through a network of branches all over the country. The company has some 300 staff in all. The board consists of six people, a part-time chairman, a chief executive, two other full time executives and two representatives of the owners. The company is jointly owned by a foreign bank and the City Property Group. The company has an internal audit department consisting of Sanjeev who is a young Chartered Accountant and Rajeev who is an accounting expert. They also have a secretary, Ritwika. They report their activities monthly in detail to the board and to the audit committees of the foreign bank and the City Property Group.

Discussion

(a) What work would the internal audit department do?

(b) In what ways may the external auditors place reliance on their work?

(c) Draw up a check list which the external auditor could use to assess the internal auditors as potentially being capable of producing work on which the external auditors may rely.

POINTS TO PONDER

- Internal control refers to the various methods and procedures adopted for the control of production, distribution and the whole system (financial and non-financial) of the enterprise.
- Basic elements of internal control include financial and other organisational plans, competent personnel, division of work, separation of operational responsibility for recording keeping, separation of the custody of assets from accounting, authorisation and managerial supervision and review.
- Internal control can be categorised as organisation, segregation of duties, physical, authorisation and approval, arithmetical and accounting, personnel, supervision and management.
- Advantages of internal control include identification of defects, flexibility, time saving, lesser risk of omission and provision for training facility.
- Disadvantages of internal control include chances of human error, costly, ignorance of unusual activity, collusion, abuse of responsibility and rigidity.
- Evaluation of internal controls is fundamental to an audit. On the basis of evaluation on the effectiveness of the internal control system, the external auditor will decide the extent or degree of his reliance on the functioning on the internal control system.
- Internal control questionnaire is basically a comprehensive list of questions, covering every aspect of the client's system, the answers to which will enable the auditor to assess the internal controls in operation.
- Internal check is arrangement of the duties of the staff members of the accounting functions in such a way that the work performed by a person is automatically checked by another.
- Factors to be considered in framing a system of internal check include work assignment, rotation of employees, compulsory leave, supervision of inter-related jobs, uses of mechanical devices, periodical review, responsibility, safeguards, supervision and reliance.
- Objectives of internal check include assigning responsibility, minimising error or fraud, detecting error or fraud, reducing clerical mistakes, enhancing work efficiency, obtaining confirmation, reducing burden of work, exercising moral pressure, ensuring reliability and obtaining supervision advantages.
- Advantages of internal check can be viewed from three different viewpoints. From business point of view, the advantages include proper allocation of work, control device, speedy work, increase in efficiency and skill, easy preparation of final accounts and creation of moral check. From the viewpoint of the owners, the advantages include reliability on accounts, orientation of accounting and economical operation. From the viewpoint of the auditor, the advantages include facilitation of audit work and attention to other important matters.
- Shortcomings of internal check include monotony, carelessness, collusion, limited application, dependence and possibility of disorder.

- The auditor is expected to apply proper judgement with reasonable care and skill to appraise the internal check system. He has to determine to what extent he would depend on internal check system, as internal check system does not reduce the liability of the auditor.
- Internal audit refers to an independent appraisal of activity within an organisation for the review of accounting, financial and other business practices. It is a separate part of internal control system.
- Basic principles of establishing internal audit in a business concern include independent status, scope of audit, clear objectives, formation of the department, time-bound programme, internal audit report, follow-up action and performance of executive action.
- Objectives behind establishment of internal audit department include accuracy in accounts, adoption of standard accounting practices, proper authority on assets, confirmation of liabilities, analysis of internal control system, prevention and detection of fraud, provision for new ideas, review of the operation of the internal control system, special investigation and review of organisational activities.
- Internal audit performs a number of functions including appraisal function, service to the organisation and other duties.
- Essential elements of internal audit include independence, staffing, relationship, due care, specific audit planning, systems control, evidence and reporting.
- Prevention of errors and frauds, early detection of errors and frauds, continuous review of internal control system, assurance regarding accuracy of books and accounts, preparation of interim accounts, early completion of annual audit, periodic physical verification and assistance to the statutory auditor are the advantages of internal audit system.
- Disadvantages of internal audit include extra cost, biased opinion, possibility of becoming ineffective, possibility of distortion and inefficient staff members.
- Area of internal audit covers review of accounting system and related internal control, examination for management of financial and operating information, examination of the effectiveness of operations and physical verification.
- External audit and internal audit can be differentiated with respect to appointment, scope, approach, responsibility, objectives and independence.
- The statutory auditor can use the work of the internal auditor after evaluation of the internal function, but the responsibility for any deficiency will be of the statutory auditor and he cannot plead that he has relied on the work done by the internal auditor.
- Auditor's independence means the judgement of the auditor is not subordinated to the wishes or directions of any person who might have engaged him or to his self-interest. The principal advantage of an independent audit lies in the society being able to get an informed, objective and unbiased opinion on the financial statements of an organisation.

REVIEW QUESTIONS

Short-answer Questions

1. Distinguish between internal control system and internal check system.
2. What is internal control questionnaire?
3. Should the statutory auditor examine the accounts already checked by the internal auditor?
4. To what extent is the internal auditor responsible for internal control?
5. How does the internal check system affect the work of an external auditor?
6. What are the precautions to be taken in the application of internal check system?
7. State briefly the matters to be included in the auditor's report in respect of the internal audit system of a large manufacturing company?
8. What are the objectives of internal audit?

Essay-type Questions

1. What do you mean by the term 'internal control'? What are the important features of a good system of internal control?
2. What is internal audit? Distinguish between internal control and internal audit? "The modern concept of internal audit envisages scope of internal audit much beyond financial audit". Explain.
3. (a) Distinguish between internal audit and statutory audit.
   (b) Can the statutory auditor rely upon the internal audit in carrying out his function as a statutory auditor?
4. Suggest a set of rules you would recommend for the internal control over the purchases of raw materials and stores of a large manufacturing concern.
5. Draft a form of questionnaire, that you would use to determine the effectiveness of the client's internal control over payrolls.
6. (a) Distinguish between internal control, internal check and internal audit.
   (b) Discuss the general considerations in framing a system of internal control in respect of purchase of goods.
7. Comment on the following statements:
   (a) "The statutory auditor is entitled to rely on the internal auditor."
   (b) "The statutory auditor should test internal control system before relying on the same."
8. (a) Discuss the objectives of internal control system.
   (b) Discuss the advantages and limitations of internal control system.
9. "In a good system of internal check, the work of one is checked indirectly by the work of another" Explain and discuss this statement with examples.
10. What system of internal check would you recommend for a manufacturing concern to prevent fraud in connection with credit purchase of raw materials.

CHAPTER 5

Vouching

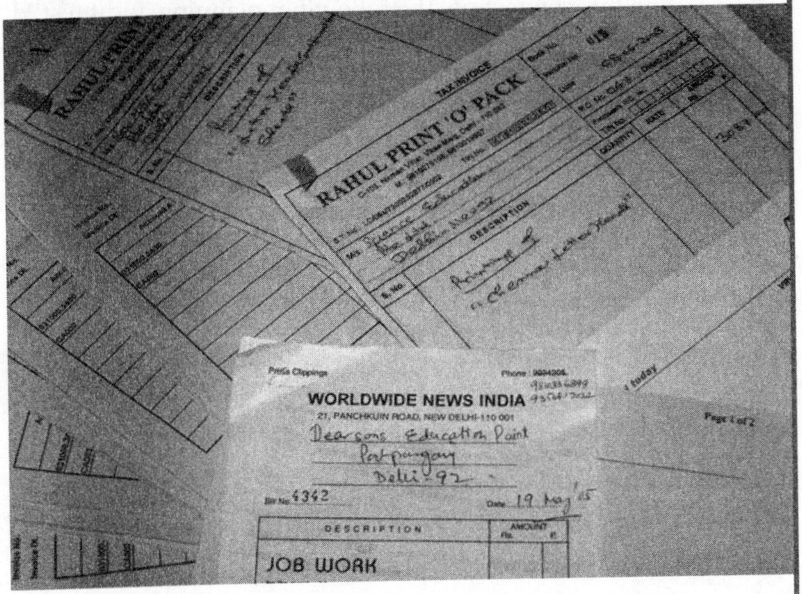

CHAPTER OUTLINE

5.1 INTRODUCTION

Having recorded the system of internal control and assessed its strengths and weaknesses, the auditor is then in a position to plan the nature and extent of the audit tests he proposes to execute in relation to the organisation's accounting transactions. The tailoring of the audit programme this way to meet individual demands of different accounting and control systems is fundamental to the concept of system audits.

A distinction will be drawn between transaction tests, to be applied where internal controls appear strong, and weakness tests, when a significant control deficiency may affect the auditor's opinion on the accounts. It is important to make this distinction correctly as the nature of the subsequent audit may be dependent upon it.

In this connection, the following 'planning audit test' diagram may be of assistance.

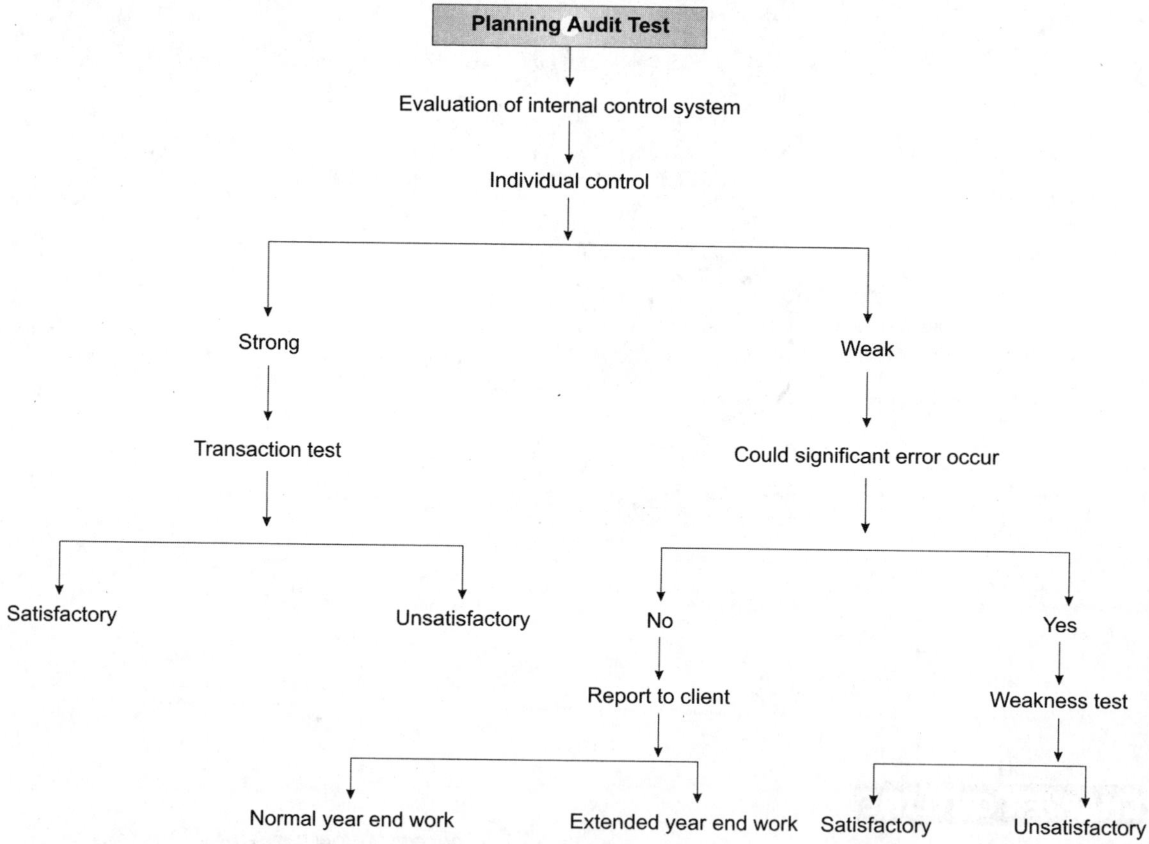

5.1.1 Transaction Tests

These are designed, where the auditor believes he is dealing with an adequate system of internal control, to test that the key aspects of the controls identified have operated consistently throughout the period under review. If the auditor has to satisfy himself of this, then he will also be able to rely upon the information being produced by the system and for this reason his tests should be concentrated on those aspects of the control system which are fundamental to its efficient and accurate operation. However, if the results of the transaction tests are unsatisfactory, if for instance one member of the enterprise's staff is not adequately performing the control function delegated to him, then the system must be regarded as being weak and an alternative, appropriate test must be designed to evaluate the materiality of that weakness.

The programme of transaction tests will need to be written out by the senior staff member responsible for the audit because this whole approach of tailoring the work to the different requirements of individual systems precludes the use of any master audit programme suitable for use under a variety of circumstances. This programme will record the exact details of the work to be performed by the audit staff; columns are provided so that the persons who are occupied in performing each part of the checking may add their initials as and when they complete it.

5.1.2 Weakness Tests

These must be adopted where the system appears weak in relation to items which are material to the validity of the accounts or alternatively have been proved weak by the result of transaction test. The test must be designed to establish whether the weakness identified has in fact led to significant error or whether this has been avoided and the only further audit action required is to report the weakness to the management.

Designing weakness tests appropriate to individual circumstances often calls for some ingenuity on the part of the auditor, but the nature of the resultant detailed tests will generally fall into one or more of the following broad classifications and should be recorded in a programme similar to that used for transaction tests.

Extended transaction tests

A greater volume of transaction tests may be specified than would be necessary under a strong control system, thus enabling the auditor to ascertain whether errors have been occurring with a frequency so as to be material to the accounts under review.

Vouching approach

Vouching means the examination of the transactions of a business, together with documentary and other evidence of sufficient validity to satisfy an auditor that such transactions are in order, have been properly authorised and are correctly recorded in the books. This means that the auditor goes behind the books of account and traces the entries to their sources and it is in this way that he can ascertain the full meaning and circumstances of the various transactions. In the absence of an effective internal control system, the entries in the books may show only such information as the book-keeper chooses to disclose and such information may be purposely or unintentionally contrary to the true facts. Therefore, only by examining external evidence can an auditor possibly ascertain the real state of affairs.

The vouching approach has its place in every audit, but extensive vouching should be restricted to circumstances of weakness and should only be adopted with caution and after careful consideration of what it will achieve. This method of audit testing is very time consuming and the auditor must always be wary lest even after extensive vouching, the state of the control systems would be such that he would still be unable to derive assurance as to the accuracy of the recording of other transactions, which he has not actually vouched.

5.2 CONCEPT OF VOUCHING

The examination of documentary evidence in support of transactions contained in the books of account is referred to as vouching. It is the technique followed in an audit for establishing authenticity of the transactions recorded in the primary books of accounts.

It essentially consists of verifying the record of transactions contained in the books of accounts with the relevant documentary evidence and the authority on the basis of which the entries were made. It also consists of examining in the process whether the amount mentioned in the voucher has been posted to an appropriate account, which would disclose the nature of the transaction on its inclusion in the final statements of account.

According to Taylor and Perry, "vouching is the examination of the evidence offered in substantiation of entries in the books, including in such examination the proof so far as possible that no entries have been omitted from the books".

According to Joseph Lancaster, "vouching is a device used to prove that various transactions for the period are fairly, truly and sincerely reflected in the books of accounts".

So, from the above definitions, it can be said that "vouching is a technique of auditing which checks the accuracy of entries made in the books of accounts with the help of available documentary evidences".

5.3 OBJECTIVES OF VOUCHING

Vouching is concerned with examining documentary evidence to ascertain the authenticity of entries in the books of accounts. It is a technique used by the auditor to judge the truth of entries appearing in the books of accounts.

Success of an audit depends on the efficiency with which vouching has been conducted. The following are the objectives for which the auditor adopts vouching techniques:

- To check that all transactions recorded in the books of accounts are supported by documentary evidence
- To verify that no fraud or error has been committed while recording the transactions
- To see that each and every transaction recorded has been adequately authorised by a responsible person
- To ensure that distinction has been made between capital and revenue items while recording the transactions
- To have greater precision in reporting the financial information as true and fair
- To ensure the reliability of the figures presented in the books of accounts
- To confirm that no transaction has been recorded in the books of accounts which are not related to the entity under audit
- To ensure the accuracy in totaling, carrying forward and recording of an amount in the accounts

5.4 IMPORTANCE OF VOUCHING

The audit normally takes place long after the transactions have taken place, and the auditor, not being in picture at the time, cannot have the benefit of direct experience of the transactions. Necessarily, he has to depend on evidence and the voucher constitutes the necessary evidence of the transaction. The auditor's basic duty is to examine the accounts, and not to merely see its arithmetical accuracy but also to see its substantial accuracy and then to make a report thereon. This substantial accuracy of the accounts and emerging financial statements can be known principally by examination of vouchers which are the primary documents relating to the transactions. If the primary document is wrong or irregular, the whole accounting statement would, in turn, become wrong and irregular. The auditor's role is to see whether or not the financial statements are wrong or irregular, and for this, vouching is simply essential. The importance of vouching was also highlighted in the case of Armitage vs Brewer & Knott (1930) wherein it was held that vouching is an important part of auditor's duty. If he shows any negligence in exercising care while vouching the books of accounts, his clients can claim damages.

In fact, the whole structure of auditing rests upon vouching. By conducting vouching, the auditor ensures the following:

- That a transaction is recorded in the proper account and revenue and expense is properly allocated to the accounting period
- That a transaction pertains to the organisation
- That there is proper authorisation for all transactions
- That all transactions, which have actually taken place, have been recorded
- That transactions have been classified and disclosed according to generally accepted accounting principles

Thus, vouching is the backbone of audit. Without vouching, auditing of financial statements cannot be conducted. The auditor's reporting on the financial statements will be farce if he avoids this part of audit.

The success of an audit will depend on the efficiency with which vouching has been applied during the process of auditing. Various frauds can be detected only if vouching is conducted in an intelligent manner. Wherever an auditor suspects a fraud, he should also check the sources of documentary evidence. Sometimes fictitious bills of expenses and purchases may be procured. Payments against these bills may be misappropriated. This type of fraud can be detected by intelligent vouching only.

Thus, it is clear from the aforesaid discussion that vouching constitutes the backbone of auditing. If vouching is conducted faithfully and effectively, it will help in establishing reliability of profit and loss account and balance sheet. So, vouching can be considered as the essence of auditing.

5.5 VOUCHING AND VERIFICATION

Vouching may be defined as the examination by the auditor of all documentary evidence, which is available to support the genuineness of transactions entered in the books of accounts. Vouching is a substantive auditing procedure designed to obtain evidence as to the completeness, accuracy and validity of the data produced by the accounting system. While obtaining evidence through vouching, the auditor aims to obtain reasonable assurance in respect of the following assertions in regard to transactions recorded in the books of account.

- Transaction is recorded in the proper account and revenue or expense is properly allocated to the accounting period.
- Transaction pertains to the concerned entity and took place during the relevant period.
- All transactions which have actually occurred have been recorded.
- Transactions have been classified and disclosed in accordance with recognised accounting policies and practices.

Thus, it is through vouching that the auditor comes to know the genuineness of transactions recorded in the books of account.

On the other hand, the term verification usually applies to the process of auditing that examines, by appropriate manner, whether assets and liabilities are properly stated in the balance sheet. The term 'verification' may also apply to items of profit and loss account for checking of the account balances and their presentation. Verification in the context of balance sheet items involves an inquiry into the ownership, valuation, existence and presentation of assets and liabilities in the balance sheet.

Regarding assets, the auditor while verifying whether the assets are owned by the client also looks into whether any charge has been created on those assets and whether the same has been appropriately disclosed. In case of liabilities, the auditor would like to see that these are actually owed by the organisation.

Therefore, vouching and verification differ in the following respects:

1. In vouching, the auditor examines the bonafides of transactions and their correct recording in the books, whereas in verification he has to ensure that assets as recorded in the balance sheet do really exist on the date of the balance sheet. Vouching cannot ensure the existence of assets. After purchase of the asset, it may be sold, destroyed or even gifted away without being recorded in the books.
2. Vouching is concerned with all items of income statement and with those balance sheet items undergoing change during the year. Verification, on the other hand, is concerned with all the items of balance sheet.
3. In vouching the auditor comes to know what should be in existence. In verification, the auditor can know the actual existence, freedom from encumbrances and proper valuation of assets.

Thus, it is clear from the above that vouching deals with the examination of transactions at their point of origin while verification usually deals with the balances contained in the balance sheet and profit and loss account.

5.6 VOUCHING AND ROUTINE CHECKING

Routine checking is a total process of accounting control, which includes the following:

- Examination of the totalling and balancing of the books of prime entry

- Examination of the posting from primary books to the ledger accounts
- Examination of totaling and balancing of the ledger accounts and of the preparation of trial balance made with those balances
- Overall examination of writing up the transactions properly.

In short, the routine checking is concerned with the ascertainment of the arithmetical accuracy of casting, posting and carry forward of balances.

A confusion sometimes arises that the concept of vouching and routine checking are similar and complementary to each other. But this is not true in actual practice. Broadly speaking, vouching includes routine checking and it is considered as a part of it. Vouching includes routine checking, checking of all totals, subtotals, carry forwards, posting and checking of all ledger accounts. The scope of routine checking is confined to the books of accounts but in case of vouching, the auditor has to go beyond the books of accounts in order to trace out the source of transaction.

5.7 CONCEPT OF VOUCHER

There is no denying the fact that without voucher, vouching cannot be conducted. Vouchers are considered as an integral part of vouching. Voucher is documentary evidence, both internal and external, which is used to support the entries made in the books of accounts of an enterprise.

A transaction is supposed to be recorded in the books of accounts only when the documentary evidence is available to support the transaction. It may be a receipt, counterfoil of a receipt, resolution passed in a meeting, cash memo, pay-in-slips, purchase invoices, minutes of a meeting etc. All such documentary evidences are known as vouchers.

Voucher can be of two types: primary and collateral vouchers.

(a) Primary vouchers When written evidence is available in original, it is known as primary vouchers. For example, purchase invoices, counterfoil of cash receipt etc.

(b) Collateral vouchers In certain cases, evidence in original is not available. Copies of such evidences are made available for the purpose of audit. These vouchers or documents are known as collateral vouchers. For example, Copies of resolution passed at a meeting, xerox copy of demand drafts etc.

On the basis of sources of documents, vouchers can again be of two types.

(a) Internal vouchers (b) External vouchers

(a) Internal vouchers Vouchers originating within the organisation are known as internal vouchers. For example, sales invoices, minutes book of board meetings, material requisition slip etc.

(b) External vouchers Vouchers originating from the outside sources are known as external vouchers. For example, mortgage deed, bank statement etc.

5.8 INTERNAL AND EXTERNAL EVIDENCE

The evidence that a voucher provides may be of various natures and can be of the following two types:

Internal evidence

It is one that has been created and used within the client's organisation and it never goes to outside party. Examples are duplicate sales invoices, employee's time reports, purchase requisitions, minute books etc. These documents are parts of the records of the concern and have been prepared in the normal course.

External evidence

It is one which emanates from outside the client's organisation. A document issued by a person with whom some business transactions had been entered into or who paid or was advanced an amount constitutes such evidence. For example, payee's receipt, lease agreement, bank statement etc. Sometimes, in certain transactions external evidence is obtained directly by the auditors, e.g. confirmation of balances from debtors and creditors.

The auditor should attempt to obtain as much external evidence as possible, since such evidence is generally more reliable than internal evidence. External evidence should be preferred, since the likelihood of its being fabricated is much less because it requires collusion with an outsider. However, when external evidences are not available or appropriate, the auditor is obliged to accept internal evidence. Every evidence whether internal or external, should be subjected to appropriate scrutiny and corroboration should be obtained, whenever possible. A lack of corroboration will require the auditor to investigate further to arrive at the fact.

5.9 GENERAL PRINCIPLES OF VOUCHING

In conducting vouching appropriately and effectively, the auditor should follow certain principles, which are stated as below.

- While vouching a transaction, the auditor must verify the authenticity of the transaction, accuracy of amount recorded and proper classification of accounts.
- The voucher, which has already been checked by the auditor should be cancelled or tick marked with a special sign, so that it may not be used again for fictitious transactions.
- It should be seen that every voucher is authorised by an officer responsible for this purpose.
- If there is any alteration in the vouchers, it must be supported by the concerned officer's initials.
- While vouching transactions, the auditor should keep in mind that the distinction is made between capital and revenue items.
- It should be seen that the date of the voucher falls within the accounting period.
- It should also be ensured that the voucher is made out in the client's name.
- The voucher should include all the relevant documents which would be expected to have been received or brought into existence on the transactions having been entered into, i.e. the voucher is complete in all aspects.

- The account in which the amount of the voucher is adjusted is the one that would clearly disclose the character of the receipt or payment posted thereto on its inclusion in the final accounts.
- All the vouchers should be numbered serially and dated.
- The amount in the receipt must be shown in words and figures. If the two differs then it should be investigated.
- If any voucher is missing, the concerned official should be asked to give proper explanation. If no satisfactory explanation is received, it should be further investigated.

5.10 TEEMING AND LADING: A CHALLENGE TO VOUCHING

Teeming and lading is a method adopted to misappropriate cash. The misappropriation of cash is activated by making a false entry relating to a transaction, which in turn is cancelled by a further entry and so on until such fraud is discovered. This method is also known as "delayed accounting of money received" as it is a method of concealment of a shortage by delaying the recording of cash receipts.

Example

Suppose, debts due from Mr. X is Rs. 50,000, from Mr. Y Rs. 1,00,000 and from Mr. Z Rs. 1,50,000. Now, say, an amount of Rs. 50,000 is being received from Mr. X in discharge of his debt in the first week of January, but no entry is made in the cash book by the cashier, who misappropriates the cash. Say, in the next month, when cash is received from Mr. Y amounting to Rs. 1,00,000, the cashier records Rs. 50,000 in the name of Mr. X and the remaining Rs. 50,000 in the name of Mr. Y. Again, in the next month, when Mr. Z pays his debt of Rs. 1,50,000, the cashier records Rs. 50,000 in the name of Mr. Y and Rs. 1,00,000 in the name of Mr. Z. Rs. 50,000 is to be shown in the balance sheet as amount due from Mr. Z. Thus, after a certain period of time, the amount due from Mr. Z has been written off as bad debt and the money received has been thus misappropriated. However, if it is detected by the auditor, immediately the cashier passes a false entry recording the receipts from Mr. Z by paying an amount of Rs. 50,000 out of his own pocket and thus the cashier utilises the money of the business for a certain period of time without any authority.

So, this type of fraud is a real challenge to the auditor. By adopting appropriate techniques of vouching, the auditor should detect this type of fraud and prevent misappropriation of cash.

For this purpose, the auditor should take the following steps as a part of vouching technique:

1. He should verify the debtors' ledger, particularly those debtors who are making part payments of their dues.
2. He may collect the balance confirmation certificate from debtors, whose accounts have been shown as due.
3. Before the commencement of the work of vouching, he should evaluate the efficiency of the internal check system regarding the receipts of cash from the customers of the organisation.
4. He should have a clear idea about the discount facility provided to the customers and the amount of bad debts to be written off.

5. If he suspects any fraud having already been committed, he should verify those transactions which have been shown in the cash book as deposited into bank and also check the bank reconciliation statement.
6. He should send the statement of accounts to the customers, whose accounts have been shown as due with a request that if a customer finds any discrepancy in the statement of account, he should contact the auditor without any delay.

5.11 VOUCHING OF DIFFERENT TYPES OF TRANSACTIONS

5.11.1 Vouching of Capital Expenditure

Capital expenditure means the expenditure relating to purchase of fixed assets. In order to vouch these types of transactions, the authenticity of the transaction, that is, whether it is properly authorised by the authority and whether the amount of transaction is duly capitalised or not should be checked.

Land and building

Documents to be checked

(i) Title deed
(ii) Mortgage deed in case of mortgaged property
(iii) Broker's note
(iv) Contract
(v) Receipts
(vi) Architect's certificate
(vii) Fixed asset register
(viii) Minutes of the directors meeting

Duty of the auditor

(i) The land and building may be freehold or leasehold. If it is freehold, it should be verified with the owner's title. But if it is leasehold, the base deed should be examined.
(ii) If the property is purchased directly from the vendor and if any contract is made with the vendor, that contract should have to be checked.
(iii) It also requires to be examined whether the ownership title of the property in favour of the client is legal or not.
(iv) The various incidental charges are required to be incurred for the purchase of land and buildings, e.g. registration expenses of the property. These expenses should be verified with proper documents and receipts and the auditor should also confirm that these expenses have been duly capitalised.
(v) If any building is constructed for the purpose of business, the contract made with the building contractor should be examined and in order to confirm the cost of construction, the certificate from the architect should be examined.

Assets acquired on H.P. system

Documents to be checked

(i) Board's minute book
(ii) Hire purchase agreement
(iii) Fixed assets register
(iv) Receipts from the vendor
(v) Bank statement

Duty of the auditor

(i) The minutes book of the Board meeting should be checked in order to confirm that the purchase of assets on hire purchase system has been approved by the Board.

(ii) The hire purchase agreement should be checked carefully and the description of the assets, cost of the assets, hire purchase charges, terms of payment and rate of interest should be noted.

(iii) It should be ensured that the concerned assets have been included in the related asset account at its cash value. It should also be checked that instalments due have been paid according to the terms of the hire purchase agreement.

(iv) It should be checked that the hire purchase charges applicable to the period from the commencement of the agreement to the end of the financial year have been charged against current profits.

(v) It should also be confirmed that the assets acquired on hire purchase basis have been included at its cash value in the balance sheet and depreciation has been calculated on the cash value from the date of the purchase. The amount due to the hire purchase vendor in respect of the capital outstanding has either been shown as a deduction from the asset concerned or as a separate amount under current liabilities.

Trademark and copyright

Documents to be checked

(i) Schedule of trademarks and copyright

(ii) Assignment deed or agreement

(iii) Contracts

Duty of the auditor

(i) A schedule of trademarks and copyright duly signed by the responsible officer should be obtained and the same should be scrutinised. It should be confirmed that all of them are shown in the balance sheet.

(ii) The written agreement in case of assignment of copyright and the assignment deed in case of transfer of trademarks should be examined.

(iii) Existence of copyright should be verified by reference to contract between the client and the other party.

(iv) It should be seen that the value has been determined properly and the cost incurred for the purpose of obtaining the trademarks and copyrights have been capitalised.

(v) It should also be ascertained that the legal life of the trade marks and copyright have not yet expired.

(vi) It should also be ensured that the amount paid for both the intangibles and assets is properly amortised having regard to appropriate legal and commercial consideration.

5.11.2 Vouching of Investments

Documents to be checked

(i) Broker's purchase note

(ii) Letter of allotment and calls

(iii) Share certificate or debenture certificate

(iv) Bank passbook

(v) Receipts

(vi) Director's meeting minute book

Duty of the auditor

(i) The auditor should examine whether investment has been made in accordance with the governing laws. Generally the organisation has its own rules regarding investment of money outside the business. It is required to be verified whether these rules have been complied with or not. Apart from this, it has to be seen that the governing provisions of the Companies Act regarding investment has been followed or not.

(ii) Investments are generally purchased through brokers. If the shares etc. are purchased through brokers, the price paid should be verified with broker's bill and the receipt.

(iii) If the investments are purchased through banks, the bank passbook should be checked.

(iv) On the basis of the Directors' meeting minute book, the auditor should confirm about the approval of the board for the purchase of investments.

(v) The auditor should verify the title of the investment through register to confirm that the investments purchased have been transferred in the name of the company.

(vi) If the investment is purchased at cum-dividend, it should be examined whether the purchase price has been shown properly under capital and revenue and the dividend receivable during the period has been accounted for or not.

5.11.3 Vouching of Borrowing from Banks

Documents to be checked

(i) Certificate from bank for securities deposited

(ii) Minutes of the Board meeting

(iii) Bank statement

(iv) Letter of loan sanction

(v) Bank passbook

Duty of the auditor

(i) Borrowing from bank may be either in the form of overdraft limits or cash credit. The auditor should confirm about the type of the loan from the letter of loan sanctioned from the bank.

(ii) Reconciliation of the balances in the overdraft or cash credit with that shown in the passbook should be done and it should be confirmed that the last mentioned balance by obtaining a certificate from the bank showing the balance in the accounts as at the end of the year.

(iii) A certificate from the bank showing particulars of securities deposited with the bank as security for the loan should be obtained. It should be confirmed that the same has been correctly disclosed and duly registered with the Registrar of Companies and recorded in the register of charges.

(iv) The auditor should verify the authority under which the loan has been raised. In the case of a company, only the Board of Directors is authorised to raise a loan or borrow from a bank.

(v) He should also confirm in the case of a company that the restrictions contained in Section 223 of the Companies Act as regards the maximum amount of loan that the company can raise has not been contravened.

(vi) It should also be ascertained that the purpose for which the loan has been raised and the manner in which it has been utilised and that this has not prejudicially affected the concern.

5.11.4 Vouching of Trading Transactions

Credit purchases

Documents to be checked

(i) Purchase invoices
(ii) Copies of orders placed
(iii) Goods received note
(iv) Copies of challans from supplier
(v) Goods inward register
(vi) Stock records

Duty of the auditor

(i) The main objective of vouching of credit purchases is to see that all purchase invoices are entered in the purchase book and the goods entered in the purchase books are actually received by the client and the client pays for only those goods, which are delivered by the supplier.

(ii) The auditor should examine the internal check system in force and should see that only credit purchases of goods are recorded in the purchase book.

(iii) It should be confirmed that the purchase of goods is sanctioned by a responsible official and only those goods are purchased in which the organisation deals with.

(iv) The goods purchased should be actually received by the client. For this purpose, the goods inward register, stock records and challan from the supplier should be verified.

(v) The auditor should be more careful while vouching the purchases made in the first month and the last month of the accounting period, because sometimes the purchases of the last year may be included in the purchase of first month of the current year or purchases of the last month of the current year may be recorded in the next year. As a result, the profit and loss account of the current year will not present true and fair position of the operating results.

Credit sales

Documents to be checked

(i) Sales invoices
(ii) Challan
(iii) Sales register/Goods outward register
(iv) Stock records
(v) Purchase order from customers

Duty of the auditor

(i) The main objective of vouching of credit sales is to see that all sales invoices are entered in the sales book and the goods sold entered in the sales book are actually disposed off by the client and the client receives for only those goods which are supplied to the customers.

(ii) The auditor should examine the internal check system in force and should see that only credit sales of goods are recorded in the sales book.

(iii) The sales register should be examined with copies of sales invoices. The sale of capital goods shall not be recorded in the sales book.

(iv) The sales tax etc. collected through sales invoices must be recorded under separate accounts.

(v) It should be verified that all sales invoices are prepared on the basis of challan and then sales invoices are entered in sales book and from there, posted to the respective customer account. No sales invoice should be left unrecorded.

(vi) Trade discount allowed to the customers should be checked. No separate entry for discount should be passed in the books.

(vii) The statement of accounts should be verified by obtaining confirmation from the customers.

(viii) The auditor should be more careful while vouching the sales made in the first month and the last month of the accounting period, because sometimes the sales of the last year may be included in the sales of the first month of the current year and sales of the last month of the current year may be recorded in the next year. As a result, the profit and loss account of the current year will not present true and fair position of the operating results.

Consignment sale

Documents to be checked

(i) Consignment day book

(ii) Account sales

(iii) Agreement between the consignor (client) and the consignee

(iv) Balance confirmation certificate from the consignee

(v) Pro-forma invoices

(vi) Goods outward book

Duty of the auditor

(i) It should be ascertained that credit has been taken only for the profit on the goods sold through the consignee before the year end. No profit should be taken for the profit on goods remaining in the hands of the consignee.

(ii) Where it is desired to show the result of each consignment, the goods sent on consignment, through consignment day book, should be debited to the consignment account. The auditor should check debits in each of consignment account by reference to the pro-forma invoice, consignment day book, goods outward book, transport documents of the goods, acknowledgement of the goods by the consignee and the account sales.

(iii) Credits in the consignment account should be verified with the help of the account sales received from the consignee.

(iv) The agreement between the consignor and the consignee should be verified to check the commission and other expenses, which are credited to consignee account.

(v) It should be ensured that the stock lying with the consignee at the year end should be taken in the balance sheet at cost on a consistent basis and credited to consignment account to arrive at the result of the consignment transactions.

(vi) Confirmation of the balance in the account of the consignee should be obtained from him.

(vii) Sometimes the goods are consigned not at cost but at an inflated price. The auditor should see that the necessary adjustments to remove the loading are made at the end of the year.

(viii) It is possible that the goods consigned are treated as ordinary sales. The auditor should see that necessary adjustments are made at the year end in respect of the unsold goods, commission and the expenses incurred by the consignee. The consignee should not be shown as a debtor for unsold goods and in valuation of stock, these goods should be included in stock at cost worked out on a consistent basis.

Goods on sale or return

Documents to be checked

(i) Receipt of approval from customer
(ii) Sales invoices
(iii) Stock records
(iv) Goods inward book
(v) Goods outward book

Duty of the auditor

(i) The auditor should see that whether a seperate record has been maintained for goods sold on approval basis.

(ii) He should ensure that the goods sent has not been included in sales unless the customer has intimated his approval or the stipulated time limit for such approval has expired.

(iii) The auditor should also check the internal control system in respect of sales on approval basis. Usually, on the receipt of approval from customers or expiry of time limit, sales invoices are prepared, a copy of which is sent to the customer.

(iv) It is also required that necessary arrangements should made to get back the goods, if within the stipulated time, the customer informs about the return of the goods.

(v) He should also verify whether the goods sent on sale or return basis has been taken in the closing stock as stock with customer, if no intimation has been received from the customer or if the time limit has not expired.

(vi) He should also get a statement from customer that the goods are lying with him on approval basis.

5.11.5 Vouching of Cash Book

Collection from debtors

Documents to be checked

(i) Sales invoices
(ii) Receipts issued to customers
(iii) Statement of customers accounts
(iv) Existing and past discount chart
(v) Correspondence with the customers

Duty of the auditor

(i) The auditor should first of all check the existing internal control system in respect of cash collection, particularly collection from customers. When cash is received from customers, a cash memo is issued; a counterfoil or carbon copy of such cash memo is retained by the receiving clerk. The auditor should verify the amount received from customers from that counterfoils or carbon copies issued.

(ii) He should also ensure that amount received from customers has been entered in the cash book on the day it is received.

(iii) He should also ensure that all these receipts are serially numbered. If any receipt is found to be missing, he should ask for clarification from the concerned officials.

(iv) It should be seen that the discount allowed to customers is authorised by a responsible officer. In addition to that, the terms and conditions of discount should be properly ascertained and the discount rates should be compared with the rates prevailing in the market.

(v) In case of suspicion, the auditor can contact the customers directly with the approval of the client to verify the receipt of cash from them.

Interest and dividend received on investments

Documents to be checked

(i) Bank statement

(ii) Dividend warrants

(iii) Schedule of securities

(iv) Agreement with party

Duty of the auditor

(i) While vouching dividends, the auditor should check dividend warrant counterfoils and covering letters received along with the cheques.

(ii) If the dividend and interest is collected through bank, the auditor should verify the amount from the bank statement. In case of warrant received and amount not yet collected by the bank, the auditor should ensure that it has been shown as cheque yet to be collected.

(iii) While vouching interest, the auditor should check the fixed interest bearing security statement. Interest on bank deposit should be checked from the bank passbook. But if interest is on the loan given to a party, it can be checked from the agreement made with the concerned party.

(vi) The auditor should ensure that all interest received and accrued have been accounted for in the books and properly shown in the balance sheet.

(v) If interest or dividend is received for the pre-acquisition period, the auditor should see whether proper adjustment has been made with the cost of investment for this pre-acquisition dividend or interest.

Bad debts recovered

Documents to be checked

(i) Notification from the court/bankruptcy trustee

(ii) Letter from collection agency

(iii) Letters from debtors

(iv) Schedule of bad debts

(vi) Bank passbook

Duty of the auditor

(i) The auditor should ascertain the total amount lying as bad debt. In some cases, the court distributes the amount recovered from the insolvent person to his creditors in proportion of their claims. In this respect, total amount of debt, treated as bad from the party concerned plays a very important role.

(ii) The auditor should ensure that all the bad debt recovery has been properly recorded in the books of accounts.

(iii) Credit manager's files are also to be checked properly for the purpose of ascertaining the actual amount recovered.

(iv) The auditor should also ensure that the amount collected on account of bad debt recovery has been deposited into the bank promptly.

(v) The amount recovered should also be counterchecked from the counterfoils or carbon copies of the receipt issued to the debtors. The auditor should also ensure that all these receipts are serially numbered.

Insurance claim received

Documents to be checked

(i) Counterfoil of the receipt

(ii) Insurance policy

(iii) Statement of claim submitted

(iv) Copy of the survey report

(v) Correspondence with the insurance company

Duty of the auditor

(i) The auditor should check the counterfoil of the acknowledgement of receipt issued by the client to know the actual amount recovered from the insurance company.

(ii) The auditor should examine the statement of the claim submitted by the client along with the insurance policy to ensure that the claim has been submitted according to the provisions in the insurance policy.

(iii) All the correspondences with the insurer on final determination of claim and payment thereof should be examined along with the copy of survey report.

(iv) The accounting treatment of the amount received should be examined in order to ensure that revenue is credited with the appropriate amount and that in respect of claim against an asset, the profit and loss account is debited with the shortfall of the claim admitted against the book value.

(v) The auditor should also see that entries in the profit and loss account has been appropriately described, if the claim was lodged in a previous year but no entries were passed then.

Cash sales

Documents to be checked

(i) Sales invoices

(ii) Cash sales summary

(iii) Copies of cash memo

Duty of the auditor

(i) The system of internal check should be examined with the objectives of finding out the defects therein, if any, whereby cash sales could be misappropriated.

(ii) The practice followed in the matter of issuing cash memos should be ascertained. Cash sales are usually verified with carbon copies of cash sales.

(iii) One of the important matters to which the auditor should pay attention is that the dates on the cash memos should tally with those on which cash collected in respect thereof has been entered in the cash book.

(iv) The computation of sales should be ascertained by the auditor in order to verify whether the price of goods sold has been calculated correctly.

(v) If a cash memo has been cancelled, its original copy should be inspected because there could be a possibility of misappropriation of the amount thereof.

(vi) If cash collections are made through automatic cash registers, the daily totals entered in the cash book should be checked with the current rolls.

Income from house property

Documents to be checked

(i) Bills issued to tenants
(ii) Tenancy agreement
(iii) Rent receipts
(iv) Statement of rent received
(v) Rent reconciliation statement

Duty of the auditor

(i) The auditor should examine the rent received from house properties with the counterfoils of the rent receipts in order to ascertain the amount of rent and the period for which it is paid.

(ii) He should check the copies of bills issued to the tenants by reference to the agreement with the tenant and charges paid by the client on behalf of tenants, e.g. electricity charges.

(iii) He should verify the statement of rent received prepared tenant-wise or property wise, if any, and check it with the rent register, if any maintained for the tenants.

(iv) He should also vouch the entries for rent received in advance or accrued rent in order to see that proper adjustment entries are passed for the amount of rent pertaining to the accounting year concerned.

(v) Reconciliation between the amount of rent received and the amount of rent receivable should be done by the auditor and if there is any difference, it should be enquired into. In this context, adjustment against deposit, if any, should also be checked.

(vi) The auditor should obtain a certificate from the responsible officer in respect of any vacant property during the year.

Remuneration paid to Directors

Documents to be checked

(i) Resolutions of the general meeting
(ii) Articles of Association
(iii) Agreement with the Directors
(iv) Director's attendance register
(v) Receipts issued by the Directors

Duty of the auditor

(i) The auditor should check the terms and conditions of appointment of Directors first by referring to the minutes of the general meeting.

(ii) He should also examine the Articles of Association in order to ascertain the mode of payment.

(iii) The agreement with the directors should also be checked to know the amount to be paid to the directors for attending board meetings and for other works by way of commission or otherwise. In this respect, the auditor should also check the Director's attendance in the board meetings as available in the attendance register.

(iv) It should be ensured that all the legal formalities as per the provisions of Sections 198, 309, 349 and 350 and Schedule XIII of the Companies Act, where applicable, have been duly complied with.

(v) Computation of the net profits and the commission payable to directors in terms of clause 4A of Part II of Schedule VI to the Companies Act should be checked thoroughly.

(vi) The amount paid to the Directors, as their remuneration should also be checked with receipts issued by the directors for this purpose.

Travelling expenses

Documents to be checked

(i) Travelling rules of the organisation
(ii) Approved tour programmes
(iii) Tour report
(iv) Board meetings minutes
(v) RBI permission letter
(vi) Air, railway tickets etc.

Duty of the auditor

(i) Before conducting vouching work of travelling expenses, the auditor should know the rules of the organisation on admissibility and rates of travelling expenses and daily allowances.

(ii) The auditor should ensure first whether the travelling expenses have been incurred only on those tour programmes, which are approved by the competent authority.

(iii) The auditor should then thoroughly check the travelling expenses bills submitted by the employees along with the supporting vouchers as may be appropriate.

(iv) The auditor should also confirm that the statement of business done or tour report has been submitted by the employees and reviewed by proper authority.

(v) In case of foreign trip, the board's resolution should be seen, to ensure that the trip has been sanctioned. The auditor should also ensure that necessary permission has been obtained from the Reserve Bank of India for foreign exchange transactions in connection with foreign trip.

(vi) It should also be checked by the auditor that advances, if any, taken by the employees for this purpose have been properly accounted for.

Cash purchases

Documents to be checked

(i) Cash memo
(ii) Cash bill
(iii) Goods inward book
(iv) Payment order
(v) Original receipts from the payee

Duty of the auditor

(i) Cash purchase is an important area where the defalcation and misappropriation of cash is made possible. For this reason, it should be carefully examined by the auditor whether proper authorisation is there for such purchase from the appropriate authority.

(ii) In case of emergency, cash purchase of goods may be made. So, the auditor should evaluate the situation under which cash purchase is made to ascertain the emergence of such purchase.

(iii) Usually purchase of stores and stationery items are made on cash basis. So the auditor should ensure that there is adequate internal control system, which will help in controlling manipulation of cash purchases.

(iv) It should be seen that the goods purchased are actually received by the storekeeper. For this purpose, cash memos can be compared with the entries in goods inward book to verify the actual goods received.

(v) The auditor can also check the discount facilities provided by the suppliers and ensure that only net amount after deducting discount availed have been entered in the books.

Salaries and wages paid

Documents to be checked

(i) Salary bills
(ii) Wage sheets or pay roll
(iii) Counterfoil of cheques
(iv) Appointment letters
(v) Service agreement
(vi) Employment registers

Duty of the auditor

(i) For the purpose of vouching salaries and wages, the auditor is required to go through the internal procedure and confirm that they are not altered since the last audit.

(ii) The additions, calculations and castings of the salary bills and wage sheets should be properly checked by the auditor.

(iii) The total amount paid for salaries and wages should be compared with the entries in the cash book. For this purpose, the auditor should compare the total of wage sheet and salary bill with the amount of cheque withdrawn. If there is any excess amount withdrawn, the auditor should ensure that it is deposited into the bank immediately.

(iv) It should be the duty of the auditor to ensure that the unclaimed salaries and wages have been deposited into bank or the concerned cheque has been cancelled.

(v) The auditor has to see whether the wage sheet and salary bill is duly certified by a responsible officer and check the employment register for the purpose of finding out dummy employees and workers.

(vi) He should further check attendance records, salary bill and wage sheets of earlier months and appointment letter of new employees. If there is an abnormal increase in the wages and salaries of a month over the previous month, he should enquire into the reasons for such increase.

Payment of sales tax

Documents to be checked

(i) Periodical sales return
(ii) Treasury challans
(iii) Sales tax assessment order
(iv) Reconciliation statement
(v) Certificate from registered dealers

Duty of the auditor

(i) The auditor should see the challan receipts of the Reserve Bank of India or State Bank of India or any other bank as per sales tax department's list in support of the payment vouchers and should ensure that the amount of tax deposited agrees with the amount of tax payable as per the return submitted.

(ii) He should also check sales tax register with the copies of invoices and confirm that proper sales tax has been charged, collected and deposited.

(iii) He should check the calculations made in the returns and ascertain that the total liability as per returns agrees with the sales tax collected and thus ensure that the sales tax payable and liability of each year are properly recorded.

(iv) He should obtain the certificates from registered dealers to ascertain that the sales tax returns agree with the sales tax collected by them for the period as shown in different invoices.

(v) Finally, the auditor should find out the total tax liability and ensure that proper provision has been made in the accounts for tax liability.

Research and development expenditure

Documents to be checked

(i) Minutes of the board meeting

(ii) Memorandum and articles of association of the client

(iii) Annual budget

(iv) Receipts and other relevant papers from the third parties

Duty of the auditor

(i) The nature of research and development work has to be ascertained first by the auditor to ensure that it is related with the normal activities of the undertaking.

(ii) The auditor should also ascertain whether the concerned research activity is authorised by the board and has relevance to the objectives of the company and ensure that no expense unrelated to the research and development programme is allowed to be debited to this account.

(iii) The auditor should check the accounting entries passed for this purpose. He should confirm that if the research expenses are paid for developing products or for inventing a new product, they are treated as deferred revenue expenditure to be written off over a period of three to five years, if successful. In case, it is established that the research effort is not going to succeed, the entire expenses incurred should be written off to the profit and loss account.

(iv) He should also ensure that if any plant and machinery have been purchased specially for the purpose of research activity, the cost thereof, less the residual value is appropriately debited to the research and development account over the years of research.

(v) The auditor should see that the tax benefit arising out of the research and development expenses is taken into account in creating tax provision.

(vi) Finally, he should ascertain the accounting policy of the concern regarding treatment of research and development expenditure and its consonance with AS-8 as issued by the Institute of Chartered Accountants of India.

Travelling salesman's commission

Documents to be checked

(i) Agreement with the salesman
(ii) Receipts issued by salesman
(iii) Statement of sales
(iv) Appointment letters of the salesman
(v) Commission statement

Duty of the auditor

(i) The auditor should see the appointment letter given to the salesman or the agreement with the salesman in order to know the rate of commission entitlement and other terms and conditions of his assignment.

(ii) An examination of the statement submitted by the salesman regarding sales should be made and checked with the sales records in order to find out the amount of sales affected by the salesman. This is required as usually sales commission is paid on the basis of sales affected through a salesman.

(iii) The auditor should also check the statement of commission submitted by the salesman in order to check the accuracy of calculation of commission payable to the salesman.

(iv) It should be ensured by the auditor that the commission is paid only on sales booked and executed within the year and the payment of commission should be vouched with the receipts signed by the salesman.

(v) The auditor should also check whether provision has been made in the accounts for commission due but not paid to the salesman.

Freight, carriage and custom duty

Documents to be checked

(i) Freight note
(ii) Transport receipts
(iii) Rate schedule of transport charges
(iv) Rate of custom duty
(v) Custom duty payment challan
(vi) Correspondence with transporters and customs authorities

Duty of the auditor

(i) The auditor should ascertain the nature of expenses first, i.e. whether they relate to the purchase of raw materials or purchase of assets or sale of goods as the accounting treatment of these expenses depend on the purpose for which they have been incurred.

(ii) He should ensure that all the expenses incurred in this connection are properly authorised.

(iii) He should ascertain the possibility of duty drawback or refund of custom duty, if any, and see whether adequate adjustments have been made in the books of account for this purpose.

(iv) The auditor should also refer to the terms and conditions of purchases and sales to know whether the expenses incurred in this connection are recoverable from the third party.

(v) He should also check the adequacy of transit insurance to cover the risk of loss due to goods lost in transit.

(vi) The auditor should also examine all the relevant documents and ensure that all the payments made in this connection have been fully accounted for.

Preliminary expenses

Documents to be checked

(i) Board's minute book
(ii) Receipts for the registration fees paid
(iii) Bills and receipts issued by the printers
(iv) Prospectus
(v) Statutory report
(vi) Other supporting papers and vouchers

Duty of the auditor

(i) The auditor should ascertain first as to whether the expenses capitalised as preliminary expenses are actually connected with the formation of the company.

(ii) The expenses incurred for the formation of the business should be approved by the Board of Directors in their meeting. It is the duty of the auditor to see whether the expenses incurred has got due approval from the authority.

(iii) The auditor should also justify the expenses from the angle of propriety aspect of the business. He should check the tightness of the amount of expenses.

(iv) The accounting policy of the concern regarding writing off of preliminary expenses should also be evaluated in order to justify the appropriateness of the policy adopted.

(v) In some cases, the approval from the shareholders is also required to be obtained for incurring expenses on account of preliminary expenses. The auditor should confirm that the required approval has been obtained from the shareholders in this regard.

(vi) The concern is also entitled to get exemption for the preliminary expenses incurred in computing business income under the Indian Income tax Act. The auditor should see whether this aspect is properly dealt with or not.

Royalty payable to a foreign collaborator

Documents to be checked

(i) Collaboration agreement
(ii) Statement of royalty payable
(iii) Permission from Reserve Bank of India
(iv) Receipts from the foreign collaborator
(v) Other supporting papers and vouchers

Duty of the auditor

(i) The auditor should go through the agreement with the foreign collaborator to note the rate of royalty, method of calculation of royalty, mode of payments etc.

(ii) He should also examine the statement showing detailed calculation of royalty payable and verify whether it has been calculated according to the agreement along with the checking of payment vouchers.

(iii) He should confirm that adequate and necessary provision has been made for the royalty accrued but not yet paid to the foreign collaborator during the year.

(iv) He should ensure that necessary permission has been obtained from the Reserve Bank of India for making payments outside the country, if royalty is required to be payable in foreign currency.

(v) The auditor should also examine that the requirement of short working facility is duly availed off.

(vi) The amount of royalty paid or payable during the year should be compared with that of the previous year and reasons for variation, if significant, should be inquired into.

Custom duty paid on import of machinery

Documents to be checked

(i) Accounts submitted by the clearing agents
(ii) Deposit account with custom authorities
(iii) Receipts issued by custom authorities for payments made
(iv) Statement of duty payable
(v) Other supporting papers and vouchers

Duty of the auditor

(i) The auditor should ensure that the custom duty paid is in connection with the import of machinery only and the machinery is purchased for the use of the business concerned.

(ii) He should verify the amount of custom duty with reference to bill of entry duty stamped by custom authority.

(iii) If the machinery is imported through clearing agents, the auditor should also refer the accounts submitted by the clearing agent in order to ensure total charges including custom duty on account of import of machinery.

(iv) The payment of custom duty should be checked with the receipts received from the custom authority.

(v) The auditor should check the accounting aspect of custom duty paid against import of machinery, i.e. whether it has been capitalised by debiting machinery account.

Insurance premium paid

Documents to be checked

(i) Insurance policy
(ii) Insurance premium receipts
(iii) Cover note issued by the insurance company
(iv) Correspondence with the insurance company
(v) Other supporting papers and vouchers

Duty of the auditor

(i) For the purpose of vouching insurance premium paid on different policies first of all the adequacy of the insurance should be examined very carefully. It should be the duty of an auditor to review the insurance policy periodically in order to ascertain the under-insurance in each of the policies undertaken.

(ii) The auditor should check the payment of insurance premium from the receipts obtained from the insurance companies.

(iii) It should be ensured by the auditor that premiums are not in arrears and the prepaid insurance has been properly adjusted against subsequent premium payable.

(iv) If the insurance premium paid against risk of fire etc. on any property, the auditor should confirm that the property belongs to the concern. However, if the premium is paid against key-man insurance policy, the auditor should evaluate the necessity of such insurance coverage.

(v) Finally, the auditor should check the entries passed for the premium paid to ensure that proper distinction has been made between fire and other natural hazards insurance with key-man insurance.

Commission paid to sole-selling agent

Documents to be checked

(i) Agreement

(ii) Receipts

(iii) Accounts sales sent by agent

Duty of the auditor

(i) The auditor should be aware regarding the percentage of commission payable to the sole-selling agent.

(ii) He should check the sales figure of account sales sent by the agent and the calculation of commission.

(iii) He should confirm whether in the agreement there is provision for adjustment of bad debt with the commission payable.

(iv) He should verify the amount of commission with reference to cash book and the receipts from the commission agent.

(v) The auditor should see that unpaid commission has been duly provided for in the accounts.

AUTHOR'S NOTE

In this chapter, a number of transactions are considered for vouching purposes, but it is not possible to consider every possible type of transaction that could be the subject of an examination question. From the transactions discussed in this chapter, it is expected that the students should be able to answer any type of transactions in the examination by following the approach adopted for vouching different transactions.

POINTS TO PONDER

- The examination of documentary evidence in support of transactions contained in the books of account is referred to as vouching. It is the technique followed in an audit for establishing authenticity of the transactions recorded in the primary books of accounts.
- Objectives for which an auditor adopts vouching technique include checking that all transactions recorded in the books of account, verifying that no fraud or error has been committed, ensuring that every transaction recorded has been adequately recorded, confirming that the figures presented in the books of accounts are reliable etc.

- Vouching is the backbone of audit. Without vouching, auditing of financial statements cannot be conducted. By conducting vouching, the auditor ensures that a transaction is recorded in the proper account, a transaction pertains to the organisation, there is proper authorisation for all transactions, all transactions have been recorded and transactions have been classified and disclosed according to generally accepted accounting principles.
- Vouching and verification are not same. Vouching deals with the examination of the transactions at their point of origin, while verification usually deals with the balances contained in the balance sheet and profit and loss account.
- Vouching includes routine checking, checking of all totals, subtotals, carry forwards, posting and checking of all ledger accounts. The scope of routine checking is confined to the books of accounts but in case of vouching, the auditor has to go beyond the books of accounts in order to trace out the source of transaction.
- Voucher is documentary evidence, both internal and external, which is used to support the entries made in the books of accounts of an enterprise. Vouchers can be of two types: primary voucher and collateral voucher.
- The evidence that a voucher provides may be of various nature and can be of two types: internal evidence and external evidence.
- For proper and effective vouching, an auditor should follow certain principles, which include authenticity of transaction, accuracy of amount recorded and proper classification of accounts. Besides, the auditor should see the date, authorisation, firm name, completeness and the accounting aspect of the transaction.
- Teeming and lading is a method adopted to misappropriate cash. Misappropriation of cash is activated by making a false entry relating to a transaction, which in turn is cancelled by a further entry and so on until such fraud is discovered.

REVIEW QUESTIONS

Short-answer Questions

1. Write the objectives of vouching.
2. What do you mean by vouchers? What are its different types?
3. Distinguish between vouching and routine checking.
4. Explain the following statements.
   (a) Vouching is the essence of auditing.
   (b) In vouching payments, the auditor does not merely seek proof that money has been paid away.
5. What do you mean by 'teeming and lading'? What is the duty of an auditor in this respect?
6. State what information would you require and what documentary evidence would you see while vouching Director's remuneration.
7. Will you accept the following as good voucher?
   (a) A bill of Rs. 5,000 submitted by a salesman for his travelling allowance

(b) A cash memo for Rs. 500 for a perambulator of a company producing rolled steel
(c) Hotel bills submitted by the sales manager amounting to Rs. 10,500
(d) A statement of account received from a debtor claiming an amount of Rs. 4,500 as balance due to him on account of unadjusted advance; the amount has been credited to the sales account
(e) Traveling allowance bills of the manager amounting to Rs. 500 for attending meeting convened by the State Government for public interest
(f) A statement of account from a clearing agent claiming Rs. 2,000 as import duty paid on behalf of the client
(g) Rent received for a house at Nagpur, the company having its office and factory at Mumbai

8. Give the type or types of evidences generally available in respect of the following:
(a) Construction work-in-progress
(b) Leasehold land
(c) Balance with bank
(d) Goods in transit
(e) Returns outward
(f) Contingent liability in respect of bills discounted
(g) Furniture and fixture
(h) Royalty paid to foreign collaborator

Essay-type Questions

1. How do you vouch the following?
(a) Custom duty paid on import of machinery
(b) Income from house property
(c) Royalty payable to a foreign collaborator
(d) Traveling expenses
(e) Interest and dividend received
(f) Directors fees paid
(g) Preliminary expenses
(h) Insurance premium paid
2. How would you as an auditor examine the following?
(a) Goods sent on sale or return
(b) Goods sent on consignment
(c) Payment of interest on share capital
(d) Shares issued at a discount
3. State what information would you require and what documentary evidence would you see while vouching the following:
(a) Freight, carriage and custom duty
(b) Commission paid to sole-selling agent
(c) Credit purchase
(d) Book debts realised
4. What is vouching? Discuss the features of vouching? State the important considerations before conducting vouching.
5. While auditing the accounts of a trading concern, how would you examine that all liabilities incurred before the close of the year in respect of wages, freight and travelers commission have been included in the accounts?
6. Discuss the principal consideration involved in the examination of debtors' and suppliers' ledger.
7. What are the special steps to be taken by the auditor in vouching the following transactions?
(a) Sales made during the last few days of the year
(b) Goods sent to debtors free of charge by way of quantitative discount

8. How will you deal with the following as an auditor?
   (a) Bonus to employees, which was hitherto being charged to profit and loss account on accrual basis, is now being accounted for on cash basis.
   (b) There is a significant fall in market price of some investments held for a long time by the concern.
   (c) Outstanding liabilities for expenses show a considerable fall as compared to last year.

CHAPTER 6

Verification and Valuation of Assets and Liabilities

CHAPTER OUTLINE

6.1 INTRODUCTION

One of the most important duties of an auditor in connection with the audit of the accounts of a concern is to verify the assets and liabilities appearing in the balance sheet. He has not only to examine the arithmetical accuracy of the transactions in the books of accounts by vouching, but also to see that the assets as recorded in the balance sheet actually exist.

If the auditor fails to verify the assets, he will be held liable as was decided in the case of "London Oil Storage Co. Ltd. vs Seear Hasluck & Co. (1904)". It was held in that case that "the auditor should verify the existence of the assets stated in the balance sheet, otherwise he will be liable for any damage suffered by the client".

6.2 MEANING OF VERIFICATION OF ASSETS

Verification means the proof of existence or confirmation of assets and liabilities on the date of balance sheet.

Verification usually indicates verification of assets of any concern, which can be done by the examination of value, ownership, existence and possession of any asset. According to Spicer and Pegler, "verification of assets implies an enquiry into the value, ownership and title, existence and possession and the presence of any charge on the assets".

So, verification is a process, which includes

- valuation of assets at its proper value
- ownership and title of the assets
- confirmation about the existence of the assets
- satisfaction about the condition that they are free from any charge or mortgage.

6.3 MEANING OF VALUATION OF ASSETS

Valuation of assets means examination of the accuracy and propriety of the valuation of those assets, which are shown in the balance sheet of any concern at the end of the financial year.

So, valuation is an operation, which includes

- obtaining all the necessary information regarding valuation
- analysing all the figures available
- confirming the fact that the valuation is being determined on the basis of generally accepted conventions and accounting principles
- ensuring that consistency of methods are followed for the valuation from year to year
- obtaining an opinion regarding the accuracy of valuation.

6.4 DIFFERENCE BETWEEN VERIFICATION AND VALUATION

Valuation of assets is a part and parcel of verification. Without proper valuation of assets, verification is not possible.

Verification includes, apart from valuation, the examination of ownership right, the existence of the asset in the business and its freeness from any sort of charge or mortgage.

6.5 IMPORTANCE OF VERIFICATION OF ASSETS

The auditor's duty is not complete only when he has vouched the entries appearing in the books. The substantiation of an entry under the date on which it is made does not prove the existence of the related asset at the date of the balance sheet, nor is the value of such asset necessary to be the same as on the date of the original entry. The auditor has the further duty of substantiating the existence and value of such items as on the date of the balance sheet. This work can be performed through proper verification of assets.

If the balance sheet contains an asset, which, in fact, does not exist or which is stated at a value different from what is considered reasonable, both the balance sheet and the profit and loss account would be incorrect. For instance, when the balance of sundry debtors include debts amounting to Rs. 5,000, that are irrecoverable and no provision has been created against such bad debts, then the amount of profit, the value of assets and the value of proprietor's fund would be shown in excess by that amount.

Auditors' duty under the Companies Act has been extended by the promulgation of the Other Companies (Auditors Report) Order '2003, issued under Section 227(4A) of the Companies Act. This order requires the auditor to state in his report some additional matters, which include matters like verification of fixed assets and stock. On these accounts, it is essential that assets should be verified with utmost care.

6.6 IMPORTANCE OF VALUATION OF ASSETS

Principally, the auditor is required to verify the original cost of asset and confirm, as far as practicable, that such a valuation is fair and reasonable. As regards the manner in which the original cost should be ascertained, there are well-defined modes of valuation, which are expected to follow.

Assets are valued either on a 'going concern' or a 'break-up value' basis. Under 'going concern' method, it is necessary to find out and calculate the cost of acquisition of the concerned assets and the rate of depreciation required to be provided. 'Break-up value' basis is considered when the company is being wound up. In this method, assets are valued at their realisable value. So, value of an asset is being determined differently in different ways.

It is thus evident that the auditor is expected to apply his knowledge and skill assessing the value of each asset with a view to confirm that it is true and fair, having regard to the principles on which assets are generally valued. In the words of Lancaster, " an auditor is not a valuer and cannot be expected to act as such. All that he can do is to verify the original cost and to ascertain as far as possible that the current values are fair and reasonable and are in accordance with the accepted commercial principles".

So, valuation forms an important part of every audit. This is because the fairness of the balance sheet depends much upon how correctly the valuation of various assets and liabilities has been made. The auditor has to see that the assets and liabilities appearing in the balance sheet have been exhibiting their proper value.

6.7 GENERAL PRINCIPLES FOR VERIFICATION AND VALUATION OF ASSETS

The following are the general principles which are required to be considered by the auditor in conducting verification and valuation of assets in an organisation:

1. ***Acquisition of individual asset*** The cost of asset acquired should be verified with their purchase agreements or ownership rights and the receipts of the seller in respect of the price paid. It should be verified that expenditure on assets newly acquired and the renewal and replacement of old assets have been correctly recorded in consistent with the method that has been generally followed in the past.

2. ***Acquisition of group of assets*** Where a concern has taken over the assets of a going concern, the agreement of purchase should be inspected and that the amount paid for them should also be ascertained.

3. ***Sale of assets*** When an asset is sold, its sale proceeds should be vouched for reference to the agreement, containing the terms and conditions of sale, counterfoil of the receipt issued to the purchaser or any other evidence which may be available.

If the sale of a fixed asset has resulted in capital profit, it should be transferred to capital reserve. However, the profit limited to the original cost or a loss should be transferred to the profit and loss account.

4. ***Depreciation*** It is now obligatory for a company to provide for depreciation out of profits in accordance with the provisions under Sub-section (1) of Section 205, before any profit can be distributed as dividend.

The law requires that depreciation should be provided in any one of the ways specified in Section 205(2) of the Companies Act.

The value of certain assets (viz. plant and machinery) is also affected by an accident or by obsolescence. Any asset which has been discarded after such a happening should be shown in the balance sheet only at realisable value.

5. ***Physical verification of fixed assets*** The existence of fixed assets, where practicable, should be verified by physical inspection or by comparing the particulars of assets as entered in the schedule attached to the balance sheet, with the asset register and also reconciling their total value with the general ledger balances.

6. ***Inspection of current assets and investments*** Wherever possible, all the securities and documents of title, cash, negotiable instruments etc. representing the assets should be inspected at the close of the last day of the accounting period. If this is not practicable and the examination is undertaken at a latter date, a careful scrutiny of transactions subsequent to the date of the balance sheet must be made to ensure that the changes in their balances that have subsequently taken place are bonafide and are supported by adequate evidence.

7. ***Charges on assets*** It should be ascertained that no unauthorised charge has been created against an asset and all the charges are duly registered and disclosed.

Where shares or securities are lodged with a bank to secure a loan or an overdraft, a certificate should be obtained from the bank showing the nature of the charges, if any.

8. ***Assets with third parties*** Where assets, e.g. government securities, shares and debentures, stock sent on consignment, goods sent on sale or approval basis etc. are in the custody of a third party other than a bank, these must be inspected.

6.8 PROBLEMS IN VERIFICATION

Without proper verification of assets and liabilities, it is not possible for the auditor to certify the balance sheet as it exhibits a true and fair view of the state of affairs of the business. It will never be possible on the part of the auditor to perform the function in his own responsibility and in accordance with his own knowledge and expertise.

Example

If the auditor is required to verify the stock-in-trade at the end of the accounting period, it will take weeks and months to complete this work. Not only that, the auditor will have to take help of experts in this line. In addition to that, there are certain assets, which have no physical existence in appearance, namely goodwill, patent, copyright, trademarks etc. In these cases, the auditor has to conduct verification on the basis of available documents.

In Kingston Cotton Mills Ltd. Case (1896), it was held that "it is no part of an auditor's duty to take stock. No one contends that it is. He must rely on others for the details of stock-in-trade". So there was no breach of duty on the part of the auditor. An auditor is not supposed to take stock himself and in the absence of suspicious circumstances he can accept a stock certificate by a trusted official of the company.

6.9 PROBLEMS IN VALUATION

The various problems which an auditor faces while conducting valuation of assets and liabilities are stated below:

(a) Character of the assets In some cases, it is not possible to identify the character of the asset for the purpose of valuation as whether it is fixed asset or current asset. The mode of valuation process of fixed asset is different from the mode of valuation process of current assets, e.g. investments.

(b) Use of assets In some situations, the same asset is available for sale and is again used in the organisation. The valuation process also depends on the nature of use of the concerned assets, e.g. stock of furniture.

(c) Estimated life The life of the fixed assets are not certain. The valuation of these assets is made on the basis of estimated life of the assets. However, the determination of estimated life is not an easy task.

(d) Eventual problems It is not possible for the auditor to take into consideration the events that have occurred after balance sheet date, which have the effect on valuation of assets.

(e) Lack of information The auditor may not be in possession of all the relevant information, which are required to be considered by the auditor in the determination of the value of assets.

6.10 WINDOW DRESSING—A CHALLENGE TO VERIFICATION

Window dressing may be defined as an artificial practice to show the current ratio position favourable. When window dressing technique is adopted in accounting statement presentations, the financial position is shown in such a way that it seems to be better than what it is. It is more of a misrepresentation than fraud.

Window dressing may be practiced in any one of the following ways:

(a) Deferring purchases, i.e. purchase of a year may be shown as of next year
(b) Making extensive drive for the collection of book debts to show the book balance favourable
(c) Recording incomes for the next year in advance in the accounts of the current year
(d) Showing borrowed capital as long-term debt capital
(e) Making provision for inadequate amount of depreciation and bad debts
(f) Charging revenue expenditure as capital expenditure
(g) Making over-and/or under-valuation of assets and liabilities
(h) Inflating the profits by entering non-existent items of purchase returns and sales return
(i) Utilising secret reserves during the depression period without making the fact known to the shareholders

The auditor should carefully verify the existence of the assets and liabilities. He should see that no attempts have been made by the client to adopt window dressing. It may sometimes happen that the client may show a particular asset in paper only, which, in fact, does not exist physically. Window dressing is a challenge to the work of verification, which should be faced by the auditor through conducting of effective verification work.

6.11 VERIFICATION AND VALUATION OF ASSETS

Verification of asset is an important audit technique. Conventionally, the scope of this technique is limited to inspection of assets and collection of information about the assets.

Through verification, the auditor should confirm the following:

- The assets are in existence on the date of the balance sheet.
- The concerned assets have been acquired for use in the business.
- The assets have been purchased under a proper authority.
- The concern has the right of ownership of the assets.
- The assets are free from any charge not disclosed in the balance sheet.
- The assets are correctly valued.
- The assets are correctly presented in the balance sheet.

Verification of assets is primarily the responsibility of the management. They are expected to have a much greater knowledge of the assets of the business as regards their condition, location etc. than that which an outsider might be able to acquire on their inspection. They are competent to determine the values of the assets at which they should be included in the balance sheet. The auditor is only expected to apply his skill and expertise estimating the value of each asset with a view to confirm that they are truly and fairly disclosed in the balance sheet.

For the purpose of applying verification techniques, we may divide the assets into the following four categories:

1. Intangible assets, viz. goodwill, patent, trademark, copyright, etc.
2. Fixed assets, viz. land and building, plant & machinery, furniture and fixtures, motor vehicles etc.
3. Current assets viz. stock-in-trade, sundry debtors, prepaid expenses and accrued incomes, cash and bank balances etc.
4. Fictitious assets viz. preliminary expenses, discount on issue of shares or debentures etc.

6.12 VERIFICATION AND VALUATION OF INTANGIBLE ASSETS

6.12.1 Goodwill

Goodwill is considered as an intangible fixed asset. The value, which is shown in the balance sheet, does not appear to be its present value, because the present value of goodwill depends upon a number of factors like financial position of the business, earning capacity at present and its future trend etc. But in actual practice, it is not valued at cost.

Valuation of goodwill

There are several methods of valuation of goodwill. However, goodwill should not be recognised in the accounts unless it is purchased. Regarding valuation of goodwill, an appropriate method is to be adopted to write the cost down out of the available profits and in this way, it should be ensured that the capital of the business is represented by tangible assets only.

Auditor's duty regarding valuation

1. The auditor should confirm that goodwill appearing in the balance sheet has not been shown in excess of its cost price.
2. The auditor should see that the goodwill is never appreciated in the books of a company.

Verification of goodwill

Goodwill is the excess price paid for a business as a whole over the book value or the computed value or the agreed value of all tangible assets purchased. It is not possible to be verified physically; hence verification of goodwill means proper checking of accounting entries passed for goodwill.

Auditor's duty regarding verification

1. The goodwill as recorded in the books of accounts should be properly examined and the same is to be verified with the balance sheet.
2. If goodwill is created on account of purchasing a running business, the auditor should verify it with the contract made between the client and the vendor.

3. Sometimes, management intends to capitalise the current expenditure by raising goodwill, which is usually high. The auditor should raise objection to this practice.
4. In case of goodwill once written off, but later on brought back in order to write off the debit balance of profit and loss account or any capital loss, the auditor should investigate the reasons for this and may refer to the resolutions adopted at the directors meeting and the approval of the shareholders.
5. The auditor should ensure that as required by Accounting Standard-10 for fixed assets, goodwill has been recorded in the books only when some consideration in money or moneys has been paid for.

6.12.2 Patent

A patent is an official document which secures to an investor the exclusive right to make, use and sell his invention.

Valuation of patent

The patent is valued at cost less depreciation. Cost is the acquisition cost, which may be purchase cost or invention cost. Also the cost of registration of patent should be included in the valuation, while the renewal fees should be charged off to revenue. Since patent suffers depreciation through effluxion of time, it is preferable to adopt fixed instalment method of charging depreciation based on its legal life.

Auditor's duty regarding valuation

1. The patent should be examined to see that the company concerned is registered as the owner of the patent.
2. It should be seen that the patent is valued at cost less depreciation. If it is found that the commercial life of the patent is shorter than its legal life, the depreciation should be spread over its commercial life only.

Verification of patent

Actual patent should be physically verified by the auditor and it should be seen that it has been duly registered. In case of joint registration of the patent with an individual, who might have developed the patented article, it should be seen that a registered assignment by the individual in favour of the company has been made.

Auditor's duty regarding verification

1. The auditor should check the patent register in order to verify that it has been properly included therein.
2. The auditor should also ensure that the legal life of the patent has not yet been expired.
3. The latest renewal certificate of the patent should also be verified by the auditor.
4. The patent may also be subject to litigation about its title. A certificate from the solicitors of the company should be obtained to ensure that it is free from encumbrances.

6.12.3 Copyright

A copyright is the exclusive legal right to produce or reproduce some kind of literary work. It is the legal protection provided to an author by which the publication of his work by others is restricted.

Valuation of copyright

Generally the value of the copyright is not fixed, as a copyright loses its value with the passage of time. In the balance sheet, it is shown at cost less amounts written off from time to time.

Auditor's duty regarding valuation

1. The auditor should see that the value of copyright is determined on proper basis including the period of copyrights.
2. It should be ensured that if any copyright does not command sale of any books, the same should be written off in that year.
3. It should be confirmed that the legal life of the copyright has not been expired.
4. The auditor should see that the copyright having no commercial value has been completely written off.

Verification of copyright

In verifying copyright, the auditor should inspect the agreement between the author and the publisher. If there are many copyrights with the business of the client, the auditor should ask for a schedule thereof from the client and verify them from the schedules.

6.12.4 Trademarks

A trademark is a distinctive mark attached to the goods offered for sale in the market so as to distinguish the same from similar goods available in the market and also to identify them with a particular trader.

Valuation of trademarks

The trademark is a symbol of the organisation's prestige. The value of trademark may be justified by reference to its renewal fees. If the trademark is purchased, the price paid for it is to be considered as the value of the trademark.

Auditor's duty regarding valuation

1. The auditor should see that trade marks are properly valued and shown in the balance sheet.
2. If the trademark has been purchased, the auditor should verify the payment made to the seller against the acquisition of trademark.
3. The auditor should ensure that all expenses incurred in the acquisition of the trade mark have been treated as capital expenditure, any renewal fees paid has been treated as revenue expenditure.

Verification of trademarks

Trademarks can be verified by examining the assignment deed duly endorsed by the office of the register of trademark. If trademarks are purchased, the assignment of interest or the assignment deed should be inspected.

Auditor's duty regarding verification

1. The auditor should see that they are registered in the name of the client and are the property of the client.
2. He should also see that proper distinction between capital and revenue expenditure is maintained. All research expense in this connection should also be capitalised.
3. In case the trademarks have been purchased from others, the auditor should check the expenditure incurred in connection with their acquisition, e.g. registration fees, payments made to vendor etc.

6.13 VERIFICATION AND VALUATION OF FIXED ASSETS

6.13.1 Land and Buildings

Almost all the business or commercial undertakings have land and buildings of their own. For the purposes of verification and valuation of land and buildings, they can be classified into two types, which are freehold and lease hold property.

1. Freehold property

Verification

(i) The auditor should inspect the title deed and see that they appear to be in order. He should obtain a certificate from the legal advisor of the client confirming the validity of the title to the property.

(ii) He should also verify that the conveyance deed has been duly registered as required by the Indian Registration Act and the particulars to be endorsed thereon have been duly endorsed.

(iii) If the property is mortgaged, the title deed would be in the possession of the mortgage. A certificate to this effect should be obtained.

(iv) In the case of property built or created by the client himself, the auditor should ensure that proper capitalisation of materials, labour and overhead is done.

Valuation

(i) The original cost and any improvement thereon should be checked with original deed and receipt. It is also seen that all expenses incurred on registration, brokerage or other legal fees have been duly capitalised.

(ii) The cost of buildings should be depreciated at appropriate value, depending upon the quality of their structure and the use, which is being made of them.

(iii) The auditor should check the expenditure on repairs so as to exclude such expenditure from capital cost.

(iv) In respect of property built by the client, contractors bill and other relevant accounts should be referred.

2. Leasehold property

Verification

(i) The auditor should inspect the lease or assignment thereof to ascertain the amount of premium, if any, paid for securing the lease and its terms and conditions.

(ii) The auditor should also see whether the lease has been duly registered.
(iii) He should also verify that all conditions prescribed by the lease are being duly complied with.
(iv) He should confirm the writing off of any legal expenses incurred to acquire the lease.

Valuation

(i) The value of the leasehold property should be checked from the lease deed. Any addition or expansion thereon should be examined by reference to the contractor's bills and other supporting papers.
(ii) The auditor should ensure that the provision for any claim that may arise under the dilapidation clause on the expiry of the lease has been made.
(iii) He should see that the cost as well as legal expenses incurred to acquire the lease is being written off at an appropriate rate over the unexpected term of the lease.
(iv) He should also check the accounting of leasehold property to ensure that it is maintained separately.

6.13.2 Building

Verification

(i) The auditor should examine the title deed of buildings to see whether the client holds the title on the balance sheet date. If the building has been mortgaged, the title deed will be in the possession of the mortgagee from whom a certificate should be obtained.
(ii) He should see the appropriate lease deed, if the building is leasehold, to ascertain the cost, amortisation etc.
(iii) He should also ensure that all conditions in the lease deed have been fulfilled by the client.
(iv) The auditor should ensure that the relevant particulars of buildings have been entered in the fixed assets register maintained by the client.

Valuation

(i) The auditor should verify the original cost of the building by reference to the deed of conveyance. If the building is constructed by the client, he should verify the original cost by reference to the contractor's bill.
(ii) He should also verify that appropriate depreciation has been provided against the building. In case no depreciation is provided on the building, a note to this effect should be given in the profit and loss account.
(iii) He should see that the buildings have been valued at cost less depreciation. In case of a company, the requirements of Schedule VI have to be complied with.
(iv) If any revaluation has taken place, the auditor should look into the basis of revaluation and ensure that the disclosure of the same has been made.

6.13.3 Plant and Machinery

Verification

(i) The auditor should call for the plant register or detailed break up schedule of plant and machinery. For the balance appearing in the balance sheet, he should identify the specific items and check the details thereof.

(ii) In the case of a company, the management is duly bound to physically verify the plant and machinery and the auditor should ask for the related working papers for his examination.

(iii) The additions and disposals during the year should be verified with reference to the purchase invoices and other appropriate documents.

(iv) The auditor should verify some of the important items of plant and machinery on test check basis.

Valuation

(i) The cost price of any plant or machinery plus any cost of installation will be vouched with supplier's invoices and other supporting documents.

(ii) The auditor should see that proper depreciation has been provided during the year.

(iii) He should check as to whether any of the items has been disposed off or sold during the year. If so, he should satisfy that it was properly authorised and the sale proceeds credited to plant and machinery account. Any capital profit made should be transferred to capital reserve.

(iv) The auditor should also verify that the plant and machinery have been properly shown under fixed assets in the balance sheet.

6.13.4 Furnitures and Fixtures

Verification

(i) The auditor should ascertain whether a register is maintained for furniture and fixtures detailing the nature of the item, its acquisition cost, location, code number etc.

(ii) He should also verify whether the furniture and fixtures bear on them the code numbers allotted.

(iii) He should inquire whether physical verification of the furniture and fixtures has been carried out by the management and if so, he should examine the working papers.

(iv) The auditor should verify physically some of the important items of furniture and fixtures on test check basis.

Valuation

(i) The auditor should satisfy that the furniture and fixtures have been properly depreciated and value written off for damaged or unserviceable items,

(ii) He should see that the cost of furniture and fixture has been properly ascertained and recorded in the books of accounts.

(iii) He should enquire whether any of the items have been disposed off or sold during the year. If so, he should check that it was properly authorised and the sale proceeds credited to furniture and fixture account. Any capital profit made therein should be transferred to capital reserve.

(iv) The auditor should also verify that furniture and fixtures have been properly shown under fixed assets in the balance sheet.

6.13.5 Motor Vehicles

Verification

(i) The auditor may call for a schedule of motor vehicles and compare it with the motor vehicles register maintained.

(ii) He should also examine the registration document for each vehicle. He should compare the registration number and description given in the registration document with the particulars shown in the ledger account or motor vehicle register.

(iii) If the vehicle is registered in the name of a person other than the client, the auditor should inspect the letter confirming the arrangement and ascertain that there is no charge on the vehicle in favour of such person.

(iv) The auditor should also check the insurance premium receipts to ensure that the vehicles are fully insured against accidents, theft etc.

Valuation

(i) The motor vehicles are to be valued at cost less depreciation.

(ii) The cost price of any motor vehicle will be vouched with supplier's invoices and other supporting documents. However, he should see that expenditures on repair have been charged to profit and loss account and not added to its cost.

(iii) The auditor should verify the adequacy of the depreciation. It is a common practice for the motor vehicles to be written off over the mileage they are expected to run.

(iv) He should also verify that the motor vehicles have been properly shown under fixed assets in the balance sheet.

6.13.6 Assets Acquired Under Hire Purchase System

Verification

(i) The existence of the assets acquired can be confirmed by physical verification of the assets by the auditor or by reviewing the working papers of physical verification of fixed assets done by the management.

(ii) The company is not the owner of the asset till the last instalment under hire purchase agreement has been paid. However, the possession right of the asset can be verified by reference to the hire purchase agreement.

(iii) A default in payment of the hire purchase instalment entitles the hire vendor to take back the possession of the asset. So, the hire purchase agreement has to be examined to ascertain the nature of encumbrances.

(iv) The auditor should also see that the asset purchased is included in the fixed asset register.

Valuation

(i) Fixed assets are generally valued at cost less depreciation. So, the auditor will have to examine the hire purchase agreement and the price list to ascertain the cash cost of the asset.

(ii) Depreciation should be deducted and the auditor should ensure that the rate normally charged by the company on same or similar assets has been applied on a consistent basis.

(iii) The auditor should confirm the proper recording of assets acquired under hire purchase agreement. The interest element in the instalments should be charged off to revenue.

(iv) The assets purchased on hire purchase agreement may also be shown at the capital value of instalments paid to date. In that case also, the depreciation at the normal rate for the full period on the cash value will have to be charged.

6.14 VERIFICATION AND VALUATION OF INVESTMENTS

In carrying out an audit of investments, the auditor should aim at collecting sufficient audit evidence in order to assure himself about the existence, ownership, valuation and possession of investment in favour of the client.

The following aspects are important in this respect:

1. *Existence*: The auditor should verify that investments shown in the balance sheet really exist on the date of the balance sheet.

2. *Ownership*: The auditor should assure himself that investments shown in the balance sheet are owned by the enterprise.

3. *Accounting records*: He should check the transactions of acquisitions, disposal etc. of the investments during the accounting period in order to verify as to whether they are properly recorded in the books of accounts.

4. *Valuation*: He should confirm that investments are stated in the balance sheet at appropriate amount in accordance with the recognised accounting principles.

5. *Disclosure*: He should also confirm that investments are properly classified and disclosed in the financial statements in accordance with the recognised accounting principles and relevant statutory requirements.

6. *Internal control*: The auditor should evaluate the internal control procedures relating to investments in order to determine the nature, timing and extent of the procedural aspects.

Almost all the business and commercial undertakings have investments of different types. In case of finance and investment companies, the amount of investment constitutes a major part of the total assets of the concern. For the purpose of verification and valuation of investments, it can be broadly classified into quoted and unquoted investments.

6.14.1 Quoted Investments

Verification

(i) The auditor should physically inspect the investments. It should be physically verified on the last date of the accounting year. If the investments are not in the possession of the entity, a certificate should be obtained from the party concerned.

(ii) The auditor should assure himself that the title of the investments are in the name of the client itself.

(iii) The purchase and sale of investments should be verified with reference to the broker's contract note, bills of cost etc.

(iv) If the amount of purchase or sale of investments are substantial, the auditor should check the price with reference to stock exchange quotations.

(v) The auditor should also examine the relevant provisions of Section 227(1 A) and see that a company not being an investment or banking company, whether so much of the assets of the company as represented by shares and debentures have been sold at a price less than that at which they were purchased by the company.

(vi) He should also confirm that the relevant provisions of the CARO, 2003 have been duly complied with in this regard.

Valuation

(i) The auditor should satisfy himself that the investments have been valued and disclosed in the financial statements in accordance with the recognised accounting policies and practices and relevant statutory requirements.

(ii) He should examine whether in computing the cost of investments, expenditure incurred on account of transfer fees, stamp duty etc. is included in the cost of investment.

The auditor may ascertain that the market value of investments are in accordance with the authentic market reports or stock exchange quotations. To judge the overall reasonableness of the amount invested, the auditor may relate the amount with the preceeding year's figure and calculate relevant ratios.

6.14.2 Unquoted Investments

Verification

(i) The auditor should ascertain the power of the enterprise to make investments by examining the memorandum of association in case of investment by a company, to ensure that the investments are not ultra-vires the company.

(ii) He should also ascertain that all the legal formalities relating to purchase of investments have been duly complied with.

(iii) Where investments are in large numbers, the auditor should obtain the schedule of securities certified by a senior officer of the company. The statement must include the name of the investment, the book value, the market price, date of purchase etc.

(iv) The auditor must verify the whole of the investment at one time. Investments are of a negotiable character and their verification at the same time removes the danger of their substitution for others.

Valuation

(i) The unquoted shares held as investments should ordinarily be valued at cost. However, if on study of the latest annual accounts of the companies, the shares of which are held as investment and the dividend records of such companies, it appears that there has occurred a permanent and material fall in the value of investments, a proper provision against such fall in values should be made. The auditor should confirm this compliance.

(ii) Unquoted shares and debentures should be shown in the balance sheet under the main head "Investments" on the asset side, indicating the mode of valuation and the aggregate amount of the unquoted shares and debentures should also be stated.

(iii) The auditor should confirm that equity and preference shares are shown separately as also fully paid up and partly paid shares being distinguished.

(iv) If the shares or debentures are held in the subsidiary of the company, the auditor should assure that the above should be shown under the sub-heading "Investment in subsidiaries".

6.15 VERIFICATION AND VALUATION OF CURRENT ASSETS

6.15.1 Stock-in-trade

Introduction

The valuation of stock is frequently the main factor in determining the results shown by the accounts. Apart from the effect on the balance sheet, incorrect stock would affect the profit of the year that has closed as well as that of next year.

Auditor's duty

The valuation of the closing stock, therefore, is an important step essential for the determination of the profits of the year, also for truly disclosing the financial position of the entity at the end of the year. An auditor being intimately connected with these aspects of financial statements, it is his duty to verify the existence of the stock-in-trade possessed by the concern at the end of the year and to ascertain that the same has been valued correctly on a consistent basis.

The precise duties in regard to verification of stock-in-trade are nowhere defined. Under the circumstances, these have to be deduced from an interpretation of the general responsibilities of auditors in regard to the statements of accounts verified by them, especially in regard to stock-in-trade.

Case Decisions

Justice Lindley, while delivering his famous judgment in the case of Kingston Cotton Mills Ltd. (1896) observed: "It is no part of the auditor's duty to take stock. No one contends that it is so. He must rely on other people for details of the stock-in-trade in hand." In the case of a cotton mill, he must rely on some skilled person for the material necessary to enable him to enter the stock-in-trade at its proper value in the balance sheet.

In the same case, Justice Lopes observed: "An auditor is not bound to be a detective or as was said to approach his work with a foregone conclusion that there is something wrong. He is a watchdog, but not a bloodhound. He is justified in believing tried servants of the company in whom confidence is placed by the company. He is entitled to assume that they are honest to rely upon their representations, provided he takes reasonable care".

In a more recent judgment in the case of Westminster Road Construction & Engineering Co. Ltd. (1932), it was held that "an auditor must make the fullest use of all materials available to him and although he is not a stock-taker and not a valuer of work-in-progress, he will be guilty of negligence, if he fails to take notice of all available evidence from which it could be reasonably deduced that the work-in-progress was over-valued".

The decisions thus appear to have settled the following three principles for the general guidance of the auditor:

1. That it is no part of the auditor's duty to take stock.
2. That for the purpose he can rely upon statements and reports made available to him in regard to the valuation of stock so long as there is no circumstance, which may arouse his suspicion, and he is satisfied.
3. That an auditor would be failing in his duty if he does not take reasonable care in verifying the statement of stock according to the information in his possession and the expert knowledge is expected of him in regard to methods of verification and stock control.

Provisions of the Companies Act

The recent changes in the Companies Act have also considerably advanced the responsibilities of auditors in this regard. Section 209 of the Act requires a company to maintain proper books of accounts. Such books of accounts must include books kept to record transactions in stock-in-trade.

The Companies (Amendment) Act of 1956 empowers the central government under Section 227 (4A) to require companies engaged in production, processing, manufacturing or mining activities to maintain books as would furnish particulars in relation to utilisation of material or labour or other items of cost as may be prescribed.

Furthermore, by Section 541 (2), proper books of accounts have been defined to include statement of annual stock-taking and of all the goods purchased and sold.

Accounting presentation

Part II of Schedule VI to the Companies Act prescribes that the figures of opening and closing balances of stock and work in progress be disclosed in the profit and loss account. Part I of the same schedule requires that the mode of valuation of stock be shown in the balance sheet. The recent amendment to Schedule VI requiring particulars of materials purchased, opening and closing stock-in-trade and also of turnover made during a particular accounting period.

Steps for verification

Verification of year end stock includes the following steps:

1. Review the procedure and arrangements for the maintenance of stock records.
2. Secure the original rough stock sheet, if available.
3. Check all additions and test fair proportions of extensions.
4. Ascertain the basis and method of valuation adopted and confirm that the same has been followed consistently.
5. Verify the cost of raw materials and stores by reference to purchase invoices.
6. Confirm that stock has been valued at 'lower of cost or market price' principle.

7. Ascertain that the goods not belonging to the client have not been included in stock-in-trade.
8. Examine the stock sheets to ascertain that they only contain goods normally dealt in by the business.
9. Find out whether there has been a complete physical stock-taking.
10. See that the stock sheets have been signed by the responsible person.

6.15.2 Work-in-Progress

As per the "Guidance Note on Audit of Inventories" (Guidance Note-2) issued by the Institute of Chartered Accountants of India in general, the audit procedures regarding verification of work-in-progress are similar to those used for stock-in-trade, i.e. stock of raw-materials as well as of finished goods. However, the auditor should pay attention to the following matters due to the difference in nature of work-in-progress as compared to the stock of finished goods and stock of raw materials:

1. The auditor has to carefully assess the degree of completion of the work-in-progress for assessing the appropriateness of its valuation.
2. He should examine the cost records and obtain expert opinion where necessary.
3. He should also obtain a certificate from the production engineer to confirm the accuracy of the cost records.
4. The elements of cost and the method of pricing of the various elements may be compared with that of the previous year and if there is a material deviation, the reasons for the same may be investigated.
5. In certain cases, physical verification of work-in-progress may not be possible due to the nature of the product and the manufacturing process involved. In such cases, the auditor should give greater emphasis on ascertaining the reliability of the system of control of work-in-progress.
6. It may also be useful for the auditor to examine the subsequent records of production.

6.15.3 Sundry Debtors

Verification

(i) Existence of book debts can be verified by examining the books of account and satisfying that the entries therein are supported by proper sales documents.

(ii) Balance of book debts should be sent to the debtors for their confirmation, which will also establish the existence of the book debts.

(iii) The examination of debtor's ledgers with related sales documents and correspondence with debtors will confirm the ownership of book debts.

(iv) The auditor should also enquire whether there is any dispute on any of the balances included in sundry debtors. In this case, the documents regarding dispute should be examined.

Valuation

(i) Usually the balances shown in the debtor's ledger supported by sales documents represent the value of book debts.

(ii) The auditor should call for the lists of book debts and debts written off and arrive at the conclusion about adequacy of write off and provision for doubtful debts.

(iii) The confirmation of balances by debtors will help establish the valuation of book debts.

(iv) It should be ensured by the auditor that sundry debtors are valued only at realisable value.

6.15.4 Bills Receivables

Verification

(i) The auditor should examine the bills receivable book and prepare a schedule of all those bills receivable, which have not yet matured before the date of the preparation of the balance sheet.

(ii) Where the number of bills is large and are kept with the bankers for collection, the auditor should obtain a detailed certificate from the bank to ascertain the clear position about the bills.

(iii) Any contingent liability in respect of the bills that are discounted or endorsed but remain outstanding at the time of audit should be maintained as a footnote of the balance sheet.

(iv) The bills which have been dishonoured before the due date of the balance sheet should not be included in the balance sheet as "bills receivable in hand" as they are no longer assets.

Valuation

(i) The auditor should see that the bills are properly drawn, stamped and duly accepted and are not overdue. In case of renewal of any bills, the auditor should compare the new bill with the old bill.

(ii) Sometimes, the bills might have matured and honoured subsequent to the date of the balance sheet, but prior to the date of the audit. The auditor should check the cash received as shown in the cash book of the next year.

(iii) If the bills have been retired before the date of the balance sheet, the proceeds thereof should be checked by reference to the cash book.

(iv) For the bills discounted prior to the date of maturity when the date of maturity is to fall after the date of balance sheet, the discount on such bills must be properly apportioned between periods covered by two separate financial years.

6.15.5 Cash at Bank

Verification

(i) The auditor should compare the balances as shown in the passbook with the balances as shown in the cash book.

(ii) The auditor should prepare a bank reconciliation statement or should check the statement prepared by the client in order to ascertain the correct bank balance.

(iii) He should obtain a balance confirmation certificate from the bank at the close of the year.

(iv) He should also obtain separate certificate for fixed deposit account, current account and savings bank account from different banks to confirm total deposits in different banks.

Valuation

(i) In order to ascertain the current position with regard to cheques issued but not yet presented or cheques deposited but not collected, the auditor should confirm through cash book and passbook figures.

(ii) Where amounts are deposited in foreign banks under exchange control regulations, the fact is to be disclosed.

(iii) Where amounts are kept in different reserve accounts in the banks in order to avail deductions under Indian Income Tax Act, the fact should also be disclosed.

(iv) The auditor should also ensure that the bank balances are properly disclosed in the balance sheet according to Schedule VI of the Companies Act.

6.15.6 Cash-in-hand

Verification

(i) The most common practice in verifying cash balance is to obtain a certificate from the accountant about the actual cash balance in hand at the date of the balance sheet.

(ii) The auditor should verify the cash in hand by actually counting it on the close of the business on the date of the balance sheet.

(iii) In certain cases, if the client is maintaining an unduly large balance of cash in hand consistently, the auditor should make a surprise check to ascertain whether the actual cash in hand agrees with the balances as shown by the books.

(iv) As far as cash in transit is concerned, the auditor should verify this balance with the help of proper documentary evidences and correspondence.

Valuation

(i) If the cash-in-hand is not in agreement with the balance as shown in the books, it should be the duty of the auditor to call for an explanation.

(ii) Often postage and other stamps are taken with the cash in the balance sheet. The auditor should confirm the balance of postage and stamps by physical counting only.

(iii) He should also check the system of making payments and safety arrangements provided for the protection of cash balance.

(iv) In case cash is maintained at the local branches and the auditor is unable to pay visit to the branch, he may ask the branch manager to deposit the balance of cash in the bank on the balance sheet date.

6.15.7 Prepaid Expenses

Verification

(i) The auditor should verify the receipts for pre-payments, i.e. expenses paid during the period for future financial periods.

(ii) The amount of prepaid expenses should be shown in the asset side of the balance sheet under current assets. The auditor should assure that it has been shown properly in the balance sheet.

(iii) Prepaid expenses for the last accounting period should be properly adjusted. The auditor should see the expenses paid in the last year pertaining to the current accounting year have been properly adjusted.

(iv) The auditor should also check the adjustments made in the next year, if possible, against the prepaid expenses made during the year.

Valuation

(i) The auditor should check the calculations for ascertaining the portion of expenses belonging to the next period by reference to the contract or other documents.

(ii) In respect of rent, rates and taxes, the auditor should check the payment vouchers and satisfy that allocation to carry forward has been made on time basis.

(iii) In respect of insurance premium, the auditor should also confirm that the carry forward allocation has been made on the basis of the terms of policy and the premium paid.

(iv) In case of prepaid sales commission, where salesmen are allowed to take payments out of future earnings, the auditor should examine the statement of sales to determine the commission earned.

6.16 VERIFICATION AND VALUATION OF FICTITIOUS ASSETS

6.16.1 Preliminary Expenses

The expenses incurred for the formation and commencement of a company is usually grouped under the heading "preliminary expenses". These include stamp duties, registration fees, legal costs, cost of printing etc.

In order to verify preliminary expenses, the auditor should take into consideration the following matters:

1. It should be seen by the auditor that no expenses other than those related to the formation of a company are included under this head.
2. The auditor should examine the contracts relating to preliminary expenses. If preliminary expenses that were incurred by the promoters have been reimbursed to them by the company, the resolution of the board and the power in the articles to make such payment should be considered.
3. The auditor can cross check the amount of preliminary expenses with that disclosed in the prospectus, statutory report and the balance sheet.
4. Being a fictitious asset, it should be written off as early as possible and the auditor should verify that the balance of preliminary expenses which has not been written off is shown in the balance sheet under the heading "miscellaneous expenditure".
5. Underwriting commission and brokerage in shares and debentures should not be included under the head "preliminary expenses". The auditor should also confirm this aspect.
6. The bills and statements supporting each item of preliminary expenses should be checked.
7. The auditor should also ensure that proper deduction has been availed against taxable income under the Income Tax Act, 1961.

6.16.2 Discount on Issue of Shares or Debentures

This refers to the expenditure or losses essentially of a revenue nature, which instead of being charged off as and when incurred, is accumulated in an account and the balance in the account is written off over a period of years during which its benefit is expected to accrue to the business.

In order to verify the discount on issue of shares or debentures, the auditor should pay attention to the following matters:

1. The auditor should confirm that it continues to appear as an asset on the right side of the balance sheet as long as the discount is not written off.
2. If during the year, any amount has been added thereto, the auditor should ask for the justification of the same.
3. Being a fictitious asset, it should be written off as early as possible. The auditor should also confirm this aspect.
4. The auditor should see that the discount on issue of shares or debentures has been shown separately under the heading 'Discount on Issue of Shares or Debentures'.
5. In issuing shares or debentures at a discount, whether the governing provisions relating to issue of shares and debentures have been duly complied with or not, should also be checked by the auditor.

6.17 VERIFICATION AND VALUATION OF CONTINGENT ASSETS

The contingent assets are those which may arise on the happening of an uncertain event. As a general practice, contingent assets are not recorded in the balance sheet because that would imply taking credit for revenue which has not accrued. But it is logical as the contingent liabilities are shown in the balance sheet the contingent assets should also be shown. The Companies Act does not require disclosure of contingent asset in the balance sheet. However, if contingent assets have a significant value, it may be advisable to disclose such assets in a note to the balance sheet.

As regards valuation of contingent assets, it may be noted that ordinarily no valuation would be required. However, if such assets were disclosed by way of a note, a proper valuation based on the related contract would be made. Where full realisation of such assets is doubtful even on the face of contingency occurring, it would be safer to value the assets on a realisable basis.

6.18 VERIFICATION AND VALUATION OF LIABILITIES

The verification of liabilities is of equal importance as that of an asset. The auditor has to satisfy himself that all liabilities whether existing or contingent have been properly determined and disclosed in the balance sheet. In case liabilities are overstated or understated, the balance sheet will not represent a fair view of the state of affairs of the company. Therefore, the auditor should ensure the following:

- That liabilities shown in the balance sheet are actually payable
- That all liabilities are properly recorded in the books

- That the recorded liabilities are payable for the legitimate operations of the business, and
- That the nature and extent of contingent liabilities has been disclosed in the balance sheet by way of a footnote.

For the purpose of applying verification technique, we may divide the liabilities into the following three categories:

- Fixed or long term liabilities, viz. share capital, debentures, long term loan from bank and other financial institutions etc.
- Current liabilities, viz. sundry creditors, bills payable, bank overdraft etc.
- Contingent liabilities viz. disputed liability of income tax suits pending for damages etc.

6.19 VERIFICATION AND VALUATION OF FIXED OR LONG TERM LIABILITIES

6.19.1 Debentures

Verification

(i) The auditor should go through the memorandum and articles of the company in order to determine the extent of borrowing power of the company and also to ascertain the limitation upon the borrowing power, if any.

(ii) A prospectus must have been issued and filed with the registrar of companies. The auditor should verify the prospectus to ensure that the terms of the prospectus have been complied with.

(iii) Balances from the register of debenture holders will have to be extracted and the total amount received from debenture holders be tallied with the total of debenture account in the general ledger.

(iv) The auditor should also examine a copy of the debenture bond to ascertain the terms and conditions on which the debentures have been issued, the particulars of assets charged as security and the method of redemption.

(v) If the debentures are mortgaged the debentures trust deed should be studied by the auditor and it should be seen that the terms and conditions of the trust deed have been fully observed by the company.

Presentation

(i) Debentures have to be shown under the head 'secured loans'.

(ii) The debentures subscribed by the directors and managers should be shown separately.

(iii) Interest accrued and due on debentures but not paid should be included along with debentures, but interest accrued but not due has to be shown under 'current liabilities'.

(iv) The nature of security provided should also be disclosed.

(v) The terms and conditions of the redemption or conversion of the debentures should be stated with the earliest date of redemption or conversion.

6.19.2 Secured Long Term Loans

A company can obtain loans from banks and other financial institutions on the basis of security provided. For the purpose of verification of long-term loans, they can be classified under two broad categories:

1. Loans against security of fixed assets
2. Loans against security of stock

1. Loans against security of fixed assets

(i) The auditor should examine the memorandum and the Articles of Association to see whether the company is empowered to borrow money against fixed assets.

(ii) He should scrutinise the loan account in the ledger and the documents relating to the fixed assets.

(iii) He should also examine the mortgage deed and find out whether the mortgage is properly executed.

(iv) He should enquire whether the lender has a right to lend money against such security.

(v) The auditor should also obtain confirmation from the lender for the amount of loan.

(vi) He should see whether principal is being repaid as stipulated and whether interest on loan is paid regularly as per the terms of loans as prescribed in CARO.

2. Loans against security of stock

(i) The auditor should inspect the receipts of the godown keeper if the loan has been taken against the godown keeper's receipts.

(ii) If the stocks are at dock or in bonded warehouse, the dock warrant or the warehouse certificate duly endorsed in favour of the lender should also be examined.

(iii) The auditor should see that the rent for the warehouse has been paid by the client regularly. If it has not been paid, adequate provision should have to be made for the purpose.

(iv) He should also obtain a certificate from the lender showing particulars of securities deposited and confirm that the same has been correctly disclosed and duly registered with registrar of companies and recorded in the register of charges.

(v) The auditor should verify the authority under which the loan has been raised. In the case of a company, only the Board of Directors is empowered to raise a loan or borrow from a bank.

(vi) He should also confirm that the restraint as contained in Section 293 of the Companies Act as regards the maximum amount of loan that a company can raise has not been contravened.

6.20 VERIFICATION AND VALUATION OF CURRENT LIABILITIES

6.20.1 Sundry Creditors

(i) The auditor will verify creditors more or less on similar lines as in the case of sundry debtors. He should take a statement of balance of the trade creditors duly signed by the authorised official and these balances should be verified with the purchase ledger balances.

(ii) He may also obtain confirmatory statements from the creditors.

(iii) He should also examine the invoices as sent by the suppliers. He should carry out test checking of purchases made during the year, particularly those made at the close of the year.

(iv) If debts have not been paid for a long time, he should enquire into the situation in detail. Sometimes it is noticed that instead of paying the creditors, the amount might have been misappropriated by the officials.

(v) If the client maintains provision in respect of discount on creditors, he should check the same with reference to the creditors account.

(vi) The purchase ledger should also be checked by the auditor with the books of original entry, invoices, credit notes etc.

(vii) For any purchase returns, he should examine the 'return outward book' and verify them with the help of credit notes as sent by the suppliers.

(viii) The auditor should pay special attention to the entries made either in the beginning or at the end of the year to check the fictitious entries in this respect.

6.20.2 Bills Payable

(i) The auditor should get a statement of bills payable and compare it with the bills payable book and bills payable account.

(ii) For the bills which have been met after the date of the balance sheet but before the date of audit, he should examine the cash book and bank passbook.

(iii) The bills payable already paid should be checked from the cash book and the auditor should examine the returned bills payable.

(iv) He should also ensure that the bills which have been paid are not recorded as outstanding.

(v) He should get confirmation in respect of amounts due on the bills accepted by the client that are held by them.

(vi) He should reconcile the total of the bills payable outstanding at the end of the year with the balance in the bills payable account.

6.20.3 Bank Overdraft

(i) The auditor should examine the overdraft agreement with the bank in order to ascertain the terms and conditions of overdraft and the maximum limit thereon.

(ii) The Memorandum of Association in case of a company should be examined to ascertain the borrowing powers of the company and any limitations thereon.

(iii) The auditor should verify the minutes of the Board meeting to assure that the bank overdraft borrowing is being authorised by the Board.

(iv) If the client is a company and if the overdraft is against any security, the auditor should see whether the charge created was registered with the registrar of companies, if required.

(v) The auditor should also obtain the confirmation certificate from the bank in respect of amount of overdraft at the close of the year.

(vi) The auditor should also check whether interest on overdraft has been duly accounted for.

(vii) The auditor should also confirm that the amount overdrawn is within the maximum limit sanctioned by the bank.

(viii) It is to be seen whether any security was offered for the overdraft in terms of agreement, depending on which the overdraft is to be classified as secured or unsecured.

6.20.4 Provision for Taxation

(i) The auditor should ascertain the tax liability and check the computation of the assessable profit and loss account. Thus, adjustments affecting taxable profit must be carefully scrutinised.

(ii) He should also go through earlier completed assessment in order to know what sort of adjustments were actually made in the past.

(iii) He should also check the amount of advance tax paid and the calculations thereof. Advance tax is required to be verified in order to provide the liability of future taxation.

(iv) If income tax return has already been filed before the date of audit, the auditor should also check the copy of the income tax return.

(v) The auditor should ensure the amount of overall provision on the date of the balance sheet having adequate regard to the figure of provision of the year, the advance tax paid, past provision made and assessment orders in respect thereof received up to the date of audit, pending appeals and refunds, if any.

(vi) He should also obtain a certificate from the tax practitioner regarding the amount of tax payable.

6.20.5 Outstanding Liabilities for Expenses

(i) The auditor should ask for the list of outstanding expenses from the client classified on the basis of nature of expenses.

(ii) He should verify the supporting documents evidencing the outstanding expenses.

(iii) He should also verify the basis of estimation of outstanding expenses, if they are provided on an estimated basis.

(iv) He should check the cash book of the previous year in order to see that the usual outstanding expenses have been paid off by the time of audit.

(v) He should also ensure that no outstanding expenses have been paid which have not been provided in the account. If paid, he should check the adjustment entries passed for this purpose.

(vi) He should compare the list of outstanding expenses of the current year with that of the previous year to identify any major deviations.

(vii) The auditor should also ensure that no usual outstanding expenses have been left out to be provided.

(viii) He should also confirm that outstanding expenses have been shown under current liabilities in the balance sheet.

6.21 VERIFICATION AND VALUATION OF CONTINGENT LIABILITIES

A contingent liability is not an actual liability but which will become a liability on the happening of an event in future. It may be converted into actual liability on an uncertain event in the future.

W. B. Meigs defines contingent liability as "the potential obligations, which may in future develop into actual liability or may dissolve without necessitating any outlay".

Accounting Standard 29 issued by the ICAI deals with the 'provisions, contingent liabilities and contingent assets'. According to it a contingent liability is

(a) a possible obligation that arises from past events and the existence of which will be confirmed only by the occurrence or non-occurrence of one or more uncertain future events not wholly within the control of the enterprise; or

(b) a present obligation that arises from past events but is not recognised because

  (i) it is not probable that an outflow of resource embodying economic benefits will be required to settle the obligation; or

  (ii) a reliable estimate of the amount of the obligation cannot be made.

Simply stated, contingent liability is not an actual liability but will become a liability on the happening of an event in the future. The examples of contingent liabilities are as follows:

- Discounting of bills receivables
- Pending suits for damages or compensation
- Disputed liability on account of income tax
- Guarantee given by the bank on behalf of the company.

As per Part I of Schedule VI of the Companies Act, 1956, a footnote may be added to the balance sheet to indicate the amount of contingent liability.

While going through the books of accounts, correspondence, minute books, bank statements and other relevant documents, the auditor may identify the existence of contingent liabilities of the concern.

From the auditing point of view, the auditor should verify that a proper disclosure about contingent liabilities is made in financial statement as required by AS-29. As per para 68 of AS-29 an enterprise should disclose for each class of contingent liability at the balance sheet date. The auditor's duty in this respect would be as follows

1. Inspect the minute book of the company to identify all contingent liabilities existing at the end of the year.
2. Scrutinise the lawyer's bill to ascertain unreported contingent liabilities.
3. Examine correspondence with the bank in respect of bill discounted but not yet matured.
4. Examine bank letters to ascertain guarantees given on behalf of other companies or individuals.
5. Scrutinise correspondence with suppliers, customers, and lawyers etc. to ascertain the existence of contingent liabilities.

6. Check the investments in the shares made by the client to identify the liabilities on partly paid up shares.
7. Find out the arrears of preference dividend on cumulative preference shares.
8. Obtain a certificate from the management that known contingent liabilities have been included in the accounts and that they have been properly disclosed.

6.22 EVENTS OCCURRING AFTER THE BALANCE SHEET DATE

Accounting Standard-4 on 'contingencies and events occurring after the balance sheet date' deals with the treatment of contingencies and events occurring after the balance sheet date in financial statements. According to this statement, events occurring after the balance sheet date are those significant events, both favourable and unfavourable, that occur between the balance sheet date and the date on which the financial statements are approved by the Board of Directors in the case of a company and in the case of any other entity by the corresponding approving authority.

Some of such events may require adjustments to assets and liabilities as at the balance sheet date or may require disclosure. These include the following:

6.22.1 Adjusting Events

Adjusting events are those significant events occurring after the balance sheet date that provide additional information materially affecting the determination of the amounts relating to conditions existing at the balance sheet date.

Example

An adjustment may be made for bad debt, which is confirmed by the insolvency of the customer, which occurs after the balance sheet date.

6.22.2 Non-adjusting Events

Non-adjusting events are those events which do not relate to conditions existing at the balance sheet date. However, disclosure of such events is generally made in case these represent unusual changes affecting the existence of the enterprise at the balance sheet date.

Example

The destruction of a major part of the factory building by a fire after the balance sheet date will not require any adjustment in the balance sheet as no conditions existed on the date of the balance sheet.

6.22.3 Other Events

There is another category which although takes place after the balance sheet date is required to be reflected in the financial statements because of statutory requirements or because of their special nature.

Example

Dividend proposed or declared after the balance sheet date in respect of the period covered by the financial statements.

6.23 PRIOR PERIOD AND EXTRAORDINARY ITEMS AND CHANGES IN ACCOUNTING POLICIES

Accounting Standard-5 on 'prior period and extraordinary items and changes in accounting policies' deals with the treatment of prior period and extraordinary items. The objective of this statement is to prescribe the classification and disclosure of certain items in the statement of profit and loss so that all enterprises prepare and present such a statement on a uniform basis. It also specifies the accounting treatment for changes in accounting estimates and the disclosure to be made in the financial statements regarding changes in accounting policies.

The net profit or loss for the period comprises the following components, each of which should be disclosed on the face of the statement of profit or loss:

(a) Profit or loss from ordinary activities

(b) Extraordinary items

Prior period items

Prior period items are income or expenses which arise in the current period as a result of errors or commissions in the preparation of the financial statements of one or more prior periods.

Extraordinary items

Extraordinary items are income or expenses that arise from events or transactions that are clearly distinct from the ordinary activities of the enterprise and therefore are not expected to recur frequently or regularly.

Any change in an accounting policy which has a material effect should be disclosed. The impact of and adjustments resulting from such change, if material, should be shown in the financial statements of the period in which such change is made, to reflect the effect of such change.

POINTS TO PONDER

- Verification means the proof of existence or confirmation of assets and liabilities on the date of balance sheet. It is a process which includes valuation of asset and liabilities, checking of ownership and title of the asset, confirmation about their existence and satisfaction about the condition that they are free from any charge.
- Valuation of assets means examination of the accuracy and propriety of the valuation of those assets, which are shown in the balance sheet of any concern at the end of the financial year.
- Valuation of assets is a part and parcel of verification. Without proper valuation of assets, verification is not possible. Verification includes, apart from valuation, the examination of ownership right, the existence of the asset in the business and its freeness from any sort of charge or mortgage.

- The auditor has the duty of substantiating the existence and value of the assets and liabilities as on the date of the balance sheet. If the balance sheet contains as asset, which, in fact, does not exist or which is stated at a value different from what is considered reasonable, both the balance sheet and the profit and loss account would be incorrect.
- Valuation forms an important part of every audit. The fairness of the balance sheet depends much upon how correctly the valuation of various assets and liabilities has been made. The auditor has to see that the assets and liabilities appearing in the balance sheet have been exhibiting their proper value.
- Basic principles to be followed for verification and valuation of assets include acquisition of assets, sale of assets, depreciation, physical verification and charges on assets.
- Without proper verification of assets and liabilities, it is not possible for the auditor to certify the balance sheet as it exhibits a true and fair view of the state of affairs of the business. But it will never be possible on the part of the auditor to perform the function in his own responsibility and in accordance with his own knowledge and expertise.
- Problems of valuation include the nature of the assets, use of the assets, estimated life of the assets, eventual problems and lack of information.
- Window dressing is an artificial practice to show the current ratio position favourable. Through window dressing the financial position is shown in such a way that it seems to be better than what it is.
- Events occurring after the balance sheet date are those significant events, both favourable and unfavourable, which that occur between the balance sheet date and the date on which the financial statements are approved by the authority.
- Prior period items are income or expenses, which arise in the current as a result of errors or commissions in the preparation of financial statements of one or more prior periods.
- Extraordinary items are income or expenses that arise from events or transactions that are clearly distinct from the ordinary activities of the enterprise and therefore are not expected to recur frequently or regularly.

REVIEW QUESTIONS

Short-answer Questions

1. What is verification of assets and liabilities?
2. Distinguish between verification and valuation.
3. Discuss the importance of verification and valuation of assets.
4. What is intangible asset? Give five examples of intangible assets.
5. What do you mean by fictitious assets? Give example.
6. What is meant by contingent liability? Discuss the auditor's duty in this regard.
7. What is goodwill? As an auditor, how would you ascertain that an amount paid for goodwill is justified?
8. Do you think that verification of assets and liabilities is necessary when vouching has been done properly?

9. "Verification forms an important part of the whole system of audit." Explain.
10. "Intangible assets are not always fictitious assets." Illustrate.
11. Discuss the problems in the valuation and verification of assets.
12. "Verification includes valuation." Comment.
13. How and in what way does verification of assets and liabilities differ from vouching?
14. What do you mean by "window-dressing of balance sheet"? State the duties of an auditor in this respect.
15. "Information and means of information are by no means equivalent terms." Comment.
16. State which of the following statements are true:
    (a) If capital expenditure is treated as revenue expenditure the profit for the year is understated, but in the long run, because of depreciation, there is no effect on profit.
    (b) Revenue expenditure includes loss arising from an event beyond one's control.
    (c) An expenditure which is not capital is revenue.
    (d) The rate of depreciation is not important since sooner or later the full cost of the asset is bound to be written off.
    (e) Under the two different methods of depreciation, the straight line method and the diminishing balance method, the life assumed is different.
    (f) Distinction between capital and revenue expenditure is relevant for short duration business.
    (g) Expenditure resulting from the acquisition of tangible asset is capital even if there is no income from that asset.
    (h) Interest included in hire-purchase price is also capital expenditure.
    (i) Verification of assets means establishing their physical existence and ownership, but not their valuation.
    (j) Trade investments are fixed assets.
    (k) It is necessary to indicate the fact if an asset is acquired on hire purchase basis.
    (l) Property let out on rent need not be depreciated.

Essay-type Questions

1. "An auditor is not a valuer though he is intimately connected with values." Discuss referring to the relevant case decisions.
2. "It has been stated that the valuation of investment for the balance sheet purpose depends largely upon the object for which investments are held." Discuss the statement.
3. How do you verify the following items?
    (a) Raw material stock
    (b) Land
    (c) Preliminary expenses
    (d) Investment
    (e) Work-in-progress
    (f) Copyright
    (g) Machine purchased on H. P. system
    (h) Patterns and designs
    (i) Freehold properties
    (j) Loans and advances
    (k) Debtors
    (l) Secured loan

4. How will you as an auditor deal with the following?
   (a) Cash
   (b) Provision for taxation
   (c) Leasehold properties
   (d) Unpaid dividends
   (e) Goods in transit
   (f) Disposal of plant
5. What are the special points to which an auditor should direct his attention for ascertaining the adequacy of provision for bad and doubtful debts in the context of proper valuation of sundry debtors?
6. "Physical presence of the auditor at the time of year end verification of stock is though not always possible, it is recommended that he should at least be present as an observer." Signify the importance of this statement and list out the important aspects which the auditor should look into to ensure an effective physical verification programme.
7. (a) What are the general considerations for valuation and verification of assets? (b) State your views on the following:
   (i) Events occurring after the balance sheet date
   (ii) Prior period and extra ordinary items

CHAPTER 7

Depreciation

CHAPTER OUTLINE

- 7.1 Definition of Depreciation
- 7.2 Purposes of Providing Depreciation
- 7.3 Causes of Depreciation
- 7.4 Basis of Charging Depreciation
- 7.5 Quantum of Depreciation
- 7.6 Distinction between Depreciation and Amortisation
- 7.7 Different Methods of Depreciation
- 7.8 Depreciation Accounting as Per AS-6
- 7.9 Accounting Disclosure Requirement
- 7.10 Legal Necessity of Provision for Depreciation
- 7.11 Provision for Depreciation for Past Years
- 7.12 Depreciation on Low Value Items
- 7.13 Depreciation on Wasting Assets
- 7.14 Change in the Method of Depreciation
- 7.15 Auditor's Duty as Regards Depreciation
- 7.16 Legal Views as Regards Depreciation

7.1 DEFINITION OF DEPRECIATION

In its broadest sense, the term 'depreciation' is used to describe a loss in value from any cause in contradistinction to 'appreciation' used in the sense of increase in value. But to an accountant, it signifies the gradual wasting away of fixed assets and a corresponding charge to the profits, to the earning of which their employment has contributed.

Accounting Standard-6 issued by the Institute of Chartered Accountants of India on "depreciation accounting" defines depreciation as "a measure of the wearing out, consumption or other loss of value of depreciable assets arising from use, effluxion of time, obsolescence through technology and market change. Depreciation is calculated so as to allocate a fair proportion of the depreciable amount in each accounting period during the expected useful life of the asset. Depreciation includes amortisation of assets whose usefulness is predetermined."

The term "depreciable amount" of a depreciable asset as per the standard is its historical cost or other amount substituted for historical cost in the financial statement less the estimated residual value.

The accounting standard recommends that the depreciable amount of a depreciable asset should be allocated on a systematic basis to each accounting period during the useful life of the asset.

7.2 PURPOSES OF PROVIDING DEPRECIATION

Depreciation is provided in the books of accounts as a charge against profit in order to fulfil the following objectives:

1. To keep capital intact

One of the effects of providing for depreciation on an asset is to retain in the business out of the profits in each year, an amount equal to the proportion of the cost of the asset employed in the business that has run off, estimated on the basis of the period of its working life and its scrap value. Thus, the original capacity of the entity, assuming that all profits have been withdrawn and losses, if any, made good, will be intact. If on the contrary, depreciation had not been charged, the net income would have been overstated over the year of the life of the asset, and if the same was withdrawn or distributed as dividends, the business would have no funds for the replacement of the asset.

2. To ascertain cost accurately

It is not possible to ascertain the true cost of production of a particular product, if proper amount of depreciation is not included therein, i.e. to charge depreciation in the profit and loss account it is essential to calculate the actual cost of production. This is because depreciation, like any other expenditure, is a charge against revenue and must be included in the accounts irrespective of the fact whether the final result of a production process is profit or loss.

3. To charge initial costs against earnings

The object of depreciation accounting is to determine on a scientific basis the proportion of the cost of a machine, which must be debited in the accounts of each year during which the machine will be used. Depreciation is an expense incurred for earning profit, which is similar to the hire of an asset, the only difference being that in case of hiring, the hire charges are paid to an outsider, while in the other, it is kept in the entity itself. Hence, unless an appropriate part of the asset value is charged against profit of the business each year, the profit earned on its working will not be correctly ascertained.

4. To prepare 'true and fair' statements of accounts

Unless depreciation is provided, the assets will be shown at an amount higher than their true value and the profit shown will be more than the real profit. In other words, the balance sheet and the profit and loss account will not reflect true and fair financial position as well as financial result of the entity.

7.3 CAUSES OF DEPRECIATION

Decline in service potential of an asset is one aspect of depreciation, which in this sense, is a physical fact. When an asset is acquired, it is considered as the prepayment of several years' depreciation, which is the basis of accounting for that asset during its estimated useful life. Therefore, acquisition of a fixed asset is seen as a bundle of services that will be provided by that asset to the business over time in future.

These bundles of future service benefits enable the owner of the asset to earn revenue by the following:

(a) Providing a place where products could be produced, stored and sold.

(b) Furnishing a means of converting raw materials into finished products, their designing and packaging (Machinery)

(c) Providing a mode of transporting goods to the customers (Trucks)

As an asset is used over time, the benefits decline with age. This is due to two factors:

- Physical factors (deterioration through use)
- Economic factors (reduction in utility through obsolescence)

Physical factors indicate the deterioration of the value of the assets due to wear and tear, time and other factors that reduce use value, and economic factors indicate the useful obsolescence arising from technological improvements and the inadequacy of the asset for the intended purpose.

From the above, it can be comprehended that the causes of depreciation arise directly through deterioration or indirectly through obsolescence.

7.4 BASIS OF CHARGING DEPRECIATION

The computation of depreciation and the amount to be charged in respect thereof in an accounting period are usually based on the following three factors:

1. Cost of the asset

Cost of an asset means the historical cost or other amount substituted for the historical cost of the depreciable asset when the asset has been revalued. Historical cost of an asset means its acquisition cost, which is the total of all costs incurred in acquiring the asset and all other incidental costs involved in bringing the asset into its working condition. When the business concern itself manufactures some assets, the cost of an asset will mean its production cost, which includes a reasonable proportion of direct costs and interest on capital borrowed to finance production.

2. Residual or scrap value of the asset

Determination of residual value of an asset is normally a difficult task. If such value is considered insignificant, it is normally regarded as nil. On the contrary, if the residual value is likely to be significant, it is estimated at the time of acquisition or at the time of subsequent revaluation of the asset. One of the bases for determining the residual value would be the realisable value of similar assets, which have reached the end of their useful lives and have operated under conditions similar to those in which the asset will be used.

3. Expected useful life of the asset

Determination of the useful life of a depreciable asset is a matter of estimation and is normally based on various factors including experience with similar types of assets.

Usually the useful life of a depreciable asset is shorter than its physical life.

(a) It is pre-determined by legal or contractual limits, such as the expiry dates of related leases.

(b) It is directly governed by extraction or consumption.

(c) It is dependent on the extent of use and physical determination on account of wear and tear, which again depends on operational factors, such as the number of shifts for which the asset is to be used, repairs and maintenance policy of the entity etc. and

(d) It is reduced by obsolescence arising out of.

- technological changes
- improvement in production process
- change in market demand for the product or service output of the asset or
- legal or other restrictions.

7.5 QUANTUM OF DEPRECIATION

The quantum of depreciation to be provided in an accounting period involves the exercise of judgment by management in the light of technical, commercial, accounting and legal requirements and accordingly may need periodical review. If it is considered that the original estimate of useful life of an asset requires any revision, the unamortised depreciable amount of the asset is charged to revenue over the revised remaining useful life.

In fact, the quantum of depreciation to be provided in the accounts depends on a number of factors, which include the following:

- The cost of the asset
- The estimated working life of the asset
- The estimated scrap value of the asset
- The risk of obsolescence
- Income tax rule regarding depreciation

Prior to Companies (Amendment) Act 1960, it was not legally compulsory to provide for depreciation before distribution of dividend. Then companies could pay dividend without providing for depreciation in pursuance of judgments in the cases-Lee vs Neuchatel Asphalt Co. Ltd. (1889) and Wilmer vs Mcnamara & Co. Ltd. (1895). However, depreciation is a charge against profit. If it is ignored while paying dividend, capital erosion could not be ruled out. The financial statements of the enterprise are also unlikely to represent a true and fair view of the state of affairs of the enterprise. So, Section 205 has been included in the act requiring every company to make provision for depreciation before payment of dividend. The act has further stipulated that if a company has failed to make provision for depreciation in past year or years, it has to provide for such arrears of depreciation in addition to depreciation for current year before paying dividend. The amount of depreciation must not be less than the amount calculated at the rates specified in Schedule XIV, which has been inserted by the Companies (amendment) Act 1988.

However, the act has given the central government power to allow a company to declare dividend without providing for depreciation, where it is necessary to pay dividend in the public interest. It is important to note that absence in the Schedule XIV of any rate of depreciation on an asset or circular of the central government in this regard will not spare a company for non-provision of depreciation before payment of dividend. In this case it will be the obligation of the company to approach the central government for approval of the basis of depreciation.

However, if the book value of an asset has already been reduced to five percent or less to its original cost, it will not be statutorily necessary to make provision for depreciation.

Provisions of the Companies Act regarding quantum of depreciation are as follows:

1. Schedule XIV of the Act specifies the rates of depreciation for various categories of assets. The schedule specifies rates for straight-line method and written-down method separately and the company is at liberty to adopt rates under any method.
2. If there is any addition to assets during the financial year, depreciation should be calculated on pro-rata basis from the date of such addition. Similarly if any asset is sold, discarded or demolished during the financial year, depreciation should be provided up to the date on which the asset is sold, discarded or demolished.
3. Schedule XIV also provides separate depreciation rates for double-shift and triple-shift machinery working under both straight-line method and written down value method.
4. The Act requires a company to make provision for depreciation arrears along with current year's depreciation if it wants to pay dividend during the year.
5. The amount of depreciation to be calculated at the rates specified in the schedule is to be viewed as minimum. If higher amount of depreciation becomes justified on the basis of bonafide technological evaluation, such higher amount may be provided with proper disclosure by way of a note forming part of annual accounts.
6. Shortfall or non-provision of depreciation should be properly disclosed by way of note in pursuance of Part II of Schedule VI of the Companies Act.
7. Apart from the written-down value method and straight-line method, depreciation can be charged on any other basis approved by the central government. Such method should, however, write off at least 95 percent of the original cost of the asset on the expiry of the specified period.

7.6 DISTINCTION BETWEEN DEPRECIATION AND AMORTISATION

Depreciation is the process of allocation of cost of fixed assets to successive profit and loss account over its useful life. The purpose of such allocation is to recover gradually the amount of capital invested in the asset so that the same can be replaced at the end of its life without further infusion of capital.

On the other hand, intangible assets, such as goodwill, trade marks and patents are written off over a number of accounting periods covering their estimated useful lives. This periodic write off is called amortisation, which is similar to depreciation of tangible assets. The term amortisation is also used for writing off leasehold premises.

The distinction between depreciation and amortisation is presented in Table 7.1.

TABLE 7.1 Distinction between depreciation and amortisation

Points of difference	*Depreciation*	*Amortisation*
1. Definition	The portion of cost of fixed tangible assets written off as expired cost is called depreciation.	The portion of cost of fixed intangible assets written off as expired cost is generally known as amortisation.
2. Residual value	While calculating depreciation, residual value of fixed assets is generally considered.	No residual value is usually considered in determination of periodic amortisation, as most of the intangible assets do not have any residual value.
3. Method	There are different methods of charging depreciation like straight-line method, reducing balance method etc.	Amortisation is generally done on the basis of fixed instalment method.
4. Determination of depreciation	The benefits to be derived out of fixed tangible assets are more or less certain. So the amount of depreciation can be determined more easily and logically.	There involves a high degree of uncertainty regarding the flow of benefit out of intangibles. The value of benefit may range from zero to a substantial amount. So the estimation of amortisation becomes subjective and less logical.

7.7 DIFFERENT METHODS OF DEPRECIATION

There are different methods of depreciation. An entity may adopt any one of the methods of depreciation for its assets. Again, it may adopt different methods of depreciation for different types of assets provided the same are adopted on a consistent basis. Even a company having plants at different locations may adopt different methods of depreciation in the same accounting year. Further it may be noted that depreciation would be charged on pro-rata basis in respect of assets acquired during the financial year.

Different methods of charging depreciation are as follows:

1. Straight line method

This is the most popular method because of its simplicity and consistency. It requires allocation of an equal amount to each period. A fixed amount of the original cost is charged as depreciation every year. Thus, the asset is written down in value each year by the same amount. Under this method, the book value of the asset may be reduced to zero. The amount of depreciation under this method is calculated as:

$$\text{Annual depreciation} = \frac{\text{Cost of the asset} - \text{Residual value}}{\text{Estimated useful life}}$$

So, depreciation under this method is the reciprocal of the estimated useful life if the scrap value is considered as nil.

2. Reducing balance method

Under this method, instead of a fixed amount, a fixed rate on the reduced balance of the asset is charged as depreciation every year. Since a constant percentage rate is being applied to the written down value, the amount of depreciation charged every year decreases over the life of the asset. This method assumes that an asset should be depreciated more in earlier years of use than later years because the maximum loss of an asset occurs in the early years of use. The fixed percentage rate, to be applied to the allocation of net costs as depreciation, can be obtained by the following formula:

$$r \text{ (rate of depreciation)} = 1 - \sqrt[n]{s/c}$$

where

n = the expected useful life in years
s = the scrap value
c = the acquisition cost

It may be noted in this context that the Companies Act, 1956 through Section 205 gives recognition to only the above two methods as the methods of depreciation, which a company can adopt for its accounting purposes.

3. Sinking fund method

Under this method, a fund is created by the regular investment of a fixed amount to accumulate the amount required to replace an asset in the future. This method is based on the concept of present value of money. The previous two methods made no attempt to generate fund for replacement of asset at the end of its useful life, In this method, an amount equivalent to depreciation charged is invested outside the business in securities and are allowed to accumulate at compound interest so as to produce the required amount to replace the asset after a specified period of time.

4. Insurance policy method

This method is similar to sinking fund method but, instead of investing the money in securities, the amount is used in paying premium on a policy taken out with an insurance company. The policy should mature immediately after the expiry of the useful life of the asset. The money that is received from the insurance company is used to replace the asset. Though the interest received is lower than that could be obtained by investing in securities, the risk of loss on realisation of securities can be avoided under this method.

5. Sum of the years' digit method

This method assumes that the depreciation charge should be more in the early years of the life of the asset. Under this method, the amount of depreciation is calculated by multiplying the cost by a fraction based on the sum of the number of periods of the useful economic life of the asset. Depreciation under this method is computed as follow:

$$\text{Depreciation} = \frac{\text{Number of year's life remaining}}{\text{Sum of years digits}} \times (\text{Cost} - \text{Salvage value})$$

where, sum of years' digits $= \frac{n(n+1)}{2}$ (n = life of the asset)

6. Annuity method

Under this method, the total amount of depreciation written off during the life of the asset equals the net cost of the asset plus interest calculated on the reducing balance. The basis of this method is to consider the time value of money and opportunity cost of capital locked up in the asset. When an amount is invested in acquiring an asset, the business has to forgo some amount of interest, which could have been earned if the money was employed in the purchase of an income-producing asset. This method of depreciation can be applied to an asset, the life of which will extend to a known period.

7. Revaluation method

This method is applied for the writing-off of a fixed asset to its current market value. To ascertain the real profit for an accounting period, it is necessary to value the assets each year at the end of the period and any decrease in the value as compared with the book value should be charged against profit as depreciation. If any profit is arising out of revaluation of assets, it should be credited to revaluation reserve account, where it will find a place on the liability side of the balance sheet. This revaluation method is a departure from historical cost accounting with regard to the valuation of assets.

8. Depletion method

This method is an accounting for natural resources rather than accounting for depreciation. Wasting assets, such as mines, quarries and the like are examples of such natural resources. The distinguishing feature of these types of assets is that they cannot be depreciated, but can gradually be depleted. Therefore, this method is applied to wasting assets only, where the output for each year depends on the quantity extracted. So, under this method, depreciation is calculated first by making an estimate in advance of the total quantity to be extracted over the life and then the cost of the asset is apportioned over the periods of the assets in proportion to the rate of extraction.

9. Machine hour rate method

This is a method of providing depreciation on annual machine hours in use as compared with total anticipated machine hours over the life of the machine. Under this method, it is necessary to estimate the total effective working hours of the machine during its whole life and to divide this total into the net cost of the machine and thus arriving at an hourly rate of depreciation. So, the depreciation charge per machine hour would be—

$$\text{Machine Hour Rate} = \frac{\text{Cost of the machine} - \text{Scrap value}}{\text{Effective working hours}}$$

But this method ignores an important aspect i.e. depreciation also takes place when a machine is not in use.

10. Depreciation and repair fund method

Under this method, total maintenance costs are estimated for the entire life of the asset and added to its net capital cost to get a composite figure, which is divided by the number of years the asset is expected to last. The resultant amount is considered as depreciation per year. The cost of repairs and maintenance are added to calculate the amount of depreciation in this method. As a result, this method can be considered one of the best methods of equalising the burden of the cost of the assets regarding its acquisition as well as its maintenance.

7.8 DEPRECIATION ACCOUNTING AS PER AS-6

AS-6 (Depreciation Accounting) issued by the Institute of Chartered Accountants of India lays down the accounting principles regarding depreciation. AS-6 provides as follows:

1. Application

The standard is applicable to all depreciable assets except the following:

- Forests, plantations and similar regenerative natural resources
- Wasting assets including expenditure on the exploration for and extraction of minerals, oils, natural gas and similar non-regenerative resources
- Expenditure on research and development
- Goodwill
- Livestock

2. Concept of depreciation

A measure of the wearing out, consumption or other loss of value of a depreciable asset arises from the following:

- Use
- Effluxion of time
- Obsolescence.

3. Depreciable assets

The assets which have the following features are termed as depreciable assets:

- Expected to be used for more than one accounting period
- Have a limited useful life
- Are held for use in production or supply of goods and services, for rental to others or for administrative purposes.

4. Useful life

As asset is considered to have a useful life under the following conditions:

- When the period over which a depreciable asset is expected to be used by the enterprise
- When the number of production or similar units expected to be obtained from the use of the asset by the enterprise.

5. Depreciable amount

Depreciable amount of a depreciable asset is its historical cost or other amount substituted for historical cost in the financial statements, less the estimated residual value.

6. Depreciation method

The method should be applied consistently from period to period. Any change in the method of depreciation should be made only if the new method has the following:

- It is required by the statute
- It is required for compliance with an accounting standard
- It would result in a more appropriate preparation or presentation of financial statements.

7. Change in the method of depreciation

Depreciation should be recalculated in accordance with the new method from the date of the asset coming to use. The deficiency or surplus should be adjusted in the accounts in the year in which the method of depreciation is changed.

Example

A company purchased machinery for Rs. 1,00,000 on 1st April 2002 and followed the diminishing balance method of depreciation @ 15%. At the end of March, 2005 it was decided to follow the straight-line method of depreciation at Rs. 15,000 per year from the very beginning. How should the company give effect to this change in the method of depreciation?

Solution

Total Depreciation from 1.4.2002 to 31.3.2005 under old method [Rs. (15,000 + 12,750 + 10,840)]	= 38,590
Total Depreciation from1.4.2002 to 31.3.2005 under new method [Rs. 15,000 × 3]	= 45,000
	Rs. 6,410

So, additional depreciation to be provided in 2004-05 is Rs. 6,410.00 debiting profit and loss account and crediting machinery account.

8. Change in useful life

Useful life of the asset should be reviewed periodically. Where there is a revision, the unamortised depreciable amount should be charged over the remaining useful life.

9. Change in the historical cost

The depreciation on the revised unamortised depreciable amount should be provided prospectively over the residual useful life of the asset.

10. Revaluation of asset

On revaluation, the provision for depreciation should be based on the following:

- The revalued amount
- The estimate of the remaining useful life

Example

X Ltd. acquired a building on 1st January 1988 at a cost of Rs. 3,20,000. The useful life of the building was estimated as 50 years and depreciation is provided on a straight-line basis. The building was revalued on 30th June 2005 for Rs. 8,40,000. Assuming no change in the remaining useful life, calculate the surplus on revaluation and depreciation to be charged in the profit and loss account of 2005.

Solution

Surplus on revaluation

Revaluation on 30th June 2005	= Rs. 8,40,000
Net book value at 30th June 2005	= Rs. 2,08,000
Surplus	= Rs. 6,32,000

This surplus of Rs. 6,32,000 should be credited directly to revaluation reserve as per AS-10.

Depreciation to be charged to the profit and loss account of 2005

Up to 30.06.2005, depreciation will be calculated on original value and from 1.7.2005 it is to be calculated on revalued figure.

(a) On historical cost (up to 30.6.2005)	= (Rs. 3,20,000/50) × ½ =	3,200
(b) On revalued amount [1.7.2005 to 31.12.2005]	= (Rs. 8,40,000/32.5) × 17.5 =	12,923
	Total =	16,123

7.9 ACCOUNTING DISCLOSURE REQUIREMENT

Clause 3(iv) of Part-II of Schedule VI to the Companies Act, 1956 provides that the profit and loss account must disclose the amount of depreciation, renewals and diminution in the value of fixed assets. If no provision has been made for depreciation in respect of a particular asset, the fact that no provision has been made should be stated and the quantum of arrears depreciation computed in accordance with Section 205(2) should be disclosed by way of a note.

The form of the balance sheet prescribed under the Companies Act, 1956 (Schedule VI Part (I)) further requires that total depreciation written off or provided in respect of each asset should be disclosed.

AS-6 requires the following information to be disclosed in the financial statements:

- The historical cost or other amount substituted for historical cost of each class of depreciable assets
- Total depreciation for the period for each class of assets, and
- The related accumulated depreciation

It also requires disclosure of information in the financial statements along with the disclosure of other accounting policies— the depreciation methods used, and depreciation rates or the useful life of the assets, if they are different from the principal rates specified in the schedule governing the enterprise.

7.10 LEGAL NECESSITY OF PROVISION FOR DEPRECIATION

On account of the provision under Section 205 that no dividend shall be declared except out of profit arrived at after providing for depreciation in accordance with the provisions of the

Act, it becomes obligatory for every company distributing dividend to make a provision for depreciation.

Sub-section (2) of Section 205 prescribes different methods that may be adopted for computing the amount of depreciation. These can be summarised as follows:

1. Method as per Income Tax Act

The charge on account of depreciation may be calculated in the manner required by Section 350, i.e. at the rates prescribed for different assets by the Income-Tax Act, 1961 and the rules framed there on in respect of depreciation.

2. Amount to be depreciated

It may be calculated at a rate arrived at by dividing 95% of the original cost of the asset to the company, by the number of years at the end of which 95% of its original cost has been provided for as depreciation.

3. Other methods as approved by central government

The provision for depreciation may be made on any other method approved by the central government, which has the effect of writing off by way of depreciation 95% of the original cost to the company of each depreciable asset at the expiry of the specified period.

4. Where no rate is available

If a company possesses a depreciable asset for which no rate for depreciation has been prescribed by the Income Tax Act, 1961 or the rules framed there on, the amount of depreciation should be computed on such basis as the central government may approve, either by any general order published in the official gazette or any special order in particular case.

7.11 PROVISION FOR DEPRECIATION FOR PAST YEARS

The provisions as contained in Section 205(1) prescribes that if a company has not provided for depreciation for any previous financial year or years ending after 28.12.1961 (the date when the Companies (Amendment) Act came into force), it shall, before declaring or paying dividend, provide for such depreciation

- either out of that financial years' profit, or
- out of the profits of any other previous financial year or years.

There are, however, two exceptions to this rule.

1. The profits of financial year or years ended before 28.12.1960 may be distributed even though in arriving at these profits, no depreciation in respect of past years had been provided.
2. A company may be permitted by the central government, if it is thought necessary, to pay dividend for any financial year without first providing for depreciation for that year or for any earlier years. The central government, would, however, exempt a company only if it finds that such a distribution is necessary in the public interest [Section 205(1)(c)].

7.12 DEPRECIATION ON LOW VALUE ITEMS

The Department of Company Affairs, Ministry of Law, Justice and Company Affairs, Government of India, issued a notification during December, 1993, which has been inserted as Notes No. 8 in Schedule XIV to the Companies Act, 1956 that "Notwithstanding anything contained in the schedule, depreciation on assets, whose actual costs does not exceed Rs. 5,000 shall be provided @100%. However, in respect of the fixed assets acquired prior to December, 1993 alternative basis of computation of depreciation is permitted."

But Note 4 to the Schedule XIV requires that, where during any financial year any addition has been made to any asset, the depreciation on such asset should be calculated on a pro-rata basis from the date of such additions. As Note 8 to Schedule XIV prescribes the rate of depreciation of 100%, pro-rata depreciation should be charged on addition of the said low value items of fixed assets also. However, the company can write off fully low value items on the consideration of materiality. Where, such an accounting policy is followed by a company, the same should be properly disclosed in the accounts.

7.13 DEPRECIATION ON WASTING ASSETS

In terms of the decision in the case Lee vs Neuchatel Asphalte Co. Ltd. (1889), there does not appear any necessity to provide depreciation on wasting assets like mines, quarries etc. In the present day context, however, it is highly doubtful whether the principle propounded in the above case would hold good.

Wasting assets exhaust by working and necessarily involve depletion of the capital employed on such assets. It is, therefore, necessary with a view to maintain the capital employed, a charge for such depletion for ascertaining a true and fair view of the financial statements. Also according to the opinion of the company law board, depreciation on wasting assets is a necessary charge for arriving at the true and fair picture of the profit and loss account and balance sheet.

7.14 CHANGE IN THE METHOD OF DEPRECIATION

According to Sec. 205(2) and 350 of the Companies Act, 1956, two methods of charging depreciation namely straight-line method and reducing balance method have been recognised. However, a company is also allowed to follow any other method of charging depreciation duly approved by the central government. Whatever method of depreciation is followed by a company, it should be followed consistently. Consistency in the method is necessary to ensure comparability of the results of the operations of the enterprise from period to period. It is to be noted that Companies Act, 1956 does not restrain a company to change the method of depreciation.

However, AS-6 issued by the Institute of Chartered Accountants of India has suggested the change in the method of depreciation only when any of the following hold:

1. The change is required by the statute or for compliance with an accounting standard.
2. The change in the method of depreciation will ensure more appropriate presentation of financial statements.

If the change in the method of depreciation has to be effected due to any of the above reasons, following procedures should be observed:

(a) The change in the method should be implemented with retrospective effect. In other words, depreciation should be recalculated in accordance with the new method from the date of the asset coming into use.

(b) The adjustment for excess or short depreciation should be treated as prior period and extra ordinary item and should be reflected in income statement accordingly.

(c) The change in the method of depreciation should be treated as change in accounting policy and should be disclosed accordingly.

7.15 AUDITOR'S DUTY AS REGARDS DEPRECIATION

Apart from fixed assets in respect of which depreciation must be provided, it also has to be provided on semi-permanent assets, e.g. patents, trade marks etc. Since the auditor is not in a position to estimate the working life of a majority of them, for this he has to rely on the opinion of persons who have a technical knowledge of the assets. He must, however, satisfy himself that an honest attempt has been made to estimate the working life of each asset, that the total provision for depreciation is adequate and that the method adopted for determining the amount to be written off is properly disclosed in the profit and loss account and the balance sheet.

In part III of Schedule VI of the Companies Act, it is provided that any amount written off as depreciation is to be regarded as a provision, but any amount so written off, which is in excess of the amount, to which in the opinion of the directors is reasonably necessary for the purpose, to be regarded as a 'reserve'. The amount should be shown as a reserve under the head "reserves and surplus" on the liabilities side of the balance sheet. It is the duty of the auditor to ensure himself that the above provisions are being followed in maintaining depreciation accounting.

So, the duties of an auditor in connection with depreciation can be stated as follows:

1. The auditor should ensure which method of depreciation, i.e. whether straight-line, method or reducing balance method as stipulated in Schedule XIV to the Companies (Amendment) Act 1988 is being followed by the company.
2. The auditor should check that depreciation has been provided at the rates not less than the rates specified in Schedule XIV to the Companies (Amendment) Act 1988.
3. He should see that if any other method of depreciation is in use, it has got the approval of the Central Government.
4. He should also make sure that the method of depreciation and the rate of depreciation, which are not in accordance with Schedule XIV, have been duly disclosed.
5. The auditor should ensure that if an asset is sold, discarded, demolished or destroyed, the excess of written down value over its sale proceeds or its scrap value has been written off in the financial year in which it is sold, discarded, demolished or destroyed.
6. The auditor should ensure that the provision for depreciation on additions, deletions etc. during the accounting year have been made on pro rata basis.

7. He should check the extra shift depreciation for double shift or triple shift, working has been computed in respect of plant and machineries in proportion of the number of days the company worked double shift or triple shift, as the case may be, bears to the total number of normal working days during the year.
8. The auditor should see that dividend has been declared only out of profits arrived at after provision for depreciation.
9. He should ensure that the amount of depreciation written off has been clearly disclosed in the profit and loss account.
10. He should see that the accounting policy of the company has clearly stated the method of depreciation in use.
11. The auditor should satisfy himself that adequate amount of depreciation has been provided. If he is not satisfied with the adequacy of amount of depreciation, he will persuade the management to make further provision for depreciation.
12. He should see the same method of charging depreciation is being followed year after year. If there is any change in the method of depreciation he will enquire into the reason and satisfy himself with its justification.
13. He will see that excess depreciation provided so far has been transferred to reserve and shown under the head 'reserves and surplus' on the liabilities side of the balance sheet.
14. The auditor should check that the following information has been disclosed in the financial statements:
    (a) The historical cost or other amount substituted for historical cost of each class of depreciable assets
    (b) Total depreciation for the period for each class of assets
    (c) The related accumulated depreciation

7.16 LEGAL VIEWS AS REGARDS DEPRECIATION

Decisions taken in different legal cases reflect the legal view regarding depreciation. Some such cases are summarised below.

Case Study

1. **Case: Wilmer vs McNamara Co. Ltd. (1895)**

   Legal view: A company could not be restrained from declaring a dividend out of current profits merely because no provision had been made for the depreciation on fixed assets.

2. **Case: Verner vs General Commercial Investment Trust Ltd. (1894)**

   Legal view: A Trust company may not make good the loss of capital. Fixed capital may be sunk and lost, yet the excess of current receipt must be kept up.

3. **Case: Bolton vs Natal Land Colonisation Co. Ltd. (1891)**

   Legal view: A company may declare a dividend out of current profits without necessarily making good the loss of capital.

4. **Case: Lee vs Neuchatel Asphalte Co. Ltd. (1889)**

   Legal view: Subject to the provisions in the articles of association, a company may distribute dividend without providing for depreciation on its wasting assets.

POINTS TO PONDER

- "Depreciation is a measure of the wearing out, consumption or other loss of value of depreciable assets arising from use, effluxion of time, obsolescence through technology and market change": AS-6.
- Depreciable amount of a depreciable asset is its historical cost or other amount substituted for historical cost in the financial statement less the estimated residual value.
- The purposes for which depreciation is provided include keeping the capital intact, ascertaining the cost accurately, charging the initial costs against earnings and preparing true and fair statements of accounts.
- Depreciation is caused basically for two factors: physical factors and economical factors i.e. directly through deterioration and indirectly through obsolescence.
- Cost of the assets, its scrap value and the expected useful life are the bases of charging depreciation.
- The quantum of depreciation depends on a number of factors, which include the cost of the asset, the estimated working life of the asset, the estimated scrap value, the risk of obsolescence and the income tax rule regarding depreciation.
- Prior to the Companies Act, 1960 it was not legally compulsory to provide for depreciation before distribution of dividend. At present, according to Section 205 of the Companies Act requires that every company should make provision for depreciation before payment of dividend.
- Different methods of charging depreciation include straight-line method, reducing balance method, sinking fund method, insurance policy method, sum of year's digits method, annuity method, revaluation method, depletion method, machine hour rate method, and depreciation and repair fund method.
- The historical cost or the amount substituted for historical cost, total depreciation for the period and accumulated depreciation of each class of assets should be disclosed in the financial statements.
- Whatever method of depreciation is followed by a company, it should be followed consistently. The change in the method of depreciation is permissible if it is required by the statute or will ensure better presentation of financial statements.
- The auditor should ensure that the company is following the method of depreciation as stipulated in Schedule XIV of the Companies Act.

- He should also make sure that the method and the rate of depreciation have been duly disclosed.
- The auditor should ensure that the provision for depreciation on additions, deletions etc. during the accounting year have been made on pro-rata basis.
- He should see the same method of charging depreciation is being followed year after year.
- He should also ensure that excess depreciation provided has been transferred to reserve and shown under the head 'reserves and surplus' on the liabilities side of the balance sheet.

REVIEW QUESTIONS

Short-answer Questions

1. What do you mean by the term 'depreciation'?
2. Is it necessary to make provision for depreciation?
3. State the main factors to be considered for determining the amount of depreciation?
4. Is it legally compulsory to charge depreciation on assets?
5. Discuss the provisions of the Companies Act regarding arrears depreciation.
6. Is there any statutory necessity to make disclosures of depreciation in company accounts?
7. What are the provisions of the Companies Act regarding depreciation on low value items?
8. Is depreciation on wasting assets a necessary charge for arriving at the true and fair picture of the financial statements of a company?

Essay-type Questions

1. Is it absolutely necessary that depreciation should be provided for before profits are distributed as dividend? What are the provisions of the Companies Act, 1956 regarding the quantum of depreciation to be provided for in the annual accounts?
2. A limited company wants to change its method of providing for depreciation from reducing balance method to fixed instalment method. Can the company do so? If so, explain as to how? In this context, discuss the view of AS-6 of ICAI and auditor's duties in regard to depreciation.
3. An enterprise purchases an item of machinery on 1.4.2002 for Rs. 1,00,000. It depreciates this item at the rate of 10% per annum on straight-line basis. On 1.4.2005, the enterprise decides to change the method of depreciation from straight-line to written down value. The applicable rate under the new method is 15%. How should the enterprise give effect to this change in the method of depreciation?
4. Discuss the accounting treatment of the following:
   (a) Change in the method of depreciation
   (b) Change in the value of the asset
5. A limited company wishes to change over from the written down value method of providing depreciation which it has hitherto been following to the straight-line method. The company seeks your opinion on this proposed action. Advise.

CHAPTER 8

Reserves and Provisions

CHAPTER OUTLINE

8.1 CONCEPT OF RESERVES

Reserves are amounts appropriated out of profits, which are not intended to meet any liability, contingency, commitment or diminution in the value of assets known to exist at the date of the balance sheet.

According to American Institute of Accountants, "the use of the term reserve is limited to indicate that an undivided portion of the asset is being held or retained for general or specific purposes".

8.2 CONCEPT OF PROVISIONS

Provisions are amounts charged against revenue to provide for the following:

(a) Depreciation, renewals or diminution in the value of assets
(b) A known liability, the amount whereof cannot be determined with substantial accuracy
(c) A claim, which is disputed

According to the Penguin Dictionary of Commerce, "a provision is the amount written off or retained by way of providing depreciation, renewals or diminution in the value of assets, or retained by way of providing for any known liability of which the amount cannot be determined with substantial accuracy".

8.3 DIFFERENCE BETWEEN RESERVES AND PROVISIONS

Reserves represent that portion of the business profits, which is meant for a use in future, in situation of emergency or contingency—general or specific. On the other hand, provisions are charges against earnings and must be shown in the profit and loss account. In the balance sheet, reserves are shown under the heading 'reserves and surplus' irrespective of the nature of reserves, capital or revenue. But, in case of provisions, that part of the provisions which represents liabilities will be shown under the heading 'current liabilities and provisions' and that part of the provisions which represents the diminution in the value of assets, e.g. provisions for depreciation, provisions for bad and doubtful debts are generally deducted from the balance of the concerned assets in the asset side of the balance sheet.

The difference between reserves and provisions is illustrated in Table 8.1.

8.4 CLASSIFICATION OF RESERVES

The net worth of the company consists of capital contribution by the shareholders as well as total undistributed profits held either to the credit of the profit and loss account or to a reserve. The reserves can again be segregated as revenue reserves and capital reserves.

As per Part I of Schedule VI, the following items are shown under the heading "reserves and surplus" in the liabilities side of the balance sheet:

- Capital reserves
- Capital redemption reserves

TABLE 8.1 Distinction between reserves and provisions

Reserves	*Provisions*
1. It is an appropriation of profit. Hence it is created by debiting profit & loss appropriation account.	1. It is a charge against profit. Hence it is debited to profit and loss account.
2. A reserve is created for an unknown liability.	2. A provision is made for a known liability.
3. Creation of reserves depends upon the financial policy of the firm.	3. Creation of provisions is a must as these are meant for meeting known liabilities.
4. The reserve is shown in the balance sheet of a company under the head "Reserves & Surplus".	4. The provisions are usually deducted from the concerned assets in the asset side of the balance sheet.
5. Past reserves can be utilised for distribution of dividend.	5. Provision can never be utilised for dividend payment. Only excess provision written back can be used for dividend distribution.
6. It is possible to create revenue only if the company earns profit. If there is a loss, no reserve cannot be created as it is an appropriation of profit.	6. Provisions are possible to be made even if there is loss as it is a charge against profit.
7. Creation of reserves is discretionary and the auditor need not devote much time for the verification of reserves.	7. Creation of provision is a must and the auditor should qualify his report if adequate provisions are not made.
8. A reserve is always reserve till it is fully utilised. Even if it is more than the requirement, it will not change its nature.	8. As per Schedule VI of the Companies Act, provision in excess of requirement can be treated as reserve.

- Other reserves specifying the nature of each reserve and the amount in respect thereof less debit balance in profit and loss account (if any)
- Securities premium account
- Surplus, i.e. balance in profit and loss account after providing for proposed allocations, namely—dividend, bonus or reserves
- Proposed additions to reserves
- Sinking fund

8.4.1 Revenue Reserve

It represents profits that are available for distribution to shareholders held for the time being for any one or more purposes, e.g. supplement divisible profits in lean years, to finance an extension of business or to generally strengthen the financial position of the company.

Since the creation of this reserve is not a must, the auditor has no duty to report on the creation, adequacy or inadequacy of such a reserve. He may advise the management on the desirability of creation and maintenance of such reserve in the interest of the business.

8.4.2 Capital Reserve

It represents reserves which are created out of capital profit. Capital profits are those profits, which do not arise in the normal course of business. So, capital reserve is created out of the profits of following nature:

(a) Profit earned on sale of fixed assets at a price in excess of cost
(b) Profit on revaluation of all assets
(c) Profit earned prior to incorporation of the company
(d) Profit on re-issue of forfeited shares.

According to the definition of capital reserve, as contained in Part-III of Schedule VI to the Companies Act, it is reserve, which does not include any amount regarded as free for distribution through the profit and loss account. In the narrowest sense, therefore the description would include only Securities premium, Capital redemption reserve, Development rebate reserve and Profit on re-issue of forfeited shares.

A capital reserve can be generally utilised for the following purposes:

- It can be utilised for issuing bonus shares, if the Articles of Association so provide.
- It can also be utilised for writing off various types of intangible and fictitious assets.

But the amount of securities premium or capital redemption reserves account can be utilised only for the purposes specified in Section 78 and Section 80 of the Companies Act.

The question whether capital reserve can be made available for the distribution of dividend or not has not been dealt specifically with by the Companies Act. However, from the decisions of the two leading cases, i.e. (1) Lubbock vs The British Bank of South America (1892) and (2) Foster vs. The New Trinidad Lake Asphalte Co. Ltd. (1901) it is learnt that the following conditions must be fulfilled before distribution of dividend out of capital reserve:

(a) The Articles of Association must authorise such distribution.
(b) The capital reserve created out of profit on sale of fixed assets should be realised in cash.
(c) The capital profit must exist after revaluation of all the assets and liabilities of the company.

So, capital reserve created out of the following incomes is not available for dividend payment:

(i) Securities premium, the distribution of which as dividend is specifically prohibited by Section 78 of the Companies Act
(ii) Capital redemption reserve
(iii) Profit on re-issue of forfeited shares
(iv) Profit prior to incorporation
(v) Profit on redeeming debentures at a discount
(vi) Profit on purchase of business.

The auditor should examine that the capital reserve is created out of capital profits only. If the capital reserves are to be utilised for distribution of dividend, he should ensure that the same is permitted by the articles of the company.

8.4.3 Capitalisation of Reserve

The term 'capital reserve' should not be confused with the term 'capitalisation of reserve'. Capitalisation of reserve is the process by which the reserve, whether capital in nature or revenue nature is permanently retained by the company by way of issuing bonus shares. It is one of the methods of financing the growth and expansion of the business and is popularly known as the 'ploughing back of profit'.

So, capital reserve and capitalisation of reserve are two different terms having the following differences between them as depicted in Table 8.2.

TABLE 8.2 Distinction between capital reserve and capitalisation of reserves

Capital reserve	*Capitalisation of reserves*
1. Capital reserve is created out of capital profit only.	1. Capitalisation of reserve is done either out of capital reserve or revenue reserve.
2. Capital reserve does not increase the capital of the company.	2. Capitalisation of reserve increases the amount of capital of the company.
3. There is no specific provision in the Companies Act regarding creation and utilisation of capital reserve.	3. SEBI has introduced detailed guidelines for the capitalisation of reserves.
4. Capital reserve is created by any type of capital profit when they arise.	4. Capitalisation of reserve is possible only out of some specific reserves.
5. Creation of capital reserve is accompanied by an increase in asset of the company.	5. Capitalisation of reserve does not increase the assets of the business. Only there is some reorganisation of capital structure of the company.

Advantages of capitalisation of reserve

Capitalisation of reserve is the process by which reserve is permanently retained by the company by way of issuing bonus shares. The shareholders as well as the company itself are benefited from the issue of bonus shares.

Advantages from the point of view of shareholders

1. The shareholders get back their undistributed profit in the shape of shares.
2. Accumulated profit can be distributed without disturbing the liquidity position of the company.
3. It will increase the number of shares in the hands of the existing shareholders without any extra payment. Thus it will increase the marketability of shares.
4. They receive profit of the company, though in kind, but in case of necessity, shares can be converted into cash by selling them in the market.

Advantages from the point of view of the company

1. The company can keep its shareholders happy without impairing the financial position and liquidity of the company.
2. Creditors can feel more protected due to increase in share capital.
3. Growth of the company is ensured by permanently keeping the reserve in the business.

4. By way of capitalisation of reserves, disparity between effective capital and book capital can be eliminated and the balance sheet can be presented in a more meaningful way.

Auditor's duty in respect of capitalisation of reserves

The auditor will ensure that the following SEBI guidelines have been duly adhered to by the company at the time of capitalising its reserves.

1. Bonus shares can be issued out of free reserves created out of genuine profits or securities premium only.
2. Reserves created out of revaluation of assets have not been utilised for the purpose of capitalisation.
3. The company has not defaulted in payment of interest and principal in respect of debentures and public deposits.
4. There has been provision in the Articles of Association authorising the company to issue bonus shares.
5. The extended capital after the issue of bonus shares has been within the limit of the authorised capital of the company.
6. In addition to the above guidelines, the auditor will also check the accounting entries to ensure himself that they have been passed properly in the books of accounts.

8.4.4 Reserve Fund

Reserves can either be retained in the business as a part of working capital or invested outside the business in marketable securities.

The term 'reserve fund' is used to describe a reserve only when the amount of reserve is invested outside the business and it is represented by the readily realisable assets.

Again, according to Part-I of Schedule VI to the Companies Act, the word 'fund' in relation to any 'reserve' should be used only where such reserve is specifically represented by earmarked investments. So, the term 'reserve fund' should not be used loosely to represent any other fund.

The auditor should see that the reserve fund has been distinctly shown in the balance sheet and the fund is represented by readily realisable and earmarked funds.

8.4.5 Sinking Fund

A sinking fund is a specific type of fund, which is created for the redemption of a long-term debt or for the replacement of an asset. This fund is created by the regular investment of an amount, which will accumulate along with the compound interest earned thereon to make available a certain amount of money at the end of a stated period.

Creation of sinking fund

Sinking fund is created by adopting any of the following two methods:

(a) Sinking fund investment method Under this method, a pre-determined amount is debited to the profit and loss account every year crediting sinking fund account and an equivalent amount should be taken out of business and invested in readily saleable securities. When the period of the fund expires, the investments are sold and the amount so realised is utilised for the concerned purpose.

(b) Sinking fund policy method Under this method, a policy for the period is taken up and the premium on the policy is debited to the profit and loss account. At the end of the policy period, the amount received is utilised for the concerned purpose. This method is adopted usually in those situations, where a certain amount is required to be received at the end of the period.

Auditor's duty regarding sinking fund

1. The auditor should ensure that the reserve fund created has been separately shown in the balance sheet.
2. He has to ensure that the purpose for which the fund is created has been clearly indicated.
3. He should also see that the creation of sinking fund for any specific purpose is authorised by the Articles of Association of the company.
4. He should also ensure that proper entries have been passed in the books of accounts to record the creation and utilisation of the fund.

8.4.6 Secret Reserve

The reserves, which is not disclosed in the balance sheet, is known as secret reserve or hidden reserve. It is called 'hidden reserve' as this reserve is not apparent on the face of the balance sheet. Obviously, if secret reserves are created, the balance sheet does not reveal the true and fair picture of the financial affairs of the company. The actual financial position of the company, in reality, is better than what is revealed on the face of the balance sheet.

Creation of secret reserve

Secret reserves can be created by adopting the measures given below.

- Charging capital expenditure as revenue expenditure
- Providing for more depreciation on fixed assets
- Making excessive provision for bad and doubtful debts
- Writing down goodwill to a nominal value
- Under-valuation of stock-in-trade
- Omitting some assets from the balance sheet
- Showing contingent liabilities as real liabilities
- Showing imaginary liabilities or overvaluing the liabilities
- Making an excessive provision for contingencies or by continuing to carry forward provisions when they are not required
- Ignoring the permanent appreciation in the value of assets
- Suppression of sales
- Inflating purchases.

Objects of creation of secret reserves

Secret reserves are usually created to serve the following purposes.

- Meet any extraordinary loss in future without disclosing the fact to the shareholders.
- Strengthen the financial position of the company

- Mislead the competitors about the financial position of the organisation
- Evade income tax and wealth tax
- Manipulate share price for some ulterior motives
- Regulate steady payment of dividend

Legal provisions

Before the Companies Act, 1956 came into force, there were no restrictions on the creation of secret reserves except that whenever secret reserves were brought back into accounts, it was necessary to disclose the amount adjusted out of such reserve.

But after the introduction of the Companies Act, 1956 it is no more possible for a company to create secret reserves. However, a banking company may continue to have secret reserves.

It is not possible to maintain secret reserves at present in a company form of organisation because of the following reasons:

1. Section 227 of the Companies Act requires the auditor of a company to state in his opinion whether the balance sheet gives a 'true and fair' view of the state of affairs of the company as at the end of its financial year. But, if secret reserves are created, it will either overstate liabilities or understate assets and as a result financial statement will not reflect a true and fair view.
2. Part I of Schedule VI to the Companies Act requires that the balance sheet will make full disclosure for reserves and provisions.
3. Part III of Schedule VI to the Companies Act also requires that a provision for depreciation, renewal or diminution in the value of assets and that in respect of a known liability, which in the opinion of directors, is in excess of the amount which is reasonably necessary for the purpose, should be credited to reserve account. As a result, it is not possible any more for a company to create secret reserves.

Auditor's duty regarding secret reserves

The auditor is required to report on whether the balance sheet reflects a true and fair view of the state of affairs of the company. If secret reserve is created, the balance sheet will not reflect a true and fair view of the state of affairs of the company. So the auditor cannot ignore the existence of secret reserve in the balance sheet. If there is secret reserve, he must find it out. His position in this respect will not change even if it is created for some good purposes, e.g. for strengthening the financial position of the business or for meeting any future contingency. The auditor should, therefore, exercise reasonable skill and care in detecting all cases of secret reserves. He will advise his client to rectify the accounts to do away with secret reserve if it exists. If his advice is ignored, he will qualify his report.

There is also some relaxation in case of banking, insurance, electricity and finance companies, which may continue to have secret reserve. But even the auditor of such companies must not remain indifferent to the secret reserve. He must ascertain the magnitude of secret reserve existing in the books and enquire into its necessity. He will allow it to continue if he is satisfied that it has been created in the best interest of the company and the amount is reasonable.

In the context of the auditors duty while he detects the existence of secret reserve, the decision in the Royal Mail Steam Packet Company case (1931) is noteworthy.

[The fact of the case was that a huge amount of secret reserve was created under the head 'Taxation Reserve' in boom years. Later, when the company suffered heavy losses, this secret reserve was used to conceal the loss. The shareholders were given to understand through annual report that the company was running profitably and they were being paid dividend out of current year's profits. The auditor was criminally prosecuted along with the chairman of the company for deceiving the shareholders. While defending himself, the auditor argued that the purpose of secret reserve was to augment profit in lean years and had he disclosed the fact of secret reserve, its purpose would have been defeated. But the auditor was held liable for committing breach of duty. It was held that 'a protected utilisation of secret reserve, in order to keep the company going, is a serious matter which ought to be disclosed to the shareholders of the company.]

Even a provision in the articles of association forbidding the auditor from disclosing the fact of secret reserve is ultra-vires and invalid as was held in the case of Newton vs Birmingham Small Arms Co. Ltd. In these judicial pronouncements, it is noted that although creation of secret reserve was permitted, its disclosure was made obligatory.

Before the Companies Act 1956 came into force, there were no restrictions on the creation of secret reserves except that whenever it was utilised, it was necessary to disclose the amount adjusted out of such reserves.

The Companies Act now prohibits the creation of secret reserves. Only the banking, insurance and electricity companies etc. are allowed to create such reserves. Therefore, the auditor should state in his report, if he finds that such a reserve has been created. In case of companies, where creation of secret reserve is permitted, he should carefully enquire into the necessity of creating such a reserve. He need not qualify his report, if he is satisfied with the purpose of creation of such a reserve and the amount involved.

Legal views as regards secret reserves

The legal views as discussed in different cases so far taken to courts of law are summarised below.

Case Study

1. **Case: Royal Mail Steam Packet Company (1931)**

   Fact of the case: A huge amount of secret reserve was created by the company under the head "taxation reserve" in boom years. Later, when the company suffered heavy losses, this secret reserve was used to conceal the loss. The shareholders were given to understand through annual report that the company was running profitably and they were being paid dividend out of current year's profit.

   Legal view: The auditor was criminally prosecuted along with the chairman of the company for deceiving the shareholders. While defending himself, the auditor argued that the purpose of secret reserve was to augment profit in lean years and had he disclosed the fact, its purpose would have been defeated. But the auditor was held liable for committing breach of duty.

It was held by Justice Wright, J that "a protected utilisation of secret reserve, in order to keep the company going, is a serious matter, which ought to be disclosed by the company".

2. **Case: Newton vs Birmingham Small Arms Co. Ltd. (1906)**

Fact of the case: In this case, the Articles of Association of the company provided that

(i) The Directors should have powers to form an internal reserve fund, which was not to be disclosed in the balance sheet and which should be utilised in whatever way the directors thought fit.

(ii) The auditor should have access to the accounts relating to such reserves, but they should not disclose any information with regard thereto to the shareholders or otherwise.

Legal view: It was held that these provisions were ultra-vires since they limit the statutory duty of the auditors.

Justice Buckley opined that, "any regulations which precluded the auditors from availing themselves of all the information to which under the Act they are entitled, as material for the report which under the act they are to make as to true and correct state of the companies affairs, are, I think, inconsistent with the Act".

8.4.7 Specific Reserve

A specific reserve is created for some definite purpose, out of the profits of the company. The purpose may be anything connected with the business, which the articles of association or the directors want to be provided for, such as dividend equalisation, replacement of fixed assets, expansion of the organisation, income tax liability for the future etc.

Though the concerned amount is carried under earmarked head, this reserve is available for distribution as dividend on the recommendation of the directors, but subject to the approval of the shareholders, since this is created by appropriation of profits.

Normally, specific reserves are created to comply with the terms of the Articles of Association or in accordance with a decision of the board of directors to meet a particular situation, which may arise in future.

Also some of the specific reserves may be required to be created under contractual obligations or legal compulsion. An example of the former would be the fund for redemption of debentures that of the latter would be the development rebate reserve, which is compulsory to be created, if the advantages of the development rebate are to be enjoyed from income tax liability. Such specific reserves take on the character of capital reserve.

Purposes of creation of specific reserve

The purposes of creation of specific reserve can be anything connected with the business, which the Articles of Association or the Board of Directors want to be provided for.

Some of the important purposes for which it is created are as follows:

1. ***Debenture redemption reserve*** In order to redeem debentures after a certain period of time, sometime debenture trust deed provides for the creation of sinking fund or debenture redemption fund. This fund is created by transferring an equal amount of profit every year to the said fund upto the specified period from profit and loss account.

2. ***Capital redemption reserve*** When preference shares are redeemed out of profit, i.e. without corresponding fresh issue of shares, an amount equal to the nominal value of shares redeemed is transferred to capital redemption reserve account from revenue profit of the company according to the provision of Section 80 of the Companies Act.

3. ***Dividend equalisation reserve*** In order to equalise the rate of dividend between lean years and boom years sometimes a reserve is created, which is known as dividend equalisation reserve. This reserve enables the company to pay dividend at a stable rate in different years irrespective of the amount of profit earned.

4. ***Foreign project reserve*** For availing deductions u/s 80HHB, a foreign project reserve account is to be created, which is equivalent to a certain percentage of profit from foreign projects earned during any financial year. The amount credited to this reserve account has to be utilised within a period of five years for the purpose of the business itself, and not for distribution of dividend.

5. ***Staff welfare reserve fund*** This reserve is created for conducting different welfare activities of the workers and employees of the organisation. The intention of this reserve is to create good image of the company amongst its employees and workers by undertaking various activities for their benefit.

Auditor's duty as regards specific reserve

Specific reserve is created out of revenue profit of the company. So, creation of this type of reserve in no way distorts the true and fair view of the financial position of the company. However, this does not mean that the auditor has no duty in respect of specific reserves, particularly for those specific reserves, which are to be created to fulfil any legal requirement. The auditor must verify its adequacy and ensure that it is not used for any purpose other than that for which it is created. If he fails to do so, he will be held guilty of negligence as was held by the Chennai High Court in the case of M.S. Krishnaswami (1952).

So, the auditor has to take the following steps in order to justify the existence of specific reserves in the balance sheet of a company.

1. ***Examination of the articles of association*** The auditor should study the Articles of Associations to examine whether there is any provision for creation of specific reserve.

2. ***Examination of the directors' meeting minute books*** He will go through the minute books of Directors' meeting to see whether the management has taken any decision for the creation of any specific reserve and if so, whether the reserve has been created according to the decision taken.

3. ***Examination of the balance sheet*** The auditor will satisfy himself that the specific reserve created has been shown in the balance sheet according to the requirement of Part I of Schedule VI of the Companies Act.

4. ***Examination of legal documents*** He will also examine the related documents, e.g. the debenture trust deed, the tax audit file etc. to ensure that adequate provision has been created according to the legal requirements and the amount credited, if utilised, has been utilised according to the legal provisions.

POINTS TO PONDER

- Reserves are amounts appropriated out of profits, which are not intended to meet any liability, contingency, commitment or diminution in the value of assets known to exist at the date of the balance sheet.
- Provisions are amounts charged against revenue to provide for depreciation, renewals or diminution in the value of assets or a known liability, the amount whereof cannot be determined with substantial accuracy or a claim, which is disputed.
- The reserves can be of either capital reserve or revenue reserve. Revenue reserve represents profits that are available for distribution to the shareholders held for the time being. Capital reserve represents reserves, which are created out of capital profit.
- Capitalisation of reserve is the process by which the reserve is permanently retained by the company by way of issuing bonus shares. It is also known as ploughing back of profit.
- Reserve can be retained in the business as a part of working capital or invested outside the business. Reserve fund is that part of reserve which is invested outside the business.
- A sinking fund is a specific type of fund, which is created for the redemption of a long-term debt or for the replacement of an asset. It is created either by sinking fund investment method or by sinking fund policy method.
- Reserves which are not disclosed in the balance sheet are known as secret reserves. At present, it is not possible for a company to create secret reserves, except banking, insurance and electricity companies.
- A specific reserve is created for some definite purpose, out of the profits of the company. The purpose may be anything connected with the business, which the Articles of Association or the directors want to be provided for. Examples of specific reserve include debenture redemption reserve, capital redemption reserve, dividend equalisation reserve etc.

REVIEW QUESTIONS

Short-answer Questions

1. What do you mean by 'capitalisation of reserve'?
2. How do you distinguish between reserve and provision?
3. What is sinking fund? How and why it is created?
4. How is secret reserve created and utilised?
5. What is the difference between 'capital reserve' and 'revenue reserve'?

Essay-type Questions

1. What do you mean by 'capital reserve'? How does the capital reserve differ from capitalisation of reserve? Can capital reserve or capitalised reserve be available for distribution of dividend? Discuss with reference to Indian Companies Act.

2. What is meant by 'capitalisation of reserves'? State the advantages of such capitalisation to the business and to the shareholders. What is the duty of an auditor in respect of capitalisation?
3. What is secret reserve? Why it is created? Discuss the duties of an auditor in regard to secret reserve with reference to provision of Indian Companies Act.
4. What is meant by 'special reserve'? What are the purposes of creation of such reserves? What are the duties of the auditor regarding special reserve?

CHAPTER 9

Company Audit

CHAPTER OUTLINE

9.1 INTRODUCTION

A company is said to be an artificial person created by law having a separate legal entity distinct from its shareholders. It cannot be directly managed by its owners, i.e. shareholders, because they are very large in number having small holding and also scattered over a wide area. As such, the management and control of the affairs of the company is done by other persons generally known as Directors. Hence, it becomes essential for a company to appoint an independent and qualified person, i.e. an auditor, to verify and certify the truth and fairness of the financial statements.

9.2 PRELIMINARIES BEFORE COMMENCEMENT OF COMPANY AUDIT

Before commencing the actual audit work of a company, the auditor should go through the following preliminaries:

1. Ensuring whether his appointment is in order

Before accepting the offer for appointment as auditor in a company, the auditor should ensure that his appointment is made according to the provisions of Section 224 and Section 225 of the Companies Act and whether all the formalities are being maintained by the company before giving him the appointment as auditor.

The auditor should go through the following:

(a) He should see whether his appointment has been made according to Section 224 (1B) of the Companies Act. For this purpose he should obtain a copy of resolution adopted at board meeting or the shareholders meeting as the case may be.

(b) If he is appointed in place of a retiring auditor he should enquire whether due notice was served to the retiring auditor. He should find out from retiring auditor about the circumstances under which he has retired and whether he should accept the appointment. This is a professional requirement as per the Chartered Accountants Act, 1949.

(c) He should, within thirty days of receipt of appointment letter, inform the Registrar in writing that he has accepted or refused to accept the appointment.

(d) If he is appointed to fill the casual vacancy caused by the death of the previous auditor, he should get the copy of the minutes of the Board meeting in this regard and also get the confirmation of death of the previous auditor.

(e) He should see that if the company has failed to appoint or re-appoint any auditor in the annual general meeting, the central government has appointed him to fill the vacancy.

(f) If he is appointed due to the resignation of the previous auditor he must see that he has been appointed in a general meeting of shareholders. The Board of Directors will have no right to appoint him under such circumstances.

(g) He should verify whether his remuneration has been fixed according to the provisions of the Companies Act.

2. Inspection of statutory books and documents

(a) Documents Before the auditor commences the work of audit, he should examine the following documents:

(i) Memorandum of Association. The auditor must do the following:

- See whether the activities of the company are consistent with the 'objective clause'
- Check whether the amount of share capital is within the limit of authorised capital
- Observe whether there is any amendment to memorandum and, if so, whether legal formalities have been complied with

(ii) Articles of Association. The auditor must go through the following points:

- The issue of share capital and its subdivisions
- The payment of underwriting commission and brokerage on shares
- The amount of minimum subscription
- Date and amount of call
- Appointments, duties and powers of auditors in addition to statutory powers and duties
- Appointment and remuneration of directors

The above is the list of few examples, which are available in the Articles of Association. The articles may contain several other items and the auditor should go through each item very carefully. If he does not go through the articles and consequently fails to audit properly, he will be held liable as was held in the case of 'Leeds Estate Building and Investment Society Ltd. vs Shepherd (1887)'.

(iii) Prospectus: In case of newly started company and company gone for public issue the auditor will examine the prospectus to see the matters like whether shares can be issued at a discount, the amount payable on application, allotment and calls, underwriting commission and brokerage etc.

(iv) Certificate of Incorporation and certificate of commencement: These certificates are required to be examined to see whether the company has been duly incorporated and it has started its business, in case of public limited company, after getting commencement of certificate.

(b) Books and registers The following is the list of books and registers required to be maintained by the companies:

- Register of Members (u/s 150)
- Index of Members (u/s 151)
- Register and Index of Debenture-holders (u/s 152)
- Register of Mortgage and Charges *(Section 143)*
- Register of Investments *[Section 49(7)]*
- Foreign Register *(Section 157* and *158)*
- Register of contracts with companies and firms in which the Directors are interested *(Section 297, 299 & 301)*
- Register of Directors, Managing Director, Manager and Secretary *(Section 303)*
- Register of Director's shareholdings *(Section 307)*

- Register of Loans *[Section 370(1C)]*
- Minute Books *(Section 193)*

3. Inspection of contracts

The auditor should inspect and examine the contracts, which have been entered into by a company with others, for example,

(a) Contracts with the vendors of any property
(b) Contracts with the brokers and underwriters for their commission
(c) Contracts with the promoters for the preliminary expenses, etc.

4. Study of previous year's balance sheet and auditor's report

The auditor should inspect the previous year's balance sheet to verify the opening balances of the current year. Moreover, according to the Companies Act, the corresponding figures of the previous year have to be given in the balance sheet of the current year. The auditor should also study the audit report of the previous year/s in order to identify the problem areas of the company.

5. Study of internal control system in operation

The study and evaluation of the internal control system in operation is important, because it serves as a basis for reliance thereon. It helps the auditor in determining the extent of the test to which auditing procedures can be restricted.

9.3 AUDIT OF SHARE CAPITAL TRANSACTIONS

Share capital may be defined as the capital raised by a company by the issue of shares. Section 86 of the Companies Act provides that the share capital of a company limited by shares shall be of two kinds only, namely,

(a) Preference Share Capital (b) Equity Share Capital

The audit of share capital is necessary on incorporation as well as when further shares are issued, and the same is explained in the following part of this section.

9.3.1 Audit of Shares Issued for Cash

While conducting audit of share capital transactions, the auditor has to check the following.

1. Ensure that the requirements as laid down in Section 69 and 149, in this connection have been duly complied with.
2. See that the issue of shares is properly authorised and that there is no over issue beyond the limit as prescribed in the memorandum.
3. See that the provision relating to rights of shareholders are duly complied with.
4. Ensure that generally accepted accounting principles are followed while preparing the accounts.

While auditing the amount of share capital, the auditor will have to follow the procedures as stated below:

1. Application stage

(i) He should check the original applications and compare the entries in the application and allotment book with the help of these applications.

(ii) He should compare entries in the application and allotment book with those in the cash book and the bank statement.

(iii) He should ensure that the amount received on application is not less than five percent of the nominal value of shares [Section 69 (3)].

(iv) He should ensure that the application money is deposited into a scheduled bank until the certificate to commence business is obtained or they are returned in accordance with the provisions of Section 69(5).

(v) He should vouch the amount refunded to unsuccessful applications with copies of letters of regret sent to them.

(vi) He should check the totals in the application and allotment book and see that appropriate journal entries have been passed accordingly.

2. Allotment stage

(i) The auditor should examine the Director's minute book to verify approvals for allotment.

(ii) He should check copies of letters of allotment and letters of regret with entries in the application and allotment book.

(iii) The money received on allotment should be vouched by comparing the entries in the applications and allotment book with the cash book or bank statement.

(iv) He should check the postings in the share register of the amount received on application and allotment with the totals in the application and allotment book.

(v) He should see that the total of shares issued does not exceed the total authorised capital according to the memorandum.

(vi) He should see that the totals have been correctly made and that proper entry has been passed for this purpose.

3. Call stage

(i) The auditor should examine the Director's minute book for verifying approval for call money.

(ii) He should check the entries in the calls book from the copies of call letters.

(iii) In order to verify the amount of calls in arrear, he should compare the total amount due on calls as per registers and the actual money received as per cash book or statement of bank account.

(iv) He should also verify the calls in advance received by the company.

(v) He should check the postings from the calls book and the cash book into the share register.

(vi) He should see that the appropriate entries have been passed in the books accordingly.

4. Other aspects

(i) The auditor should see that the shares issued by the company are within the amount of authorised capital of the company.

(ii) He should see that the allotment of shares has been made in conformity with the conditions as stipulated in the prospectus.

(iii) If the shares are issued through underwriters, the auditor should see the contracts with the underwriters to ascertain whether the terms and conditions have been complied in full by the underwriters. In this respect, he should also see that the commission given to the underwriters does not exceed the statutory limit.

9.3.2 Audit of Shares Issued for Consideration Other Than Cash

Shares may be issued for consideration other than cash under the following circumstances:

1. Issue of shares against purchase consideration to the vendor for the business taken over by the company.
2. Issue of shares against services rendered to the underwriters, promoters or any other special service rendering agencies by way of payment of their remuneration or for any expenses incurred by them.
3. Issue of shares to the existing shareholders as bonus shares.

In order to issue shares for consideration other than cash, the auditor should follow the procedures as explained in the following segment.

1. Issue of shares to vendors/promoters

(a) Examination of contract The auditor should examine the contract entered into by the company with the vendors/promoters to know the amount of purchase consideration and the mode of payment. For the purchase consideration settlement, the mode of payment would be according to the prospectus. So, the auditor should also examine the prospectus to see the mode of payment.

(b) Checking of Director's minute book The decision regarding issue of shares to the vendors/promoters are taken at the Board meeting. The resolution passed by the Directors for allotment of shares to vendors/promoters should be confirmed from the minute book.

(c) Filing of contracts with the Registrar Such contracts are required to be filed with the registrar of companies within 30 days from the date of allotment.

(d) Allotment of shares to the nominees If shares have been allotted to the nominees of the vendors/promoters, the auditor should examine the vendor's/promoter's authority given to them in their favour.

2. Issue of shares to underwriters

(a) Examination of the contract The auditor should examine the contract with the underwriters. It is required to know the terms and conditions of the contract between the company and the underwriters.

(b) Examination of the prospectus The auditor should also examine the prospectus of the company to see the mode of payment. The auditor should verify whether the right for the payment of commission in the form of shares has been mentioned in the prospectus or not.

(c) Director's minute book He should examine the resolution of the directors by reference to the Director's minute book.

(d) Examination of the articles of association He may confirm the amount of underwriting commission from the Articles of Association. In fact, in the Articles of Association the maximum limit of underwriting commission that can be given to the underwriters and the mode of payment and procedure to be followed are mentioned.

3. Issue of bonus shares

(a) Examination of the Articles of Association The auditor should examine the Articles of Association to ascertain whether the articles permit capitalisation of profit and also whether the company had a sufficient number of un-issued shares for allotment as bonus shares.

(b) Assurance about the compliance of SEBI Guidelines The auditor should ensure that SEBI Guidelines (Chapter XV of the SEBI [D & IP] guidelines, 2000) relating to issue of bonus shares have been complied with.

(c) Checking of allotment book The auditor should trace the allotment of shares as per particulars contained in the allotment book or sheets into the register of members.

(d) Confirmation about the fulfilment of legal requirements The auditor should confirm that all statutory requirements relevant to the issue of shares have been complied with. The company has to file the particulars of the bonus shares allotted with the Registrar together with a copy of the resolution on the basis of which allotment of bonus shares has been made.

(e) Inspection of the minute book of shareholders The auditor should inspect the minute book of shareholders for the resolution authorising declaration of the bonus and Director's minute for the resolution appropriating profits for being applied in payment of shares to be allotted to shareholders as bonus shares.

(f) Checking of accounting entries The auditor should also check the accounting entries passed for issue of bonus shares and confirm that they are in conformity with the legal requirements and basic accounting principles.

4. Issue of sweat equity shares

As per explanation to Section 79A of the Companies (Amendment) Act, 1999, the term "Sweat Equity Shares" means the equity shares issued by the company to its employees or Directors at a discount or for consideration other than cash for providing know-how or making available rights in the nature of intellectual property rights or value additions, by whatever name called.

The auditor should cover the following aspects while checking the issue of sweat equity share transactions:

(a) Authorised by a special resolution The issue of sweat equity shares is authorised by a special resolution passed by the company in the general meeting.

(b) Details about share issues are specified The resolution specifies the number of shares, current market price, consideration, if any, and the class or classes of Directors or employees to whom such equity shares are to be issued.

(c) Minimum time gap for issue Not less than one year has, at the date of the issue, elapsed since the date on which the company was entitled to commence business.

(d) SEBI guidelines The sweat equity shares of a company, whose equity shares are listed on a recognised stock exchange, are issued in accordance with the regulations by the SEBI.

(e) Issue out of already issued share type The sweat equity shares issued by the company should be of a class of shares already issued by the company.

9.3.3 Shares Issued at a Discount

According to Section 79 of the Companies Act, a company can issue shares at a discount subject to the fulfilment of the following conditions:

- The issue should be authorised by an ordinary resolution of the company and sanctioned by the central government.
- No such resolutions shall be sanctioned by the company law board in case the maximum rate for discount exceeds 10% unless the Board is of the opinion that a higher rate of discount is justified by the special circumstances of the case.
- The issue should be made within two months of the sanction by the company law board, but not earlier than one year after the date of commencement of business.
- The shares should be of a class already issued by the company.

Auditor's duty

1. The auditor should confirm that all the conditions *of Section 79* have been duly complied with.
2. He should also see that the amount of discount, not yet written off, is shown separately in the balance sheet under the head "miscellaneous expenditure".
3. The auditor should check that the appropriate entries have been passed in the books of accounts.

9.3.4 Shares Issued at a Premium

According to Section 78 of the Companies Act, a company can issue shares at a premium subject to the fulfilment of the following conditions:

(a) Where a company issues shares at a premium, whether for cash or otherwise, a sum equal to the aggregate amount or value of the premium on those shares shall be transferred to an account, to be called the "Securities Premium Account"- Section 78 (1).

(b) The securities premium account may be applied by the company in the following matters:

- In paying up un-issued shares of the company to be issued to members of the company as fully paid bonus shares
- In writing off the preliminary expenses of the company
- In writing off the expenses of, or the commission paid or discount allowed on any issue of shares or debentures of the company
- In providing for the premium payable on the redemption of any redeemable preference shares or of any debentures of the company-Section 78 (2)

Auditor's duty

1. The auditor should examine the prospectus, the Articles of Association and the minutes book of the Directors to ascertain whether they permit the issue of shares at a premium and, if so, the rate.
2. He should check the amount of premium received.
3. He should also check that the share premium received has been taken to the 'Securities Premium Account' and shown on the liabilities side of the balance sheet under the head "reserves and surplus".
4. He should see that the 'Securities Premium Account' if utilised has been utilised for the purposes as specified in Section 78.

9.3.5 Calls in Arrear

Calls in arrear refer to that portion of the share capital, which has been called up, but not yet paid by the shareholders. When a shareholder fails to pay the amount due on allotment and/or calls, the allotment account and/or calls account will show debit balance equal to the total unpaid amount of each instalment. Generally such amount is transferred to a special account called 'calls in arrear' Account.

The balance of 'calls in arrear account' at the end is shown in the balance sheet as a deduction from respective share capital account.

Interest on calls in arrear may be collected by the directors from the shareholders if the Articles of Association so provide. If the company has adopted 'Table A', then it can charge interest @ 5% p.a. from the due date to the actual date of collection of call money.

Auditor's duty

1. The amount due from shareholders in respect of calls in arrears should be verified by reference to the share register.
2. If any calls are due from directors, they should be shown separately in the balance sheet.
3. Often the articles provide that interest be charged on calls in arrears, the adjustment of interest in such a case should be verified.
4. The auditors should also check that the appropriate entries have been passed in the books of accounts and ensure that calls in arrear are properly shown in the balance sheet.

9.3.6 Calls in Advance

A company, if permitted by the articles, may accept from members, either the whole or part of the amount remaining unpaid on any shares held by him as calls in advance. But the amount so received cannot be treated as a part of the capital for the purpose of any voting rights until the same becomes presently payable and duly appropriated (Section 92 of the Companies Act).

A company, if so authorised by the articles, may pay dividend in proportion to the amount paid upon each share, where a larger amount is paid up on some shares than that on other (Section 93 of the Companies Act).

Interest may be paid on calls in advance if Articles of Association so provide. If the company has adopted 'Table A', then it is required to pay interest @ 6% p.a. from the date of receipt to the due date (Article 18 of Table A). Such interest is a charge against profit. However, such interest can be paid out of capital, when profits are not available for such payment.

Auditor's duty

1. The auditor should see that the provisions regarding payment of calls in advance exist in the articles.
2. He should see that calls in advance have not been treated as part of the share capital and are shown separately in the balance sheet.
3. He should ensure that the payment of interest on calls in advance does not exceed the percentage stated in the articles.
4. He should vouch the receipt of such amount and the payment of interest thereon by inspecting the relevant entries in the cash book or passbook.

9.3.7 Forfeiture of Shares

If a shareholder fails to pay the calls made on him, the Directors may have the power of forfeiting the shares held by him. The Directors are empowered, subject to the fulfilment of certain conditions, to remove his name from the register of members and to treat the amount already paid by him forfeited to the company.

But it should be noted that shares could be forfeited only if the articles authorise the directors to do so. Forfeiture shall be void, if it is contrary to the provisions of the articles. Forfeiture of shares can ordinarily be made only for non-payment of calls, but the articles may provide for forfeiture on grounds other than non-payment of calls.

Conditions to be fulfilled before forfeiting shares

1. ***Notice to the shareholder*** Before forfeiting any shares, the defaulting member must be served with a notice requiring him to pay the unpaid amount of call together with interest. The notice must mention the day on or before which the payment is to be made and also mention that in the event of non-payment, the shares will be liable to forfeiture.

2. ***Resolution of the board*** If the requirements of the above notice are not complied with, the shares may be forfeited by a resolution of the directors.

Auditor's duty

1. The auditor should ascertain that the articles authorise the board of directors to forfeit the shares and that the power has been exercised by the board in the best interest of the company.
2. He should verify the amount of call which was outstanding in respect of each of the share forfeited.
3. He should also ascertain that the procedure in the articles has been followed, viz. the notice given (14 days, according to Table A) to the defaulting shareholders, warning them that in the event of non-payment by a specified date, the shares shall be forfeited.

4. The auditor should verify the entries recorded in the books of account consequent upon forfeiture of shares to confirm that the premium, if any, received on the issue of shares has not been transferred to the forfeited shares account.

9.3.8 Re-issue of Forfeited Shares

A forfeited share is merely a share available to the company for sale and remains vested in the company for that purpose only. Re-issue of forfeited shares is not allotment of shares but only a sale. When shares are re-issued, return of the forfeited shares need not be filed under Section 75(1) of the Companies Act, 1956.

The share, after forfeiture in the hands of the company, is subject to an obligation to dispose it off. In practice, forfeited shares are disposed off by auction. These shares can be re-issued at any price so long as the total amount received for those shares is not less than the amount in arrear on those shares.

Auditor's duty

1. The auditor should ascertain that the Board of Directors has the authority under the articles to re-issue forfeited shares.
2. He should refer to the resolution of the Board of Directors when re-allotting forfeited shares.
3. He should vouch the amount collected from person to whom the shares have been allotted and also check the entries recorded for this purpose.
4. The auditor should see that the total amount received on the shares, including that received prior to forfeiture, is not less than the par value of shares.
5. He should also verify that the surplus resulting on the re-issue of shares is credited to the capital reserve account.

9.3.9 Issue of Right Shares

According to Section 81 of the Companies Act, 1956, the new shares that are offered in the first instance to the existing equity shareholders of the company are known as "right shares", because they are so offered to the existing shareholders as a matter of their right.

Where at any time after the expiry of two years from the formation of a company or at any time after the expiry of one year from the allotment of share of the company made for the first time after its formation, whichever is earlier, the company proposes to issue further shares, then such further shares shall be offered to the existing equity shareholders of the company, in proportions, as nearly as possible to their present holding of shares. The existing shareholders shall have to exercise their right within fifteen days or such further time as may be mentioned. Thereafter they may accept such offer, may decline to accept or may transfer their right to their nominees.

Auditor's duty

1. The auditor should ensure that the provisions of Section 81 have been duly complied with.
2. He should satisfy that appropriate resolution was passed either by the Board or the general meeting depending upon the circumstances of the issue.
3. He should see that consideration money was duly received.

4. He should also check to ensure that the guidelines issued by SEBI have been duly followed.
5. He should examine the filing of the return of allotment with the registrar.
6. He should satisfy that the allotment was made on pro rata basis.

9.3.10 Buying Back of Equity Shares

The Companies (Amendment) Act, 1999 contains provisions regarding buying back of own securities by a company. The word 'security' includes both equity and preference share. But preference share can also be redeemed, perhaps the provision is intended for equity share only.

As per Section 77A of the Companies Act

1. A company may purchase its own shares or other specified securities out of
   - its free reserves
   - the securities premium account, or
   - the proceeds of any earlier issue other than from issue of shares made specifying for buy back purposes.
2. No company shall purchase its own shares or other specified securities, unless
   - the buy-back is authorised by its articles
   - a special resolution has been passed in general meeting of the company authorising the buy-back
   - the buy-back is less than 25% of the total paid up capital (both equity and preference) and free reserves of the company
   - the debt-equity ratio is not more than 2: 1 after buy-back
   - all the shares or other specified securities are fully paid up
   - the buy-back of the shares or other specified securities listed on any recognised stock exchange is in accordance with the regulations made by SEBI
   - the buy back in respect of shares or other specified securities, other than those in point except the last point as above, is in "accordance with the guidelines as may be prescribed.
3. Every buy-back shall be completed within 12 months from the date of passing the special resolution or a resolution passed by the board.
4. A solvency certificate should be filed before making buy-back.
5. The company shall, after completion of the buy-back, file with the registrar and the SEBI, a return containing such particulars relating to the buy-back within 30 days of such completion.

As per Section 77AA of the Companies Act

In case shares are bought back out of free reserves, then a sum equal to the nominal value of shares bought back shall be transferred to a reserve account to be called the "capital redemption reserve account" and details of such transfer shall be disclosed in the balance sheet. This account, as per SEBI guidelines, shall be allowed to be used for issue of fully paid bonus shares.

As per Section 77B of the Companies Act

No company shall, directly or indirectly, purchase its own shares or other specified securities

- through any subsidiary company including its own subsidiary companies
- through any investment company or group of investment companies
- if a default, in repayment of deposit or interest thereon, in redemption of debentures or preference shares or in payment of dividend or repayment of a term loan or interest thereon to any financial institution or bank, is subsisting
- in case it has not complied with provisions of Section 159, Section 207 and Section 211.

Auditor's duty

1. The auditor should ensure that the provisions of Section 77A has been complied with.
2. He should vouch that amount of consideration was duly paid.
3. He should satisfy that appropriate resolution was passed in general meeting of the company authorising the buying-back option.
4. He should also ensure that the guidelines issued by SEBI have been duly followed.
5. He should examine the filing of the return after completion of the buy-back with the registrar and the SEBI.
6. The auditor should also verify that the proper accounting entries have been passed immediately after the buy-back.

9.3.11 Employees Stock Option Scheme (ESOPS)

'Employees Stock Option' means the option given to the whole-time directors, officers and employees of a company to purchase or subscribe at a future date, the securities offered by the company at a pre-determined price. Section 2 (15A) of the Companies Amendment Act, 2000 has allowed the companies to offer stock option scheme to their employees subject to SEBI Guidelines, 2000 in this regard.

SEBI guidelines on ESOPS

1. Issue of stock options at a discount to the market price would be regarded as another form of employee compensation and would be treated as such in the financial statement of the company regardless of the quantum of discount.
2. The issue of ESOPS would be subject to approval of shareholders through a special resolution.
3. In cases of employees being offered more than 1% of shares, a specific disclosure and approval would be necessary in the annual general meeting.
4. A minimum period of one year between grant of options and its vesting must be prescribed. After one year, the period during which the option can be exercised would be determined by the company.
5. The operation of the ESOP scheme would have to be under the superintendence and direction of a compensation committee of Board of Directors in which there would be a majority of independent directors.

6. ESOP would be open to all permanent employees and to the directors of the company but not to the promoters and large shareholders. With the specific approval of the shareholders, the scheme would be allowed to cover the employees of a subsidiary or a holding company.
7. Directors report shall contain the following disclosures:
   - The total number of shares covered by the ESOP as approved by the shareholders
   - The pricing formula
   - Options granted, options vested, options exercised, options forfeited, extinguishments or modification of options, money realised by exercise of options, total number of options in force, employee-wise details of options granted to senior managerial personnel and to any other employee who receives a grant in any one year of options amounting to 5% or more of options granted during that year
   - Fully diluted earnings per share (EPS) computed in accordance with international accounting standards.

Auditor's duty

1. The auditor will see whether the company has strictly adhered to the above conditions as stipulated in SEBI guidelines in connection with ESOP.
2. He will vouch the receipt of cash against issue of shares under option exercised by checking the entries in the cash book and bank statements.
3. He will judge the reasonableness of the price at which options were given.
4. He will see that paid up capital has not exceeded the authorised capital due to exercise of option.
5. He should ensure that discount on issue under option has been treated as employee compensation and has been charged to the profit and loss account.
6. The auditor will see that the fact of ESOP has been adequately disclosed in the balance sheet.

9.3.12 Issue and Redemption of Preference Shares

1. Issue of preference shares

A company limited by shares, if authorised by its articles, may issue preference shares, which are liable to be redeemed at the option of the company before or on a predetermined date. However, after the commencement of the Companies (Amendment) Act, 1996 no company limited by shares shall issue any preference share which is irredeemable or is redeemable after the expiry of a period of 20 years from the date of its issue.

Auditor's duty

1. The auditor should see that the issue of redeemable preference shares is properly authorised by the articles.
2. He should vouch the issue and check the necessary records made to the books of account in this connection.
3. So long as the shares are not redeemed, the terms of redemption, if any, must be stated in the balance sheet along with the earliest date of redemption.

4. He should vouch the receipts of issue price from the cash book and the share registers.

2. Redemption of preference shares

Section 80 of the Companies Act describes the conditions to be fulfilled for the purpose of redemption of preference shares:

(a) The shares to be redeemed are fully paid up.

(b) The shares are to be redeemed out of profit available for distribution as dividend or out of proceeds of a fresh issue made for the purpose of redemption.

(c) The premium on redemption, if any, is to be provided for either out of the securities premium account or out of divisible profits of the company.

(d) If the shares are to be redeemed out of profits, otherwise available for dividend, an amount equal to the nominal amount of shares to be redeemed has to be transferred to the capital redemption reserve account.

Auditor's duty

1. The auditor should see that the redemption of preference shares is in accordance with the provision of Section 80 of the Companies Act.
2. In case the shares are redeemed out of fresh issue, the auditor should verify the articles and the minutes of the director's meeting.
3. In case the shares are redeemed out of divisible profits, he should see that the nominal value of shares redeemed has been transferred to the capital redemption reserve account.
4. The auditor should also ensure that the capital redemption reserve account is treated as part of capital and not applied except for paying up un-issued share capital of the company to be issued to members as fully paid up bonus shares.

9.3.12 Alteration of Share Capital

A company having a share capital, if so authorised by its articles, may alter its share capital by an ordinary resolution without confirmation of the court, in any of the manners authorised by Section 94. Each alteration made should be noted in every copy of the Memorandum or Articles issued subsequent to the date of alteration *(Section 40)*.

Auditor's duty

1. The auditor should verify that the alteration of capital is authorised by the articles.
2. He has to inspect the minutes of the shareholders authorising the alteration.
3. He has to see that the procedures prescribed by the articles in this regard has been duly complied with.
4. He should verify that the share capital account is correctly presented in the balance sheet.
5. He has to inspect the director's resolution in regard to allotment, consolidation, conversion or sub-division passed pursuant to the resolution of the members.
6. He should examine the cancelled share certificates, if any, and match the same with the counterfoils of new certificates issued.

7. He should check the required journal entries being incorporated in the accounts to give the effect of alteration to share capital.
8. The auditor should see that the necessary intimation to the Registrar contemplated by Section 95 has been sent.

9.3.13 Reduction of Share Capital

The provisions of Section 100 to 105 of the Companies Act, 1956 describes the procedures of reduction of share capital. Reduction of capital may be affected in the following ways:

1. Reduction without the consent of the court

In the following cases, a company need not obtain the confirmation of the court for reducing its share capital:

- Where redeemable preference shares are redeemed in accordance with the provision of Section 80
- When any share is forfeited for non-payment of calls
- Where there is a surrender of shares
- When un-issued shares are cancelled.

2. Reduction with the consent of the court

The Act has neither prescribed the manner in which the reduction of share capital is to be carried out nor has it prohibited any method of affecting the reduction if a companyfulfills the following.

(a) It is authorised by its Articles.
(b) It has passed a special resolution for the purpose.
(c) It has obtained the confirmation of the court.
(d) It may reduce its share capital in any one of the following ways:
  - Reduce or extinguish the liability on any of its shares in respect of share capital not paid up
  - Cancel any paid up share capital, which is lost or is not represented by the available assets
  - Pay off any paid up share capital which is in excess of the needs of the company.

Auditor's duty

1. The auditor should verify that special resolution for this purpose has been passed in the general meeting of the shareholders and the proposal has been circulated in advance to the members.
2. He should confirm that the reduction of capital is authorised by the articles of association.
3. He should examine the order of the court confirming the reduction, if the reduction is in accordance with the consent of the court.
4. He should also inspect the Registrar's certificate as regards reduction of capital.
5. The auditor should vouch the journal entries passed to record the reduction of share capital.
6. He should verify the adjustments made in the member's accounts in the register of members.

7. He should confirm that the words "and reduced", if required by the order of the court, have been added to the name of the company in the balance sheet.
8. The auditor should also verify that the Memorandum of Association of the company has been suitably altered.

9.3.14 Share Transfer

Large-size companies, having numerous shareholders and having their shares quoted in the recognised stock exchanges, often face the problem of frequent and large-scale share transfer. There is a possibility of errors and mistakes or even fraud taking place in the process for which the company may have to pay damages. Therefore, the management often appoints auditors for carrying out this special assignment, though the arrangement for this audit may be concurrent with the ordinary audit.

Auditor's duty

1. The auditor should inspect the articles regarding the prescribed form of transfer and other provisions, particularly the time limits laid down by the articles.
2. He should scrutinise transfer forms, noting specially that:
    - in every case, the application for transfer was made in the prescribed form and the prescribed authority had stamped the date on which it was presented to it
    - each transfer form is properly executed and bears the appropriate stamp duty
3. He should vouch the entries in the share transfer journal by reference to the transfer form.
4. He should verify postings from the transfer journal to the register of members.
5. The auditor should also inspect letters of indemnity for lost certificates and ensure that duplicate certificates have been issued by proper authority.
6. Where part of the shares has been transferred, the auditor should verify the issue of balance certificates to the transferors and confirm that the distinctive number of shares has been correctly stated.
7. The auditor should verify by reference to the minute's book that the Board has approved all the transfers recorded in the transfer journal.
8. He should reconcile the amount of transfer fees collected with the total number of transfers and verify that the amount of transfer fees have been accounted for.
9. He should also reconcile the total number of shares of different classes issued by the company with the total amount of capital issued and its sub - divisions by extracting balances of shares held by different members from the members' register.
10. Finally, the auditor should confirm that the shares transferred by the Directors have been entered in the register of Directors' share holding.

9.4 AUDIT OF DEBENTURES

Debentures are considered as one of the important sources of external fund to a company. A company may issue debentures to raise funds, provided it is empowered to do so. Memorandum and Articles of Association assigns powers to the company in this regard. Debentures are not considered a part of the capital of the company. Debenture holders are merely the creditors of the company. They have the right to receive interest at a fixed percentage irrespective of the quantum of profit earned by the company in a particular period. The audit procedure of debentures is explained in the following part of this section.

9.4.1 Issue of Debentures

Debentures may be issued at par or at a premium or at a discount. When the debentures are issued at a premium, the amount of premium collected should be credited to premium on debenture account. Subsequently, this balance is transferred to capital reserve account, as it is a capital profit. Where the debentures are issued at a discount, the amount of discount allowed should be debited to discount on issue of debenture account. The balance in this account will appear in the balance sheet until written off.

Auditor's duty

1. The auditor should verify that the prospectus had been duly filed with the registrar before the date of allotment of debentures.
2. He should check the allotment of debentures by reference to the director's minute book.
3. He should also check the amount collected in the cash book with the counterfoils of receipts issued to the applicants and also cross check the amount into the application and allotment book.
4. The auditor should verify the entries on the counterfoils of debentures issued with the debentures register.
5. He should examine the debenture trust deed and note the conditions contained therein as to issue and repayment.
6. If the debentures are covered by a mortgage of charge, it should be verified that the charge has been correctly recorded in the register of mortgage and charges and it has also been registered with the registrar of companies.
7. Where debentures have been issued as fully paid up to vendors as a part of the purchase consideration, the contract in this regard should be checked.
8. Compliance with SEBI guidelines should also be ensured.

9.4.2 Redemption of Debentures

A company can issue redeemable as well as irredeemable debentures. If debentures are redeemable, it can be done in any of the following three ways:

- By way of periodical drawing
- By way of payment on fixed date
- By payment whenever the company desires to do so.

Auditor's duty

1. The auditor should inspect the debentures or the trust deed for the terms and conditions of the redemption of debentures.
2. The auditor should also refer to the Article of Association.
3. He should see the Directors' minute book authorising the redemption of debentures.
4. He should also vouch the redemption with the help of debenture bonds cancelled and the cash book.

5. The auditor should also examine thoroughly the accounting treatment given to the redemption.

9.4.3 Interest on Debentures

A predetermined fixed rate of interest is payable on debentures irrespective of the fact that the company has been able to earn any profit or not. Debenture-holders are the creditors of the company, not the owners. They have no voting rights and cannot influence the management for the affairs of the company, but their claim of interest rank ahead of the claim of the shareholders.

Auditor's duty

1. The repayment of interest should be vouched by the auditor with the acknowledgement of the debenture-holders, endorsed warrants and in case of bearer debentures with the coupons surrendered.
2. The auditor should reconcile the total amount paid with the total amount due and payable with the amount of interest outstanding for payment.
3. Interest on debentures is payable, whether or not any profit is made. Therefore, a provision should be made that unless it has been specially agreed with the debenture-holders, interest in such a case would be waived by them. The auditor should also consider this aspect.
4. The auditor should also consider the disclosure part of the interest on debentures. He should ensure that the interest paid on debenture, like that on other fixed loans, must be disclosed as a separate item in the profit and loss account.

9.4.4 Re-issue of Redeemed Debentures

A company may issue debentures previously redeemed, either by re-issuing the debentures or issuing others in their place. But re-issue is not possible, if the articles or a contract or resolution, recorded at a general meeting, or terms of issue or some other act of the company expressly or impliedly manifest the intention that, on redemption, the debentures shall be cancelled.

However, there are re-issue of redeemed debentures, or the issue of others in their place are treated as a new issue for the purpose of stamp duty and the rights and privileges attaching to the debentures that re-issued shall be the same as if the debentures had never been redeemed.

On these considerations, it is necessary for the auditor to verify the re-issue of debentures in the same manner as those issued for the first time.

Auditor's duty

The auditor will verify the following:

1. Whether the articles permit such re-issue
2. Whether the terms and conditions of debenture impose any restriction on re-issue of debentures after they have been redeemed
3. Whether the company has passed any resolution in the general meeting for re-issue of redeemed debenture

4. Whether Section 121 of the Companies Act, which empowers the holders of re-issued debentures hold same rights and priorities as the original holders, have been complied with
5. Whether particulars of re-issued debentures have been clearly shown in the balance sheet
6. Whether fresh stamp duty has been paid on re-issued debentures.

9.4.5 Issue of Debentures as Collateral Security

Debentures may be issued to creditors, bankers or any other person, without receiving any cash thereon. It acts as a collateral security and becomes real debentures in the event of the default of the loan. Usually the nominal value of such debentures is more than that of the amount of loan.

Auditor's duty

1. The auditor should see that such debentures do not appear on the liabilities side of the balance sheet, but are shown by way of a note under the heading loan.
2. The auditor should ensure that necessary entries made in the register of mortgages and that the necessary papers are filed with the registrar of companies.
3. He should also examine the loan agreement and confirm that it has been approved by the board.
4. He should also check whether the debentures are automatically cancelled as soon as the loan is repaid.

9.5 AUDIT OF HOLDING COMPANY

A holding company is that company which holds whole or more than half of the equity shares in one or more companies and thus assumes controlling interest in such companies by acquiring majority voting powers in them. The development of holding companies is quite marked in recent years and there are many such business organisations today, even international in character, controlling large number of companies in countries all over the world.

According to Section 4 of the Companies Act, 1956 a holding company is that which fulfills the following requirements.

(a) Holds more than 50 percent of the nominal value of the equity share capital of another company.
(b) Controls the composition of the board of directors of the other companies.
(c) Controls more than half of the total voting power of the other companies.
(d) Has a subsidiary, which is the subsidiary of the holding company's subsidiary.

9.5.1 Legal Requirements Regarding Accounts of Holding Companies

The various provisions of the Companies Act related to holding company accounts are given in Sections 212, 213 and 214 and Schedule VI, Part I. These include the following

1. Preparation of balance sheet

The balance sheet of the subsidiary shall be made:

- At the end of the financial year of the subsidiary if it coincides with the financial year of the holding company, or
- At the end of the financial year of the subsidiary last before that of the holding company, in case the financial year of the subsidiary does not coincide with that of the holding company.

2. Disclosure of special items in the balance sheet

The following items should be specifically mentioned in the balance sheet of the holding company related to its subsidiary:

- The aggregate amount of loans and advances to subsidiary company
- The aggregate amount of investment in shares or debentures or bonds in subsidiary company
- Secured loans and advances from subsidiaries
- Unsecured loans and advances from subsidiaries
- The aggregate amount of liabilities due to subsidiary companies.

3. Preparation of profit and loss account

The profit and loss account of the subsidiary must be made out within the period to which the accounts of the holding company relate. But where the financial year of the subsidiary does not coincide with that of the holding company, the financial year of the subsidiary shall not end on a day which precedes the day on which holding company's financial year ends by more than six months.

4. Statement of profit and loss

A statement should be there specifying how the profits of the subsidiary company or aggregate profits or losses of the subsidiary have been taken into accounts of the holding company. Such statement would also specify how and to what extent, losses, if any, of the subsidiaries have been brought into the accounts of the holding company. Such statement shall be signed by the persons by whom the balance sheet of the holding company is required to be signed.

5. Documents to be attached

The holding company shall at the end of the financial year attach to its balance sheet the following documents in respect of its subsidiary company:

- A copy of the balance sheet of the subsidiary
- A copy of the profit and loss account
- A copy of the report of its board of directors
- A copy of the report of its auditors
- A statement of the holding company's interest in the subsidiary
- A statement containing any change in the holding company's interest in the subsidiary or any material change of the subsidiary in its fixed assets, investments, money borrowed etc.
- A report attached to the balance sheet if the board of directors of the holding company is unable to obtain information on any of the specified matters.

6. Inspection of books of accounts

The holding company may, by resolution, authorise a particular representative to inspect the books of accounts of any of its subsidiaries during business hours.

7. Investigation

The members of the holding company may request the central government to appoint a person to investigate into the affairs of its subsidiaries.

8. Exemptions

The central government may exempt the holding company from the application of the provision with regard to attachment of various documents to the balance sheet. It is also empowered to extend the financial year so that it may coincide in both the cases.

9.5.2 Consolidation of Accounts

Holding companies attach to their own balance sheet a consolidated balance sheet to give a more detailed and clear picture of their subsidiaries. Such consolidated balance sheet is definitely more useful than the separate balance sheet of each of the subsidiaries. For this purpose, the whole group is regarded as one undertaking and hence the total assets as well as liabilities of all the companies in the group are presented in one balance sheet. The profit and loss account of the whole group is also presented in a similar fashion.

Accounting Standard 21 on 'Consolidated Financial Statements' issued by the Institute of Chartered Accountants of India on consolidation of accounts prescribes the accounting principles to be followed by the holding companies in consolidating the balance sheet and profit and loss account with that of the financial statements of the subsidiaries.

The following points should be kept in mind while consolidating the accounts of the holding company:

1. Date of consolidation

The date of the balance sheets of all the companies should be the same. If it is not so, efforts should be made to make adjustments so that the financial position of all the companies should be shown as on a particular date in the consolidated balance sheet.

2. Valuation of assets and liabilities

The basis for the valuation of assets or of bringing liabilities into account should be similar in all cases.

3. Share of subsidiaries

The shares of subsidiaries have to be adjusted by replacing them with the actual assets and liabilities of the subsidiary companies.

4. Minority interest

In case a part of the shares of subsidiary companies is held by persons other than the holding company, their total interest should be shown as liabilities in the consolidated balance sheet.

5. Inter-company loans

The loans taken by the subsidiaries amongst themselves should be shown in the consolidated balance sheet as inter-company debt. However, it has to be set off.

6. Inter-company profits

Inter-company profits, if any, should also be adjusted by deducting it from the profit and loss account and the related assets, if they are added therein. Thus, in the consolidated balance sheet, stock and such other type of assets should be combined together at cost.

7. Profits or losses of minorities

The proportion of profits or losses belonging to outside shareholders should be properly adjusted. They should be deducted from the consolidated profit and loss account and at the same time shown as liabilities in the consolidated balance sheet, as they do not belong to the holding company.

Auditor's duty

The duties of an auditor of a holding company with regard to its subsidiaries have not been extended by the Companies Act, 1956. He has to perform the same type of duties as provided under the Act as in the case of other companies. The additional care which he has to take is to see that the provisions of Sections 212, 213 and 214 as mentioned earlier have been duly complied with.

However, the auditor of a holding company has to see whether the financial statements of the holding company is consolidated with the financial statements of its subsidiaries by following the principles as prescribed in the AS-21 and, if not, he has to report accordingly.

In addition to above, the auditor of a holding company has to pay attention to the following points:

1. He should examine the contract of purchase and vouch the purchase consideration, if he finds that during the year under audit, the company has purchased shares in a subsidiary company. He also sees that the shares have been registered in the name of the holding company.
2. He should examine and verify the inter-company transactions carefully. He should ascertain that all such transactions have been properly recorded in the books of accounts of the holding company.
3. He must verify the valuation of shares in the subsidiary company held by the holding company. Due attention should also be given to any provisions with regard to valuation of shares contained in the memorandum and articles of the company.
4. He must vouch the dividends received from the subsidiary companies and see that they have been properly dealt with in the accounts.
5. He must examine that the requirements of Schedule VI of the Companies Act with regard to the disclosure of certain items related to the accounts of subsidiary companies separately in the balance sheet of the holding company have been duly complied with.
6. He must see that the balance sheet gives a true and fair view of the financial state of affairs of the company.

9.6 AUDIT OF PRE-INCORPORATION PROFIT

In many cases, a new company is formed to acquire exclusively an existing business unit and take it over as a going concern, from a date prior to its own incorporation. In such cases, the business unit is purchased first and the registration of the acquiring company takes place later.

The profit earned during the pre-incorporation period is called 'pre-incorporation profit (loss)'. Legally, this profit is not available for dividend, since a company cannot earn profit before it comes into existence. Profit earned before incorporation of a company is a capital profit and its accounting treatment is totally different from post-incorporation profit.

Accounting Treatment of Pre-incorporation Profit/Loss

Pre-incorporation profit

Any profit prior to incorporation may be dealt with as follows:

- Credited to capital reserve account
- Credited to goodwill account to reduce the amount of goodwill arising from acquisition of business
- Utilised to write down the value of fixed assets acquired.

Pre-incorporation loss

Any loss prior to incorporation may be dealt with as follows:

- Debited to goodwill account
- Debited to capital reserve account arising from acquisition of business
- Debited to a suspense account, which can be written-off later.

Auditor's duty

1. The auditor should examine the methods of calculating such profits and profits subsequent to incorporation.
2. He should ensure that such profits are not distributed as dividend to shareholders as these are in the nature of capital profits.

9.7 SPECIFIC PROVISIONS FOR ACCOUNTS IN THE COMPANIES ACT

The provisions in the matter of books of account, which a company is required to maintain, are contained in Section 209 of the Companies Act, 1956. They are briefly summarised as follows:

1. Books to be maintained

Every company shall keep at its registered office proper books of accounts, with respect to the following.

(a) All sums of money received and expended by the company and the matters in respect of which the receipt and expenditure takes place

(b) All sales and purchase of goods by the company

(c) The assets and liabilities of the company, and

(d) In the case of a company pertaining to any class of companies engaged in production, processing, manufacturing or mining activities, such particulars relating to utilisation of material and labour or to other items of cost as may be prescribed in such class of companies as required by the central government to include such particulars: Section-209 (1).

2. Place of preservation of books

All the books are usually required to be kept at the registered office in India. All or any of the above stated books of accounts might be kept at such other place instead of registered office in India as the Board of Directors may decide. The company must file with the registrar a notice in writing giving the full address of the other place: Section 209 (1).

3. Books of branch offices

Where a company has a branch office, whether in or outside India, the company shall be deemed to have complied with the aforementioned provisions, if the company maintains proper books of account relating to transactions affected at the branch office and also arranges to obtain from the branch proper summarised returns, at intervals of not more than three months, for being kept at the registered office or the other place: Section 209 (2).

4. Method of accounts

For the purpose of Sub-section (1) and (2), proper books of account shall not be deemed to be kept with respect to the matters specified therein:

(a) If they are not kept such books as are necessary to give a true and fair view of the state of affairs of the company or branch office, as the case may be and to explain its transactions and

(b) If such books are not kept on accrual basis and according to the double entry system of accounting: Section 209 (3).

5. Inspection of books of accounts

The books of accounts and other books and papers shall be kept open for inspection by any director during business hours: Section 209 (4).

6. Period of preservation

The books of accounts of every company relating to a period of not less than eight years immediately preceding the current year together with vouchers relevant to the entry in such books of accounts shall be preserved in good order. In case of a company incorporated less than eight years before the current year, the books of accounts for the entire period preceding the current year shall be preserved: Section 209 (4A).

7. Penalty

If the managing director or manager and, in the absence of any of them, any director of the company fails to take reasonable steps to secure compliance with the requirements of law aforementioned or by a willful act causes any default by the company, he shall be punishable for each offence with imprisonment for a term which may extend to six months or a fine which may extend to Rs. 10,000 or both: Section 209 (5).

9.8 PAYMENT OF INTEREST OUT OF CAPITAL

Under the provisions of Section 208 of the Companies Act, 1956 a company which has raised money by issue of shares to meet the cost of construction of any work or building or provision of any plant which cannot be made profitable for a long time, can pay interest on paid up capital for a period and subject to the conditions specified in Sub-sections (2) to (7) of Section 208.

The interest paid, being a part of the capital expenditure incurred in bringing into existence assets, should be added thereto. Until so added, it must be shown as a separate item in the balance sheet under the head 'miscellaneous expenditure'.

Auditor's duty

1. The auditor should ascertain that the payment is authorised by the articles or by a special resolution.
2. He should verify that the sanction of the central government for making such payment has been obtained.
3. He should confirm that the interest has been paid only for such period as has been authorised by the central government and does not extend beyond the next half-year following during which the construction was completed or the plant was provided.
4. He should verify that the rate of interest does not exceed 12% or such other rate that the central government has notified in the official gazette.
5. The auditor should also check that the amount of interest paid out of capital has been added to the cost of the assets created.

9.9 SPECIAL REQUIREMENTS OF COMPANY AUDIT

The company audit is compulsory in nature and governed basically by the provisions of the Companies Act. While conducting audit in a company form of organisation, the auditor should take into consideration certain requirements of company audit as dictated by the provisions of the companies act.

The special requirements to be kept in mind by the auditor while conducting company audit are described below:

9.9.1 Verification of the Constitution and Power

A company can function within the limits prescribed by the documents on the basis of which it has been registered. It raises its capital from the public on certain conditions. On this account, it is essential that the auditor, prior to starting the audit of a company, shall examine the following:

1. Memorandum of Association

It is a charter containing particulars of business activities that the company can undertake and the powers it can exercise in regard thereto. If a company enters into a transaction, which is ultra-vires, the shareholders may restrain the management from charging the loss, if any, that has been suffered thereon, to the company. If the auditor fails to detect and report the transactions, which are ultra-vires the company, he would be guilty of negligence.

2. Articles of Association

These are rules and regulations for the internal management of the company and they define the rights of different classes of shareholders, conditions under which calls can be made, the maximum and the minimum number of Directors, their qualifications, disqualifications and removal etc. The terms and conditions of these provisions have relevance to the examination of transactions that the auditor is required to carry out. He should, therefore, study the articles and include extracts from them in his permanent audit file. The auditor, who fails to take note of the provisions in the articles in the verification of statements of accounts, would be guilty of professional negligence.

3. Prospectus

It is a formal document which a public company must issue before it makes the allotment of shares under Section 56. It must contain all the terms and conditions on which subscription to the shares are sought to be obtained from the public. In case the company fails to carry out any of these undertakings, or if any statement made by it ultimately is proved to be false, the shareholder has the right to claim refund of the amount paid by him. The auditor should, therefore, study carefully all the conditions and stipulations made in the prospectus and in case any of them has not been carried out, draw the attention of shareholders thereto.

9.9.2 Knowledge About Authority Structure of the Company

With a view to carry out the audit effectively, it is necessary that the auditor should know the authority structure of the company. Under Section 291 of the Act, the Board of Directors of a company are entitled to exercise all such powers and to do all such acts and things, as the company is authorised to do.

Section 292 specifies five types of decisions that can be taken by the Board of Directors only in Board's meetings. These include the following:

- Making calls on partly paid shares
- Issue of debentures
- Borrowing money other than on debentures
- Investing the fund of the company and
- Making loans

Apart from the above, the Board also carries out a number of other functions. Such functions include the following:

(a) Adopting of accounts before the same to be submitted to the auditor for their report—Section 215

(b) Appointment of the first auditors and filing of casual vacancy-Section 224

(c) Investment in shares of companies within the limits-Section 372A

(d) Entering into contracts with persons who are directors of the company or related to or associated with the directors as specified in Section 297 of the Companies Act.

However, the Board shall not exercise any power or do any act or thing which is directed or required by any legislation or by the memorandum or articles of the company, to be exercised or done by the company, in a general meeting.

Following are some of the matters, which only the shareholders can sanction in a general meeting:

(a) Appointment and fixation of remuneration of auditors in the annual general meeting—Section 224

(b) Declaration of Dividend—Regulation 85, Table A

(c) Appointment of relative of directors to an office or place of profit in the company—Section 314

(d) Sale, lease or disposal of the whole of the company's undertakings or a substantial part of it and donations above a certain limit—Section 293(1).

Some matters which require the sanction of the central government e.g. for sanctioning loans to directors by a company other than a banking or a finance company, can not be exercised by the board of directors or the shareholders.

9.10 COMPANY AUDITOR

An auditor is a person who is appointed to conduct an independent examination of books, accounts and supporting vouchers to report on the reliability and fairness of profit and loss account and balance sheet. He is a professional man having specialised knowledge and expertise in all branches of accounting.

In order to ensure that the person conducting the audit of accounts of company have sufficient knowledge in accounting, the Companies Act requires him to be a chartered accountant within the meaning of the Chartered Accountants Act, 1949. Apart from being well versed in accounting, the auditor should be honest, tactful, methodological, cautious and careful. Lord Justice Lindley in his famous case London and General Bank (1895) held that "an auditor must be honest, i.e. he must not certify what he does not believe to be true and he must take reasonable care and skill before he believes what he certifies is true". Learned Judge Lopes in Kingston Cotton Mill case remarked, "an auditor need not be over-cautious or always suspicious. He is a watchdog but not a bloodhound. He is justified in believing the tried servants of the company and entitled to rely upon their representation provided he takes reasonable care."

9.10.1 Appointment of Auditors

The provisions regarding appointment of the auditors are contained in Section 224 of the Companies Act.

1. First auditor

Section 224(5) provides for the appointment of first auditors, by the Board of Directors within one month of the date of registration of the company. The auditor or auditors so appointed shall hold office till the conclusion of the first annual general meeting.

But the company may at a general meeting remove such an auditor and appoint another in his place, on a nomination being made by any member of the company, notice being given to the members of the company, not less than 14 days before the date of the meeting.

If the first auditor is not appointed by the directors, within one month of registration, the company in general meeting may appoint the first auditor. The auditor of a company is normally appointed by the shareholders by passing a resolution at the annual general meeting. Once appointed, he holds office from the conclusion of that meeting to the conclusion of the next annual general meeting.

An auditor once appointed may be reappointed in the next annual general meeting or a new auditor may be appointed in his place. It is obligatory on the part of a company to annually make such an appointment, as well as to give, within seven days of the appointment, intimation to every auditor so appointed or reappointed.

2. Subsequent auditors

Subsequent auditors of a company are appointed every year by the shareholders in annual general meeting by passing an ordinary resolution. According to Section 224(1), "Every company shall, at each annual general meeting, appoint an auditor to hold office." Section 224 (1A) requires the auditor so appointed to communicate his acceptance or refusal to the registrar within the period of 30 days of the receipt from the company intimating his appointment.

If the auditor so appointed does not accept the appointment, the vacancy can neither be treated as casual vacancy nor a vacancy by resignation. The research committee of the Institute of Chartered Accountants of India has clearly expressed this opinion on the strength of the provisions of the Companies Act which vest the general power with shareholders and the delegation of powers to the board of directors is not permitted. Therefore, another general meeting has to be convened to appoint new auditor.

3. Appointment by central government

According to Section 224(3), where at an annual general meeting, no auditors are appointed or re-appointed, the central government may appoint a person to fill the vacancy. Within seven days of the power of the central government becoming exercisable, the company shall give notice of that fact to the central government. Failure to give such notice will make the company in default with a fine, which may extend to Rs. 5,000.

4. Appointment against a casual vacancy

If due to death, insanity or insolvency etc, a casual vacancy of the auditor arises, the board of directors can fill the same u/s 224(6). The auditor appointed against such a vacancy will hold office till the conclusion of the next annual general meeting.

5. Appointment by special resolution

The Companies (Amendment) Act, 1974 introduced Section 224A, which provides that in the case of a company in which 25%, or more, of the subscribed share capital is held, whether individually or collectively by

(a) a public financial institution or a government company or any state government or
(b) any financial or other institution established by any Provincial or State Act in which a state government holds not less than 51% of the subscribed share capital or
(c) a nationalised bank or an insurance company carrying on general insurance business the appointment of the auditor shall be made by a special resolution.

If the company fails to pass a special resolution, it shall be deemed that no auditor has been appointed by the company at its annual general meeting and the central government will be empowered to make an appointment.

6. Appointment of auditors of government or certain other companies

Section 619 provides that the auditor of a government company shall be appointed or reappointed by the central government on the advice of the comptroller and auditor general of India.

The amendment act also introduced another section, i.e. Section 619B which extends the provision of Section 619 to a company in which the central government or state government or any government company or any government corporation hold either singly or jointly not less than 51% of the paid up share capital.

A person should keep these provisions in mind while accepting an appointment as the auditor of a company since the onus of complying with the provisions of section 619B lies with the concerned companies. All the same it would be necessary on the part of the auditors appointed or re-appointed under Section 224 of the Act to ensure, before accepting the appointment/ re-appointment that the company concerned is in fact outside the ambit of Section 619B of the Act.

9.10.2 Tenure of Appointment

Section 224 (1) of the Companies Act provides that an auditor is appointed from the conclusion of one annual general meeting until the conclusion of next annual general meeting. But, if the annual general meeting is not held within the period prescribed by Section 166, the auditor will continue in office till the annual general meeting is actually held and concluded. So, if an annual general meeting is adjourned, his tenure will extend till the conclusion of the adjourned meeting.

9.10.3 Re-appointment of Retiring Auditor

According to the provisions of Section 224(2), retiring auditor, by whatsoever authority appointed, shall be automatically re-appointed by passing an ordinary resolution except in the following circumstances:

- Where he is not qualified for re-appointment
- Where he has given to the company a notice in writing of his unwillingness to be re-appointed
- Where a resolution has been passed at the meeting, appointing somebody else instead of him or providing expressly that he shall not be re-appointed
- Where a notice has been given of an intended resolution to appoint some person in the place of retiring auditor, and by reason of death, incapacity or disqualification of that person, the resolution can not be proceeded with.

The re-appointment will not be automatic. Also, the non-reappointment of the retiring auditor in the annual general meeting is not removal of the auditor. It will be considered simply as retirement.

The auditor will also not be re-appointed in the following two special cases:

1. Where he holds the audit of specified number of companies or more than that on the day of appointment in terms of Section 224 (1B) of the Companies Act.
2. Where 25%, or more, of the subscribed capital of the company is held by public financial institution(s), government companies etc. or a combination of them, unless the retiring auditor is appointed by a special resolution.

The rights of retiring auditor are as follows:

(a) He has the right to receive the notice of the resolution.

(b) He has the right to make a written presentation to the company and request its notification to members of the company.

(c) The auditor has the right to get his representation circulated among the members.

(d) He has the right to get his representation read out at the meeting, if it has not been sent to the members because of delay or default on the part of the company.

9.10.4 Ceiling on Number of Audits

The Companies (Amendment) Act, 1974 added two new sub-sections 224(1B) and 224(1C) on ceiling on number of audits. The objective of these sections is to prevent concentration of audits in few hands. These sections were further amended in 1988 and finally revised in the year 2000.

According to Section 224(1B), an individual cannot be the auditor of more than 20 companies at a time. Further, out of these 20 companies not more than 10 should be companies having a paid up share capital of Rs. 25 lakhs or more. In case of a partnership firm of auditors, the ceiling is 20 companies per partner of the firm and if a partner is also a partner in any other firm, the overall ceiling in relation to such a partner will be 20.

Example

In a firm of chartered accountants, say, there are three partners— X, Y and Z. The overall ceiling of the firm will be 3 x 20 = 60 company audit, out of which not more than 3 x 10 = 30 companies may have paid up share capital of Rs. 25 lakhs or more.

Again, say X is also a partner of another firm of chartered accountants. In that case, in these two firms, total number of company audit he can undertake as a partner of the firms is limited to 20 only subject to the ceiling of 10 large company audits i.e. companies having a paid up share capital of Rs. 25 lakhs or more. It is his affair that how he will allocate these 20 company audits between these two firms.

Section 224(1C) has been amended by the Companies (Amendment) Act, 1988 to disallow the appointment of person, who are in full time employment elsewhere, as company auditor. Even in case of partnership, such a partner shall be excluded from counting the number of audits per partner.

According to the recent amendments in the Companies Act in the year 2000, the above provisions are applicable in case of public limited companies only. So, private limited companies are excluded in computing the ceiling of number of audits.

However, the Institute of Chartered Accountants of India has issued a notification [No. 1- CA (7)/53/2001] in the gazette of India dated 19th May 2001 to include private companies also within the ceiling of 20 companies. According to the notification, "a member of the Institute in practice shall be deemed to be guilty of professional misconduct, if he holds at any time appointment of more than specified number of audit assignment of the companies including private companies."

9.10.5 Remuneration of Auditor

- In case of an auditor appointed by the Board of Directors or the central government, his remuneration may be fixed by the Board of Directors or the central government as the case may be.
- In all other respect, it must be fixed by the company in general meeting or in such manner as the company in general meeting may determine.

'Remuneration' includes any sum paid by the company in respect of the auditor's expenses in carrying out his duties. Obviously, the general meeting can disperse without deciding the amount of the remuneration of the auditor. However, it must provide the manner in which the remuneration can be determined.

If an auditor renders services other than the audit work, he will be entitled to get additional remuneration for such work. A special disclosure of all amount paid to the auditor in whatever capacity is required to be made in the profit and loss account as any of the following

(a) As auditor
(b) As adviser, or in any other capacity, in respect of
 - taxation matters,
 - company law matters,
 - management services, and
(c) In any other manner.

The aforesaid manner of disclosure is required by Part II of Schedule VI to the Act.

Where the auditor is re-appointed in the next annual general meeting, the amount fixed for the previous year continues to be the remuneration of the auditor, unless specific changes are made.

9.10.6 Qualification of an Auditor

Section 226 of the Companies Act prescribes the qualification and disqualification of Company Auditors. According to Section 226(1), "a person shall not be qualified as auditor of a company unless he is a chartered accountant within the meaning of the Chartered Accountants Act, 1949."

It further provides that a firm whereof all the partners practicing in India are qualified for appointment as auditors may be appointed by firm's name to be the auditor of the company. In this connection, it may be noted that under the Chartered Accountants Act, 1949 only a chartered accountant having a certificate of practice can be engaged in the public practice of the profession of accountancy. Therefore, only a practicing chartered accountant can be appointed as an auditor of a company.

In addition to above, a person, holding a certificate under the law in force in the whole or any portion of a Part B State immediately before the commencement of the Part B States (Laws) Act, 1953 or of the Jammu and Kashmir (Extension of Laws) Act, 1956 as the case may be, entitling him to act as an auditor of the companies in the territories which, immediately before 1st November, 1956 were comprised in that state or any portion thereof, shall also be entitled to be appointed to act as an auditor of companies registered anywhere in India.

Thus, the auditor of a company must either be (1) a practising chartered accountant, or (2) the holder of a certificate in erstwhile Part B States entitling him to act as an auditor of companies.

9.10.7 Disqualification of an Auditor

Section 226(3) provides the disqualification of auditors. According to it, none of the following shall be qualified for appointment as an auditor of a company:

1. A body corporate
2. An officer or employee of the company
3. A partner or an employee of an officer or employee of the company

4. A person who is indebted to the company for an amount exceeding Rs. 1,000 or who has given any guarantee or provided any security in connection with the indebtness of any third person
5. A person holding any security of the audit company when such security carries voting right.

A person shall not be qualified for appointment as an auditor of a company if he is, by virtue of Section 226(3), disqualified for appointment as an auditor of any other company which is that company's subsidiary or holding company or a subsidiary of that company's holding company.

Disqualification may come to an auditor if he ceases to be a member of the Institute of Chartered Accountants of India or adjudged as having unsound mind or is an undischarged insolvent.

If after his appointment, an auditor becomes disqualified subject to any of the points listed above, he shall be deemed to have vacated his office as such.

9.10.8 Removal of Auditors

An appointed auditor may be removed from his office either in accordance with the provisions of the Companies Act or as per restrictions imposed by the Chartered Accountants Act.

Removal as per the Companies Act

The removal of the auditor in accordance with the provisions of the Companies Act depends upon the option of the concerned company. He may be removed before the expiry of his term or after the expiry of his term. The service of the first auditor appointed by the board and supposed to hold office till the conclusion of the first annual general meeting can be terminated beforehand by way of passing a resolution in a general meeting. However, the removal of any subsequent auditor before the expiry of his term is difficult in the sense that it requires the approval of the central government as per Section 227 (7). So, the central government has to be convinced about the unsuitability of the existing auditor to continue as auditor.

The Companies Act lays down clear procedures about the removal of auditors in Section 224 and Section 225.

1. *Removal before the expiry of the term*

(a) Under Section 224(5)(a), it is provided that the company can remove in a general meeting the first auditor appointed by the board of directors.

(b) Under Section 224(7), it is provided that except the first auditor, auditors appointed u/s 224 could be removed before the expiry of the term in a general meeting, only after obtaining previous approval of the central government.

2. *Removal after the expiry of the term*

The auditor can be removed after the expiry of his term of office, as per the procedures laid down in Section 225.

According to the Section, for removal of a retiring auditor or appointing another auditor in his place, the following procedures must be observed:

(a) Special notice must be given by a member of the intended resolution to be passed at an annual general meeting

(b) On receipt of such a notice, the company shall forward a copy thereof to the retiring auditor

(c) The retiring auditor then may make written representation to the company not exceeding a reasonable length and request their notification to the members of the company.

The company shall, unless the representations received by it are too late to do so,

- state the fact of the representation in any notice of the resolution given to members of the company and
- send a copy of the representation to every member of the company to whom notice of the meeting is sent.

If a copy of the representation is not sent as aforesaid, because they are received too late or because of the company's default, the auditor may require that the representation shall be read out at the meeting. However, these are not required, if it is established that the above rights are abused by the auditor.

Removal as per Chartered Accountants Act

An auditor may also be removed from his office due to his professional misconduct. Following are some of the important clauses of the Chartered Accountants Act, 1949, which mention the professional misconduct for which a chartered accountant may be removed from his office:

1. If a Chartered Accountant accepts the position as an auditor previously held by another chartered accountant without first communicating to him in writing
2. If a chartered accountant is grossly negligent in the conduct of his professional duties
3. If a chartered accountant is engaged in any business or occupation other than the profession of accountancy unless permitted by the council of the Institute
4. If a chartered accountant contravenes any of the provisions of the act and regulation made thereunder etc.

9.10.9 Status of the Company Auditor

The auditor of a company can be considered a servant of the company, an agent of the shareholders as well as an officer of the company.

1. A servant of the company

Like any other employee or director of a company, an auditor also renders his services to the company. The employees get remuneration from the company for their services. The auditor is receiving remuneration from the company, (not termed as audit fees) for the services rendered by him for the company. Hence, like employees of the company, the auditor may also be considered as a servant of the company.

But if payment to auditor by the company makes him a servant of the company, it will create a lot of confusion. Then the doctor who is paid by the patient is to be treated as servant of the client. So, it would not be logical to treat the auditor as servant of the company.

2. An agent of the company

Except in certain special situations where an auditor is appointed by the Directors or the central government, an auditor is normally appointed by the shareholders. Not only that, the auditor checks the accounts on behalf of the shareholders and he has to submit his report to the shareholders. It therefore appears that an auditor is an agent of the shareholders.

Lord Cranworth in the course of his judgment in the case Spackman vs Evans also said, " The auditor may be the agent of the shareholders, so far as it relates to the audit of the accounts. For the purpose of the audit, the auditors will bind the shareholders".

However, according to the Law of Agency, "he who does through another does by himself". It means that any act of the agent will be purported to be the act of the principal. But this relationship does not exist between the shareholders and the auditors. Again, under the same law, the knowledge of an agent regarding a matter is also taken as the knowledge of the principal. So far as company auditor is concerned, he is not supposed to intimate the shareholders any information other than the actual results and financial position through financial statements.

Therefore, a company auditor cannot be treated as an agent of the shareholders. He can best be described as the representative of the shareholders under certain circumstances.

3. An officer of the company

An auditor is an officer of the company under Section 2(30) of the Companies Act for the purpose of the following sections:

(a) Section 477: Powers to summon persons suspected of having property of the company.
(b) Section 478: Power to order public examination of promoters, directors, officers etc.
(c) Section 539: Penalty for falsification of books
(d) Section 543: Power of the court to assess damages against delinquent directors, officers etc. in course of winding up procedure
(e) Section 545: Prosecution of delinquent officers and members of the company
(f) Section 621: Offences against act to be cognizable only on complaint by registrar, shareholder or government
(g) Section 625: Payment of compensation in cases of frivolous or vexatious prosecution
(h) Section 633: Power of the court to grant relief in certain cases

Except for the above sections, an auditor shall not be considered as an officer under the Companies Act, 1956.

In addition to that there are many legal decisions where a company auditor has been termed as an officer of the company. In London and General Bank case, it was held by Justice Lindley that it seems impossible to deny that for some purposes and to some extent, an auditor is an officer of the company. It was also held in the famous Kingston Cotton Mills Co. Ltd. case that the auditors are officers of the company.

But an officer is bound by the service rules of the company and is required to work as per the directions given to him. But independence in the work of an auditor is a well-established principle. He needs to be independent of management in order to make his report reliable to the shareholders and other interested parties like bankers, creditors etc. Therefore, the auditor must work according to his own judgment and independent thought even though that may not suit the desire of management. So, to treat the auditor as an officer of the company is contrary to the basic philosophy of audit.

The position of an auditor is, therefore, a bit controversial. Sometimes he may appear to be an agent of the shareholders and sometimes he may be considered an officer of the company. But an auditor is an independent person rendering professional services to the company in return of fees. He can neither be an agent of the shareholders nor be an officer of the company, nor is he a servant of the company.

9.10.10 Auditor's Rights, Duties and Liabilities

The auditor of a company has statutory rights, duties and liabilities under the Companies Act.

Rights of a company auditor

An auditor of a company is required to report on the truth and fairness of the financial statement of the company. To perform his duties effectively, he requires some rights and powers. In case of sole-proprietor or partnership firm, the rights and duties of an auditor are determined by the agreement entered into by him with the sole proprietor or the partnership firm as the case may be. But the Companies Act, 1956, has specifically laid down the rights and duties of a statutory auditor of a joint stock company. These rights and duties are absolute and cannot be curtailed in any way. Any resolution or provision in the articles in this regard will be null and void. It was held in the case of Newton vs Birmingham Small Arms Co. Ltd. that any resolution precluding the auditor from of any information to which he is entitled to as per Companies Act is inconsistent with the Act.

The Companies Act provides the following rights to the auditor to enable him to discharge his duties properly:

1. ***Right of access to books and vouchers*** Section 227(1) of the Companies Act, 1956 provides that the auditor of a company shall have the right of access, at all times, to the books and vouchers of the company whether kept at the head office or elsewhere. This right of the auditor is the fundamental basis on which the auditor can proceed to examine and inspect the records of the company for the purpose of making his report.

2. ***Right to obtain information and explanations*** Section 227(1) also entitles the auditor to require from the officer of the company such information and explanations as the auditor may think necessary for the performance of his duties. Corresponding to the right to ask for information and explanations, Section 221 of the Act also makes it obligatory for the concerned officers of the company to furnish without delay the relevant information to the auditor.

3. ***Right to visit branch offices and access to branch accounts*** Section 228(2) of the Companies Act gives specific rights to the company auditor where the accounts of any branch office are audited by another person. The company auditor has the right to visit branch office, if he deems it necessary to do so for the performance of his duties and has the right of access to books and accounts along with vouchers maintained by the branch office.

4. ***Right to receive branch audit reports*** The company auditor has also the right to receive the audit report from the branch auditor for his consideration and deal with it in

such a way, as he considers necessary while preparing his audit report on the accounts of the company.

5. ***Right to receive notices and to attend general meeting*** Section 231 of the Companies Act entitles the auditors of a company to attend any general meeting of the company and to be heard on any part of the business, which concerns him as the auditor. He is also entitled to receive all notices and communications relating to any general meeting of the company.

6. ***Right to make representation*** Pursuant to Section 225, the retiring auditor is entitled to receive a copy of the special notice intending to remove him or proposing to appoint any other person as auditor. The retiring auditor sought to be removed has a right to make his representation in writing and request that the same be circulated amongst the members of the company. In case, the same could not be circulated, the auditor may require that the representation shall be read out at the general meeting.

7. ***Right to sign audit report*** According to Section 229 of the Companies Act, only the person appointed as auditor of the company, or where a firm is so appointed only a partner in the firm practising in India, may sign the auditor's report.

8. ***Right to seek legal and technical advice*** The auditor of a company is entitled to take legal and technical advice, which may be required in the performance of conduct of audit or discharge of his duties (London and General Bank Case).

9. ***Right to be indemnified*** For different purposes, an auditor is considered to be an officer of the company. As an officer, he has the right to be indemnified out of assets of the company against any liability incurred by him in defending himself against any civil or criminal proceedings by the company, if he is not held guilty by the law.

10. ***Right to receive remuneration*** On completion of his work, an auditor is entitled to receive his remuneration. The rights of the auditor cannot be limited by any resolution of the members passed in the general meeting (Homer vs Quitler).

Right of lien of company auditor

The right of 'lien' means right of one person to retain the property of another person who owes money to the former. The right of lien of an auditor of a limited company indicates his right to retain documents and records of the company for his unpaid fees. The Companies Act is silent about the right of lien of auditors on clients' documents and records. Also there are many conflicting legal judgments regarding this issue. The Institute of Chartered Accountants of England and Wales has issued a guideline in this regard.

Based on that guideline, the auditor's lien can be discussed under the following heads:

1. ***Lien on books of accounts*** In the case Herbert Alfred Burliegh vs Ingram Clark Ltd. (1901), it was held that while an auditor acts as an accountant preparing books of accounts, he should have lien on such books of accounts for unpaid fees. But if he merely audits the books of accounts, he will not enjoy any right of lien on them.

But allowing auditor to enjoy right of lien on books of accounts prepared by him will conflict Section 209 of the Companies Act which make it mandatory for every company to keep its books of accounts at its registered office or at such other place in India as the directors think fit. So, the auditor's lien would not be upheld on books of accounts, which the company has to keep in its possession as per the provisions of the Companies Act.

2. *Lien on working papers* Audit working papers are those documents and records, which the auditors prepare in connection with his audit work. In fact, this question of ownership in respect to the working papers arose in the case of Sockockingky vs Bright Graham & Co. (1938) in England. The question was whether the auditor had a right to retain the working papers as if it were their own property even after the payment of the audit fees. The court gave judgment in favour of the auditors on the ground that they were independent contractors and not agents of the client.

3. *Lien on communication documents* An auditor may communicate with third parties either as an agent on behalf of the client or independently in connection with his work. In this case, the communication documents will belong to the client. However, if the auditor makes correspondence with third parties not as an agent, but as a professional man for discharging his duties, the correspondence with the third parties will be his property.

4. *Lien on client's money* The auditor should not have any lien on client's money, which may be kept with him. This is simply because he does not work on the money. He may be required to keep the money as a trustee only. So, if the auditor appropriates client's money towards his outstanding fees, he will be held liable.

5. *General or special lien* An auditor has only lien on the particular document in respect of which he has rendered his professional service, but he has not yet been paid. He cannot have general lien, i.e. he cannot retain other documents with which he has not been concerned.

Duties of a company auditor

The duties of a company auditor can be described by classifying it in the following categories:

1. *Statutory duties*

(a) Duty to report: According to Section 227 of the Companies Act, 1956, it is the duty of the company auditor to make a report to the members of the company on the accounts examined by him and on balance sheet and profit and loss account laid before the company in its general meeting.

(b) Duty to enquire: Sub-section (1A) of Section 227 of the Companies Act specifies six matters, which are required to be looked into by a company auditor. The statement on qualifications in the auditor's report issued by the ICAI clarifies that the auditor is not required to report on the matters specified in Sub-section (1 A), unless he has any special comments to make on any of the items referred to therein.

(c) Duty to follow CARO: Under Section 227(4A) of the Companies Act, the central government has the power to direct by a general or special order that in the case of specified companies, the auditor's report shall include a statement on such matters as may be specified in its order. In accordance with the provision, the central government issued revised order in 2003, namely Companies (Auditor's Report) Order. The auditor has the duty to follow the order.

(d) Other duties under the Companies Act: The auditor has the following other duties under the Companies Act:

(i) Duty of the auditor or a partner of a firm of chartered accountants practising in India to sign audit report (Section 229)

(ii) Duty of the auditor to report on prospectus on the accounting part (Section 56)

(iii) Duty to assist the inspector appointed by the central government to investigate the affairs of the company (Section 240)

(iv) Duty to report on profit and loss account for the period from the last closing date to the date of declaration of insolvency by the directors and also on balance sheet (Section 488)

(v) Duty to certify the statutory report of the company in respect of shares allotted, cash received in respect of such shares and the receipts and payments of the company [Section 165(4)]

2. ***Contractual duties*** A professional accountant may be hired by a company for purposes other than the statutory audit. In all such cases, the duty of the auditor will depend upon the terms and conditions of his appointment.

3. ***Duty to have reasonable care and skill*** An auditor of a company must be honest and must exercise reasonable care and skill to perform his audit work, otherwise he may be sued for damages. It was observed in Kingston Cotton Mills Case (1896) that the auditor should perform his audit work with such care, skill and caution that a reasonably competent, careful and cautious auditor will use.

4. ***Duty of an auditor regarding mandatory accounting standards*** According to the decision of the Council of the Institute of Chartered Accountants of India, it has been resolved that while discharging their functions, it is the duty of the members of the Institute, to ensure that the mandatory accounting standards are followed in the presentation of the financial statements covered by their audit report. In the event of any deviation from the standards, it is also the duty of the auditor to makes adequate disclosure in their reports so that the users of such statements may be aware of such deviations.

Section 227 (3) (d) of the Companies Act also states that the auditor's report shall state whether the company's balance sheet and profit and loss account comply with the accounting standards referred to in Section 211 (3C).

5. ***Duty to the profession itself*** Every profession has its own code of conduct and professional ethics. The Institute of Chartered Accountants of India has also issued the required code of conduct and professional ethics, which has to be maintained by the members of the Institute. So, it is the duty of the company auditor to follow code of conduct and his professional ethics.

Liabilities of company auditor

The auditor holds a position of great responsibility and has to perform certain duties, statutory or otherwise, assigned to him. In performing his duties, he has to exercise reasonable care and skill. His client expects him to follow the generally accepted auditing standards and he may be held liable in case he does not act with reasonable care and skill required from him in a particular situation.

The liabilities of an auditor can be described by classifying them under the following categories, as depicted in the given flow chart.

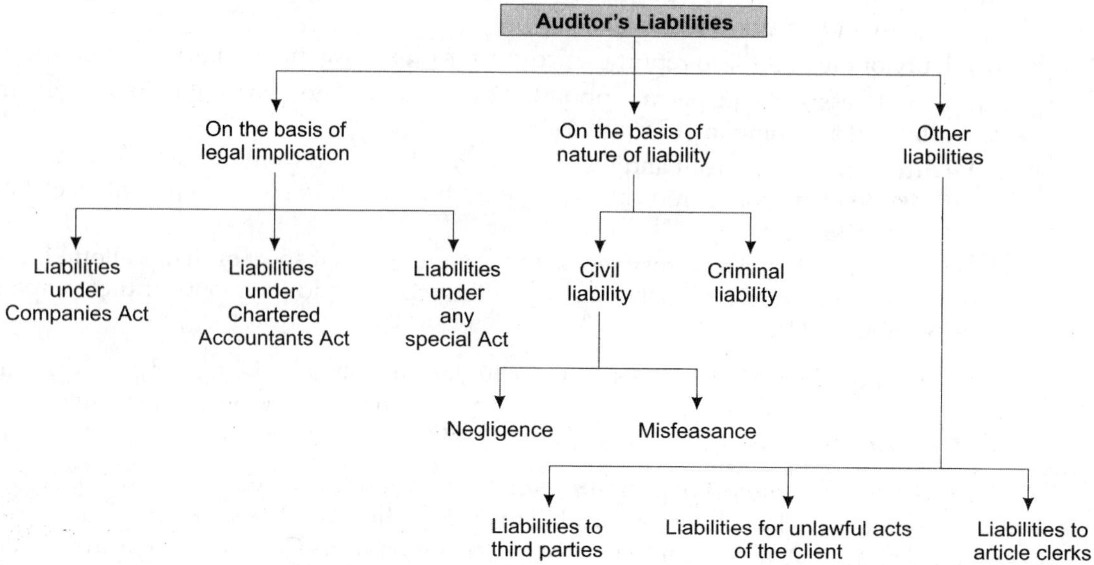

Liabilities on the basis of legal implications On the basis of legal implication, liabilities may be divided into three categories, namely,

1. *Liabilities under the Companies Act*: Under the Companies Act, the liability of an auditor may arise in the following cases:

(a) Misappropriation and retention of client's money: If an auditor has misappropriated or retained or become liable or accountable for any money or property of the company, or has been guilty of any misfeasance or breach of trust in relation to the company, the court may compel him to repay or to restore the money or property of or any part thereof with interest at certain rate or to contribute such sum to the assets of the company by way of compensation (Section 543).

(b) Mis-statements in the prospectus: He shall be liable with regard to mis-statements in the prospectus of the company under Section 62. The auditor is liable to pay compensation to every person who subscribes for any shares or debentures on the faith of the prospectus issued by the company for any loss or damage he may have sustained.

(c) False statement in returns, reports etc.: He shall be liable if he makes a false statement with material particulars in returns, reports or other statements knowing it to be false or omits any material fact knowing it to be material (Section 628),

(d) Intentional false evidence: He shall be liable if he gives false evidence intentionally upon any examination upon oath or solemn affirmations, authorised under this Act or in any affidavit, deposition or solemn affirmations, in or about the winding up of any company under this act (Section 629).

(e) Liability for delinquency: The liquidators may prosecute an auditor as an officer of the company during the course of winding up of the company for delinquency (Section 545).

(f) Wilful default in report making: He will be held liable if he wilfully makes a default in making his report to the shareholders according to the provisions of Sections 227 and 229 (Section 233).

(g) Destruction, alteration of books etc.: If he is found guilty of destruction, mutilation, alteration, falsification or hiding of any books, papers or securities or if he makes any false or fraudulent entry in any register, books of accounts or documents of the company, he may be held liable (Section 539).

(h) Authorising false statement in the prospectus: If he authorises the issue of the prospectus of a company containing a false and untrue statement, he will be held liable (Section 63).

(i) Party to the issue of prospectus: He may be held liable if he is party to the issue of prospectus including statement purporting to be made by him as an expert, unless he is not interested in the formation or promotion or in the management of the company (Sections 57, 58 and 59).

(j) Inducing fraudulently to invest money: He will be liable if he induces a person fraudulently to invest money by knowingly or recklessly making a statement or promise which is false or misleading, or if he dishonestly conceals the material fact (Section 68).

2. *Liabilities under the Chartered Accountants Act*: Liability of chartered accountant, acting as an auditor, may be in the form of disciplinary proceedings under the Chartered Accountants Act, 1949. It may arise on account of professional misconduct on the part of the auditor.

There are separate provisions for professional misconduct in relation to (a) chartered accountants in practice (b) members of the institute in service and (c) members of the institute in general.

The Council, under Section 21, refers the case of professional misconduct on the part of the members to the disciplinary committee. The latter holds the enquiry and reports its findings to the council. In case the council finds, on the basis of its report that the member is guilty of professional misconduct, it gives chance to the member to explain his conduct. On the basis of hearing, the council takes necessary actions. But if the misconduct on the part of the member is other than that specified in the first schedule of the Chartered Accountants Act, 1949 the council has to refer the case to the High Court with its recommendations thereon.

3. *Liabilities under any special act*: In addition to the Companies Act and the Chartered Accountants Act, the auditors are also held liable under different special acts, which are stated below:

(a) Under Banking Regulation Act, 1940:

(i) Under Section 46 of the Banking Regulations Act, 1940, if an auditor in any return, balance sheet or other document, wilfully makes a statement, which is false in any material particulars, knowing it to be false, or wilfully omits to make a material statement, he will be held responsible.

(ii) Under Section 45G, an auditor of a banking company may be publicly examined in the winding up proceedings. On such examination, the high court may make an order, if he is not found fit to act as an auditor, that he will not act as auditor of any company for such period not exceeding five years as may be specified in the order.

(b) Under the Life Insurance Corporation Act: Under Section 104 of the Life Insurance Corporation Act, 1956 an auditor may be sentenced to imprisonment or fine, or both, if he gives a false statement knowingly in any return, report or other such forms to be issued under the act.

(c) Under the Indian Penal Code: Under Section 197 of the Indian Penal Code, if any person including auditor issues or signs a certificate required by law to be given or signed, or relating to any fact of which such certificate is by law admissible in evidence, knowing or believing that such certificate is false in any material point, he shall be punishable in the same manner as if he gave false evidence.

(d) Under the Income Tax Act: Under Section 278 of the Income Tax Act, 1961, if any person including an auditor abets or induces in any manner another person to make and deliver an account, statement or declaration relating to any income chargeable to tax which is false and which he either knows to be false or does not believe to be true, he shall be punishable.

Liabilities on the basis of nature of liability On the basis of nature of liability, it can be divided into two groups:

1. *Civil liability*: The civil liability of an auditor can be for (a) negligence or (b) misfeasance. In these cases, he may be called upon to pay damages as decided by the court.

(a) Liability for negligence: An auditor is appointed to perform certain duties. To the extent of his duties as an auditor, he acts as an agent of his client. In this capacity, he must exercise reasonable care and skill to perform his duties for which he is employed. If he acts negligently on account of which the client has to suffer loss, the auditor may be held liable and may be called upon to make good the damages, which the client suffered due to his negligence.

It should be noted that if an auditor fails to discover frauds, he might not be failing in his duty. In fact, fraud and other irregularities may not be disclosed by an annual audit and even a detailed audit may not discover certain types of fraud. Under such circumstances, whether the auditor will be held responsible that depends on the fact that whether the auditor should have been able to discover that fraud if he applies reasonable care and skill. If he could, he will be held responsible, otherwise not.

(b) Liability for misfeasance: The term 'misfeasance' implies breach of trust or breach of duty. An auditor has to perform certain duties, which may arise out of a contract with the client as in the case of sole-proprietor or partnership or it may be statutory as laid down under various statutes. The duties of a company auditor have been statutorily laid down in the Companies Act, 1956. If the auditor does not perform his duties properly and as a result his client suffers, he may be held liable for misfeasance.

It should be noted that according to Section 543, the court might assess damages against delinquent Director or other officers of the company, including an auditor for misfeasance or breach of trust. In the case of an auditor, who also comes within the definition of officer in Section 2(30) for the purpose of this section, if he is guilty of neglect of duty or misfeasance, so as to cause loss to the company in any way, proceedings may be taken under this section against him either independently or other officers or jointly with them.

2. *Criminal liability*: An auditor of a company can be held guilty of criminal offences, if he wilfully makes a false statement in any report, return, certificate or balance sheet.

Under Section 628 of the Companies Act, "if an auditor in any report, certificate, balance sheet, prospectus, statement or other document required by or for the purpose of any of these acts, makes a statement (a) which is false in any material particular, knowing it to be false or (b) omits any material fact, knowing it to be material, he will be held liable on criminal offence.

Again, Section 197 of the Indian Penal Code provides that whoever issues or signs any certificate required by law to be given or signed or relating to any fact which such certificate is by law admissible in evidence, knowing or believing that such certificate is false in any material point, shall be punishable in the same manner as he gave false evidence.

Other liabilities The other liabilities of an auditor may include the following:

1. *Liability to third parties*: There are several persons who completely rely upon the financial statements entitled by the auditor and enter into transactions with the company without any further enquiry. These parties may include creditors, the bankers, the tax authorities, the prospective investors etc.

In general, the auditor is not liable to third parties since no contractual obligation exists between the auditor and the third parties. Since they do not appoint him, he owes no duty to them and hence there is no question of any liability to them. He cannot be held liable unless he owes any duty to the persons, who hold him able for damages caused.

The third parties, however, can hold him liable, if there has been any fraud on the part of the auditor. Even if there is no contractual obligation between the auditor and the third parties, the latter can sue the auditor if the report of the auditor is of such a nature as amounts to fraud.

2. *Liability for unlawful act of the client*: An auditor may obtain knowledge about the unlawful acts or defaults committed by his client during the course of his audit. The question arises whether he should inform the proper authorities about it and whether he can be held liable if he does not do so. It is a difficult question indeed since it involves breach of confidence placed on him by his client.

Under such circumstances, he must act very carefully. He must not act in such a way, which unnecessarily injures the confidence of his client on him. If required, he should terminate his association with the client rather than open himself to such liability.

3. *Liability to article clerks*: The auditor may be held liable to his article clerks in the following circumstances:

(a) If he does not act honestly with his article clerk

(b) If he removes any of his article clerks without any prior notice

(c) If he does not pay the required amount of monthly stipend to the article clerks

(d) If he gives a false certificate of payment of stipend to his article clerks.

The auditor, however, cannot be held liable to his article clerks to pay compensation to them in case their services are terminated by the auditor. The question of payment of compensation to a retrenched or dismissed worker arises under the Industrial Dispute Act, 1956 only, which is not applicable to article clerks.

9.11 SPECIAL AUDITOR

1. Circumstances

Power has been given to the central government under Section 233A of the Companies Act, 1956, to direct a special audit, where the government is of the opinion that:

- the affairs of any company are not being managed in accordance with sound business principles or prudent commercial practices, or
- any company is being managed in a manner likely to cause serious injury or damage to the interest of the trade, industry or business to which it pertains or
- the financial position of any company is such as to endanger its solvency.

The central government may, at any time, direct that a special audit of the company's account for such period or periods as may be specified, be carried out.

2. Qualification

A chartered accountant as defined in Clause (b) of Sub-section (1) of Section 2 of the Chartered Accountants Act, 1949, whether such accountant is in practice or not, or the company's auditor himself may be appointed to conduct such special audit. This appointment is made by the central government.

3. Rights, powers and duties of special auditor

The special auditor shall have the same rights, powers and duties in relation to the special audit as an auditor of a company has under Section 227 of the Companies Act.

However, instead of making his report to the members of the company, the special auditor must submit his report to the central government. The report of the special auditor shall, as far as may be, include all the matters required to be included in an auditor's report, under Section 227 and if the central government so directs, shall also include a statement on any other matter which may be referred to him by the government.

4. Remuneration of special auditor

The remuneration of special auditor is fixed by the government, but is payable by the company. If the company fails to pay the remuneration, it can be recovered in the same way as land revenue.

9.12 BRANCH AUDITOR

1. Qualification

Section 228 of the Companies Act governs the audit of branch offices. Where a company has a branch office in India, the accounts of that office shall be audited by the company's auditors or by a person qualified under Section 226.

If the branch is situated outside India, audit can be conducted, in addition to persons mentioned above, by an accountant duly qualified to act as an auditor in accordance with the laws of the country in which the branch office is situated.

2. Appointment

If it is decided in the general meeting of the company to have the accounts of a branch audited by auditor other than the auditor of the company, Section 228(3) requires that the meeting should appoint any qualified person as auditor of the branch or authorise the board of directors to appoint a qualified person as auditor for the branch in consultation with the main auditor of the company.

3. Rights, powers and duties of branch auditor

The branch auditor shall have the same rights, powers and duties in relation to the branch audit as an auditor of a company has under Section 227 of the Companies Act (Section 228(3)(b)).

The branch auditor shall prepare a report on the accounts of the branch office examined by him and forward the same to the auditor of the company, who shall, in preparing the audit report, deal with the same in such manner as he considers necessary (Section 228 (3)(c)).

4. Remuneration of the branch auditor

The branch auditor shall receive such remuneration and shall hold his appointment subject to such terms and conditions as may be fixed either by the company in general meeting or by the Board of Directors if so authorised by the company in general meeting (Section 228 (3)(d)).

5. Exemptions from branch audit

Under Section 228(4) of the Companies Act, the central government is empowered to give exemptions from branch audit. The central government is also empowered to withdraw these exemptions.

9.13 JOINT AUDITOR

Sometimes, two or more firms are appointed to conduct the audit of a company. This is the usual case with large companies like insurance and banking companies having a wide geographical network. In such a situation, the following matters assume importance:

- The audit work has to be shared by the joint auditor
- There should be proper co-ordination of work of the joint auditors
- Proper attempt should be made to resolve the differences of opinion among the joint auditors

The Companies Act, 1956 does not contain any specific provisions regarding joint audit. However, the Institute of Chartered Accountants of india has issued AAS-12 on the 'responsibility of joint auditors'. According to this statement, the functions and duties of joint auditors can be stated as follows:

1. Division of work

Where joint auditors are appointed, they should, by mutual discussion, divide the audit work among themselves. In some cases due to the nature of the business of the entity under audit, such a division of work may not be possible. In such situation, the division of work may be with reference to items of assets and liabilities or income and expenditure or with reference to periods of time. The division of work among joint auditors as well as the areas of work to be covered by all of them should be adequately documented and preferably communicated to the entity.

2. Co-ordination

Where, in the course of his work, a joint auditor comes across matters, which are relevant, to the areas of responsibility of other joint auditors, and which deserve their attention, he should communicate the same to all the other joint auditors in writing.

3. Responsibility of joint auditor

In respect of audit work divided among the joint auditors, each joint auditor is responsible only for the work allocated to him.

Each auditor should bring to the attention of the other joint auditors matters requiring discussion, disclosure or application of judgment, by submitting a report or a note prior to the finalisation of audit. If any such matter were brought to the attention of the other joint auditors by an auditor after the audit report has been submitted, the other joint auditors would not be responsible in respect of those matters.

It is the responsibility of each joint auditor to determine the nature, timing and extent of audit procedures to be applied in relation to the area of work allocated to him.

4. Audit report

Normally, the joint auditors are able to arrive at an agreed report. However, where the joint auditors are in disagreement with regard to any matters to be covered by the report, each one of them should express their own opinion through a specific report. A joint auditor is not bound by the views of the majority of the joint auditors regarding matters to be covered in the report and should express his opinion in a separate report in case of disagreement.

9.14 LEGAL VIEWS ON AUDITOR'S LIABILITY

The legal views as discussed in different cases so far taken to courts of law can be summarised as follows:

Case Study

1. **Case: Leeds Estate Building and Investment Co. vs Shepherd (1887)**

   Fact of the case: In this case, the auditor had not discovered that certain payments relating to dividends, directors fees and bonus were irregular. This was because he had not concerned himself with the company's articles. He was held liable for damages.

   Legal view: This case had established that it is not sufficient for an auditor to concern himself with the arithmetical accuracy of the books and accounts. He has a duty to ensure that the transactions are in order. When an auditor takes over a company audit, one of his first actions is to obtain a copy of the memorandum and articles and note important points therein affecting the account.

2. **Case: London and General Bank Limited (1895)**

   Fact of the case: The company, in this case, had not made adequate provision for bad debts. The auditor had discovered that the debts were doubtful and had clearly reported the situation to the directors, but, when the directors failed to make provisions, instead of reporting the facts equally clearly to the shareholders, he simply made the statement that "the value of the assets is dependent upon realisation". It was held that the auditor had failed in his duty to convey information clearly in his report, and he was made liable for certain dividends improperly paid.

   Legal view: This case is important because it was stated unequivocally that an auditor has a duty to convey facts clearly to shareholders. "A person whose duty is to convey information to others does not discharge that duty by simply giving them so much information as is calculated to induce them, or some of them, to ask for more."

   This case established the fact that an auditor who shrinks from fully and clearly disclosing all the material facts known to him is putting himself at risk. The court also discussed the basic duty of an auditor. It was laid down that he must exercise reasonable care and skill, but that he is in no way acts as an insurer and does not guarantee the accounts.

3. **Case: Kingston Cotton Mill Co. Ltd. (1896)**

   Fact of the Case: In this case, the accounts had been manipulated by the over-valuation of stock by the managing director, who had certified the stock valuation to the auditor. It was held in the Court of Appeal that it was not the duty of the auditor to take stock, and that in the absence of suspicious circumstances he was not guilty of negligence in accepting the certificate of a responsible official with regard to the value of stock.

   Legal view: As far as the main question is involved, whether the auditor could place total reliance on the stock certificate of a responsible official with regard to the value of stock in the absence of suspicious circumstances, this case is now of historical interest only. The Companies Act also requires that the auditors should state whether the accounts show a true and fair view. The professional accountancy bodies have issued statements regarding detailed audit work to be carried out in relation to stock verification and valuation and attendance by the auditor at stock taking. It does not seem that the auditor could now simply accept a stock certificate from a responsible official where stock was a material item and then plead this case in justification when defending the inevitable action for misfeasance or negligence.

4. **Case: Irish Wollen Co. Ltd. vs Tyson (1900)**

   Fact of the case: The auditor was found to have been negligent in that he had failed to discover that the company's liabilities were understated due to the suppression of creditor's invoices. This fraud would have been discovered if the auditor had either checked the ledger balances against the creditor's statements or scrutinised the dates entered in the first few weeks of the next period.

   Legal view: This case again shows the courts refusing to accept that an auditor had discharged his duties by checking the arithmetical accuracy of the entries in the books. He must exercise due skill and care in checking the validity of these entries. Auditors would now always carry out the tests omitted in this case, checking balances against creditors' statements and testing the correctness of the "cut-off" procedure carefully.

5. **Case: The London Oil Storage Co. Ltd. vs Seear, Hasluck & Co. (1904)**

   Fact of the case: This was another case where the auditors had concerned themselves only with the entries in the books, and not with verification procedure. The balance sheet showed cash balances of almost £ 800, which agreed with the books, but the actual balance was only £ 30, the difference having been misappropriated. The auditor was held to have been negligent in not verifying the balance. However, damages of only five guineas were awarded against the auditor because the court held that the director responsible for supervising the fraudulent employee was the person primarily responsible for the loss.

   Legal view: There are two important aspects to this case. The first is that the court again held that auditors have a duty to verify assets and not merely to check book-keeping entries. The second, and very important, or aspect is that auditors are responsible for the loss resulting directly from their negligence and thus are not responsible where the loss has resulted from other causes.

6. **Case: Arthur E. Green & Co. vs the Central Advance & Discount Corporation Ltd. (1920)**

   Fact of the case: The case concerned the failure of the company to make adequate provision for bad debts. The auditors relied upon the bad debt provisions made by the managers, despite the fact that many debts not provided for were old and some were even statue-barred. The auditors were found to have been negligent.

   Legal view: The decision indicates that the auditors must exercise proper skill and care in carrying out their own tests to establish the value of material assets. They are not adequately performing their duties by relying on a certificate provided by a responsible official.

7. **Case: The City Equitable Fire Insurance Co. Ltd. (1924)**

   Fact of the case: This case concerned various alleged frauds in relation to the accounts of the company. The most important of these with regard to auditing principles was that securities owned by the company were deposited with its stock brokers. The auditor accepted a certificate from the stock brokers in respect of such securities for a very material amount. Had they insisted on inspecting the securities, these could not have been produced as they had been pledged by the stock brokers. An additional complication was that the chairman of the company was also a partner in the firm of stock-brokers.

   The auditors escaped liability because the company had a clause in its articles, which provided that the directors, auditors and officers of the company should be indemnified by the company except in the case of willful default.

   Legal view: The importance of this case was that it demonstrated the importance of auditors' actually inspecting documents of title held by third parties. Only where such documents are held by one of the major banks or are not very substantial and are held in the ordinary course of a business by another independent third party should the auditor accept a certificate. Moreover, if the auditor entertains the slightest doubt of the desirability of accepting a certificate, it would always be wise to insist on actual inspection.

8. **Case: Westminster Road Construction and Engineering Co. Ltd. (1932)**

   Fact of the case: This case concerned misfeasance by the auditor of a company, which had subsequently gone into liquidation. The auditor was held to have been negligent for failing to detect the omission of liabilities from the balance sheet in circumstances where their omission should have been apparent, and for failing to detect the over-valuation of work-in-progress in circumstances where there was available evidence to have enabled him to do so.

   Legal view: This case again underlined the need for sound verification procedures and, with regard to the work-in-progress, underlined the need for the auditor to make use of all available records and information.

9. **Case: S. P. Catterson and Sons Ltd. (1937)**

   Fact of the case: In this case, the company had a poor system of dealing with sales in that the same invoice book was used for both cash sales and credit sales, this led to defalcations. The auditors had drawn the attention of the directors to the shortcomings of the system, but no action had been taken. The auditor was acquitted of negligence on the grounds that the primary responsibility for exercising control vested with the directors.

   Legal view: The auditors had reported about the weaknesses in the system rightly to the directors. This should now be done formally in internal control letters (letters of weaknesses). So, the auditor was not held liable.

10. **Case: Thomas Gerrand & Sons Ltd. (1967)**

    Fact of the case: The accounts of this company had allegedly been manipulated in the following ways:

    (i) The stock figures were inflated.

    (ii) Purchases relating to the current period were charged in the succeeding period.

    (iii) Sales made after the accounting date were credited in the earlier period. The auditors were found liable for misfeasance in respect of dividends paid by the company where, had the accounts not been manipulated, no profits would have been available. The auditors' negligence arose primarily from their failure to follow up the alternations of the purchase invoices. They had discovered the alterations, but accepted explanations too easily.

    Legal view: Two main conclusions can be drawn from this case: firstly, the need for sound audit tests on the year end cut-off procedures and secondly, the fact that once auditors have discovered suspicious circumstances. In this case the alteration of the dates on the invoices they have a duty to probe the matter thoroughly, and must not be easily satisfied by explanations provided by Directors or officers.

POINTS TO PONDER

- As in case of a company, the ownership is separated from management it becomes essential for a company to appoint an independent and qualified auditor to verify and certify the truth and fairness of the financial statements.
- Before commencing the actual audit work of a company, the auditor should go through certain preliminaries, which include ensuring whether his appointment is in order or not, inspecting the statutory books and documents, inspecting contracts with third parties, studying previous year's balance sheet and audit report and studying of internal control system of the company.
- While conducting audit of share capital transactions, the auditor has to ensure that the legal requirements have been duly complied with, to see that the issue of share is properly authorised and that there is no overissue beyond the prescribed limit, to check that the rights of the shareholders are duly protected and to ensure that the generally accepted accounting principles are followed while recording the transactions relating to issue.
- Shares can be issued on consideration other than cash as issue of shares to the vendors or promoters or issue of shares to underwriters, issue of sweat equity shares etc.
- Shares can be issued at par or at a discount or at a premium. There can be calls in arrear or calls in advance in case of issue of shares. Shares can be forfeited for non-payment of share call and forfeited shares can also be reissued.
- Shares can be issued to the existing shareholders as right shares, to the employees under employees stock option scheme or even shares can be bought back form the shareholders.
- A company limited by shares may issue preference shares, which are liable to be redeemed at the option of the company on a predetermined date. At present, no company limited by shares shall issue any preference shares, which are irredeemable or is redeemable after the expiry of a period of 20 years from the date of its issue.
- A company having a share capital may alter its share capital and each alteration made should be noted in the memorandum and articles issued subsequent to the date of alteration.
- A company can reduce its share also in a number of ways, which include reduction without the consent of the court and with the consent of the court.
- Large-size companies often face the problem of frequent and large scale share transfer and there is every possibility of errors and mistakes taking place in the process for which the company appoints auditors for carrying out this special assignment.
- In addition to shares, a company can issue debentures for procuring fund. Debentures can be issued at par, at a premium or at a discount. The debentures are redeemable after a certain period of time. A predetermined fixed rate of interest is payable on debentures irrespective of the fact that the company has been able to earn any profit or not.
- Debentures may be issued to creditors, bankers or any other person, without receiving any cash thereon. It acts as a collateral security and becomes real debentures in the event of the default of the loan.

- Accounting Standard 21 on 'consolidated financial statements' issued by the ICAI prescribes the principles to be followed by the holding companies in consolidating the balance sheet and profit and loss account with that of the financial statements of the subsidiaries. The auditor of a holding company has to see whether the financial statements of the holding company is consolidated with the financial statements of its subsidiaries by following the principles as prescribed in AS- 21.
- The profit earned during the pre-incorporation period is called 'pre-incorporation profit'. Legally, this profit is not available for dividend, since a company cannot earn profit before it comes into existence.
- Every company shall keep at its registered office proper books of accounts as prescribed in Section 209 of the Companies Act. The books are usually to be kept at the registered office for at least last eight years.
- The special requirements of company audit include the verification of the constitution and power of the company and knowledge about the authority structure of the company.
- The provisions regarding the appointment of the auditors are contained in Section 224 of the Companies Act. The first auditors are usually appointed by the Board of Directors and subsequent auditors are appointed by the shareholders in the annual general meeting. In some cases, auditors are appointed by the central government or by passing a special resolution.
- Usually a retiring auditor shall be automatically reappointed by passing an ordinary resolution. An individual auditor cannot be the auditor of more than 20 companies at a time. The remuneration of the auditors is fixed by the appointing authority.
- The auditor of a company must be either a practicing chartered accountant or the holder of a certificate in erstwhile Part B States entitling him to act as an auditor of companies.
- An appointed auditor may be removed from his office either in accordance with the provisions of the Companies Act or as per restrictions imposed by the Chartered Accountants Act.
- The auditor of a company can be considered a servant of the company, an agent of the shareholders as well as an officer of the company.
- Rights of the company auditor includes right of access to books and vouchers, right to obtain information and explanations, right to visit branch offices and to receive branch audit report, right to receive notices to attend general meeting, right to sign audit report and right to receive remuneration.
- Duties of a company auditor include statutory duties, contractual duties, duty to have reasonable care and skill, duty regarding accounting standards and duty to the profession itself.
- The auditor is liable under the Companies Act, under the Chartered Accountants Act and under other special acts. He has civil liabilities as well as criminal liabilities. He is liable to third parties and to the article clerks.

REVIEW QUESTIONS

Short-answer Questions

1. Write short notes on:
   (a) Issue of shares at premium
   (b) Payment of interest out of capital
   (c) Reduction of share capital
2. What are the points you will consider at the time of examining the issue of right shares?
3. State how an auditor should outline the programme suitable for a share transfer audit.
4. How will you examine the following items while auditing the accounts of a limited company?
   (a) Re-issue of forfeited shares
   (b) Profit prior to incorporation
5. How are the first auditors of a limited company appointed?
6. Explain in brief the legal provisions as well as the Schedule VI requirements regarding auditors' remuneration.
7. Describe the qualifications of an auditor according to the Chartered Accountants Act, 1949.
8. Discuss the status of an auditor in the company.
9. How will you examine the following items while auditing the accounts of a limited company?
   (a) Redemption of preference shares
   (b) Forfeiture of shares
10. State the circumstances when a person will be disqualified for being appointed as company auditor.
11. How is the auditor of a government company appointed?
12. Discuss the auditors' liability to third party?

Essay-type Questions

1. What are the steps to be taken by a statutory auditor before commencement of an audit of a company?
2. Mention important items for which auditor would refer to each of the following:
   (a) Board's meeting minutes book
   (b) Shareholders' meeting minutes book
3. What are the points to which you would direct your attention, while accepting an appointment as an auditor of a company? State under what circumstances, an appointed auditor can be removed from his office?
4. State clearly the rights and duties of an auditor.
5. Under the Companies Act, an auditor may be held liable both for negligence and misfeasance. Do you agree? Give reasons for your answer.

6. Under what circumstances, an auditor can be appointed by the following:
   (a) The Board of Directors
   (b) The shareholders
   (c) The central government
7. (a) Discuss the circumstances in which bonus shares can be issued by a company.
   (b) Enumerate the procedures to be followed
   (c) Explain the duties of the auditor in relation to the above
8. State the procedures an auditor should follow to verify the issue of share capital for the following.
   (a) Cash
   (b) Consideration other than cash
   (c) Employees as 'sweat equity share'
9. Explain the statements:
   (a) Information and means of information are by no means equivalent terms.
   (b) An auditor is liable for any damages sustained by a company by reason of falsification, which might have been discovered by exercise of reasonable care and skill in the performance of audit.
10. Discuss the rights of lien of an auditor of a limited company.

ANNEXURE

Schedule VI to the Companies Act, 1956

PART I—FORM OF BALANCE SHEET

The balance sheet of a comapny shall be either in horizontal form or vertical form.

A—Horizontal Form

Balance sheet of .... (here enter the name of the company)
As at .... (here enter the date as at which the balance sheet is made out)

Instructions in accordance with which liabilities should be made out	*Liabilities*			*Assets*		*Instructions in accordance with which assets should be made out*
	Figures for the previous year Rs (b)	*Figures for the current year Rs (b)*		*Figures for the previous year Rs (b)*	*Figures for the current year Rs (b)*	
*Terms of redemption or conversion (if any) of any redeemable preference capital to be stated, together with earliest date of redemption or conversion. Particulars of any option on unissued share capital to be specified. †Particulars of the different classes of preference shares to be given. ‡Specify the source from which bonus shares are issued, e.g. capitalisation of profits or reserves or from Share Premium Account.			***Share Capital** Authorised ... shares of Rs ... each †Issued (distinguishing between the various classes of capital and stating the particulars specified below, in respect of each class) ... shares of Rs ... each. †Subscribed (distinguishing between the various classes of capital and stating the particulars specified below, in respect of each class), (c) ... shares of Rs ... each. Rs ... called up. Of the above shares ... shares are allotted as fully paid-up pursuant to a contract without payments being received in cash. ‡Of the above shares ... shares are allotted as fully paid-up by way of bonus shares.			
			***Fixed Assets** Distinguishing as far as possible between expenditure upon (a) goodwill, (b) land, (c) buildings, (d) leasehold, (e) railway sidings, (f) plant and machinery, (g) furniture and fittings, (h) development of property, (i) patents, trade marks and designs, (j) livestock, and (k) vehicles, etc.			*Under each head the original cost and the additions thereto and deductions therefrom during the year, and the total depreciation written off or provided up to the end to the year to be stated. Where the original cost aforesaid and additions and deductions thereto, relate to any fixed asset which has been acquired from a country outside India, and in consequence of a change in the rate of exchange at any time after the acquisition of such asset, there has been an increase or reduction in the liability of the company, as expressed in Indian currency, for making payment towards the whole or a part of the cost of the asset or for repayment of the whole or a part of money borrowed by the company from any person, directly or indirectly, in any foreign currency specifically for the purpose of acquiring the assets (being in either case the liability existing immediately before the date on which the change in the rate of

Contd.

Contd.

<table>
<tr>
<td>†Any capital profit on reissue of forfeited shares should be transferred to Capital Reserve

*Additions and deductions since last balance sheet to be shown, under each of the specified heads.

The word "fund" in relation to any "Reserve" should be used only where such Reserve is specifically represented by ear-marked investments.</td>
<td>Less: Calls unpaid
(i) By managing agent of secretaries and treasurers and where the managing agent or secretaries and treasurers are a firm, by the partners thereof, and where the managing agent or secrataries and treasurers are a private company, by the directors or members of that company.
(ii) By directors.
(iii) By others.
†Add: Forfeited shares (amount originally paid-up).

*Reserves and Surplus
1. Capital Reserves.
2. Capital Redemption Reserve.
3. Share Premium Account (cc)
4. Other reserves specifying the nature of each reserve and the amount in respect thereof.
Less: Debit balance in profit and loss account (if any) (h)
5. Surplus, i.e. balance in profit and loss account after providing for proposed allocations, namely—
Dividend, bonus or reserves.
6. Proposed additions to reserves.
7. Sinking funds</td>
<td></td>
<td>exchange takes effect), the amount by which the liability is so increased or reduced during the year, shall be added to, or, as the case may be, deducted from the cost, and the amount arrived at after such addition or deduction shall be taken to be the cost of the fixed asset.

Explanation 1—This paragraph shall apply in relation to all balance sheets that may be made out as at the 6th day of June, 1966, or any day, thereafter and where, at the date of issue of the notification of the Government of India, in the Ministry of Industrial Development and Company Affairs (Department of Company Affairs), G.S.R. No, 129, dated the 3rd day of January, 1968, any balance sheet, in relation to which this paragraph applies, has already been made out and laid before the company in Annual General Meeting, the adjustment referred to in this paragraph may be made in the balance sheet made out after the issue of the said notification.

Explanation 2—In this paragraph, unless the context otherwise requires, the expressions "rate of exchange", "foreign currency" and "Indian currency" shall have the meanings respectively assigned to them under Sub-section (1) of Section 43A of the Income-tax Act, 1961 (43 of 1961), and Explanation 2 and Explanation 3of the said sub-section shall, as far as may be, apply in relation to the said paragraph as they apply to the said Sub-section (1).

In every case where the original cost cannot be ascertained, without unreasonable expense or delay, the valuation shown by the books shall be given. For the purposes of this paragraph, such valuation shall be the net amount at which an asset stood in the company's books at the</td>
</tr>
</table>

Contd.

Contd.

*Loans from directors, the managing agents, secretaries and treasurers, manager should be shown separately. Interest accrued and due on Secured Loans should be included under the appropriate sub-heads under the head 'Secured Looans' *The nature of the security to be specified in each case. Where loans have been guaranteed by managing agents, secretaries and treasurers, managers and/or directors, a mention thereof shall also be made and also the aggregate amount of such loans under each head. †Terms of redemption or conversion (if any) of debentures issued to be stated together with earliest date of redemption or conversion.	**Secured Loans** *1. Debentures *2. Loans and advances from banks. *3. Loans and advances from subsidiaries. *4. Other loans and advances.		commencement of this Act after deduction of the amounts previously provided or written off for depreciation or diminution in value, and where any such asset is sold, the amount of sale proceeds shall be shown as deduction. Where sums have been written off on a reduction of capital or a revaluation of assets, every balace sheet (after the first balance sheet) subsequent to the reduction or revaluation shall show the reduced figures and with the date of the reduction in place of the original cost. Each balance sheet for the first five years subsequent to the date of the reduction, shall show also the amount of the reduction made. Similarly, where sums have been added by writing up the assets, every balance sheet subsequent to such writing up shall show the increased figures with the date of the increase in place of the original cost. Each balance sheet for the first five years subsequent to the date of writing up shall also show amount of increase made.
†Loans from directors, the managing agents, secretaries and treasurers, manager should be shown separately. Interest accrued and due on Unsecured Loans should be included under the appropriate sub-heads under the head 'Unsecured Loans'. Where loans have been guaranteed by managing agents, secretaries and treasurers, managers and/or directors, a mention thereof shall also be made and also the aggregate amount of such loans under each head. **See* note (d) at foot of Form.	**Unsecured Loans** 1. Fixed deposits. †2. Loans and advances from subsidiaries. †*3. Short-term loans and advances: (a) From Banks. (b) From others. 4. Other loans and advances: (a) From Banks (b) From others.	**Investments** Showing nature of investments and mode of valuation, for example cost or market value and distinguishing between 1. Investment in Government or Trust Securities 2. *Investments in shares, debentures or bonds (showing separately shares, fully paid-up and partly paid-up and also distinguishing the different classes of shares and showing also in similar details investments in shares, debentures or	*Explanation*—Nothing contained in the preceding two paragraphs shall apply to any adjustment made in accordance with the second paragraph. *Aggregate amount of company's quoted investments and also the market value thereof shall be shown. Aggregate amount of company's unquoted investment shall also be shown. All untilised monies out of the issue must be separately disclosed in the balance sheet of the company indicating the form in which such unutilised funds have been invested.

Contd.

Contd.

		bonds of subsidiary companies. 3. Immovable properties. 4. Investments in the capital of partnership firms. 5. Balance of unutilised monies raised by issue.	
The name(s) of small scale industrial under-taking(s) to whom the company owes any sum together with interest outstanding for more than 30 days, are to be disclosed.*	**Current Liabilities and Provisions** *(A) Current Liabilities* 1. Acceptances. 2. Sundry creditors. (i) Total outstanding dues of small scale industrial under takings(s); and (ii) Total outstanding dues of creditors other than small scale industrial undertaking(s). 3. Subsidiary companies. 4. Advance payments and unexpired discounts for the portion for which value has still to be given, e.g. in the case of the following classes of companies— Newspaper, Fire insurance, theatres, clubs, banking, steamship companies, etc. 5. Investor Education and Protection Fund shall be credited by the following amounts namely— (a) Unpaid dividend; (b) Unpaid application money received by the companies for allotment of securities and due for refund; (c) Unpaid matured deposits; (d) Unpaid matured debentures;	**Current Assets, Loans and Advances** *(A) Current Assets* 1. Interest accrued on investments. 2. Stores and spare parts. 3. Loose tools. ‡4. Stock-in-trade. **5. Works-in-progress. †6. Sundry debtors— (a) Debts outstanding for a period exceeding six months. (b) Other debts. Less: Provision (7A) Cash balance on hand. *(7B) Bank balance— (a) with scheduled banks; and (b) with others.	‡Mode of valuation of stock shall be stated and the amount in respect of raw material shall also be stated separately where practicable. **Mode of valuation of works in progress shall be stated. In regard to sundry debtors particulars to be given separately of— (a) debts considered good and in respect of which the company is fully secured; and (b) debts considered good for which the company holds no security other than the debtors's personal security; and (c) debts considered doubtful or bad. Debts due by directors or other officers of the company or any of them either severally or jointly with any other person or debts due by firms or private companies respectively in which any director is a partner or a director or a member to be separately stated. Debts due from other companies under the same management within the meaning of Sub-section (1B) of Section 370, to be disclosed with the names of the companies. The maximum amount due by directors or other officers of the company at any time during the year to be shown by way of a note. The provisions to be shown under this head should not exceed the amount of debts stated to be considered doubtful or bad and any surplus of such provision, if already created, should be shown at every closing under "Reserves and Surplus" (in the Liabilities side) under a separate sub-head "Reserve for Doubtful or Bad Debts".

Contd.

Contd.

	(e) Interest accrued on (a) to (b) above 6. Other liabilities (if any). 7. Interest accrued but not due on loans.		*In regard to bank balances. particulars to be given separately of— (a) the balances lying with scheduled banks on current accounts, call accounts, and deposit accounts; (b) the names of the bankers other than scheduled banks and the balance lying with each such banker on current accounts, call accounts and deposit accounts and the maximum amount outstanding at any time during the year from each such banker and (c) the nature of the interest, if any, of any director or his relative or the managing agent, secretaries and treasurers, of any associate of the latter in each of the bankers (other than Schedules Banks) referred to in (b) above.
	B. Provisions 8. Provision for taxation. 9. Proposed dividends. 10. For contingenecies. 11. For provident fund scheme. 12. For insurance, pension and similar staff benefit schemes. 13. Other provisions.	*#(B) Loans And Advances* 8.(a) Advances and loans to subsidiaries. (b) Advances and loans to partbership firms in which the company or any of its subsidiaries is a partner. 9. Bills of exchange. 10. Advances recoverable in cash or in kind or for value to be received, e.g., rates, taxes, insurance, etc. 11. Balances on current account with managing agents or secretaries and treasurers. 12. Balances with customs, port trust, etc. (where payable on demand).	All unutilised monies out of the issue must be separately disclosed in the Balance Sheet of the company indicating the form in which such unutilised funds have been invested. #The above instructions regarding 'Sundry Debtors' apply to 'Loans and Advances' also.
*The period for which the dividends are in arrear or if there is more than one class of shares, the dividends on each such class are in arrear, shall be stated. The amount shall be stated before dedcution of income-tax, except that in the case of tax-free dividends the amount shall be shown free of income-tax and the fact that it is so shown shall be stated. **The amount of any guarantees given by the company on behalf of directors or other officers of the company shall be stated and where practicable, the general nature and amount of each such contingent liability, if material, shall also be specified.	A foot note to the balance sheet may be added to show separately— 1. Claim against the company not acknowledged as debts. 2. Uncalled liability on shares partly paid. 3. *Arrears of fixed cumulative dividends. 4. Estimated amounts of contracts remaining to be executed on capital account and not provided for. 5. **Other money for which the company is contingently liable.	**Miscellaneous Expenditure** (to the extent not written off or adjusted) 1. Preliminary expenses. 2. Expenses including commission or brokerage on underwriting or subscription of shares or debentures. 4. Interest paid out of capital during construction (also stating the rate of interest). 5. Development expenditure not adjusted. 6. Other items (specifying nature).	
		Profit and Loss Account	*Show here the debit balance of profit and loss account carried forward after deduction of the uncommitted reserves, if any.

Notes

General Instructions for Preparation of Balance Sheet

(a) The information required to be given under any of the items or sub-items in this form, if it cannot be conveniently included in the balance sheet itself, shall be furnished in a separate Schedule or Schedules to be annexed to and to form part of the balance sheet. This is recommended when items are numerous.

(b) Naye Paise can also be given in addition to Rupees, if desired.

(c) In the case of subsidiary companies the number of shares held by the holding company as well as by the ultimate holding company and its subsidiaries must be separately stated.

The auditor is not required to certify the corrections of such shareholdings as certified by the management

(d) The item "Share Premium Account" shall include details of its utilisation in the manner provided in section 78 in the year of utilisation.

(e) Short-term loans will include those which are due for not more than one year as at the date of the balance sheet.

(f) Depreciation written off or provided shall be allocated under the different asset heads and deducted in arriving at the value of fixed assets.

(g) Dividends declared by subsidiary companies after the date of the balance sheet should not be included unless they are in respect of period which closed on or before the date of the balance sheet.

(h) Any reference to benefits expected from contracts to the extent shall not be made in the balance sheet but shall be made in the Board's report.

(i) The debit balance in the profit and loss account shall be shown as a deduction from the uncommitted reserves, if any.

(j) As regards Loans and Advances, amounts due by the managing agents or secretaries and treasurers, either severally or jointly with any other persons, to be separately stated; the amounts due from other companies under the same management within the meaning of sub-section (1B) of section 370 should also be given with the names of the companies; the maximum amount due from every one of these at any time during the year must be shown.

(k) Particulars of any redeemed debentures which the company has power to issue should be given.

(l) Where any of the company's debentures are held by nominee or a trustee for the company, the nominal amount of the debentures and the amount at which they are stated in the books of the company shall be stated.

(m) A statement of investments (whether shown under "Investment" or under "Current Assets" as stock-in trade) separately classifying trade investments and other investments should be annexed to the balance sheet showing the names of the bodies corporate (including separately the names of the bodies corporate under the same management) in whose shares or debentures, investments have been made (including all investments, whether existing or not, made subsequent to the date as at which the previous balance sheet was made out) and the nature and extent of the investment so made in each such body corporate; provided that in the case of an investment company, that is to say, a company whose principal business is the acquisition of shares, stock, debentures or other securities, it shall be sufficient if the statement shows only the investments existing on the date as at which the balance sheet has been made out. In regard to the investments in the capital of partnership firms, the names of the firms (with the names of all their partners, total capital and the shares of each partner), shall be given in the statement.

(n) If, in the opinion of the Board, any of the current assets, loans and advances have not a value on realisation in the ordinary course of business at least equal to the amount at which they are stated, the fact that the Board is of that opinion shall be stated.

(o) Except in the case of the first balance sheet laid before the company after the commencement of the Act, the corresponding amounts for the immediately preceding financial year for all items shown in the balance sheet shall be also given in the balance sheet. The requirement in this behalf shall, in the case of companies preparing quarterly or half-yearly accounts, etc. relate to the balance sheet for the corresponding date in the previous year.

(p) The amounts to be shown under sundry debtors shall include the amounts due in respect of goods sold or services rendered or in respect of other contractual obligations but shall not include the amounts which are in the nature of loans or advances.

(q) Current accounts with directors, managing agents, secretaries and treasurers and manager, whether they are in credit, or debit, shall be shown separately.

(r) A small-scale industrial undertaking has the same meaning as assigned to it under clause (j) of Section 3 of the Industries (Development and Regulation) Act, 1951.

B—Vertical Form

Name of the company ....
Balance Sheet as at ....

(1)	(2)	Schedule No. (3)	Figures as at the end of current financial year (4)	Figures as at the end of previous financial year (5)
I Sources of Funds				
1. Shareholders' funds				
(a) Capital			....	
(b) Reserves and surplus			....	....
2. Loan funds			....	
(a) Secured loans			....	....
(b) Unsecured loans			....	....
		TOTAL	....	....
II Application of Funds				
1. Fixed assets				
(a) Gross block			....	
(b) Less depreciation			....	....
(c) Net block			....	....
(d) Capital work-in-progress			....	....
2. Investments			....	....
3. Current assets, loans and advances				....
(a) Inventories			....	
(b) Sundry debtors			....	....
(c) Cash and bank balances			....	....
(d) Other current assets			....	....
(e) Loans and advances			....	....

Contd.

Contd.

Less			....
Current liabilities and provisions			
(a) Liabilities		....	
(b) Provisions		....	....
Net current assets		....	
4. (a) Miscellaneous expenditure to the extent not written off or adjusted		....	....
(b) Profit and loss account		....	....
TOTAL		....	....

Notes

1. Details under each of the above items shall be given in separate Schedules. The Schedules shall incorporate all the information required to be given under A—Horizontal Form read with notes containing general instruction for preparation of balance sheet.
2. The Schedules, referred to above, accounting policies and explanatory notes that may be attached shall form an integral part of the balance sheet.
3. The figures in the balance sheet may be rounded off as under:—

Where the turnover of the company in any financial year is:	Round off permissible
(i) less than one hundred crore rupees	to the nearest hundreds or thousands, or decimals thereof.
(ii) one hundred crore rupees or more but less than five hundred crore rupees	to the nearest hundreds or thousands, lakhs or million, or decimals thereo.

4. A footnote to the balance sheet may be added to show separately contingent liabilities.

PART II

Requirements as to Profit and Loss Account

1. The provisions of this Part shall apply to the income and expenditure account referred to in Sub-section (2) of Section 210 of the Act, in like manner as they apply to a profit and loss account, but subject to the modification of references as specified in that sub-section.
2. The profit and loss account–
   (a) shall be so made out as clearly to disclose the result of the working of the company during the period covered by the account; and
   (b) shall disclose every feature, incuding credits or, receipts and debits or expenses in respect of non-recurring transactions or transactions of an exceptional nature.
3. The profit and loss account shall set out the various items relating to the income and expenditure of the company arranged under the most convenient heads and in particular, shall disclose the following information in respect of the period covered by the account:—

(i) (a) The turnover, that is, the aggregate amount for which sales are effected by the company, giving the amount of sales in respect of each class of goods dealt with by the company and indicating the quantities of such sales for each class separately.

(b) Commission paid to sole selling agents within the meaning of Section 294 of the act.

(c) Commission paid to other selling agents.

(d) Brokerage and discount on sales, other than the usual trade discount.

(ii) (a) In the case of manufacturing companies—

1. The value of the raw materials consumed, giving item-wise break-up and indicating the quantities thereof. In this break-up, as far as possible, all important basic raw materials shall be shown as separate items. The intermediates or components procured from other manufacturers may, if their list is too large to be included in the break-up, be grouped under suitable headings without mentioning the quantities, provided all those items which in value individually account for 10 per cent or more of the total value of the raw material consumed shall be shown as separate and distinct items with quantities thereof in the break-up.
2. The opening and closing stocks of goods produced, giving break-up in respect of each class of goods and indicating the quantities thereof.

(b) In the case of trading companies, the purchases made and the opening and closing stocks, giving break-up in respect of each class of goods traded in by the company and indicating the quantities thereof.

(c) In the case of companies rendering or supplying services, the gross income derived from services rendered or supplied.

(d) In the case of a company, which falls under more than one of the categories mentioned in (a), (b) and (c) above, it shall be sufficient compliance with the requirements herein if the total amounts are shown in respect of the opening and closing stocks, purchases, sales and consumption of raw material with value and quantitative break-up and the gross income from services rendered is shown.

(e) In the case of other companies, the gross income derived under different heads.

Note 1—The quantities of raw materials, purchases, stocks and the turnover, shall be expressed in quantitative denomination in which these are normally purchased or sold in the market.

Note 2—For the purpose of items (ii)(a), (ii)(b), and (ii)(d), the items for which the company is holding separate industrial licences, shall be treated as separate classes of goods, but where a company has more than one industrial licence for production of the same item at different places or for expansion of the licensed capacity, the item covered by all such licences shall be treated as one class. In the case of trading companies, the imported items shall be classified in accordance with the classification adopted by the Chief Controller of Imports and Exports in granting the import licences.

Note 3—In giving the break-up of purchases, stocks and turnover, items like spare parts and accessories, the list of which is too large to be included in the break-up, may be grouped under suitable headings without quantities, provided all those items, which in value individually account for 10 per cent or more or the total value of the purchases, stocks, or turnover, as the case may be, are shown as separate and distinct items with quantities thereof in the break-up.

(iii) In the case of all concerns having works-in-progress, the amounts for which such have been completed at the commencement and at the end of the accounting period.

(iv) The amount provided for depreciation, renewals or diminution in value of fixed assets.

If such provision is not made by means of a depreciation charge, the method adopted for making such provision.

If no provision is made for depreciation, the fact that no provision has been made shall be stated and the quantum of arrears of depreciation computed in accordance with Section 205(2) of the Act shall be disclosed by way of a note.

(v) The amount of interest on the company's debentures and other fixed loans, that is to say, loans for fixed periods, stating separately the amount of interest, if any, paid or payable to the managing director, the managing agent, the secretaries and treasurers and the manager, if any.

(vi) The amount of charge for Indian incom-tax and other Indian taxation on profits, including, where practicable, with Indian income-tax any taxation imposed elsewhere to the extent of the relief, if any, from Indian income-tax and distinguishing, where practicable, between income-tax and other taxation.

(vii) The amounts reserved for—

(a) repayment of share capital and

(b) repayment of loans.

(viii) (a) The aggregate, if material, of any amounts set aside or proposed to be set aside, to reserves, but not including provisions made to meet any specific liability, contingency or commitment known to exist at the date as at which the balance sheet is made up.

(b) The aggregate, if material, of any amounts withdrawn from such reserves.

(ix) (a) The aggregate, if material, of the amounts set aside to provisions made for meeting specific liabilities, contingencies or commitments.

(b) The aggregate, if material, of the amounts withdrawn from such provisions, as no longer required.

(x) Expenditure incurred on each of the following items, separately for each item—

(a) Consumption of stores and spare parts.

(b) Power and fuel.

(c) Rent.

(d) Repairs to buildings.

(e) Repairs to machinery.

(f) (1) Salaries, wages and bonus

(2) Contribution to provident and other funds.

(3) Workmen and staff welfare expenses to the extent not adjusted from any previous provision or reserve.

Note—Information in respect of this item should also be given in the balance sheet under the relevant provision or reserve account.

(g) Insurance.

(h) Rates and taxes, excluding taxes on income.

(i) Miscellaneous expenses.

Provided that any item under which the expenses exceed 1 per cent of the total revenue of the company or Rs. 5,000, whichever is higher, shall be shown as a separate and distinct item against an account head in the profit and loss account and shall not be combined with any other item to be shown under 'Miscellaneous expenses'.

(xi) (a) The amount of income from investments, distinguishing between trade investments and other investments.

(b) Other income by way of interest, specifying the nature of the income.

(c) The amount of income-tax deducted if the gross income is stated under sub-paragraphs (a) and (b) above.

(xii) (a) Profits or losses on investments showing distinctly the extent of the profits or losses earned or incurred on account of membership of a partnership firm to the extent not adjusted from any previous provision or reserve.

Note—Information in respect of this item should also be given in the balance sheet under the relevant provision or reserve account.

(b) Profits or losses in respect of transactions of a kind, not usually undertaken by the company or undertaken in circumstances of an exceptional or non-recurring nature, if material in amount.

(c) Miscellaneous income.

(xiii) (a) Dividends from subsdiary companies.

(b) Provisions for losses of subsidiary companies.

(xiv) The aggregate amount of the dividends paid, and proposed and stating whether such amounts are subject to deduction of income-tax or not.

(xv) Amount, if material, by which any items shown in the profits and loss account are affected by any change in the basis of accounting.

4. The profit and loss account shall also contain or give by way of a note detailed information, showing seperately the following payments provided or made during the financial year to the directors (including managing directors), the managing agents, secretaries and treasurers or manager, if any, by the company, the subsidiaries of the company and any other person—

(i) managerial remuneration under Section 198 of the Act paid or payable during the financial year to the directors (including managing directors), the managing agent, secretaries and treasurers or manager, if any;

(ii) expenses reimbursed to the managing agent under Section 354;

(iii) commission or other remuneration payable separately to a managing agent or his associate under Section 356, 357 and 358;

(iv) commission received or receivable under Section 359 of the Act by the managing agent or his associate as selling or buying agent of other concerns in respect of contracts entered into by such concerns with the company;

(v) the money value of the contracts for the sale or purchase of goods and materials or supply of services, entered into by the company with the managing agent or his associate under Section 360 during the financial year;

(vi) other allowances and commission including guarantee commission (details to be given);

(vii) any other perquisites or benefits in cash or in kind (stating approximate money value where practicable;

(viii) pensions, etc.—

(a) pensions,

(b) gratuities,

(c) payments from provident funds, in excess of own subscriptions and interest thereon.

(d) compensation for loss of office.

(e) consideration in connection with retirement from office.

4A. The profit and loss account shall contain or give by way of a note a statement showing the computation of net profits in accordance with Section 349 of the Act with relevant details of the calculation of the commissions payable by way of percentage of such profits to the directors (including managing directors), the managing agents, secretaries and treasurers or manager (if any).

4B. The profit and loss account shall further contain or give by way of a note detailed information in regard to amounts paid to the author, whether as fees, expenses or otherwise for services rendered—

(a) as auditor;

(b) as adviser, or in any other capacity, in respect of:

(i) taxation matters;

(ii) company law matters;

(iii) management services; and

(c) in any other manner.

4C. In the case of manufacturing companies, the profit and loss account shall also contain, by way of a note in respect of each class of goods manufactured, detailed quantitative information in regard to the following, namely

(a) the licensed capacity (where licence is in force);

(b) the installed capacity and

(c) the actual production.

Note 1—The licensed capacity and installed capacity of the company as on the last date of the year to which the profit and loss account relates, shall be mentioned against items (a) and (b) above, respectively.

Note 2—Against item (c), the actual production in respect of the finished products meant for sale shall be mentioned. In cases where semi-processed products are also sold by the company, separate details thereof shall be given.

Note 3—For the purposes of this paragraph, the items for which the company is holding separate industrial licences shall be treated as separate classes of goods but where a company has more than one industrial licence for production of the same item at different places or for expansion of the licensed capacity, the item covered by all such licences shall be treated as one class.

4D. The profit and loss account shall also contain by way of a note the following information, namely—

(a) value of imports calculated on CIF basis by the company during the financial year in respect of (i) raw materials; (ii) components and spare parts; (iii) capital goods;

(b) expenditure in foreign currency during the financial year on account of royalty, know-how, professional consultation fees, interest, and other matters;

(c) value of all imported raw materials, spare parts and components consumed during the financial year and the value of all indigenous raw materials, spare parts and components similarly consumed and the percentage of each to the total consumption;

(d) the amount remitted during the year in foreign currencies on account of dividends with a specific mention of the number of non-resident shareholders, the number of shares held by them on which the dividends were due and the year of which the dividends related;

(e) earnings in foreign exchange classified under the following heads, namely:

(i) export of goods calculated on FOB basis;

(ii) royalty, know-how, professional and consultation fees;

(iii) interest and dividend;

(iv) other income, indicating the nature thereof.

5. The central government may direct that a company shall not be obliged to show the amount set aside to provisions other than those relating to depreciation, renewal or diminution in value of assets, if the central government is satisfied that the information should not be disclosed in the public interest and would prejudice the company, but subject to the condition that in any heading stating an amount arrived at after taking into account the amount set aside as such, the provision shall be so framed or marked as to indicate that fact.

6. (1) Except in the case of the first profit and loss account laid before the company after the commencement of the act, the corresponding amounts for the immediately preceding financial year for all items shown in the profit and loss account shall also be given in the profit and loss account.

(2) The requirement in sub-clause (1) shall, in the case of companies preparing quarterly or half-yearly accounts, relate to the profit and loss account for the period which entered on the corresponding date of the previous year.

PART III

Interpretation

7.(1) For the purposes of Parts I and II of this Schedule, unless the context otherwise requires:

(a) the expression "provision" shall, subject to Sub-clause (2) of this clause, mean any amount written off or retained by way of providing for depreciation, renewals or diminution in value of assets, or retained by way of providing for any known liability of which the amount cannot be determined with substantial accuracy;

(b) the expression "reserve" shall not, subject as aforesaid, include any amount written off or retained by way of providing for depreciation, renewals or diminution in value of assets or retained by way of providing for any known liability;

(c) the expression "capital reserve" shall not include any amount regarded as free for distribution through the profit and loss account; and the expression "revenue reserve" shall mean any reserve other than a capital reserve;

and in this sub-clause the expression "liability" shall include all liabilities in respect of expenditure contracted for and all disputed or contingent liabilities.

(2) Where—

(a) any amount written off or retained by way of providing for depreciation, renewals or diminution in value of assets, not being an amount written off in relation to fixed assets before the commencement of this Act; or

(b) any amount retained by way of providing for any known liability;

is in excess of the amount which in the opinion of the directors is reasonably necessary for the purpose, the excess shall be treated for the purposes of this Schedule as a reserve and not as a provision.

8. For the purposes aforesaid, the expression "quoted investment" means an investment in respect which there has been granted a quotation or permission to deal on a recognised stock exchange and of the expression "unquoted investment" shall be construed accordingly.

PART IV

Balance Sheet Abstract and Company's General Business Profile

I. Registration Details

Registration No.	☐☐☐☐☐	State Code	☐☐	(Refer Code List)

Balance Sheet Date	☐☐	☐☐	☐☐
	Date	Month	Year

II. Capital Raised During the Year (Amount in Rs. Thousands)

Public Issue	Right Issue
☐☐☐☐☐☐☐	☐☐☐☐☐☐☐
Bonus Issue	**Private Placement**
☐☐☐☐☐☐☐	☐☐☐☐☐☐☐

III. Position of Mobilisation and Deployment of Funds (Amount in Rs Thousands)

Total Liabilities | Total Assets

Sources of Funds

Paid-up Capital | Reserves & Surplus

Secured Loans | Unsercured Loans

Application of Funds

Net Fixed Assets | Investments

Net Current Assets | Misc. Expenditure

Accumulated Losses

IV. Performance of Company (Amount in Rs Thousands)

Turnover | Total Expenditure

+ – Profit/Loss Before Tax | + – Profit/Loss After Tax

(Please tick appropriate Box + for Profit, - for Loss)

Earning per Share in Rs | Dividend Rate %

V. General Names of Three Principal Products.Services of Company (as per monetary terms)

Item Code No. (ITC Code)

Product Description

Item Code No. (ITC Code)

Product Description

Item Code No. (ITC Code)

Product Description

Note: For ITC Code of Products please refer to the publication Indian Trade Classfication based on harmonised commodity description and coding system by Ministry of Commerce, Directorate General of Commercial Integence & Statistics, Calcutta-700 001.

Code List: State Codes

State Code	*State Name*	*State Code*	*State Name*	*State Code*	*State Name*
01	Andhra Pradesh	02	Assam	03	Bihar
04	Gujarat	05	Haryana	06	Himachal Pradesh
07	Jammu & Kashmir	08	Karnataka	09	Kerala
10	Madhya Pradesh	11	Maharashtra	12	Manipur
13	Meghalaya	14	Nagaland	15	Orissa
16	Punjab	17	Rajasthan	18	Tamil Nadu
20	Uttar Pradesh	21	West Bengal	22	Sikkim
23	Arunachal Pradesh	24	Goa	52	Andaman Islands
53	Chandigarh	54	Dadra Islands	55	Delhi
56	Daman & Diu	57	Lakshadweep	58	Mizoram
59	Pondicherry				

CHAPTER 10

Divisible Profits and Dividends

CHAPTER OUTLINE

10.1 MEANING OF DIVISIBLE PROFIT

The portion of profit, which can legally be distributed to the shareholders of the company by way of dividend, is called the 'divisible profit'.

The term 'divisible profit' has nowhere been defined in the Companies Act, neither the act states what is meant by 'profit'. Only Section 205 of the act lays down that no dividend can be declared or paid by a company except out of current profits or past undistributed profits or both, arrived at after providing for depreciation or money provided by the government for payment of dividend in pursuance of a guarantee given by the government.

10.2 MEANING OF DIVIDEND

The dictionary meaning of 'dividend' is "sum payable as interest on loan or as profit of a company to the creditors of an insolvent's estate or an individual's share of it." But in commercial usage, however, dividend is the share of the company's profit distributed among the members. So, corporate earnings and profits not retained in the business and distributed among the shareholders is known as dividend. The term 'dividend' is also used to include distribution of the company's assets, in cash or in specie, which remain with the liquidator after he has realised all the assets and discharged all the liabilities, in the event of its winding up.

In Commissioner of Income Tax vs Girdhar Das & Co. (P) Ltd. 1967 case, the Supreme Court defined the expression 'Dividend' as follows:

"As applied to a company which is a going concern, it ordinarily means the portion of the profit of the company which is allocated to the holders of shares in the company. In case of winding up, it means a division of the realised assets among creditors and contributories according to their respective rights."

Before introduction of Sub-section (14A) in Section 2 of the Companies Act, the term was not defined. At present, according to this section, dividend includes any interim dividend. This definition assumes that the term should be understood only in its commercial sense.

The Institute of Chartered Accountants of India has defined dividend in its Guidance Notes on *Terms used in Financial Statements* as "a distribution to shareholders out of profits or reserves available for this purpose".

10.3 CONCEPT OF PROFIT

The main objective of any business organisation is profit, but the term 'profit' does not have any exact meaning in the accountant's language. Profit may be defined "as the increase in the net value of assets of a business over their net value at the commencement of a given period which has arisen other than by capital adjustment".

According to the viewpoint expressed by the court in the case Spanish Prospecting Co. Ltd. (1911), "the profit of an enterprise can be ascertained by computing the market value of its net assets at two accounting dates. The increase or decrease in the net worth is the profit or loss for the intervening period".

The Institute of Chartered Accountants of India has defined 'profit' in its Guidance Notes on Terms used in Financial Statements as "the excess of revenue over related costs".

10.4 PROFIT VS DIVISIBLE PROFIT

All the profits of a company cannot be said to be divisible. Only those portions of the profit, which can be legally distributed to the shareholders of the company in the form of dividends, are called as divisible profits. A number of factors are required to be considered for the determination of divisible profit. Out of different important factors, the following four considerations govern the determination of divisible profit to a great extent:

- Accounting principles
- Provisions of the Companies Act
- Provisions of the Memorandum and Articles of Association
- Legal judgments

10.5 PRINCIPAL DETERMINANTS OF DIVISIBLE PROFIT

Several matters influence the determination of divisible profits. These arise from the provisions of law, case laws, provisions in the articles of association of the company and the principles and policies involved in the determination of true and fair amount of profit.

Section 205 of the Companies Act contains provisions relating to declaration of dividend and ascertainment of divisible profit. There are also certain provisions elsewhere in the act connected with the question of divisible profit. All these provisions are stated in the following paragraphs.

1. Profit after providing for depreciation

Dividend can be paid by a company only out of current profits and past profits remaining undistributed, both arrived at after providing for depreciation in accordance with the provisions of the Companies Act. However, the central government may, if it thinks necessary to do so in the public interest, allow any company to declare or pay dividend for any financial year out of the profits of the company for that year or any previous financial year or years without providing for depreciation.

As to how much depreciation should be provided for determining the divisible profit, Section 205(2) provides that depreciation must be provided in any of the following ways:

(a) To the extent specified in Section 350

(b) In respect of each item of depreciable asset, for such an amount as is arrived at by dividing 95% of the original cost by the specified period

(c) On any other basis approved by the central government by which 95% of the original cost of each such depreciable asset can be written off on the expiry of the specified period

(d) In respect of other depreciable assets for which no rate of depreciation has been laid down by the act or the rules made there under, on such basis as may be approved by the central government by general or special order

2. Grant by the government

Dividend can also be paid out of money made available by the central or state government for the payment of dividend in pursuance of a guarantee given by the government.

3 Arrear depreciation

If there is any arrear depreciation is respect of past years, it must be provided for out of current or past profits, before paying dividend for any financial year. In other words, where a company has not provided for depreciation for any financial year after the commencement of the Companies (Amendment) Act, 1960, this should be done before any dividend is declared. Such arrears of depreciation may be provided out of current profits or the profits of the previous financial years, remaining undistributed.

4. Past losses

Any past loss of the company must be set off against current or past profits or on both to the extent required by the Companies Act, before paying dividend for any financial year. Where a company has incurred any loss in any previous financial year or years falling after the commencement of the Companies (Amendment) Act, 1960, then the lower of the following two amounts should be set off:

- The amount of the loss
- The amount of depreciation provided for that year or those years.

The amount should be set off against the following.

(i) The profits of the company for the year for which dividends are proposed to be declared or paid, or

(ii) The profits of the company for any previous financial year or years arrived at after providing for depreciation

(iii) Both (i) and (ii) mentioned above.

5. Exemption from depreciation

The central government may in the public interest allow any company to pay dividend out of current or past profits without making provisions for depreciation.

6. Transfer of profits to reserves

The current profit of a company arrived at after providing for depreciation can be applied for the payment of dividend only after transferring to reserves such a percentage of profit not exceeding 10% as may be prescribed by the central government.

After the commencement of the Companies (Amendment) Act, 1974 a company is required to transfer a prescribed percentage of its profit to its reserves before declaring dividend. However, there is no bar on a company to voluntarily transfer a higher percentage of its profits to the reserves in accordance with such rules as may be made by the central government in this context.

Table 10.1 depicts the prescribed rates of profit to be transferred to reserve according to the Transfer to Reserve Rules, 1984 as framed by the central government:

TABLE 10.1 Prescribed rates of profit to be transferred to reserves

Rate of proposed dividend	Amount to be transferred to reserves
Exceeding 10%, but not 12.5%	Not less than 2.5% of current profit
Exceeding 12.5%, but not 15%	Not less than 5% of current profit
Exceeding 15%, but not 20%	Not less than 7.5% of current profit
Exceeding 20%	Not less than 10% of current profit

However, no amount is required to be transferred to reserves, where the rate of proposed dividend is 10% or less.

7. Dividend from reserves

Dividend can be paid out of the accumulated past profits of a company kept in reserves in accordance with the rules framed by the central government in this regard or with the previous approval of the central government: Section 328(3). Section 205(3) inserted by the Companies Act, 1974 requires that dividend can be declared out of reserves only in accordance with the rules framed by the central government in this behalf. However, where a company wishes to declare a dividend otherwise than as per these rules, it may do so with the prior approval of the central government. The credit balance, if any, showcased in the profit and loss account will be available for declaration of dividend without restriction if such balance was carried after charging depreciation, tax etc. in the previous year(s).

The rules framed by the central government in this regard provide that in the event of absence or inadequacy of profits in any year, dividend may be declared by the company out of accumulated past profits provided the following conditions are satisfied:

(a) The rate of dividend declared does not exceed the average of the rates at which dividend was declared by it in the five years immediately preceding that year or 10% of its paid-up capital, whichever is less.

(b) The total amount to be drawn from the accumulated profits earned in previous years and transferred to the reserves does not exceed an amount equal to one-tenth of the sum of its paid-up capital and free reserves and the amount so drawn must first be utilised to set off the losses incurred in the financial year before any dividend in respect of preference or equity shares is declared.

- The balance of reserves after such withdrawal does not fall below 15% of its paid-up share capital.
- The amount in no way possible should be used to pay interim dividend.

8. Distribution of profit out of capital redemption reserve account

If capital redemption reserve is created against redemption of preference shares, no dividend can be paid from this reserve in future (Section 80).

9. Premium on redemption

The premium payable on redemption of preference shares shall be provided for out of the profits of the company or out of the securities premium account (Section 80).

10. Other determining factors

(a) Provision for taxation No part of the net profit from business can be appropriated for payment of dividend without making necessary provision for taxation, as payment of income tax from business earnings is a legal obligation.

(b) Dividend out of capital profit Except securities premium, profit from forfeiture of shares and profits prior to incorporation, capital profits can be applied for payment of dividend, subject to certain conditions, which include the following:

- Such profits must be realised profits
- The Articles of Association of the company shall not contain any prohibitive provision relating to distribution of such profits as dividend and
- Such profits must remain as a surplus after revaluation of all the assets of the company.

(c) Capital losses, intangible assets and ficticious assets According to the accounting and commercial principles capital losses, intangible assets and ficticious assets should be written off from profits over a reasonable period and a company should have definite policies in respect of such writing off. Application of profit for payment of dividend can arise only after such regular annual write off.

(d) Transfer of additional profits to reserve The Directors of a company are empowered to transfer to reserves any additional amount of profit or carry forward any amount of profit, as they consider necessary, after statutory transfer of profits to reserves. Dividend can be paid only from the balance amount of profit.

10.6 COMPANIES ACT RELATING TO PAYMENT OF DIVIDEND

The provisions of the Companies Act relating to payment of dividend are as follows:

1. Dividend shall only be payable in cash. But this will not prohibit capitalisation of profits or reserves of a company for the purpose of issuing fully paid-up bonus shares or paying up any unpaid amount of shares held by the members of the company: Section 205(3).
2. Dividend payable in cash may be paid by cheque or dividend warrant. This has to be sent by post directly to the registered address of the shareholders entitled to the payment of the dividend or in the case of joint holders to the registered address of that one of the joint shareholders which is first named in the register of members or to such person and to such address as the shareholder or the joint shareholders may in writing direct: Section 205(4)(b).
3. The department of company affairs has clarified through its Circular No. 5/99 dated 12.5.1999 that dividend can also be transmitted electronically to the shareholders after obtaining their consent in this regard and asking them to nominate specific bank account number to which dividend due to them should be remitted.
4. Dividend has to be paid to the registered holder of share or to his order or to his banker. In case a share warrant has been issued in respect of the share in pursuance of Section 114, dividend shall be paid to the bearer of such warrant or to his banker Section 206.

5. Dividend has to be paid or the dividend warrant has to be posted within 30 days from the date of declaration of dividend, subject to certain exceptions: Section 205(4)(1).
6. Where a dividend has been declared by a company but has not been paid or the warrant in respect thereof has not been posted within 30 days from the date of the declaration to any shareholder entitled to the payment of the dividend, every Director of the company shall, if he is knowingly a party to default, be punishable with simple imprisonment for a term which may extend to three years and shall also be liable to a fine of Rs. 1000 for every default during which such default continues: Section 207.

   But the above provision is not applicable in the following circumstances:
   (a) Where the dividend could not be paid by reason of the operation of any law
   (b) Where a shareholder has given direction to the company regarding the payment of the dividend and those directions cannot be complied with
   (c) Where there is a dispute regarding the right to receive the dividend
   (d) Where the dividend has been lawfully adjusted by the company against any sum due to it from the shareholder
   (e) Where, for any other reason, the failure to pay the dividend or to post the warrant within the period aforesaid was not due to any default on the part of the company
7. Any dividend, when declared, the amount thereof shall have to be deposited in a separate bank account within five days of declaration. The amount of dividend deposited in a separate bank account as above shall be used for the payment of interim dividend. Section 205(1A).

10.7 COMPANIES ACT REGARDING UNPAID AND UNCLAIMED DIVIDEND

The provisions of the Companies Act regarding unpaid (unclaimed) dividend are as follows:

1. Where, after the commencement of the Companies (Amendment) Act, 1974 a dividend has been declared by a company but has not been paid or claimed within 30 days from the date of the declaration, to any shareholder entitled to the payment of the dividend, the company shall, within seven days from the date of expiry of the said period of 30 days, transfer the total amount of dividend which remains unpaid or unclaimed to a special account to be opened by the company in that behalf in any scheduled bank to be called "unpaid dividend account". Section 205A(1).
2. If the default is made in transferring the total amount referred to in Sub section (1) or any part thereof to the unpaid dividend account of the concerned company, the company shall pay from the date of such default, interest at the rate of 12% per annum and the interest accruing on such amount shall be used for the benefit of the members of the company in proportion to the amount remaining unpaid to them. Section 205A(4).

3. Any money transferred to the unpaid dividend account of a company in pursuance of this section, which remains unpaid or unclaimed for a period of seven years from the date of such transfer shall be transferred by the company to the fund known as Investors Education and Protection Fund established under Sub-section (1) of Section 205C. Section 205A(5).
4. If a company fails to comply with any of the requirements of this section, the company and every officer of the company, who is in default, shall be punishable with fine which may extend to Rs. 5000 for every day during which the failure continues. [Section 205A(8)].
5. Any person claiming to be entitled to any money transferred under Sub-section (5) of Section205A to the general revenue account of the central government may apply to the central government for an order for payment of the money claimed, and the central government may, if satisfied, whether on a certificate by the company or otherwise that such person is entitled to the whole or any part of the money claimed, make an order for the payment to that person of the sum due to him after taking such security from him as it may think fit. Section 205B.

10.8 PAYMENT OF DIVIDEND OUT OF CAPITAL PROFIT

Capital profits are those profits which arise from capital sources and not from normal trading activity of a business. Capital profits are not frequently earned in a business. These profits are earned from capital transactions and assets revaluation.

Following are the examples of capital profits:

- Profit prior to incorporation
- Premium received on the issue of shares or debentures
- Profit on forfeiture of shares and re-issue of forfeited shares
- Profit made on sale of fixed assets
- Profit on revaluation of fixed assets
- Profit on redemption of debentures at a discount

Section 205 of the Companies Act provides that dividend can only be paid out of profits. Profits can be both revenue profits and capital profits. So the Companies Act does not provide any general restriction on the distribution of capital profit as dividend. But the following capital profits are not available for distribution of dividend:

1. Premium on issue of shares

As per Section 78 of the Companies Act, premium on issue of shares is available only for certain specified purposes and not for payment of dividend.

2. Profit on re-issue of forfeited shares

As per Part I of Schedule VI of the Companies Act, the amount of profit made on forfeiture of shares has to be shown by adding to the called up share capital of the company in its balance sheet and the amount of such profit finally left after re-issue of forfeited shares has to be transferred to capital reserve.

3. Profit prior to incorporation

A company comes into legal existence only from the date of incorporation. So, the profit earned during the period when the company was not in existence can not be legally distributed as profit of the company.

4. Profit from redemption of debentures at a discount

A capital profit earned from the redemption of debentures at a discount is not available for distribution as dividend as was held in the case Wall vs London and General Provincial Trust Co. Ltd. (1930).

10.9 PAYMENT OF DIVIDEND OUT OF CAPITAL

According to the Companies Act, no dividend can be paid out of capital as it expressly provides in Section 205 that the dividend is payable only out of current profit or past undistributed profits, arrived at after providing for depreciation. Therefore, if the memorandum or the articles of association even empower the company to declare dividend out of capital, such power becomes automatically invalid. [Verner vs General and Commercial Investment Trust Ltd. (1894)]

In the following circumstances, payment of dividend may amount to payment of dividend out of capital:

1. If dividend is paid out of the sale proceeds of fixed assets
2. If profits are inflated by the following
   - Charging revenue expenditure to capital
   - Making lower provisions for depreciation or liabilities
   - Overvaluing closing stock or investments
   - Excluding revenue expenditure from accounts
   - Increasing profit by any other way
3. If a deficiency of capital exists and dividend is paid without making good such deficiency.

Payment of dividend out of capital indicates returning to the shareholders part of the paid-up share capital as dividend. The payment of dividend out of capital has the following consequences:

(a) The Directors may have a right of indemnity against the members who knowingly received dividend out of capital. But they lose that right where the directors represent that the dividend was paid out of profits (Moxham vs. Grant –1990).

(b) In the absence of suspicious circumstances, the Directors are never wrong in accepting the reports and valuation of trusted officers of the company (Kingston Cotton Mills Co. – 1896).

(c) The Directors are personally liable to make good the amount, which they have knowingly paid as dividend out of capital (London and General Bank – 1895).

(d) When the payment of dividend out of capital is subsequently made good out of profit, the Directors can escape liability (Boaler vs The Watchmakers' Alliance and others – 1903).

(e) An auditor cannot be held liable for negligence of duty for his inability to detect payment of dividend out of capital, if he has exercised reasonable skill and care and there is no suspicious circumstances for detection of deliberate enhancement of profit (Kingston Cotton Mills Co. Ltd. – 1896).

10.10 GENERAL GUIDELINES FOR DISTRIBUTION OF DIVIDEND

Following guidelines govern the distribution of profit as dividend by a company in general way :

1. Dividend can be declared and paid only if the cash position of the company is satisfactory.
2. Shareholders' capital must not be utilised for the payment of dividend.
3. A dividend should not be paid without making an adequate provision for depreciation on fixed assets.
4. Capital profits may be distributed as dividend only if the following conditions are satisfied:
   (a) The Articles of Association of the company permit such a payment
   (b) Such capital profits have been realised
   (c) The surplus remains even after the revaluation of all the other assets
5. If there is a debit balance in the profit and loss account, dividend should not be distributed.
6. If goodwill or other assets have been excessively written down in the past, the excess may be written back tŏ profit and loss account and dividend can be distributed out of such profit.
7. The company should adopt a steady dividend pay-out ratio. It need not distribute the whole of the profit amongst its shareholders as dividend.
8. Provision of the Companies Act, Income-tax Act and the decisions of significant legal cases have to be observed and complied with while declaring dividend.
9. Capital losses, intangible assets and ficticious assets should be written off over a period of time gradually to strengthen the financial position of the company.
10. The provisions of the Memorandum and Articles of Association must be complied with before distributing profit as dividend.

10.11 ARTICLES OF ASSOCIATION REGARDING DIVIDEND

The provisions of the Articles of Association of a company should also be considered before distribution of profit as dividend along with the provisions of the Companies Act. But, it may be noted in this regard that no provisions as contained in the Articles of Association superceed the provisions of the Companies Act. If a company has no articles of its own, then it has to follow the privisions as contained in Table A as a substitute of articles of association.

Regulations 85 to 94 of Table A of the Companies Act describe the provisions regarding distribution of dividend by a company, which are given below:

1. ***Clause 85*** The company in general meeting may declare dividends, but no dividend shall exceed the amount recommended by the Board of Directors.

2. ***Clause 86*** The Board may from time to time pay to the members such interim dividends as appear to be justified by the profits of the company.

3. ***Clause 88*** Subject to the rights of persons, if any, entitled to shares with special rights as to dividends, all the dividends shall be declared and paid according to the amount paid or credited as paid on the shares, in respect whereof, the dividend is paid, but if and so long as nothing is paid upon any of the shares of the company, dividends may be declared and paid according to the amounts of the shares.

All dividends shall be apportioned and paid proportionately to the amount paid or credited on the shares.

4. ***Clause 89*** The Board may deduct from any dividend payable to any member all sums of money, if any, presently payable by him to the company on account of calls etc.

5. ***Clause 91*** Any dividend, interest or other money payable in cash may be paid by cheque or warrant sent through post directed to the registered address of the shareholders.

Every such cheque or warrant shall be made payable to the order of the persons to whom it is sent.

6. ***Clause 92*** Any one of two or more joint holders of shares may give effectual receipts for any dividends or bonuses payable in respect of such shares.

7. ***Clause 93*** Notice of any dividend that may have been declared shall be given to the persons entitled to share therein in the manner mentioned in the Act.

8. ***Clause 94*** No dividend shall bear interest against the company.

10.12 AUDITOR'S DUTY AS REGARDS PAYMENT OF DIVIDEND

Once dividend is declared, it constitutes an item of liability of the business. As specified above that Regulation of Clause 85 of Table A of 1st schedule states that no dividend shall be paid in excess of the amount of dividend declared. But this does not mean that the company should pay less than what is declared. Accordingly, a company may be sued by the shareholders for such payment as was held in the case Savern vs Wye Railway Co. (1896).

The duties of an auditor in connection with the payment of dividend are as follows :

1. He should examine the documents of the company to ascertain the various rights and privileges of the various categories of the members.
2. He should also examine the minutes of both director's and shareholder's meeting regarding such payments.
3. He should verify the rate of dividend and justify the rate in the context of the amount of profit earned.
4. He should see that the unclaimed dividends have been transferred to a separate bank account.
5. He should obtain the register of members to justify whether dividend warrants have been sent to the appropriate persons.

6. He should verify the articles of association to verify the authority for such payment.
7. He should confirm that the declaration of dividend does not affect adversely the working capital position of the company.
8. He should see that the provisions of the Companies Act relating to declaration and payment of dividend (Section 205) have been duly complied with before declaration and payment of dividend.
9. He should ensure the basic principles of accounting and provisions regarding transfer of reserves have been duly adhered to while arriving at the distributable profit.
10. He should also consider the rate of interim dividend declared by the company and confirm that it has been considered in the declaration and payment of the final dividend.

10.13 PAYMENT OF INTERIM DIVIDEND AND THE ROLE OF AUDITORS

Interim dividend is a dividend which is paid in respect of a year before the declaration of the final dividend. This means that it occurs between two annual general meetings and the declaration is done by the Directors instead of the shareholders.

Sub-section (1A) of Section 205 empowers the Board of Directors of a company to declare interim dividend. Clause 86 of Table A of Schedule 1 to the Companies Act provides that the board may from time to time pay to the members such interim dividend as appeared to be justified from the profits of the company. Generally, the Articles of Association of a company gives this power to the board of directors. Till the passing of the Companies (Amendment) Act, 2000, there was no provision in the Companies Act (except Regulation 86 of Table A) relating to interim dividend. The Companies (Amendment) Act, 2000 has introduced Sub-section (14A) in Section 2 whereby 'interim dividend' is now part of dividend and accordingly all provisions of the Companies Act relating to dividends have become applicable to interim dividend also.

To put things beyond doubt, Section 205 has also been amended to provide for the following:

1. The Board of Directors may declare interim dividend and the amount of dividend including interim dividend shall be deposited in a separate bank account within five days from the date of declaration of such dividend.
2. The amount of dividend including interim dividend so deposited above shall be used for the payment of dividend including interim dividend.
3. The provisions contained in Sections 205, 205A, 205C, 206, 206A and 207, as far as may be, also apply to interim dividend.

Often an auditor's advice is sought in the matter of payment of interim dividend. Following points are required to be considered by the auditor while giving advice to the management :

1. Interim profit and loss account should be prepared, if posssible by a fair estimate of the closing stock.
2. Where the closing stock value at the end of the interim period cannot be fairly ascertained, a rough estimate of profit can be made by applying the gross profit percentage to sales and deducting from such gross profit the expenses to date.

3. All adjustments on account of bad and doubtful debts, depreciation, outstanding liability, prepaid expenses etc. should be duly made to ascertain the fair profit for the interim period.
4. The proportion of interim profit to be applied to the payment of interim dividend should always be on the conservative approach after consideration of the forecasts for the future months and the allowances required for contingencies.
5. A good cash balance should not be taken as an indicator of profit for the purpose of interim dividend. However, cash is also another decision factor.
6. Future requirement of cash for expenses, asset replacement, loan repayment and working capital requirement should be fairly estimated. A good cash position does not always justify the payment of interim dividend, as the future cash requirement for those purposes may be quite substantial.
7. It is the final dividend which has to be declared after the closing of the accounting year at a rate reasonably higher than the rate of interim dividend. Hence, it should be seen whether the company would be able to declare final dividend at a higher rate or not.

In paying interim dividend, the Directors undertake certain amount of risk, because an interim dividend is in fact a dividend in respect of the whole year and for the year if there is a loss, the payment of interim dividend will amount to payment of dividend out of capital, where there are inadequate balances of reserves and surplus.

10.14 LEGAL VIEWS AS REGARDS DIVIDEND

Case Study

1. **Case: Lee vs Neuchatel Co. Ltd. (1889)**

   Fact of the case: The Articles of Association of the company provided for the distribution of profit on preference shares and ordinary shares at the rate of 7% and 4% respectively. For that the consent of the shareholders is a must. Moreover, the Articles of Association of the company contained a clause which does not bind the directors to make reserve for replacement or renewal of any property. The Directors decided to declare dividend out of profits of the company to the preference shareholders without making good the loss of depreciation of wasting assets, i.e. mines and other assets of the company. One of the ordinary shareholders Mr. Charles John Lee brought an action against the Directors of the company restraining them to pay dividend without making good the depreciation of assets of the business.

   Legal view: It was held that the company may distribute dividend without making good the depreciation on wasting assets, if it is authorised by its Articles of Association to do so. In fact, the object of charging depreciation is for the replacement of assets, but when the wasting assets are subject to exhaustion the company is formed to go into liquidation, the question of replacement does not arise.

2. **Case: Bolton vs Natal Land and Colonisation Co. Ltd. (1892)**

   Fact of the case: The business of the company consisted of buying, selling, letting, cultivating and otherwise dealing with land in South Africa. In the year 1892, the company, under peculiar circumstances debited to its profit and loss account £ 70,000 as bad debt and credited in the same profit and loss account with an equal amount arising from revaluation in the value of land, over and above the cost price. Accordingly, the profit and loss account was balanced. Subsequently, the company earned working profit and declared dividend from the said source in respect of the arrear dividend of 1885.

   Legal view: An action was brought before the court against the company restraining it to capitalise a part of the reserve that has been created by revaluation of assets of the company. The basic reason behind such action was that the profits of the business are not realised. But it was held that surplus of capital assets resulting from bonafide revaluation of assets, even though it is unrealised, may be available for issuing bonus shares. The application of this decision cannot be made possible in India after the introduction of the Indian Companies Act, 1956.

3. **Case: Foster vs The New Trinidad Asphelte Co. Ltd. (1901)**

   Fact of the case: The company along with the assets of the other company took over a debt of £ 1,00,000 secured by promissory note, at its formation. At that time, the debt was considered valueless. Later on, the debt was paid in full together with an interest accrued amounting to £ 26,258. 16s. The directors proposed to distribute the amount as dividend as the directors treated the said amount as capital profit. But one shareholder, brought an action before the court restraining the company to pay dividend on the ground that the decrease in the value of other assets should have been considered.

   Legal view: It was held in this case that the question of what is profit available for dividend depends upon the results of the whole accounts taken fairly for the year, capital as well as profit and loss, and though dividends may be paid out of earned profits in proper cases, notwithstanding a depreciation of capital, a realised accretion to the estimated value of one item of capital asset cannot be deemed to profit divisible among the shareholders without reference to the result of the whole account fairly taken.

4. **Case: Ammonia Soda Co. Ltd. vs Arthur Chamberlain and others (1918)**

   Fact of the case: An action was brought by the company against the former two Directors, asking them to refund to the company a sum amounting to £ 1268. 14s. 4d. which was illegally paid as dividend during the years from 1912 to 1915. The company was incorporated as a private limited company in July 1908. Thereafter by a special resolution, passed in October 1911, it was converted into a public limited company. The company's profit and loss account showed a debit balance amounting to £ 19,028. 5s. 4d. The directors were entrusted to value the land, and accordingly it was valued at £ 79,166 and the addition of expenses for the innovation of new bed of rockself amounting to £ 20,542. 2s. 4d. was added to the value of land. The sum was credited to reserve account and was used to write-off the following:

   (i) The debit balance of the profit and loss account amounting to £ 12,970. 18s. 3d.

(ii) Goodwill for £ 1,500

(iii) Cash bonus for £ 1,980

And the balance £ 4,091. 4s. 5d. was transferred to reserve account. During half year ended 31.01.1912, the company made net profit of £ 7,348. 13s. and the value of the land was increased in the balance sheet to the extent of £ 16,450. 18s. 3d. and thus eliminating the credit balance for £ 4091. 4s. 5d. which was left to the credit of the reserve account. During the years 1912 to 1915 dividends amounting to £ 1,268. 14s. 4d. were paid to the preference shareholders.

Legal view: The court decided that the assets of the business may be written up as a result of bonafide revaluation and that the current profits may be divided without making good past losses of the business. But the decision of this case in no way holds good in India after the introduction of Section 205(1)(b) of the Indian Companies Act, 1956.

5. **Case: Stapley vs Red Brothers (1924)**

Fact of the case: The company had written off the balance of goodwill account £ 51,000 out of reserve. In a later year, the profit having been found inadequate for both setting off the debit balance of the profit and loss account and paying dividend on preference shares including arrear dividend, the Directors decided to write up goodwill by £ 40,000, being the conservative value of goodwill and credit the sum to reserve account which could be utilised for writing off the debit balance £ 25,500 of the profit and loss account and paying the dividend. A shareholder, thereupon, moved the court for an injunction to restrain the directors from writing back £ 40,000 which was previously written off out of reserves created from profit.

Legal view: It was held that a company could write up at a fair value the goodwill, which was written off excessively in the earlier years and utilise the sum for writing off the debit balance of the profit and loss account and distribute the current profit as dividend.

POINTS TO PONDER

- The portion of profit, which can legally be distributed to the shareholders of the company by way of dividend, is called the divisible profit.
- According to ICAI Guidance Notes dividend is a distribution to shareholders out of profits or reserves available for this purpose.
- According to ICAI Guidance Notes profit is the excess of revenue over related costs. All the profits of a company cannot be said to be divisible. Only those portions of the profit, which can be legally distributed to the shareholders of the company in the form of dividend, are called divisible profit.
- The principal determinants of divisible profit are depreciation, grant by the government, arrear depreciation, past losses, transfer of profits to reserves, cash position of the company and taxation aspect.

- Dividend shall only be payable in cash. It can be paid by cheque or dividend warrant. It has to be paid to the registered holder of share or to his order or to his banker. Dividend has to be paid within 30 days from the date of declaration of dividend and the amount shall have to be deposited in a separate bank account within 5 days of declaration.
- If dividend is unpaid or unclaimed, the company shall, within 7 days from the date of expiry of the said period of 30 days, transfer the total amount of dividend to a special account called unpaid dividend account.
- Capital profits are those profits, which arise from capital sources and not from normal trading activity of a business. Companies Act does not provide any general restriction on the distribution of capital profit as dividend. But premium on issue off shares, profit on re-issue of forfeited shares, profit prior to incorporation and profit from the redemption of debentures at a discount are not available for distribution of dividend.
- According to the Companies Act, no dividend can be paid out of capital. Payment of dividend out of capital indicates returning to the shareholders part of the paid-up share capital as dividend.
- The provisions of the Articles of Association of a company should also be considered before distribution of profit as dividend along with the provisions of the Companies Act. Regulations 85 to 94 of Table A of the Companies Act describe the provisions regarding distribution of dividend by a company.
- The auditor should see that the provisions of the Companies Act relating to declaration and payment of dividend have been duly complied with before declaration any payment of dividend.
- Interim dividend is a dividend, which is paid in respect of a year before the declaration of the final dividend. The Companies Act provides that the board from time to time pay to the members such interim dividend as appeared to be justified from the profits of the company.
- The auditor should consider the rate of interim dividend declared by the company and confirm that it has been considered in the declaration and payment of the final dividend. He should also ensure that the basic principles of accounting have been duly adhered to while arriving at the distributable profit.

REVIEW QUESTIONS

Short-answer Questions

1. What is dividend?
2. What is interim dividend? When does the question of interim dividend arise?
3. State with reasons whether you, as an auditor, would approve the payment of dividend out of capital.
4. Can dividend be paid out of current profits without writing off intangible and ficticious assets?
5. Can dividend be paid out of profit arising out of forfeited and re-issue of shares?

Essay-type Questions

1. State the provisions of the Companies Act, 1956 regarding the declaration and payment of dividend.
2. Can dividend be paid under the following circumstances:
   (a) Out of current profit without making good past losses
   (b) Out of a capital profit
   (c) Out of past profit when there is neither profit nor loss in the current year
   (d) Realised capital profits
3. State the provisions of the Companies Act, 1956 regarding declaration and payment of Interim dividend. What would be the duty of an auditor in connection with such dividend?
4. What do you understand by 'divisible profit'? State what considerations should be borne in mind before declaring dividend.
5. While examining the accounts of a company, you find the following items on credit side of profit and loss account:
   (a) Profit on revaluation of land
   (b) Bounties received from central government
   (c) Excess depreciation charged in the previous year now written back
   (d) Unclaimed dividend

   Would you have any objection as auditor in passing the accounts of the company? State with reasons.

CHAPTER 11

Audit Report and Certificate

CHAPTER OUTLINE

11.1 DEFINITION OF REPORT

A report is a statement of collected and considered facts, so drawn up as to give clear and concise information to persons who are not in possession of full facts of the subject matter of the report.

According to Joseph Lancaster, "a report is a medium of expressing an opinion to persons concerned in order to give a clear and summarised information based on collected facts and figures".

In short, a report is a statement of opinion regarding an event or series of events.

11.2 DEFINITION OF AUDIT REPORT

The document through which the auditor conveys his opinion about the fairness of the financial statements is called auditor's report. An auditor, under Section 227(2) of the Companies Act, 1956, is required to make a report to the shareholders of the company whether the books of accounts examined by him exhibit 'true and fair' view of the state of affairs of the business.

The auditor submits his report to his client giving clear and concise information of the result of audit performed by him. The fact or information contained in the auditor's report is not available from any other source. Auditor's report is the end product of his audit work. By submitting the report, the auditor completes his duty as imposed by the respective statutes.

The statutory auditor of a company has to express his professional opinion about the truth and fairness of the state of affairs of the company as shown by the balance sheet and of the profit or loss as shown by the profit and loss account in addition to several other information in his report.

An auditor's report is, therefore, a written statement of the auditor, containing his independent professional opinion about the truth and correctness of accounts and financial statements examined by him and other specific information, which the auditor submits to his client at the conclusion of audit.

11.3 VALUE OF AUDIT REPORT

The auditor's report is of great value not only to the members of the company, i.e. the shareholders, but also to those persons who are interested in the affairs of the business, i.e. investors, creditors, employees, government and other financial institutions that require the audited balance sheet and profit and loss account for the purpose of granting loans and for a number of reasons beneficial to them. The most important value of the auditor's report is reflected through its checking and verifying procedure as to accuracy and fairness of the facts and figures that appear in the books of account of the company. The audit report does not add anything more than what is inserted.

The basic purpose of audit is to secure the interest of different groups of people in the organisation. Based on the audit report, these groups of people such as shareholders, bankers, creditors etc. can decide their course of action in respect of the organisation with which they are concerned. In fact, these groups of people are all outsiders and they have no other alternatives but to rely upon the auditor's report to know the actual state of affairs of the company. So, the auditor's report is extremely important to these groups of people. It serves their interest in the following ways:

- The shareholders can have the idea from audit report about how well their company is being managed by their representatives, i.e. the Board of Directors.
- The creditors and the bankers can understand from audit report how far their loan to the business is safe and secure.
- The prospective investors and creditors can know from auditor's report whether it would be prudent to invest in the organisation.
- The management can also take various decisions for more efficient running of the organisation based on the auditor's report.
- The determination of purchase consideration in case of purchase or sale of the organisation is facilitated by the auditor's report.
- Very often the government grants and subsidies are based on the auditor's report.
- To settle insurance claim, the insurance companies generally want audited financial statements along with the auditor's report.
- The income tax authority very often depends upon the auditor's report in respect of various income tax matters.

In view of changing socio-economic conditions where the society demands more disclosure of accounting information, the auditor should insist on more disclosure by his clients to appraise the actual financial position of the business. It is a fact that the auditor makes his report on the available information supplied to him. So, his tests and examinations are confined to available information supplied to him. He has nothing to do, but to report if certain items appear suspicious to him.

11.4 ESSENTIALS OF GOOD AUDIT REPORT

The essentials of good audit report are as follows :

1. Simplicity

Simplicity should be one of the important characteristics of good audit report. It should be as clear as understandable. It implies that ambiguous terms and facts should not be included in the audit report.

2. Clarity

The term 'clarity' implies cleanness in audit report. This indicates that the audit report should not conceal material information which are required in evaluating and appraising the performance of the business.

3. Brevity

The term 'brevity' signifies the conciseness in audit report. Repetition of facts and figures should be avoided in order to control the length of the report.

4. Firmness

The report should clearly indicate the scope of work to be done and should cleary indicate whether the books of account exhibit 'true and fair' view of the state of affairs of the business.

5. Objectivity

The report should be based on objective evidence. Opinion formed on the basis of information and evidences which are not measured in terms of money should not be incorporated in the audit report.

6. Consistency

Consistency in presenting accounting information is the basis of good audit report. A good audit report should take into consideration whether consistency, as to the method of stock valuation and depreciation charges, has been adhered to.

7. Accepted principles

The audit report should be based upon the facts and figures that are kept in accordance with generally accepted accounting and auditing principles.

8. Disclosure principles

The audit report should be unbiased. It should disclose all the facts, all the truth.

9. Relevance

The report should disclose all relevant information, which are supposed to be known by the users, but are not included in the financial statements disclosures.

10. Reference to AAS

It should preferably state the auditing standards and practices adopted by the auditor while conducting audit. Such a reference in the report will assure the users that the audit has been carried out in accordance with Auditing and Assurance Standards.

11.5 SCOPE OF AUDIT REPORT

Sub-sections (2) and (3) of Section 227 of the Companies Act, 1956 provide that it is the duty of the auditor to report to the members of the company on the accounts examined by him and on the balance sheet and profit and loss account and every other document declared by the act to be part of or annexed to the balance sheet and the profit and loss account, laid before the company in general meeting during the tenure of his office, also that the report shall confirm the position, envisaged in the undermentioned manner in which the requirements are to be met.

Sub-section (2) specifically requires that the auditor should report whether in his opinion and to the best of his information and according to the explanations given to him, the said accounts give the information required by the Companies Act, 1956 in the manner so required and the balance sheet gives a true and fair view of the company's affairs at the end of the financial year and the profit and loss account gives a true and fair view of the profit and loss for the financial year.

Sub-section (3) requires that the auditor shall report on the following matters:

- Whether he has obtained all the information and explanations which to the best of his knowledge and belief were necessary for his audit
- Whether in his opinion, proper books of accounts as required by law have been kept by the company, so far as appears from his examination of those books and proper returns adequate for the purpose of his audit have been received from branches not visited by him

- Whether in his opinion, the balance sheet and the profit and loss account comply with the accounting standards referred to in Sub-section (3C) of Section 211 of the Companies Act, 1956
- Whether the company's balance sheet and profit and loss account dealt with by the report are in agreement with the books of accounts and returns
- Whether the report on the accounts of any branch office audited under Section 228 by a person other than the company's auditor has been forwarded to him as required by Section 228(3)(c) and how he has dealt with the same in preparing the auditor's report

The duty of any auditor for making a report on the statement of account also extends to matters reported upon by the Directors to the shareholders in so far as information which is required to be given by the Act in the statements of account or can be given in a statement annexed to the accounts are contained in the report of Directors (Provision in Section 222). For instance, the opinion of the Board of Directors as regards current assets, loans and advances, when contained in the Director's report, must be considered by the auditor.

11.6 SIGNING OF THE AUDIT REPORT

According to Section 229 of the Companies Act, only the person appointed as the auditor of the company or where a firm is so appointed, only a partner in the firm practising in India may sign the auditor's report.

The Department of Company Affairs, Government of India, in a communication dated 29th July, 1972 has expressed the view that when a single chartered accountant is practising, there cannot be any question of any firm name. Further, it is stated that Section 229 of the act clearly provides that if a firm of chartered accountants is appointed as auditor, only a partner in the firm may sign the auditor's report or sign or authenticate any other document required by law to be signed by the auditor. The practice of merely affixing the 'firm name' on the report or such other document is the correct approach in the eye of law.

According to Section 233 of the Companies Act, if an auditor's report or any document of the company is signed or authenticated otherwise than in conformity with the requirements of Section 229, the auditor concerned and the person, if any, other than the auditor who signs the report or signs or authenticates the document shall, if the default is wilful, be punishable with a fine which may extend upto Rs. 10,000.

According to Section 230 of the Companies Act, the auditor's report must be read before the shareholders of the company in general meeting and should be kept open for the inspection to every member of the company.

According to Section 232, it is no part of duty of the auditor either to send a copy of his report to or allow inspection thereof by each member of the company individually, or to see that the report is read before the company in general meeting. For non-compliance with any of the requirements of Section 225 to 231, the company and every officer of the company who is in default, will be liable to a fine, which may extend upto Rs. 5,000.

11.7 CONTENTS OF AUDIT REPORT

As per the provisions of Section 227 of the Companies Act, 1956 the following matters are required to be included in the auditor's report of a company:

1. Whether in his opinion and to the best of his information and according to the explanations given to him :
   (a) The accounts of the company examined by him give the information required by the Companies Act in the manner so required.
   (b) The accounts give a true and fair view of the state of company's affairs as at the end of its financial year in the case of the balance sheet.
   (c) The accounts also give a true and fair view of the profit or loss of the company for its financial year in the case of the profit and loss account.
2. Whether he has obtained all the information and explanations which to the best of his knowledge and belief were necessary for the purpose of his report.
3. Whether in his opinion, proper books of accounts as required by law have been kept by the company so far as appears from his examination of those books.
4. Whether proper returns adequate for the purpose of his audit have been received from branches not visited by him.
5. Whether the report on the accounts of any branch office audited by a person other than the main auditor of the company has been forwarded to him.
6. The method used to deal with the branch auditor's report in preparing his audit report.
7. Whether the profit and loss account and balance sheet of the company are in agreement with the books of accounts and returns.
8. Whether in his opinion the balance sheet and the profit and loss account comply with the accounting standards.
9. Where any of the matters in the auditor's report is answered in the negative or with a qualification, the reasons for such should also be stated.
10. A statement on such matters as may be specified in the central government orders. Presently the company auditors are required to make a statement on the matters specified in the CARO, 2003 issued by the central government, so far as they are applicable to a particular class of company.

11.8 COMPANIES (AUDITOR'S REPORT) ORDER, 2003

In addition to the provisions regarding Auditor's Report in Section 227 of the Companies Act, in respect of certain types of companies, the Companies (Auditor's Report) Order (CARO), 2003 issued by the central government is applicable. These orders have been issued by the central government in exercise of its power under Section 227(4A) of the Act.

The new order of 2003 has further enlarged the scope of audit of the companies replacing the previous order of 1988. The order is reproduced as follws:

Title This order may be called the Companies (Auditor's Report) Order, 2003.

Area of application It shall apply to every company including a foreign company as defined in Section 591 of the Companies Act, 1956.

It shall not apply to the following.

(a) A Banking Company as defined in Clause (C) of Section 5 of the Banking Regulation Act

(b) An Insurance Company as defined in clause (21) of Section 2 of the Act
(c) A company licensed to operate under Section 25 of the Act
(d) A private limited company with a paid up capital and reserves of not more than fifty lakh rupees and one which has not accepted any public deposit and does not have loan outstanding ten lakh rupees or more from any bank or financial institution and does not have a turnover exceeding five crore rupees

Effective date It came into force on the 1st day of July 2003.

Matters to be included in auditor's report:

1. Re: Fixed assets

(a) Records of fixed assets Whether the company is maintaining proper records showing full particualrs, including quantitative details and situation of fixed assets.

(b) Physical verification Whether these fixed assets have been physically verified by the management at reasonable intervals, whether any material discrepancies were noticed on such verification and if so, whether the same have been properly dealt with in the books of accounts.

(c) Disposal of fixed assets If a substantial part of the fixed assets have been disposed off during the year, whether it has affected the going concern.

2. Re: Stock-in-trade

(a) Regular physical verification Whether physical verification of inventory has been conducted by the management at reasonable intervals.

(b) Adequate physical verification Are the procedures of physical verification of stock followed by the management reasonable and adequate in relation to the size of the company and the nature of its business? If not, the inadequacies in such procedures should be reported.

(c) Material discrepancies Whether the company is maintaining proper records of inventory and whether any material discrepancies were noticed on physical verification of stocks as compared to book records, and if so, whether the same have been properly dealt with in the books of accounts.

3. Re: Loan obtained/granted

(a) Terms and conditions of loan Has the company either granted or taken any loans, secured and unsecured, to/from companies, firms or other parties covered in the register maintained u/s 301 of the Companies Act, 1956? If so, give the number of parties and amount involved in the transactions.

(b) Terms and conditions of loan Whether the rate of interest and other terms and conditions of loans given or taken by the company, secured or unsecured, are prima facie prejudicial to the interest of the company.

(c) Regularity Whether payment of the principal amount and interest is also regular.

(d) Recovery of loan If overdue amount is more than one lakh, whether reasonable steps have been taken by the company for recovery/payment of the principal and the interest.

4. Re: Adequacy of internal control

Is there an adequate internal control procedure commensurate with the size of the company and the nature of its business, for the purchase of inventory and fixed assets and for the sale of goods? Whether there is a continuing failure to correct major weaknesses in internal control.

5. Re: Special transactions

(a) Recording Whether transactions that need to be entered into a register in pursuance of Section 301 of the Act have been so entered.

(b) Reasonable prices Whether each of these transactions has been made at prices which are reasonable having regard to the prevailing market prices at the relevant time.

This information is required only in case of transactions exceeding the value of five lakh rupees in respect of any party and in any one financial year.

6. Re: Acceptance of deposits

In case the company has accepted deposits from the public, whether the directives issued by the Reserve Bank of India and the provisions of Sections 58A and 58AA of the Companies Act and the rules framed there under, where applicable, have been complied with. If not, the nature of contraventions should be stated.

7. Re: Internal audit system

In the case of listed companies and/or other companies having a paid up capital and reserves exceeding Rs.50 lakhs as at the commencement of the financial year concerned, or having an average annual turnover exceeding five crore rupees for a period of three consecutive financial years immediately preceding the financial year concerned, whether the company has an internal audit system commensurate with its size and nature of its business.

8. Re: Maintenance of cost records

Where maintenance of cost records has been prescribed by the central government u/s 209 (1) (d) of the Companies Act, 1956 whether such accounts and records have been made and maintained.

9. Re: Statutory obligations

(a) Provident fund and employees state insurance etc Is the company regular in depositing undisputed statutory dues including provident fund, investors' education and protection fund, employees' state insurance, income tax, sales tax, wealth tax, custom duty, excise duty, cess and any other statutory dues with the appropriate authorities? If not, the extent of arrears of outstanding statutory dues as at the last day of the financial year concerned for a period of more than six months from the date they became payable shall be indicated by the auditor.

(b) Pending disputes In case dues of sales tax/income tax/custom tax/wealth tax/ excise duty/cess have not been deposited on account of any dispute, then the amount involved and the forum where the dispute is pending may please be mentioned.

10. Re: Accumulated loss/cash loss

Whether in case of a company which has been registered for a period not less than five years, its accumulated losses at the end of the financial year are not less than fifty percent of its net worth and whether it has incurred cash losses in such financial year and in the financial year immediately preceding such financial year also.

11. Re: Default in repayment

Whether the company has defaulted in repayment of dues to financial institutions or bank or debenture holders. If yes, the period and the amount of default to be reported.

12. Re: Secured loans and advances

Whether adequate documents and records are maintained in cases where the company has granted loans and advances on the basis of security by way of pledge of shares, debentures and other securities. If not, the deficiencies to be pointed out.

13. Re: Chit fund

Whether the provisions of any special statute applicable to chit fund have been duly complied with.

14. Re: Nidhi/mutual benefit fund/societies

In respect of nidhi/mutual benefit fund/societies:

1. Whether the net-owned funds to deposit liability ratio is more than 1:20 as on the date of the balance sheet.
2. Whether the company has complied with the prudential norms on income recognition and provisioning against sub-standard/default/loss assets.
3. Whether the company has adequate procedures for appraisal of credit proposal/ request, assessment of credit needs and repayment capacity of the borrowers.
4. Whether the repayment schedule of various loans granted by the nidhi is based on the repayment capacity of the borrower and would be conducive to the recovery of the loan amount.

15. Re: Investments

If the company deals or trades in shares, securities, debentures or other investments, whether proper records of the transactions and contracts have been maintained and also whether timely entries have been made therein, whether the shares, securities, debentures, and other investments have been held by the company in its own name extent to the exemption, if any, granted under Section 49 of the Companies Act.

16. Re: Guarantee for loans

Whether the company has given any guarantee for loans taken by others from bank or financial institutions, the terms and conditions whereof are prejudicial to the interest of the company.

17. Re: Term loan

Whether term loans were applied for the purpose for which the loans were obtained.

18. Re: Uses of fund

Whether the funds raised on short-term basis have been used for long-term investment and vice versa; if yes, the nature and amount is to be indicated.

19. Re: Preferential allotment

Whether the company has made any preferential allotment of shares to parties and companies covered in the register maintained under Section 301 of the Companies Act and if so whether the price at which shares have been issued is prejudicial to the interest of the company?

20. Re: Creation of securities

Whether securities have been created in respect of debentures issued.

21. Re: Public issue

Whether the management has disclosed on the end use of money raised by public issues and the same has been verified.

22. Re: Fraud

Whether any fraud on or by the company has been noticed or reported during the year. If yes, the nature and amount involved is to be indicated.

23. Re: Reasons for qualifications

Reasons to be stated for unfavourable or unqualified answers where, in the auditor's report, the answer to any of the questions referred to above points (1 to 22) is unfavourable or qualified, the auditor's report shall also state the reasons for such unfavourable or qualified answer, as the case may be. Where the auditor is unable to express any opinion in answer to a particular question, his report shall indicate such fact together with the reasons why it is not possible for him to give an answer to such question.

11.9 FORMS OF AUDIT REPORT

International Auditing Guidelines issued by the International Federation of Accountants (first issued in 1983 and revised in 1989) provide guidance on the form and content of the auditor's report to be issued after the examinations of financial statements.

As per the guidelines, the basic elements of the report are as follows.

1. Title

An appropriate title such as 'Auditor's Report' helps the reader to identify the report and to distinguish it from reports issued by others.

2. Address

The report should be properly addressed. Like in the case of a statutory audit of a company, the report is addressed to the shareholders and in case of special audit, it is addressed to the government.

3. Identification of financial statements

The financial statements can be identified by including the name of the entity and the date and period covered by the financial statements.

4. Reference to auditing standards and practices

Such a reference ensures the compliance of the resolution of the ICAI and assures the readers that the accounting and auditing standards have been complied with.

5. Opinion on the financial statements

The report should clearly state the auditor's opinion on the financial position and operational result of the entity.

6. Signature

The report should be signed in the name of the firm or personal name of the auditor or both.

7. Address of the auditor

The report should give the address of the firm.

8. Dating of the report

It should be properly dated.

11.10 AUDIT REPORT AND AUDIT CERTIFICATE

When an auditor certifies a financial statement, it implies that the contents of the statement are reliable as the auditor has vouched the exactness of the data. The term 'certificate' is, therefore, used to mean confirmation of the truth and correctness of something after a verification of certain exact facts. An auditor may therefore, certify the circulating figures of a newspaper or the value of imports and exports of a company.

Thus, auditor's certificate confirms the correctness of the statements prepared by the client. By certifying the statements, the auditor gives guarantee about the genuineness of the statements. So, before certifying a statement, an auditor is required to be thorough and meticulous in examining the truthfulness of each and every content in it. If it is revealed subsequently that the statement certified by the auditor is not correct, he will be held responsible regardless of utmost care and skill exercised by him in checking its contents.

The term 'certificate' should not be confused with the term 'report'. A report is a statement of opinion regarding an event or series of events. So, an auditor's report is his expression of opinion regarding the fairness of financial statements in reflecting the financial result and the financial position of the organisation. The auditor only draws his conclusion about the general reliability of financial statements. He does not give guarantee in his report that the accounts are free from errors and frauds. He does not owe any responsibility while reporting on accounts, provided he exercises reasonable skill and care in his audit work.

So, while a certificate affirms the truth and correctness of a fact, figure or a statement, a report is generally a statement of facts or an expression of opinion regarding the truth and fairness of the facts, figures and statements.

11.11 TYPES OF AUDITOR'S REPORT

Auditor's report can be of the following types:

1. Clean report

An audit report is clean, when there is no qualified or adverse opinion or disclaimer of opinion in the report. A clean report indicates that the auditor is satisfied with all the points required to be stated in his report and states them in the affirmative, adding no reservation anywhere.

An auditor makes a clean or unqualified report when he is satisfied with various matters, such as follows:

- He has got reasonable evidence in support of all material transactions.
- All entries have been passed according to generally accepted accounting principles.
- The financial statements correspond to the books of accounts.
- All relevant information have been disclosed.

2. Qualified report

When an auditor expresses an opinion in his report with a reservation or states anything in the negative, but its nature is such that it does not materially affect the true and fair picture shown by the accounts, then the auditor's report is said to be a qualified report.

3. Adverse report

When the auditor expresses an adverse or negative opinion in his report about the principal point in the report for which audit is mainly intended, the report is called an adverse report. So, an adverse report is the report in which the auditor categorically states that the profit and loss account and the balance sheet do no exhibit a true and fair view of the state of affairs and working results of the concern. An adverse report should be given by the auditor, only when he has strong and convincing evidence to support his conclusion. He should disclose all the reasons of adverse report. Generally in extreme cases like excess provision for depreciation, charging fictitious expenses etc. compel the auditor to give negative or adverse report.

4. Disclaimer of opinion

When an auditor is unable to express an opinion due to certain reasons and states this in his report, it becomes a report with a disclaimer of opinion. A disclaimer of opinion is always required to be supported by the justified facts.

It may not be possible for an auditor to collect all information, which are necessary for expressing an opinion on the financial statements. Though these situations are rare, it may arise because of incomplete accounts submitted by the client or negligence on the part of the client to furnish the required information or explanations. When the auditor is to submit such inconclusive audit report because of reasons beyond his control, such report is called a report with disclaimer.

5. Piecemeal report

Auditor's opinion in his report may not be on the entire financial statements. Such opinion may relate to some of the items contained in the statements on which only he can satisfactorily express opinion after audit. Such an opinion as a part of the financial statement is a piecemeal opinion and the auditor's report containing such opinion is called a piecemeal report.

11.12 QUALIFIED AUDIT REPORT

When the auditors are satisfied with the truth and correctness of the financial statements of accounts without any qualifications, they give a clean, clear or unqualified report. In some cases, the auditor is unable to give such an opinion for one or more of a large variety of reasons. In these cases an auditor is said to give a qualified report.

When an auditor expresses his opinion in his audit report subject to some observations, he is said to have qualified his report. In other words, his assertions in the qualified report regarding fairness of financial statements depend upon some conditions. As for example, if the auditor does not agree with his client regarding treatment of an item such as grant received or provision for gratuity, he may qualify his report stating 'subject to above, we report the balance sheet shows a true and fair view----------'. While qualifying his report, the auditor should keep in his mind the materiality of the matter. Unless the amount is significant, the auditor need not qualify his report. The reasons of qualification should always be clearly stated in the report.

The principal source materials on qualified auditor's reports are:

- The Companies Act, 1956
- Auditing and Assurance Standards
- Accounting Standards

A qualified audit report is a disadvantage to a concern for several reasons.

- It has legal consequences, notably in restricting dividend payments.
- It may lead to the accounts being seen as less reliable by contact groups such as banks and other lenders and potential buyers of the business.
- It reflects badly on the Directors.

There are several types of qualifications. These include the following:

1. Limitation of scope

Limitation of scope means a limitation of scope of the auditors' work that prevents them from obtaining sufficient evidence to express an unqualified opinion. Consider the following examples:

(a) A limitation imposed on the auditor—for example, if he were not permitted to carry out an audit procedure considered necessary. The Directors may not permit a debtors' circulation or may not allow the auditor to attend a stock take.

(b) A limitation outside the control of both the auditors and the directors. Perhaps necessary records existed but have been destroyed by fire or the auditor was prevented from attending stock take by a breakdown.

2. Disagreement

It means that the auditors do not agree with the accounting treatment or disclosure of some item in the accounts. The financial statements may have an accounting policy, e.g. inclusion of overheads in finished goods stock on a global percentage of overheads to prime cost, when the auditor considers that a more complex apportionment is essential for true and fair view.

3. Material and pervasive

This term applies when the possible effect of the limitation of scope is so material or pervasive that the auditors are unable to express an opinion on the financial statements. Similarly when the matter giving rise to the disagreement is so material and pervasive that the financial statements are seriously misleading.

4. Less material

Less material means when the effect of the limitation is not so material or pervasive as to require a disclaimer. Similarly when the disagreement is not so material or pervasive as to require an adverse opinion.

5. Adverse opinion

An adverse opinion is one where the auditors state that the financial statements do not give a true and fair view.

6. Disclaimer

A disclaimer of opinion occurs when the auditors conclude that they have not been able to obtain sufficient evidence to support, and accordingly are unable to express, an opinion on the financial statements.

7. Possible adjustments

The wording of the opinion should indicate that it is qualified as to the possible adjustments to the financial statements that might have been determined to be necessary had the limitation not existed.

8. Exclusion of certain points

The opinion is qualified by stating that the financial statements give a true and fair view except for the effects of any adjustments that might have been found necessary, had the limitation not affected the evidence available to the auditors.

11.13 TYPES OF AUDIT CERTIFICATE

The professional accountants are sometimes required to issue certificates on many occasions. In fact, the types of certificates depend on the purpose for which they are intended. The major types of certificates include the following:

1. Certificate for tax computation

The chartered accountants are sometimes required to certify certain incomes and expenses for obtaining exemptions from income tax, which is computed on the basis of provisions as contained in the Income Tax Act, 1961. The forms and contents of these types of certificates are usually provided under income tax rules, as the appropriate wordings of the certificate depend on the nature and circumstances of individual cases.

2. Certificate of import and export

Import and Export Trade Control Rules and Procedures provide that the applicant applying for import or export licence must furnish a certificate of import and/or export from a qualified accountant in practice. These certificates include the value of goods imported or exported, goods consumed by the entity out of imported goods, goods supplied by the entity for export out of own source and from other sources and the unutilised value of licence on hand.

3. Certificate of circulation

The Audit Bureau of Circulations Ltd. which is an association of advertisers and publishers, gives report of circulation figures of publication of its members. The association issues circulation certificate on the basis of audit report of the member. The auditor has to certify the circulation figure on the basis that he has checked and verified the books regarding newsprint consumption, distribution and unsold stock of publications as per the guidelines issued under A.B.C. Audit Procedure.

11.14 AUDITOR'S REPORT AND 'TRUE AND FAIR VIEW'

The expression 'true and fair view' is central to auditing and yet it is an abstraction whose meaning is far from clear. In fact, the true and fair view is a Companies Act concept and is therefore a legal notion. However, neither the Companies Act nor the court has ever attempted to define it.

Investigation and discovery of anything is assisted by breaking down or classifying the thing into parts. We therefore will breakdown true and fair view into parts, beginning with true.

1. Truth

In practice the word 'true' is difficult to pin down as it also incorporates a high level of abstraction. However in accounting terms we can consider synonyms like—in accordance with fact or reality, not false or erroneous, representing the thing as it is.

Numerous accounts items can be seen in this light. For example, 'freehold land at cost Rs.2, 00,000.

It is either true or false that

- Freehold land exists
- The freehold land is the property of the company that holds a good title
- The freehold land did cost the company Rs.2, 00,000
- All the freehold land belonging to the company is included

On the other hand, the matter may not be as simple as it seems. For example,

(a) Good title may be a matter of opinion.

(b) Historical cost may be a matter of opinion—is legal cost included? Subsequent costs (drainage, fencing) may be considered capital or revenue.

A dictionary definition of true also includes 'in accordance with reason or correct principles or received standard' which brings us back to generally accepted accounting principles and the accounting standards.

2. Fair view

The word view is important in that accounts cannot give a view in an abstract way. The view given cannot be divorced from the perceptions of a reader/user of the accounts. Again, the idea of fairness involves a number of thoughts including the following:

(a) Expectation Any user has certain expectations from a set of accounts. He presumes that the accounts will conform to generally accepted accounting principles and the accounting standards.

(b) Relevance The fair view from the point of view of a user must mean that the view given by the accounts will be relevant to the informational needs of the user.

(c) Objectivity It consists of extremely verifiable facts, rather than subjectively considered opinions. In practice, as we have seen under 'truth', most accounting figures are subjective or contain a substantial subjective element.

(d) Freedom from bias The producer of accounts (directors, managers) should not allow personal preferences to enter into their accounts preparation work. For example, a desire to show a favourable profit should not influence a manager's assessment of the expected life of the fixed assets, or the saleability of stock. In practice, all human activities are influenced by personal experience and prejudice. The important thing is to be aware of this and for an auditor to be aware of the tendency to bias in all financial reporting.

3. Beyond simple conformity

The users of accounts expect accounts to conform to generally accepted accounting principles and accounting standards. However, simple rigid conformity can give a misleading view. For example, inclusion of profit from overseas branches may mislead shareholders when those profits are not available to the shareholders because of exchange control restrictions.

4. Least as good

At one time the prudence convention was so highly esteemed that shareholders and auditor's expectations went no further than making sure that the true position was at least as good as that shown by the balance sheet. Despite modern insistence on fairness up and down, the least-as-good syndrome lurks in every accountant's subconscious.

5. Accounting principles

The accounting principles and policies used should be

- in conformity with accounting standards
- generally accepted
- widely recognised and supported
- appropriate and applicable in the particular circumstances.

In most areas, more than one policy will satisfy these criteria. For example, there are several different acceptable methods for depreciation and therefore several different measures of profit, all of which may give a true and fair view.

6. Disclosure

Accounting is an aggregating and summarising process. A thousand transactions in a year can be summarised in a relatively few lines in a setting of accounts. The overall results and final position can only be appreciated by aggregating transactions and balances into suitable classes and categories. Too much aggregation can hide individual figures or subclasses that ought properly to be disclosed. On the other hand, too much disaggregation causes confusion between the wood and the trees and a general indigestibility.

7. Materiality

The elusive accounting principle of materiality is intimately bound up with the true and fair view. An item is material if its disclosure or non-disclosure would project any difference to the view received by the user of the accounts. Fairness is therefore a function of materiality.

The Companies Act, 1956 has introduced the words "true and fair" in place of the words "true and correct" as appearing in the Companies Act, 1913. This is an important change and has far-reaching effects.

The phrase "true and correct" means that the financial statements are arithmetically correct and that they correspond to the figures in the books of accounts. But it does not specifically mean that the financial statements are representing the actual state of affairs and actual working results. In fact, at present the auditor is supposed to verify whether the books of accounts show a true and fair view of the state of affairs of the company as well as the true and fair view of the financial result of the company.

The phrase "true and fair" thus signifies in the auditor's report that the financial statements are representing a fair and actual financial position of the company and profit and loss for the period. It means that the financial statements are disclosing all the relevant information as are required by various provisions of the Companies Act.

The major criticism of the phrase 'true and correct' was that in an accounting sense, there was insufficient distinction between the words 'true' and 'correct'. As such, every figure in the accounts could be justified and substantiated as both true and correct but, at the same time, the figures together could present a view to the reader of the accounts which could be misleading or even totally false when the accounts were read as a whole.

It was for this reason that the word 'fair' was used to replace 'correct', despite the inherent vagueness and absence of precision that the former word implies. The word 'fair', by definition, requires a judgement which can only be determined subjectively. This subjectivity and the related exercising of judgement provide the term with its true strength, at the same time it provides the auditor with his greatest challenge.

An auditor's assessment of whether accounts give a true and fair view, lacking as it does any legal or professional definition, necessitates a consideration of the accounts as a whole and the forming of an opinion concerning the overall impression conveyed by the accounts to the auditor and therefore to a reader. It also involves consideration of the substance of the information disclosed in the accounts as well as its form. In fact, the phrase 'true and fair' attempts to explain that accounts cannot be exact in all aspects due to the subjectivity of certain items, such as the valuation of closing stock and the provision for doubtful debts. The word 'fair' implies that the user should take an overall view of the financial statements and base interpretations on the figures as a set rather than an individual item. The word 'true' implies that the figures are decided on the facts as seen by the directors and the auditor but that other persons may draw different conclusions from the same facts. There is no attempt to make accounts precise in terms of mathematical accuracy as this is not possible due to need of estimation in certain cases. However, an attempt is made to ensure that the financial statements fairly reflect the company's result for the period and its state of affairs at the balance sheet date.

In view of this discussion, it can be stated that the concept 'true and fair' that are used in the auditor's report is not appropriate in present day dynamic and complex nature of business environment. So, it is advocated that the audit report which should be free from criticism as to nature and pattern of disclosing material information should not use these equivocal words 'true and fair'. It is expected that the Companies Act should be duly amended for taking special care in this matter.

11.15 SPECIMEN OF CLEAN AUDIT REPORT

To
The Shareholders
XYZ Co. Ltd., Kolkata
Dear Members,

I/we have audited the annexed balance sheet of XYZ Co. Ltd. as at 31st March, 200x and also the profit and loss account of the company for the year ended on that date and report that—

I/we have obtained all the information and explanations which to the best of my/our knowledge and belief were necessary for the purpose of audit.

In my/our opinion proper books of accounts as required by law have been kept by the company so far as appears from my/our examination of such books and proper returns adequate for the purpose of my/our audit have been received from the branches not visited by us.

The accounts of Chennai branch office have been adudited u/s 228 of the Companies Act by Subrata Renuka and Co. The report of the said accounts which has been forwarded to us has been dealt with by us, in the manner we have considered necessary, while preparing this report.

The balance sheet and the profit and loss account dealt with in this report are in agreement with the books of accounts.

In my/our opinion and to the best of my/our information and according to the explanations given to me/us, the said accounts, together with the notes thereon, give the information required by the act in the manner so required and give a true and fair view :

(i) In the case of the balance sheet of the state of the affairs of the company as at 31st March, 200X and

(ii) In the case of profit and loss account of the profit of the company for the year ended on that date.

For. G. G. Basu & Co.
Kolkata
Date

Chartered Accountants
Signature
B. B. Basu (Partner)

11.16 SPECIMEN OF QUALIFIED AUDIT REPORT

To
The Shareholders
ABC Co. Ltd. Mumbai
Dear Members,

We have audited the annexed balance sheet of the ABC Co. Ltd. as at 200X and also the profit and loss account for the year ended on that date. We report that—

We have obtained all the information and explanations, which to the best of our knowledge and belief were necessary for the purpose of audit.

In our opinion, proper books of accounts as required by law have been maintained by the company, kept in accordance with the accounting standards, so far as it appears from our examination of the books subject to the comments given here under:

(i) The stocks of the company have been valued at a current replacement price, which is higher than the cost price to the extent of Rs. 1,03,000.

(ii) Provisions for bad and doubtful debts has not been taken into consideration which should have been taken in view of the fact that some of the debts are quite old and time-barred.

(iii) In the absence of stock registers, adjustments relating to the balances on the register have been accepted on the basis of the decisions of the management.

The balance sheet and profit and loss account dealt with by the report are in agreement with the books of accounts and returns.

Subject to the qualifications given above, in our opinion and to the best of information available and according to the explanations given to us, the said accounts, with the notes thereon and documents attached thereto give the information required by the law and accounting standards and gives a true and fair view:

(i) in the case of the balance sheet of the state of affairs of the company as at 200x and

(ii) in the case of the profit and loss account of the profit for the year ended on that date.

Mumbai
Date

For S. K. Basu & Co.
Chartered Accountants
Signature
S. K. Basu (Partner)

11.17 LEGAL VIEWS AS REGARDS AUDIT REPORT

Case Study

1. **Case: Allen Craig & Co. (London) Ltd. (1934)**

   Fact of the Case: The company made loss in each year of its existence, and there was a deficiency of assets to meet liabilities of over £ 40,000. In submitting the accounts for the year to 30th June, 1924 the auditor sent a letter to the company drawing attention to the serious position of the company, this being quite apart from the normal audit report. In 1927, in submitting the accounts for the years to 30th June, 1925 and 1926 respectively, the auditor sent further letters, showing that there was a deficiency as regards creditors of nearly £ 11,000.

   The liquidator of the company took out a summon for misfeasance against the former managing director and the auditors asking for a declaration that such parties were liable for the debts of the company incurred after 30th June, 1925.

Legal View: It was held that the duty of the auditors, after having signed the report to be annexed to a balance sheet, is confined only to forwarding that report to the secretary of the company. It will be for the secretary or the directors of the company to convene a general meeting and send the balance sheet and report to members entitled to receive it. The auditor, in no way, will be held liable in this situation.

2. **Case: London and General Bank Ltd. (1895)**

   Fact of the Case: The company, in this case, had not made adequate provision for bad debts. The auditor had discovered that the debts were doubtful and had clearly reported the situation to the directors. But when the directors failed to make provisions, instead of reporting the fact equally clearly to the shareholders, he simply made the statement that "the value of the assets is dependent upon the realisation." It was held that the auditor had failed in his duty to convey information clearly in his report and he was made liable for certain dividend improperly paid.

   Legal view: This case underlined the dangers of equivocal statements in audit report. In the course of his judgement, Justice Lindley, L. J. said, "information 'and means of information are by no means equivalent terms. An auditor who gives shareholders means of information does so at his peril and runs the very serious risk of being held, judicially, to have failed to discharge his duty".

   It was held in this case that an auditor has a duty to convey facts clearly to shareholders. The auditor whose duty it is to convey information to others does not discharge that duty by simply giving them so much information as is calculated to induce them or some of them to ask for more.

POINTS TO PONDER

- A report is a statement of collected and considered facts, so drawn up as to give clear and concise information to persons who are not in possession of full facts of the subject matter of the report.
- An audit report is a written statement of the auditor containing his independent professional opinion about the truth and fairness of accounts and financial statements examined by him.
- The essentials of good audit report include simplicity, clarity, brevity, firmness, objectivity, consistency, relevance and reference to auditing and assurance standards.
- Only the person appointed as the auditor of the company or where a firm is so appointed, only a partner in the firm practicing in India may sign the audit report.
- In addition to the provisions regarding auditor's report in section 227 of the Companies Act, in respect of certain types of companies, The Companies (Auditor's Report) Order, 2003 issued by the central government is also applicable.
- The basic elements of the audit report are title, address, identification of financial statements, reference to the auditing standards, opinion on the financial statements, signature, address of the auditor and dating of the report.

- Audit certificate should not be confused with the audit report. Audit certificate confirms the correctness of the statements prepared by the client. But audit report is the auditor's expression of opinion regarding the fairness of the financial statements in reflecting the financial result and the financial position of the organization.
- Audit report can be basically of four types, which are clean report, qualified report, adverse report and disclaimer of opinion.
- When the auditors are satisfied with the truth and correctness of the financial statements of accounts without any qualifications, they give a clean report. In some cases, the auditors are unable to give such an opinion for one or more of a large variety of reasons. In these cases, an auditor is said to give a qualified report.
- The concept 'true and fair' view that are used in the auditor's report is not appropriate in present day dynamic and complex nature of business environment. So, the audit report, which should be free from criticism as to nature and pattern of disclosing material information, should not use these equivocal words 'true and fair'.
- The audit report is of great value not only to the shareholders of the company, but also to those persons who are interested in the affairs of the business, i.e., the employees, investors, creditors, government and other financial institutions.
- The auditor should report whether in his opinion and to the best of his information and according to the explanations given to him, the balance sheet gives a true and fair view of the company's affairs at the end of the financial year and the profit and loss account gives a true and fair view of the profit and loss for the financial year.

REVIEW QUESTIONS

Short-answer Questions

1. What do you mean by 'auditor's report'?
2. What is piecemeal report?
3. Distinguish between auditor's report and auditor's certificate.
4. Is there any difference between an adverse and a qualified report?
5. "Information and means of information are by no means equivalent terms." Explain.
6. What are the contents and format of an audit report?

Essay-type Questions

1. What is meant by Auditor's Report? Discuss the characteristics of a good audit report. What is the value of Auditor's Report ?
2. State the matters required by the Companies Act, 1956 to be stated in auditor's report to the shareholders on the accounts of a company audited by such auditor.
3. What is a Clean Report? Give a specimen of a clean report of the auditor.
4. What is a Qualified Report? Give a specimen of a qualified report of the auditor.
5. How many types of audit reports may be submitted by a company auditor and in what circumstances? Discuss briefly.

6. Under Section 227 (4A) of the Companies Act (1988), some additional information is to be given by the auditor in his report to the shareholders. State those matters.
7. What are the events that may occur after the preparation of balance sheet? Do you think that those events should be incorporated in auditor's report?

CHAPTER 12

Audit of Banks

CHAPTER OUTLINE

12.1 Introduction
12.2 An Overview of Banking Institutions in India
12.3 Legislation Relevant to Audit of Banks
12.4 Approach to Bank Audit
12.5 Stages in Audit of Banks
12.6 Audit Procedures
12.7 Advances
12.8 Income Recognition
12.9 Bank Audit Report

12.1 INTRODUCTION

A well-organised and efficient banking system is a pre-requisite for economic growth. Banks play an important role in the functioning of organised money markets. They act as a conduit for mobilising funds and channelising them for productive purposes. The Indian banking system, like the banking system in other countries, has played a significant role in the economic growth of the country. In order to meet the banking needs of various sections of the society, a large network of bank branches has been established. The volume of operations and the geographical spread of banks in India are steadily on the rise.

12.2 AN OVERVIEW OF BANKING INSTITUTIONS IN INDIA

Presently, there are four types of banking institutions in India. These are:

- Commercial banks
- Regional rural banks
- Co-operative banks
- Development banks (more commonly known as 'term-lending institutions')

Besides, the Reserve Bank of India (hereinafter referred to as RBI) acts as the central bank of the country.

Commercial banks are by far the most wide spread banking institutions in India. Typically, commercial banks provide the following major products and services.

Acceptance of deposits Acceptance of deposits from the public is one of the most important functions of a commercial bank. Commercial banks accept deposits in various forms like term deposits, savings bank deposits, current account deposits, etc.

Granting of advances This again is an important function of commercial banks. Advances granted by commercial banks take various forms such as cash credit, overdrafts, purchase or discounting of bills, term loans, etc.

Remittances Remittances involve transfer of funds from one place to another. Two of the most common modes of remittance of funds are drafts and telegraphic/mail transfers (TT/MT). Electronic funds transfer is another mode of remittance, which facilitates almost instantaneous transfer of funds between two centres electronically.

Collections The customers can lodge various instruments such as cheques, drafts, pay orders, travellers cheques, dividend and interest warrants, tax refund orders, etc. drawn in their favour and the trade bills drawn by them on their buyers with their bank for collection of the amount from the drawee. Banks also collect instruments issued by post offices, like national savings certificates, postal orders, etc.

Electronic Clearing Service (ECS) is also in vogue. ECS takes two forms: ECS credit or ECS debit.

Cash management product A derivative of the collection business, this facility is provided for expeditious transfer of funds collected by a customer at the specified centres in the country to his central account with the use of computer/satellites. It is particularly useful for large units which have their sales/collection network in a very wide geographical area.

Issuance of letters of credit and guarantees These are two important services rendered by banks to customers engaged in business, industrial and commercial activities. A letter of credit (LC) is an undertaking by a bank to the payee (the supplier of goods and/or services) to pay to him, on behalf of the applicant (the buyer) any amount up to the limit specified in the LC, provided the terms and conditions mentioned in the LC are complied with. The guarantees are required by the customers of banks for submission to the buyers of their goods/services to guarantee the performance of contractual obligations undertaken by them or satisfactory performance of goods supplied by them.

Merchant banking business Many bank branches act as collection agents for issue business for merchant bankers. The customers and the banks have to agree to the modalities of the scheme, like names of branches authorised as collecting branches, the procedure for retaining the subscription and its remittance periodically, the documents required by the customer from the collecting branches, etc.

Credit cards The processing of applications for issuance of credit cards is usually entrusted to a separate division at the central office of a bank. The dues against credit card are collected by specified branches. Most cards issued by banks are linked to one of the international credit card networks like VISA, Master or Amex.

Technology-based services Some banks have started providing internet banking services. Besides, some banks also provided remote log-in facility to their selected clients. In this facility, a terminal is provided to the customer at their work place. He is given an access code through which he can gain access to his account at the branch and if the arrangements so provide, operate his account.

Dividend/Interest/Refund warrants Many entities require facilities for distribution of funds to their shareholders and others. For this purpose, they issue warrants in favour of shareholders/others payable at designated branches of specified banks, with prior arrangements with the banks concerned. The aggregate amount of the warrants or other instruments issued is deposited by the entity with a nodal branch. The designated branches pay the warrants when presented to them.

Safe-keeping services Banks provide services for safe keeping of the scrips and valuables of customers in their vaults. A receipt is issued to the customer by the branch at the time of deposit of the items and an acknowledgement is obtained from him at the time of delivery.

Lockers This facility is provided to the customers for safe keeping of their valuables in lockers. The branch has no knowledge of the contents of the locker. Only the account holder or his authorised representative can operative on the locker.

Handling government business Banks act as agents for receipts and payments on behalf of various government departments. There are authorised branches to handle the specified type of work. Normally, a specified branch acts as a nodal branch for a particular segment of the government business within a given geographical area.

Depository participant services The depository system is meant to facilitate quick transfer of stock market securities in a dematerialised form from the seller to the buyer by using satellite connectivity. Each participatory branch has to get itself registered with a depository. The customer has to open an account with the branch, which provides the DP services.

Automated Teller Machines (ATMs) Operations on ATMs are through a card, which contains information about the cardholder in a magnetic form. The cardholder has to use the password to carry out any transaction through ATM. Earlier, ATMs were used merely as cash dispensing machines but now-a-days, other services like issue of drafts, deposit of cash and instruments, balance enquiry etc. are also being provided by many banks. ATMs may be on-site or off-site.

Exchange of notes Banks exchange mutilated notes from the public for good quality notes. These mutilated notes are periodically sent to the RBI, which gives equivalent credit to the branch concerned.

Commercial banks operating in India can be divided into two categories based on their ownership, i.e. public sector banks and private sector banks. However, irrespective of the pattern of ownership, all commercial banks in India function under the overall supervision and control of the RBI.

12.3 LEGISLATION RELEVANT TO AUDIT OF BANKS

Different acts are relevant to audit of different types of banks. An auditor should know the specific provisions of the act(s) applicable to the type of bank under audit.

Following are the important acts relevant for bank audit:

- Nationalised banks are governed by the provisions of the relevant Banking Companies (Acquisition and Transfer of Undertakings) Act, 1980. Certain provisions of the Banking Regulation Act, 1949 also apply to nationalised banks.
- Non-nationalised banking companies are governed by the provisions of the Banking Regulation Act, 1949 and those provisions of the Companies Act, 1956 which are not inconsistent with the provisions of the Banking Regulation Act, 1949.
- The Co-operative Societies Act, 1912 or the Co-operative Societies Act of the state in which they are situated, as well as part V of the Banking Regulation Act, 1949, governs co-operative banks.
- The Regional Rural Banks Act, 1976, governs regional rural banks. The provisions of the State Bank of India Act, 1955 and State Bank of India (Subsidiary Banks) Act, 1959 apply to State Bank of India and its subsidiaries respectively. Certain specified provisions of the Banking Regulation Act, 1949 are also applicable to regional rural banks as well as to State Bank of India and its subsidiaries.

Besides the above, the provisions of the Reserve Bank of India Act, 1934 also affect the functioning of banks. This Act gives wide powers to the Reserve Bank of India to give directions to banks.

12.3.1 Legal Provisions Relating to Accounts

Section 29 of the Banking Regulation Act deals with the obligations of banks regarding maintenance of accounts and preparation of financial statements. According to the provisions of this section-

- Every bank has to prepare a balance sheet and a profit and loss account as on March 31st every year in the forms set out in the Third Schedule to the Act or as near thereto as the circumstances admit.
- The financial statements of banks are to be signed by the manager or the principal officer and by at least three directors.
- In case of banking companies, the provisions of the Companies Act, 1956 relating to financial statements are also applicable to the extent they are not inconsistent with the requirements of the Banking Regulation Act, 1949.
- As per the Third Schedule to the Banking Regulation Act, the balance sheet of a bank is to be prepared in vertical form and assets and liabilities will be classified as in the following manner.

TABLE 12.1 Classification of assets and liabilities

Capital and liabilities	*Assets*
Capital Reserves and surplus	Cash and balances with RBI Balances with banks and money at call and short notice
Deposits	Investments
Borrowings	Advances
Other liabilities and Provisions	Fixed assets
	Other assets

- Contingent liabilities and bills for collection are also to be disclosed.
- The profit and loss account is also required to be prepared in vertical form and it will show the main items of income (interest earned and other income), expenditure (interest expended, operating expenses and provisions) and appropriations.

Apart from the requirements of the Third Schedule to the Banking Regulation Act, 1949 the financial statements of a bank have to include additional disclosures required by Reserve Bank of India from time to time. The RBI has issued detailed notes and instructions for compilation of balance sheet and profit and loss account of banks. These notes and instructions are very useful to the auditor.

Legal Provisions Relating to Audit

The legal provisions relating to bank auditors are as follows:

Appointment of auditors

The auditor of a bank has to be a person who is duly qualified under law to be an auditor of a company. So, Section 226 of the Companies Act applies in case of appointment of auditor of a bank. Previous approval of RBI is required for appointment of auditor of a bank. The following are the appointing authorities of auditors of banks:

TABLE 12.2 Appointing authorities of auditors for banks

Bank	*Appointing authority*
Nationalised Banks	Board of Directors
Banking Companies	Shareholders in AGM
State Bank of India	RBI in consultation with Central government
Subsidiaries of State Bank of India	State Bank of India
Regional Rural Banks	Concerned bank with the approval of central government

A detailed procedure is followed for appointment of central auditors as well as branch auditors of nationalised banks including State Bank of India and its subsidiaries. Each nationalised bank usually appoints four to six statutory central auditors and one auditor for each of its branches.

Procedure of appointment

Central statutory auditors The statutory central auditors are appointed by the bank concerned on the basis of the names recommended by RBI from out of a panel of auditors. The RBI formulates required norms on the basis of which a panel is prepared by the Comptroller and Auditor General of India.

Branch auditors For the appointment of branch auditors in case of nationalised banks including State Bank of India and its subsidiaries, RBI maintains a panel which is prepared by ICAI. ICAI invites applications for this purpose for empanelment. On the basis of these applications, ICAI prepares and sends the panel to RBI.

The remuneration of statutory central auditors as well as branch auditors is fixed on the basis of certain norms laid down by RBI.

Rights and liabilities of auditors

The auditor of a bank has the same rights and liabilities as those of a company auditor with the following exceptions.

Re: Right The rights and powers of the auditors of a co-operative bank are governed by the relevant Co-operative Societies Act.

Re: Liabilities If a person, in any return, balance sheet or other document, wilfully and knowingly makes a statement, which is false in any material particular or wilfully omits to make a material statement, he is liable for punishment with imprisonment for a term which may extend to three years and is also liable to fine under Section 46 of the Banking Regulation Act.

Special audit

In addition to the normal audit, a special audit of a bank can be ordered by RBI under Section 30 (1B) of the Banking Regulation Act. If the RBI is of the opinion that it is necessary to do so in public interest or in the interest of the bank or its depositors, it can give the order for special audit.

For conducting the special audit, RBI may either appoint any person who is qualified to act as a company auditor or direct the statutory auditor of the bank to conduct the special audit.

12.4 APPROACH TO BANK AUDIT

Banks have the following characteristics, which distinguish them from most other commercial enterprises.

Rigorous internal control system They have custody of large volumes of monetary items, including cash and negotiable instruments, whose physical security has to be ensured. This applies to both the storage and the transfer of monetary items and makes banks vulnerable to misappropriation and fraud. They, therefore, need to establish formal operating procedures, well-defined limits for individual discretion and rigorous systems of internal control.

Complex accounting system They engage in a large volume a variety of transactions in terms of both number and value. This necessarily requires complex accounting and internal check system.

Greater decentralisation of authority They normally operate through a wide network of branches and departments, which are geographically dispersed. This necessarily involves a greater decentralisation of authority and dispersal of accounting and control functions, with consequent difficulties in maintaining uniform operating practices and accounting systems, particularly when the branch network transcends national boundaries.

Off-balance-sheet items They often assume significant commitments without any transfer of funds. These items, commonly called ' off-balance-sheet' items, may not involve accounting entries and, consequently, the failure to record such items may be difficult to detect.

Regulatory requirements They are regulated by governmental authorities and the resultant regulatory requirements often influence accounting and auditing practices in the banking sector.

Special audit considerations arise in the audit of banks because of the following:

1. ***Risk attachment*** The particular nature of risk associated with the transactions undertaken by banks.

2. ***Scale of banking operation*** The scale of banking operations and the resultant significant exposures, which can arise within short periods of time.

3. ***Statutory requirement effect*** The continuing development of new services and banking practices, which may not be matched by the concurrent development of accounting principles and auditing practices.

The auditor should consider the effect of the above factors in designing his audit approach.

12.5 STAGES IN AUDIT OF BANKS

As in the cases of any other audit, the audit of banks involves the following stages:

- Preliminary work
- Evaluation of internal control system
- Preparation of audit programme for substantive testing and its execution
- Preparation and submission of audit report

12.5.1 Preliminary Work

AAS 20. Knowledge of business requires that in performing an audit of financial statements, the auditor should have or obtain knowledge of the business sufficient to enable the auditor to identify and understand the events, transactions and practices that in the auditors judgment, may have a significant effect on the financial statements or on the examination or audit report. The auditor's level of knowledge for an engagement would include a general knowledge of the economy and the industry within which the entity operates, and a more particular knowledge of how the entity operates. Knowledge of the business provides a frame of reference within which the auditor exercises professional judgment and assists him in assessing risks and identifying problems, planning and performing the audit effectively and efficiently, and evaluating the audit evidence.

The auditor should accordingly acquire a knowledge of the regulatory environment in which the bank operates. Thus, the auditor should familiarise himself with the relevant provisions of applicable law(s). He should be well acquainted with the provisions of the Banking Regulation Act, 1949, as well as any other applicable law(s) (e.g. Companies Act, 1956 in the case of audit of a banking company) particularly in so far as they relate to preparation and presentation of financial statements and their audit. The auditor should also have an understanding of the various guidelines issued by the RBI in so far as such guidelines have a bearing on his work.

The auditor should also acquire knowledge of the economic environment in which the bank operates. Similarly, the auditor needs to acquire good working knowledge of the services offered by the bank. In acquiring such knowledge, the auditor needs to be aware of the many variations in the basic deposit, loans and treasury services that are offered and continue to be developed by banks in response to market conditions. To do so, the auditor needs to understand the nature of services rendered through instruments such as letters of credit, acceptance, forward contracts, and other similar instruments. A bank's lone portfolio may have large concentration of credit to highly specialised industries, e.g. hire purchase and leasing, software, infrastructure etc. Evaluating the nature of these may require knowledge of the business and reporting practices of those industries. Besides, there are a number of risks associated with banking activities, which, though not unique to banking, are sufficiently important in that they serve to shape banking operations. An understanding of the nature of these risks may help the auditor in perceiving the risk inherent in different aspects of a bank's operations and thus assist him in determining the degree of reliance on internal control and the nature, timing and extent of his other audit procedures.

The auditor should also obtain an understanding of the accounting system of the bank and the terminology used by the bank to describe various types of transactions and operations. Most banks have well-designed accounting and procedures manual which can serve as an important source of information on these aspects.

In the case of joint auditors, it would be preferable that each joint auditor also obtains a general understanding of the books and records, etc. relating to the work of other joint auditors.

In addition to the above, the auditor should also undertake the following:

- Review relevant instructions issued by the bank, particularly those relating to closing of annual accounts. These instructions contain standardised accounting procedure required to be followed at head office, at regional offices, zonal offices and branches.
- Review the audit report for the previous year including the long term audit report. In case of branch auditors, the audit report on the financial statements of the branch for the previous year or for the audit last conducted should be reviewed. The purpose of this review is to understand the nature of observations/comments made on the financial statements and for enquiring into the follow-up action taken on matters contained in such report.
- Review the revenue audit reports, internal audit reports, inspection reports and concurrent audit reports pertaining to the bank/branch, as the case may be.

The above review would help the auditor in gaining an understanding of the nature and volume of operations and the structure of assets and liabilities of the bank/branch as also of the nature of adverse feature observed in the past.

12.5.2 Evaluation of Internal Control System

Internal control evaluation is an important element of audit process. In the case of audit of banks, it assumes even greater importance due to the enormous volume of transactions entered into by banks. Evaluation of design and operation of internal control system enables the bank auditors to perform more effective audits. The auditor should, therefore, study and evaluate the design and operation of internal controls. This would assist him in determining the nature, timing and extent of substantive procedures in various areas, depending upon whether the internal controls are adequate and observed in practice.

12.5.3 Preparation of Audit Programme for Substantive Testing and Its Execution

Having familiarised himself with the requirements of audit, the auditor should prepare an audit programme for substantive testing which should adequately cover the scope of his work. In framing the audit programme, due weightage should be given by the auditor to areas where, in his view, there are weaknesses in the internal controls. The audit programme for central auditors would be different from that of the branch auditors. At the branch level, basic banking operations are to be covered by the audit. On the other hand, the central auditors have to deal with consolidation of branch returns (both audited and unaudited), investments and items normally dealt with at the head office.

The auditor should ensure that the work is executed in accordance with the audit programme by persons having the requisite skills and competence.

12.5.4 Preparation and Submission of Audit Report

The audit report is the end product of the audit. It is through the medium of the audit report that the auditor conveys his observations/comments on the financial statements. The form and content of the audit report should be determined by the auditor taking into account his terms of engagement and applicable statutory, regulatory and professional requirements.

12.6 AUDIT PROCEDURES

Banking is a dynamic activity, which has constantly been undergoing changes. In recent years particularly there has been a perceptible change in the nature, volume and spread of transactions of banks. Apart from a significant increase in the volume of transactions of banks, the non-traditional functions of banks, e.g. investment, merchant banking, foreign exchange activities etc. have acquired a considerable significance during this period. The auditors of bank should familiarise themselves thoroughly with the changes in operations of banks as also changes in environment having an effect on bank's activities. They should adopt audit techniques and procedures that respond effectively to the changes in circumstances. Apart from verifying the assets and liabilities, the auditors should also apply appropriate audit techniques to those transactions, which have material impact on the financial statements of banks. Thus, apart from verification of year-end balances, the auditors should also evaluate the effectiveness of design and operation of internal controls, review the follow-up action on weaknesses pointed out in reports of internal auditors, concurrent auditor etc. carryout a selective verification of transactions which have taken place during the year, and apply appropriate analytical procedures in forming their opinion. For example, apart from verification of year-end cash balance, an auditor may also look into any abnormal pattern of cash holdings at the branch. Similarly, in respect of advances, he may examine whether the account is being conducted regularly, whether interest is being paid as per schedule, and so on. While verifying income, the auditor may compare the yield on advances with the corresponding figures for the previous year. The auditor may also compare the first half-yearly results with the second half-yearly results. It may, however, be emphasised that the exact nature, timing and extent of audit tests to be performed is a matter of professional judgment of the auditor.

It may be emphasised that it is the duty of an auditor to exercise reasonable skill, care and caution in examining whether the financial statements present a true and fair view, including whether they reflect the substance of various transactions and not merely their legal form. An auditor has to exercise reasonable care and skill but he need not proceed with suspicion unless the circumstances are such as to arise suspicion or ought to arise suspicion in a professional man of reasonable competence.

An important issue relating to the audit procedures that the auditor should perform when he encounters circumstances that cause him to suspect, or when he determines, that a fraud has occurred, e.g. when the auditor becomes aware of certain frauds on going through the vigilance reports. Reference to the management note on nature of frauds committed during the year or in the immediately preceding year in the bank would also be of help to branch auditor while conducting the audit.

The RBI has wide powers to control advances by banks and to give directions to banks. In exercise of these powers, the RBI issues, from time to time, directions to banks on accounting and operational matters. These directions relate to a wide range of functions of banks, from interest rate structure to treatment and/or disclosure of specific items in balance sheet and profit and loss account of banks. Considering the specific duties of statutory auditors of banks as laid down in the relevant legislation, they cannot be expected to examine compliance with all the directions. However, as a part of their audit, they should examine compliance with those directions of the Reserve Bank of India, which have a direct and material effect on the balance sheet or profit and loss account of a bank. In this regard, it may be noted that the Board of Directors of each bank also monitors compliance with the directions of the RBI. As such, a reference to the minutes of board meetings may be useful to the auditor.

It should, however, be recognised that even where the statutory auditor of a bank examines and reports on compliance with the directions of the RBI as aforesaid, he is not bound by these directions in forming his opinion about the true and fair view of the financial statements of the bank. The responsibility for forming and expressing an opinion on the financial statements is that of the statutory auditor. He should, therefore, exercise his professional judgment in forming an opinion, which is appropriate in the facts and circumstances of the particular case.

12.7 ADVANCES

In a bank branch, advances usually constitute the maximum amount of assets. Normally banks sanction advances against security of tangible assets. The bank may also require that the borrower should furnish guarantees of third parties for repayment of the advances. In some cases, the banks also grant advances without any security.

12.7.1 Legal Provisions Regarding Advances

According to the Banking Regulation Act, certain restrictions are imposed against the granting of advances by the banks. These are the following:

Section-20

A bank cannot make any loans or advances on the security of its own share. A bank is also not permitted to enter into any commitment for granting any loan or advance to or on behalf of the following.

(a) Any of its directors

(b) Any firm in which any of its directors is interested as a partner, manager, employee or guarantor

(c) Any company (except its own subsidiary or a company registered under section 25 of the Companies Act, 1956 or a government company) of which, or of a subsidiary of the holding company of which, any of its directors is a director, manager, employee or guarantor or in which he holds substantial interest

(d) Any individual in respect of whom any of its directors is a partner or guarantor

Section-20A

A bank is prohibited from remitting the whole or any part of the debts due to it by certain persons (any director of the bank, any firm or company in which any such director is a director, partner or guarantor, and any individual of whom any director of the bank is a partner or guarantor) without the prior approval of RBI.

Section-21

The RBI has the power to determine the policy in relation to advances to be followed by banks generally, or by any bank in particular and can give directions to bank regarding the purposes for which advances may or may not be given, the margins to be maintained, maximum amount of advances to any one party, the rate of interest and other terms and conditions of advances.

12.7.2 Prudential Norms of RBI Relating to Advances

The RBI has prescribed the prudential norms relating to advances classification on the basis of record of recovery, creation of provision for doubtful advances and timing of recognition of income on doubtful advances. The important features of these norms can be stated as follows:

Classification of advances

Advances are to be classified into two broad categories, standard advances and non-performing Advances.

A **standard advance** is an advance, which does not disclose any problems and does not carry more than the normal risk attached to the banking business.

A **non-performing advance** is an advance other than a standard advance. Non-performing advances are to be further classified into three sub-categories—sub-standard advances, doubtful advances and loss advances.

A **sub-standard advance** is one, which has been classified as NPA (non-performing assets) for a period not exceeding 12 months.

A **doubtful advance** is one, which has remained in the sub-standard category for 12 months.

A **loss advance** is one, which has been identified by the bank or by its internal or external auditors or by RBI inspection but the amount has not been written off.

When advances become NPA

Once an advance is classified as NPA, adequate provision against the same has to be created. In addition to that income from such advances has not to be recognised until realised. Following norms have been prescribed to determine when an advance will become NPA.

1. ***Term loans*** A term loan account should be identified as NPA if interest and/or any instalment of principal remain overdue for a period of more than 90 days. This is applicable for all term loans except agricultural advances.

2. ***Cash credits and overdrafts*** A cash credit or overdraft account should be treated as NPA if it remains out of order. Cash credit or overdraft account becomes out of order in the following circumstances:

(a) If the outstanding balance in the principal operating account remains continuously in excess of the sanctioned limit for 90 days as on the date of the balance sheet.

(b) Though the outstanding balance is less than the sanctioned limit, there are no credits continuously for 90 days as on the date of the balance sheet.

(c) The credits are not enough to cover the interest debited during the same period.

3. ***Bills purchased/discounted*** A bill purchased/discounted should be treated as NPA if the bill remains overdue for a period of more than 90 days.

4. ***Agricultural advances*** A loan granted for short duration crops is to be treated as NPA, if the instalment of principal and/or interest thereon remains overdue for two crop seasons.

A loan granted for long duration crops (longer than one year) will be treated as NPA if the instalment of principal and/or interest thereon remains overdue for one crop season.

5. *Other accounts* Credit facilities other than those mentioned above should be treated as NPA if any amount in respect of such a facility will remain overdue for a period of more than 90 days.

Provision for non-performing advances:

The banks are required to make provisions against sub-standard advances, doubtful advances and loss advances. The norms in this regard are as follows.

1. *Loss advances* The entire advances should be written off. If the advances are permitted to remain in the books for any reason, 100% of the outstanding should be provided for.

2. *Doubtful advances* Provision has to be made for unsecured as well as secured portion as follows:

(a) 100% to the extent to which the advance is not covered by the realisable value of the security to which the bank has valid recourse and the realisable value of which is estimated on a realistic basis should be provided for.

(b) Provision in respect of the secured portion should be made as follows:

TABLE 12.3 Provision for doubtful advances

Period for which the advance has been considered as doubtful	*Percentage of provision*
Up to one year	20
One to three years	30
More than three years	
a) Outstanding stock of NPA as on March 31, 2004	60 with effect from March 31, 2005 75 with effect from March 31, 2006 100 with effect from March 31, 2007
b) Advances classified as doubtful-more than three years on or after April 1, 2004	100 with effect from March 31, 2005

3. *Sub-standard advances* A general provision of 10% of the total outstanding should be made. The unsecured exposures, which are identified, as sub-standard would attract additional provision of 10%, i.e. a total of 20% on the outstanding balance.

4. *Standard advances* A general provision of a minimum of 0.25 % should be made on standard advances on global loan portfolio basis. However, the provisions on standard advances should not be deducted for arriving at net NPA.

Provision for bad and doubtful debts

The central auditor should examine the adequacy of provisions in respect of each of the categories under which advances are shown in the balance sheet of a bank. In evaluating such adequacy, the auditor should specifically consider the guidelines issued by the RBI in this regard. The norms prescribed by the RBI provide a uniform and objective manner of determining the required provision.

According to the Guidance Note on bank audit issued by ICAI, these norms should be considered as the minimum quantum of provision and if the situation demands a higher provision in the context of the threats to recovery, such higher provision should be made. So, the norms regarding the provisions for doubtful debts as prescribed by the RBI do not influence the judgment of the auditor regarding the risks of non-recovery of advances and also the amount of provision required. The provisions of the Banking Regulation Act also support the necessity of auditor's judgment regarding provision for doubtful debts. According to Section 15 of the said Act, the provision for doubtful debts is to be made to the satisfaction of auditors in the context of payment of dividends.

12.8 INCOME RECOGNITION

In line with the international practices and as per the recommendations made by the committee on the financial system, the RBI has introduced, in a phased manner, prudential norms of income recognition of the banks so as to move towards greater consistency and transparency in the published accounts.

The basis of income recognition in case of bank can be summarised in the following way:

12.8.1 Income from Advances

In respect of advances against term deposits, National Savings Certificates eligible for surrender, Indira Vikas Patras, Kisan Vikas Patras and life insurance policies, interest may be recognised on due dates even when any amount in respect of such advances is overdue for the prescribed period. However, this interest can only be recognised if there is adequate margin available in the account.

Fees and commissions earned by the bank as a result of re-negotiation or rescheduling of outstanding advances should be recognised on an accrual basis over the period of time covered by the re-negotiated or rescheduled period of credit.

12.8.2 Income from Non-performing Assets

Interest, fee, commission etc. pertaining to non-performing assets should not be recognised in the profit and loss account unless the same has been realised. Interest realised on a non-performing asset may be taken to the profit and loss account if the credits in the accounts towards interest are not out of fresh/additional credit facilities sanctioned to the borrower concerned.

If any advance becomes NPA as at the close of any year, the amount of fees, interest, commission etc. credited to the profit and loss account in the corresponding financial year should be reversed or provided for, if the same has not been realised. In the case of assets given on finance lease, the finance charge component of finance income which was accrued and credited to income account in the last accounting year before the asset became non-performing but which remains, should be reversed or provided for in the current accounting period.

Banks are permitted to debit interest to an NPA account and take the same interest to suspense account or to maintain only a record of such interest in pro-forma account.

The bank should adopt a uniform and consistent policy regarding appropriation of partial recoveries in NPAs towards interest due and principal where there is no clear agreement between the bank and the borrower in this aspect.

12.9 BANK AUDIT REPORT

The bank auditor has to make his report directly to the bank. The contents of the auditor's report in the case of different types of banks are somewhat different. The report of the auditor of a nationalised bank is to be verified, signed and transmitted to the central government. The auditor has also to forward a copy of the audit report to the bank concerned and to the RBI.

In addition to the matters, which the auditor is required to state in his report under the Companies Act, the auditor of a bank has also to state the following in his report:

1. In case of banking companies the auditor should include in his report the following:
   (a) Whether or not the information and explanations required by him have been found to be satisfactory.
   (b) Whether or not the transactions of the company which have come to the notice have been within the powers of the company.
   (c) Whether or not the returns received from branches of the company have been found adequate for the purposes of his audit.
   (d) Whether the profit and loss account shows a true balance of profit or loss for the period covered by such account.
   (e) Any other matter, which he considers should be brought to the notice of the shareholders of the company.
2. In case of nationalised banks the auditor of a nationalised bank, State Bank of India or its subsidiary, is required to report to the central government and has to state the following in his report:
   (a) Whether in his opinion the balance sheet is a full and fair balance sheet containing all the necessary particulars and is properly drawn up so as to exhibit a true and fair view of the affairs of the bank and in case he had called for any explanation of information, whether it has been given and whether it is satisfactory.
   (b) Whether or not the transactions of the bank, which has come to his notice, have been within the powers of the bank.
   (c) Whether or not the returns received from the offices and branches of the bank have been found adequate for the purpose of his audit.
   (d) Whether the profit and loss account shows a true balance of profit or loss for the period covered by such account.
   (e) Any other matter, which he considers should be brought to the notice of the central government.

12.9.1 Long Form Audit Report (LFAR)

Apart from the audit report on the financial statements, the auditor of a nationalised bank, State Bank of India and any of its subsidiaries or a banking company including a foreign bank has also to prepare a Long Form Audit Report (LFAR).

The LFAR highlights certain important aspects of the working of a bank and its branches. Guidance notes issued by ICAI on audit of banks also deals with LFAR. In case of branches, the auditors have to answer a detailed questionnaire formulated by the RBI.

Where any of the comments made by the auditor in his LFAR is adverse, he should consider whether a qualification in his main report is necessary. It should not however be assumed that every adverse comment in the LFAR would necessarily result in a qualification in the main report. In deciding whether a qualification in the main report is necessary, the auditor should use his judgments in the facts and circumstances of each case.

The various important aspects of long form audit report as recommended by the institute's guidance note are discussed as follows:

1. ASSETS

(a) Cash The auditor should report on major and persistent deviations from the norms fixed by the controlling authority for the balances of cash held at the branch. The auditors are also required to verify whether all excess balances have been reported to the controlling authorities by the branch as per the required norms and within the specified time frame.

The auditor should examine the adequacy of the insurance cover for cash in hand and cash in transit with reference to the cash balances generally carried by the branch. He should also enquire whether the insurance policy is in force. Where the bank has obtained a global insurance policy in respect of cash in hand and cash in transit at all branches, the auditor should report this fact.

Each branch is generally required to maintain records showing details of key and the key-holders. The auditor should ascertain whether instruction of the controlling authority in this regard have been complied with by the branch.

The auditors have to verify whether the procedure prescribed by the controlling authorities has been followed in relation to checking of cash balances at periodic intervals by the branch.

In the normal course, cash balances are expected to be verified on a daily basis and recorded in the cash book both in figures and in words under the signature of the branch manager and another authorised signatory, since cash is generally under dual charge at the branch level.

A general scrutiny should be made on the cash book to ascertain whether, in accordance with the instruction, cash has been physically verified and agrees with the books maintained, with due authentication of such balances by the authorised signatories in the relevant books.

(b) Balances with RBI, SBI and other banks The auditor should insist on production of bank confirmation certificates as a part of his audit procedure. He should mention the name of the banks and the year-end outstanding balances, which remain unconfirmed by the other banks.

The auditor should scrutinise the reconciliation statements and report his observations, stating the extent of major transaction of the nature specified in the questionnaire.

The auditor should obtain the details of old outstanding balances and examine whether any such balance has remained unexplained/unadjusted. Such details need to be furnished in the LFAR, giving the break-up as outstanding between six months and one year, one year and above.

Where any of the items of a material amount appearing in the reconciliation statements remain unresponded/unadjusted for an unreasonably long period, the auditor should state in respect of such item, the nature, amount and the period for which it has remained unresponded/unadjusted.

(c) Money at call and short notice

(i) The auditor should examine the balances held at the branch in the above account with reference to general or specific authority from the controlling authority.

(ii) He should also examine whether the instructions/guidelines laid down by the controlling authority in this regard have been complied with.

(d) Investments

For branches in India:

(i) The auditor should ensure physical verification of investments held by the branch on behalf of the head office/other branches. Where any of such investment is not made available to the auditor for physical verification, the auditor should report the nature and amount of the relevant investments.

(ii) The auditor should ensure that income received on investments held by the branch on behalf of the head office/other branch is promptly reported to the head office/other branch.

(iii) The auditor should verify that income received/accrued on investment held by it on behalf of head office is recognised as income of the branch only if specific instructions are received from the controlling authorities of the bank in this regard. The auditor should report cases where income is accrued/received and recognised as income of the branch contrary to the instructions of the controlling authorities of the bank.

The auditor should verify the cases where investments have been matured or overdue and have not been encashed. The auditor should report the nature, amount, maturity date and reasons for which the overdue investments are not encashed.

The auditor in his audit procedure has to verify whether the guidelines relating to transaction in securities have been complied. If any deviation is observed, the same has to be reported with details.

The auditor should enquire the mode of valuation of investments followed by the branch and examine whether it is following the guidelines issued by the RBI. The auditor should also obtain from the branch management a statement showing the basis of valuation of investments and state such valuation in his report.

For branches outside India:

The audit procedure should ensure physical verification of investments available with the branch, including those held by it on behalf of head office/other branches. Where any of such investment is not made available to the auditor for physical verification and there is no certificate/acknowledgement of its having being deposited/lodged with another office/branch etc. the auditor should report the nature and amount of the relevant investments.

The auditor should enquire into the mode of valuation of investments followed by the branch and examine whether it is consistent with the practice as laid down by the relevant regulatory authority of the country in which the branch is located. In case of any deviation, the auditor should report this fact stating the nature of deviation, basis of valuation and amount of relevant investments.

The auditor should verify the cases where investments have matured or are overdue but have not been encashed. The auditor should report the nature, amount, maturity date and reason for which the overdue investments have not been encashed.

(e) Advances

Advances should be examined as follows:

- The auditor should check all large advances and test check other advances to ascertain whether the branch has complied with the instructions and/or the procedure prescribed by the head office regarding preparation of proposals for grant/review/renewal of advances, enhancement of limits etc. In this regard, the auditor should also examine whether the procedure adopted for preparation of the proposals is such that the proposals are recommended after due consideration of all the relevant factors like latest financial statements, past dealings, repayment capacity etc. of the parties.
- The auditor should examine the documents prescribing the limits of advances, e.g. operations manual, circular from the head office etc. where, in the course of examination of advances, the auditor comes across any cases of credit facilities sanctioned beyond the aforesaid limits, he should state this fact. He should also examine whether such cases have been reported to higher authorities as per the procedure laid down in this behalf. If not, he should report the fact along with the relevant details.
- The auditor should scrutinise the documents executed in respect of the advances examined by him. In case the auditor comes across cases where credit facilities have been realised by the branch without execution of all the documents, he should state this fact giving details of relevant cases.
- The auditor should verify that the advances given against lien of deposits have been properly granted by making lien on deposit and in accordance with the guidelines prescribed by the controlling authority.
- The auditor should ascertain whether there is a system of intimating the borrower well in advance of the due date for review and for obtaining the latest financial statements and other supporting papers required for review. The auditor should also examine whether there is a system of recording any adverse features in the operation of the account experienced by the branch or observed by internal auditors, inspectors etc. in the review note. He should analyse and report the accounts overdue for review/renewal for classification between six months and one year and over one year.
- The auditor should ascertain whether stock/book debt statements, quarterly information statements and other periodic operational data and financial statements etc. are received from the borrowers on a regular and timely basis. He should also ascertain whether effective system of scrutiny of such statements, data etc. exists.
- The auditors in the course of audit should verify whether there is any system of obtaining stock audit report periodically and branch has complied with such system. In case of non-compliance of the system, the auditor should report the same.

- The auditor should ascertain from the branch management, cases of advances where limits have been granted or renewed beyond the stipulated limit and list out the names of the borrowers and the year-end outstanding balances where the borrowers have not furnished their audited accounts and auditor's reports prior to the sanction/renewal of the limits.
- The auditor should obtain from the branch management a statement of inspections due and inspections actually made. The auditor should also scrutinise the relevant inspection reports.
- In case of lease finance activities, the auditor should ascertain whether the guidelines prescribed by the controlling authority of the bank relating to security creation, asset inspection, insurance etc. are complied with. The auditor should also ascertain that the branch has complied with the accounting norms prescribed by the controlling authorities of the bank relating to leasing activities. The auditor may also note that Accounting Standard- 19 on "Leases" issued by the ICAI is considered by the controlling authorities in the accounting guidelines prescribed by it. Any adverse comment, if any should be reported.
- The auditor in the course of his audit should verify whether credit card dues are recovered promptly and proper action has been taken by the branch in the cases where the dues are not recovered.
- The auditor should generally examine whether the advances have been promptly classified in accordance with the guidelines. If the auditor does not agree with the classification of advances by the branch, the details of such advances with reasons should be incorporated/suggested with suitable changes in the memorandum of changes.
- The auditor should obtain from the branch management a list of cases where legal action for recovery of any advances or recalling of advances was authorised by the board. The auditor should also examine previous reports in this regard. Cases where action was required to be taken by the branch management pursuant to authorisation/directions of the board but has not been taken by the branch management for an unduly long period of time, should be pointed out.
- The auditor is required to examine and report whether the branch has been submitting promptly the information regarding non-performing assets to the controlling authority as per the procedure laid down in this behalf.
- The auditor should ascertain the procedure for identifying accounts, which has become doubtful for recovery. He should then examine whether appropriate steps were initiated and the claims lodged. In addition, the auditor should also obtain a year-wise break up of outstanding claims from the management to determine the recoverability of the same.
- The auditor should ensure that the securities charged to the bank in case of non-performing assets are valued by approved valuers at least once in three years and consider such value whilst arriving at the provisioning figure in respect of doubtful and loss assets.
- The auditor should verify the cases of compromise/settlement and write-off during the year. The auditor should ensure that the branch has complied with the recovery policy prescribed by the controlling authorities. If any adverse feature has been

observed by the auditor such as acting beyond the delegated authority of the branch etc. the same should be reported.

(f) Other assets Other assets include the following:

(i) Stationery and stamps: Auditing of stationery and stamps include the following steps:

- The branch auditor should familiarise himself with the internal control system for issue and custody of stationery comprising security paper. Since misuse of unissued security paper or unsystematic issue thereof may lead to adverse consequences for the bank.
- If the auditor comes across the cases of missing/lost items of stationery, it should be reported with the details of missing/lost items of stationery.

(ii) Suspense accounts/Sundry assets: The auditor should obtain from the branch management, details of old outstanding entries in suspense or other similar accounts as at the year end. The auditor should also ascertain from the branch management the reasons for delay in adjusting the outstanding entries. The auditor may review the steps being taken by the branch management for clearing outstanding entries.

Where, in the course of audit, the auditor comes across unusual items in the suspense or other similar accounts, he should report the details of such items, indicating their nature and the amounts involved.

2. Liabilities

(a) Deposits The auditor while scrutinising deposit accounts should confirm whether the controlling authority has prescribed any guidelines with respect to conduct and operations of inoperative accounts. If yes, then he should ascertain whether the branch has followed the same. In cases, where the guidelines are not being followed, details of the deposits should be given.

In cut-off procedure, if the auditor notices any unusual large movements in the aggregate deposits held at the year end, the auditor should obtain suitable clarifications from the management for the same and verify the same.

(b) Other liabilities The auditor should obtain from the management and check the list of old outstanding items comprised in bills payable account, sundry deposits accounts etc. The number and aggregate amount of items outstanding for over three years should be reported. Where, in the course of audit, the auditor comes across any unusual items in the bills payable, sundry deposits or other similar accounts, he should report the details of such items, indicating their nature and the amounts involved.

(c) Contingent liabilities In respect of contingent liability, the auditor is primarily concerned with seeking reasonable assurance that all contingent liabilities are identified and properly disclosed.

To this end, the auditor should, generally follow the audit procedure given as follows:

(i) Ascertain whether there are adequate internal controls to ensure that transactions giving rise to contingent liability are executed by persons authorised to do so and in accordance with the laid down procedures.

(ii) Ascertain whether the accounting system of the bank provides for maintenance of adequate records in respect of such obligations and whether the internal controls ensure that the contingent liabilities are properly identified and recorded.

(iii) Perform substantive audit tests to establish the completeness of the recorded obligations. Such tests include confirmation procedures as well as examination of relevant records in appropriate cases.

(iv) Review the reasonableness of the year-end amount of contingent liabilities in the light of previous experience and knowledge of current year's activity.

(v) Obtain representation from the management that all contingent liabilities have been disclosed and that the disclosed contingent liabilities do not include any contingencies which are likely to result in a loss and which, therefore, require consequent adjustments of assets and liabilities.

3. Profit and loss account

While reporting significant discrepancies in his main report, the branch auditor should elaborate the same in the LFAR. Where the auditor finds discrepancies in recording of interest/discount incomes in a large number of cases, he should also assess their effect on his planned audit procedures.

The auditor may refer to the instructions regarding charging of interest on non-performing advances as may have been issued by the controlling authorities.

The auditor should verify that the adjustments of the discrepancies have been done in accordance with the guidelines laid down by the controlling authority. Where the auditor finds discrepancies in recording of interest on deposits in a large number of cases, he should also assess their effect on his planned audit procedures.

The auditor should perform a systematic verification of the overdue deposits. He should check whether the branch estimates and provides interest on overdue/ matured term deposits. If yes, the auditor may assess the overall reasonableness of the figures of interest expense on overdue deposits by working out the ratio of interest on different types of deposits to the average quantum of respective liabilities during the year. The auditor may then compare this rate with the actual rate of interest provided on the relevant deposits as per the financial statements and enquire into the difference, if material. The auditor may also compare the average rate of interest paid on the relevant deposits with the corresponding figures for the previous year and analyse any material differences.

The auditor should request the management to co-relate the interest and other income to the relevant aggregate of average advances and make a comparison of the figures for the year under audit with those of the earlier years and explain any divergent trends noticed between the figures upon co-relation thereof.

4. General

(a) Books and records

In case books of accounts are maintained manually: If the auditor has any observations as to the books of accounts maintained manually not having been properly maintained, he should point out in the LFAR the relevant defects, specifying the books of accounts in respect of which he has noticed these defects.

The branch auditor should carry out a general scrutiny of the books and report if they are mutilated, torn or otherwise destroyed. He should also examine whether overwriting, cutting or rubbing of the figures or alteration of books of accounts without proper authentication, is a regular feature.

In case of computerised branches:

- The auditor should verify whether the hard copies of the accounts have been printed regularly, as changes are not traceable in soft copies.
- The auditor should report the extent of computerisation and the areas of operation covered.
- The auditor should check whether there exists a proper security system.
- The auditor should verify whether any contingency and disaster recovery plans are in place for loss/encryption of data. In case no plans are in place, it should be reported.

(b) Reconciliation of control and subsidiary records The auditor is expected to list out the heads of account and indicate the balances as per the general ledger control account and those as per the subsidiary records. Where the subsidiary records have not been balanced or are incomplete, the relevant particulars should be reported indicating the dates up to which the control and subsidiary records are balanced.

(c) Inter-branch accounts The auditor should ensure the following:

- The auditor should verify that the branch forwards on a daily basis to the designated cell/head office, a statement of debit/credit transaction in relation to other branches. If it is not forwarding, the auditor should report the same with illustrative list of days on which the statement is not forwarded.
- The auditor should verify that the balance in the head office account is shown in the statements sent by the branch on a daily basis and as at the year end are in agreement with the head office account in the general ledger. If these are not in agreement, the auditor should report the difference with the reasons.
- The auditor should obtain the outstanding debit balance in the head office account in respect of inter-branch transactions with the details thereof.
- The auditor should in case of unmatched transaction verify whether the branch expeditiously comply with/respond to the communications from the designated cell/head office to reconcile the items. If at the year end there are any unresponded/uncomplied queries or communication, he should report the same in the LFAR with details thereof.
- In case of transaction for which double responses have been received in the head office account, the auditor has to report the same with details thereof.
- The auditor should verify and report any old/large outstanding debit entries lying in the branch adjustments as at the year end, which remain unexplained.

(d) Audits/Inspections

- The auditor should see whether the branch is covered for concurrent audit or any other audit/inspection during the year. If such audit/inspection has not been conducted the same should be reported.
- The auditor should make a written request to the branch management for furnishing him the latest available reports of the statutory auditors and of the concurrent audit or stock audit or internal audit, as also of the RBI where inspection or special audit has taken place for the branch. The auditor should scrutinise the contents of such

reports and take a note of relevant major adverse comments. In case adverse features are observed to persist at the branch or where no remedial action has been initiated or taken by the branch management, he should report the same.

Frauds:

- The auditor is expected to report on major frauds discovered and recorded by the bank.
- In case the auditor observes weaknesses in the internal control system, which has resulted in frauds, or where the modus operandi is common, he may give his suggestions for overcoming such weaknesses.

Miscellaneous:

- Where the auditor's examination indicates possibility of window dressing, he should report the fact of possibility of window dressing along with a general description of the nature of relevant transactions and the amounts involved.
- The auditor should verify that the branch maintains records of all fixed assets acquired and held by it irrespective of whether the values thereof or depreciation thereon have been centralised. The documents of title if available with the branch, should be verified and in case these are not available evidence from the management should be taken.

Besides covering specific issues in response to the questions in the questionnaire, the branch auditor may report on other significant areas, which, in his opinion, deserve to be highlighted in his report.

POINTS TO PONDER

- A well-organised and efficient banking system is a pre-requisite for economic growth. The Indian banking system has played a significant role in the economic growth of the country.
- Presently, there are four types of banking institutions in India. These include commercial banks, regional rural banks, co-operative banks and development banks. Besides, the Reserve Bank of India acts as the central bank of the country.
- Different acts are relevant to audit of different types of banks. Important acts for bank audit includes the Banking Companies Act, 1980, the Banking Regulation Act, 1949, the Co-operative Societies Act, 1912, the Regional Rural Banks Act, 1976 and the State Bank of India Act, 1955. Besides, the provisions of the Reserve Bank of India Act, 1934 also effect the functioning of the banks.
- Every bank has to prepare a balance sheet and a profit and loss account as on March 31st every year in the forms set out in the Third Schedule to the Banking Regulation Act. Apart from the requirements of the third schedule of the above act, the financial statements of a bank have to include additional disclosures required by Reserve Bank of India from time to time.
- The auditor of a bank has to be a person who is duly qualified under law to be an auditor of a company. A detailed procedure is followed for appointment of central auditors as

well as branch auditors of nationalised banks including State Bank of India and its subsidiaries.

- Banks have the special characteristics, which distinguish them from other commercial enterprises. These include rigorous internal control system, complex accounting system, greater decentralisation of authority off-balance items and regularity requirements.
- As in the cases of any other audit, the audit of banks involves a number of stages which include preliminary work, evaluation of internal control system, preparation of audit programme for substantive testing and its execution and preparation and submission of audit report.
- In a bank branch, advances usually constitute the maximum amount of assets. According to the Banking Regulation Act, certain restrictions are imposed against the granting of advances by the banks.
- The RBI has prescribed the prudential norms relating to advances classification on the basis of record of recovery, creation of provision for doubtful advances and timing of recognition of income on doubtful advances.
- Advances are to be classified into two broad categories, standard advances and non-performing advances. Non-performing advances include sub-standard advances, doubtful advances and loss advances.
- The bank auditor has to make his report directly to the bank. The report of the auditor of a nationalised bank is to be verified, signed and transmitted to the central government. The auditor has also to forward a copy of the audit report to the bank concerned and to the RBI.
- Apart from the audit report on the financial statements, the auditor of a nationalised bank, State Bank of India and any of its subsidiaries or a banking company including a foreign bank has also to prepare a long-form audit report.

REVIEW QUESTIONS

Short-answer Questions

1. What is long-form audit report?
2. How is an auditor of banking company appointed?
3. What are the acts relevant for bank audit?
4. What do you mean by special audit in case of bank?
5. What are the rights and liabilities of a bank auditor?
6. What are the different types of advances of a bank according to RBI prudential norms?
7. When does an advance become NPA?
8. "Verification of advances is an important function of an auditor of a bank." Explain.
9. "In the case of a bank only a balance sheet audit is carried out." Justify.
10. Explain in brief the specific problems, which the auditor has to look into in every bank.

Essay-type Questions

1. State, in brief, the contents of an audit report of a bank.
2. Describe the prudential norms of RBI relating to advances.
3. State, in brief, the relevant legal provisions in case of audit of banks.
4. Describe the main features of internal check suitable for a bank.
5. State the special features of a bank audit.
6. Discuss the different stages of conducting bank audit.
7. State the legal requirements of making provisions for non-performing assets.
8. State the duties of a bank auditor in writing long form audit report in respect of the following aspects:
    - Cash
    - Investments
    - Advances
    - Deposits
    - Contingent liabilities
    - Books and records
    - Inter-branch accounts
    - Audit and inspection
    - Frauds
    - Stamps and stationeries.
9. State the practices that should be followed by the bank in respect to the following:
   i) Provision for doubtful debts and ii) Income recognition.
10. Discuss briefly important areas you will review as an auditor in conducting the audit of a bank.

ANNEXURE

The Third Schedule to the Banking Regulation Act, 1949

FORM 'A'

Form of Balance Sheet

Balance Sheet of .... (here, enter name of the banking company)

Balance Sheet as on 31st March_(Year)

(000's omitted)

	Schedule	As on 31.3._ (current year)	As on 31.3._ (previous year)
Capital & Liabilities			
Capital	1		
Reserves & Surplus	2		
Deposits	3		
Borrowings	4		
Other liabilities and provisions	5	....	....
Total		....	....
Assets			
Cash and Balances with Reserve Bank of India	6		
Balances with banks and money at call and short notice	7		
Investments	8		
Advances	9		
Fixed assets	10		
Other assets	11	....	....
Total		....	....
Contingent liabilities	12		
Bills for collection			

Schedule 1—Capital

	As on 31.3._ (current year)	As on 31.3._ (previous year)
I. For Nationalised Banks		
Capital (Fully owned by Central Government)		
II. For Banks incorporated outside India		
Capital (The amount brought in by banks by way of start-up capital as prescribed by RBI should be shown under this head.)		
Amount of deposit kept with RBI under sub-section 2 of section 11 of the Banking Regulation, Act, 1949	....	....
Total	....	....
III. For Other Banks		
Authorised Capital		
(.... Shares of Rs. .... each)		
Issued Capital		
(.... Shares of Rs. .... each)		
Subscribed Capital		
(.... Shares of Rs. .... each)		
Called-up Capital		
(.... Shares of Rs. .... each)		
Less: Calls unpaid		
Add: Forfeited shares	....	....

Schedule 2—Reserves & Surplus

	As on 31.3._ (current year)	As on 31.3._ (previous year)
I. Statutory Reserves		
Opening Balance		
Additions during the year		
Deductions during the year		
II. Capital Reserves		
Opening Balance		
Additions during the year		
Deductions during the year		
III. Share Premium		
Opening Balance		
Additions during the year		
Deductions during the year		
IV. Revenue and other Reserves		
Opening Balance		
Additions during the year		
Deductions during the year		
V. Balance in Profit and Loss Account	....	....
Total (I, II, III, IV and V)	....	....

Schedule 3—Deposits

	As on 31.3._ (current year)	As on 31.3._ (previous year)
A. I. Demand Deposits		
(i) From banks		
(ii) From others		
II. Savings Banks Deposits		
III. Term Deposits		
(i) From banks		
(ii) From others	....	....
Total (I, II and III)	....	....
B. (i) Deposits of branches in India		
(ii) Deposits of branches outside India	....	....
Total	....	....

Schedule 4—Borrowings

	As on 31.3._ (current year)	As on 31.3._ (previous year)
I. Borrowings in India		
(i) Reserve Bank in India		
(ii) Other banks		
(iii) Other institutions and agencies		
II. Borrowings outside India	....	....
Total (I & II)	....	....
Secured borrowings included in I & II above—Rs		

Schedule 5—Other Liabilities and Provisions

	As on 31.3._ (current year)	As on 31.3._ (previous year)
I. Bills payable		
II. Inter-office adjustments (net)		
III. Interest accrued		
IV. Others (including provisions)		
Total	....	....

Schedule 6—Cash and Balances with Reserve Bank of India

	As on 31.3._ (current year)	As on 31.3._ (previous year)
I. **Cash in hand** (including foreign currency notes)		
II. Balances with Reserve Bank of India		
(i) in Current Account		
(ii) in other Accounts		
Total (I & II)	....	....

Schedule 7—Balances with Banks and Money at Call & Short Notice

	As on 31.3._ (current year)	As on 31.3._ (previous year)
I. In India		
(i) Balances with banks		
(a) in Current accounts		
(b) in other Deposit accounts		
(ii) Money at call and short notice		
(a) with banks		
(b) with other institutions	....	....
Total (i & ii)	....	....
II. Outside India		
(i) in Current accounts		
(ii) in other Deposit accounts		
(iii) Money at call and short notice	....	....
Total (i, ii & iii)	....	....
Grand Total (I & II)	....	....

Schedule 8—Investments

	As on 31.3._ (current year)	As on 31.3._ (previous year)
I. Investments in India in		
(i) Government securities		
(ii) Other approved securities		
(iii) Shares		
(iv) Debentures and Bonds		
(v) Subsidiaries and/or joint ventures		
(vi) Others (to be specified)	....	....
Total	....	....
II. Investments outside India in		
(i) Government securities (including local authorities)		
(ii) Subsidiaries and/or joint ventures abroad		
(iii) Other investments (to be specified)	....	....
Total	....	....
Grand Total (I & II)	....	....

Schedule 9—Advances

	As on 31.3._ (current year)	As on 31.3._ (previous year)
A. (i) Bills purchased and discounted		
(ii) Cash credits, overdrafts and loans repayable on demand		
(iii) Term loans	....	....
Total	....	....
B. (i) Secured by tangible assets		
(ii) Covered by Bank/Government Guarantees		
(iii) Unsecured	....	....
Total	....	....
C.I Advances in India		
(i) Priority sectors		
(ii) Public sector		
(iii) Banks		
(iv) Others	....	....
Total	....	....
C.II Advances outside India		
(i) Due from banks		
(ii) Due from others		
(a) Bills purchased and discounted		
(b) Syndicated loans		
(c) Others	....	....
Total	....	....
Grand Total (C.I. & C.II)	....	....

Schedule 10—Fixed Assets

	As on 31.3._ (previous year)	As on 31.3._ (current year)
I. Premises		
At cost as on 31st March of the preceding year		
Additions during the year		
Deductions during the year		
Depreciation to date		
II. Other Fixed Assets (including furniture and fixtures)		
At costs as on 31st March of the preceding year		
Additions during the year		
Deductions during the year		
Depreciation to date	....	....
Total (I & II)	....	....

Schedule 11—Other Assets

	As on 31.3._ (current year)	As on 31.3._ (previous year)
I. Inter-office adjustments (net)		
II. Interest accrued		
III. Tax paid in advance/tax deducted at source		
IV. Stationery and stamps		
V. Non-banking assets acquired in satisfaction of claims		
VI. Others*	....	....
Total	....	....

*In case there is any unadjusted balance of loss the same may be shown under this item with appropriate foot-note.

Schedule 12—Contingent Liabilities

	As on 31.3._ (previous year)	As on 31.3._ (current year)
I. Claims against the bank not acknowledged as debts		
II. Liability for party paid investments		
III. Liability on account of outstanding forward exchange contracts		
IV. Guarantees given on behalf of constituents		
(a) In India		
(b) Outside India		
V. Acceptances, endorsements and other obligations		
VI. Other items for which the bank is contigently liable		
Total	....	....

FORM 'B'

Form of Profit & Loss Account for the Year Ended 31st March_(Year)

(000's omitted)

	Schedule	*Year ended 31.3._ (current year)*	*Year ended 31.3._ (previous year)*
I. Income			
Interest earned	13		
Other income	14	....	....
Total		....	....
II. Expenditure			
Interest expended	15		
Operating expenses	16		
Provisions and contihencies		....	....
Total		....	....
III. Appropriations			
Net profit/loos (–) for the year			
Profit/loss (–) brought forward		....	....
Total		....	....
Transfer to statutory reserves			
Transfer to other reserves			
Transfer to Government/Proposed dividend			
Balance carried over to balance sheet		....	....
Total		....	....

Schedule 13—Interest Earned

	Year ended 31.3._ (current year)	*Year ended 31.3._ (previous year)*
I. Interest/discount on advances/bills		
II. Income on investments		
III. Interest on balances with Reserves Bank of India and other inter-bank funds		
IV. Others		
Total	....	....

Schedule 14—Other Income

	Year ended 31.3._ (current year)	Year ended 31.3._ (previous year)
I. Commision, exchange and brokerage		
II. Profit on sale of investments		
Less: Loss on sale of investments		
III. Profit on revaluation on investments		
Less: Loss on revaluation of investments		
IV. Profit on sale of land, buildings and other assets		
V. Profit on exchange transactions		
Less: Loss on exchange transactions		
VI. Income earned by way of dividends etc. from subsidiaries, company and/or joint ventures abroad/in India		
VII. Miscellaneous income		
Total	....	....

Note: Under items II to V, loans figures may be shown in brackets.

Schedule 15—Interest Expended

	Year ended 31.3._ (current year)	Year ended 31.3._ (previous year)
I. Interest on deposits		
II. Interest on Reserve Bank of India/inter-bank borrowings.		
III. Others		
Total		

Schedule 16—Operating Expenses

	Year ended 31.3._ (current year)	Year ended 31.3._ (previous year)
I. Payments to and provisions for employees		
II. Rent, taxes and lighting		
III. Printing and stationery		
IV. Advertisement and publicity		
V. Depreciation on bank's property		
VI. Directors' fees, allowances and expenses		
VII. Auditors' fees and expenses (including branch auditor' fees and expenses)		
VIII. Law charges		
IX. Postage, telegrams, telephones, etc.		
X. Repairs and maintenance		
XI. Insurance		
XII. Other expenditure		
Total		

NOTES AND INSTRUCTIONS FOR COMPILATION OF AND ADDITIONAL DISCLOSURES IN FINANCIAL STATEMENTS OF BANKS

PART A

Notes and Instructions for Compilation

Vide its circular DBOD. No.BP.BC.78/C.686/1991-92 dated February 6, 1992, RBI issued detailed notes and instructions for compilation of the balance sheet and profit and loss account of banks in the formats prescribed in the Third Schedule to the Banking Regulation Act, 1949. Since then, RBI has issued a number of further instructions through its various circulars. A compilation of the these notes and instructions is given below.

General Instructions

1. The formats of Balance Sheet and Profit and Loss Account cover all items likely to appear in these statements. In case a bank does not have any particular item to report, it may be omitted from the formats.
2. Corresponding comparative figures for the previous year are to be disclosed as indicated in the formats. The words 'current year' and 'previous year' used in the formats are only to indicate the order of presentation and may not appear in the balance sheet.
3. Figures should be rounded off to the nearest thousand rupees. Thus a sum of Rs 19,75,821.20 will appear in the balance sheet as Rs 19,76.
4. Unless otherwise indicated, the term 'bank/s' in the these statement will include banking companies, nationalised banks, State Bank of India, associate banks and all other institutions including co-operatives carrying on the business of banking, whether or not incorporated or operating in India.
5. The Hindi version of the balance sheet will be a part of the annual report.

Balance Sheet

Item	*Notes and instruction for compilation*
Schedule 1—Capital **Nationalised Banks** Capital (Fully owned by Central Government)	The capital owned by Central Governmetn as on the date of the Balance Sheet including contribution from Government, if any, for participating in World Bank Projects should be shown.
Banking companies incorporated outside India	(i) The amount brought in by banks by way of start-up capital as prescribed by RBI should be shown under this head. (ii) The amount of deposit kept with RBI, under Sub-section 2 of Section 11 of the Banking Regulation Act, 1949 should also be shown.
Other Banks (India) Authorised Capital (..... Shares of Rs .... each) Issued Capital (..... Shares of Rs .... each) Subscribed Capital	Authorised, Issued, Subscribed, Called-up capital should be given separately. Calls-in-appears will be deducted from Called-up capital while the paid-up value of forfeited shares should be added thus arriving at the paid-up capital. Where necessary, items which can be combined should be shown under one head, for instance 'Issued and Subscribed Capital'.

(..... Shares of Rs .... each) Called-up Capital (..... Shares of Rs .... each) Less: Calls unpaid Add: Forfeited shares Paid up Capital	*Notes—General* The changes in the above items, if any, during the year, say fresh contribution made by Government, fresh issue of capital, capitalisation of reserves, etc. may be explained in the notes.
Schedule 2—Reserves and Surplus	
I. Statutory Reserves	Reserves created in terms of section 17 or any other section of Banking Regulation Act must be separately disclosed.
II. Capital Reserves	The expression 'capital reserves' shall not include any amount regarded as free for distribution through the profit and loss account. Surplus on revaluation should be treated as Capital Reserves. Surplus on translation of financial statements of foreign branches (which includes fixed assets also) is not a revaluation reserve.
III. Share Premium	Premium on issue of share capital may be shown separatelu under this head.
IV. Revenue and other Reserves	The expression, 'Revenue Reserve' shall mean any reserve otehr than capital reserve. This item will include all reserves, other than those separately classifed. The expression 'reserve' shall not include any amount written off or retained by way of providing for depreciation, renewals or diminution in value of assets or retained by way of providing for any known liability. Investment Fluctuation Reserve should be shown as a separate item under the head 'Revenue and Other Reserves' Banks should transfer maximum amount of the gains realised on sale of investment in securities to the gains realised on sale of investment in securities to the IFR. Transfer to IFR shall be as an appropriation of net profit 'below the line' after appropriation to statutory reserve.
V. Balance of Profit	Includes balance of profit after appropriations. In case of loss the balance may be shown as a deduction. *Notes—General* Movements in various categories of reserves should be shown as indicated in the schedule.
Schedule 3—Deposits	
A.I. Demand Deposits	
(i) from banks	Includes all bank deposits repayable on demand.
(Ii) from others	Includes all demand deposits of the non-bank sectors. Credit balances in overdraft, cash credit accounts, deposits payable at call,

	overdue deposits, inoperative current accounts, matured time deposits and case certificates, certificates of deposits, etc. are to be included under this category.
II. Savings Bank Deposits	Includes all savings bank deposits (including inoperative savings bank accounts).
III. Term Deposits	
(i) from banks	Includes all types of bank deposits (including inoperative savings bank accounts).
(i) from others	Includes all types of deposits of the non-bank sector repayable after a specified term. Fixed deposits, cumulative and recurring deposits, cash certificates, certificates of deposits, annuity deposits, deposits mobilised under various schemes, ordinary staff deposits, foreign currency non-resident deposits accounts, etc. are to be included under this category.
(B) (i) Deposits of branches in India	
(ii) Deposits of branches outside India	The total of these two items will agree with the total deposits. *Notes—General* (a) Interest payable on deposits which is accrued but not due should not be included but shown under Other Liabilities. (b) Matured time deposits and case certificates, etc. should be treated as demand deposits. (c) Deposits under special schemes should be included under term deposits if they are not payable on demand. When such deposits have matured for payment they should be shown under demand deposits. (d) Deposits from banks will include deposits from the banking system in India, co-operative banks, foreign banks which may or may not have a presence in India.
Schedule 4—Borrowings	
I. Borrowings in India	
(i) Reserve Bank of India	Includes borrowings/refinance obtained from RBI.
(ii) Other banks	Includes borrowings/refinance obtained from commercial banks (including co-operative banks).
(iii) Other institutions and agencies	Includes borrowings/refinance obtained from IDBI, 'EXIM Bank, and other institutions, agencies (including liabitlity against participation certificates, if any).

II. Borrowins outside India	Includes borrowings of Indian branches abroad as well as borrowings of foreign branches.
Secured borrowings included above	This item will be shown separately. Includes secured borrowings/ refinance in India and outside India. *Notes—General* (i) The total of I & II will agree with the total borrowings shown in the balance sheet. (ii) Inter-office transactions should not be shown as borrowings. (iii) Funds raised by foreign branches by way of certificates of deposits, notes, bonds, etc., should be classified, depending upon documentation, as 'deposits', 'borrowings'. etc. (iv) Refinance obtained by banks from Reserved Bank of India and various institutions are being brought under the head 'Borrowings'. Hence, advances will be shown at the gross amount on the assets side.
Schedule 5—Other Liabilities and Provisions	
I. Bills payable	Includes drafts, telegraphic, transfers, traveller's cheques, mail transfers payable, pay slips, banker's cheques and other miscellneous items.
II. Inter-Office adjustments	The inter-office adjustments balance, if in credit, should be shown under this head. Only net position of inter-office accounts, inland as well as foreign, should be shown here. In working out the net position, credit entries outstanding for more than five years in inter-branch accounts should be segregated and transferred to a separate Blocked Account.
III. Interest accrued	Includes interest accrued but not due on deposits and borrowings.
IV. Others (including provisions)	Includes net provision for income tax and other taxes like interest tax (less advance payment, tax deducted at source, etc.), surplus in aggregate in provisions for bad debts provision account, surplus in aggregate in provision for depreciation in securities, contingency funds which are not disclosed as reserves but are actually in the nature of reserves, proposed dividend as reserves but are actually in the nature of reserves, proposed dividend/transfer to Government, other liabilities which are not disclosed under any of the major heads such as unclaimed dividend, provisions and funds kept for specific purposes, unexpired discount, outstanding charges like rent, conveyance, etc. Certain types of deposits like staff security deposits, margin deposits, etc. where the repayment is not free, should also be included under this head. Provisions toward standard assets need not be netted from gross advances but shown separately as 'Contingent Provisions against Standard Assets' under this head.

	Amount of subordinated debt raised as Tier II capital should be shown in Schedule 5 as well as by way of explanatory notes/remarks in the balance sheet. The Blocked Account arising from transfer of credit entries in inter-branch accounts outstanding for more than five years should be shown under this head. *Notes—General* (i) For arriving at the net balance of inter-office adjustments all connected inter-office accounts should be aggregated and the net balance only will be shown, representing mostly items in transit and unadjusted items. (ii) The interest accruing on all deposits, whether the payment is due or not, should be treated as a liability. (iii) It is proposed to show only pure deposits under the head 'deposits' and hence all surplus provisions for bad and doubtful debts, contingency funds, secret reserves, etc., which are not netted off against the relative assets, should be brought under the head 'Others (including provisions)'.
Schedule 6—Cash and Balances with Reserve Bank of India	
I. Cash in hand (including foreign currency notes)	Includes case in hand including foreign currency notes and also of foreign branches in the case of banks having such branches.
II. Balances with Reserve Bank of India (i) in Current Account (ii) in other Accounts	
Schedule 7—Balances with Banks and Money at Cell and Short Notice	
I. In India (i) Balalnces with banks (a) in Current accounts (b) in other Deposit accounts	Includes all balances with banks in India (including co-operative banks). Balance in current accounts and deposit accounts should be shown separately.
(ii) Money at cell and short notice (a) with banks (b) with other institutions	Includes deposits repayable within 15 days or less than 15 days' notice lent in the inter-bank calll maney market.
II. Outside India (i) Current accounts (ii) Deposit accounts	Includes balances held by foreign branches and balances held by Indian branches of the outside India. Balances held with foreign branches by other branches of the bank should not be shown under this head but should be included in inter-branch accounts. The amounts held in 'current accounts' and 'deposit accounts' should be shown separately.

(iii) Money at call and short notice	Includes deposits unusually classified in a foreign countries as money at call and short notice.
Schedule 8—Investments	
I. Investments in India	
(i) Government securities	Includes Central and State Government securities and Government treasury bills. These securities should be shown at the book value.
(ii) Other approved securities	Securities other than Government Securities, which according to the Banking Regulation Act, 1949, are treated as approved securities, should be included here.
(iii) Shares	Investments in shares of companies and corporations not included in item (ii) should be included here.
(iv) Debentures and Bonds	Investments in debentures and bonds of companies and corporations not included in item (ii) should be included here.
(v) Investments in subsidiaries/joint ventures	Investments in subsidiaries/joint ventures (including RRBs) should be included here.
(vi) Others	Includes residual investments, if any, like gold, commercial paper and other instruments in the nature of shares/debentures/bonds.
II. Investments outside India	
(i) Government securities (including local authorities)	All foreign Government securities including securities issued by local authorities may be classified under this head.
(ii) Subsidiary and/or joint ventures abroad	All investments made in the share capital of subsidiaries floated outside India and/or joint ventures abroad should be classified under this head.
(iii) Others	All other investments outside India may be shown under this head. *Notes—General* Indicate the gross value of investments in India and outside India, the aggregate of provisions for depreciation separately on investments in India and outside India, and the net value of investments in India and outside India, the total of which will be carried to balance sheet. The gross value of investments and provisions need not, however, be shown against each of the categories specified in the Schedule. The break-up of net value of the investments in India and outside India (gross value of investments less provision) under each of the specified category need only be shown.
Schedule 9—Advances	
A.(i) Bills purchased and discounted. (ii) Cash credits, overdrafts and loans repayable on demand	In classification under Section 'A', all outstandings—in India as well as outside—less provisions made (excluding those for standard assets), will be classified under three heads as indicated and both secured and unsecured advances will be included under these heads.

	Outstandings in credit card operations should be shown as part of advances under the head 'cash credits', overdrafts and loans repayable on demand.
(iii) Term loans	Including overdue instalments.
B.(i) Secured by angible assets (includes advances against book debts)	All advances or part of advances which are secured by tangible assets may be shown here. The item will include advances in India and outside India.
(ii) Covered by Bank/Government Guarantees	Advances in India and outside India to the extent they are covered by guarantees of Indian and foreign governments and India and foreign banks and DICGC & ECGC are to be included.
(iii) Unsecured	All advances not classified under (i) & (ii) will be included here. Total of 'A' should tally with total of 'B'.
C.I Advances in India (i) Priority sectors (ii) Public sector (iii) Banks (iv) others C.II Advances outside India (i) Due from banks (ii) Due from others (a) Bills purchased and discounted (b) Syndicated loans (c) Others	Advances should be broadly classified into 'Advances in India' and 'Advances outside India'. Advances in India will be further classified on the sectoral basis as indicated. Advances to sectors which for the time being are classified as priority sectos according to the instructions of the Reserve Bank are to be classified under the head 'Priority sectors'. Such Advances should be excluded from item (ii) i.e., advances to public sector. Advances to Central and State Government and other Government undertakings including Government Companies and Corporations which are, according to the statutes, to be treated as public sector companies are to be included in the category 'Public Sector'. All advances to the banking sector including co-operative banks will come under the head 'Banks'. All the remaining advances will be included under the head 'Others' and typically this category will include non-priority advances to the private, joint and co-operative sectors. *Notes—General* (i) The gross amount of advances including refinance but excluding rediscount and provisions made to the satisfaction of auditors should be shown as advances. (ii) Term loans will be loans not repayable on demand. (iii) Consortium advances would be shown net of share from other participating banks/institutions. (iv) All interest-bearing loans and advances granted to staff should be shown under 'advances'. However, all non-interest bearing loans and advances to staff should be included in item (v) 'Others' under the head 'Other Assets' in Schedule 11.
Schedule 10—Fixed Assets	
I. Premises (i) At cost as on 31st March of the preceding year	Premises wholly or partly owned by the banking comapny for the purpose of business including residential premises should be shown against 'premises'. In the case of premises and other fixed assets,

(ii) Additions durign the year (iii) Deductions during the year (iv) Depreciation to date	the previous balance, additions thereto and deductions therefrom during the year as also the total depreciation written off should be shown. Where sums have been written off on reduction of capital or revaluation of assets, every balance sheet after the first balance sheet subsequent to the reduction or revaluation should show the revised figures for a period of five years with the date and amount of revision made
II. Other Fixed Assets (including furniture and fixtures) (i) At cost as on 31st March of the preceding year (ii) Additions during the year (iii) Deductions during the year (iv) Depreciation to date	Motor vehicles and all other fixed assets other than premises but including furniture and fixtures should be shown under this head.
Schedule 11—Other Assets	
I. Inter-office adjustments (net)	The inter-office adjustments balance, if in debit, should be shown undet this head. Only net position of inter-office accounts, inland as well as foreign, should be shown here. For arriving at the net balance of inter-office adjustment accounts, all connected inter-office accounts should be aggregated and the net balance, if in debit, only should be shown representing mostly items in transit and unadjusted items. Banks should arrive at the category-wise position of unreconciled entries outstanding in the inter-branch accounts for more than six months as on March 31 and make provision equivalent to 100 per cent of the aggregate net debit under all categories. While doing so, it may be ensured that: (i) credit balance in Blocked Account created in terms of instructions contained in circular No. DBOD. BP.BC. 73/21.04.018/98 dated July 27, 1998 is also taken into account; and (ii) the net debit in one category is not set-off against net credit in another cetegory.
II. Interest accrued	Interest accrued but not due on investments and advances and interest due but not collected on investments will be the main components of this item. As banks normally debit the borrowers' account with interest due on the balance sheet date, usually there may not be any amount of interest due on advances. Only such interest as can be realised in the ordinary course should be shown under this head.
III. Tax paid in advance/tax deducted at source	The amount of tax deducted at source on securities, advance tax paid, etc. to the extent that these items are not set off against relative tax provisions should be shown against this item.

IV. Stationery and stamps	Only exceptional items of expenditure on stationery like bulk purchase of security paper, loose leaf or other ledgers, etc. which are shown as quasi-asset to be written off over a period of time should be shown here. The value should be on a realistic basis and cost escalation should not be taken into account, as these items are for internal use.
V. Non-banking assets acquired in satisfaction of claims	Immovable properties/tangible assets acquired in satisfaction of claims are to be shown under this head.
VI. Others	This will include items like claims which have not been met, for instance, clearing items, debit items representing additions to assets or reduction in liabilities which have not been adjusted for technical reasons, want of particulars, etc. All interest-bearing loans and advances granted to staff should be included under 'advances'. However, all non-interest bearing loans and advances to staff should be included here. Items which are in the nature of expenses which are pending adjustments should be provided for and the provision netted against this item so that only realisable value is shown under ths head. Accrued income other than interest may also be included here. Outstandings in credit card operations should be shown as part of 'advances' instead of clubbing these under 'other assets'.
Schedule 12—Contingent Liabilities	
I. Claims against the bank not acknowledged as debts	
II. Liability for party paid investments	Liability on partly paid shares, debentures, etc. will be included in this head.
III. Liability on account of outstanding forward exchange contracts	Outstanding forward exchange contracts may be included here.
IV. Guarantees given on behalf of constituents (i) In India (ii) Outside India	Guarantees given for constituents in India and outside India may be shown separately.
V. Acceptances, endorsements and other obligations	This item will include lettters of credit and bills accepted by the bank on behalf of the customers.
VI. Other items for which the bank is contigently liable	Arrears of cumulative dividends, bills rediscounted, commitments under underwriting contracts, estimated amounts of contracts remaining to be executed on capital account and not provided for, etc. are to be included here.
Bills for Collection	Bills and other items in the course of collection and not adjusted will be shown against this item in the summary version only. No separate schedule is proposed.

Profit and Loss Account

Item	Notes and instructions for compilation
Schedule 13—Interest Earned	
I. Interest/discount on advances/bills	Includes interest and discount on all types of loans and advances like cash credit, demand loans, overdrafts, export loans, term loans, domestic and foreign bills purchased and discounted (including those rediscounted), overdue interest and also interest subsidy, if any, relating to such advances/bills.
II. Income on investments	Includes all income derived from the investment portfolio by way of interest and dividend.
III. Interest on balances with RBI and other inter-bank funds	Includes interest on balances with Reserve Bank and other banks, call loans, money market placements, etc.
IV. Others	Includes any other interest/discount income not included in the above heads.
Schedule 14–Other Income	
I. Commission, exchange and brokerage	Includes all remuneration on services such as commission on collections, commission/exchange on remittances and transfers, commission on letters of credit and guarantees, letting out of lockers, commission on Government business, commission on other permitted agency business including consultancy and other services, brockerage, etc. on securities. It does not include foreign exchange income.
II. Profit on sale of investments Less: Loss on sale of investments III. Profit on revaluation of investments Less: Loss on revaluation of investments IV. Profit on sale of land, buildings and other assets Less: Loss on sale of land, buildins and other assets	Includes profit/loss on sale of securities, furniture, land and buildings, motor vehicles, gold, silver, etc. Only the net position should be shown. If the net position is a loss, the amount should be shown as a deduction. The net profit/loss on revaluation of assets may also be shown under this item. Profit on sale of investments in held-to-maturity category should be first taken to the Profit & Loss Account and thereafter be appropriated to the 'Capital Reserve Account' Profit or loss on sale of investments in available-for-sale and held-for-trading categories should be taken to the Profit & Loss Account.
V. Profit on exchange transactions Less: Loss on exchange transactions VI. Income earned by way of dividends etc. from subsidiaries, companies and/or joint ventures abroad/in India	Includes profit/loss on dealing in foreign exchange, all income earned by way of foreign exchange, commission and charges on foreign exchange transactions excluding interest which will be shown under interest. Only the net position should be shown. If the net position is a loss, it is to be shown as a deduction.
VII. Miscellaneous income	Includes recoveries from constituents for godown rents, income from bank's properties, security charges, insuracnce, etc. and any other miscellaneous income. In case any item under this head exceeds one percentage of the total income, particulars may be given in the notes.

Schedule 15—Interest Expended	
I. Interest on deposits	Includes interest paid on all types of deposits including deposits from banks and other institutions.
II. Interest on Reserve Bank of India/inter-bank borrowings	Includes discount/interest on all borrowings and refinance from Reserve Bank of India and other banks.
III. Others	Includes discount/interest on all borrowings/refinance from financial institutions. All other payments like interest on participation certificates, penal interest paid, etc., may also be included here.
Schedule 16—Operating Expenses	
I. Payments to and provisions for employees	Includes staff salaries/wages, allowances, bonus, other staff benefits like provident fund, pension, gratuity, liveries to staff, leave fare concessions, staff welfare, medical allowance to staff, etc.
II. Rent, taxes and lighting	Includes rent paid by the banks on buildings, and other municipal and other taxes paid (excluding income tax and interest tax), electricity and other similar charges and levies. House rent allowance and other similar payments to staff appear under the head 'Payments to and provisions for employees'.
III. Printing and stationery	Includes books, and forms and stationery used by the bank and other printing charges which are not incurred by way of publicity expenditure.
IV. Advertisement and publicity	Includes expenditure incurred by the bank for advertisement and publicity purposes including printing charges of publicity matter.
V. Depreciation on bank's property	Includes depreciation on bank's own property, motor cars and other verhicles, furniture, electric fittings, vaults, lifts, leasehold properties, non-banking assets, etc.
VI. Directors' fees, allowances and expenses	Includes sitting fees and all other items of expenditure incurred on behalf of directors. The daily allowance, hotel charges, conveyance charges, etc. which though in the nature of reimbursement of expenses incurred may be included under this head. Similar expenses of local Committee members may also be included under this head.
VII. Auditors' fees and expenses (including branch auditor' fees and expenses)	Includes the fees paid to the statutory and branch auditors for professional services rendered and all expenses for performing their duties, even though they may be in the nature of reimbursement of expenses. If external auditors have been appointed by banks themselves for internal inspections and audits and other services, the expenses incurred in that context including fees may not be included under this head but shown under 'other expenditure'.
VIII. Law charges	All legal expenses and reimbursement of expenses incurred in connection with legal services are to be included here.

IX. Postage, telegrams, telephones, etc.	Includes all postal charges like stamps, telegram, telephones, teleprinter, etc.
X. Repairs and maintenance	Includes repairs to bank's property, their maintenance charges, etc.
XI. Insurance	Includes insurance charges on bank's property, insurance premium paid to DICGC, etc. to the extent they are not recovered from the concerned parties.
XII. Other expenditure	All expenses other than those not included in any of the other heads, like, license fees, donations, subscriptions to papers, periodicals, entertainment expenses, travel expenses, etc., may be included under this head. In case any particular item under this head exceeds one percentage of the total income, particulars may be given in the notes.
Provisions and Contingencies	Includes all provisions made for bad and doubtful debts, provisions for taxation, provisions for diminution in the value of investments, transfers to contingencies and other similar items. The provisions required to be created on account of depreciation in the available for sale category in any year should be debited to Profit & Loss Account and an equivalent amount (net of tax benefit, if any, and net of consequent reduction in the transfer to Statutory Reserve) or the balance available in Investment Fluctuation Reserve Account, whichever is less, should be transferred from the Investment Fluctuation Reserve Account to Profit & Loss Account. In the event provisions created on account of depreciation in the available for sale category are found to be in excess of the required amount in any year, the excess should be credited to Profit & Loss Account and an equivalent amount (net of taxes, if any, and net of transfer to Statutory Reserve as application to such excess provision) should be appropriated to the Investment Fluctuation Reserve Account to be utilised to meet future depreciation requirement for investments in this category. The amount debited to Profit & Loss Account for provision and the amount credited to Profit & Loss Account for reversal of excess provision should be debited and credited respectively under the head 'Expenditure—Provisions & Contingencies'. The amounts appropriated from Profit & Loss Account and the amount transferred from the Investment Fluctuation Reserve to Profit & Loss Account should be shown as 'below the line' items after determining the profit for the year.

PART B

Additional Disclosures in Financial Statements

Apart from complying with the presentation and disclosure requirements of the Third Schedule to the Banking Regulation Act, 1949, read with the notes and instructions for their compilation issued by RBI, banks have to also make the following disclosures in the 'Notes on Accounts' pursuant to the requirements of RBI.

1. Capital adequacy ratio
2. Capital adequacy ratio—Tier I capital
3. Capital adequacy ratio—Tier II capital
4. Amount of subordinated debt raised as Tier II capital

   This item should be shown by way of explanatory notes/remarks in the balance sheet as well as in Schedule 5 relating to 'Other Liabilities and Provisions'.
5. Percentage of shareholding of the government of India in the nationalised banks.
6. Gross value of investments in India and outside India, aggregate of provisions for depreciation separately on investments in India and outside India, and the net value of investments in India and outside India.
7. Percentage of net NPAs to net advances.

   Net NPAs mean gross NPAs as reduced by (i) balance in Interest Suspence Account, (ii) DICGC/ECGC claims received and held pending adjustment, (iii) part payments received and kept in Suspence Account, and (iv) provisions held for loan losses.
8. Movements in NPAs

   The disclosures should include the balances of Gross NPAs (after deducting provisions held, interest suspense account, DICGC claims received and part payments received and kept in Suspence Account) at the beginning of the year, reductions/additions to the NPAs during the year and the balances at the end of the year.
9. The amount of provisions made towards NPA, depreciation in the value of investments and income-tax during the year.

   Provisions for NPAs should be disclosed in the following format.

   Opening balance (as on 1 April ....)
   Add: Provisions made during the year
   Less: Write off, write back of excess provisions
   Closing balance (as on 31 March ....)

   Provisions for depreciation on investments should be disclosed in the following format.

   Opening balance (as on 1 April ....)
   Add: Provisions made during the year
   Less: Write off, write back of excess provisions
   Closing balance (as on 31 March ....)

   These provisions along with other provisions and contingencies should tally with the aggregate of the amount held under 'Provisions and contingencies' in the profit and loss account.
10. Maturity pattern of investment securities

    Banks may follow the maturity buckets prescribed in the guidelines on Asset-Liability Management System contained in Circular DBOD.BP.BC.8/21.04.09/99 dated February 10, 1999, for disclosure of maturity pattern. The maturity buckets prescribed in the aforesaid circular may also be followed in respect of items 11-13 below.
11. Maturity pattern of loans and advances.
12. Maturity pattern of deposits

13. Maturity pattern of borrowings
14. Maturity pattern of foreign currency assets and liabilities
    The maturity profile of the bank's foreign currency assets and liabilities should be given.
15. Lending to sensitive sectors.
    Banks should disclose lending to sectors which are sensitive to asset price fluctuations. These should include advances to sectors such as capital market, real estate, etc. and such other sectors to be defined as 'sensitive' by RBI from time to time.
16. Interest income as a percentage to working funds
    Working funds mean total assets on the date of balance sheet (excluding accumulated lossed, if any)
17. Non-interest income as a percentage to working funds
18. Operating profit as a percentage to working funds
    Operating profit means total income minus interest expense and operating expenses.
19. Return on assets means net profit divided by average of total assets as at beginning and end of the year.
20. Business (deposit plus advances) per employee
    This means fortnightly average of deposits (excluding inter-bank deposits) and advances divided by number of employees as on the date of balance sheet.
21. Profit per employee
22. Information in respect of restructuring, etc. undertaken during the year
    (a) Total amount of loan assets subjected to restructuring, etc.
    (b) The amount of standard assets subjected to restructuring, etc.
    (c) The amount of sub-standard assets subjected to restructuring, etc.
23. Information in respect of corporate debt restructuring undertaken during the year
    (a) Total amount of loan assets subjected to restructuring to CDR.
    (b) The amount of standard assets subjected to CDR.
    (c) The amount of sub-standard assets subjected to CDR.
    (d) The amount of doubtful assets subjected to CDR.
24. Details of financial assets sold during the year to SC/RC for Asset Reconstruction
    (a) No. of accounts
    (b) Aggregate value (net of provisions) of accounts sold to SC/RC
    (c) Aggregate consideration
    (d) Additional consideration realised in respect of accounts transferred in earlier years
    (e) Aggregate gian/loss over net book value.
25. Issuer composition of non-SLR investments

(Rs in crore)

No.	Issuer	Amount	Extent of private placement	Extent of 'below investment grade' securities	Extent of 'unrated' securities	Extent of 'unlisted' securities
(1)	(2)	(3)	(4)	(5)	(6)	(7)
1.	PSUs					
2.	Fis					
3.	Banks					
4.	Private corporates					

5. Subsidiaries/Joint ventures					
6. Others					
7. Provision held towards depreciation		XXX	XXX	XXX	XXX
Total*					

Notes:

1. Total under column 3 should tally with the total of investments included under the following categories in Schedule 8 to the balance sheet:

   Shares

   Debentures & Bonds

   Subsidiaries/joint ventures

   Others
2. Amounts reported under column 4, 5, 6 and 7 above may not be mutually exclusive.

26. Non performing non-SLR investments

The criterion for classifying a non-SLR investments as non-performing is similar to that used in classifying an advance as non-performing. As far as an investment in equity shares is concerned, it should be classified as non-performing in the event it is valued at Re 1 due to non-availability of the latest balance sheet of the issuer. If any credit facility availed by the issuer is classified as NPA by the bank, investment in any of the securities issued by that issuer should be treated as a non-performing investment.

The disclosure of non-performing non-SLR investments is to be made in the following format:

Particulars	*Amount (Rs. Crore)*
Opening balance	
Additions during the year since 1st April	
Reductions during the above period	
Closing balance	
Total provisions held	

27. Detail of Repo/Reverse Repo transactions done during the year

(Rs in crore)

	Minimum outstanding during the year	*Minimum outstanding during the year*	*Daily average outstanding during the year*	*As on March 31*
Securities sold under repos				
Securities purchase under reverse repos				

28. Total investments made in equity shares, convertible bonds and debentures and units of equity oriented mutual funds and aggregate advances against shares.
29. Category-wise country exposures
    (a) The risk category-wise country exposures, and
    (b) the extent of aggregate provisions held thereagainst.
30. Disclusures regarding forward rate agreements/interest rate swaps

(a) The notional principal of swap agreements;

(b) nature and terms of the swaps including information on credit and market risk and the accounting policies adopted for recording the swaps;

(c) quantification of the losses which would be incurred if counterparties failed to fulfil their obligation under the agreement;

(d) collateral required by the entity upon entering into swaps;

(e) any concentration of credit risk arising from the swaps. Examples of concentration could be exposures to particular industries or swaps with highly geared companies; and

(f) the 'fair' value of the total swaps book. If the swaps are linked to specific assets, liabilities or commitments, the fair value would be the estimated amount that the entity would receive or pay to terminate the swap agreement at balance sheet date. For a trading swap, the fair value would be its mark to market value.

CHAPTER 13

Audit of Insurance Companies

CHAPTER OUTLINE

13.1 AUDIT OF COMPANIES CARRYING ON LIFE INSURANCE BUSINESS

Due to liberalisation, the economic policies of India have witnessed a significant transformation during the last decade. A new regulatory framework in the insurance sector has brought sweeping changes not only in terms of number of participants, but also in terms of portfolio of insurance business and the way business is conducted.

The conduct of life insurance business is unique in the sense that the concept of 'life fund' and consequential segregation of *shareholders fund* from *life fund* and conditionalities of financial transactions between these two funds are not present in the conduct of any other business. This uniqueness brings about issues relating to recognition of revenue, preparation and presentation of accounts, valuation of assets and liabilities and measurement of taxable income requiring addressal in specific manner.

The changing environment has made a strong case for better regulation on the insurance sector. An independent authority named, "Insurance Regulatory and Development Authority" was constituted in the year 1999 to protect the interest of holders of insurance policies and to regulate, promote and ensure orderly growth of the insurance industry.

With the arrival of new participants in life insurance business, the organisational structure may differ from one insurance company to another. The Life Insurance Corporation of India (LICI) has a four--tier structure, i.e. head office, regional offices, divisional offices and branch offices, each tier being responsible for performing the functions assigned by the head office.

13.1.1 Important Statutory Provisions for Audit

The important statutory provisions relevant to the audit of life insurance companies are included in the following Acts and Rules:

1. The Insurance Act, 1938
2. The Insurance Rules, 1939
3. The Income Tax Act, 1961
4. The Companies Act, 1956
5. The Life Insurance Corporation Act, 1956.

13.2 AUDIT OF COMPANIES CARRYING ON GENERAL INSURANCE BUSINESS

The Indian economic environment is undergoing a significant transformation in view of liberalisation reforms introduced since early 1990s. In the wake of liberalisation reforms, the privatisation of insurance sector is not only intended to mobilise long-term funds but also to make the insurance business more competitive and thus meet the fundamental security needs of various sections of the society.

The opening up of the insurance sector enabled entry of various new participants and expanded the scope of insurance coverage. With the arrival of new participants in general insurance business, the organisation structure may differ from one insurance company to another. Most of the companies carrying on general insurance business have a four-tier structure, i.e. head office, regional office, divisional office and branch offices. Each tier of the structure is responsible for performing the functions assigned to it by the Head Office.

General insurance business usually involves fire, marine or miscellaneous insurance business, whether carried on singly or in combination of one or more of them. Some common types of miscellaneous insurance include motor vehicle insurance, credit insurance, burglary insurance, loss of profit insurance, health insurance etc.

13.2.1 Important Statutory Provisions for Audit

The important statutory provisions relevant to the audit of general insurance companies are included in the following Acts and Rules:

1. The Insurance Act, 1938
2. The Insurance Rules, 1939
3. The Income Tax Act, 1961
4. The Income Tax Rules, 1962
5. The Companies Act, 1956
6. The General Insurance Business (Nationalisation) Act, 1972
7. The Motor Vehicles Act, 1988
8. Employees' State Insurance Act, 1948

13.3 APPLICABILITY OF ACCOUNTING STANDARDS

The Accounting Standards as issued by the Institute of Chartered Accountants of India are applicable to the preparation of financial statements of a company carrying on Insurance Business, subject to Paragraph 1 of Part 1 of Schedule B to the IRDA (Preparation of Financial Statements and Auditor's Report of the Insurance Companies) Regulations, 2000.

The applicability of Accounting Standards to the insurance companies are discussed below.

Accounting Standard-3

According to the IRDA (Preparation of Financial Statements and Auditor's Report of Insurance Companies) Regulations, 2000, the receipts and payments account of an insurer should be prepared using the 'Direct Method' as mentioned in Accounting Standard-3 on cash flow statements.

Accounting Standard-4

Accounting Standard-4 on 'Contingencies and Events Occurring After the Balance Sheet Date' that deals with accounting treatment of contingent losses and gains and events occurring after the balance sheet date excludes from its applicability the liabilities of companies carrying on insurance business in view of special considerations applicable to such liabilities. The Standard excludes, from its applicability, the liabilities arising out of policies issued and not other liabilities which do not arise out of policies issued by the insurance companies such as liabilities arising out of income tax dispute. Thus, the Standard applies to such other liabilities.

Accounting Standard-9

Accounting Standard-9 on 'Revenue Recognition' does not apply to revenue of insurance companies arising from insurance contracts, in view of the fact that revenue recognition from insurance contracts requires special considerations. The Standard is applicable to the insurance companies only in respect of income not earned from the insurance contracts such as interest, dividend, rent etc.

Accounting Standard-13

Under paragraph 2 (c) of Accounting Standard-13 on 'Accounting for Investments' it has been provided that the Standard does not deal with the investments of insurance enterprises.

Accounting Standard-17

So far as the applicability of Accounting Standard-17 on 'Segment Reporting' is concerned, the Regulations have disregarded the applicability clause contained in the Standard by providing that irrespective of the fact that the securities of the company are traded or not, Accounting Standard-17 would be applicable to an insurer carrying on life or general insurance business.

13.4 BOOKS AND REGISTERS TO BE MAINTAINED

An insurance company is required to maintain the following books of accounts and returns:

13.4.1 Registers

1. Register of policies

Under Section 14 of the Insurance Act, 1938 every insurer is required to maintain a register or record of policies containing the details regarding every policy issued by the insurer, name and address of the policy holder, the date of effect of the policy, record of any transfer, assignment or nomination of which insurer has a notice.

2. Register of claims

Every insurer is also required to maintain a register or record of claims containing the details on date of claim made, name and address of the claimant, date of discharge of each claim and in case the claim is rejected, the date of rejection along with grounds thereof.

13.4.2 Books of Accounts

The insurance companies generally maintain the following books of accounts:

- Cash book (for receipts and payments)
- Ledger
- Subsidiary records (Account of claims, premium, commission, assets, liabilities etc.)
- Control register

In addition to that the provisions under Section 209 of the Companies Act, 1956 regarding books of accounts are also applicable to the insurance companies.

13.5 SUBMISSION OF REPORTS AND RETURNS

Under Section 18 of the Insurance Act, 1938 every insurer is required to furnish to the Authority, a certified copy of every report on the affairs of the concern, which is submitted to the members or policyholders of the insurer immediately after its submission to the members of policyholders, as the case may be.

The audited accounts and statements referred to in Section 11 or Section 13(5) and the abstracts and statements referred to in Section 13 shall be printed and four copies thereof shall be furnished as returns to the Authority, in the case of the accounts and statements referred to in Section 11 or Section 13(5) within six months and in case of the abstracts and statements referred to in Section 13 within nine months from the end of the period to which they refer.

13.6 AUDIT OF ACCOUNTS

Under Section 12 of the Insurance Act, 1938 the financial statements (balance sheet, profit and loss account and appropriations thereof) and revenue accounts of every insurer are required to be audited annually. Section 2(4) of the Insurance Act, 1938 defines the term 'auditor' as a person qualified under the Chartered Accountants Act, 1949 to act as an auditor of a company.

The provisions of Section 12 of the Insurance Act, 1938 apply only in a case where the financial statements of the insurer are not subject to audit under the Companies Act, 1956. A company carrying on life and general insurance business is, therefore, subject to audit requirements laid down under the Companies Act, 1956.

Further, Section 12 of the Insurance act, 1938 does not cover the requirement for audit of the Receipts and Payments Account of an insurer. But the IRDA Act, 1999 inserted a new sub-section (1A) in Section 11 of the Insurance Act, 1938, overriding sub-section (1) of Section 11, prescribing the financial statements to be prepared by an insurer. The new sub-section requires that after the commencement of the IRDA Act, 1999 every insurer, in respect of insurance business transacted by him and in respect of his shareholders funds, should, at the end of each financial year, prepare a balance sheet, a profit and loss account, a separate account of receipts and payments and a revenue account in accordance with the regulations made by the Authority.

The Authority, in exercise of the powers conferred by the Insurance Act, 1938 issued the IRDA (Preparation of Financial Statements and Auditor's Report of Insurance Companies) Regulations, 2000. These Regulations also require the auditor of an insurance company to report whether the receipts and payments account of the insurer is in agreement with the books of accounts and returns. The auditor is also required to express an opinion as to whether the receipts and payments account has been prepared in accordance with the provisions of the relevant statutes and whether the receipts and payments account give a true and fair view of the receipts and payments of the insurer for the period under audit. It implies that the auditor is required to audit the receipts and payments account of the insurer.

The IRDA Act, 1999 also inserted the third proviso to section 2C (1) of the Insurance Act, 1938. The proviso requires that no insurer other than an Indian insurance company can commence any class of insurance business after the commencement of the IRDA Act, 1999. Under the circumstances, an Indian insurance company would be subject to the audit requirements laid down under the Companies Act, 1956.

Qualification of auditor

A chartered accountant fulfilling the requirements of the Companies Act, 1956 can be appointed as an auditor of an insurer. According to section 226 of the Companies Act, 1956 a chartered accountant or a firm of chartered accountants or a restricted state auditor can be appointed as auditor of a company.

However, the following persons cannot be appointed as auditor of a company:

(a) A body corporate

(b) An officer or employee of the company

(c) A person who is a partner, or who is in the employment of an officer or employee of the company

(d) A person who is indebted to the company for an amount exceeding rupees one thousand or who has given any guarantee or provided any security in connection with the indebtedness of any third person to the company for an amount exceeding rupees one thousand

(e) A person holding any security of the company carrying voting rights

It may be noted that the Insurance Act, 1938 mentions that the auditor of an insurer should be a chartered accountant qualified under the Chartered Accountants Act, 1949. Therefore, a restricted state auditor cannot be appointed as an auditor of an insurance company and only chartered accountants can be appointed as auditors of insurance companies.

A person is not qualified for appointment as auditor of a company if he is disqualified for appointment as auditor of any other body corporate which is that company's subsidiary or holding company or a subsidiary of that company's holding company or would be so disqualified if the body corporate were a company.

It may also be noted that in case of indebtedness in excess of the specified limit as mentioned above, the chartered accountant concerned becomes disqualified to audit any branch of the insurer and the disqualification is not only confined to appointment as auditor of the particular branch to which the debt is owed.

Appointment of auditor

The Insurance Act, 1938 is silent on the procedure for appointment of auditors of insurance companies. Therefore, the provisions of the Companies Act, 1956 would apply in so far as appointment of auditor is concerned. The auditor of an insurance company is to be appointed at the annual general meeting of the company. The approval of the Authority is required before the appointment is made. The central statutory auditors of insurance companies are appointed by the insurance company concerned on the basis of the names recommended by the Authority from out of a panel of auditors. For this purpose, the Authority formulates detailed norms on the basis of which the panel is prepared.

Remuneration of auditor

The remuneration of auditor of insurance company is fixed in accordance with the provisions of section 224 of the Companies Act, 1956, i.e. the remuneration of the auditor is fixed by the company in general meeting or in such manner as the company in general meeting may determine.

Powers of auditor

The auditor of an insurance company has the same power as those of a company auditor in the matter of access to the books of accounts, documents and vouchers. He is also entitled to require from the officers of the insurance company such information and explanations as he may think necessary for the performance of his duties. In the case of an insurance company, he is entitled to receive notice relating to any general meeting. He is also entitled to attend any general meeting and to be heard there on any part of the business, which concerns him as the auditor.

Auditor's report

The authority has prescribed the matters to be dealt with by the auditor's report under Schedule C of IRDA (Preparation of Financial Statements and Auditor's Report of Insurance Companies) Regulations, 2000.

The auditors are required to make a report to the members of the company in which they have to deal with the following matters:

I. (a) Whether they have obtained all the information and explanations which, to the best of their knowledge and belief, were necessary for the purposes of their audit and whether they have found them satisfactory

(b) Whether proper books of account have been maintained by the insurer so far as it appears from an examination of those books

(c) Whether proper returns, audited or unaudited, from branches and other offices have been received and whether they were adequate for the purpose of audit

(d) Whether the balance sheet, revenue accounts and profit and loss account dealt with by the report and the receipts and payments account are in agreement with the books of account and returns

(e) Whether the actuarial valuation of liabilities is duly certified by the appointed actuary including a statement to the effect that the assumptions for such valuation are in accordance with the guidelines and norms, if any, issued by the Authority, and/or the Actuarial Society of India in concurrence with the Authority.

II. The auditors are also required to express their opinion on the following.

(a) (i) Whether the balance sheet gives a true and fair view of the surplus or the deficit for the financial year/period

(ii) Whether the revenue accounts give a true and fair view of the surplus or the deficit for the financial year/period

(iii) Whether the profit and loss account gives a true and fair view of the profit or loss for the financial year/period

(iv) Whether the receipts and payments account gives a true and fair view of the receipts and payments for the financial year/period

(b) Whether the financial statements stated in (a) have been prepared in accordance with the requirements of the Insurance Act, 1938, the Insurance Regulatory and Development Authority Act, 1999 and the Companies Act, 1956, to the extent applicable and in the manner so required

(c) Whether investments have been valued in accordance with the provisions of the Act and Regulations

(d) Whether the accounting policies selected by the insurer are appropriate and are in compliance with the applicable Accounting Standards and with the accounting principles, as prescribed in these Regulations or any order or direction issued by the Authority in this behalf

III. The auditors are required to further certify the following:

(a) They have reviewed the management report and there is no apparent mistake or material inconsistency with the financial statements; and

(b) The insurer has complied with the terms and conditions of the registration stipulated by the Authority.

IV. The auditors are required to sign a certificate certifying

(a) that they have verified the cash balances and the securities relating to the insurer's loans, reversions and life interests and investments;

(b) the extent, if any, to which they have verified the investments and transactions relating to any trusts undertaken by the insurer as trustee; and

(c) that no part of the assets of the policyholders' funds has been directly or indirectly applied in contravention of the provisions of the Insurance Act, 1938 relating to the application and investments of the policyholders' funds.

13.6.1 Other Important Provisions Relating to Audit

Every insurance company in the management report has to furnish a responsibility statement in connection with the existence and effective operation of an internal audit system. It implies that every insurance company should have in place an internal audit system commensurate with its size and nature of the business.

Section 40B and 40C of the Insurance Act, 1938 provides for the limitations on expenses of management in life and general insurance companies, the rules in respect of which have been specified under Insurance Rules, 1939. Every insurer is required to incorporate in the revenue account a certificate signed by the chairman and two directors and by the principal officer of the insurer, and by the auditor certifying that all expenses of management, wherever incurred, directly or indirectly, in respect of the business referred to in this section have been fully debited in the Revenue Account as expenses.

13.6.2 Audit at Branch/Divisional Office Level and at Head Office Level

Under the restructuring of the insurance sector, insurance business can be run by Life Insurance Corporation of India or by General Insurance Corporation of India or public sector companies or private operators. The concept of divisional office may not be relevant in case of private operators but may continue to be of relevance in case of Life Insurance Corporation of India and General Insurance Corporation of India. Wherever the reference is made to the divisional office, it may be understood as branches or any other offices where those operations are carried out in case of private companies.

Further, the Life Insurance Corporation of India and General Insurance Corporation of India may call for trial balances or other relevant returns from the branches and then the same may be consolidated at the head office level. There is a significant difference in the scope of audit at a branch or divisional office of an insurance company and at head office as well as other controlling offices such as regional offices. The difference stems from the fact that the insurance business—receiving premiums and selling claims—as well as most other insurance related operations take place at the branch level or divisional office level.

In the normal course, the head office and the regional offices do not conduct any insurance business except reinsurance transactions. They are generally responsible for administrative and policy decisions which are executed at the branch/divisional office level.

Audit at branch/divisional level

Audit of branches of insurance companies is required under Section 228 of the Companies Act, 1956. It is, thus, obligatory for an insurance company to get the financial statements of each of its branch offices audited except branches under the Companies (Branch Audit Exemption) Rules, 1961.

The branch auditor has the same powers and duties in respect of audit of financial statements of the branch as those of the central statutory auditors in relation to audit of head office.

The branch auditors furnish their audit reports on the branch financial statements to central statutory auditors with a copy to the management of the company. Branch returns include balance sheet, profit and loss account, revenue account and other information relevant for preparation of financial statements of the insurance company such as particulars of premiums/claims and also include the returns from unaudited branches. Audited as well as unaudited branch returns are consolidated at the head office. The returns pertaining to a region may be sent by the branches or divisional office to the regional office concerned and are consolidated there. The returns received from various regions may then be consolidated at the head office.

Audit at the head office level

The central statutory auditors, apart from examining consolidation of branch returns, look into specific matters, which are normally not dealt with at the branch level. These may include the following:

- Depreciation on assets like premises etc., where the recording of the relevant fixed assets is centralised at the head office
- Valuation of investments and provisions for diminution in value thereof
- Provisions in respect of non-performing loans and doubtful elements of other current assets
- Accounting for reinsurance transactions

- Provisions for gratuity, pension and other retirement benefits
- Provision for payment of bonus or ex-gratia in lieu of bonus
- Provision in respect of losses arising from frauds discovered
- Provision for taxation
- Provision for audit fee
- Provisions to meet any other specific liabilities or contingencies the amount of which is material
- Transfers to reserves
- Dividends
- Any other matters dealt with at the head office

Another area, which is of utmost importance for the central statutory auditors in the present day context, is that related to inter-office reconciliation. Such reconciliation is mostly centralised at the head office. Each company has laid down methods and procedures for reconciling the transactions between the various offices of the company.

The central statutory auditors also have to consider the observations made in the branch auditors' reports. They have to judge whether the observations appearing in the branch auditors' reports, though considered material at the branch level are material in the context of the financial statements of the company as a whole.

13.7 PREPARATION FOR THE AUDIT

Following are the stages through which the auditors of insurance companies can prepare themselves for conducting audit:

1. Preliminary work

The auditor's knowledge for an engagement would include general knowledge of the economy and the industry within which the entity operates. The auditor should, accordingly, acquire knowledge of the regularity environment in which an insurance company operates. He should familiarise himself with the relevant provisions of the applicable laws and ascertain the scope of his duties and responsibilities in accordance with such laws.

2. Evaluation of internal control system

Evaluation of the internal control system assumes greater importance in case of audit of insurance companies due to the enormous volume of transactions entered into by these companies. The auditor should study and evaluate the design and operation of internal control.

3. Preparation of audit programme

The auditor should prepare an audit programme for substantive testing which should adequately cover the scope of his work. In framing the audit programme, the auditor should give due importance to the areas where, in his view, there are weaknesses in internal controls. The audit programme for central statutory auditors would be different from that of branch auditors. The central statutory auditors have to deal with consolidation of branch accounts, investments and items normally dealt with at head office level, while the branch auditors have to deal with basic operations.

4. Communication with the previous auditor

The objective of communicating with the previous auditor is to provide the proposed auditor with an opportunity to know the reasons for the change. When communicating with the previous auditor, the incoming auditor should find out whether there is any professional or other reason why he should not accept the appointment.

5. Letter of engagement

An audit engagement letter is aimed at documenting and confirming the acceptance of appointment as auditor. The branch auditor should send an audit engagement letter to the appointing authority before the commencement of the audit.

6. Co-ordination with branch management

Co-ordination between the auditor and the branch management is essential for an effective audit. The branch auditor should send a formal communication to the branch management specifying the books, records and other information that would be required while conducting the audit.

13.8 INTERNAL CONTROLS

The existence and effective operation of an adequate system of internal control is an essential pre-requisite for efficient and effective functioning of any enterprise. Specific internal control procedures are to be followed in an enterprise depend upon variety of factors. However, as in the case of other enterprises, the generic internal controls in insurance companies generally fall under following categories:

13.8.1 Segregation and Rotation of Duties

One of the fundamental features of an effective internal control system is the segregation and rotation of duties in a manner conducive to prevention and timely detection of frauds and errors.

The functions, typically, segregated are as follows:

- Authorisation of transactions
- Execution of transactions
- Physical custody of related assets
- Maintenance of records and documents.

13.8.2 Authorisation of Transactions

The management of an enterprise delegates authority to different levels and to particular persons in the enterprise to execute specified kinds of transactions in accordance with the prescribed conditions. Authorisation may be general or it may be specific with reference to a single transaction. It is necessary to establish procedures, which provide assurance that authorisations are issued by persons acting within the scope of their authority and that the transactions conform to the terms of the authorisations.

The following procedures are usually established in insurance companies for this purpose:

- The financial and administrative powers of key officials are approved and noted in the Board meetings and other committee meetings.
- The financial and administrative powers of each official are fixed and communicated to all persons concerned.
- All financial decisions at any level are required to be reported to the next higher level for confirmation and information.
- Any deviation from the laid down procedures requires confirmation from/ intimation to higher authorities.
- Branch managers have to send periodic confirmation to their controlling authority on compliance of the laid down systems and procedures.

13.8.3 Maintenance of Adequate Records and Documents

The prime objective of accounting controls is to ensure that the transactions are recorded at correct amounts and in the accounting periods in which they are executed and that they are classified under appropriate accounts. The procedures adopted by insurance companies to achieve these objectives are quite similar to other commercial enterprises and include the following:

- All records are maintained in accordance with the prescribed regulations and furnish the information as required.
- Books are reviewed periodically by responsible official and balanced and reconciled where necessary.
- Inter-office transactions are reconciled within a specified time frame.
- Records are duly updated to ensure accountability and safeguarding of assets.
- Proper returns are received from branches at the corporate level for necessary accounting and reconciliation.

13.8.4 Accountability for and Safeguarding of Assets

Accountability of assets starts at the time of their acquisition and continue until their use and disposal. It is achieved by maintenance of records of assets and their periodic comparison with the related assets. To safeguard the assets, it is also necessary that the access to assets is limited to authorised personnel. This covers not only direct physical access, but also indirect access through preparation and processing of documents that authorise the use or disposal of assets. Significant controls in this regard generally followed in the insurance companies are as follows:

- All the assets held physically/by custodians are duly verified/confirmed on a periodic basis and verified with the underlying records as stated above. Any discrepancies need to be promptly dealt with.
- The assets are reviewed for impairment at the time of verification as stated above to reflect to the appropriate valuation in respect thereof.
- Sensitive items such as cash on hand, cheque books, electronic fund transfer access control to be under the responsibility/custody of at least two officers who have been instructed the importance of such responsibility.

POINTS TO PONDER

- The concept of life insurance business is unique in the sense that the concept of life fund and consequential segregation of shareholders fund from life fund and conditionalities of financial transactions between these two funds are not present in the conduct of any other business.
- The important statutory provisions relevant to the audit of life insurance companies include the Insurance Act, the Insurance Rules, the Income Tax Act, the Companies Act and the Life Insurance Corporation Act. In addition to that the accounting standards as issued by the Institute of Chartered Accountants of India are also applicable to the preparation of financial statements of the insurers.
- General insurance business usually involves fire, marine or miscellaneous business, whether carried on singly or in combination of one or more of them. Some common types of miscellaneous insurance include motor vehicle insurance, credit insurance, burglary insurance, loss of profit insurance, health insurance etc.
- The important statutory provisions relevant to the audit of general insurance companies include the Insurance Act, the Insurance Rules, the Income Tax Act, the Income Tax Rules, the Companies Act, the General Insurance Business (Nationalisation) Act and the Motor Vehicles Act. In addition to that the Accounting Standards as issued by the Institute of Chartered Accountants of India are also applicable to the preparation of financial statements of the insurers.
- An insurance company is required to maintain a number of books of accounts and registers, which include register of policies, register of claims, cash book, ledger subsidiary records and control registers.
- Every insurer is required to furnish to the authority a certified copy of every report on the affairs of the concerns, which is submitted to the members or policyholders of the insurer.
- The financial statements and the revenue accounts of every insurer are required to be audited annually. A chartered accountant fulfilling the requirements of the Companies Act can be appointed as an auditor of an insurer. The auditor is to be appointed at the annual general meeting and his remuneration is also fixed at that meeting. The auditor of an insurance company has the same power as those of a company auditor and the auditor is required to make a report to the members of the company.
- In the management report, every insurance company has to furnish a responsibility statement in connection with the existence and effective operation of an internal audit system.
- It is obligatory for an insurance company to get the financial statements of each of its branch offices audited except the exempted branches. The branch auditors furnish their audit reports to the central statutory auditors. The central statutory auditors have to consider the observations made in the branch auditor's report.
- The central statutory auditors, apart from examining consolidation of branch returns, look into specific matters, which are normally not dealt with at the branch level.
- The auditors of insurance companies can prepare themselves for conducting audit by following a number of stages, which include preliminary work, evaluation of internal

control system, preparation of audit programme, communication with the previous auditor and co-ordination with the branch management.

- The existence and effective operation of an adequate system internal control is an essential pre-requisite for efficient and effective functioning of any insurance business. The generic internal controls in insurance companies include segregation and rotation of duties, authorisation of transactions, maintenance of adequate records and documents and accountability for and safeguarding of assets.

REVIEW QUESTIONS

Short-answer Questions

1. What are the Acts and Rules that govern the accounts of companies carrying on general insurance business?
2. What are the registers to be maintained by an insurance company?
3. Name the books of accounts required to be maintained by a company carrying on life insurance business.
4. Who can be appointed as auditors of an insurance company?
5. How the auditor of a company carrying on life insurance business is appointed?
6. How is the remuneration of the auditor of a company carrying on general insurance business fixed?
7. State the powers of an auditor of an insurance company.
8. State the important matters, that the central statutory auditor looks into, while conducting audit at the head office level.

Essay-type Questions

1. State the important provisions of the IRDA regulations, 2000 governing the audit of an insurance company.
2. State the applicability of Accounting Standards to the preparation of financial statements of insurance companies.
3. What are the provisions of the Insurance Act, 1938 regarding submission of reports and returns by the insurance companies?
4. State the provisions as contained in Schedule C of IRDA Regulations, 2000 regarding Auditor's Report of an insurance company.
5. How do the auditors prepare themselves before undertaking audit of an insurance company?
6. Discuss, in detail, the internal control procedures, that should be adopted by an insurance company.

Reference: Guidance Notes issued by the Institute of Chartered Accountants of India on Life Insurance Business and General Insurance Business.

ANNEXURE

Extracts From
The Insurance Regulatory and Development Authority (Preparation of Financial Statements and Auditor's Report of Insurance Companies) Regulations, 2002
Schedule B

PART I

Accounting Principles for Preparation of Financial Statements

1. **Applicability of Accounting Standards:** Every Balance Sheet, Receipts and Payments Account [Cash Flow statement] and Profit and Loss Account [Shareholders' Account] of the insurer shall be in conformity with the Accounting Standards (AS) issued by the ICAI, to the extent applicable to the insurers carrying on general insurance business, except that:

   Accounting Standard 3 (AS 3), Cash Flow Statements—Cash Flow Statement shall be prepared only under the Direct Method. Accounting Standard 13 (AS 13), Accounting for Investments, shall not be applicable. Accounting Standard 17 (AS 17), Segment Reporting, shall apply to all insurers irrespective of the requirements regarding listing and turnover mentioned therein.

2. **Premium:** Premium shall be recognised as income over the contract period or the period of risk, whichever is appropriate. Premium received in advance, which represents premium income not relating to the current accounting period, shall be disclosed separately in the financial statements.

   A reserve for unexpired risks shall be created as the amount representing that part of the premium written which is attributable to, and to be allocated to the succeeding accounting periods and shall not be less than as required under Section 64 V (I) (ii) (b) of the Act:

   Premium Received in Advance, which represents premium received prior to the commencement of the risk, shall be shown separately under the head 'Current Liabilities' in the financial statements.

3. **Premium Deficiency:** Premium deficiency shall be recognised if the sum of expected claim costs, related expenses and maintenance costs exceeds related reserve for unexpired risks.

4. **Acquisition Costs:** Acquisition costs, if any, shall be expensed in the period in which they are incurred.

   Acquisition costs are those costs that vary with and are primarily related to the acquisition of new and renewal insurance contracts. The most essential test is the obligatory relationship between costs and the execution of insurance contracts (i.e. commencement of risk).

5. **Claims:** The components of the ultimate cost of claims to an insurer comprise the claims under policies and specific claims settlement costs. Claims under policies comprise the claims made for losses incurred, and those estimated or anticipated under the policies following a loss occurrence.

   A liability for outstanding claims shall be brought to account in respect of both direct business and inward reinsurance business. The liability shall include:

   (a) Future payments in relation to unpaid reported claims:

   (b) Claims Incurred But Not Reported (FBNR) including inadequate reserves [sometimes referred to as Claims Incurred But Not Enough Reported (IBNER)],

   which will result in future cash/asset outgo for settling liabilities against those claims. Change in estimated liability represents the difference between the estimated liability for outstanding claims at the beginning and at the end of the financial period.

The accounting estimate shall also include claims cost adjusted for estimated salvage value if there is sufficient degree of certainty of its realisation,

Actuarial Valuation of claim liability—in some cases: Claims made in respect of contracts where the claims payment period exceeds four years shall be recognised on an actuarial basis, subject to regulations that may be prescribed by the Authority.

In such cases, certificate from a recognised actuary as to the fairness of liability assessment must be obtained. Actuarial assumptions shall be suitably disclosed by way of notes to the account.

6. Procedure to determine the value of investments: An insurer shall determine the values of investments in the following manner:–

   (a) *Real Estate—Investment Property*: Investment Property shall be measured at historical cost *Less* accumulated depreciation and impairment loss, residual value being considered zero and no revaluation being permissible.

The insurer shall assess at each balance sheet date whether any impairment of the investment property has occurred. An impairment loss shall be recognised as an expense in the Revenue/Profit and Loss Account immediately.

Fair value as at the balance sheet date and the basis of its determination shall be disclosed in the financial statements as additional information.

   (b) *Debt Securities:* Debt securities including government securities and redeemable preference shares shall be considered as 'held to maturity' securities and shall be measured at historical cost subject to amortisation.

   (c) *Equity Securities and Derivative Instruments that are traded in active markets:* Listed equity securities and derivative instruments that are traded in active markets shall be measured at fair value as at the balance sheet date. For the purpose of calculation of fair value, the lowest of the last quoted closing price of the stock exchanges where the securities are listed shall be taken.

The insurer shall assess on each balance sheet date whether any impairment of listed equity security (ies)/derivative(s) instruments has occurred.

An active market shall mean a market, where the securities traded are homogenous, availability of willing buyers and willing sellers is normal and the prices are publicly available.

Unrealised gains/losses arising due to changes in the fair value of listed equity shares and derivative instruments shall be taken to equity under the head 'Fair Value Change Account'. The 'Profit on sale of investments' or 'Loss on sale of investments', as the case may be, shall include accumulated changes in the fair value previously recognised in equity under the heading Fair Value Change Account in respect of a particular security and being recycled to Profit and Loss Account on actual sale of that listed security.

For the removal of doubt, it is clarified that balance or any part thereof shall not be available for distribution as dividends. Also, any debit balance in the said Fair Value Change Account shall be reduced from the profits/free reserves while declaring dividends.

The insurer shall assess, at each balance sheet date, whether any impairment has occurred. An impairment loss shall be recognised as an expense in Revenue/Profit and Loss Account to the extent of the difference between the remeasured fair value of the security/investment and its acquisition cost as reduced by any previous impairment loss recognised as expense in Revenue/Profit and Loss Account. Any reversal of impairment loss, earlier recognized in Revenue/Profit and Loss Account shall be recognised in Revenue/Profit and Loss Account.

   (d) *Unlisted and other than actively traded Equity Securities and Derivative Instruments:* Unlisted equity securities and derivative instruments and listed equity securities and derivative instruments that are not regularly traded in active market will be measured at historical costs. Provision shall be made for diminution in value of such investments. The provision so made shall be reversed in subsequent periods if estimates based on external evidence show an increase in the value of the investment over its carrying amount. The increased carrying amount of the investment due to the reversal of the provision shall not exceed the historical cost.

For the purposes of this regulation, a security shall be considered as being not actively traded, if as per guidelines governing mutual funds laid down from time to time by SEB1, such a security is classified as 'thinly traded'.

7. Loans: Loans shall be measured at historical cost subject to impairment provisions. The insurer shall assess the quality of its loan assets and shall provide for impairment. The impairment provision shall not be lower than the amounts derived on the basis of guidelines prescribed from time to time by the Reserve Bank of India, that apply to companies and financial institutions.
8. Catastrophe Reserve: Catastrophe reserve shall be created in accordance with norms, if any, prescribed by the Authority. Investment of funds out of catastrophe reserve shall be made in accordance with prescription of the Authority.

PART II

Disclosures Forming Part of Financial Statements

A. The following shall be disclosed by way of notes to the Balance Sheet:

1. Contingent Liabilities:
   (a) Partly-paid up investments
   (b) Underwriting commitments outstanding
   (c) Claims, other than those under policies, not acknowledged as debts
   (d) Guarantees given by or on behalf of the company
   (e) Statutory demands liabilities in dispute, not provided for
   (f) Reinsurance obligations to the extent not provided for in accounts
   (g) Others (to be specified)
2. Encumbrances to assets of the company in and outside India.
3. Commitments made and outstanding for Loans, Investments and Fixed Assets.
4. Claims, Less reinsurance, paid to claimants in/outside India.
5. Actuarial assumptions for determination of claim liabilities in the case of claims where the claims payment period exceed four years.
6. Ageing of claims—distinguishing between claims outstanding for more than six months and other claims.
7. Premiums, Less reinsurance, written from business in/outside India.
8. Extent of premium income recognised, based on varying risk pattern, category wise, with basis and justification, therefore, including whether reliance has been placed on external evidence.
9. Value of contracts in relation to investments, for:
   (a) Purchases where deliveries are pending;
   (b) Sales where payments are overdue.
10. Operating expenses relating to insurance business: basis of allocation of expenditure to various classes of business.
11. Historical costs of those investments valued on fair value basis.
12. Computation of managerial remuneration.
13. Basis of amortisation of debt securities.
14. (a) Unrealised gain/losses arising due to changes in the fair value of listed equity shares and derivative instruments are to be taken to equity under the head 'Fair Value Change Account' and on realisation reported in profit and loss account.
    (b) Pending realization, the credit balance in the 'Fair Value Change Account' is not available for distribution.

15. Fair value of investment property and the basis therefore.
16. Claims settled and remaining unpaid for a period of more than six months as on the balance sheet date.

B. *The following accounting policies shall form an integral pan* of *the financial statements:*

1. All significant accounting policies in terms of the accounting standards issued by the ICAI. and significant principles and policies given in Part I of Accounting Principles. Any other accounting policies followed by the insurer shall be stated in the manner required under Accounting Standard AS 1 issued by the ICAI.
2. Any departure from the accounting policies as aforesaid shall be separately disclosed with reasons for such departure.

C. *The following information shall also be disclosed:*

1. Investments made in accordance with any statutory requirement should be disclosed separately together with its amount, nature, security and any special rights in and outside India.
2. Segregation into performing/non-performing investments for purpose of income recognition as per the directions, if any, issued by the Authority.
3. Percentage of business sector-wise.
4. A summary of financial statements for the last five years, in the manner as may be prescribed by the Authority.
5. The Authority may prescribe accounting Ratios as.
6. Basis of allocation of Interest, Dividends and Rent between Revenue Account and Profit and Loss Account.

PART III

General Instructions for Preparation of Financial Statements

1. The corresponding amounts for the immediately preceding financial year for all items shown in the Balance Sheet, Revenue Account and Profit and Loss Account should be given.
2. The figures in the financial statements may be rounded off to the nearest thousands.
3. Interest, dividends and rentals receivable in connection with an investment should be stated as gross value, the amount of income tax deducted at source being included under 'advance taxes paid'.
4. Income from rent shall not include any notional rent.
5. (I) For the purposes of financial statements, unless the context otherwise requires-
   - (a) the expression 'provision' shall, subject to note II below mean any amount written off or retained by way of providing for depreciation, renewals or diminution in value of assets, or retained by way of providing for any known liability or loss of which the amount cannot be determined with substantial accuracy;
   - (b) the expression 'reserve' shall not, subject to as aforesaid, include any amount written off or retained by way of providing for depreciation, renewals or diminution in value of assets or retained by way of providing for any known liability;
   - (c) the expression capital reserve shall not include any amount regarded as free for distribution through the profit and loss account; and the expression 'revenue reserve' shall mean any reserve other than a capital reserve;
   - (d) The expression "liability" shall include all liabilities in respect of expenditure contracted for and all disputed or contingent liabilities.

   (II) Where:
   - (a) any amount written off or retained by way of providing for depreciation, renewals or diminution in value of assets, or

(b) any amount retained by way of providing for any known liability is in excess of the amount which in the opinion of the directors is reasonably necessary for the purpose, the excess shall be treated for the purposes of these accounts as a reserve and not as a provision.

6. The company should make provisions for damages under lawsuits where the management is of the opinion that the award may go against the insurer.
7. Extent of risk retained and reinsured shall be separately disclosed.
8. Any debit balance of Profit and Loss Account shall be shown as deduction from uncommitted reserves and the balance if any, shall be shown separately.

PART IV

Contents of Management Report

There shall be attached to the financial statements, a management report containing, inter alia, the following duty authenticated by the management:

1. Confirmation regarding the continued validity of the registration granted by the Authority;
2. Certification that all the dues payable to the statutory authorities have been duly paid;
3. Confirmation to the effect that the shareholding pattern and any transfer of shares during the year are in accordance with the statutory or regulatory requirements;
4. Declaration that the management has not directly or indirectly invested outside India the funds of the holders of policies issued in India;
5. Confirmation that the required solvency margins have been maintained;
6. Certification to the effect that the values of all the assets have been reviewed on the date of the Balance Sheet and that in his (insurer's) belief the assets set forth in the balance sheets are shown in the aggregate at amounts not exceeding their realisable or market value under the several headings - 'Loans', 'Investments', 'Agents balances', 'Outstanding Premiums', 'Interest, Dividends and Rents outstanding', 'Interest, Dividends and Rents accruing but not due', 'Amounts due from other persons or Bodies carrying on insurance business', 'Sundry Debtors', 'Bills Receivable', 'Cash' and the several items specified under 'Other Accounts';
7. Disclosure with regard to the overall risk exposure and strategy adopted to mitigate the same;
8. Operations in other countries, if any, with a separate statement giving the managements estin,ate cf country risk and exposure risk and the hedging strategy adopted;
9. Ageing of claims indicating the trends in average claim settlement time during the preceding five years;
10. Certification to the effect as to how the values, as shown in the balance sheet, of the investments and stocks and shares have been arrived at, and how the market value thereof has been ascertained for the purpose of comparison with the values so shown;
11. Review of asset quality and performance of investment in terms of portfolios, i.e. separately in terms of real estate, loans, investments, etc.
12. A responsibility statement indicating therein that:
    (i) in the preparation of financial statements, the applicable accounting standards, principles and policies have been followed along with proper explanations relating to material departures, if any;
    (ii) the management has adopted accounting policies and applied them consistently and made judgements and estimates that are reasonable and prudent so as to give a true and fair view of the state of affairs of the company at the end of the financial year and of the operating profit or loss and of the profit or loss of the company for the year; .

(iii) the management has taken proper and sufficient care for the maintenance of adequate accounting records in accordance with the applicable provisions of the Insurance Act 1938 (4 of 1938)/Companies Act, 1956 (1 of 1956), for safeguarding the assets of the company and (or preventing and detecting fraud and other irregularities;

(iv) the management has prepared the financial statements on a going concern basis;

(v) the management has ensured that an internal audit system commensurate with the size and nature of that business exists and is operating effectively.

13. A schedule of payments, which have been made to individuals, firms, companies and organisations in which Directors of the insurer are interested.

PART V

Preparation of Financial Statements

1. An insurer shall prepare the Revenue Account, Profit and Loss Account [Shareholders' Account] and the Balance Sheet in Form B-RA, Form B-PL, and Form B-BS, or as near thereto as the circumstances permit.

Provided that an insurer shall prepare Revenue Accounts separately for fire, marine and miscellaneous insurance business and separate schedules shall be prepared for Marine Cargo, Marine-Other than Marine Cargo and the following classes of miscellaneous insurance business under miscellaneous insurance and Jingly application of AS 17, Segment Reporting, shall stand modified.

(a) Motor

(b) Workmen's Compensation/Employers' Liability

(c) Public/Product Liability

(d) Engineering

(e) Aviation

(f) Personal Accident

(g) Health Insurance

(h) Others

2. An insurer shall prepare separate Receipts and Payments Account in accordance with the Direct Method prescribed in AS 3, Cash Flow Statement, issued by the 1CAI.

FORM B-RA

Name of the Insurer:

Registration No. and Date of Registration with the IRDA

Revenue Account for the Year Ended 31st March, 20–

Particulars	Schedule	Current Year (Rs '000)	Previous Year (Rs '000)
1. Premiums earned (Net) Profit/Loss on sale/redemption of Investments	1		
3. Others (to be specified)			
4. Interest, Dividend & Rent-Gross			
Total (A)			
1. Claims Incurred (Net)	2		
2. Commission	3		
3. Operating Expenses related to Insurance Business	4		
Total (B)			
Operating Profit/(Loss) from Fire/Marine/ Miscellaneous Business C =(A – B)			
Appropriations			
Transfer to Shareholders' Account			
Transfer to Catastrophe Reserve			
Transfer to Other Reserves (to be specified)			
Total (C)			

FORM B-PL

Name of the Insurer:

Registration No. and Date of Registration with the IRDA

Profit and Loss Account for the Year Ended 31si March, 20–

Particulars	Schedule	Current Year (Rs.'000)	Previous Year (Rs.'000)
1. Operating profit/loss)			
(a) Fire Insurance			
(b) Marine Insurance			
(c) Miscellaneous Insurance			
2. Income from investments			
(a) Interest, Dividend & Rent-Gross			
(b) Profit on sale of investments			
Less: Loss on sale of investments			

3. Other income (to be specified)			
Total (A)			
4. Provisions (Other than taxation)			
(a) For diminution in the value of investments			
(b) For doubtful debts			
(c) Others (to be specified)			
5. Other expenses			
(a) Expenses other than those related to Insurance Business			
(b) Bad debts written off			
(c) Others (To be specified) Total (B)			
Profit Before Tax Provision for Taxation			
Appropriations			
(a) Interim dividends paid during the year			
(b) Proposed final dividend			
(c) Dividend distribution tax			
(d) Transfer to any Reserves or Other Accounts (to be specified)			
Balance of profit/loss brought forward from last year			
Balance carried forward to Balance Sheet			

Notes to Form B-RA and B-PL

(a) Premium income received from business concluded in and outside India shall be separately disclosed.

(b) Reinsurance premiums whether on business ceded or accepted are to be brought into account gross (i.e. before deducting commissions) under the head reinsurance premiums.

(c) Claims incurred shall comprise claims paid, specific claims settlement costs wherever applicable and change in the outstanding provision for claims at the year-end.

(d) Items of expenses and income in excess of one percent of the total premiums (*less* reinsurance) or Rs 500,000 whichever is higher, shall be shown as a separate line item,

(e) Fees and expenses connected with claims shall be included in claims.

(f) Under the sub-head 'Others' shall be included items like foreign exchange gains or losses and other, items.

(g) Interest, dividends and rentals receivable in connection with an investment should be stated as gross amount, the amount of income tax deducted at source being included under 'advance taxes paid and taxes deducted at source'.

(h) Income from rent shall include only the realised rent. It shall not include any notional rent.

FORM B-BS

Name of the Insurer:

Registration No. and Date of Registration with the IRDA

Balance Sheet as at 31st March, 20–

Particulars	*Schedule*	*Current Year (Rs '000)*	*Previous Year (Rs '000)*
Sources of funds			
Share capital	5		
Reserves and surplus	6		
Fair value change account.			
Borrowings	7		
Total			
Application of funds			
Investments	8		
Loans	9		
Fixed assets	10		
Current assets			
Cash and Bank Balances	11		
Advances and Other Assets	12		
Sub-Total (A)			
Current liabilities	13		
Provisions	14		
Sub-Total (B)			
Net current assets (C) = (A – B)			
Miscellaneous expenditure (to the extent not written off or adjusted)	15		
Debit balance in profit and loss account			
Total			
Contingent liabilities			
1. Partly paid-up investments			
2. Claims, other than against policies, not acknowledged as debts by the company			
3. Underwriting commitments outstanding (in respect of shares and securities)			
4. Guarantees given by or on behalf of the Company			
5. Statutory demands/liabilities in dispute, not provided for			
6. Reinsurance obligations to the extent not provided for in accounts			
7. Others (to be specified)			
Total			

Schedule 1—Premium Earned [Net]

Particulars	Current Year (Rs '000)	Previous Year (Rs '000)
Premium from direct business written *Add:* Premium on reinsurance accepted *Less:* Premium on reinsurance ceded Net Premium Adjustment for change in reserve for unexpired risks **Total Premium Earned (Net)**		

Note: Reinsurance premiums whether on business ceded or accepted are to be brought into account, before deducting commission, under the head of reinsurance premiums.

Schedule 2—Claims Incurred [Net]

Particulars	Current Year (Rs '000)	Previous Year (Rs '000)
Claims paid Direct *Add:* Re-insurance accepted *Less:* Re-insurance Ceded Net Claims paid *Add:* Claims Outstanding at the end of the year *less:* Claims Outstanding at the beginning Total Claims Incurred		

Notes:

(a) Incurred But Not Reported (IBNR) Incurred but not enough reported (IBNER) claims should be included in the amount for outstanding claims.

(b) Claims includes specific claims settlement cost but not expenses of management.

(c) The surveyor fees, legal and other expenses shall also form part of claims cost.

(d) Claims cost should be adjusted for estimated salvage value if there is a sufficient certainty of its realisation.

Schedule 3—Commission

Particulars	Current Year (Rs '000)	Previous Year (Rs '000)
Commission paid Direct *Add:* Re-insurance Accepted *Less:* Commission on Reinsurance Ceded Net Commission		

Note: Profit/commission, if any. are to be combined with Re-insurance accepted or Re-insurance ceded figures.

Schedule 4—Operating Expenses Related to Insurance Business

Particulars	Current Year (Rs '000)	Previous Year (Rs '000)
1. Employees' remuneration & welfare benefits		
2. Travel, conveyance and vehicle running expenses		
3. Training expenses		
4. Rents, rates & taxes		
5. Repairs		
6. Printing & stationery		
7. Communication		
8. Legal & professional charges		
9. Auditors' fees, expenses etc,		
(a) as auditor		
(b) as adviser or in any other capacity, in respect of		
(i) Taxation matters		
(ii) Insurance matters		
(iii) Management services; and		
(c) in any other capacity		
10. Advertisement and publicity		
11. Interest & Bank Charges		
12. Others (to be specified)		
13. Depreciation		
Total		

Note: Items of expenses and income in excess of one percent of1he total premiums (*Less* reinsurance) or Rs 5,00,000, whichever is higher, shall be shown as a separate line item.

Schedule 5—Share Capital

Particulars	Current Year (Rs '000)	Previous Year (Rs '000)
1. *Authorised Capita/:* Equity Shares of Rs... each		
2. *Issued Capital:* Equity Shares of Rs. each		
3. *Subscribed Capital:* Equity Shares of Rs. each		
4. *Called-up Capital*		
Equity Shares of Rs. ..each		
Less: Calls unpaid		
Add Equity Shares forfeited (Amount originally paid up)		
Less: Par Value of Equity Shares bought back		
Less: Preliminary Expenses		
Expenses including commission or brokerage on Underwriting or subscription of shares		
Total		

Notes:

(a) Particulars of the different classes of capital should be separately stated.

(b) The amount capitalised on account of issue of bonus shares should be disclosed.

(c) In case any part of the capital is held by a holding company, the same should be separately disclosed.

Schedule 5a—Share Capital-pattern Of Shareholding [As Certified By The Management]

	Shareholder	Current Year		Previous Year	
		Number of Shares	*% of Holding*	*Number of Shares*	*% of Holding*
Promoters • Indian • Foreign Others **Total**					

Schedule 6—Reserves and Surplus

Particulars	*Current Year (Rs '000)*	*Previous Year (Rs '000)*
1. Capital Reserve		
2. Capital Redemption Reserve		
3. Share Premium		
4. General Reserves		
Less: Debit balance in Profit and Loss Account *Less:* Amount utilized for Buy-back		
5. Catastrophe Reserve		
6. Other Reserves (to be specified)		
7. Balance of Profit in Profit & Loss Account		
Total		

Note: Additions to and deductions from the reserves should be disclosed under each of the specified heads.

Schedule 7—Borrowings

Particulars	*Current Year (Rs '000)*	*Previous Year (Rs '000)*
1. Debentures/Bonds		
2. Banks		
3. Financial Institutions		
4. Others (to be specified)		
Total		

Notes:

(a) The extent to which the borrowings are secured shall be separately disclosed stating the nature of the security under each sub-head.

(b) Amounts due within 12 months from the date of Balance Sheet should be shown separately

Schedule 8—Investments

Particulars	Current Year (Rs '000)	Previous Year (Rs '000)
Long-term investments		
1. Government securities and Government guaranteed bonds including Treasury Bills		
2. Other Approved Securities		
3. Other Investments		
(a) Shares		
(aa) Equity		
(bb) Preference		
(b) Mutual Funds		
(c) Derivative Instruments		
(d) Debentures/Bonds		
(e) Other Securities (to be specified)		
(f) Subsidiaries		
(g) Investment Properties-Real Estate		
4. Investments in Infrastructure and Social Sector		
5. Other than Approved Investments		
Short term investments		
1. Government securities and Government guaranteed bonds including Treasury Bills		
2. Other Approved Securities		
3. Other Investments		
(a) Shares		
(aa) Equity		
(bb) Preference		
(b) Mutual Funds		
(c) Derivative Instruments		
(d) Debentures/Bonds		
(e) Other Securities (to be specified)		
(f) Subsidiaries		
(g) Investment Properties-Real Estate		
4. Investments in Infrastructure and Social Sector		
5. Other than Approved Investments		
Total		

Notes:

(a) Investments in subsidiary/holding companies, joint ventures and associates shall be separately disclosed, at cost.

(i) Holding company and subsidiary shall be construed as defined in the Companies Act, 1956.

(ii) Joint Venture is a contractual arrangement whereby two or more parties undertake an economic activity, which is subject to joint control.

(iii) Joint control is the contractually agreed sharing of power to govern the financial and operating policies of an economic activity to obtain benefits from it.

(iv) Associate is an enterprise in which the company has significant influence and which is neither a subsidiary nor a joint venture of the company.

(v) Significant influence (for the purpos:e of this schedule) -means participation in the financial and operating policy decisions of a company, but not control of those policies. Significant influence may be exercised in several ways, for example, by representation on the board of directors, participation in the policymaking process, material inter-company transactions, interchange of managerial personnel or dependence on technical information. Significant influence may be gained by share ownership, statute or agreement. As regards share ownership, if an investor holds, directly or indirectly through subsidiaries, 20 percent or more of the voting power of the investee, it is presumed that the investor does have significant influence, unless it can be clearly demonstrated that this is not the case. Conversely, if the investor holds, directly or indirectly through subsidiaries, less than 20 percent of the voting power of the investee, it is presumed that the investor does not have significant influence, unless such influence is clearly demonstrated. A substantial or majority ownership by another investor does not necessarily preclude an investor from having significant influence.

(b) Aggregate amount of company's investments other than listed equity securities and derivative instruments and also the market value thereof shall be disclosed.

(c) Investments made out of Catastrophe reserve should be shown separately.

(d) Debt securities will be considered as 'held to maturity' securities and will be measured at historical cost subject to amortisation.

(e) Investment Property means a property [land or building or part of a building or both held to earn rental income or for capital appreciation or for both, rather than for use in services or for administrative purposes.

(f) Investments maturing within twelve months from balance sheet date and investments made with the specific intention to dispose of within twelve months from balance sheet date shall be classified as short-term investments.

Schedule 9—Loans

Particulars	*Current Year (Rs '000)*	*Previous Year (Rs '000)*
1. Security-wise classification		
Secured		
(a) On mortgage of property		
(aa) In India (bb) Outside India		
(b) On Shares, Bonds, Govt. Securities		
(c) Others (to be specified) *Unsecured*		
Total		
2. Borrower-wise classification		
(a) Central and State Governments		
(b) Banks and Financial Institutions		
(c) Subsidiaries		
(d) Industrial Undertakings		
(e) Others (to be specified)		
Total		
3. Performance-wise classification		
(a) Loans classified as standard		
(aa) In India (bb) Outside India		

(b) Non-performing loans \ *less* provisions		
(aa) In India		
(bb) Outside India Total		
4. Maturity-wise classification		
(a) Short Term		
(b) Long-Term		
Total		

Notes:

(a) Short-term loans shall include those, which are repayable within 12 months from the date of balance sheet. Long term loans shall be the loans other than short-term loans.

(b) Provisions against non-performing loans shall be shown separately.

(c) The nature of the security in case of all long term secured loans shall be specified in each case. Secured loans for the purposes of this schedule, means loans secured wholly or partly against an asset of the company.

(d) Loans considered doubtful and the amount of provision created against such loans shall be disclosed.

Schedule 10—Fixed Assets

(Rs. '000)

Particulars	*Cost/Gross Block*				*Depreciation*				*Net Block*	
	Opening	*Additions*	*Deductions*	*Closing*	*Uplo Last year*	*For The Year*	*On Sales/Adj-usiments*	*To Date*	*As at Year end*	*Previous Year*
Goodwill										
Intangibles (specify) land-Freehold leasehold										
Property Buildings furniture & Fittings										
Information Technology Equipment										
Vehicles										
Office Equipment										
Others (Specify nature)										
Total										
Work in progress										
Grand Total										
Previous Year										

Note: Assets included in land, building and property above exclude Investment Properties as defined in note (e) to Schedule 8.

Schedule 11—Cash and Bank Balances

Particulars	*Current Year (Rs '000)*	*Previous Year (Rs '000)*
1. Cash (including cheques, drafts and stamps)		
2. Bank Balances		
(a) Deposit Accounts		
(aa) Short-term (due within 12 months)		
(bb) Others		
(b) Current Accounts		
(c) Others (to be specified)		
3. Money at Call and Short Notice		
(a) With Banks		
(b) With other Institutions		
4. Others (to be specified)		
Total		
Balances with non-scheduled banks included in 2 *and* 3 *above*		

Note: Bank balance may include remittances in transit. If so, the nature and amount should be separately stated.

Schedule 12—Advances and Other Assets

Particulars	*Current Year (Rs '000)*	*Previous Year (Rs '000)*
Advances		
1. Reserve deposits with ceding companies		
2. Application money for investments		
3. Prepayments		
4. Advances to Directors/Officers		
5. Advance tax paid and taxes deducted at source (Net of provision for taxation)		
6. Others (to be specified)		
Total (A) Other Assets		
1. Income accrued on investments		
2. Outstanding Premiums		
3. Agents' Balances		
4. Foreign Agencies Balances		
5. Due from other entities carrying on insurance business (including reinsurers)		
6. Due from subsidiaries/holding		
7. Deposit with Reserve Bank of India [Pursuant to Section 7 of Insurance Act, 1938]		
8. Others (to be specified)		
Total (B)		
Total (A+B)		

Notes:

(a) The items under the above heads shall not be shown net of provisions for doubtful amounts. The amount of provision against each head should be shown separately.

(b) The term 'officer' should conform to the definition of that term as given under the Companies Act, 1956.

(c) Sundry Debtors will be shown under the item 8 (others).

Schedule 13—Current Liabilities

Particulars	*Current Year (Rs '000)*	*Previous Year (Rs '000)*
1. Agents' Balances		
2. Balances due to other insurance companies		
3. Deposits held on re-insurance ceded		
4. Premiums received in advance		
5. Unallocated Premium		
6. Sundry creditors		
7. Due to subsidiaries/holding company		
8. Claims Outstanding		
9. Due to Officers/Directors		
10. Others (to be specified)		
Total		

Schedule 14—Provisions

Particulars	*Current Year (Rs '000)*	*Previous Year (Rs '000)*
1. Reserve for Unexpired Risk		
2. For taxation (*Less* advance tax paid and taxes deducted at source)		
3. For proposed dividends		
4. For dividend distribution tax		
5. Others (to be specified)		
Total		

Schedule 15—Miscellaneous Expenditure (To the Extent Not Written Off or Adjusted)

Particulars	*Current Year (Rs '000)*	*Previous Year (Rs '000)*
1. Discount Allowed in issue of shares/debentures		
2. Others (to be specified)		
Total		

Notes:

1. No item shall be included under the head 'Miscellaneous Expenditure' and carried forward unless:
   (a) some benefit from the expenditure can reasonably be expected to be received in future, and
   (b) the amount of such benefit is reasonably determinable.
2. The amount to be carried forward in respect of any item included under the head 'Miscellaneous Expenditure' shall not exceed the expected future revenue/other benefits related to the expenditure.

Schedule

Auditor's Report

The report of the auditors on the financial statements of every insurer shall deal with the matters specified herein:

1. (a) That they have obtained all the information and explanations which, to the best of their knowledge and beliefs were necessary for the purposes of their audit and whether they have found them satisfactory;
   (b) Whether proper books of account have been maintained by the insurer so far as appears from an examination of those books;
   (c) Whether proper returns, audited or unaudited, from branches and other offices have been received and whether they were adequate for the purpose of audit;
   (d) Whether the Balance sheet, Revenue account, Profit and Loss account and the Receipts and Payments Account dealt with by the report are in agreement with the books of account and returns:
   (e) Whether the actuarial valuation of liabilities is duly certified by the appointed actuary including to the effect that the assumptions for such valuation are in accordance with the guidelines and norms, if any, issued by the Authority and/or the Actuarial Society of India in concurrence with the Authority.
2. The auditors shall express their opinion on:
   (a) (i) Whether the balance sheet gives a true and fair view of the insurer's affairs as at the end of the financial year/period; (ii) Whether the revenue account gives a true and fair view of the surplus or the deficit for the financial year/period; (iii) Whether the profit and loss account gives a true and fair view of the profit or loss for the financial year/period; (iv) Whether the receipts and payments account gives a true and fair view of the receipts and payments for the financial year/period;
   (b) The financial statements slated at (a) above are prepared in accordance with the requirements of the Insurance Act, 1938 (4 of 1938), the Insurance Regulatory and Development Authority Act, 1999 (41 of 1999) and the Companies Act, 1956 (1 of 1956), to the extent applicable and in the manner so required.
   (c) Investments have been valued in accordance with the provisions of the Act and these Regulations.
   (d) The accounting policies selected by the insurer are appropriate and are in compliance with the applicable accounting standards and with the accounting principles, as prescribed in these Regulations or any order or direction issued by the Authority in this behalf.
3. The auditor shall further certify that:
   (a) they have reviewed the management report and there is no apparent mistake or material inconsistencies with the financial statements;
   (b) the insurer has complied with the terms and conditions of the registration stipulated by the Authority.
4. A certificate signed by the auditors [which shall be in addition to any other certificate or report which is required by law to be given with respect to the balance sheet] certifying that:
   (a) they have verified the cash balances and the securities relating to the insurer's loans, reversions and life interests (in the case of life insurers) and investments;
   (b) to what extent, if any, they have verified the investments and transactions relating to any trusts undertaken by the insurer as trustee; and
   (c) no part of the assets of the policyholders' funds has been directly or indirectly applied in contravention of the provisions of the Insurance Act, 1938 relating to the application and investments of the policyholders' funds.

CHAPTER 14

Investigation

CHAPTER OUTLINE

14.1 INTRODUCTION

In addition to regular audit of the books of accounts of an enterprise, there may be the requirement of thorough examination of the accounts and records of past several years to fulfill certain objectives from time to time. In order to carry out thorough examination of books of accounts and records of an enterprise, investigation is undertaken. Investigation implies an enquiry into the accounts and business records to attain certain specific objective. In most cases, the purpose of such enquiry is to ascertain the true financial position of the concern or its normal profit-earning capacity or the extent of fraud. Thus, investigation is a special type of examination of accounts and records carried on by an investigator with a pre-determined objective according to the requirement of the situation and entail something beyond the verification of accuracy of figures in the financial statements.

14.2 DEFINITION

An investigation may be defined as a special examination of and enquiry into books of accounts and other related records with a view to establishing a fact or to evaluating a state of affairs or to determining causes for a happening in a business. For example, an investigation may be conducted into the accounts of a firm whose business is to be acquired by a company or investigation may be required to establish the extent of a suspected fraud.

In the opinion of Taylor and Perry, "investigation involves enquiry into facts behind the accounts, i.e. into the technical, financial and economic position of the business organisation."

So, investigation is a special type of examination of accounts and records carried on by the investigator with a pre-determined purpose in accordance with the necessity of the situation and are concerned with something more than the verification of accuracy of the figures of the financial statements.

14.3 OBJECTIVES OR PURPOSES OF INVESTIGATION

The need of investigation may arise in many cases, but these are some of the circumstances where investigation is most frequently called for:

1. For purchasing any business

Investigation can be conducted by a person on behalf of his client, when the client intends to purchase an existing business.

2. For admission of a new partner

Investigation into the affairs of a partnership firm can be made by any person on behalf of the incoming partner of an existing partnership business.

3. For seeking avenues of investment

In order to measure the financial solvency position of any business, investigation can be done. The financial solvency is measured through investigation on behalf of a person who seeks avenues of investment.

4. For granting loan or financial assistance

Investigation can also be undertaken on behalf of a bank or other financial institutions proposing to extend or grant loans to its client or alter the terms and conditions of the same.

5. For suspected fraud

If the owner or the management suspects fraud, they can appoint an investigator to detect the fraud activated by the employees.

6. For abnormal fluctuation of profit

Investigation can be conducted on behalf of the owner or the management of a business in order to ascertain the reason of abnormal fluctuation in profit in the organisation.

7. For settlement of tax liability

Investigation can be undertaken for the settlement of tax liability or in some cases for the detection of undisclosed income of the assessee.

8. For settlement of insurance claim

In case of fire or other hazards, the organisations have to submit claim to the insurance company to recover the loss. The insurance company can appoint an investigator to determine the exact amount of loss for settlement of claim.

9. For valuation of goodwill and shares

The shares and goodwill of the business are required to be valued on different occasions. In order to calculate the fair value of shares and goodwill, investigation can be undertaken.

10. For judging sickness of a business unit

Government may consider to take over a sick industrial unit and for this purpose, it may give appointment to an investigator to investigate into the affairs of the sick unit.

11. For the provisions of the Companies Act

Section 235 to Section 251 of the Companies Act provide regulations for the investigation of any company under different specific situations.

12. For justifying negligence of the auditor

In some cases, the auditor is held liable for negligence in his duty. But before accusing auditors for negligence, the case has to be properly investigated.

13. For complaint by the shareholders

Investigation can also be undertaken by the management on the basis of complaints made by the shareholders.

14. For the affairs of a trust

Investigations are sometimes required to be conducted on behalf of the beneficiaries of any trust into the affairs of a trust for suspected fraud.

15. For the liquidation of the business

Investigation of suspected fraud or misfeasance against the Directors on behalf of the liquidator of a company could also be undertaken.

14.4 FEATURES OF INVESTIGATION

"An investigation is an examination of accounting records undertaken for a special purpose; in effect it is an audit of which the scope is limited or extended in accordance with the requirement of the particular purpose. Its objective is usually to discover and display the facts in such a manner as will enable the parties for whom it is undertaken to draw conclusions and make their decisions accordingly."

On the basis of analysis of the above definition, the following inherent features of investigation can be identified:

- Investigation is normally conducted with certain specific objectives.
- It involves critical examination and verification of specific records.
- There are no statutory provisions or rules prescribed for investigation except in case of companies. It is voluntary and contractual in nature.
- It is not only confined to examination of financial aspects of an organisation, but also concerned with the policy matters.
- It is undertaken with certain suspicion, depending on the nature of the objective for which it is undertaken.
- In most of the cases, the future courses of action have to be outlined by the investigator.
- In addition to the detailed analysis and study of the books of accounts and records, personal examination of individuals may also be undertaken.
- The scope of investigation may be limited to a certain specific objective or extended to cover a number of objectives according to the requirements of the situation.
- The investigator reports to the person/s who is/are responsible for his appointment.
- In the report, the factual information has to be given in analytical as well as descriptive manner.

14.5 TERMS OF REFERENCE

In the case of a private investigation, e.g. one undertaken on behalf of a prospective purchaser of a business, the investigating accountant must obtain precise instructions from his client as to his terms of reference the purpose of investigation, the amount of detailed work required etc. These terms of references must be set out clearly in a letter of engagement.

In the case of investigation governed by statute, e.g. reports for prospectus, the reporting accountant must be fully conversant with the statutory regulations and must also obtain necessary instructions where that would be applicable.

14.6 WORKING METHODS

Having clearly established the purpose of the investigation, the investigator will first make such preliminary inquiries as are necessary to ascertain the information that is required to enable him to plan his investigation.

He will then draft an outline report, detailing the headings, which he will use in his final report. These will vary according to the nature of investigation being undertaken, but if a business were being investigated on behalf of a prospective purchaser, the headings could be as follows:

- The business and its history
- Management and the staff
- Sales and marketing
- Purchasers and suppliers
- Trading results as per audited accounts
- Future prospects and trends
- Assets and liabilities
- Conclusions and recommendations

After drafting the outline report, the investigator will undertake the detailed work necessary to complete the investigation. This will normally be mainly composed of interviews and discussions with relevant persons and work on the accounts and records, but on every investigation he will need to exercise his judgment as to exactly understand the work to be undertaken. Detailed working papers will be prepared and from those working papers the final report will be written. These working papers must be carefully preserved. In the event of a dispute arising and negligence being alleged against the investigating accountant, these working papers would be vital evidence in litigation. When the investigation is completed, the draft report will be finalised.

14.7 DUTIES OF AN INVESTIGATOR

The procedures to be followed in an investigation depend on the nature of investigation, its purpose and the circumstances of the case in which the investigation was undertaken. In all the cases of investigation, certain precautionary measures are required to be taken by the investigator. These measures are considered as the duties of the investigator, which he should follow in discharging his duties in conducting investigation. These duties are given below.

1. Obtaining written instruction about scope and objectives of investigation

Before starting an investigation, the investigator should obtain from the client clear written instruction about the scope of his work and purposes of investigation. If the client is interested to impose any restriction or limitation to his work, he should also get it in writing so that he may exactly determine the scope of his work and the nature of his duties.

The period to be covered in the investigation should also be confirmed by the investigator from his client clearly in writing. The period is very important because the investigator can accordingly restrict his examination of transactions and records to that period only.

2. Framing investigation programme

Based on the objectives, scope and period to be covered, an effective investigation programme should be chalked out. The investigation programme should be flexible, so that the investigator may make required changes in the programme during actual investigation. Such flexibility in the programme is necessary, since many steps in an investigation depend on the results of the earlier steps.

3. Collection of information about the business

It is not possible for the investigator to give correct interpretation and reporting of the fact, if he does not have the detailed knowledge of the activities of the enterprise for which he is to conduct investigation. So, before starting his work of investigation, the investigator should collect all relevant information about the activities of the enterprise.

4. Enquiry about the reputation of the enterprise

The investigator should make enquiries and collect information about the reputation of different individuals working in the organisation. Information should also be obtained about the goodwill of the enterprise. This information will help the investigator a lot in preparing his report.

5. Taking expert advice

The investigator should take the assistance of experts during the course of his examination, if required, and consult experts on matters in which his knowledge is not adequate.

6. Reliance on accounts and records

If the books of accounts and required records have been properly maintained and the accounts have been audited, the work of the investigator becomes simplified as he is entitled to rely upon the audited accounts and properly maintained records.

So, usually the investigator should avoid duplication of work and concentrate more on such procedures as will be more purposeful for investigation. But the fact that the investigator has depended on the audited books of accounts should be included in the investigation report.

7. Preservation of working papers

It is the duty of the investigator to maintain his working papers properly. A complete record of work carried out, records examined, relevant information and evidence collected etc. should be kept in his file together with important statements, schedules and documents. These working papers will help him at the time of finalisation of report. These working papers can also be valuable documents in his defense, in case the affected parties subsequently challenge his findings.

8. Maintenance of secrecy and confinement to purpose

The investigator should always keep in mind the purpose of investigation, as the purpose of investigation will determine which records and figures should be examined in detail, which need not be examined, for which cases detailed checking may be avoided, what information he should seek from sources other than books and records and what procedures should he adopt in his investigation work. On the other hand, secrecy is the basic necessity of any investigation. So, the investigator should keep the details of the investigation very secret.

9. Maintenance of minimum standard of work

The investigator must be honest and he should approach his work with reasonable care, skill and diligence. He should not allow himself to be influenced by others, as total independence is required in investigation. So, the investigator should always keep himself free from the influence of interested persons.

10. Proper and correct reporting

The investigation report should be clear and unambiguous. The investigator should analyse the data and evidence collected by him. He must take great care to see that his report does not contain any wrong information. So, before signing his report, he should carefully check the content of his report with preserved working papers and notes. This is very important as incorrect report may mislead his client and invite legal action against him.

14.8 INVESTIGATION REPORT

The report on the investigation must be carefully prepared. It should be simply worded, very clear in its meaning and as concise as practicable in the given circumstance. It must, however, give full consideration to all the factors affecting the decision to be made.

The form of the report will normally be an introduction setting out the terms of reference and the nature of the enterprise being investigated. A main section will be there setting out the facts ascertained and detailing the work performed, and a final section setting out the conclusions and the recommendations. It should be remembered that the main points of the report are not obscured by details; any voluminous statistics should be relegated to appendices and referenced to the relevant part of the report.

Investigation report should contain all important and relevant matters. He must present in his report what is essential, ignoring what is not essential. Facts and only facts should be presented and nothing based on estimates should be given. The investigator should mention in his report the instructions given to him by his client with regard to the investigation. He must mention the limits, if any, put in the scope of his work.

14.9 QUALITIES OF AN INVESTIGATOR

An investigating accountant should combine sound auditing techniques, considerable experience, sound judgment and a good understanding of a variety of business enterprises. Because of the demanding nature of the work, it will usually be found that partners and senior staff will personally perform a higher proportion of the work on investigation than on audits.

The investigator must approach his work methodically. He must work honestly and diligently. He must keep the interest of his client at the top and must work with a feeling of some service to the client. The subject of the investigation is highly technical in nature and usually a senior accountant with profound knowledge and experience suitable for the job. He need not be a chartered accountant, but he must have sound knowledge of accounting and auditing and practical knowledge about the various affairs of different types of enterprises. He must be a man of competence and ability to understand different critical matters clearly. He must possess the ability to grasp things easily and express them in clear words. While conducting the investigation, he must exert utmost care, skill and reasonable diligence keeping in mind all through the purpose of investigation.

14.10 DIFFERENCE BETWEEN INVESTIGATION AND AUDITING

The difference between audit and investigation is outlined in Table 14.1.

TABLE 14.1 Distinction between audit and investigation

Points of difference	*Audit*	*Investigation*
1. Interested parties	Audit is conducted on behalf of the shareholders or proprietors.	Investigation is usually carried out on behalf of outsiders who intend to purchase the business or who wish to lend money and thus want to know the earning capacity or the financial position of the concern.
2. Legal aspects	Audit is compulsory for a corporate business according to the Companies Act.	Investigation is not compulsory.
3. Inter-dependence	Audited accounts are not audited again except in case of special audit u/s 233 A.	Investigation may be conducted even though the accounts have been audited.
4. Duration	The audit of accounts is usually for a year or six months.	Investigation may cover a period extending over three to seven years.
5. Depth of work	Audit is a kind of test checking.	Investigation is a thorough examination of the books of accounts.
6. Subject matter	Audit includes an examination of the books of accounts.	Investigation is not only an examination of accounts, but also inquiry into other factors, i.e. it goes beyond the books of accounts.
7. Computation of net profit	Audit is not concerned with the alteration of figures and introduction of adjustments to have net profits from different points of view.	Net profit or the actual earning capacity of the concern is ascertained by making certain adjustments in the net profit as calculated.
8. Purpose	Audit is conducted to know the true and fair view of the books of accounts.	Investigation is conducted to know the financial position and the earning capacity of the concern.

14.11 TYPES OF INVESTIGATIONS

There are many types of investigations, but certain main classes can be identified. Following are some of the areas where the investigation is mostly called for:

1. Investigation on behalf of a person or company who wants to purchase a running business.
2. Investigation on behalf of a person who is interested to join as a partner in a partnership firm.
3. Investigation on behalf of a person who wants to lend money to a business or is interested to know its financial position.
4. Investigation on behalf of the owner/shareholder of the business who suspects a fraud.
5. Investigation on behalf of the tax authority for assessing actual tax liability.

6. Investigation on behalf of prospective shareholders who wish to make a valuation of shares of a limited company.
7. Investigation on behalf of government into the affairs of a sick company.
8. Investigation under the Indian Companies Act, i.e. the statutory investigation.

All these cases are discussed separately in detail as follows:

14.11.1 Investigation on behalf of a Person or Company Wanting to Purchase a Running Business

The purchaser of an existing running business may be interested to know the earning power and the future prospects of the business. He would like to know the worth of the business and how much he should pay for the purchase of that business. Investigation has got a higher responsibility in this case, as his client would take the decision on the basis of the report of the investingator.

Therefore, the investigator should pay due attention on the following points:

1. Preliminary matters

(a) Letter of engagement The purpose and scope of the investigation would be agreed with the client. Such matters as who could be approached for information, the amount of detailed work to be undertaken and the approximate fee authorised, would be settled. These would be formally confirmed in a letter of engagement.

(b) Outline report Initial discussions would be held with the auditors, if any, and the management of the business being investigated. The history and the nature of the business would be considered. The outline report would then be drafted and the detailed work to be undertaken would be planned.

2. Detailed work of investigation

(a) Inquiries The investigator would hold exhaustive discussions of relevant matters with the management, senior staff and the auditors, if any, of the business. He would also make any necessary inquiries of third parties.

(b) Accounts The accounts of the business for an agreed period would be obtained and considered. The period selected is often three years, as that allows trends to be established and comparisons to be made without going back to periods that are so remote to be irrelevant. The investigator would form an opinion as to the reliability of the accounts.

The investigator would make the necessary adjustments to the accounts under review. These adjustments would be of two types:

(i) Correctness to accounts: Assets would be adjusted to their true values. Slow moving or obsolete stocks would be written down. Bad debts would be written off. Any liabilities omitted would be brought in. Any other relevant correction would be made.

(ii) Adjustment to accounts: When items relating to the past have no relevance to the future, appropriate adjustments would be made. Details of all adjustments would be shown in appendices to the accounts.

Once the accounts for the relevant years has been adjusted, they would be set out in columnar form so that trends would be clearly shown. To assist the making of comparisons, the important percentages and ratios would be inserted.

The important percentages and ratios, which are required to be calculated in this respect may include the following:

- Percentage of gross profit on turnover
- Percentage of net profit on turnover
- Ratio of stock to cost of sales
- Ratio of debtors to turnover
- Ratio of creditors to purchases
- Ratio of current assets to current liabilities
- Ratio of liquid assets to liquid liabilities

(c) Consideration apart from the accounts The scope of the investigator would not normally be confined to the accounts. Therefore, he would consider all other relevant matters, which include the following:

- The economic prospects for the trade or industry
- The trends and mix of sales
- Any local planning matters affecting the business
- The probable effects of any proposed legislation
- Actual competition of rival businesses, or the threat of future competition
- Whether there could be difficulty in renewing any important contract
- Whether premises are leasehold, when the leases are due for renewal and whether they can be renewed and if so, on what terms
- The state of the fixed assets and their potential future life
- The competence and age of the key staff and
- Any relevant matters concerning the tax position of the business

3. Report

Once the detailed work had been completed, the report would be finalised. The final section on the result of the investigation and the conclusions to be drawn from them would be written, and the report would be submitted to the client.

14.11.2 Investigation on Behalf of a Person Who Wants to be the Partner in a Partnership Firm

A person admitted to the partnership becomes the co-partner and the co-owner of the properties of the firm. Hence, the incoming partner would like to know the profitability, sound financial position of the business, efficiency and the extent of the use of the capacity of the fixed capital in the firm.

Under these circumstances, an investigator is required to take a note of the objective of the firm and the terms, conditions, provisions of the partnership deed, nature of the business and the existing partner's capital balance and their profit sharing ratio.

In addition to the above noted points, the investigator should pay due attention to the following points:

1. Quality of the existing partners

Partnership business is basically dependent on the trustworthiness of the partners. Before being admitted into a partnership firm as a new partner, the character and quality of the existing partners should be first evaluated.

2. Reason for admission

The investigator should know the reasons for taking new partner in the firm. The reasons for the admission of a new partner could be that the business is expanding or that an existing partner is retiring, but it could be that the business is undercapitalised or facing some other trading difficulty.

3. Examination of the partnership deed

The terms of the partnership agreement or if there is no written agreement, the present arrangements and effects of the Partnership Act should be examined with regard to the following matters:

(a) The term for admitting the new partner particularly with regard to the treatment of goodwill and the valuation of asset

(b) The provisions regarding the appropriation of profits, including whether there are arrangements for the accounts to be audited to establish agreed profits

(c) The provisions for dealing with the dissolution of the partnership on the death or retirement of a partner, particularly with regard to the treatment and the valuation of assets

(d) The rights of the individual partners and the provisions for dealing with disputes.

4. Analysis of profitability and prospect

The prospects for the partnership firm, given the general economic trends for the profession, industry or trade in which it is operating and such special factors as its reliance on any large customers or contracts should also be examined by the investigator.

5. Ascertainment of financial position

The investigator will analyse the financial position of the firm on the basis of different aspects such as liquidity, solvency, adequacy of working capital, collection from customers and net worth of the business. He should ensure that all the assets and liabilities as disclosed in the latest balance sheet have been properly valued.

6. Justification of premium for goodwill to be brought in

The investigator will check the method of valuation of goodwill of the firm. He will ensure that the method adopted is logical and suitable in the given circumstances and also ensure that earning capacity (past and expected) is duly considered in the valuation of goodwill.

7. Justification of the amount of capital to be brought in

The investigator will check the basis of computation of capital contribution to be made by the incoming partner and will ensure that the amount of capital of the incoming partner is consistent in proportion of the capital of the old partner.

8. Examination of financial position of old partner

As in partnership business, all partners are individually as well as collectively liable for all the liabilities of the firm, the investigator will also inquire into the financial position of the existing partners. If the financial positions of the existing partners are not sound, the incoming partner will be in trouble in the near future.

9. Enquiry into the administration set up of the firm

The investigator will see that the salaries paid to the partners are inconsistent with their duties and technological skill. If the incoming partner is going to be admitted replacing a partner having some sort of technical expertise, he will see whether the business will be affected due to the loss of expertise of the partner retiring and if so, what actions have been taken by the firm to compensate it.

10. Ensuring trustworthiness and confidence

The success of the partnership firm depends upon the trustworthiness and confidence among the partners to a great extent. So, it is the duty of the investigator to verify the relationship among the partners and ensure that the incoming partner will be able to adjust himself with the existing partners.

14.11.3 Investigation on Behalf of a Person Who Wants to Lend Money to a Business or is Interested to Know Its Financial Position

Bank and other non-banking financial institutions are the prime sources from where one can borrow money. If a person approaches a bank or other financial institutions for money, the financial agencies would first of all like to examine thoroughly the present financial position of the customer. In this situation, the audited balance sheets of the customers of the last few years serve the purpose to a great extent. However, in those cases, where the money to be lent is a big amount, usually an investigator is appointed to investigate into the financial position of the customer and to advise whether the money should be lent to the customer or not. Investigation may also be conducted on behalf of a private moneylender.

The investigator will undertake the following procedures for this purpose:

1. Purpose of the loan

The investigator should know the purpose of the loan and should ensure that the loan amount applied for is adequate for the purpose for which it is intended to be used. It is obviously foolish for a loan to be sanctioned where it will not be adequate for the stated purpose.

2. Borrowing power of the customer

The investigator will see whether the required loan is within the legal borrowing power of the business. This is particularly important where a limited company is involved.

3. Repayment capacity of the borrower

He will also check whether the projected profits and cash flow of the business will enable it to meet both the interest on the loan and also the capital repayment. It must be remembered that, while assets may provide security, the lender will only want to invoke the sale of assets as a last resort. The loan should not be made, even if assets provide adequate security, unless there are reasonable grounds for anticipating that it can be repaid in the ordinary course of business.

4. Security against the loan

The investigator should check the extent to which the loan can in fact be secured by fixed or floating charges over the assets of the business. The security offered should be examined with respect to value, title, and realisability.

5. Adequacy of insurance coverage

The investigator should verify the adequacy of the insurance cover of the business, with regard to the assets, loss of profit, indemnity and other relevant matters. The insurance policies should be checked to see whether all assets have been adequately insured or not and whether up-to-date premiums have been paid on all policies.

6. Terms of loan and its repayment

The investigator should go through the terms of loan and its repayment schedule and ensure that the proposed borrower will be able to satisfy the terms of loan and be able to repay the loan within the stipulated time period.

7. Present loan liabilities of the borrower

The investigator should further verify and collect a complete information regarding the existing liabilities of the borrower against loan and other borrowings of the business, their duration and interest rate.

8. Profitability of the business

The ability of the borrower to pay interest and principal in time will largely depend upon the profitability of the business. So, the profit and loss account of the business for the last few years should be reviewed and profitability trend should also be assessed.

9. Study of feasibility report

If the loan is required for any capital expenditure of the borrower, the feasibility report should be studied very carefully. He will check whether the project will be viable and will give adequate return to the prospective borrower.

10. Cash flow analysis

The borrower should be asked to submit a projected cash flow statement indicating the method of repayment of loan along with the amount of interest on the basis of time schedule. This statement should be checked very carefully to assess the justifiability of loan sought.

14.11.4 Investigation on Behalf of the Owner/Shareholder of the Business Suspecting a Fraud

Investigation is conducted, sometimes, to detect a suspected fraud. Fraud is generally activated by those employees who handle cash and goods. The investigator should know from his client the nature of fraud suspected and the names of the suspected persons. There is more possibility of fraud, if the internal check system is ineffective. The investigator should thoroughly study the internal check and control system of the organisation.

Fraud takes two main forms which are manipulation of the accounts and defalcation of money or goods by employees of a company or other enterprise.

In the case of manipulation of accounts, the classic way in which this is contrived is the inflation or over-valuation of stock, the suppression of creditors or the inclusion of sales which are either non-existent or relate to the following accounting period. However, there are numerous possibilities, such as creation of non-existent assets or the manipulation of accounts with other companies within a group or with associated companies. The investigator must bring great skill, experience and thoroughness to ensure that every aspect of the business is both genuine and properly accounted for.

In case of defalcations, the exact nature of the investigation will depend upon the circumstances of the case. However, it will always be necessary to evaluate carefully the system of internal control in the areas affected.

The most frequent asset to be the subject of fraud is of course cash, and where cash has been misappropriated, the following checks will normally be carried out by the investigator:

1. Nature and duties of suspected employees

The investigator should know the authority exercised by the defaulting employee and the exact nature and extent of his duties.

2. Checking of cash book

The cash book must be cast and checked fully with the bank statements. It must be ensured that all receipts were banked promptly. The original pay-in slips retained by the bank should be obtained and checked with the counterfoils, as discrepancies could indicate "teeming and lading". Certificate of opening and closing bank balances should be obtained direct from the bank.

3. Vouching of payments

Payments should be vouched with paid cheques and other appropriate evidences, to ensure that the names on the cheques are the same as those in the cash book. Duplicates of any missing voucher must be obtained. It must also be considered whether any cash payments are abnormal and if so, they must be vouched with the utmost care.

4. Vouching of petty cash expenses

Payments, which are not made through banks, are made through petty cash. The investigator should also vouch the petty cash payments. Cash received on account of unusual receipts such as sale of waste materials should be thoroughly checked, as these provide good chances of misappropriation.

5. Checking of payments of wages and salaries

The correctness of payments for wages and salaries must be checked. With regard to wages, great care should be taken to ensure that no fictitious names have been included in the payroll.

6. Checking of debtors ledger

Posting to the debtors' ledger must be checked, and it must be scrutinised for payments on account, which could indicate "teeming and lading". The validity of write-offs of bad debts and allowances given to debtors must be established. A positive circularisation of debtors should be carried out.

7. Vouching of cash sales

Cash sales must be properly vouched. Particular attention should be paid to the adequacy of the system of control relating to cash sales and any weakness should be reported.

8. Checking of payments to creditors

Payments to creditors should be vouched with purchase invoices to ensure that no invoices have been paid twice. The genuineness of purchase invoices must be established by checking them against goods records. It should also be seen that all purchases of goods have been properly authorised and relate to the business of the client.

9. Checking of personal accounts of employees

The personal accounts of the employees showing unusual amount of debit balance for a long period of time should be checked. It is usually seen that executives are in the habit of drawing advances before any tour but do not bother to submit voucher and refund the surplus money after the tour.

10. Checking of handling of cheques

The investigator should also enquire as to who is authorised to sign the endorsement of the cheques to avoid any misappropriation.

The investigator should follow step-by-step above mentioned checking procedure. In order to trace fraud regarding misappropriation of cash, detailed procedure of vouching and verification should be adopted by the investigator.

14.11.5 Investigation to Find Out the Possible Reasons of Shortfall in Working Capital of a Company

Working capital is that portion of capital, which is employed in the business for its day-to-day operations. It is the amount of investment made in various current assets like stock, sundry debtors, cash etc. Sometimes the net concept of working capital also becomes relevant, which is the excess of current assets over current liabilities. But when a company speaks of shortfall of working capital, it generally implies scarcity of cash resources.

Scarcity of cash resources may arise due to various reasons like lengthy operating cycle, diversion of working capital for procurement of fixed assets, wrong dividend policy etc. The investigator will cover the following areas in his investigation to find out the reasons for shortfall in cash or working capital:

1. Nature of the business

The investigator will verify whether the investment in current assets is consistent with the nature of the business of the company. For this purpose, he will ascertain the current assets to total assets ratio of the company and compare it with the average ratio of the industry to which the company belongs. The industry average may be made available from the publication of Reserve Bank of India or from the publication of the Chamber of Commerce and Industry. This may perhaps reveal that the root of the problem lies in the inadequate investment in current assets.

2. Scale of operation

The investigator should see whether scale of operation has increased with corresponding increase in working capital of the company. This may be found out by analysing the trend of current assets to sales ratio of the company for the last five to six years. Overtrading, i.e. the situation of increased scale of operation without matching working capital may increase the profitability in the short-run but will ultimately disrupt the normal operation of the business.

3. Material storage policy

The investigator will evaluate the material storage policy of the company. For this purpose, he will find out the average period during which raw materials remain in store and compare it with the industry average. The average period of material storage can be ascertained by dividing the average inventory with average daily consumption. He will also examine the store ledger to locate the slow-moving and obsolete items of materials in which working capital may remain blocked.

4. Processing period

He will find out the processing period and see whether the processing period is reasonable or not. The processing period can be found out by dividing the average work-in-progress with daily average factory cost of production. The processing time may be lengthy due to various reasons like defective production planning, supervisory incompetence, outdated technology, fall in demand of the product in the market or shortage of cash required for further inputs. The investigator may require the help of some technical expert in this area.

5. Finished goods storage period

The investigator should assess the finished goods storage period and try to justify the length of the period. The average storage period can be found out by dividing the average finished stock with average daily cost of goods sold. This period may be long due to wrong production policy, fall in demand of the product, marketing incompetence etc. The actual reason has to be identified by the investigator by careful and thorough study.

6. Credit period allowed

He will ascertain the credit period allowed to debtors. The period is found out by dividing average debtors with average daily credit sales. It indicates how long capital remains blocked in debtors on an average. He will also conduct age analysis of individual debtor accounts involving large amounts. This will help him to find out whether working capital shortage is due to sluggishness in debt collections. It should also be checked whether any fictitious sales has artificially kept the working capital high.

7. Credit period enjoyed

The investigator will also ascertain the credit period enjoyed by the company from its suppliers. This will be measured by dividing the average credit balance with daily credit purchase. It may so happen that credit period enjoyed by the company is much shorter than the credit period allowed to debtors, thus resulting in scarcity of cash resources.

8. Price level

The investigator will compare the price level of those inputs for last three to five years, which form significant part of cost of production and see whether there is any significant increase in price level. Increased cost of production is supposed to be followed by increase in selling price. But since there is a time gap between purchase of material, and the realisation of cash from sale will have an impact on working capital, so, further introduction of working capital is required to cope with the situation.

9. Capital expenditure

He will see whether capital expenditure incurred during last two-three years is more than the amount of depreciation charged during this period. If there is no introduction of additional long-term fund, capital expenditure over the amount of depreciation will impair working capital position of the firm.

10. Cash flow statement

The investigator will prepare cash flow statement and fund flow statement of the company for last two-three financial years and see whether cash position and working capital position have been impaired due to payment of dividend and tax out of unrealised profit, repayment of loan, purchase of assets etc. Both these statements prepared simultaneously for an in-depth analysis of change in cash and working capital position of the company.

14.11.6 Investigation on Behalf of Tax-authority for Assessing Actual Tax Liability

Such investigations are carried out where the tax authority suspects that the taxpayer has understated his income in his returns. The tax authority may have various grounds for suspicion, for example, they may have discovered sources of income, which have not been disclosed; they may know that the tax-payer is living in a style, which exceeds his known income; or they may have been given some information about the tax-payer's affairs by an informer.

These types of investigation have no set rules. The investigator must use his initiative and experience with regard to the circumstances of the particular case. All potential sources of information relating to both the client's business at private affairs must be used. In relation to the business, the investigator will use his auditing experience to test for possible manipulations. In relation to the client's private affairs, the investigator must do his utmost to ensure that he establishes the client's income from all sources as accurately as possible.

The investigator must obtain all the relevant documents relating to the whole period of investigation. These would include the following:

- All business records and accounts audited or un-audited
- Copies of the client's tax return for the period, if available
- Bank passbooks for all the accounts of the client and the client's spouse and dependents
- All records of the client's income for the period
- Schedules of investments and income thereon and details of rights at bonus issue
- Schedules of all other assets and liabilities, with details of acquisition and disposals during the period
- Details of all legacies and gifts received, and any other non-recurring receipts and expenditure
- Details of insurance and premiums paid
- Estimates of the living and personal expenses of the client and his family for the whole period of the investigation

Once the investigator has assembled and shifted all the relevant documents and has received all the available information and explanations from the client, he must prepare the appropriate accounts to show his client's true total and taxable income for the period. If there is no sufficient information available to prepare proper accounts, it will be necessary to rely on statements reconciling the client's total wealth at the commencement of the period with his total wealth at the end of the period, and treating any unexplained increase in wealth as additional taxable income.

The investigator should ensure that the client approves and signs the statement before it is submitted to the tax authority. If he feels that the client is being less than honest, he should warn the client of the possible consequences of misleading the income. The report should be exhaustive, and should indicate the evidence relied on by the investigator, including the assumptions made and any deficiencies in the information available.

14.11.7 Investigation on Behalf of Prospective Shareholder Who Wishes to Make a Valuation of Shares of a Limited Company

Sometimes professional accountants are required to investigate the value of shares of private limited companies and the shares of public limited companies, which are not quoted in the stock exchange. The valuation of the shares of a public limited company listed on the stock exchange is easy, but the shares of a private limited company or of a public limited company not quoted in the exchange cannot be purchased and sold in the open market, hence its valuation is quite difficult.

Where the client is proposing to purchase a minority shareholding in an unquoted company, the same consideration will apply as where a business is being purchased in deciding whether the company is a basically sound vehicle for investment.

However, as the shares are not readily marketable and the holding is to be a minority one, certain additional factors must be taken into consideration by the investigator, which are stated as follows:

1. State of control

The investigator should see whether the company is absolutely under the control of certain Directors and their associates. There are obvious risks in being a minority shareholder in a company, which is under the absolute control of a small group of people.

2. Right to transfer the shares

The investigator should go through the Articles of Association of the company to know the provisions as contained therein regarding the right of the shareholders to transfer shares. Otherwise, should the purchaser later wish to sell the shares, it may be found that there are restrictions on the right of the shareholder to transfer shares freely to the highest bidder.

3. Influence to hold a particular size of the shares

The investigator will also check whether there are provisions in the Articles of Association giving influence to holding of a particular size. For instance, powers to block certain actions by the majority could be conferred on holders of, say, more than 25% of the voting shares.

4. Prices of shares recently transferred

In valuing the shares, the investigator will of course take into account the price of any shares recently transferred, but it must be recognised that such transfers do not establish the value of the shares. Moreover, little weight should be attached to them unless they were arm's length transactions between unassociated persons. The size of the holding being transferred must of course also be considered.

5. Past dividend policy

Past dividend policy must be taken into account in deciding what return on the investment is likely to be received, as any indications that have been given by the Directors for future dividend policy.

6. Possibility for quotation of shares

Enquiries should be made as to whether there is any possibility that the company might seek quoted company status. A quotation would almost certainly increase the value of the shares, because shares in unquoted companies are usually at a substantial discount as against similar quoted shares because of their lack of marketability.

7. Fair valuation of shares

The fair value of shares may be calculated by one of the following two methods:

(a) Net asset value method In this method, the gross value of assets of the company is ascertained. From the gross asset value, all the external liabilities are subtracted to get the net asset value. If this net asset value figure is divided by the number of shares of the company, value per share is obtained.

(b) Yield method Under this method, the value of shares is obtained by comparing the rate of return of the company with the average rate of return of the industry to which this particular company belongs. If the rate of return is more than the normal rate of return of the industry, the paid up value of shares increases proportionately and the resulting value is regarded as the market value of shares.

14.11.8 Investigation on Behalf of Government into the Affairs of a Sick Company

A state government or central government may be considering the takeover of a sick company and for this purpose, it may give appointment to an investigator to investigate into the affairs of the sick company. Investigation in such a case involves detailed examination of records for several years, collection of information from different sources and analysis of facts and figures.

An investigation into the affairs of such a company will involve the following major steps:

1. Investigation of documents, books and records

The investigator should examine the different documents, books and records including the books of accounts in order to know the existing position of the business along with different aspects of the business including legal, financial, social, economical and other aspects, which directly or indirectly influenced the functioning of the organisation. The important documents, books and records mainly include the following:

- The Memorandum and the Articles of Association
- Audited financial statements
- Different budgets including cash budget
- Stock records
- Debtors and creditors ledger
- Bank statements

- Records for working capital requirement
- Records of cost structure of different products

2. Collection of information from different sources

The investigator should collect information for his proper investigation from different sources including the management of the organisation. He should gather information about the weaknesses and threats of the business from the management. He should also meet the bankers and other financial institutions to know the financial position of the organisation as reflected in its dealings with those institutions. The investigator should also meet with the trade union leaders to identify the basic problems of the organisation. He should visit the Chamber of Commerce and Industry to know the prospects of the organisation and the industry to which it belongs.

3. Measurement of the degree of sickness

The investigator should then measure the degree of sickness of the company with the help of some standard accounting ratios on the basis of last few years' financial statement.

Following are the most accepted ratios for the measurement of sickness:

- EBIT to Sales Ratio
- OCF to Sales Ratio
- EBIT to Total Assets Ratio
- OCF to Total Assets Ratio
- OCF to Net Worth

(EBIT = Earning before interest and taxes, OCF = Operating Cash Flow)

4. Identification of the causes of sickness

After measuring the degree of sickness, the investigator must try to find out the reasons for sickness of the company. Sickness of a company may be due to various reasons, out of which some of the reasons are inborn in nature. The company under investigation may be born sick for reasons as given below.

- Selection of wrong technology
- Selection of improper place of business
- Selection of wrong product-mix
- Adoption of defective production policy.

Again, the company may be started healthy but subsequently may become sick due to a number of reasons, which include the following

- Change in the government policy of the country
- Change in the economic scenario of the country
- Change of market condition of the product
- Lack of management effectiveness
- Adoption of wrong market strategy.

A company may become sick because of innumerable reasons and the investigator will have to identify the actual causes of sickness.

5. Possible remedies

The investigator will then find out the possible remedies for the survival of the sick company. These remedial measures can be of long-term and short-term basis. He will also ascertain the fund requirement for the implementation of the revival programme. The requirement of fund can again be for working capital purpose or for the purpose of acquiring fixed assets. Usually the revival measures include the following suggestions:

- Modernisation and technology upgradation
- Sound financial management and policy
- Deployment of surplus worker
- Re-organisation of capital structure
- Change of product-mix and design.

6. Socio-economic justification for the continuation of the business

Before taking over any sick industrial unit, the government should consider the aspects of socio-economic factors for the continuation of the business. Socio-economic factors include the following:

- Development of the local economy
- Employment of workers
- Tax revenue of the government
- Economic aspects of persons related to the business and
- Environment effect of the business activities.

7. Reporting

On the basis of the above study and evaluation of the position of the sick business unit, the investigator should write his report. The report should be written carefully stating all the relevant information including the symptoms of sickness, the causes of sickness, the suggested programme of revival and socio-economic justification for the continuation of the business. Finally, he should offer his opinion as to whether the government should take over the unit or whether the revival of the sick unit is possible in other ways without taking over it.

14.11.9 Investigation under the Indian Companies Act, i.e. the Statutory Investigation

Section 235 to Section 251 of the Companies Act, 1956 deals with the Statutory Investigation.

Under Section 235, the central government may appoint one or more competent persons as inspectors or investigators to investigate into the affairs of any company and to report to the central government in the prescribed manner.

The central government may direct for investigation under the following situations:

1. On application by members of the company

According to Section 236, when members apply for investigation, they must support their application by evidence and give a security not exceeding Rs. 1000 towards the cost of investigation. Investigation is possible only in the following cases:

(a) In case of a company having share capital, on the application of 2,000 members holding not less than one-tenth of the total voting power (Section 235(a))

(b) In the case of a company without share capital, on application of not less than one-fifth of the members (Section 235(b))

2. On the report by the Registrar of companies

If the Registrar of companies finds the following:

(a) That the company has not furnished the required information or explanation asked for

(b) The information or explanations supplied by the company to him is unsatisfactory

(c) The company has not made a full disclosure of facts

(d) The business of the company is carried on for a fraudulent or unlawful purpose

3. Investigation of company's affairs in other cases

According to Section 237 without prejudice to its power under Section 235, the central government

(a) shall appoint one or more competent persons as inspectors to investigate the affairs of a company and to report thereon in such manner as the central government may direct, if the company by special resolution or by the court order declares that the affairs of the company ought to be investigated by an inspector appointed by the central government, and

(b) may do so if, in the opinion of the supervising authority, there are circumstances suggesting:

- (i) that the business of the company is being conducted with an intention to defraud its creditors, members or any other persons, or otherwise for a fraudulent or unlawful purpose or in a manner oppressive of any of its members or that the company was formed for any fraudulent or unlawful purpose.
- (ii) that persons concerned in the formation of the company or the management of its affairs have in connection therewith been guilty of fraud, misfeasance or other misconduct towards the company or towards any of its members, or
- (iii) that the members of the company have not been given all the information with respect to its affairs which they might reasonably expect, including information relating to the calculation of the commission payable to a managing or other directors or the manager of the company.

Restrictions on appointment No firm, body corporate or other association shall be appointed as an inspector under Section 235 or 237 (Section 238).

Investigation on ownership of company Under Section 247, the central government may appoint one or more inspector to investigate and report on the membership of a company for the purpose of determining the true persons:

(a) Who are or have been financially interested in the success or failure, whether real or apparent, of the company

(b) Who are or have been able to control or materially influence the policy of the company

The expenses of this type of investigation will be borne by the central government out of money provided by parliament unless the government may order the recovery of the expenses from persons on whose application the investigation was ordered.

Power of the inspector According to the provision as contained in Section 240 of the Companies Act, the inspector enjoys the following powers:

1. The inspector can demand the production of any book, papers etc. from any officer, employees or the agents of the company or the related bodies corporate.
2. He can examine on oath from an officer, employee or the agent of a related body corporate.
3. The inspector has the power with the prior approval of the central government, summon any other person and examine him on oath.
4. The inspector can even seize, if so authorised by a magistrate, the books and papers of the company or of any related body corporate and retain them if he is of opinion that these books, papers etc. will be destroyed, altered, mutilated or removed. He can retain them till the conclusion of the investigation.

Inspector's report According to Section 241 of the Companies Act, every inspector has to prepare and submit an interim report if necessary and a final report to the central government. He has to submit his report also to the following:

(a) The members of the company, where he was appointed on their application
(b) The court, if he was appointed on its order

The central government may publish the report and the interested parties may get the copy of the report on the payment of the prescribed fee.

Sections 242 to 244 state that if the inspector's report shows that if any person has committed any offence for which he is criminally liable, the government may take steps to prosecute him for the offence.

Section 246 states that the inspector's report shall be admissible in any legal proceedings as evidence of the opinion of the inspector in relation to any matter contained in the report.

Section 250A states that an investigation can be initiated even if the company has passed a special resolution for voluntary winding up or if an application has been made for an order under Section 397 and 398 of the Act.

14.12 LEGAL VIEWS AS REGARDS INVESTIGATION

Case Study

1. **Case: Colmer vs Merrett, Son and Street (1914)**

   Fact of the case: Mr. Colmer, an engineer, claimed damages from the defendant, the auditor, for the losses sustained by him by investing heavy sum of money on the reliance of his report.

   In fact, the auditor was given only three days' time to prepare the annual accounts. Therefore, he did not undertake the complete audit or investigation. The report was based on approximation.

Legal view: It was held that assessment of financial position along with the preparation of annual accounts for the purpose of investigation was not possible within a period of two or three days. The investigating auditor had taken only the ready-made information into consideration. He had not checked the truth and fairness of the accounting records. So, he was held liable for gross negligence in his duty.

2. **Case: Regina vs Wake and Stone (1954)**

   Fact of the case: The prospectus of the defendant company Wake and Stone contained the figures for stock and work-in-progress which was duly certified by the auditor of the company, and the figure was subsequently proved to be false, deceptive and misleading. A case was filed by the plaintiff against the company and its auditor for inflating the stocks and work-in-progress figure. It was pleaded on behalf of the auditor that he relied on the statement given by the managing director.

   Legal view: Both the managing director and the auditor were found guilty. But the nature of punishment in two cases was different. Because the managing director was sentenced to imprisonment and the auditor was fined £ 200 or in the alternative six month's imprisonment for having signed the report for the prospectus recklessly.

3. **Case: Short & Compton vs Brackett (1904)**

   Fact of the case: The plaintiff sued for the fees for having investigated the books of the defendant firm in respect of the proposed admission of partner in the firm. It was subsequently revealed that an employee of the firm defrauded the firm by defalcation of wage sheet. The important point to be noted in this case is that a part of the fraud was made by an employee during the period of investigation. A counter sue was made by the defendant against the plaintiff to the original case for alleged negligence in failure to discover the fraud.

   Legal view: It was proved by the court that when the plaintiff checked the wage sheet, it was correct at that time. Therefore, the counter claim was dismissed by the court.

POINTS TO PONDER

- An investigation may be defined as a special examination of and enquiry into books of accounts and other related records with a view to establishing a fact or to evaluating a state of affairs or to determining causes for a happening in a business.
- The need for investigation may arise in many cases including cases for purchasing a business, for admission of a business, for seeking avenues of investment, for granting loans, for suspected fraud, for settlement of tax liability, for judging sickness of a business unit and for many other purposes.
- Investigation is normally conducted with certain specific purposes. There are no statutory provisions prescribed for investigation except in case of companies. Investigation is not confined to examination of financial aspects of an organisation, but also concerned with the policy matters.

- The procedures to be followed in an investigation depend on the nature of the investigation, its purpose and the circumstances of the case in which the investigation was undertaken.
- In all the cases of investigation, certain precautionary measures are required to be taken by the investigator, which are considered as the duties of the investigator. These duties include obtaining written instruction about scope and objectives of investigation, framing investigation programme, collection of information about the business, taking expert advice, preservation of working papers and proper and correct reporting.
- The report on the investigation must be carefully prepared. It should be simply worded, very clear in it's meaning and as concise as practicable. It should contain all important and relevant matters. The investigator must mention the limits, if any, put in the scope of his work.
- An investigator should combine sound auditing techniques, considerable experience, sound judgment and a good understanding of a variety of business enterprises. He should be methodical. Honest and diligent.
- Audit and investigation are not same. Audit is conducted to know the true and fair view of the books of accounts. But investigation is conducted to know the financial position and earning capacity of the concern.
- Investigation can be of different types. But whatever may be the type of investigation, an investigator has to consider certain points in conducting investigation, which include preliminary matters, detailed work of investigation and reporting.
- Preliminary matters include letter of engagement and outline report. Detailed work of investigation includes inquiries and accounts and other considerations apart from the accounts. After completion of detailed work, the report would be finalised. The final section on the result of the investigation and the conclusions to be drawn from them would be written and the report would be submitted to the client.

REVIEW QUESTIONS

Short-answer Questions

1. What is investigation?
2. Are investigation and audit the same?
3. How can misappropriation of cash and goods be checked?
4. Discuss in brief the powers of inspector.
5. What are the important purposes of investigation?

Essay-type Questions

1. What is investigation? Distinguish investigation from audit.
2. What do you understand by 'investigation'? Explain the general procedure followed in an investigation.
3. A fraud is suspected in a business house and you are asked to carry out an investigation. Explain briefly how you would proceed in this matter.

4. What special points should be borne in mind by you in carrying out an investigation on behalf of a person who wants to purchase business as a going concern?
5. What are the points to be borne in mind in carrying out an investigation on behalf of a banker who wants to lend money to a borrower, which is a company?
6. Mention the circumstances under which an investigation of a company can be ordered by the central government? What should be the procedure of investigation in such a case?
7. The Directors of a private limited company of which you are an auditor ask you to fix the value of its equity shares. Discuss the factors you would consider to evaluate the shares.
8. What are the general powers and duties of an investigator appointed by the central government? Discuss the investigator's report according to the Companies Act.
9. A going concern having become sick has approached the state government for taking over the undertaking. You have been asked to investigate into the affairs of the concern. Chalk out the procedure of this investigation as an investigator.
10. You are appointed to find out the possible reasons of shortfall in the working capital of a company. Discuss how you would investigate the matter.

CHAPTER 15

New Areas of Auditing

CHAPTER OUTLINE

15.1 Introduction
15.2 Cost Audit
15.3 Management Audit
15.4 Human Resource Audit
15.5 Operational Audit
15.6 Forecast Audit
15.7 Social Audit
15.8 Tax Audit
15.9 Forensic Audit
15.10 Environmental (Green) Audit
15.11 Audit Committee
15.12 Accounting Standards
15.13 Auditing and Assurance Standards

15.1 INTRODUCTION

Auditing in its modern form has adopted a multidimensional approach. At present, the scope of auditing is not restricted to only financial audit under the Companies Act. The purpose of auditing has been extended to cost accounts, managerial policies, operational efficiencies, system applications, social implications of business organisations and environmental aspects too. Even non-business organisations avail the services of qualified auditors and get their accounts audited. At present, the field of audit also covers the following:

1. Checking cost accounting records and verifying the cost accounting principles that have been adopted in preparing and presenting cost accounting data, i.e. cost audit.
2. Comprehensive examination and review of managerial policies and operational efficiency, i.e. management audit.
3. Checking the performance of the organisation and comparing it with the overall performance of the industry in which the organisation belongs, i.e. performance audit.
4. Critical examination and analysis of the contribution of the organisation for the benefit of the society, i.e. social audit.
5. Evaluation and measurement of efficiency of the human resources in the organisation and comparing it with the expected utilisation of the human resources as a whole, i.e. human resource audit.

15.2 COST AUDIT

Under Section 233B of the Companies Act, the central government may, if it considers necessary, direct by an order that a cost accountant within the meaning of the Cost and Works Accountants Act, 1959 shall conduct the cost audit in such manner as may be specified.

Thus, the central government may order an audit of cost accounts for specified companies and that audit is to be conducted by a cost accountant. This cost audit is in addition to the financial audit conducted by an auditor appointed under Section 224 of the Companies Act. If the central government orders for the cost audit, it requires the company concerned to conduct cost audit every year till further orders.

Definition

Cost audit was first time introduced in 1965 in India, when the central government added Clause (d) to Section 209 and 233B of the Companies Act. Cost audit is an effective means of control in the hands of management and it is a check on behalf of the shareholders of the company, consumers and the government.

In fact, cost audit is an audit process for verifying the cost of manufacture or production of any article, on the basis of accounts as regards utilisation of material or labour or other items of costs, maintained by the company.

According to the definition provided by the Institute of Cost and Works Accountants of London, "Cost audit is the verification of the correctness of cost accounts and adherence to the cost accounting plans."

Smith and Day define cost audit as "the detailed checking of costing system, techniques and accounts to verify correctness and to ensure, adherence to the objectives of cost accounting."

So, from the above-mentioned definitions, we can say in simple words "cost audit is the detailed checking as well as the verification of the correctness of the costing techniques, systems and cost accounts".

Objectives

Every branch of study or knowledge has got its objectives. It is quite natural that cost audit should have some objectives. Without objectives, no branch of study can be developed.

Following are the main objectives of cost audit:

1. To detect any error or fraud which might have been done intentionally or otherwise
2. To ensure that the cost accounting procedures which have been laid down by the management is strictly followed
3. To verify the accuracy of costing data by checking the arithmetical accuracy of cost accounting entries in the books of accounts
4. To have full control on the working of costing department of the organisation and to suggest ways and means for its smooth running
5. To introduce an effective internal cost-audit system in order to reduce the burden of detailed checking work of the external auditor
6. To help the management in taking correct and timely decisions on cost of production and cost variations
7. To verify the adequacy of the books of accounts and records relating to cost
8. To value accurately the value of work-in-progress and closing stock
9. To advise the management for adoption of alternative courses of action by preparing cost plan
10. To report to appropriate authority as to the state of cost affairs of the organisation

Advantages

From the discussion of the objectives of cost audit, it appears that it not only serves the management of the business and the shareholders but it also serves the consumers as well as the society in a broader sense. The advantages of cost audit can be described in the following way:

1. *To the management*

- It helps in controlling different elements of cost.
- It can assess the profitability of the organisation.
- It helps to have a better inter-firm comparison.
- It is a basis of evaluation of the inter-divisional performance.
- It helps in obtaining licenses for either expansion or diversification of the various product lines of the business.
- It can also check to control high inflationary trend of cost.
- It helps the management in finding out the correct cost of production.

- It can increase the productivity by detecting the weaker areas of cost of production.
- The inefficiencies of the employees working in the cost department may be revealed.
- Errors and frauds may be detected through efficient conduct of cost audit.

2. *To the shareholders*

- It gives guarantee of the proper maintenance of cost records.
- It can stop the capital erosion by constant watch on better plant utilisation, discontinuing uneconomic product lines and elimination of wastage.
- Through cost audit, the decision makers get timely and proper information, which results in better performance by the organisation.
- Cost audit also ensures fair return to shareholders on their investments.

3. *To the consumers*

- Cost audit helps in the fixation of fair prices.
- It helps the consumers indirectly in increasing their standard of living.

4. *To the government*

- It forms a basis for the assessment of income tax.
- It helps the government in fixing and regulating prices.
- It gives guidelines to improve working of uneconomic industrial units.
- It gives information to the government regarding fraudulent intentions of any company.

5. *To the society*

- Cost audit provides guidelines to the industries for improving its workings and thus renders a great service towards the society.
- It saves the customers from exploitation by revealing them the actual cost and to know whether the market price of product is fair or not.
- It helps the industries to improve their efficiencies and production and to reduce the prices of the product.

Disadvantages

Cost audit may have some limitations. In fact, these limitations do not relate to the objectives for which it has been introduced. It may arise due to its limited scope of application in the related field of operation. However, cost audit is criticised on the following grounds:

1. It introduces unnecessary interference in the normal working of companies.
2. It leads to duplication of work because large areas of working of financial and cost audit are common.
3. It may be considered as a burden to the company because of the additional cost to be incurred on cost audit.
4. Conduct of cost audit by outsiders may be harmful to the interest of the company itself as the secrecy in cost accounts may not be maintained.
5. By introducing cost audit in certain industries, more restrictions have been imposed on the functioning of the organisations by the government.

Appointment

According to Sub-section (2) of Section 233(B), a cost auditor shall be appointed by the board of directors of the company in accordance with the provisions of Sub-section (IB) of Section 224 and with the previous approval of the central government. Further, it has been provided that before the appointment of any cost auditor is made by the board, a written certificate shall be obtained by the Board from the auditor proposed to be appointed to the effect that the appointment, if made, will be in accordance with the provisions of sub-section (IB) of Section 224.

Such a company is required under Clause (d) of sub-section (I) of Section 209 of the Companies Act to include in its books of accounts the particulars referred to therein. The cost audit is in addition to and independent of the normal financial audit carried out pursuant to the appointment under Section 224 of the Act. The cost auditor shall have the same powers and duties as are prescribed under Section 227(1) of the Act for the auditors appointed under Section 224.

A firm of cost accountants can be appointed as cost auditor if all the partners of the firm are practicing cost accountants and the firm itself has been constituted with the previous approval of the central government as required by the regulations framed under the Cost and Works Accountants Act, 1959.

Qualification

Under the provisions of Section 233B such an audit is to be conducted by a cost accountant within the meaning of the Cost and Works Accountants Act, 1959.

But if the central government is of opinion that sufficient number of cost accountants within the meaning of the Cost and Works Accountants Act, 1959 are not available for conducting the audit of the cost accounts of companies generally, that government may, by notification in the official gazette, direct that for such period as may be specified in the said notification, such chartered accountant within the meaning of the Chartered Accountant's Act, 1949, possessing the prescribed qualifications, may also conduct the audit of the cost accounts of companies, and thereupon a chartered accountant possessing the prescribed qualifications may be appointed to audit the cost accounts of the company.

Disqualification

A person will be considered disqualified to be appointed as cost auditor in the following cases:

1. If he is disqualified according to the provisions of Sections 226(3) and 226(4) of the Companies Act as applicable in case of appointment of company auditor.
2. If he is holding appointment as the statutory auditor under Section 224 of the Companies Act.
3. On becoming subject to any of the disqualifications mentioned in 1 and 2 above after being appointed as the cost auditor.

Cost-audit report

According to Sub-section (i) of Section 233(B), the auditor appointed under that section is expected to conduct the audit in such manner as may be specified in the order issued by the central government. Further, as per Section 233(B)(4), the cost auditor must forward his report to the central government and to the company within 120 days of the closing of the year to which the audit is related. The report is to be given in the form prescribed for the purpose.

The central government has issued Cost Audit (Report) Rules, 1968 specifying the form of the report and the additional information, which should be included therein in the form of annexure. The rules have also set down the various points on which the auditor should make his observations and give his conclusions. The rules have been superceded by a Cost Audit (Report) Rules, 1996.

The auditor must further report on the adequacy of cost accounting records maintained by the company as prescribed by the government under Section 209(1)(d) of the act to confirm that they give a true and fair view of the cost of production, processing, manufacturing or mining activities, as the case may be. If the auditor's report contains any qualification, the company must furnish to the central government full explanation on any such qualification within 30 days of the receipt of such report.

In the cost audit report, the cost auditor is supposed to mention the following points:

1. Whether proper records of fixed assets, in details are mentioned or not
2. Whether the assets have been properly revalued during the year and what was the basis of revaluation
3. Whether all the assets are properly verified and discrepancies, if any, are properly dealt with in the books of accounts
4. Whether Proper accounting records as required by Section 209(l)(d) have been kept or not

If there is any additional information that the auditor would like to furnish, he may include in the annexure to the report.

15.2.1 Financial Audit and Cost Audit

The difference between financial and cost audits are shown in Table 15.1.

TABLE 15.1 Distinction between financial and cost audit

Points of difference	*Financial audit*	*Cost audit*
1. Concept	Financial audit is an audit of financial accounts, supporting vouchers or documents and financial statements.	Cost audit is an audit of cost accounts, cost statements and cost accounting plans.
2. Inter-relationship	It is not necessary for a financial auditor to examine cost accounts except for the purpose of valuation of inventory.	As the source of cost accounts is financial accounts, the cost auditor has to make a detailed checking of expenses.
3. Objectives	The primary objective of financial audit is to check whether necessary accounts, records and documents have been maintained by the concern and whether the profit and loss account and the balance sheet give a true and fair view of the profit and loss and state of affairs respectively.	The primary objective of cost audit is to verify whether costs have been ascertained on the basis of cost accounting principles, whether cost records have been properly maintained and whether the cost of production and sale has been correctly worked out.

Contd.

Contd.

4. Nature	Financial audit is somewhat a post-mortem examination. It looks back to the past.	Even though cost audit also refers to the past, it creates thinking for the future. It is therefore forward-looking to a great extent.
5. Verification of stock	The financial auditor has only to see whether all categories of stock have been included in the accounts in true quantities and values.	The cost auditor has not only to check the cost of each item of stock, but also to check whether the stocks are maintained at proper level or not.
6. Purpose	Financial audit is essentially an audit on behalf of the proprietors or shareholders.	Cost audit is a tool in the hands of the management. Statutory cost audit is, however, conducted as per order of the central government.
7. Compulsion	Financial audit is compulsory for each company in each financial year as per the Companies Act.	As per the Companies Act, statutory cost audit is only required for the year if it is so ordered by the central government.
8. Submission of report	The financial auditor submits his report to his clients. In case of company, such report is required to be submitted to the shareholders.	Cost auditor also submits his report to his clients. In case of statutory cost audit, such report is required to be submitted to the central government.

15.2.2 Ceiling on Number of Audits

Section 233B (2) of the Companies Act provides that the cost auditor shall be appointed by the Board of Directors of the company as per the provisions of Section 224 (1B) and with the previous approval of the central government. According to Section 224 (1B), the number of audits that an auditor or a firm of auditors can undertake has certain maximum ceiling. This ceiling is as follows:

1. ***In case of a firm of cost accountants*** Twenty companies (other than private companies) for every partner of the firm who is not in full time employment. Not more than ten out of the twenty companies should have a paid up share capital of Rs. 25 lakh or more.

2. ***In case of an individual cost accountant who is in full-time employment*** Twenty companies (other than private companies) of which not more than ten should have a paid up share capital of Rs. 25 lakh or more.

3. ***In case of an individual cost accountant who is not in full-time employment*** There is no limit on the number of companies that such a person can audit.

The Board of Directors should obtain a written certificate from the person proposed to be appointed as cost auditor that he is not violating the aforesaid ceiling.

15.2.3 Phases or Stages of Cost Audit

The stages or phases of the cost audit may be classified under two broad categories. These include efficiency audit and propriety audit.

(a) Efficiency or performance audit

Definition

The efficiency audit provides the means to appraise the performance of the enterprise and diagnose the weaknesses or ills of the enterprise. Therefore, efficiency audit may be defined as that part of cost audit, which determines whether the resources of the business flow into remunerative or paying channels. Thus, efficiency audit is concerned with the diagnosis and review of the organisations environment, measuring return on investment, cash flow performance etc. and comparing these measures with the standard and determining the management system of control and techniques.

In other words, efficiency audit makes an appraisal of how efficiently different activities of the business, consisting of both operational and financial activities, have been performed and it prescribes the remedies for shortcomings or inefficiencies. Hence, efficiency audit is also known as 'performance audit'.

Objectives

Efficiency or performance audit involves an appraisal of the performance of a business concern. Performance audit mainly looks into operational and financial performance and overall performance of a business. The performance audit does not end in finding out good or bad points, it must tell the management the reasons of the bad points so that the management can take appropriate remedial measures.

The main purposes of the efficiency audit are as follows:

1. To determine the operational weaknesses and general ills of the organisation
2. To highlight or to evaluate the important facts in each of the functions analysed
3. To evaluate and compare the optimum return on capital employed in the business
4. To ensure that the investment techniques aim at giving optimum levels
5. To ensure the improvement of organisational efficiency

Steps

Efficiency audit can be conducted by following the steps as follows:

- Diagnosis of weak areas of the business
- Study of the business environment for the marketability of its products
- Profitable utilisation of physical assets
- Effective utilisation of human resources
- Review of functional and operational efficiency of the business

Scope

Performance audit involves an appraisal of the performance or efficiency of an enterprise. Performance audit reviews how efficiently various plan have been formulated and how far the actual performance meets the target as planned. Performance audit analyses the variances of actual expenditure from the budgeted figures. It also checks the results of capital investments and tries to find out how efficiently the capital has been utilised. Performance audit is, therefore, a check of efficiency of the different aspects of an organisation. It helps the management to improve the overall performance of the organisation.

The important aspects of an organisation, which a performance auditor evaluates, include the following:

- Sales value and sales quantity
- Actual production and total cost of production
- Levels of inventory and its management
- Capital employed and its utilisation
- Profitability of the concern
- Solvency and liquidity position of the concern.

By comparing the actual figures with the budgeted figures, standards and figures of the past periods, by proper analysis of the data and by inter-firm comparison, performance audit evaluates the performance of the organisation.

Advantages

Performance audit has the following advantages:

1. Performance audit gives an insight into the quality of performance. Performance audit gives us the idea as to whether the goals and objectives of the organisation have been kept in view and whether the plans and budgets have been followed in the operation of the business activities.
2. Due to the existence of performance audit, all employees of the organisation become aware of efficient discharge of duties, otherwise the performance auditor will detect their inefficiencies. This moral check on employees is of immense value to the organisation.
3. The defects and limitations in plans, budgets and standard setting are also detected in performance audit. On the basis of audit observations, these defects and limitations can be eliminated.
4. By conducting performance audit, the errors, defects and inconsistencies in different areas of management can be identified. So, proper actions can be taken to remove these defects and inconsistencies.
5. The performance auditor gives the management proper advice for the removal of existing defects and inefficiencies and in that way helps the management to improve future performance of their activities.

Disadvantages

The performance audit has the following limitations:

1. Performance audit is a post-mortem audit, i.e. examination of the events of what have already been occurred. In reality, this practice does not give better result.
2. If the management control system of the organisation is effective, there cannot be any necessity of performance audit.
3. Conducting of performance audit requires high cost. So, this type of audit is not suitable for small organisations.
4. In performance audit errors and defects are highlighted long after it occurrs. Such errors or defects may not be in existence when it is reported to the management.
5. Performance audit creates an unhealthy atmosphere in the organisation due to the competition among the employees in achieving the desired performance.

(b) Propriety audit

Definition

The term 'propriety' means 'justness' or 'rightness'. When this term is applied in the area of auditing, it signifies the audit of rightness of expenditure incurred or the rightness of optimum result or rightness of selecting alternative plan of action.

Therefore, 'propriety audit' may be defined as an appraisal of rightfulness of executive actions and plans. In the conduct of propriety audit, the role of cost auditor resembles the advisory function rather than executive function. So, propriety audit refers to the assessment of rightness of plans and policies of management in connection with various financial events or transactions of the business.

Functions

The function of the cost auditor in the context of propriety audit may be stated as follows:

1. To check that expenditure incurred is planned
2. To appraise whether those expenditures are likely to give optimum result
3. To see that the size and channels of expenditure are rightful and expected to give optimum result
4. To see that any alternative plan of action can bring about an improvement or current operation as well as return from capital expenditure

In case of company form of organisations, there is separation of ownership from management. The persons entrusted with the responsibility of management come for a short period of time. After the expiry of their tenure of service, they leave the organisation without taking any responsibility for the adverse effect on business of their past activities which might have been undertaken for their self interest only. In this context, the propriety audit is of great help as it acts as a restriction on undertaking any transaction for personal benefit of an executive. That is why, the government has also amended the Companies Act requiring the auditor to report not only on the fairness of the financial statements but also on the propriety of transactions of some particular nature.

Objectives

The objectives of propriety audit are to check the following:

- Whether there is a revenue leakage
- Whether funds have been misappropriated
- Whether there is wastage or misuse of any kind
- Whether legal or financial conditions have been overlooked or flouted in dealing with the affairs of the company
- Whether adequate safety of assets has been ensured
- Whether transaction have been entered into for the interest of the entity

Advantages

Propriety audit has the following advantages:

1. In propriety audit wastes, misuse of assets and frauds are detected. So, guilty persons can be punished. The loopholes in the internal control systems of the organisation can also be adequately plugged to minimise these in future.

2. If financial considerations or standards of propriety are flouted in any decision, propriety audit brings these to the notice of the authority. So, decision-makers always remain very alert and well-judged decisions result in the organisation.
3. This audit also checks whether or not all the activities of the organisation have been carried on prudently, profitably and in the best interest of the organisation. If anything is pointed out adversely in the audit report, appropriate corrective action can be taken against it.
4. If any asset of the organisation is inadequately protected, propriety audit brings this to light. Accordingly, measures can be taken to protect the asset from loss or damage.
5. Inefficiency, extravagance, personal interest on any matter, etc. are detected in propriety audit. So, adequate preventive measures can be taken against these features.
6. Propriety audit may cause useful corrections in financial and general administration. For this, administrative efficiency of the organisation may increase.
7. Without the consideration of propriety in some important matters, financial audit and cost audit will be of little value. These audits can be really effective when propriety audit in certain areas becomes part of them.
8. The shareholders of a company or the proprietors of a business are the maximum beneficiaries from propriety audit, because propriety audit in commercial organisations mainly serve their interests.
9. Not only the shareholders or the proprietors, but also all those connected with the business are benefited from propriety audit as this audit keeps an eye on financial discipline in the day-to-day management of the business, which is also beneficial to the society at large.
10. Propriety audit is indispensable in government departments and in government or public transitions, because their activities, transactions, expenditure and decisions are supposed to be in public interest.

Traditional audit and propriety audit

TABLE 15.2 Distinction between traditional and propriety audit

Points of difference	*Traditional audit*	*Propriety audit*
1. Objective	In traditional audit, all business transactions are checked with the help of vouchers and documents to ascertain whether the financial statements prepared gives a true and fair view of the financial result and financial position of the enterprise.	In propriety audit, the matters to be observed are whether the transactions entered into and all the business activities including the decision taken by the management are in conformity with the standards of propriety.
2. Fund utilisation	It is not the purpose of traditional audit to discover wastes and misuse of fund.	Discovery of wastes and misuse of fund is the main purpose of propriety audit.

Contd.

Contd.

3. Accepted standard	If an expense is duly approved by the appropriate authority and supported by valid vouchers, it meets the accepted standard of traditional audit.	Mere approval and existence of supporting vouchers against an expense will not satisfy the auditor in propriety audit. The auditor has to verify whether the expense is necessary and the amount incurred is reasonable or not.
4. Function	It is not within the function of traditional audit to see whether the business is being managed prudently and profitably.	It is the function of the propriety audit to see whether the business is being managed prudently and profitably.
5. Verification of assets	In traditional audit all assets described in the balance sheet are verified in respect of existence, title, custody and value of the assets.	In propriety audit what is particularly required to be seen in the case of assets is whether all the assets are adequately protected or not.
6. Detection of fraud	Detection of fraud and misappropriation of fund is not the primary object of traditional audit. It is a secondary object only.	Detection of fraud or misappropriation of fund is one of the primary objects of propriety audit.

15.3 MANAGEMENT AUDIT

It has been advocated in recent years that accountants should become more concerned with the efficiency of their clients, rather than concentrating their attentions almost exclusively on the accuracy of accounting records and financial statements relating to past periods. This could entail a professional firm's undertaking what has become known as management, operations or efficiency audit in addition to fulfilling its basic statutory duties.

Management audit reveals irregularities and defects in the working of management and suggests the ways to improve the efficiency of the management. It concentrates on results and does not examine whether procedures have been followed or not.

Definition

Management audit is an audit to examine, review and appraise the various policies and functions of the management on the basis of certain standards. It attempts to evaluate the performance of various management processes of an organisation.

According to Taylor and Perry, "management audit is the comprehensive examination of an enterprise to appraise its organisational structure, policies and procedures in order to determine whether sound management exists at all levels, ensuring effective relationships with the outside world".

According to the Institute of Internal Auditors, management audit is"a future oriented, independent and systematic evaluation of the activities of all levels of management for the purpose of improving organisational profitability and increasing the attainment of the other organisational objectives".

So, from the above definitions, it can be simply stated that "management audit is that type of audit which examines, reviews and appraises the various policies and actions of the management on the basis of established norms and standards."

Objectives

The following are the main objectives of management audit:

1. To reveal any irregularity or defect in the process of management and to suggest improvements to obtain the best results
2. To assist all levels of management from top to bottom through constant watch of all operations of the organisation
3. To review the performance of the management through close observation of inputs and outputs
4. To assist management in achieving co-ordination among various departments
5. To assist management in establishing good relations with the employees and to elaborate duties, rights and liabilities of the entire staff
6. To recommend changes in the policies and procedures for a better future
7. To ensure most effective relationship with the outsiders and the most efficient internal organisation
8. To recommend for better human relation approach, new management development and overall organisational plans and objectives

Importance

Management audit is concerned with assessment of efficiency and soundness of management to lead the business to its goal. It critically reviews all aspects of management performances and prescribes ways and means for its improvements.

Management audit is very important for its usefulness and is outlined as follows:

1. ***Reviews plans and policies*** In an organisation, the management holds periodical meetings for the review of their performance and for the assessment of their operations to know as to whether these are performed according to the plans and policies adopted by them. But if the plans and policies are defective, the assessment will be of no use. Hence, there should be some independent review of the plans and policies as formulated by the management. The functions are performed by the management auditors.

2. ***Identification of management weaknesses*** Management audit properly spots the inefficiencies and weaknesses of the management. It assesses the soundness of plans adopted and the adequacy of control system for making the plans successful.

3. ***Proper advice to the management*** Management audit does not rest simply on identifying diseases. To make proper prescription for removal of these diseases is one of the major functions of management auditors.

4. ***Advising the prospective investors*** Management audit can also be useful to a prospective investor who is considering to make a big investment in an organisation. The management auditor engaged by him can collect such information from the organisation as will be useful in evaluating the investment decision.

5. *Taking over of sick industry* Before deciding to take over a sick organisation, the government can order a management audit in that organisation and learn the actual causes of sickness. On the basis of the recommendations from the management auditors, the government can take proper steps accordingly.

6. *Helping in foreign collaboration* In case of industrial collaboration, the foreign collaborators can collect useful information about the management and the future of the collaborating unit through management audit and can take right decision.

7. *Guides the bank in sanctioning loan* Before granting loan or participating in the equity capital of a company, a bank or financial institution may get management audit conducted to ensure that their investment in the company would be safe and secured in the hands of the management.

8. *Guard against shortsighted project* As the tenure of the directors is very short, they become prone to taking decisions keeping in view only short run profit ignoring its adverse effect on the company in the long run. Management audit can act as a guard against such possibility.

Scope

The following are the important areas that come within the normal terms of reference of management audit:

1. Whether the basic aims and objectives of the enterprise are being fulfilled in practice
2. Whether the enterprise is being successful in adapting itself to technological change
3. Whether the management structure is suitable
4. Whether management is efficient at all levels and to what extent economies are possible
5. Whether the policies with regard to staff recruitment and training are adequate, and whether staff morale is satisfactory
6. Whether there is a proper communication system both upwards and downwards throughout the enterprise including a proper management information system
7. Whether the enterprise's share of the market is increasing or declining and how it compares with its main competitors
8. Whether the return on capital employed is satisfactory and how it compares with other companies in the same industry
9. Whether the management has been able to establish good relations with the employees and how it compares with other companies
10. Whether its relationship with the outside world is effective and whether its corporate image in the eyes of outsiders is satisfactory

Steps

Management auditors are appointed for getting their suggestions for improving efficiency of the entire organisation or the specific areas assigned to them. Management audit, therefore, comprises three basic steps. These are as follows:

- Examination of management performance
- Reporting defects and irregularities
- Presenting suggestions for improvement

These basic steps can further be broken down into the following stages:

(i) Study of the activities
(ii) Detailed diagnosis
(iii) Determination of purpose and relationship
(iv) Looking for deficiencies
(v) Analytical balance
(vi) Testing of effectiveness
(vii) Searching for problems
(viii) Ascertainment of solutions
(ix) Determination of alternatives
(x) Seeking out methods of improvement.

The auditors conducting management audit begin their work with discussions with the management executives and employees, then they note down their findings and make out their probable recommendations on the basis of those findings. Finally, they submit their final report along with their recommendations.

Advantages

The importance of management audit can be conceived of if the advantages of the management audit can be studied properly. There is no denying the fact that the management audit is result-oriented. It provides us the following advantages:

1. It helps the management in preparing plans, objectives and policies and suggests the ways and means to implement those plans and policies.
2. The inefficiencies and ineffectiveness on the part of the management can be brought to light.
3. The techniques of management audit are not only applicable to all factors of production, but also to all elements of cost.
4. Proper management audit techniques can help the business to stop capital erosion.
5. It increases the overall profitability of a concern through constant review of solvency, profitability and efficiency position of the concern.
6. It helps the top management in arriving at correct management decisions without any delay.
7. It helps the management in strengthening its communication system within and outside the business.
8. It can help management in the preparation of budgets and resources management policies.
9. It can also help the management in training of personnel and marketing policies.

Disadvantages

The disadvantages of management audit can briefly be stated as follows:

1. The introduction of management audit technique involves heavy expenditure.
2. Managers will hesitate to take initiative, as the management auditor will always pinpoint some shortcomings in the action.
3. Managers will always try to keep the records up-to-date rather than improving efficiency and reducing the costs.
4. Due to ineffectiveness and inefficiency of the management auditor, in all cases, management audit cannot provide result-oriented service.
5. Management auditors are sometimes engaged in some activities detrimental to social objects of auditing, for example, evasion of tax.

Appointment

A group of auditors should be appointed to conduct management audit, as it is not expected that an individual auditor should have all the expertise in all fields of management to conduct this type of audit effectively. Hence a group is formed taking experts from each area of management field for this purpose. The internal auditors must also be included in this group as they are familiar with internal affairs of the organisation and management.

Management audit involves an appraisal of activities of the management of the organisation. So, the auditors must study the organisational activities and its plan of action in detail. Not only that, the management auditors should get full co-operation from the top-level management to enable them to conduct the audit effectively. But the effectiveness of management audit will depend on the scope of audit, which the management has to decide.

Qualities of management auditors

The task of performing the management audit cannot be assigned to an ordinary person. The management auditor should have sufficient experience and knowledge about the functions of management. In fact, he should have the ability to understand different management activities of the organisation viz. internal control system, production planning and control, personnel management techniques etc. The different qualities that the management auditor should possess are stated below:

1. The management auditor should have the ability to understand the problems of the organisation.
2. He should have a clear understanding as to the nature, purposes and objectives of the organisation.
3. He should have the ability to determine the progress of the organisation.
4. He should be tactful in dealing with different employees and officers of the organisation.
5. He should have pleasing and dynamic personality.
6. He should have general understanding of different types of laws, particularly the Income Tax Act and the Companies Act.
7. He should have a sound knowledge in preparing various reports, presented to management.
8. He should be able to assess and examine the internal control system of the organisation.
9. He should be familiar with various principles of management, viz. planning, control, management by exceptions etc.
10. He should have a good knowledge of financial statement analysis techniques like fund flow analysis, ratio analysis, standard costing etc.

Management auditor's report

After conducting management audit, the management auditors are required to prepare a report to be submitted to the management of the organisation. On the basis of findings and definite information, the auditors prepare a report making recommendations for improvement in the functioning of the management. He should not hesitate in criticising the management. His recommendations should be constructive and adequate for the improvement of the overall efficiency of the management.

Nevertheless the report must be clear and unambiguous, either making the point that efficiency is such that no change is advocated, or if reorganisation is considered advisable, then the management auditor must be sufficiently confident of his own ability to have assessed the situation that he can make adequate proposals which will lead to improvement and increased profitability.

Difference between management audit and cost audit

Cost audit is the detailed checking as well as the verification of the correctness of the costing techniques, systems and cost accounting data.

On the other hand, management audit is the detailed examination of an organisation to appraise its organisational structure, policies and procedures of management in order to determine the existence of effectiveness of management system in the organisation.

TABLE 15.3 Difference between management and cost audit

Points of difference	*Management audit*	*Cost audit*
1. Scope of audit	Management audit is a comprehensive review of all aspects of management functions.	Cost audit is the verification of correctness of cost accounting data, costing techniques and system.
2. Legal compulsion	Management audit is not a statutory requirement.	In certain industries cost audit is compulsory and a statutory requirement.
3. Qualification of auditor	The management auditor must be a person having wide expertise in the field of management and accountancy.	The cost auditor must possess prescribed qualifications as per the provisions of the Companies Act.
4. Area of audit	The management auditor critically examines the policies, procedures and the techniques of management adopted and report on their effectiveness.	The cost auditor checks the cost accounting data only.
5. Periodicity	It covers wide area of activities of the management and may be for more than one financial year.	The cost audit is conducted for every financial year separately.
6. Submission of audit report	There is no time limit for the submission of management audit report.	There is a stipulated time limit within which cost audit report has to be submitted.
7. Regularity	Management audit is not a regular feature. Whenever need arises, the management may decide to conduct management audit.	It is a regular feature and required to be conducted year after year.
8. Accountability	The management auditor is accountable to the management only.	The cost auditor is accountable to the shareholders as well as to the central government.

Difference between management audit and financial audit

Management audit is an examination of efficiency of management at all levels throughout the organisation in order to ascertain whether sound management prevails, thus facilitating the most effective relationship with the outside world and the most efficient organisation.

On the other hand, financial audit is an audit of financial accounts, supporting vouchers or documents and financial statements.

Financial audit and management audit may be distinguished in the following lines as given in Table 15.4.

TABLE 15.4 Difference between financial and management audit

Points of difference	*Financial audit*	*Management audit*
1. Concept	Financial audit is an examination of financial accounts and financial statements.	Management audit is a comprehensive and constructive examination of the efficiency of management at all levels throughout the organisation.
2. Objectives	The primary objectives of financial audit are to ascertain whether all the transactions have been properly accounted for in the books of accounts and whether the financial statements of the concern give a true and fair view of the financial result and financial position.	The primary objectives of management audit are to make an evaluation of the efficiency of management at different levels and make useful suggestions for removal of inefficiencies of management functions.
3. Continuity	Financial audit is required to be done every year.	Management audit is not required to be conducted every year.
4. Scope	The scope of financial audit is quite narrow.	The scope of management audit is much broader.
5. Efficiency of employees	The efficiency of employees is not assessed in financial audit.	The efficiency of the employees is assessed in management audit.
6. Auditor	Only professional accountants are competent to perform financial audit.	Management audit can be performed by a group of experts, consisting of management experts, professional accountants, engineers etc.
7. Cost involvement	Financial audit involves less cost.	Management audit is quite costly.
8. Duration	Financial audit covers the accounts of only one year.	Management audit covers accounts and other aspects of management activities for a number of years.

15.4 HUMAN RESOURCE AUDIT

Concept of human resource

Of all the elements that result in profit generation of an organisation, the most important factor is the human resource factor. The growth and development of the organisation including increase in productivity, profitability and expansion of the organisation is dependent on the performance and efficiency of all the workers and employees of the organisation in general and the dynamism on the part of the top management in particular. All these human factors, which contribute to the growth and expansion of the business, either directly or indirectly, may be termed as 'human assets or human resources'.

Concept of human resource accounting

Touche Ross and Co., a Canadian CPA firm has introduced for the first time the concept of human resource accounting as a part of its management information system in the belief that a good human resource accounting system can provide information of vital importance for both short term as well as long-term decision-making and performance measurement.

According to Eric Flamholtz, "accounting for people as an organisational resource involves measuring the costs incurred by business firms and other organisations to recruit, select, hire, train and develop human assets".

Dr. B. K. Basu defines human resource accounting as "a method of accounting that deals with recording the cost that are incurred for the development and welfare of the human resources of the organisation as well as to record the expected future earning from each employee".

Concept of human asset audit

The decision of the investor to invest in the company is greatly influenced by the working of the managerial staff of the company. So, disclosure of information regarding human capital in the annual report of the company may help a lot to the investors in forming an opinion whether to invest or not. This may remove the standing criticism of the financial reporting that 'one of the outstanding omissions is information concerning the human capital employed'.

But before including human capital employed as a part of annual account it has to be ensured that the human capital as included is reliable and computed on the basis of generally accepted principles for the valuation of human capital. In order to get reliable value of human resources, the necessity of human resource audit is felt. The human resource audit examination should not relate to the rightness to the process of valuation of the asset, but it should see that the information upon which the calculations are based upon are reliable and authentic.

So, the definition of human resource audit may be given in the following way:

"Examination of the human asset figure that appears in the balance sheet through checking, inspecting and appraising the various facts and figures which are based on the estimated value of human assets is called human resource audit."

Steps for human resource audit

Following steps may be suggested for the purpose of audit of human resources:

1. The nature of the organisation should be thoroughly examined to know whether it is a firm of professionals or of the general business.
2. Interview with the top managerial personnel should be taken to acquire information regarding the valuation of human resources.
3. It should be seen that provision for depreciation of human assets has been adequately provided.
4. It should be confirmed that the correct value has been placed in the balance sheet.
5. The internal control system as regards various information of human resources should be reviewed to evaluate its effectiveness.
6. It should also be ensured that all contingencies that have the effect on the valuation of human resources are duly considered in the value measurement of human resources.

Problems of human resource audit

Though the auditor is not an expert for the human resource valuation, he has to be intimately connected with the measurement of human resources. For this, the auditor has to appraise the values that are placed in the balance sheet either in the form of investment against human resources or in the form of net value of human assets. But there are certain problems, which may be encountered by the auditor while verifying the value of human resources. These are as follows:

1. It is not possible to determine the value of an individual with perfection. Therefore, the audit procedure under this system of audit is bound to give unrealistic approach to the direction.
2. It is difficult for the auditors to measure the value of the employees who are trained by the methods suggested by the accountants or the valuers.
3. As there is a scope for a subjective judgment in valuing the resource, the audit procedure may not give the guarantee as to the reliability of the data.
4. It is difficult for the auditor to collect the required correct information upon which the human resource valuation is based.
5. As the concept of audit under the name, 'human resource audit' has not attained much popularity and its use is not found so far widely in organisations, the auditor may be put into the dilemma as to the course of action to be followed for the purpose of audit.

Advantages of human resource audit

In spite of the existence of various problems that stand on the way of conducting an efficient audit of human resources, the audit procedure adopted for this purpose may provide the following advantages:

1. The audited figure may be taken by the management as reliable for taking any decision on the matter.
2. The actual audit of this figure may help the auditor to give his audit report about the true and fair view of the state of affairs of the business.

3. It may invite the investor to invest more funds in the business.
4. Thorough enquiry as to allocation of resources amongst various competiting opportunities made by the company can be made possible through this system of audit.
5. The audit of human asset may rightfully justify whether expenditure incurred in this regard is reasonable.
6. The audited figure of human resource may form a valuable basis in the preparation of social accounts.

15.5 OPERATIONAL AUDIT

Definition

The dictionary meaning of the term 'operation' means 'working' or 'performs functions'. Therefore the term 'operational audit' implies audit of the working of the business or it may be defined as an audit of functions performed by the business.

According to Federal Financial Officers' Institute, Canada, "operational audit is a systematic independent appraisal activity within an organisation for a review of the entire departmental operations as a service to management".

Dr. B. K. Basu defines operational audit as "the audit of measuring effectiveness of the working of the business as well as functions performed in financial and operational areas of an organisation".

On review of the definitions, it appears that at present the scope of application of operational audit has been extended in financial and accounting areas too in addition to other areas of operations in an organisation.

Objectives

The objectives of operational audit in particular may be stated as follows:

1. To appraise or evaluate the objectives of the business and see whether they are properly set.
2. To evaluate the policies of the company to judge whether they are adequately framed or not.
3. To analyse the measure of devices as laid down in the policies for the accomplishment of objectives.
4. To determine the work force of the organisation and ensure that the productivity of the available work force is satisfactory.
5. To evaluate the structure of the organisation to know the rights, duties and responsibilities of different persons engaged in different operations.
6. To appraise or evaluate the different control techniques used by the organisation for the satisfactory completion of the operations.

Scope of audit

The approaches of operational audit may be classified under the following two broad heads:

(a) Organisation In the related field of organisational areas, the auditor of operation is concerned with the following aspects:

(i) Examination of the administration of different departments of the organisation
(ii) Examination of various functions within the organisation
(iii) Evaluation of the performance of the employees of the organisation
(iv) Anticipation of future performance of the organisation through preparation of budget
(v) Improvement of the product of the organisation
(vi) Improvement of the organisational structure of the concern

(b) Function As to the functional approach of the operational audit, it is important to note that the auditor in operation is concerned with the following:
(i) All activities of the organisation from the beginning to its end
(ii) The performance of workers working in operational areas
(iii) Appraisal of function through all the units involved in the process of operation
(iv) Examination of workflow
(v) Assistance to management through overview
(vi) Evaluation of plans and procedures adopted by the management

Advantages

The advantages of operational audit may be stated as below:

1. It increases the productivity and profitability of the organisation.
2. It can alert the management before resulting losses.
3. It can characterise both financial and operating areas by the state of mind of the auditor.
4. It protects the interest of the shareholders.
5. It can train up inefficient employees working in different key operating areas of the business.
6. It may protect capital erosion through constant watch and review of different operating areas.

Disadvantages

1. The application of this system of audit involves greater amount of cost.
2. The required qualities as are expected from the auditor may not be found in actual practice.
3. If the auditor's report is ignored, the auditor cannot function properly.
4. The operational audit programme, unlike the financial audit programme, is difficult to prepare.

15.6 FORECAST AUDIT

Definition

The term 'forecasts' are derived through a combination of judgment and science in which history, plans, reactions, aspirations, constraints and pressure all play a part. Forecasts are based on management's assumptions of future events, some of which are explicit and some of which are implicit. But, there is no assurance that the forecast will be achieved.

So, forecast audit may be defined as a critical examination and review of the forecasts of profit, sales and cash flow of the organisation made by the management for the general understanding of all concerned, interested in the affairs of the business, by applying reasonable care, skill and judgment.

Objectives

There is no doubt that budgeting and planning help the management to ensure a better control on the financial aspect of the organisation. However, a higher control is required to ensure the potentiality of the planning. This is possible through 'forecast audit', which ensures the following:

(a) It can stop capital erosion mainly arising from payment of dividend and tax out of inflated as well as unrealised profit.

(b) It ensures the continuity of the organisation by regular check up of the different key areas of the accounting processes.

(c) It can strengthen the 'integrity of the capital structure' of the business.

(d) It can alert the business against any uncertainties.

Steps in confirming the forecasted figures

For the purpose of confirming the forecasted figures as prepared by the management, the auditor should verify the same with reference to the following:

1. ***Determination of the range of probabilistic consideration*** The auditor should check the probabilistic consideration with reference to the authenticity of the available information, which justifies the probabilities.

2. ***Adhering to the generally accepted accounting principles*** The auditor should verify those forecasted figures by reference to principles of accountancy.

3. ***Exercise of reasonable care and skill*** It is the reasonable care and skill which form the basis of judgment power. With the aid of this judgment power, the auditor may check the reliability of information upon which is based the forecast figure.

4. ***Better information system*** All channels of information should be thoroughly examined and verified to form a basis for information, which is the basic of forecast figure.

5. ***Adhering the objectives of the business*** The auditor should see that the forecast figures are not contrary to the objectives and plans of the organisation.

6. ***Proper documentation*** The auditor should check whether the forecasting provides proper documentation of both the forecast and the forecasting process.

7. ***Comparison*** The auditor for the purpose of attaining precision and designing the forecast model should compare the forecast with the results attained. This may enable him to take corrective steps to verify the figures more accurately and efficiently.

8. ***Approval*** The auditor should examine properly whether the financial forecast bears proper authorisation from the top management.

Problems of conducting forecast audit

The problems that are faced by the auditor in the conduct of the forecast audit can be stated as follows:

1. The inherent risk in the conduct of an audit is an important problem of forecast audit.
2. The ambiguity in the client's instruction relating to the liability of the auditor.
3. The exercise of reasonable care and skill in estimating the forecast figure, which is based on subjective and objective consideration, is really very difficult to concentrate upon.
4. Another problem lies with the fact that the auditor has to make his report on the available information furnished by the organisation.
5. It is really very difficult to examine the concept of 'materiality' relating to an item that is included in the profit forecast. It is a fact that there is no boundary line to judge what is material and what is immaterial.
6. Another problem is that the estimation always depends upon the assumption of which forecast is made. But some assumptions inevitably will not materialise and unanticipated events and circumstances may occur.

TABLE 15.5 Difference between annual audit and forecast audit

Points of difference	*Annual audit*	*Forecast audit*
1. Nature of audit	The auditor conducts the audit work on the past records.	The auditor conducts his audit work on the future events.
2. Audit report	The audit report is realistic.	The audit report is unrealistic.
3. Supporting evidence	Effective checks can be made possible on the supporting documents.	There is no supporting evidence on which checks are to be made.
4. Liability of auditor	The liability of the auditor is clearly defined.	It is difficult to define the liability of the auditor.
5. True and fair view	The use of the words true and fair view in audit report justifies the propriety of happenings.	The auditor cannot certify the uncertainties as being true and fair.
6. Risk factor	The risk factor in the conduct of an audit of this type is minimum.	It involves greater amount of risk.
7. Audit approach	The audit work approaches through the books of accounts.	The audit work approaches through the evaluation of the administrative control.

15.7 SOCIAL AUDIT

Concept of social responsibility

Corporate entities are now regarded as a great social force. They are not expected to be only engaged in profit earning activities and paying dividend to the shareholders. They have an important role to play in the social well-being. They have high responsibility to the society. Such responsibilities can be identified in two directions as follows:

1. ***Internal social responsibility*** It includes the following:
   (a) Extending staff benefits comprising indirect monetary benefits like provident fund, gratuity, bonus, insurance, leave salary, medical benefits, housing facility, recreation and entertainment for employees and workers and other benefits
   (b) Keeping the environment of the factory and its surrounding area clean and non-hazardous
   (c) Paying the statutory dues in time
   (d) Supplying quality products at fair prices
   (e) Giving fair return to investors commensurate with risk

2. ***External social responsibility*** It includes the following:
   (a) Community development through creation and maintenance of roads, parks, playgrounds and provision for drinking water facilities
   (b) Tree plantation for the improvement of environment
   (c) Growth and expansion of the business and thereby creating new job opportunities
   (d) Setting up plants in backward areas

Concept of social accounting

In recent years a school of thought has developed a new concept, which advocates that as large companies have responsibilities to persons other than their shareholders, information relevant to such groups should be provided.

For instance, it has been suggested that information should be given dealing with such matters as follows:

- Remuneration of employees and fringe benefits
- Retirement arrangements for employees
- Health and safety measures
- Staff training programmes
- Industrial relations
- Pricing policies in respect of goods and services provided
- Quality control over products sold
- Integrity of advertising campaigns
- Pollution controls
- Energy conservation

Social accounting is a system of accounting, which indicates how and in what way a business organisation performs the above-mentioned obligations for the society. So, social accounting can be defined as "a method of measurement and reporting, internal and external, of the information concerning the impact of an entity and its activities on society".

According to the National Association of Accountants of USA (NAA), social accounting is the "identification, measurement, monitoring and reporting of the social and economic effects of an institution on society. It is intended for both internal managerial and external accountability purposes and is an outgrowth of changing values that have led society to redefine its notion of a corporation's social responsibility".

Concept of social audit

The term 'social accounting' and 'social audit' are used sometimes in the literature interchangeably. But social accounting is concerned with the development of measurement system to monitor social performance, and social audit is the use of an independent auditing system to verify a firm's records of social performance. John Crowhurst in his book *Auditing: A Guide to Principles and Practice* has clearly explained these two terms. According to him, 'Social accounting is the process of determination of social performance of an organisation', while 'social audit' is the enquiry into the corporate social accounting records by an outside agency that can opine with a view to attestation and authentication of such results and reports.

So, social audit may be defined as "assessment of the performance of an industry as a whole vis-à-vis its total responsibility." But social responsibility now a days is not a total concept relating to an industry. Each organisation forming part of an industry is considered to have specific social responsibility. Social audit may, therefore, be rightly defined as "the assessment of social performance of an organisation."

Objectives of social audit

Social audit is a very new and growing area of audit. Modern accountants have developed several approaches and techniques for the effective conduct of social audit. Social audit techniques, in fact, are to be framed by the accountants taking the following objectives of social audit into consideration:

1. To make an assessment of social performance by an organisation
2. To inform the management of an organisation of the accuracy and fairness of its social accounts
3. To evaluate the socio-economic contributions made by an industry
4. To bring to light for public knowledge how far an organisation has discharged its responsibility to the society
5. To advise the management in the preparation of social accounts
6. To evaluate with the help of financial data various social actions of an organisation and describe them in properly analysed form in the absence of socio-economic performance statement
7. To check whether various social actions of an organisation have been evaluated under proper categories like products, employees, local community, environment, public in the social income statement
8. To examine the correctness of 'value added statements' when the contribution of an enterprise to the national economy is described through such statements
9. To verify the assets shown in the social balance sheet and check their values

10. To examine the correctness of amount shown as social equity in the liability side of the social balance sheet

Importance

Social audit is a new concept and has emerged out of the growing awareness of the responsibility of the business towards the society. In the changing socio-economic scenario, the social audit has assumed a special significance. In fact society now demands something more from the auditing profession. Apart from expecting the traditional services from audit, i.e. ensuring reliability and fairness of accounts, the society now requires audit to become social oriented for safeguarding the interest of various elements of the society. So, social audit is very important in the present business environment. The importance of social audit can be stated in the following way:

1. ***Assessment of social contribution*** Social audit assesses the social performance of a business enterprise. Only through social audit one can get a correct picture of the contributions made by an enterprise to the society.

2. ***Presentation of annual social accounts*** In order to conduct social audit, social accounts are also required to be prepared. Attention is given at present for the development of suitable social accounting system with standards for measurement of social performance and presentation of annual social accounts.

3. ***Guide to the management*** The social auditors may guide the management in the measurement of social performance, proper keeping of social accounting records and presentation of social statements. Their specialised knowledge may be of immense value to the management.

4. ***Contribution of the industry*** Social audit has also an important role to play in relation to an industry, as it can successfully assess the overall contribution made by an industry to the society and the national economy.

5. ***Allocation of scarce resources*** To ensure effective allocation of scarce resources, evaluation of different social projects should be done from the viewpoint of their social costs and social benefits. This evaluation is done through social audit.

Social audit in India

When the central government issued manufacturing and other companies (auditor's report) order in 1975 and when it is implemented as social audit by company law board by the introduction of Section 227(4A) of the Companies Act, 1956, it becomes compulsory for the company auditor to give report on several additional matters of social importance. A number of audit experts described these steps by the central government as the introduction of social audit in India. But it is not at all a social audit, as social audit is not an audit for expressing auditor's opinion on the matters of internal control, propriety and compliance. However, this can be considered a right step in keeping the companies aware of their social responsibility and accountability to the society.

For the first time in India, the Tata Iron and Steel Company published the report of their social audit committee in the year 1980. The committee had to make an assessment of the social performance of the company in the light of specific provision contained in the

Articles of Association regarding its responsibility to the society. But the report of the committee was mere description of socio-economic contributions made by the company. No socio-economic activity-wise operating statement showing costs and benefits of various social actions was prepared.

In India, audit of social accounts is not yet in practice and the term 'social audit' is still in a conceptual stage in our country. There are two basic reasons for this situation:

1. There is no statutory provision in any act attempted to make it compulsory the keeping of social accounting and conducting the audit thereof.
2. In our country, no standard for the preparation of statement of social performance and socio-economic operating statement have yet been developed.

So, in India, the concept of social audit is still a vision in reality.

15.8 TAX AUDIT

Definition

Statutory audit is conducted mainly keeping in view the information requirement of the shareholders. But there are also other parties who are interested in the financial information of the organisation. One such interested party is the tax authority, who wants to know the correct income of the assessee for the tax provisions point of view. With this objective, the Income Tax Act of 1961 has included a number of provisions, which require audit of statements prepared for tax purposes.

So, the term 'tax audit' refers to the audit of income and expenses or specific claims of deductions and exemptions that are required to be computed as per the provisions of the Income Tax Act. Tax Audit is a specific requirement under the Income tax Act. It is required in addition to financial audit, which does not fulfill the specific requirement of the tax authority.

Types of tax audit

There are three types of tax audit under the Income Tax Act. These are as follows:

1. Compulsory tax audit under Section 44AB
2. Tax audit for claiming exemptions or deductions
3. Selective tax audit under Section 142(2A)

Tax auditor

Only an accountant as defined in the explanation to Section 288(2) of the Income Tax Act can conduct a tax audit under any of the provisions of the act. A person eligible for the appointment as auditor of a company under Section 226(2) of the Companies Act, 1956 is also included in the definition of accountant. A chartered accountant, to conduct tax audit, must however be a practicing chartered accountant holding a certificate of practice as required under the Chartered Accountants Act, 1949.

In the case of companies, the tax audit can be conducted by the statutory auditor or by any other chartered accountant in practice.

The appointment of tax auditor can be made by the management of the organisation. Thus, in case of a company, the Board of Directors or the officer so authorised by it can appoint the tax auditor. Similarly, a sole proprietor or a partner of a firm or any other authorised person can appoint the tax auditor.

Compulsory tax audit under Section 44AB

Since the assessment year 1985–86, certain provisions under Section 44AB of the Income tax Act, 1961 was inserted to provide that certain persons have to get compulsory tax audit of their accounts. This section provides that every person (a) carrying on business, if his total sales or gross receipts in the previous year exceeds Rs. 40 lakhs, or (b) carrying on profession, if his gross receipts exceeds Rs. 10 lakhs in the previous year, shall get his accounts of the previous year audited by an 'accountant' before the 'specified date' and obtain before that date the report of such audit in the prescribed form duly signed and verified by such accountant. 'Specified date' means 31st day of December of the assessment year, where the assessee is a company and 31st day of October of the assessment year in any other case.

So, unlike statutory audit, tax audit under this section is not confined to company only. The approach of tax auditor is similar to that of statutory auditor. He applies the same generally accepted principles for conducting audit and can rely on the technique of selective verification. However, he is to keep in mind the requirement of Income Tax Act and various judicial pronouncements in this area of application.

Penalty for non-compliance

Section 271B of the Income tax Act, 1961 prescribes a penalty of a sum equal to 0–5% of the total sales or gross receipts, as the case may be, or Rs. 1,00,000, whichever is lower, for a person, where he fails to get his accounts audited as per Section 44AB or to furnish such report with his return of income. But, if a person can show reasonable cause against his failure, no such penalty may be imposed.

Tax audit report

The tax auditor is required to express his opinion in the tax audit report about the tax computation method adopted by the enterprise. He has to express in his report the following:

1. Whether or not the financial statements give a true and fair view of the profit or loss and the state of affairs, if the accounts of the assessee are not subjected to audit under any other law
2. Whether or not the prescribed particulars contained in the statement annexed to the audit report are true and correct

Rule 6G of the Income Tax Rules prescribe the formats in which the auditor has to submit his audit report. The various formats are as follows:

(a) Form 3CA+ 3CD In the case of a person who carries on business or profession and who is required under any other law to get his accounts audited, the tax auditor has to give his report in Form 3CA and annex with the audit report a statement of particulars in form 3CD.

(b) Form 3CB+ 3CD In the case of a person who carries on business but whose accounts are not audited under any other law, the tax auditor has to give the audit report in Form 3CB and annex thereto a statement of particulars in Form 3CD.

15.9 FORENSIC AUDIT

Companies (Auditors' Report) Order, 2003 requires auditors to report, amongst others, whether any fraud on or by the company has been noticed or reported during the year. If yes, the nature and the amount involved are to be indicated. In this context, the techniques of forensic auditing have gained importance.

Definition

The term 'forensic auditing' has not been defined anywhere. However, since the object is to relate the findings of audit by gathering legally tenable evidence and in doing so the corporate veil may be lifted to identify the fraud and the persons responsible for it.

Forensic auditing aims at legal determination of whether fraud has actually occurred. In the process, it also aims at naming the person(s) involved with a view to take legal action.

Forensic audit involves examination of legalities by blending the techniques of propriety, regularity and investigative and financial audits. The objective is to find out whether or not true business value has been reflected in the financial statements and in the course of examination to find whether any fraud has taken place.

Objectives

Objective of forensic audit is to find whether or not a fraud has taken place. Forensic auditor shall have to examine voluminous and in totality, records and witnesses, if permitted by law. Proper documentation is vital in substantiating the findings. The outcome shall focus on the following, in case of frauds:

- Proving the loss
- Proving the responsibility for the loss
- Proving the method/motive
- Establishing guilty knowledge
- Identifying other beneficiaries

Application

Forensic accounting and audit may be applied in the following areas besides fraud detection:

- Conducting due diligence especially for segment-wise profitability analysis
- Business valuation
- Management auditing
- Assessing loss before settling insurance claims

Techniques

Forensic auditing should focus on significant transactions both as reflected in the financial statements and off balance sheet items. The techniques used mainly are as follows:

1. *For financial statement items*

(a) Critical point auditing: This technique aims at filtering out the systems of fraud from regular and normal transactions in which they are mixed or concealed. For this purpose, financial statements, books, records etc. are analysed mainly to find out the following:

- Trend-analysis by tabulating significant financial transactions
- Unusual debits/credits in accounts normally closing to credit/debit balances respectively
- Discrepancies in receivable or payable balances/inventory as evidenced from the non-reconciliation between financial records and corresponding subsidiary records
- Accumulation of debit balances in loosely controlled accounts
- False credits to boost sales with corresponding debits to non-existent personal accounts
- Cross debits credits and inter account transfers
- Weaknesses/inadequacies in internal control/check system

(b) Propriety audit: Propriety audit is conducted by supreme audit institutions to report on whether all expenditure sanctioned and incurred are need-based and all revenues due to the concern have been realised in time and credited to the account. In conducting the propriety audit, 'value for money audit' technique aims at lending assurance that economy, efficiency and effectiveness have been achieved in the transactions for which expenditure has been incurred or revenue collected is usually applied. Financial frauds are results of wasteful, unwarranted and unfruitful expenditure or diversion of fund by the investigated entity to another entity.

2. *For off-balance sheet transactions* There are certain transactions which are neither discussed prima facie in the financial statements nor suitable disclosures made. Since these are intangible in financial statement, the auditor may not consider these as significant or material, no statement/qualification is normally made in auditor's report. These may encompass the following:

- Significant purchases/sales of raw materials and/or finished goods with only a particular dealer or group companies of such vendor
- Pattern of consumption of major raw materials/components, indicating excess consumption
- Over/under invoicing for capital goods, raw materials/components or services as compared to normal prices for the same
- Alteration of contractual terms, to pass on otherwise accrued benefit, to holding/group companies
- Diversion of funds through group companies and setting off such debits as expenditure in accounts with proper authorisation before closure of accounts to avoid detection
- Cost over-runs in major capital expenditure without corresponding benefit or convincing reasons
- Justification for non-maintenance of certain basic records, on technical grounds, but with intention to defraud.

TABLE 15.6 Distinction between statutory audit and forensic audit

Points of difference	*Statutory audit*	*Forensic audit*
1. Objective	The basic objective of statutory audit is to express opinion as to the true and fair presentation of financial statements.	The objective of forensic auditing is to determine correctness of the accounts or whether any fraud has actually taken place.
2. Techniques	Usually both the substantive and compliance techniques of auditing are adopted.	As techniques of auditing, analysis of past trend and substantive or in-depth checking of selected transactions are adopted.
3. Period covered	Normally all the transactions for the particular accounting period are covered.	There is no such limitation in this type of audit. Accounts may be examined in detail from the beginning.
4. Verification of assets	Under this type of audit, verification of assets relies on the management certificate/representation of management.	Under this type of audit, independent verification of suspected/selected items are carried out.
5. Off balance sheet items	These items are considered to vouch the arithmetic accuracy and compliance with procedures.	Regularity and propriety of these transactions/contracts are examined.
6. Adverse findings	In case of adverse findings, the auditor expresses negative or qualified opinion.	Legal determination of fraud and naming persons behind such frauds are the results of adverse findings.

15.10 ENVIRONMENTAL (GREEN) AUDIT

Environmental audit is an excellent management tool for relating productivity to pollution. The Environment (Protection) Act, 1986 under the Rule 14 requires an industry to submit annual environmental statement by the 30th of September every year, from 1993 onwards, to the relevant State Pollution Control Board. Rule 14 is applicable to any industry or organisation, which possesses or requires consent or authorisation under Water (Prevention & Control of Pollution) Act, 1974, Air (Prevention & Control of Pollution) Act, 1981 and/or Hazardous Waste (Management & Handling) Rules, 1989.

Definition

Environmental audit is the examination of the correctness of environmental accounts. In broader sense, environmental auditing is the examination of accounts of revenues and costs of environmental and natural resources, their estimate, depreciation and values recorded in the books of accounts.

In the words of N. Rajaraman, "environmental auditing is a series of activities undertaken on the initiative of an organisation's management to evaluate its environmental performance".

The International Chamber of Commerce defines environmental auditing "as a basic management tool comprising a systematic, documented, periodic and object evaluation of how well environmental organisation, management and equipment are performing with the aim to safeguard the environment".

So, environmental audit is an excellent management tool to assess the activities of an industry from a pollution angle and measure the efficiency and the adequacy of control measures.

Objectives

The following are some of the objectives of environmental auditing:

- To see that the natural resources are properly utilised
- To control the costs incurred on procuring the natural resources and to ensure that they have been properly classified
- To see that natural resources have been properly shown in a nation's balance sheet as they are the nation's valuable assets
- During production process, when natural resources are utilised, some adverse environmental effects are produced and pollution is created. So, the objective of such an audit is to see that proper steps are taken to control or to prevent such adverse effects like pollution
- To ensure that the natural resources are utilised for industrial development and for national progress
- To see that proper steps have been taken for maintaining health and welfare of the community and also for disposal of harmful wastes and social risks

Approach

Establishment of an effective environmental audit programme requires careful planning and attentions to the goals and objectives established for the audit programme of each company.

The requirement of environmental audit will undoubtedly vary from one plant to another and there is not necessarily any one single approach. In principle, such audits are carried out by a small qualified and independent team of experts who would visit a particular plant site basically to check on the environment management and performance of the plant in question. Since there is a process of self-analysis for the industry, the industries themselves can conduct this audit under the guidance of expert professionals. Environmental audit software can also assist the industry in performing this task.

The following steps are required to be followed while approaching towards environmental audit:

Step 1: Preparatory activities The first step is to constitute a multidisciplinary audit team having expertise in general environmental matters (policy, regulations, environmental management) as well as in specific environmental issues (ecology, environmental toxicology, fate and behaviour of potential containment), abatement technologies and operational aspects.

After forming an audit team, the next task is to enable the team to assemble pre-visit information. The industry records would contain background information on the nature of the operations and environmental matters relevant to the plant. For example, the production details, water cess payable, energy consumption, and raw materials related information are available in the industry records. On the basis of information available, the audit team will identify the main areas for consideration, develop a visit programmme and allocate specific tasks to team members.

So, preparatory activities related tasks include the following:

1. *Imparting education on environmental audit*: Imparting education to management and plant personnel on environmental audit is the primary task. To ensure the success of an audit programme, support and commitment of the senior management should be obtained. Management should realise that environmental audit is one of the very important pragmatic tools.

2. *Review of background information*: Gathering and reviewing of background information relating to the corporate environment as a whole and also awareness of acts and rules, consent compliance, performance of pollution control system, solid waste management, safety measures etc. is needed. In other words, the objective and scope of environmental audit should be unambiguously outlined.

3. *Composition of audit team*: Being a multi-disciplinary approach, environmental audit depends upon involving right people for the task. The audit team may include engineers and technologists, biologists and personnel from other industries doing similar activities. Experienced environmental engineer should act as coordinator.

4. *Time frame*: Time frame for the audit should be carefully formulated so that all the activities are completed within a reasonable time.

5. *Preparing the questionnaire*: To conduct the audit, necessary questionnaires and other tools should be designed to collect and analyse the relevant information. In other words, appropriate audit tools should be designed and tested before the commencement of actual audit.

Step-2: On site visit The key elements of the visit are inspection of the facilities and interviews with the employees. The interview includes senior, middle and junior level staff of relevant departments. It has been helpful to conduct interviews in accordance with protocol before hand, using a flexible checklist.

The audit studies the process flow sheet and carries out a material balance for water and raw material used. Each process is to be broken up into individual sub-processes. The quantities and water entering and leaving the process are estimated from

- the chemical process engineering calculations,
- the plant records, or
- actual measurement conducted at the site.

The objective for preparing material balance is to relate water and raw material usage to per unit production. Similarly, air, solid and hazardous wastes generated are also estimated for individual processes. The quantities of various types of pollutants, thus estimated, are summed overall and the processes to arrive at a figure for pollution is generated per unit of each product. Based upon the above, it is possible to detect inefficiencies in production processes and undue wastage of raw material and water. Therefore, productivity of the industry can be related to pollution generation and resource utilisation.

So, on site activities related tasks include

- Interviewing site personnel working at various sites
- Inspecting the site, the operations and the equipments
- Reviewing safety measures
- Reviewing operating and administrative records and documents etc.

As with statutory and cost audit, environmental management also needs a functional internal control system. These internal controls are incorporated in a facility's environmental management system. They include the organisational monitoring and record keeping procedures, formal planning documents for the prevention and control of accidental release, internal inspection programmes, physical controls such as containment of released materials and a variety of other control system elements. The audit team gains information of all significant control system elements from numerous sources through use of formal questionnaires, observations and interviews.

Step-3: Post-visit activities Post-visit activities related tasks include the following:

- Identifying and evaluating waste reduction options and develop waste reduction action plan
- Determining potential solutions and preparing recommendations
- Preparing the interim audit report
- Assigning the responsibilities for corrective actions and establishing time-scales
- Implementing corrective actions
- Conducting follow-up to the corrective actions.

Based upon the plant visit and the information collected, an interim audit report is prepared. A typical environmental audit report contains the following:

- General information of the industry
- Water budget, i.e. quantity used in production processes, cooling water, domestic water etc.
- Raw materials balance for processes and consumption per unit produced
- Air and water pollution generated from various processes
- Solid and hazardous wastes generated from various processes and disposal techniques used for them
- Cost analysis of pollution prevention
- Future investment for environmental protection and abatement of pollution

Step-4: Final report preparation Within a short time, the audit team produces an interim report for comments by the site management. Recommendation and findings are discussed in a group discussion. The final report is then prepared and submitted to the industry.

Stages of environmental audit

As green consciousness is growing and developing, more companies are beginning to evaluate both, its commercial implications and the impact of their operations. The environmental audit is essentially a management tool. It implies that companies should not wait for restrictive legislation to bring about changes.

Environmental audit comprises the following stages:

- Existing legislative requirements, health and safety practices and forthcoming regulatory developments are analysed
- Internal procedures and external requirements are examined, compared and constructed. The implications of external requirements on production processes and equipments are assessed and the impact in terms of waste and emission are evaluated
- The organisation structure, administration and communication process of the company are analysed to determine the extent to which management is informed of the environmental impact of the company's activities. Gaps are identified and remedies suggested.

Environmental audit practice in India

The development of environmental audit can be traced back to the early 1970s. Oil spill off the British South Coast, Bhopal Gas Leak, Chernobyl disaster, pollution of different rivers etc. has led to increased concern in industrial environmental management. The United States Environmental Protection Agency published their environmental audit policy in 1986, followed by International Chamber of Commerce booklet on Environmental Auditing (1988) and UNEP published their technical report on Environmental Audit.

In India, recognising the importance of Environmental Audit and its procedure was first notified under the Environment (Protection) Act, 1986 by the Ministry of Environment of Forests. Under this Act, every person carrying on an industry, operation or process requiring consent under Section 25 of the Water (Prevention & Control of Pollution) Act, 1974 or under Section 21 of the Air (Prevention & Control of Pollution) Act, 1981 or both or authorisation under the Hazardous Wastes (Management and Handling) Rule of 1989 issued under the Hazardous (Protection) Act, 1986 is required to submit an environmental audit report. The environmental audit report has been renamed as Environmental Statement in 1993. This statement is required to be submitted to the concerned Pollution Control Boards.

The environmental statement should not be treated as a substitute for environmental audit, rather as a database for environmental audit. The analysis of the data and necessary suggestions for improvement in the environment and efficiency is not outlined in the environmental statement. Most of the developed countries like the USA, the UK, Canada, Australia etc. have already taken up environmental audit for their corporate sector. As of now, any disclosures on the environmental matters in the annual report of an Indian company are voluntary in nature. Environmental audit is conducted by a very limited number of companies in India.

15.11 AUDIT COMMITTEE

Section 292 requires the setting up of an audit committee by every public company having a paid-up capital of Rs. 5 crore or more. An audit committee is a committee of the board of directors of a company entrusted with the task of overseeing the financial reporting process of the company. This committee will consider various issues relating to the audit function and review the company's financial and risk management policies.

15.11.1 Requirements Under the Companies Act

According to Section 292 of the Companies Act, following are the requirements of the audit committee:

- The audit committee should consist of not less than three directors, with two-thirds of the total strength being other than managing or whole time directors.
- The committee should ensure compliance of internal control systems.
- The committee should have discussions with the auditors periodically about internal control systems and the scope of audit including the observations of the auditors and review the half-yearly and annual financial statements before submission to the Board of Directors.
- The auditors, the internal auditor (if any) and the finance director should attend the meetings of the committee but shall not have the right to vote.
- The committee should have the authority to investigate into any relevant matter and should have full access to information contained in the records of the company. The committee can also seek external professional advice, if required.
- If the Board of Directors does not accept the recommendations of the committee, it should record the reasons and communicate such reasons to the shareholders.
- The chairman of the committee should attend the annual general meetings of the company to provide any clarification on matters relating to audit.

15.11.2 Requirements of Listing Agreement

All entities listed on a stock exchange in India have to set up an audit committee in compliance with clause 49 of the listing agreement. The main features of this requirement are as follows:

Composition of the committee

A qualified and independent audit committee should be set up and should comply with the following:

- Audit committee members should have a minimum of three Directors who shall be the non-executive directors of the company and two-thirds of them shall be independent.
- The chairman of the committee should be an independent director.
- All members of the audit committee should be financially literate and at least one member shall have accounting or related financial management expertise.
- The chairman should be present at annual general meeting to answer the shareholders' queries.
- The audit committee should invite such of the executives as it considers appropriate to be present at the meeting of the committee, but on occasions it may also meet without the presence of any executives of the company.

Meeting of the committee

It has been stipulated that the audit committee should meet at least four times in a year, with a gap of not more than four months as against earlier requirement of three meetings, one in every six months and one at the time of accounts finalisation.

Powers of the audit committee

The audit committee should have sufficient powers in discharging its duties effectively including the following:

- To investigate any activity within its terms of reference
- To obtain outside legal or other professional advice
- To seek information from any employee
- To secure attendance of outsiders with relevant expertise, if required

Functions of audit committee

The audit committee should perform the following functions:

1. Oversight of the company's financial reporting process and the disclosure of its financial information to ensure that the financial statements are correct, sufficient and credible
2. Recommending the appointment and removal of external auditor, fixation of audit fee and also approval for payment for any other services
3. Reviewing with management the annual financial statements before submission to the Board, focussing mainly on the following:
    - Any changes in accounting policies and practices
    - Major accounting entries based on exercise of judgment by management
    - Qualifications in draft audit report
    - Significant adjustments arising out of audit
    - The going concern assumption
    - Compliance with accounting standards
    - Compliance with stock exchange requirements and legal requirements concerning financial statements
    - Any related party transactions
4. Reviewing with the management and the external and internal auditors, the adequacy of internal control system
5. Reviewing the adequacy of internal audit function, including the structure of internal audit department and frequency of internal audit
6. Discussion with the internal auditors on any significant findings and follow-up there on
7. Reviewing the findings of any internal investigations by the internal auditors into matters where there is suspected fraud or irregularity or a failure of internal control systems of a material nature and reporting the matter to the Board
8. Discussion with external auditors before the commencement of audit about the nature and scope of audit as well as post-audit discussion to ascertain any area of concern
9. Reviewing the company's financial and risk management policies
10. Looking into the reasons for substantial defaults in the payment to depositors, debenture-holders, shareholders and creditors

Audit committee has been entrusted with the additional responsibility of the compulsory review of the following-

- Management discussion and analysis
- Statement of significant related party transactions
- Management letter issued by the statutory auditors
- Reports of the internal auditor in the matter of internal control weaknesses
- Appointment/removal/terms of remuneration of chief internal auditor.

15.12 ACCOUNTING STANDARDS

Concept

Accounting standards are the written policy documents issued by the government or other regulatory body or expert institute covering various aspects of recognition, measurement, treatment, presentation and disclosure of accounting transaction in the financial statements.

Companies (Amendment) Act, 1999 has inserted new Sub-section (3C) in Section 211 which defines "accounting standards to mean standards of accounting recommended by the Institute of Chartered Accountants of India, constituted under the Chartered Accountants Act, 1949, as may be prescribed by the central government in consultation with the National Advisory Committee on accounting standards established under Section 415(1)".

All over the world, accounting standards are drafted, framed and implemented by professional accounting bodies. While accounting standards in India are framed by Accounting Standard Board of the Institute of Chartered Accountants of India, International Accounting Standards (IAS) are pronounced by the International Accounting Standard Committee comprised of representatives of member institutes of professional accountants.

Objective/Importance

The objective of accounting standards is to standardise the diverse accounting policies and practices with a view to eliminate, to the extent possible, the non-comparability of financial information and to produce reliable accounting statements acceptable in the country.

The use of accounting standards is well established and no one can deny the importance of accounting standards. It is utmost necessary that these statements are compiled on the basis of accounting standards. Legislative attempts have been made to have accounting standards prescribed under different statutes. For example, Companies (Amendment) Act, 1999 lay down prescribing accounting standards.

The globalisation of business, promotion of external trade, internationalisation of financial institutions etc. necessitated the development of accounting standards. So the importance of accounting standards can be described in the following way:

1. ***Globalisation of business*** Business is a global entity in these days. Multinational companies are working in different countries with different currency, rules and accounting practices. If every country is allowed to follow its own practice, external trade cannot flourish. A lot of confusion will be created. The smooth and fair flow of the global business needs international accounting standards.

2. ***Uniform presentation of accounts*** Financial accounting is not a very exact science. To some extent it is the subject of interpretation. The presence of different concepts, conventions, customs, traditions and practices created confusion and checked free, fair and smooth flow of financial activities. It necessitated uniformity in the concepts, conventions and practices.

3. ***Removal of ambiguity*** Accounting is one of the important parts of business activities. It does not show the actual financial status of the business by indicating net profit or loss only, but it also forecasts the future trend of the business. But certain accounting terms and practices are ambiguous and confusing, e.g. valuation of stock, methods of depreciation etc. Accounting standards are needed to remove these different types of ambiguity.

4. ***Prevention of accounting scandals*** Ambiguity, confusion and inexactness in the meaning of accounting terminology generate accounting scandals leading to the failure of the business. As such, standardisation of accounting terminology is necessary for preventing misuse of accounting terminology.

5. ***Internationalisation of financial institutions*** In these days banks and financial institutions have assumed global status. Their activities are not restricted within their countries alone. Banks have got their branches in the foreign countries also. The successful implementation of these activities needed that the financial accounting must be standardised internationally.

Accounting standards and the auditor

While discharging their attest function, the auditors are required to ensure that the accounting standards issued and made mandatory by the Institute of Chartered Accountants of India are implemented in the presentation of financial statements covered by their audit reports. In the event of any deviation from the standards it will also be their duty to make adequate disclosure in their reports so that the users of the financial statements are made aware of such deviations.

According to amendment made in Section 227 of the Companies Act, 1999 additional duties has been given to the auditors to state in their reports whether in their opinion, the profit and loss account and the balance sheet comply with the accounting standards provided in Section 211 (3C) and also the reasons for any adverse comments or qualifications in this regard.

15.13 AUDITING AND ASSURANCE STANDARDS

Concept

In India the Institute of Chartered Accountants of India issues the auditing procedures/ practices and these are called Auditing and Assurance Standards (AAS), previously known as Standard Auditing Practices (SAP). The AAS will apply whenever an independent audit is carried out; that is, in the independent examination of financial information of any entity, whether profit oriented or not and irrespective of its size or legal form when such an examination is conducted with a view to express an opinion thereon.

In fact, AAS are the benchmarks by which the quality of audit performance can be measured and the achievement of objectives can be documented. By using standards an auditor can determine the professional qualities necessary for effective audit performance. In simple words, AAS are auditing standards which prescribe the way the auditing should be conducted.

Objectives/Importance

AAS refer to general guidelines given by the professional bodies of accountants for conducting audit. They indicate principles and techniques of auditing to be followed by the auditors while conducting audit in different audit environment. Based on the collective deliberations and views, the professional bodies prescribe principles and techniques of auditing. The aims of prescribing these guidelines are to ensure sound and effective auditing practices.

Various professional bodies of accountants in different countries have issued pronouncements on accepted auditing practices for the guidance of their members. These pronouncements on auditing practices relate not only to financial audit but also other types of audit namely propriety audit, internal audit, peer review etc. In India the Institute of Chartered Accountants of India has been issuing a series of statements of AAS on independent financial audit.

So, the importance of AAS can be outlined in the following way:

1. ***Codification of auditing practices*** These professional pronouncements attempt to codify the auditing practices expected to be applied while conducting audit.

2. ***Ensure effective auditing practices*** These professional principles and techniques of auditing are generally accepted as standard. The objective of prescribing these guidelines is to ensure sound and effective auditing practices.

3. ***Guidance to the auditor*** These standards refer to general guidelines given by the professional bodies of accountants for conducting audit. They indicate the principles and techniques of auditing to be followed by the auditors while conducting audit.

4. ***Uniform presentation of accounts*** Auditing is not a very exact science. To some extent it is the subject of interpretation. The presence of different concepts, conventions, customs, traditions and practices created confusion and checked free, fair and smooth flow of auditing activities. It necessitated uniformity in the concepts, conventions and practices.

5. ***Prevention of accounting scandals*** Ambiguity, confusion and inexactness in the meaning and interpretation of auditing terminology generate accounting scandals leading to the failure of the business. As such, standardisation of auditing terminology is necessary for preventing misuse of auditing terminology.

AAS and the auditor

It is the duty of the auditor to ensure that the audit is conducted in accordance with AAS and if there is any material departure from the standards, the auditor should report thereon. The auditor becomes liable to the disciplinary preceding of the Institute of Chartered Accountants of India under Clause (9) of Part I of Second Schedule to the Chartered Accountants Act, 1949.

The auditors in their audit report have to mention that they have conducted the audit in accordance with the "generally accepted auditing standards". The generally accepted auditing standards in Indian context means the Auditing and Assurance Standards as issued by the Institute of Chartered Accountants of India.

POINTS TO PONDER

- Auditing is a multidimensional subject. The scope of auditing is not only restricted to financial audit under the Companies Act. The purpose of audit has been extended to cost accounts, managerial policies, operational efficiencies, system applications, social implications of business and environmental aspects too.
- Cost audit is an audit process for verifying the cost of production of any article, on the basis of accounts as regards utilisation of materials or labour or other items of costs maintained by the company. The basic objective of cot audit is to detect any error or fraud, which might have been done intentionally and to report to appropriate authority as to the state of cost affairs of the organisation. But it introduces duplication of work because large area of working of financial and cost audit are common and the cost secrecy cannot be maintained.
- Efficiency audit provide the means to appraise the performance of the enterprise and diagnose the weaknesses of the enterprise. It mainly looks into operational and financial performance and overall performance of a business. Hence, efficiency audit is also known as performance audit.
- Propriety audit is defined as an appraisal of rightness of executive actions and plans. In propriety audit waste and misuse of assets and frauds are detected. So, guilty persons can be punished.
- Management audit is an audit to examine, review and appraise the various policies and functions of the management on the basis of certain standards. It attempts to evaluate the performance of various management processes of an organisation. The basic objective of management audit is to assist all levels of management through constant watch of operation and to recommend changes in the management policies and procedures for better future.
- Human resource audit is the examination of the human asset figure that appears in the balance sheet through checking, inspecting and appraising various facts and figures, which are based on the estimated value of human assets. As the concept of audit under this name has not attained much popularity and its use is not found so far widely in organisations, the auditor may be put into dilemma as to the course of action to be followed for the purpose of this audit.
- Operational audit is a systematic independent appraisal activity within an organisation for a review of the entire departmental operations as a service to management. The basic objective of this audit is to appraise the different control techniques used by the organisation for the satisfactory completion of the operations.
- Forecast audit may be defined as a critical examination and review of the forecasts of profit, sales and cash flow of the organisation made by the management for the

understanding of all concerned interested in the affairs of the business by applying reasonable care, skill and judgment.

- Social audit is the assessment of the performance of an industry as a whole towards the fulfillment of social obligations. It is a very new and growing area of audit. The basic objective of social audit is to verify the assets shown in the social balance sheet and check their values.
- Tax audit refers to the audit of income and expenses or specific claims of deductions and exemptions that are required to be computed as per the provisions of the Income Tax Act. Tax audit is a specific requirement under the Income Tax Act. It is required in addition to financial audit, which does not fulfill the specific requirements of the tax authority.
- Forensic audit involves examination of legalities by blending the techniques of propriety, regularity and investigative and financial audit. The objective of this audit is to find out whether or not true business value has been reflected in the financial statements and in the course of examination to find out whether any fraud has taken place.
- Environmental audit is the examination of the correctness of environmental accounts. It is the examination of accounts of revenues and costs of environmental and natural resources, their estimate, depreciation and values recorded in the books of accounts.
- As of now, any disclosures on environmental matters in the annual report of an Indian company are voluntary in nature. Environmental audit is conducted by a very limited number of companies in India.
- Section 292 requires the setting up of an audit committee by every public company having a paid up capital of rupees five crore or more. An audit committee is a committee of the board of directors of a company entrusted with the task of overseeing the financial reporting process of the company. All entities listed on a stock exchange in India have to set up an audit committee in compliance with clause 49 of the listing agreement. The main function of the audit committee is to oversight the company's financial reporting process and disclosure of its financial information to ensure that the financial statements are correct, sufficient and credible.
- Accounting standards are the written policy documents issued by the government or other regularity body or expert institute covering various aspects of recognition, measurement, treatment, presentation and disclosure of accounting transactions in the financial statements. Accounting standards in India are framed by Accounting Standard Board of the Institute of Chartered Accountants of India.
- In India the Institute of Chartered Accountants of India issues the auditing practices and these are called Auditing and Assurance Standards. In fact, Auditing and Assurance Standards are the benchmarks by which the quality of audit performance can be measured and the achievement of the objectives can be documented. It is the duty of the auditor to ensure that the audit is conducted in accordance with the requirements of theses standards and if there are any deviations from the standards, the auditor should report thereon.

REVIEW QUESTIONS

Short-answer Questions

1. Define 'propriety' audit. What are its objectives?
2. Define 'efficiency' audit. What are its objectives?
3. Who can conduct cost audit under the Companies Act, 1956?
4. Do you justify the introduction of social audit in India?
5. What is tax audit? Who can be appointed as tax auditor?
6. Write short notes on compulsory tax audit.
7. What do you mean by human resource audit?
8. Define performance audit. What is its importance?
9. What are the contents of cost audit report?
10. Define operational audits. What are its objectives?

Essay-type Questions

1. What is social audit? Give your views on the objectives of social audit. Discuss the position of social audit in Indian scenario?
2. Define 'propriety audit'. Distinguish between traditional audit and propriety audit. What are the benefits of propriety audit? Is there any provision for such audit in case of companies under the Companies Act, 1956?
3. Discuss the concept and objective of cost audit. What are the advantages of cost audit from the viewpoint of the management? Distinguish between cost audit and management audit.
4. What is management audit? State the uses, limitations and importance of management audit.
5. Define human resource audit. State its advantages and limitations. How does it differ from human resource accounting?

CHAPTER 16

Professional Ethics and Misconduct

CHAPTER OUTLINE

16.1 INTRODUCTION

The 'code of conduct' is essentially a set of professional ethical standards regulating the relationship of chartered accountants with their clients, employers, employees, fellow members of the group and the public in general. According to the International Federation of Accountants, the ethical requirements of any accountancy body should be based on integrity, objectivity, independence, confidentiality, high technical standards, professional competence and above all on ethical behaviour. The Chartered Accountants Act, 1949 and the Schedules to the Act set out the acceptance forms of behaviour of the members of the profession.

The conduct of the chartered accountants is judged under provisions contained in the Chartered Accountants Act, 1949 and the Schedules thereto, setting out different forms of behaviour, which would constitute professional and other misconducts under the Act.

16.2 MEANING OF PROFESSIONAL ETHICS

The term 'ethics' refers to the moral principles. It gives rise to certain standard of conduct of behaviour, based on moral foundation. 'Professional ethics' are those moral standards of conduct for the members of a profession.

The code of conduct of the Institute of Chartered Accountants of India defines professional ethics of a chartered accountant as "his behaviour with their clients, employers, employees, fellow members of the group and the public as a whole".

16.3 MEANING OF PROFESSIONAL MISCONDUCT

The term 'professional misconduct' has been defined in Section 22 of the Chartered Accountants Act, 1949 as follows:

"Professional misconduct shall be deemed to include any act or omission specified in any of the schedules, but nothing in this section shall be construed to limit or abridge in any way the power conferred or duty cast on the council under Section 21(1) to enquire into the conduct of any member of the institute under any other circumstances."

16.4 SCHEDULES TO THE CHARTERED ACCOUNTANTS ACT, 1949 RELATING TO PROFESSIONAL MISCONDUCT

There are two schedules to the Chartered Accountants Act, listing instances of professional misconduct. The first schedule, which has three parts, contains instances of professional misconduct, which are adjudicated by the council of the ICAI. The second schedule has two parts that requires action of the High Court.

16.4.1 The First Schedule

Part I

Professional misconduct in relation to chartered accountants in practice

A Chartered Accountant in practice shall be deemed to be guilty of professional misconduct, if he does the following:

Clause 1: Allows others to practice in his name This clause prevents unqualified persons from practicing in the name of qualified chartered accountants. Only a qualified partner or a qualified employee of a practicing chartered accountant can practice in his name.

Clause 2: Pays or allows to pay profit on his profession to persons other than CA According to this clause, no commission, no brokerage or fees can be paid to third parties nor the profits of his profession can be shared with the persons other than CA.

Example

Fact

Mr. A, a practicing chartered accountant, has accepted the assignment of preparing a project report for a chemical factory jointly with a chemical engineer.

Legal view

As per Clause 2 of the First Schedule (Part-I) of the Chartered Accountants Act, 1949 a chartered accountant cannot share the fees of his professional activities with a person other than a member of the Institute.

In the above case, Mr. A will be held guilty of professional misconduct, if he shares the fee for the preparation of the project report of the chemical factory. However, he will not be held guilty of professional misconduct if in the joint assignment with that chemical engineer, his extent of responsibility is specific and his professional fee is separate.

Clause 3: Accepts or agrees to accept profit of profession from persons other than CA This clause states that a chartered accountant in practice cannot share the profits of persons belonging to other professions, (e.g.) lawyer, auctioneer, broker or other agents, who is not a member of the institute.

Example

Fact

Mr. B, a chartered accountant in practice, and a lawyer agree to pay to each other 10% of the gross fees received by them from clients referred to each by the other. It is also agreed that both of them will maintain a record in respect of such clients and the accounts will be settled at the end of the financial year.

Legal view

As per Clause 3 of the First Schedule (Part-I) of the Chartered Accountants Act, 1949 the chartered accountant is guilty of professional misconduct as he agreed to receive a share in the profits of a person who is not a member of the ICAI.

Clause 4: Enters into partnership with a person other than a CA in practice According to this clause, a practicing chartered accountant can take another person as a partner only if he fulfills any of the following criteria:

(a) He is a chartered accountant in practice.
(b) He resides outside India, but in spite of his residence abroad is entitled to be registered as a member.
(c) His qualifications are recognised by the central government or the council of the Institute for the purpose of permitting such partnership.
(d) He shares the fees and profits of the profession both in and outside India.

Example

Fact

Mr. C, a chartered accountant in practice, enters into a partnership with a non-chartered accountant. However, the firm does not undertake any professional assignment and is dissolved after a few months.

Legal view

According to Clause 4 of the First Schedule (Part- I) of the Chartered Accountants Act, 1949 Mr. C is guilty of professional misconduct, because a chartered accountant is restricted to enter into professional partnerships with non-chartered accountants. It is immaterial whether any professional assignment has been undertaken or not.

Clause 5: Secures any professional business through the services of a person not qualified to be his partner This clause prohibits a member to procure professional business through third parties or through such means and practices as are not opened to him. The purpose of this clause is to impose check on ugly competition amongst the chartered accountants in practice, thereby lowering the dignity of the profession.

Clause 6: Solicits clients by circular, advertisement, personal communication or interview or by any other means This clause bans all forms of canvassing for professional work by a chartered accountant in practice, including issue of circulars, advertisements or personal communication or through interviews. He should secure and retain clients by his own skill and intelligence.

Example

Fact

Mr. D, a chartered accountant in practice, responds to an advertisement released by a private company in a newspaper inviting applications for appointment as auditors.

Legal view

As per Clause 6 of the First Schedule (Part-I) of the Chartered Accountants Act, 1949 Mr. D is guilty of professional misconduct. A chartered accountant in practice cannot respond to advertisements inviting applications for appointment as auditors unless the same is sought by certain specified institutions like central government regulated institutions, World bank or the audit services are to be provided abroad.

Clause 7: Advertises his professional attainment or services or uses any designation other than CA on professional documents, visiting cards, letter heads or signboard, unless it is a degree recognised by the central government or by the Council of the Institute This clause prohibits a chartered accountant in practice to publicise his professional attainment in any manner.

Example

Fact

Mr. E, who recently started his practice, has put up a signboard outside his office describing himself as a "Chartered Accountant and Management Consultant".

Legal view

As per Clause 7 of the First Schedule (Part-I) of Chartered Accountants Act, 1949 a chartered accountant in practice is not allowed to use any designation other than "Chartered Accountant".

In the above case, Mr. E has violated the provision of this clause by describing himself on his office signboard as "Chartered Accountant and Management Consultant". Hence, Mr. E will be held guilty of professional misconduct.

In the above case, Mr. E will be held guilty of professional misconduct, as he has related his professional fees to the valuation of the business goodwill.

Clause 8: Accepts audit work without intimating the ex-auditor In act, this clause serves as a safeguard for the new auditors. It enables them to know well in advance the circumstances, which have led to his appointment, and retirement of the existing auditor.

Example

Fact

Mr. F, a practicing chartered accountant, has been appointed as the auditor of a company for the first time. He accepts the assignment without communicating with the retiring auditor.

Legal view

Clause 8 of the First Schedule (Part-I) of the Chartered Accountants Act, 1949 requires an auditor to communicate with the retiring auditor, before accepting a position as auditor.

More than being a matter of courtesy, this communication will enable the newly appointed auditor to know whether it will be justified for him to accept this assignment. Communication with the previous auditor will also enable him to know whether there is any under-cutting of fees in which case he should also refuse to accept the assignment. So, in the above case, Mr. F has not communicated with the retiring auditor of the company in which he is appointed as auditor. So, he will be held guilty of professional misconduct.

Clause 9: Accepts jobs without maintaining legal provisions regarding appointment of auditors of the Companies Act This clause states that an auditor should ascertain first whether his appointment is in order or not. Only then, he should accept the appointment. Sections 224 and 225 of the Companies Act provide the required provisions for the appointment of company auditor.

Example

Fact

Mr. G, a chartered accountant in practice, accepts the audit of a company on the basis of an ordinary resolution passed at the annual general meeting of the company. The company attracts the provisions of Section 224A of the Companies Act, 1956.

Legal view

Section 224A of the Companies Act, 1956, requires that in the case of a company in which not less than 25 per cent of the subscribed share capital is held by certain specified institutions, the appointment or re-appointment of the auditor shall be made by a special resolution. In the above case, therefore, the appointment is not valid. The chartered accountant, i.e. Mr. G is guilty of professional misconduct for not having ascertained compliance with Section 224A as per Clause 9 of the First Schedule (Part-I) of the Chartered Accountants Act, 1949.

Clause 10: Charges or accepts fees on a percentage basis of profit or which are contingent upon the findings or results According to this clause, the basis of calculation of professional fees should not be related to the profits or results of an assignment except in cases permitted under any regulations made under this act. The basis should be related to time, skills and responsibilities involved in the assignment.

Example

Fact

Mr. H, a practicing chartered accountant, who is appointed to value the goodwill of a running business for the purpose of its takeover, charged his fees on the basis of a predetermined percentage of the value of goodwill.

Legal view

Clause 10 of the First Schedule (Part-I) of the Chartered Accountants Act, 1949 restrains a chartered accountant from charging fees contingent upon his findings. This clause has been included, as the professional fees of a chartered accountant should always be based on time, skill and the responsibilities involved in the assignment. It helps in maintaining the dignity of the profession.

In the above case, Mr. H will be held guilty of professional misconduct, as he has related his professional fees to the valuation of the business goodwill.

Clause 11: Engages himself in any occupation without permission This clause prohibits a chartered accountant to engage himself in any trade or business other than that of a chartered accountant. It helps in maintaining the dignity of the profession.

However, Regulation 191 of the Chartered Accountants Regulations (1988) allows a chartered accountant in practice to act, subject to the control of the council, as a liquidator, trustee, executor, administrator, arbitrator, receiver, adviser or representative for costing, financial or taxation matters.

Apart from the above regulation, the general and the specific regulation of the council of the Institute of Chartered Accountants of India have specified the activities in which a chartered accountant can engage himself.

The following is the list of occupations covered by the general resolutions, where no prior permission is required to be obtained from the council of the Institute:

1. Employment under chartered accountants in practice or firm of chartered accountants.
2. Private tutorship
3. Authorship of books and articles
4. Holding of life insurance agency license for the purpose of getting only renewal commission
5. Attending classes and appearing for any examination
6. Holding of public elected offices such as that of MP, MLA, etc.

7. Honorary office-bearership of charitable, educational or other non-commercial organisation
8. Part-time tutorship under the coaching centres of the Institute
9. Evaluation of papers, acting as paper-setter, head-examiner or a moderator for any examination
10. Editorship of professional journal
11. Acting as Public notary, Justice of peace and the like
12. Acting as surveyor or loss assessor under the Insurance Act, 1938

Apart from the above, the following is the list of occupations covered by specific resolution, where prior approval is required to be obtained from the Council of the Institute:

1. Full-time or part-time employment in business concerns provided that the member or his relatives do not hold substantial interest in such a concern
2. Full-time or part-time employments in non-business concerns
3. Office of the Managing Director or a full-time Director of a body corporate within the meaning of the Companies Act, 1956 provided that the member or his relatives do not hold a substantial interest in such a concern
4. Interest in family business concerns or concerns in which interest has been acquired as a result of relationship and in the management of which no active part is taken
5. Interest in agricultural and allied activities carried on with the help, if required, of hired labour
6. Interest in any educational institution
7. Part-time or full time lectureship for courses other than those relating to the institutes examination conducted under the auspices of the institute or the regional councils or their branches
8. Part-time or full-time tutorship under any educational institution other than the coaching centre of the Institute
9. Editorship of journals other than professional journals
10. Any other business or occupation for which the executive committee considers that permission may be granted.

Example

Fact

Mr. I, a practicing chartered accountant and part-time lecturer of a college, has accepted a joint authorship of a book on Cost and Management Accounting along with a colleague who is a cost accountant.

Legal view

Clause 11 of the 1st Schedule of the Chartered Accountants Act, 1949 prohibits a practicing chartered accountant to engage in any business or occupation other than the profession of chartered accountancy. However, there are some occupations, which do not affect the dignity of a chartered accountant, which are included in the general resolution as well as in the special resolution of the Council of the Institute of Chartered Accountants.

In the above case, Mr. I will not be held guilty of professional misconduct if he has already taken prior permission for part-time lectureship in college from the Institute. He is not required to take prior permission for co-authorship of book. It is important to note in this regard that the general resolution is in fact silent about co-authorship. But it is implied from the spirit of the resolutions that co-authorship with another dignified member of the society will not tarnish the image of a chartered accountant.

Clause 12: Accepts work as to constitute undercutting of fees This clause prohibits a chartered accountant to undertake an audit assignment at terms which are lower than those offered by another chartered accountant in practice, provided there is no change in the workload and the degree of skill and responsibility involved. The purpose of this clause is to avoid competition among the members of the Institute.

Clause 13: Allows others not being a member of the Institute or a member not being his partner to sign on his behalf or on behalf of his firm According to this clause, a chartered accountant in practice cannot allow anyone except his partner to sign financial statements on his behalf or on behalf of his firm.

Part II

Professional misconduct in relation to members of the Institute in service

A member of the Institute (other than a member in practice) shall be deemed to be guilty of professional misconduct, if he

(a) pays or allows to pay any person any share in the emoluments of his employment
(b) accepts or agrees to accept any part of fees or gain from a lawyer, a chartered accountant or broker engaged by such employer by way of commission or gratification
(c) discloses confidential information except as and when required by law or except as permitted by the employer.

Part III

Professional misconduct in relation to the members of the Institute in general

A member of the Institute, whether in practice or not, shall be deemed to be guilty of professional misconduct, if he

(a) includes in any statement, return or form to be submitted to the council any particulars knowing them to be false
(b) not being fellow styles himself as a fellow
(c) does not provide information as required by the council.

Example

Fact

Mr. J, a chartered accountant, in an application submitted by his articles clerk to the council of ICAI for permission to pursue another course, confirms that the normal working hours of his office are from 10.30 am to 5.30 pm and hours during which the articles clerk is required to attend the classes are from 6 am to 9.40 am. However, the articles clerk attends the classes from 10 am to 3 pm on all weekdays for one year.

Legal view

Since the application seeking permission submitted to ICAI contains false information, the chartered accountant is guilty of professional misconduct.

16.4.2 The Second Schedule

Part I

Professional misconduct in relation to Chartered Accountants in practice requiring action by a High Court

A chartered accountant in practice shall be deemed to be guilty of professional misconduct, if he does the following:

Clause 1: Discloses information about the client without his consent or otherwise than as required by any law This clause prohibits an auditor to disclose any information regarding the affairs of his client to a third party, except with the consent of his client or as required by law.

Example

Fact

Mr. K, a chartered accountant in practice, becomes aware of the components of the product produced by a company during the course of his audit. He describes the same in detail to another company in which he is also conducting audit, without knowing the fact that the said company would take the advantage of this information. He is, however, aware that the former company has taken great pains to keep its product contents a top secret.

Legal view

According to Clause 1 of the Second Schedule (Part-1) of the Chartered Accountants Act, 1949 an auditor cannot disclose any information regarding the affairs of his client to a third party except with the consent of his client. So, Mr. K is guilty of professional misconduct for divulging information regarding his client's business without the consent of the client.

Clause 2: Certifies or submits report on financial statement without audit According to this clause, a chartered accountant in practice cannot sign reports on financial statements or accounts examined by outsiders. He can, however, certify the statements examined by another chartered accountant in practice. This exception is necessary to enable two or more firms of chartered accountants to conduct joint audit.

Clause 3: Certifies an estimate of earnings contingent upon future transactions This clause prohibits a chartered accountant in practice to certify the accuracy of a statement showing forecasted earnings. However, he can render assistance in the preparation of forecasted cash flows, budgets or similar statements.

Clause 4: Expresses opinion on financial statement of any business in which he has substantial interest, without disclosing it This clause imposes restrictions on the chartered accountant to express his opinion on financial statements of any business in which he is directly or indirectly interested. If he does so, he must also disclose about his interest in his report.

Example

Fact

Mr. L, a chartered accountant in practice, accepts tax audit of a concern in which he is a Director.

Legal view

Mr. L is guilty of professional misconduct. The Companies Act disqualifies a chartered accountant from acting as auditor of a company of which he is a director. Though this provision is not applicable to tax audit, the council of the ICAI has opined that this restriction should be applied to all kinds of audit.

Clause 5: Fails to disclose any material fact known to him, which is not disclosed in financial statement According to this clause, a chartered accountant is expected to disclose in his report any material fact, which is known to him, but has not been disclosed in the financial statement in order to safeguard the interest of the public.

Clause 6: Fails to report on any material misstatement known to him to appear in a financial statement This clause in fact is complementary to the above Clause 5. In addition to disclose of any omission of a material fact from the financial statement, the auditor should also report a material mis-statement contained therein.

Clause 7: Is grossly negligent in the conduct of his professional duties According to this clause, a chartered accountant is expected to show his skill and expertise so much as is expected from a man of his caliber and status. The gross negligence on his part means utter carelessness. What constitutes gross negligence is a matter of the actual circumstances of the individual case.

Clause 8: Fails to obtain sufficient information to warrant the expression of an opinion This clause prohibits a chartered accountant to express an opinion on the financial statement unless he is able to obtain sufficient evidence in this regard. The clause also requires the auditor to express a negative opinion if the qualifications in his report are so material as to render a positive opinion on the true and fair nature of the financial statements meaningless.

Clause 9: Fails to invite attention to any material deviation from the generally accepted procedures of audit This clause requires that an auditor should follow the normal procedure of audit. If he has departed from it, he must state the fact in his report.

Clause 10: Fails to keep money of the client in a separate banking account or to use such money for the intended purposes According to this clause, an auditor should not misuse the money deposited to him by his clients for some specific purposes. If he misuses it, it will amount to breach of trust.

Part II

Professional misconduct in relation to members of the Institute in general requiring action by a High Court

A member of the Institute, whether in practice or not, shall be deemed to be guilty of professional misconduct, if:

(a) He contravenes any of the provisions of the Act or the regulations made thereunder

(b) He is guilty of such other act or omission as may be specified by the council by notification in the gazette of India.

Example

Fact

Mr. M, a practicing chartered accountant, does not maintain any record of his professional receipts.

Legal view

Here, Mr. M is guilty of professional misconduct. As per a notification of the council of the ICAI, a chartered accountant in practice is required to maintain proper books of account in respect of his professional practice.

16.5 ENQUIRY INTO CHARGES OF MISCONDUCT OF CHARTERED ACCOUNTANTS

Section 21 of the Chartered Accountants Act, 1949 lays down the procedure of enquiry relating to the professional misconduct of chartered accountants. It has been summarised as follows:

1. Initial processing of complaint or information

On receipt of information by, or a complaint made, the council of the Institute considers whether there is *a prima facie* case against the member concerned for any professional or other misconduct.

The member against whom the complaint has been lodged, may, within 14 days of the service of the copy of complaint to him or within such time as extended by the authority, make a written statement in his defense. If the council is of the view that a *prima facie* case exists, it shall refer the case to the disciplinary committee. However, if there does not exist any *prima facie* case against the respondent, the complainant and the respondent are informed accordingly.

2. Inquiry by disciplinary committee

The disciplinary committee holds an inquiry in all matters referred to it by the council, in such manner as may be prescribed. The respondent can defend himself before the committee either in person or through a legal practitioner or through any other member. Thereafter, the committee shall submit the report of the result of its enquiry to the council of the institute.

3. Consideration of the report by the council

The report of the disciplinary committee is considered by the council along with the written presentation, if any, made by the member. The council, if necessary, refers the matter again to the disciplinary committee for its further enquiry and report. If the council finds from the report of the committee that the member is not guilty of misconduct, its findings are recorded accordingly and the case is terminated. But, if the council finds that the member is guilty, it issues a notice to the concerned member asking him to state why a disciplinary action should not be taken against him.

4. Action taken

If the council finds that the member is guilty of professional misconduct specified in the first schedule, the member is given an opportunity of being heard and may thereafter be either reprimanded or his name be removed from the register of members for not exceeding five years by the council. If the council decides that the misconduct is such that the member's name should be excluded from the register of members for a period exceeding five years or permanently, it has to forward the case to the High Court with its recommendation thereof.

But, if the misconduct of a member is such that it does not fall within the scope of the first schedule to the act, the council must refer the case to the high court with its recommendations, unless, on receipt of the report of the disciplinary committee, it finds that the member is not guilty of any misconduct. On a case being referred to the High Court, the High Court may decide the case as it deems fit.

5. Appeals against the order of the council

A member who has been reprimanded or whose name has been removed from the register of members may prefer an appeal to the High Court against such an order of the council. The appeal must be filed within 30 days of the date on which the order is communicated to the concerned member. However, the High Court may accept an appeal even after the expiry of the said period, if it is satisfied that the delay was caused by a sufficient cause.

POINTS TO PONDER

- Ethics refers to the moral principles. It gives rise to certain standard of conduct of behaviour, based on moral foundation.
- Professional ethics are those moral standards of conduct for the members of a profession. The code of conduct of the ICAI defines professional ethics of a chartered accountant as his behaviour with their clients, employers, employees, fellow members of the group and the public as a whole.
- Professional misconduct shall be deemed to include any act or omission specified in any of the schedules, but nothing in this section shall be construed to limit or abridge in any way the power conferred or duty cast on the council under section 21 (1) to enquire into the conduct of any member of the Institute under any other circumstances. : Section 22.
- There are two schedules to the Chartered Accountants Act, listing instances of professional misconduct. The first schedule, which has three parts, contains instances of professional misconduct, which are adjudicated by the council of the Institute. The second schedule has two parts that require action of the High Court.
- Part One of the first schedule deals with the professional misconduct in relation to chartered accountants in practice. This part includes total thirteen clauses.
- Part Two of the first schedule deals with the professional misconduct in relation to members of the institute in service.
- Part Three of the first schedule deals with the professional misconduct in relation to the institute in general.

- Part One of the second schedule deals with the professional misconduct in relation to chartered accountants in practice requiring action by a High Court. This part includes total ten clauses.
- Part Two of the second schedule deals with professional misconduct in relation to members of the Institute in general requiring action by a High Court.
- Enquiry into the charges of misconduct of chartered accountants follows certain procedures. The procedures include initial processing of complaint or information, inquiry by the disciplinary committee, consideration of the report by the council, action taken and appeals against the order of the council.

REVIEW QUESTIONS

Short-answer Questions

1. Discuss the reasons as to why the conduct of a chartered accountant in practice is considered material if he
   (a) solicits professional work
   (b) engages in undercutting
   (c) accepts appointment as an auditor without communicating with the previous auditor
   (d) charges fees, which are contingent upon the results.
2. In view, of the provisions of the Chartered Accountants Act, 1949 state and justify your views on the following cases
   (a) Whether you would accept offer of appointment as auditor of a firm in which your brother is a partner?
   (b) Whether the chartered accountant employed in your firm can sign the balance sheet of a concern in the name of your firm?
   (c) Whether you can put up a signboard showing your designation as a "Chartered Accountant, Income-Tax Practitioner and Company Law Adviser"?

Essay-type Questions

1. Define 'Professional Misconduct' and state how professional misconduct and professional ethics are related. Give few instances of professional misconduct with case decisions.
2. Enumerate the instances of professional misconduct of a chartered accountant in practice, which, however, does not require action by the high court.

CHAPTER 17

Special Audit

CHAPTER OUTLINE

17.1 INTRODUCTION

The main aspects of the auditor's work are common to all types of audit, but as every organisation will have its own peculiar facets, it will be necessary for the auditor to apply his skill and judgment individually in carrying out his audit work. There are, however, certain types of organisations which will require special treatment, either owing to the exceptional nature of work or to their being covered by statutes which require the investigation and presentation of certain information.

While framing audit programme concerning the audit of specialised enterprises, the auditor should ask himself the following questions:

- Are there any special statutory regulations covering the enterprise?
- Are there any special regulations governing the accounts?
- What is the enterprise's basic internal regulatory document?
- What is the nature of the enterprise's business, and what transactions arise from its business?
- What are its main sources of income and expenditure?
- What are its main assets and liabilities?
- Are there any special audit points that should be considered?

Hence, audits requiring special treatment are discussed in the following sections of this chapter.

17.2 AUDIT OF CHARITABLE SOCIETIES

A charitable society performs its operations for rendering social services. Its main sources of revenue are donations and legacies. The object of audit of this type of society is to ensure that its revenue is being utilised for the purpose for which the society has been established and it is being operated in conformity with its rules and regulations.

The auditor should pay attention to the following points while auditing the accounts of a charitable institution:

17.2.1 General Matters

1. Study of the constitution

The constitution of the charitable institution has to be studied first and important rules and regulations are to be noted down for consideration of detailed auditing of the institution.

2. Examination of activities

The activities of the institution should be identified and it should be examined whether these activities are within the constituted objectives of the institution.

3. Review of internal control system

The internal control system regarding the cash receipts and cash disbursement should be reviewed.

4. Inspection of the minute book

The auditor should inspect the minute book of the meetings of the managing committee and identify the resolutions having bearing on accounts and audit.

5. Study of financial power of executives

The financial power of different executives and officers as well as the members of the managing committee should be noted.

17.2.2 Receipts

1. Subscriptions and donations

Subscriptions and donations, which are the main sources of income of a charitable institution, should be checked and verified with reference to entries in the cash book with the help of receipts counterfoil, registers of subscription and donations, list of members, rates of subscription for different classes of membership and other relevant documents.

2. Grants

Grants received or receivable from the government or any local authority should be checked with the help of relevant correspondence, minute book etc.

3. Interest and dividend

Interest and dividend from the deposits and investments should be checked with the relevant vouchers. In addition to that, the interest on such deposits and dividends, either ex-dividend or cum-dividend should be checked to see whether these are recorded properly in the books of accounts.

4. Rent and other income from house property

Rent and other income from properties of the institution should be checked with the help of counterfoils of receipts and other relevant documents.

5. Receipts from charity show etc.

Receipts from charity shows or other special functions should be checked with the counterpart of the tickets sold, statement of cash collection and entries in the cash book.

17.2.3 Payments and Expenses

1. Distinction between capital and revenue expenditure

The auditor should see that proper distinction has been made in the accounts between capital expenditure and revenue expenditure.

2. Vouching of expenses

He should check all expenses with reference to the entries in the cash book with the help of bills, receipts etc. In addition to that, special attention should be given for the checking of expenses relating to charity shows and other functions.

3. Grants made by the institution

Grants made by the institution constitute the major expenses of the institution. So the auditor should pay special attention to check these payments. The auditor should ensure that all grants have been made for admissible purposes and they are properly authorised.

4. Purchase and sale of assets and investments

Purchase and sale of movable as well as immovable properties and investments should be verified with the help of relevant documents. The auditor should assure himself about their existence through physical verification at a particular point of time.

17.2.4 Assets and Liabilities

1. Verification of assets and liabilities

The auditor should verify all assets and liabilities with the help of relevant documents. He would confirm about their physical existence either through physical verification or through confirmation from the concerned parties.

2. Utilisation of fund

In this type of organisation, different types of funds are created for some specific purposes. The auditor should ensure the proper utilisation of these funds for the purposes specified.

17.2.5 Income Tax

Taxability of income

The auditor should see whether the income of the institution is exempt from income tax according to the provisions of Section 11 of the Income Tax Act, 1961 and, if so, whether refund of income tax deducted at source from interest income, if any, has been claimed from the tax authority.

17.2.6 Financial Statement

True and fair view

The auditor should examine the financial statements and see whether they give a true and fair view of the surplus or deficit and of the state of affairs of the institution.

17.3 AUDIT OF CINEMA HALLS

The main purpose of a cinema hall is to provide entertainment to the public. The number of cinema halls in our country has increased in recent years. The cinema halls are now providing not only the opportunity of viewing movies, but also restaurant and bar facilities are also available in cinema halls in big cities. As a result, the requirement of maintaining proper accounts of cinema hall activities and its regular audit has also increased to a large extent.

The auditor should pay attention to the following points while auditing the accounts of a cinema hall:

17.3.1 General Matters

1. Study of the status

The legal status of the cinema hall has to be studied first, i.e. whether it is a sole-proprietorship concern or a partnership firm or a company.

2. Review of internal control system

The internal control system regarding the cash receipts and cash disbursements should be reviewed.

3. Inspection of the minute book

The auditor should inspect the minute books of the meetings of the Board of Directors/ partners and note down the relevant resolutions having bearing on accounts and audit.

4. Study of financial power of executives

The financial power of different executives and employees of the hall should be noted.

5. Review of previous audit report

The auditor should review the previous audit reports and note down the qualifications and observations made in those reports.

17.3.2 Receipts

1. Sale of tickets

The system of control over sale of tickets is required to be examined by the auditor. A statement of total tickets sold and the total receipts for the day with each booking clerk are reconciled with the number of tickets sold.

2. Issue of free passes

The auditor should also check that all the free passes are issued only with proper authorisation.

3. Deposit of entertainment tax

The auditor should examine whether the entertainment tax collected by the hall is deposited in a separate bank account and he should also examine whether the tax is paid to the authorities concerned regularly and as per the regulations.

4. Rent and income from other sources

Rent and other income from different sources of the cinema hall, e.g. letting out of shops, offices and other spaces in the hall compound should be vouched with the help of counterfoils of receipts and other relevant documents.

5. Receipts from advertisements

The auditor should examine the system of collection of charges on account of hoarding in the compound as well as on account of screening of short films, trailers, slides etc.

17.3.3 Payments and Expenses

1. Distinction between capital and revenue expenditure

The auditor should see that proper distinction has been made in the accounts between capital expenditure and revenue expenditure.

2. Vouching of expenses

He should vouch all expenses with reference to the entries in the cash book with the help of bills, receipts etc.

3. Payment to distributors

He should verify the film hire charges and other payments to distributors. He should examine a sample of these transactions in depth with reference to the agreements, correspondence, bill etc.

4. Depreciation of fixed assets

The auditor should examine whether proper depreciation has been charged on projection equipments, furniture and other fixed assets.

17.3.4 Assets and Liabilities

1. Verification of assets and liabilities

All assets and liabilities of the hall should be either verified physically along with the documentary evidence or through confirmation from third parties.

2. Advances to distributors

The auditor should examine the advances to distributors remaining unadjusted at the end of the accounting period and verify whether provision or write-off is required.

17.3.5 Income Tax

Tax assessment

The auditor should check the assessment of tax aspect of the hall in order to verify that whether the tax return in submitted on regular basis along with the amount of tax.

17.3.6 Financial Statement

True and fair view

The auditor should see whether the financial statements give a true and fair view of the profit or loss and of the balance sheet of the cinema hall.

17.4 AUDIT OF CLUBS

Clubs are associations of group of persons with common interest and these are basically established with non-profit motive. The main activities of the clubs include provision for amusement and recreation and constructive work for the welfare of the society. From the legal point of view, clubs can be of two types: government registered clubs and unregistered clubs.

Government registered clubs are required to get their accounts audited at regular intervals for renewal of their registration. Besides, in order to avail different government grants the clubs are required to submit audited accounts. But this is not required for unregistered clubs.

The auditor should pay attention to the following points, while conducting audit of accounts of a club.

17.4.1 General

1. Study of the constitution

First of all, the auditor shall acquaint himself with rules, regulations, by-laws and constitution of the club, particularly in respect of accounts.

2. Inspection of the minute book

The auditor should inspect the minute book of the executive committee and take note of resolutions passed having bearing on accounts and audit.

3. Noting of financial power of executives

The financial powers of different executives and of different committees have to be noted.

4. Review of internal control system

The auditor should also study the internal check and internal control system in respect of purchases, receipts, stock of foodstuff etc.

17.4.2 Receipts

1. Subscriptions and entrance fees

The main source of income of a club is subscription from the members. The auditor should vouch all the receipts from entrance fees and subscriptions from members with the help of counterfoils of receipts and register of members.

2. Arrear subscriptions

Any subscriptions in arrear should be verified from the schedule received from the club, which should be certified by the executive committee. He should also look into the reasons for non-payment of subscriptions and steps taken for their recovery.

3. Sale of refreshment etc.

He should vouch the sale of refreshments, wines, cigars and billiard room and swimming receipts etc. He should also see that proper records are maintained for the stock of refreshments, wines, cigars, swimming costumes etc.

4. Donations

If donations are received by the club, it should be ensured that such donations are utilised by the club for the specified purposes for which it is received.

5. Receipts from cultural functions

Receipts from special functions or cultural functions should be vouched with the counterfoils of tickets, statement of collections etc. Expenses of the functions should also be checked with the related vouchers.

17.4.3 Payments and Expenses

1. Distinction between capital and revenue expenditure

The auditor should see that proper distinction has been made in the accounts between capital expenditure and revenue expenditure.

2. Vouching of expenses

He should vouch all expenses with reference to the entries in the cashbook with the help of bills, receipts etc. He should vouch the payments made on account of purchases of crockery, wines, furnitures etc.

3. Depreciation of fixed assets

The auditor should examine whether proper depreciation has been charged on all assets of the club including furniture, sports equipments and crockery.

17.4.4 Assets and Liabilities

1. Verification of assets and liabilities

The auditor should verify all assets and liabilities with the help of relevant documents. He should confirm about their physical existence either through physical verification or through confirmation from the concerned parties.

2. Creation of reserve fund

The club has to create a number of reserve funds for different purposes. The auditor should ensure that proper appropriation of surplus generated has been made for this purpose.

17.4.5 Income Tax

Taxability of income

The auditor should check the tax liabilities of the club as regards sales tax and income tax. He should verify that whether the tax return is submitted on regular basis along with the amount of tax.

17.4.6 Special Accounts

1. Special services to the members

The auditor should vouch debits to members for special services, e.g. billiards, tennis court reservations, dinners etc. with the member's signatures in the respective registers.

2. Individual activity accounts

Individual accounts maintained for various activities like games and sports, social functions, charity shows, etc. should be carefully examined and the arrangement for meeting the expenses of teams for participation of the club in different tournaments should be particularly checked.

17.4.7 Financial Statements

True and fair view

The auditor should examine the financial statements and see whether they give a true and fair view of the surplus or deficit and of the state of affairs of the club.

17.5 AUDIT OF CO-OPERATIVE SOCIETIES

The co-operative movement in India is not a recent event. The co-operative sector in India has been developed as a result of government initiative and effective measures. In our country, the Co-operative Societies Act was passed in the year 1912. The co-operative societies in India are established and governed by this Act.

To monitor the day-to-day activities of the society, a group of members are selected to form the 'management committee'. This committee usually consists of chairman, secretary and treasurer. In every annual general meeting, the members of this committee are elected.

On the basis of liability of members, co-operative societies can be of two types: limited liability societies and unlimited liability societies.

The provisions regarding the maintenance of books of accounts and records are also governed by the Indian Co-operative Societies Act, 1912. According to Section 17 of this Act, the accounts of these types of societies are required to be audited by the auditors of the department of co-operative societies. A chartered accountant can also conduct audit of this type of society. It may be noted in this context that the Companies Act, 1956 is not at all relevant and applicable in case of audit of co-operative societies. In general, three types of audits are conducted in a co-operative society, namely continuous audit, annual audit and re-audit. The auditors of co-operative societies are appointed by the registrar of co-operatives.

The auditor should pay attention to the following points, while auditing the accounts of a big co-operative society.

17.5.1 General

1. Study of the Act

The auditor should go through the Co-operative Society Act, 1912 and the rules and regulations relating to accounts to see that the books of account are kept with the provisions as contained in the act.

2. Inspection of the minute book

The auditor should obtain the minutes of the board meeting to see any specific resolutions relating to accounts. He should also see that the resolutions of the meetings of the board have been properly implemented.

3. Review of the internal control system

The auditor should review the internal control system to see whether it is commensurate and compatible with the requirements of co-operative society. He should examine its effectiveness in preventing frauds and misapplication of assets.

4. Restrictions on functions of the society

The auditor should examine the compliance of the following restrictions as imposed by the Act:

(a) If the liability of members is limited by share, no member other than a co-operative society can hold a number of shares exceeding the prescribed number of shares as per the Act.

(b) No member of a society registered with limited liabilities can transfer his shareholdings violating the regulations of the Act.

(c) A registered society cannot give loan to a person other than a member.

(d) A registered society can take loan from non-members only to such extent as may be prescribed by the provisions of the Act.

17.5.2 Receipts

1. Recovery of loan

The auditor should see that the receipts of instalment money have been properly entered in the cash book and accordingly the member's account is credited to that extent.

2. Interest on loan

The auditor should check the interest receipt by reference with the agreement of loan with the borrower.

17.5.3 Payments and Expenses

1. Loan payments

The auditor should vouch the payment of loan granted with the agreement of loan with the borrower as well as from the money receipts of the borrower.

2. Provisions for depreciation

The auditor should see that adequate provisions for depreciation have been provided for all the fixed assets owned by the society.

3. Appropriation of profit

He should ensure that proper appropriation of profits to different funds viz. reserve fund and welfare fund have been made as per the provisions contained in the Act.

4. Payment of dividend

The auditor should confirm that dividend declared and paid to the members are in accordance with the rules and regulations of the society and see that the dividend should not exceed the permissible limit.

17.5.4 Assets and Liabilities

1. Capital structure

The auditor should examine the capital structure of the society. He should ensure that no individual member should hold more than the prescribed limit of the authorised share capital of the society.

2. Loan obtained

He should vouch the loan from central co-operative banks and other financial institutions by reference to cash book, correspondences and other documentary evidences.

3. Investment of surplus

The auditor should see that the surplus funds of the society are invested either in government securities or in such banks as deposits as approved by the registers of societies.

4. Physical verification of assets

The auditor should verify physically the assets of the society. He should verify cash and investment by reference with cash counting and statement of investments.

5. Overdue debts

He should verify whether or not there are any overdue debts and whether or not assets and liabilities have been properly valued.

6. Irregularity in granting loan

He should examine whether there is any material impropriety or irregularity in sanctioning loan to any member or in the realisation of loans from any member.

17.5.5 Income Tax

Taxability of income

The central government is empowered to exempt any registered co-operative society from income tax, stamp duty and registration fees. The auditor will see whether necessary application has been made to the central government for arrangement of their exemption.

17.5.6 Financial Statement

True and fair view

The auditor should verify whether books of accounts have been maintained as per rules framed and whether financial statements have been prepared in accordance with the prescribed form.

17.6 AUDIT OF EDUCATIONAL INSTITUTIONS

Educational institutions include schools, colleges, training centres and universities. The main activities of these types of institutions are more or less similar to each other. As a result, the types of problems the auditor usually faces in conducting audit of these types of institutions are also same. However, on the basis of financial support and affiliation from the government, the educational institutions can be divided into four types, which include the following:

- Government institutions
- Government aided and affiliated institutions
- Government affiliated institutions
- Private institutions

On the basis of the nature of the institutions, the activities and mode of maintenance of books of accounts and records may also differ and the auditor will take into consideration these deviations at the time of his audit.

The auditor should pay attention to the following points, while auditing the accounts of educational institutions:

17.6.1 General

1. Study of the constitution

The auditor should go through the trust deed or regulations to find out provisions affecting accounts and should ensure that the books of accounts are kept with the provision as contained in the deed or regulation.

2. Inspection of the minute book

The auditor should inspect the minutes of the meetings of the managing committee or governing body, noting resolutions affecting accounts, and ensure that these have been duly complied with, specially the decisions as regards the operation of bank account and sanctioning of expenditure.

3. Review of the internal control system

The auditor should check the names entered in the students fee register for each term with the respective class registers, showing names of students on rolls and check the amount of fees charged. In this way, he should ensure that there operates a system of internal check which is effective.

17.6.2 Receipts

1. Tuition fees received

The auditor should check the fees received by comparing counterfoils of receipts granted with entries in the cash book and should trace the collection in the fees register to confirm that the revenue from this source has been duly accounted for.

2. Admission fees received

He should check admission fees with admission slips signed by the head of the institution and confirm that the amount has been credited to a capital fund, unless the managing committee has taken a decision to the contrary.

3. Government grants

He should verify the grant from the government or any local authority with the memo of grant. If any expense has been disallowed for purposes of grant, the auditor should ascertain the reasons thereof.

4. Fine for late payments etc.

The auditor should check that the fine for late payment or absence etc. have been either collected or duly accounted for under the proper authority.

5. Income from other sources

The auditor should check income from other sources viz. rental income from landed property, interest and dividends from investments etc. with reference to documentary evidence available.

17.6.3 Payments and Expenses

1. Distinction between capital and revenue expenditure

The auditor should see that proper distinction has been made between capital expenditure and revenue expenditure in the accounts.

2. Vouching of expenses

He should check all expenses with reference to the entries in the cash book with the help of bills, receipts etc.

3. Purchase of fixed assets

Purchase of fixed assets should be verified with the help of relevant documents. The auditor should assure himself about their existence through physical verification at a particular interval of time.

4. Depreciation of fixed assets

The auditor should examine whether proper depreciation has been charged on the fixed assets of the institute including furniture and buildings.

17.6.4 Assets and Liabilities

1. Arrears on account of fees

The auditor should report on any old and heavy arrears on account of fees, hostel rents etc. to the managing committee.

2. Caution money and other deposits

The auditor should confirm that caution money and other deposits paid by the students on admission have been shown as liability in the balance sheet and not transferred to revenue, unless they are not refundable.

3. Accumulated investments

He should note the investments representing endowment funds for prizes are kept separate and any income in excess of the cost of prizes has been accumulated and invested with the original fund.

4. Maintenance of different funds

The auditor should verify the annual statements of account and while doing so, he should ensure that separate statements of accounts have been prepared as regards poor students fund, games fund, library fund etc.

17.6.5 Income Tax

Tax liability on income

The auditor should confirm that the refund of taxes deducted from income from investment has been claimed and recovered since the institutions are generally exempted from income tax liability.

17.6.6 Financial Statements

True and fair view

The auditor should examine the financial statements and see whether they give a true and fair view of the surplus or deficit and of the state of affairs of the institution.

17.7 AUDIT OF HOTELS

The business of running a hotel is very different from running any other organisation. It is a service oriented business and may have some element of production of foodstuff and sales thereof. However, this business is characterised by handling of liquid cash, stocking and providing a large variety of items, keeping watch on customers to ensure that satisfactory services are being provided to them etc.

In view of these, the following matters deserve special attention of the auditor in auditing hotel businesses:

1. Internal control

The Internal control system of the hotel should be reviewed first. The auditor should ensure that effective internal control is in operation and for this purpose he should evaluate the following:

(a) Effectiveness of arrangement regarding receipts and disbursement of cash
(b) Purchase procedure and stocking of various commodities and provisions
(c) Billing procedures for the customers

2. Cash collections

Control of cash assumes great importance in any hotel. The auditor should reconcile the total sales reported with the total bills issued. Billing may be done room-wise as well as customer-wise. The auditor should see that there exists numerical control over the bills to ensure that all bills are included in the total.

3. Stocks

The stocks in any hotel are both portable and saleable; particularly the food and beverage stock. It is, therefore, extremely important that all movements and transfer of such stocks should be properly documented. Control over stocks can be imposed from the point of two directions

(a) Control over movements The area where stocks are kept should be locked under the supervision of the departmental manager. The auditor should see that the movements of goods in or out of the stores takes place only after proper authorisation and recording.

(b) Control over valuation Although valuation of stocks are made by the experts appointed by the management, it is important that the auditor satisfies himself that the amount included for such stocks are reasonable. The auditor can also attend the physical stocktaking and check certain pricing calculations.

4. Fixed assets

The accounting of fixed assets is likely to differ from hotel to hotel. Certain hotels may consider its utensils as a stock item while others may treat it as fixed assets. A comprehensive definition of the stock should be there and the auditor should see whether the same has been clearly followed or not. Regarding auditing of fixed assets, the auditor should ensure the following:

(a) All the fixed assets are physically verified and properly valued at the end of the accounting period.
(b) Adequate provisions have been made for depreciation on all fixed assets for the accounting year.

5. Compliance with statutory provisions

A number of statutory provisions are required to be complied with in running a hotel business. All types of hotels are governed by various rules and regulations by different authorities, which include the following

(a) Foreign Exchange Regulatory Authority In large hotels, it is very common to have facility of exchanging foreign currency into Indian rupees. There are provisions for foreign exchange transactions.

(b) Department of Tourism The Department of Tourism also prescribes various conditions to be fulfilled by the hotels.

(c) Local authority Approval of the local authority and license are required for running hotel business. The auditor should see that various applicable regulations and conditions are duly complied with by the hotel.

6. Dealings with travelling agents

It is very common that the hotels get their bookings through travel agents or other booking agencies. The auditor should ensure that money is recovered from travel agents as per the terms of credit allowed. Commission, if any, paid to travel agents should be checked by reference to the agreement.

7. Vouching of receipts and expenses

The auditor should vouch all receipts and expenses with reference to the entries in the cash book with the help of documentary evidence. He should pay special attention to the following points:

(a) Consumption shown in various physical stock accounts may be traced to customers bill on a sampling basis, wherever practicable, to ensure that all issues have been billed or accounted for.

(b) All payments made to foreign collaborator, if any, are in accordance with the terms of agreement.

(c) Expenses and receipts may be compared with the figures of the previous year having regard to the average occupancy of visitors and changes in the rates.

(d) Special receipts on account of letting out of the auditorium space and other spaces for shops and for special exhibitions etc. should be verified with reference to the respective agreements.

(e) Customer's ledger should be examined on a sample basis but in depth to check that all charges that should be made to the customers are in fact made.

(f) Proper reserves are required to be maintained for redecoration and renovation of buildings and other structural facilities.

8. Other points

In addition to the above important points regarding the workings of the hotel, the auditor should also take into consideration the following points:

(a) Taxability of income The auditor should check the assessment of tax aspect of the hotel in order to verify that whether the tax return is submitted by the hotel on regular basis along with the amount of tax.

(b) Deposit of sales and entertainment tax The auditor should examine whether the sales and entertainment tax collected by the hotel is duly deposited to the proper authorities with the prescribed limit of time.

(c) True and fair view The auditor should also see whether the financial statements give a true and fair view of the profit or loss and of the balance sheet of the hotel for the accounting period.

17.8 AUDIT OF HOSPITALS

The hospitals are usually established with the fund provided by the government, local authorities, municipalities and similar other types of funds. On the basis of ownership, hospitals can be government hospitals or private hospitals or a joint venture of public-private partnership. As the nature of activities of a hospital are totally different from that of other organisations or institutions, the audit programme to be followed for conducting audit of these types of organisations will also differ.

The auditor should pay attention to the following points, while auditing the accounts of a hospital:

17.8.1 General Matters

1. Legal status

The auditor should see relevant documents to ascertain the legal status of the hospital. He should examine the constitution of the management and provisions affecting annual accounts for consideration of auditing techniques to be used.

2. Inspection of the minute book

If there is a managing committee or a governing body, the auditor should go through the minutes of their meetings in order to note decisions concerning financial matters, specially, engagement of staff, acquisition and sale of fixed assets and investments, delegation of authority regarding expenditure etc. and to see that the resolution affecting accounts have been duly complied with.

3. Internal check system

The auditor should examine the internal check as regards the issue and receipts of stores, linen, apparatus, clothing, instruments etc. so as to ensure that purchases have been properly recorded in the stock register and that issues have been made only against proper authorisation.

4. Examination of activities

The activities of the hospital should be identified and the auditor should ensure that all the activities as decided to be undertaken are being actually performed by the hospital.

17.8.2 Receipts

1. Cash collections

The auditor should check the cash collections as entered in the cashbook, with the receipt counterfoils and other evidence. He should also check the bill registers of patients to see that the bills have been correctly prepared.

2. Free bed facility

He should see that bills have been issued to all patients from whom any amount was recoverable according to the rules of the hospital. He should also ensure that free bed facilities were extended to the patients only in terms of hospital regulations.

3. Income from property and investments

The auditor should refer to the properties and investment registers to see that all the incomes that should have been recovered by way of rent from properties, dividend and interest on securities etc. have been collected.

4. Legacies and donations

He should also ascertain that legacies and donations received for a specific purpose have been so utilised.

5. Grants received

The auditor should verify that the grants received, if any, have been duly accounted for. He should also ensure that the refund in respect of taxes deducted has been claimed.

6. Income from other sources

The auditor should verify the income of the hospital from any other sources, with reference to the source of income, e.g. x-ray lab, blood testing lab etc.

17.8.3 Payments and Expenses

1. Distinction between capital and revenue expenditure

The auditor should see that proper distinction has been made in the accounts between capital expenditure and revenue expenditure.

2. Purchase and sale of assets

Purchase and sale of movable as well as immovable properties should be verified with the help of relevant documents. The auditor should assure himself about their existence through physical verification at a particular point of time.

3. Vouching of expenses

The auditor should vouch all the expenses including the capital expenditure He should verify that the capital expenditure has been incurred only with the prior sanction of the managing committee.

4. Depreciation on fixed assets

He should see that depreciation at appropriate rates has been written off against all the fixed assets.

17.8.4 Assets and Liabilities

1. Verification of assets and liabilities

The auditor should see that all fixed assets have been acquired under proper authority and that proper registers are maintained to record their particulars. He should also confirm about their physical existence either through physical verification or through confirmation from the concerned parties.

2. Stock-in-trade

The auditor should obtain inventories of stocks and stores at the end of the year and check a percentage of them physically. He should also verify stock register in respect of stock and stores such as medicines, test tubes, cleaning materials etc. and see that management has carried out a periodical inspection of all such store items.

17.8.5 Income Tax

Taxability of income

The auditor should see whether the income of the hospital is exempt from income tax according to the provisions of the Income Tax Act, 1961 and, if so, whether refund of income tax deducted at source, if any, has been claimed from the tax authority.

17.8.6 Financial Statement

True and fair view

The auditor should examine the financial statements and see whether they give a true and fair view of the financial results as well as of the financial position of the hospital.

17.9 AUDIT OF LIBRARIES

The activities of a library are unique and totally different from other types of organisations. The basic objective of a library is to impart education to the public at a minimum cost, i.e. by charging only membership fees and annual fees. In case of library, the main cost is the cost for purchase of books.

Libraries are usually established with the help of government grants. The capital expenditure regarding purchase of books are met basically from the money received as grant. Other revenue expenditures are met from the collections of membership fees and annual charges.

The auditor should pay attention to the following points, while auditing the accounts of a library:

17.9.1 General Matters

1. Study of the constitution

The constitution of the library is to be studied first in order to ascertain whether it is a registered society or public trust. The auditor should examine the relevant bye-laws or trust deed in order to ascertain the powers and duties of the management.

2. Inspection of the minute book

The auditor should go through the minute books of the managing committee in order to ensure that resolutions affecting the accounts have been duly complied with.

3. Internal check system

He should also evaluate the internal check system in respect of collection of fees, disbursement on account of payment of salaries to the staff, purchase of books, issue of books to the members, sale of magazines and journals and security against unauthorised movement of books.

17.9.2 Receipts

1. Collection of fees

The auditor should check whether collection of admission fees as well as membership fees are made according to the bye-laws and rules of the library He should vouch the amount of fees collected with reference to the entries passed in the book and the counterfoil of receipts.

2. Security deposits

He should ensure that proper registers are maintained to record the security deposit received from members. He should also check the entry in such register with counterfoil of the receipt book.

3. Government grants etc.

The auditor should verify the receipts of the grant from government or local authorities and its utilisation for the specific purposes mentioned in letters issued by them.

4. Sale proceeds of magazines etc.

He should also vouch the sale proceeds of magazines and journals and check whether the sale proceeds have been properly accounted for or not.

5. Arrear fees

Any arrear fees should be verified from the schedule received from the library, which should be certified by the managing committee. He should also look into the reasons for non-payment of fees and steps taken for their recovery.

6. Donations

If donations are received by the library, it should be ensured that such donations are used by the library for the specified purpose for which it is received.

17.9.3 Payments and Expenses

1. Distinction between capital and revenue expenditure

The auditor should see that proper distinction has been made in the accounts between capital expenditure and revenue expenditure.

2. Vouching of expenses

He should vouch all expenses with reference to the entries in the cash book with the help of bills, receipts etc. He should also vouch the payments made on account of purchase of books and periodicals.

3. Books distributed to poor students

Sometimes libraries accumulate funds for the purchase of books, which are usually distributed to the poor students. The auditor should see that the fund created for the purpose has been effectively utilised for the purchase of books and those books are distributed to the poor students.

4. Depreciation on fixed assets

The auditor should examine whether proper depreciation has been charged on furniture and fixtures, books and other fixed assets of the library.

17.9.4 Assets and Liabilities

1. Physical verification of assets

The auditor should ensure that physical verification of furniture, fixtures and books is done at reasonable intervals and if there is any material discrepancy, it has been properly adjusted in the books of accounts.

2. Maintenance of proper assets registers

Books are the main assets of a library. The total books owned by a library should be properly recorded in the books registers maintained for this purpose. For other assets including furniture and fixtures also, separate asset registers are to be maintained.

3. Investments of surplus

The auditor should see that the surplus funds of the library are invested in those securities or banks as decided by the managing committee or it has been utilised for the purchase of new books.

17.9.5 Taxability of Income

Income tax

The auditor should confirm that the refund of taxes deducted from income from investment has been claimed and recorded since the libraries are usually exempted from income tax liability.

17.9.6 Financial Statement

True and fair view

The auditor should examine the financial statements and see whether they give a true and fair view of the surplus or deficit and of the state of affairs of the library.

17.10 AUDIT OF NURSING HOMES

The activities of nursing homes are similar to that of hospitals. However, there is a basic difference between the objectives of a nursing home and that of a hospital. Hospitals are usually owned either individually or jointly by the government or local authority and these are established to provide services to the common public at a minimum cost. Hospitals are non-profit-seeking concerns. On the other hand, nursing homes are usually privately owned and are formed either as sole-proprietorship business or partnership business or as a company.

The auditor should pay attention to the following points, while auditing the accounts of a nursing home:

17.10.1 General Matters

1. Study of the rules and regulations

The rules and regulations of the nursing home should be studied first and important provisions are to be noted down for consideration of detailed auditing of the nursing home.

2. Review of the internal check system

The internal check system regarding the cash receipts and cash payments should be reviewed.

3. Verification of adequacy of internal control system

The auditor should verify the adequacy of internal control system in respect of the following:

(a) Billing and collection procedures from the patients

(b) Purchasing of medicines, equipments, provisions and other store items

(c) Issuing of medicines, equipments and other store items and their proper recording

17.10.2 Receipts

1. Billing system

The auditor should vouch the copies of the bill issued to the patients with reference to the patients' registers. He has to check the number of bills on selective basis with respect to period of bed occupation, category of bed hired, cost of medicines used and charges for other facilities provided.

2. Cash collections

The auditor should check the cash collections as entered in the cash book with copies of patients' bills, counterfoils of receipts issued etc.

3. Income from other sources

The auditor should see by reference to the property and investment register that all incomes which should have been received by way of rent on properties, interest on investments etc. have been duly accounted for.

17.10.3 Payments and Expenses

1. Vouching of expenses

He should check all expenses with reference to the entries in the cash book with the help of bills, receipts etc. He should also ensure that they have proper sanctions of the authority.

2. Salaries and wages

The auditor should vouch the payments to doctors, nurses, caretakers and other employees with reference to salary bills, appointment letters or contract. He should also see that the appointments and increments have sanction of the appropriate authority.

3. Distinction between capital and revenue expenditure

He should see that proper distinction has been made in the accounts between capital expenditure and revenue expenditure.

4. Depreciation of fixed assets

The auditor should examine whether proper depreciation has been charged on different operation theatre equipments, furniture and fixtures and other fixed assets of the nursing home.

5. Writing off of special equipments

Some of the assets, which are used in nursing home, are required to be written off before the expiry of its expected life due to the nature of the assets. The auditor should enquire into all these cases of writing off of equipments and see that they have approval of the competent authority.

17.10.4 Assets and Liabilities

1. Ownership and records of assets

The auditor should inspect the bonds, share certificates and title deeds of the properties and compare their particulars with those entered in the investment register. He should ensure that the title of those assets is in the name of the nursing home.

2. Physical verification of assets

All the assets of the nursing home should be either verified physically along with the documentary evidence or through confirmation from the third parties.

3. Control over stocks

The auditor should verify the stock register of medicines with reference to purchase invoices and issue requisitions and see that book stock of medicine physically exists.

4. Purchase and sale of assets

Purchase and sale of fixed assets and properties as well as investments should be verified with the help of proper documents and the auditor should ensure that the competent authority approves these purchases and sales.

5. Advances to suppliers

The auditor should examine the advances to suppliers remaining unadjusted at the end of the accounting period and verify whether provision or write-off is required.

17.10.5 Tax Assessment

Income tax

The auditor should check the assessment of tax aspect of the nursing home in order to verify that whether the tax return is submitted on regular basis along with the amount of tax.

17.10.6 Financial Statement

True and fair view

The auditor should see whether the financial statements give a true and fair view of the profit or loss and of the balance sheet of the nursing home.

17.11 AUDIT OF TRAVEL AGENCIES

Travel agents perform a number of services including reservation of seats, execution of travel formalities and documents, arrangements for transit passengers, booking of hotel accommodation, sponsoring package trips and excursions etc.

The exact nature of audit programme of a travel agency will depend upon the nature of the organisation. The auditor should determine whether the concern is a limited company or a partnership or a sole-proprietorship. The special points, which may be included in the audit programme of a travel agency, are given as follows:

17.11.1 Evaluation of Internal Control System

The following may be carefully looked into.

1. Procedure relating to receipts of requests

The auditor should evaluate the internal control system relating to the receipts of requests for booking through rail, sea and air etc. and for cancellation thereof.

2. Procedure relating to receipts of deposits

He should also check the internal control procedures relating to the receipts of deposits with non-credit customers for expenses incurred on their behalf and adjustments of such accounts.

3. Procedure regarding bookings

He should evaluate the internal control technique regarding bookings with the hotels and agreement about commission on bookings.

4. Procedure for raising bills

The auditor should also evaluate internal control procedures for raising bills against services rendered and internal checks against non-inclusion of certain services in the bills.

5. Examination of terms of agreement

The auditor should examine the terms of agreement with railway authorities, airlines and shipping lines regarding the types of services to be obtained.

6. Nature of additional services

The auditor should also examine the nature of additional services rendered to the customers going abroad and to the foreign tourists.

7. Procedure for cash collection

He should examine thoroughly the procedure relating to receipts and deposit of cash collection.

17.11.2 Checking of Arithmetical Accuracy

The arithmetical accuracy of books of accounts, e.g. cash book, petty cash book, ledgers, journal, commission register etc. has to be examined by the auditor by checking posting, casting, cross-casting and balancing.

17.11.3 Vouching and Verification

Apart from usual procedures, the following aspects may be paid special attention:

1. Vouching of expenses

The auditor should vouch the expenses to ensure that those expenses, which are reimbursable, have been collected from the customers.

2. Vouching of receipts

The auditor should vouch the receipts for services against bill to ensure that any concessions or rebates are given under proper authority. The log books of tourist cars and buses should be checked on a sample basis and it should be verified that appropriate bills have been raised.

3. Vouching of depreciation

The auditor should examine whether proper depreciation has been provided on different tourist cars and other assets of the agency.

4. Reconciling the physical stock of tickets

He should reconcile the physical stock of unsold tickets on the basis of previous years' balances, tickets received, tickets sold and the amount collected or charged to customers.

5. Scrutinising the personal ledgers

He should scrutinise the personal ledger of different customers and clients for possible bad debts and dummy accounts.

6. Confirming account balances

He should confirm the account balances with the air, rail and shipping lines and other clients on the basis of letters of confirmation received from them. He should also confirm the balances of deposits with different authorities, if any.

7. Examining the basis of commission computation

The auditor should ensure that only the commission in respect of journeys undertaken is treated as income, and in respect of future journeys, even if the client has paid the fare in full, the commission is not treated as income.

8. Vouching of travel tax

The auditor should vouch the collection and payment of travel tax levied by the government and it has to be ensured that the tax has been collected at appropriate rates and deposited to the proper authority regularly.

9. Reconciling commission income

The auditor should reconcile total commission earned on the basis of total fares involving various types and the respective rates of commission.

17.11.4 Examination of Statutory Requirements

The auditor should ensure that specific statutory requirements of the relevant authorities concerning grant of license etc. to act as a travel agent are duly complied with.

17.12 AUDIT OF COLLEGE HOSTELS

A college hostel provides boarding facilities to the students of the college. Usually these hostels are maintained by the college authority on no profit no loss or subsidised basis. Generally, a cash book is maintained to record day to day cash receipts and cash payments. Most of the transactions usually are conducted on cash basis. At the end of the year, a receipts and payments account is prepared to know the financial position of the hostel.

In order to conduct audit in a college hostel, the auditor should pay attention to the following points:

17.12.1 General Matters

1. Study of the rules and regulations

The rules and regulations of the college hostel should be studied first and important provisions should be noted down for consideration of detailed auditing of the hostel.

2. Activities of the hostel

The activities of the hostel should be identified. The auditor should know that whether the college hostel is providing only the accommodation facility or both food and accommodation facilities.

3. Hostel capacity and boarder's eligibility

The auditor should check the number of seats in the hostel and also verify whether only eligible students are accommodated in the hostel.

17.12.2 Receipts

1. Hostel fees

The auditor should vouch the receipts of hostel fees with the register of students. He should also ensure that hostel fees have been recovered from all the students on the basis of period of his stay in the hostel.

2. Arrear hostel fees

He should see whether arrear hostel fees have been properly recorded in the books of accounts and reflected in the statement of affairs of the hostel, if at all prepared.

3. Advance hostel fees

The auditor should also check that advance hostel fees have been received according to the provisions of the hostel regulations and they have been properly accounted for in the books of accounts.

4. Recovery of unrealised fees

He should ensure that effective action is taken against those students who are regular defaulters in payment of hostel fees.

5. Donations and government grants

If donations and government grants are received by the college hostel, it should be ensured by the auditor that such donations and grants are used by the hostel authority for the specified purposes for which it is received.

17.12.3 Payments and Expenses

1. Internal control for food procurement

The auditor should check the system of internal control for procurement of food supply. If it is supplied by the contractors, the auditor should ensure that the selection of contractors is being made by following the appropriate procedures.

2. Payments to contractors

The auditor should vouch the payments made to contractors with reference to the contractor's invoices and goods received note. He should also see that the bill is duly certified by the storekeeper and hostel superintendent.

3. Vouching of petty expenses

The auditor should vouch the petty expenses and also see that all the vouchers of expenses are duly sanctioned by the hostel superintendent.

4. Depreciation of fixed assets

He should see that depreciation at appropriate rates has been written off against all the fixed assets of the hostel.

5. Purchase and sale of fixed assets

Purchase and sale of all fixed assets during the accounting period should be checked by the auditor in order to check that these transactions were duly authorised by the proper authority.

17.12.4 Assets and Liabilities

1. Stock register

The auditor should check the stock registers of various main items of foodstuff like rice, wheat, mustard oil etc. He should also check that all entries of issue are supported by store requisition duly signed by the head cook and authorised by hostel superintendent.

2. Verification of fixed assets

The auditor should check that proper registers are maintained to record the particulars of all fixed assets owned by the hostel. He should also confirm their existence through physical verification.

3. Security deposits from students

The auditor should confirm that security deposits have been received from all the boarders as caution money and they are refunded only at the time of vacation of the accommodation.

17.12.5 Financial Statements

1. Preparation of receipts and payments account

The auditor should check the receipts and payments account prepared by the hostel authority and check all the items from the cash book entries. Sometimes income and expenditure accounts are also prepared by the big hostels to know the results of the operation of the hostel. The auditor should also check the accuracy of the account and the financial results ascertained thereon.

2. Classification of capital and revenue expenditure

The auditor should also confirm that proper classification has been made between capital expenditure and revenue expenditure so that the operating result as ascertained in the Income and Expenditure Account gives a true and fair picture of the financial result of the hostel.

17.13 AUDIT OF PUBLISHING CONCERNS

Before conducting audit of a publishing concern, the auditor should make a clear distinction between publishers of books, where stocks will present valuation problem but where advertising revenue is not a factor, and publishers of weekly and monthly journals, where advertising revenue is of great importance.

17.13.1 Audit of Book Publishers

When the audit of book publishers is being undertaken the auditor should pay attention to the following main points:

1. Account for each book published

An account should have been opened for each book published. This should have been credited with the income and debited with all relevant expenditure and should therefore show the profit or loss on the publication of the book. These accounts must be thoroughly vouched.

2. Valuation of the stock of books

The auditor must pay careful attention to the quantities and valuation of the stock of books in hand at the year end. He must ensure that the valuation never exceeds the cost of publication. Moreover, not all the books are successful and care must be taken to ensure that slow-moving stocks are written down to their realisable value.

3. Royalty due to authors

Royalty due to authors must be properly recorded, and the auditor must check the author's accounts. For this purpose, it is obviously important that the auditor inspects the relevant contracts.

4. Ascertainment of actual sales

The auditor must ensure that the records clearly distinguish between true sales and books dispatched on sale or return. With regard to the latter, great care must be exercised to ensure that profit is not taken or recognised until the books are sold.

17.13.2 Audit of Weekly or Monthly Journals

When the audit relates to weekly or monthly journals the auditor should pay attention to the following main points:

1. Records of sales income

The records of sales income must be examined and tested. It should be seen that all production is reconciled with sales and agreed returns and allowances. The authority for all discounts and allowances given must be established. Copies of the journals sent on sale or return must be accounted for, and credit must not be taken until sales are confirmed.

2. Advertising income

The records of advertising income must be vouched with the relevant agreements, and also tested against the actual advertisements appearing. Where advertising income has been received in advance before the year end, it must be seen that this has been carried forward into the following accounting period to which it relates.

3. Vouching of expenditure

All expenditures, including payment to contributors, must be vouched with the relevant evidence.

4. Action against defamation

The possibility of actions against the concern for defamation should be investigated and the insurance position checked.

Special note: Apart from the normal audit of the financial statements referred to above, separate audits will be carried out periodically to enable the auditor to certify the circulation.

17.14 CONCLUDING REMARKS

It is not possible to consider every possible type of entity that could be the subject of an examination question, but it is proposed in this chapter to set out the more important points relating to a number of enterprises. Students should see to establish for themselves the approach that they would adopt in tackling such questions.

POINTS TO PONDER

- The main aspects of the auditor's work are common to all types of audit. As every organisation will have its own peculiar facets, it will be necessary for the auditor to apply his skill and judgment individually in carrying out his audit work.
- The auditor should consider a number of points while conducting audit of different types of organisations, which include general matters, receipts and incomes, payments and expenses, assets and liabilities, taxability of income and the financial statements.
- A charitable society performs its operations for rendering social services. Its main sources of revenue are donations and legacies. The object of audit of this type of society is to ensure that its revenue is being utilised for the purpose for which the society has been established and it is being operated in conformity with its rules and regulations.
- The main purpose of a cinema hall is to provide entertainment to the public. The cinema halls are now providing not only the opportunity of viewing movies, but also restaurant and bar facilities are also available in the cinema halls in big cities. As a result, the requirement of maintaining proper accounts of cinema hall activities and its regular audit has also increased to a large extent.
- Clubs are the associations of group of persons with common interest and these are basically established with non-profit motive. The main activities of the clubs include provision for amusement and recreation and constructive work for the welfare of the society. Government registered clubs are required to get their accounts audited at regular intervals for renewal of their registration. This is not required for unregistered clubs.
- The co-operative societies in India are established and governed by the Co-operative Societies Act, 1912. To monitor the day-to-day activities of the society, a group of members are selected to form the management committee. The accounts of these types of societies are required to be audited by the auditors of the department of co-operative societies.
- Educational institutions include schools, colleges, training centres and universities. The main activities of these types of institutions are more or less similar to each other. On the basis of the nature of the institutions, the activities and mode of maintenance of books of accounts and records may also differ and the auditor will take into consideration these deviations at the time of his audit.

- The business of running a hotel is very different from running any other organisation. It is a service oriented business and may have some element of production of foodstuff and sales thereof. However, this business is characterised by handling of liquid cash, stocking and providing a large variety of items, keeping watch on customers to ensure that satisfactory services are being provided to them.
- The hospitals are usually established with the fund provided by the government, local authorities, municipalities and similar other types of funds. On the basis of ownership, hospitals can be government hospitals or private hospitals or a joint venture of public-private partnership. As the nature of activities of a hospital are totally different from that of other organisations, the audit programme to be followed for conducting audit of these types of organisations will also differ.
- The activities of a library are unique and totally different from other types of organisations. The basic objective of a library is to impart education to the public at a minimum cost. In case of library, the main cost is the cost of books. Libraries are usually established with the help of government grants. The capital expenditure regarding purchase of books are met mainly from the money received as grant. Other revenue expenditures are met from the collections of membership fees and annual charges.
- The activities of nursing homes are similar to that of hospitals. However, there is a basic difference between the objectives of a nursing home and a hospital. Hospitals are usually owned either individually or jointly by the government or local authority and these are established to provide services the common public at a minimum cost. Hospitals are non-profit seeking concerns. On the other hand, nursing homes are usually privately owned and are formed either as sole-proprietorship business or partnership business or as a company.
- Travel agents perform a number of services including reservation of seats, execution of travel formalities and documents, arrangements for transit passengers, booking of hotel accommodation, sponsoring package trips and excursions etc. The exact nature of audit programme of a travel agency will depend upon the nature of the organisation.
- A college hostel provides boarding facilities to the students of the college. Usually these hostels are maintained by the college authority on no profit no loss or subsidised basis. Generally, a cash book is maintained to record day to day cash receipts and cash payments. Most of the transactions usually are conducted on cash basis. At the end of the period, a receipts and payments account is prepared to know the financial position of the hostel.
- In conducting audit of a publishing concern, the auditor should make a clear distinction between publishers of books, where stock will present valuation problem but where advertising revenue is not a factor and publishers of weekly and monthly journals, where advertising revenue is of great importance.

REVIEW QUESTIONS

Short-answer Questions

1. In framing the audit programmes of specialised enterprises, what additional factors are required to be considered by the auditor?
2. Draft an audit programme covering eight special points for examining the accounts of
   (a) Sports club
   (b) Medical college
   (c) Travelling agent
   (d) College hostel
   (e) Publishing concern

Essay-type Questions

1. Draft an audit programme for examining the accounts of either a hotel or a cinema hall.
2. Prepare audit programme of any one organisation of following two:
   (a) Nursing home
   (b) Co-operative society.
3. What special points should the auditor consider in conducting audit in the following institutions
   (a) Charitable institution
   (b) Educational institution

CHAPTER 18

Audit of Sole-proprietorship and Partnership Firm

CHAPTER OUTLINE

18.1 INTRODUCTION

There are different types of business organisations from the point of view of their formation and legal aspects. Amongst the different types of business organisations the important types are the sole-proprietorship business and partnership business forms of organisation. Unlike company form of organisation, there is no compulsion in conducting audit for these two types of organisations as a matter of legal requirement, because under these two types of organisations, the owners have direct control over the day-to-day management and accounts are being prepared under the direct control and supervision of the owners. But it does not indicate that there is no requirement of audit to be conducted in these types of organisations. These organisations appoint auditors and get their accounts audited due to the various advantages they can derive by conducting an audit.

18.2 AUDIT OF SOLE-PROPRIETORSHIP BUSINESS

There is no legal requirement that a qualified auditor should audit the books of accounts of the sole-proprietorship business. It is up to the choice of the sole proprietor to get his accounts audited by a qualified auditor. But the sole-proprietors having large business houses are found to get their accounts audited due to the inherent advantages of audit.

Usually following are the reasons behind the audit of the proprietorship business.

1. To know about the adequacy of books of accounts

The sole proprietor is confirmed about the adequacy of the books of accounts maintained by him through the conduct of an audit.

2. To know the true and fair view of the accounts

The sole proprietor can assure himself by conducting audit that the books of accounts maintained by him exhibit a true and fair view of the state of affairs of the business.

3. To detect and prevent errors and frauds

In order to detect and prevent errors and frauds committed by the staff members, auditing can be undertaken. If there is an audit, errors and frauds can be detected and located at any early date.

4. To implement moral check on employees

The auditing of accounts keeps the employees regular and careful in their work, as they know that their auditor will complain against them if there is any error or fraud or if the accounts are not prepared up to date.

5. To settle insurance claim

In case of fire, theft or other hazards, the insurance company may settle the claim on the basis of the audited accounts of the client.

6. To borrow money from banks etc.

Money can be borrowed easily from bank and other financial institutions on the basis of audited balance sheet. Usually, in most of the cases, the banks and other financial institutions grant loans on the basis of previous audit report.

7. To file income tax return

In order to present reliable accounts to the income tax authority, auditing is undertaken. Generally the income tax authorities accept the profit and loss account that has been prepared and audited by a qualified auditor and they do not go into the details of the accounts.

8. To value assets and goodwill

If the business is to be sold as a going concern, there may not be much difficulty regarding the valuation of assets and goodwill, if the accounts have already been audited by a qualified auditor.

9. To bring uniformity in accounts

If the accounts have been prepared on a uniform basis for the purpose of auditor's satisfaction, accounts of one year can be compared with other years and if there is any discrepancy, the cause may be enquired.

10. To get advice from the auditor

The proprietor may consult the auditor and seek his advice for efficient keeping of his accounts.

18.2.1 Appointment of Auditor for Sole-proprietorship Business

The audit of accounts of the sole-proprietorship business is not governed by any specific statute. Hence, the appointment of auditor in this type of organisation depends upon the contract entered into by the proprietor with the auditor. Normally it is expected that the contract for appointment should be in writing and it should include the details of work to be undertaken by the auditor in conducting his audit because an auditor is required in some cases to prepare the accounts also, in addition to his audit work. All these assignments and other terms and conditions of the appointment should be clearly stated in the contract. In this context, it is important to note that the newly appointed auditor should correspond with the previous auditor intimating him about the acceptance of audit assignment. The remuneration of the auditor of this type of organisation usually depends upon the nature and volume of work and should also be included in the contract.

18.2.2 Steps to be Taken Before Commencement of New Audit in a Sole-proprietorship Business

In order to conduct audit in a sole-proprietorship business, the auditor should take the following steps before the commencement of new audit:

1. Ascertain the scope of work

First of all, the auditor should ascertain the precise nature and scope of his audit work. In case of sole-proprietorship business, in fact, the scope and area of work depends on the contract between the owner and the auditor.

2. Knowledge about the business

In order to conduct audit efficiently, the auditor should clearly understand the nature of the business and activities undertaken by the business organisation. The nature and activities of the business will help the auditor to get a clear idea about the different types of transactions in the organisation.

3. Knowledge about the accounting system

The auditor should collect from the proprietor a list of all books of accounts maintained in order to record the transactions of the organisation and assure himself that those books of accounts are maintained in actual practice.

4. List of principal officers

The auditor should also obtain list of the principal officers of the organisation. He should also acquire knowledge about the extent and scope of authority of each of them.

5. Knowledge of technical details

He should also acquire some knowledge about the technical details, if any, of the business. This will enable him to grasp the nature of transactions, which will be the subject matter of audit.

6. Communication with the previous auditor

If the auditor is being appointed in place of another auditor, it becomes his professional duty to communicate with the auditor, in whose place he is appointed.

7. Instruction to the proprietor

After completing the aspects as stated above, the auditor should issue clear instructions to the proprietor of the business to keep the accounts ready for audit and to prepare necessary schedules and annexure for the finalisation of audit work.

8. Preparation of audit programme

Finally, the auditor will prepare an audit programme, which will outline the procedures to be followed in conducting his audit work effectively.

18.3 AUDIT OF PARTNERSHIP FIRM

Like the audit of sole-proprietorship business, there is no legal obligation in case of partnership firm of business organisation that the books of accounts are to be audited by a qualified auditor. Even in the Indian Partnership Act, 1932 there are no specific provisions containing any instructions to get the accounts audited by a qualified auditor. But there are certain situations which usually occur in case of partnership business, which demand that the books of accounts of the firm should be audited by a duly qualified auditor. In this type of business, there may be the possibility of friction or dissatisfaction among the partners of the firm regarding the accounts maintained. In order to avoid this situation, many firms generally contain in their partnership deed a clause to the effect that the books of accounts should be audited by a qualified auditor.

Usually following are the reasons behind the audit of a partnership firm.

1. Settlement of dispute

The audit of accounts by an independent auditor may minimise or settle the misunderstandings and disputes among the partners. If there is no understanding among the partners, the growth and expansion of the business will not be activated. So, auditing of accounts may bring a peaceful atmosphere in the organisation, which is the key to the future development of the business.

2. Protection of sleeping partners

The audit of accounts of the partnership firm may protect the interest of the sleeping partners of the business. As the sleeping partners do not take active part in the day-to-day management of the business, they can depend on the audited accounts about the truth and fair view of the business.

3. Borrowing facilities

The audited accounts are very helpful in securing loan from bank and other financial institutions. In most cases, normally banks and other financial institutions grant loans on the basis of audited accounts of the applicants.

4. Assessment of tax

The income tax department seldom feels discontent on the certified accounts presented for the assessment of tax. As a result, in order to present reliable accounts to the income tax authority, auditing is undertaken.

5. Settlement of accounts

The audited accounts are very helpful in the settlement of disputes arising from retirement and death of partners and dissolution of the partnership firm. So, the audited accounts facilitate the settlement of the accounts of the retired or deceased partner.

6. Presentation as evidence

The audited accounts may be considered as reliable evidence in the court of law. So, in deciding the judgment against any case, the audited accounts can play an important role.

7. Valuation of goodwill of the firm

Valuation of goodwill in case of partnership firm arises as a result of changes in the constitution of the partnership firm. For the purpose of valuation of goodwill, the most important factor is the profit of the business. Therefore, the audited profit figure may be of great benefit in this regard.

8. Improvement of business

The firm may be greatly benefited as regards its improvement in managerial operation and keeping up-to-date records if the suggestions of the auditor are taken into consideration.

18.3.1 Appointment of Auditor for Partnership Firm

Like sole-proprietorship business, the audit of accounts of the partnership firm is not governed by any specific statute. Even in the Partnership Act, 1932 there are no specific provisions regarding the appointment of auditor in a partnership firm. In these types of organisations, the auditor is appointed as per agreement among the partners or as per the provision of the partnership deed. Normally it is expected that the contract for appointment of an auditor should be in writing and it should include the details of work to be undertaken by the auditor in conducting the audit. Under this type of audit the auditor has to check merely the compliance of the provisions of the partnership deed, those provisions of the Partnership Act, which have a bearing on the financial transactions and accounts. All these assignments and other terms and conditions of the appointment should be clearly indicated in the contract. The remuneration of the auditor of this type of organisation usually depends upon the nature and volume of transactions and should also be included in the contract.

18.3.2 Steps to be Taken Before Commencement of New Audit in a Partnership Firm

Before the conduct of an audit of the accounts of the partnership firm, the auditor should first of all obtain from his client a clear-cut instruction as to his scope of work and nature of assignment. For this purpose, he should confirm that his contract for appointment is in writing and in order. In the absence of any such clear-cut instruction, the auditor is required to perform complete audit, otherwise he may be held liable for the damages caused to the business for his failure to conduct complete audit.

However, the following steps may be suggested as a part of the conduct of an audit of partnership firm:

1. Knowledge about partnership deed

The auditor should carefully go through the partnership deed for knowing the different aspects of the partnership business viz. amount of capital contributed by the partners, profit sharing ratio, valuation of goodwill etc.

2. Observation of internal check system

He should observe the operation of the system of internal check and check whether the system is effectively implemented or not.

3. Knowledge about sleeping partners

He should collect the names of the sleeping partners and verify whether their interest is justified by the working partners.

4. List of books of accounts

The books of accounts maintained by the firm should be collected and the auditor should observe the nature of usual transactions that are recorded in the books of accounts.

5. Provisions of the partnership deed

The auditor should carefully note the provisions of the partnership deed regarding the maintenance of accounts of the firm and for taxation purpose whether the partnership firm will be treated as such or as an association of persons.

6. Contracts with the third parties

He should verify the contracts that are entered into with the third parties by reference to agreement deed and other documentary evidences.

7. Knowledge about the business

In order to conduct audit effectively, the auditor should clearly understand the nature of the business and activities undertaken by the firm. This will help him to get clear idea about the different types of transactions in the organisation.

8. Ascertain the scope of work

The auditor should ascertain the precise nature and scope of his audit work. In case of partnership firm audit, the scope and area of work depends upon the terms of contract entered in between the firm and the auditor.

9. Knowledge about the accounting system

The auditor should know the accounting system adopted by the organisation to ensure that all the transactions not agreed by the partners are incorporated in the books of accounts according to the provisions of the Partnership Act, 1932.

10. Knowledge of technical details

He should also acquire some knowledge about the technical details, if any, of the business. This will enable him to set the idea about the nature of transactions of the business.

11. Communication with the previous auditor

In case of fresh appointment, professional ethics requires that the newly appointed auditor should communicate with the previous auditor.

12. Preparation of audit programme

Finally, the auditor will prepare an audit programme, which will outline the procedures to be followed for conducting his audit work effectively.

18.4 SALIENT FEATURES OF AUDIT OF ACCOUNTS OF SOLE-PROPRIETORSHIP AND PARTNERSHIP FIRM

The audit of sole-proprietorship business and partnership firm is not legally compulsory. Sole-proprietorship business is not governed by any specific Act. So, there is no question of any legal provision of audit of sole-proprietorship business. Although the Partnership Act, 1932 governs the partnership business, it does not contain any legal provision for compulsory audit of partnership business.

The important features of the audit of accounts of sole-proprietorship or partnership businesses are as follows:

1. Legal compulsion of audit

Audit of sole-proprietorship or partnership business is not compulsory. It is basically voluntary in nature and conducting audit of these types of businesses depends on the wish of the proprietor or the partners. However, in case of partnership firm, the partnership deed may contain provision for regular audit of accounts.

2. Scope of audit

As there is legal provision regarding the scope or area of audit under these types of businesses, it depends on the terms of appointment of the auditor. As a result, an auditor of such a business is required to get clearly in writing from his client as to what area he has to cover exactly.

3. Application of legal provision

In case of audit of sole-proprietorship or partnership business, there is no statutory provision relating to recognition of income or expenditure, valuation of assets and liabilities, presentation of financial statements etc. Therefore, in those matters only basic accounting and commercial principles are required to be applied. However, in case of partnership business the partnership deed may contain certain provisions on accounting and financial matters in addition to matters of mutual interests of partners. In the absence of agreement amongst the partners on certain matters of mutual interest, the provisions of the Partnership Act will apply.

4. Qualification of an auditor

There is no statutory provision regarding the qualification of an auditor of a sole-proprietorship or partnership business. Therefore, the auditor of such organisations need not be a chartered accountant. But a chartered accountant usually conducts audit of these types of organisations, because audit by a chartered accountant is advantageous to the organisation. However, the partnership deed may provide for audit by a chartered accountant.

18.5 RIGHTS, DUTIES AND LIABILITIES OF THE AUDITOR OF A SOLE-PROPRIETORSHIP OR PARTNERSHIP FIRM

There is no specific provision in any statute, which contains the rights or duties or liabilities of an auditor of a sole-proprietorship or partnership business. In fact, the rights, duties and liabilities of an auditor of these types of organisations are the results of the agreement between the auditor and the firm itself.

Auditor's right

The auditor enjoys no statutory right, in case of audit of accounts of sole-proprietorship or partnership firm. However, for audit of accounts of these types of organisations the auditor has the right to get all the books of accounts, vouchers, supporting documents, relevant records and necessary information and explanations from the management, i.e. he must be provided all the facilities, which are required for the effective discharge of his duties. In addition to that, the auditor has the right to take expert advice on any technical point and give advice for the proper maintenance of books of accounts and of course he should have the right to receive the agreed remuneration after successful completion of his work.

Auditor's duties

An auditor of a sole-proprietorship or partnership organisation has no statutory duties to perform in conducting audit. But there is a contractual relationship between the auditor and his client. The auditor is also an agent of his client. Therefore, it is his duty under common law to exercise reasonable skill, care and caution in the performance of his work. It is his ethical duty to maintain confidentiality of all such information relating to the client's business as he acquires this information in the course of his work. Moreover, his work is not complete, unless he gives a report to his client informing the outcome of audit or audit findings. Such a report should include the following points:

- Whether he could get all such books, records, vouchers and other documents, and obtain all such information and explanations from the management, as are necessary for the purpose of his audit.
- Whether the balance sheet and the profit and loss account of the organisation are in complete agreement with the books of accounts as maintained by the firm.
- Whether the books of accounts are adequate according to the nature and size of the business and whether these have been written correctly and properly.
- Whether the balance sheet and the profit and loss account give a true and correct view of the state of affairs and of the profit or loss of the business respectively.

The auditor should not hide any material information when he gives his report. In his report he should mention all frauds and material errors discovered by him in clear and unambiguous language. These are his duties relating to audit report. If the auditor has worked as an accountant, he should indicate the fact and the nature of his work in his report.

Auditor's liabilities

An auditor of a sole-proprietorship or partnership organisation has no specific statutory liability. However, as per common law an auditor is liable to his client for damages if he is negligent in the performance of his duties and by such negligence his client suffers loss. But, the nature of his work is an important determinant of the extent of his liability. If he is appointed for maintaining the books of accounts and records, he will not be held liable for the errors and fraud activated through the books of accounts and records in his individual capacity. In that case, he will be considered as servant of the company.

18.6 POSITION OF AUDITOR OF A SOLE-PROPRIETORSHIP OR PARTNERSHIP FIRM

The position of an auditor of a firm or individual is totally different from that of a company. In the case of a company, audit is compulsory under the Companies Act. The Act lays down how the statutory auditor can be appointed and what are his specific duties and responsibilities, which cannot be curbed in any manner by the Directors, the shareholders or by the Articles of Association.

The position of an auditor of an individual or firm is, on the other hand, completely different. Here, the auditor is mostly guided by the agreement between him and the individual or the partners, as the case may be, and by any expressed provision in the partnership deed. There is no specific statute, which lays down the duties and liabilities of the auditor of an individual or firm. Hence, it is said that the auditor of an individual or a firm has no statutory obligation to comply with.

But whatever be the difference between the auditor of a company and the auditor of an individual or firm, the statement quoted above is not correct. It is true that the auditor of an individual or firm is outside the purview of the Companies Act, but it is equally true that even he has certain statutory obligations as the following points reveal:

1. Law of Agency

There is an agent-principal relationship between the auditor and his client and hence an auditor is required to protect the interest of his client and performs his duties with utmost care and skill as required by the law of agency.

2. Contract Act

Once an auditor is given an offer to work as an auditor for an individual or firm in consideration for a fee and the auditor accepts the offer, there is a binding contract under the Contract Act, and the auditor is under statutory obligation to fulfil the terms of the contract.

3. Chartered Accountants Act

The Chartered Accountants Act, 1949 requires a chartered accountant in practice not to be negligent in his professional duty. Negligence in duty attracts disciplinary proceedings under the said Act.

4. Indian Penal Code

For giving false information or evidence etc. an auditor is liable for fraud under the Indian Penal Code.

5. Income Tax Act

Where an auditor of an individual or firm by the terms of appointment acts like an accountant on matters of income tax, he must guard against certain liabilities, which may arise under the Income Tax Act.

From the above, it is clear that the auditor of an individual or firm is also not free from statutory obligation.

18.7 REPORTS ON ACCOUNTS OF INDIVIDUAL OR PARTNERSHIP FIRM

There is no statutory form of auditor's report in the case of sole-proprietor and partnership firm. Often the auditors of sole-proprietors and partnership firms have nothing to say on the audited accounts except "Examined and found correct" or "Audited and found correct". This form of reporting is not recommended, as it gives no indication of the extent of the examination of accounts that has been undertaken by the auditor.

Having realised the need of a clear and appropriate report by the professional accountants on the accounts of sole-proprietor and partnership firm, the Institute of Chartered Accountants in England and Wales issued a statement on the subject.

According to the statement of the Institute, the audit report of a sole-proprietorship firm or a partnership firm should highlight the following aspects:

1. Undertaking of accounting and auditing work for sole-proprietor and partnership firm is a matter of instruction of each particular client. Responsibility of the professional accountant is governed by the scope of work assigned to be done and by the nature and extent of the records to be made available.
2. The accountants should make it clear to the client at the engagement stage the responsibility he is accepting in relation to the accounts. This could be done by the

issue of an 'engagement letter' or by maintaining a proper record of the client's instructions.

3. The report should bear a specific mention of the extent of responsibilities accepted by them, opinion on accounts to truth and fairness should be expressed in the report only if such accounts have been audited.
4. Where accountants have been instructed to prepare accounts but not to audit, the report on the accounts prepared should be titled as "Accountant's Report" and should be so carefully worded as to exclude the possibility of misunderstanding about the nature of the job.
5. Where an audit has not been carried out, care should be taken that any reference to the accountant's fees in the accounts or in footnotes or in correspondence with the client does not indicate them as audit fees.
6. Accountants should not allow their names to be associated with the accounts, even though unaudited, which they believe give a misleading view.
7. Accountants, when instructed to prepare accounts, should see that the accounts conform to accepted accounting principles.
8. Reports on accounts prepared without audit should not be extended to include expression of opinion or to disclaim responsibility for any particular item.
9. Where the instruction is to conduct audit, the same should be carried out on the principles of auditing. The accountant should see that he has audited the accounts and also should state whether such accounts present a true and fair view.
10. Accounts prepared with or without audit should be approved by the client before the report is signed.

18.8 COMPARISON OF COMPANY AUDIT WITH THE AUDIT OF SOLE-PROPRIETORSHIP AND PARTNERSHIP FIRM

The distinction between audit of company with the audit of sole-proprietorship and partnership firm is given in Table 18.1.

TABLE 18.1 Distinction in the audit of different kinds of companies

Point of distinction	*Company audit*	*Partnership firm audit*	*Sole-proprietorship audit*
1. Legal requirement	Company audit is compulsory under the Companies Act.	Partnership firm audit is not compulsory under the Partnership Act.	Audit of sole-proprietorship business is not compulsory under any Act.
2. Qualification of auditor	Only a chartered accountant having a full time certificate of practice can be appointed as auditor in a company.	There is no statutory provision regarding qualification of an auditor of a partnership firm.	The auditor of a sole-proprietorship business can be any person as there is no prescribed qualification in this respect.

Contd.

Contd.

3. Area of audit	Nature and area of audit in this case is totally governed by the provisions of the Companies Act.	Nature and area of audit depends on the terms of appointment.	The sole proprietor will decide about the nature and area of audit and should be Included in the appointment letter.
4. Status of the auditor	The company auditor is on the one hand an agent of the shareholders and on the other hand he is treated as an officer of the company.	The auditor of a partnership firm is only an agent of the partners.	The auditor is an agent of the proprietor. He cannot be treated as an officer of the organisation.
5. Rights and duties	The company auditor has specific statutory rights and duties under the Companies Act.	The auditor of a firm has no specific statutory rights and duties; only the common law will apply.	The auditor of a sole-proprietorship business also has no specific statutory rights and duties. Only the common law will apply in this case.
6. Auditor's report	The contents of the auditor's report are clearly specified in the Companies Act and required to be submitted to the shareholders only.	There is no statutory provision relating to auditor's report. He has to submit the report to the partners.	No statutory provision is there concerning an auditor's report. He submits his report to the proprietor.
7. Auditor's independence	No Director or shareholder can interfere in his rights and duties as he has independence in his work.	The auditor has much less independence in his work and the partners can interfere in his rights and duties.	The proprietor can also interfere in the rights and duties of the auditor.
8. Liabilities of auditors	The auditor of a company has specific statutory liabilities under the Companies Act.	The auditor of a partnership firm has no specific statutory liabilities. But, he is liable to the partners for negligence of duty under the common law.	The auditor of a sole-proprietorship business has no specific statutory liabilities. He is liable only to the proprietor for negligence of duty under the common law.
9. Appointment of auditor	The auditors are appointed by the shareholders in the annual general meeting.	The auditor is appointed as per the agreement among the partners or as per provisions of the partnership deed.	The auditor is appointed by the proprietor and no legal provision exists for the appointment of an auditor in a sole-proprietorship business.

Contd.

Contd.

10. Nature of work	In a company audit, the auditor has to check whether the provisions of the Companies Act relating to the books of accounts and other records, basic accounting policies, certain financial transactions, preparation and presentation of financial statements etc. have been duly followed or not.	The auditor has to check merely the compliance of the provisions of the partnership deed, those provisions of the Partnership Act, which have bearing on financial transactions and accounts.	No law or internal documents regulate the affairs of a sole-proprietorship business. The proprietor can keep accounts according to his own requirements and can appoint the auditor to check only those specific areas as he feels necessary.

18.9 LEGAL VIEWS AS REGARDS AUDIT OF INDIVIDUAL AND FIRM

Case Study

1. **Case: Leech vs Stokes Bros. & Prim (1937)**

   Fact of the case: The defendants had prepared accounts for a number of years for a firm of solicitors for the purpose of submission to the inspector of taxes. No balance sheet was ever prepared. The instructions were given by one of the partners, Dublin, and on his death, a new partner employed another accountant to audit the accounts, as a result of which defalcations by the cashier of client's money were discovered. Action for damages on the ground of negligence was brought against the defendants.

   Legal view: The negligence alleged were as follows:

   - Failure to prepare a balance sheet
   - Failure to vouch or test certain fees brought into the accounts
   - Failure to reconcile the bank account and cash

   The defendants were able to prove that they were not employed to audit the accounts but only to prepare a profit and loss account for income tax.

   The courts found that there was no negligence in not preparing a balance sheet or in not refusing to prepare a profit and loss account until the books were written up to enable them to prepare a balance sheet.

2. **Case: Smith vs Sheard (1906)**

   Fact of the case: The plaintiff had incurred losses owing to the defalcations of an employee. The actual contract with the accountant was in question. The defendant denied that he had ever agreed to audit the books; he was only instructed to check the postings in order to make out a balance. But in sending the bill of charges, his clerk had inadvertently used the word "audit", instead of "auditing of postings". The accounts and balance sheet sent in did not contain any signature or certificate.

Legal view: It was held that the accountant was liable for damages. The jury found that there was a contract to audit, though the decision was very much against the opinion of the judge.

3. **Case: Trustee of Apfel vs Annan, Dexter and Co. (1926)**

   Fact of the case: The trustee in bankruptcy of Apfel sought to recover damages from the defendants in that they had failed to discover that large sums had been converted to their own use by the sons of the bankrupt. The plaintiff alleged that the defendants were employed as auditors. The defendants replied that they were employed only as accountants to prepare such accounts as were necessary for the purpose of income tax returns. The form of certificate used was "prepared from the books of Mrs. Adele Apfel, and in accordance therewith" but the account of charges and the covering letter referred to "the audit of your accounts" and "auditing".

   Legal view: It was held that the work the defendants were instructed to do and the work they actually did, was accountancy for a specific purpose, and that they were not liable for the loss. It was suggested in this case that the accountants should have discovered the frauds if they had examined into the books for the months following the date to which the accounts were made up. But the learned judge pointed out that they had no right to examine the books for the year following that for which they were engaged, and ought not to be prejudiced by what might have come to light if they had examined the later records.

POINTS TO PONDER

- Unlike company form of organisation, there is no compulsion in conducting audit for sole-proprietorship and partnership firms. As the owners of these types of organisations have direct control over the day-to-day management and accounts, legally it is not required to conduct audit.
- The sole-proprietorship and partnership firms having large business houses are found to get their accounts audited due to the inherent advantages of audit.
- The audit of accounts of the sole-proprietorship and partnership firms is not governed by any specific statute. Hence the appointment of auditor in these types of organisations depends upon the contract entered into between the owner/s with the auditor.
- In order to conduct audit in a sole-proprietorship and partnership firm, the auditor should take a number of preparatory steps, which includes ascertainment of the scope of audit, knowledge about the business and accounting system, list of principal officers, knowledge of technical details, communication with the previous auditor, instruction to the proprietor and preparation of audit programme.

- Before the conduct of an audit of the accounts of the sole-proprietorship firm or partnership firm, the auditor should first of all obtain from his client a clear-cut instruction as to his scope of work and nature of assignment. In the absence of any such clear-cut instruction, the auditor is required to perform complete audit, otherwise he may be held liable for the damages caused to the business for his failure to conduct complete audit.
- Audit of sole-proprietorship and partnership firm is not compulsory. As a result, auditor of such a business is required to get clearly in writing from his client as to what area he has to cover exactly. Usually the auditor of such organisations need not be a chartered accountant.
- There is no specific provision in any statute, which contains the rights and duties or liabilities of an auditor of a sole-proprietorship or partnership business. In fact, the rights, duties and liabilities of an auditor of these types of organisations are the results of the agreements between the auditor and the firm. In the absence of agreement his rights, duties and liabilities are governed by the common law.
- The position of an auditor of a firm or individual is totally different from that of a company. Though there is no specific rule that governs the activities of an auditor of a firm or individual, he is not free from statutory obligations.
- There is no statutory form of auditor's report in the case of sole-proprietorship and partnership firm.

REVIEW QUESTIONS

Short-answer Questions

1. Is the audit of sole-proprietorship business compulsory?
2. Is the audit of partnership business compulsory?
3. "The auditor of an individual or a firm has no statutory obligation to comply with." Comment.
4. Can an auditor be appointed by a partner or his legal representative to audit the accounts of a firm?

Essay-type Questions

1. Discuss the appointment, scope of work, rights and duties of an auditor of a sole-proprietorship business.
2. What are the advantages of the audit of a partnership firm? What special points should be included in the audit report in respect of such an audit?
3. Describe the steps to be taken by the auditor before commencement of a new audit of a partnership firm.
4. State the special points to be considered while conducting audit on behalf of the following perons:

- A sleeping partner
- A retiring partner
- The legal representatives of a deceased partner

5. Does the audit of accounts of a partnership firm differ from that of a company? If so, in what respect?

CHAPTER 19

Audit of the Accounts of Government and Public Sector Undertakings

CHAPTER OUTLINE

19.1 INTRODUCTION

The audit of government accounts and the accounts of public sector undertakings has a special significance and importance in view of the public accountability of government and innumerable transactions involving large sums of public money. Government audit is totally different from audit of commercial firms and the audit of public sector undertakings has the features of both commercial audit and government audit.

19.2 AUDIT OF PUBLIC SECTOR UNDERTAKINGS

Special statutes have been set up for audit of several public sector undertakings. In many of such undertakings the C&AG has to conduct statutory audit. In some of the undertakings though professional accountants conduct the statutory audit, the C&AG is empowered to conduct separate audit, independent of statutory audit. Moreover, in government companies, which are governed by the Companies Act, the C&AG has the power to direct the manner in which the accounts shall be audited by the statutory auditor and the C&AG can conduct test audit or supplementary audit in government companies.

In fact, public sector undertakings are of three different types, which are as follows:

- Departmental commercial undertakings
- Statutory corporations
- Government companies

Departmental commercial undertakings are those concerns, which are directly controlled by a ministry or department of the government. Examples of these are Indian Railways, Post and Telegraph, Bharat Sanchar Nigam Limited etc. Statutory corporations have been set up by special Acts of parliament and they are governed by such Acts. Examples of such corporations are the Life Insurance Corporation of India, the Reserve Bank of India, the State Bank of India, and the nationalised banks. Government companies are the third type of public sector undertakings. These companies are registered under the Companies Act and are also governed by the said Act. There are innumerable central and state level public sector undertakings in our country.

19.2.1 Some Special Features of Public Sector Undertakings

The public sector undertakings differ from private sector undertakings in many ways and it is necessary to keep them in mind before actually undertaking the audit of such undertakings. Some important features of public sector undertakings affecting audit are as follows:

1. Different forms

These undertakings have been set up mainly in three forms, viz. departmental commercial undertakings, statutory corporations and government companies. All these three forms differ substantially from the point of view of their establishment, operations and operational autonomy.

2. Governing Acts and provisions

Majority of these undertakings have been set up as government companies under the Companies Act, 1956 just like any other company in the private sector. These companies are governed by the provisions of the Companies Act. A few undertakings have been set up as departmental undertakings and their operational autonomy is quite limited as they are under the direct control of the government. Statutory corporations are governed by the special statute and Act.

3. Profit motive

These undertakings are desired to observe business and commercial principles and are also required to earn profits. However, the profit motive cannot be the overriding factor in their case as it is in private companies.

4. Managerial personnel

Several managerial personnel in these undertakings come from the government departments and not from the commercial or industrial fields. As a result, the approach of the management is not the same as we find in case of private commercial undertakings.

5. Accountability

The autonomy of the management of these undertakings is severely restricted due to stricter control and accountability of the management to the government and to the parliament and several other agencies. The managing director of a public sector undertaking is not as free to act as in case of a private undertaking.

6. Government policy

For several matters, the management of these undertakings is guided and directed by the concerned ministry. The minister concerned controls them formally as well as informally. The government is empowered to lay down policies, issue directions, appoint or replace top officials, approve capital expenditures beyond a prescribed limit, sanction borrowings and investments etc.

7. Reporting

Every undertaking is required to submit its annual report in detail in the parliament every year. There is a parliamentary committee known as committee on public undertakings, which examines their workings in detail. On the basis of the report submitted to the parliament, action has to be taken on it within the stipulated period. The report on action taken is also submitted in the parliament.

8. Audit

The professional accountants normally undertake the audit of these undertakings, but the Comptroller and Auditor General of India has the power to conduct an efficiency-cum-propriety audit of these undertakings.

19.3 DISTINCTION BETWEEN AUDIT OF PUBLIC SECTOR UNDERTAKINGS AND AUDIT OF PRIVATE SECTOR UNDERTAKINGS

The auditor should keep in mind the distinction between the audit of private sector undertakings and that of public sector undertakings. This is quite necessary, as the professional accountants are required to audit the accounts of both types of undertakings.

The auditor of a private sector undertaking is, in general, required to undertake the verificatory audit and has to give his opinion as to whether the profit and loss account and the balance sheet exhibit true and fair state of affairs of the undertakings. He has nothing to do with the impropriety of the actions of the management. He is not required to question the points of inefficiency of the management.

The auditor of a public sector undertaking has to adopt some of the techniques of the government audit and at the same time should follow the standard practices and techniques of audit of a private concern. It seeks to verify whether the expenditure conforms to the various provisions of the law and the rules and whether every officer has exercised the same vigilance in respect of expenditure incurred from public money, as a person of ordinary prudence would exercise in respect of expenditure of his own money. It also seeks to verify whether the expenditure was necessary and whether the individual items of expenditure give the best results.

It has been found in practice that the auditors of the public sector undertakings have been adopting bolder approach as compared to those of private sector undertakings. A qualified report by the auditors of private sector undertakings is given only in very exceptional circumstances and is rare. But it is not so in case of public sector undertakings.

We have three forms of public sector undertakings as already mentioned earlier. They are departmental commercial undertakings, statutory corporations and the government companies. Let us discuss the provisions and procedures of audit of these different types of undertakings separately.

19.3.1 Audit of Departmental Commercial Undertakings

Several central government commercial undertakings have been set up in the country as departmental commercial undertakings. They are administered as a part of the department, like any government department. The departmental commercial undertakings have been defined as those, which are maintained mainly for the purpose of rendering services or providing supplies of certain special kinds on payment for the services rendered or the articles supplied. They are required to work to a financial result determined through accounts maintained on commercial principles. The examples of these undertakings are: Indian Railways, Indian Security Press, Chittaranjan Locomotive Works, Post and Telegraph Department etc.

The main features of departmental commercial undertakings are as follows:

- The enterprise is financed by annual appropriations from the treasury and a major share of its revenue is paid into the treasury.
- The enterprise is subject to the budget, accounting and audit controls applicable to other government activities.
- The enterprise is generally organised as a major sub-division of one of the central departments of government.
- The employees of these types of enterprises are civil servants.
- The enterprise possesses the sovereign immunity of the state and may be sued without the consent of the government.

Under Article 149 of the Constitution of India, the Comptroller and Auditor General of India is empowered to conduct audit of departmental undertakings. The audit is primarily in the nature of commercial audit, but it is extended to include the examination of the regularity and propriety of transactions, authority of expenditure etc. The commercial audit of the C&AG mainly aims at verifying the adoption of commercial principles in the preparation and presentation of statements showing financial result and financial position of the undertaking, the completeness and accuracy of the preparation and presentation, the correctness of the allocation of expenditure between capital and revenue, the fairness of the valuation of the assets and liabilities, the adequacy of the provisions for depreciation, bad debts etc.

The function of the auditor in this case is also to ensure that the subsidiary accounts are so prepared as to render it possible to compare the relative efficiency of government trading and manufacturing institutions with one another or with similar non-government institutions. The audit of such undertakings is more than the verificatory audit and efforts are made to analyse the workings of these undertakings in details so that weaknesses, if any, may be brought to light and remedial measures may be taken in future.

19.3.2 Audit of Statutory Corporations

A few statutory corporations have also been set up in the country to undertake the commercial and industrial activities. For the establishment of these corporations, special Acts have to be enacted through Parliament. There are several corporations in financial areas, such as Reserve Bank of India, State Bank of India and Life Insurance Corporation of India. Some of these corporations such as Oil and Natural Gas Commission, Air India etc. are also working in the non-financial areas.

The main features of statutory corporations are given below.

- It is generally established by a special law defining its powers, duties and obligations.
- It is wholly owned by the state.
- As a body corporate it has a separate entity for legal purposes.
- Statutory corporations are usually independently financed.
- It is not ordinarily subject to the budget, accounting and audit laws and procedures, applicable to non-corporate agencies.

The enabling statutes of these corporations have made provision for the audit of these corporations. In some cases, the auditor general is fully empowered to undertake their audit and in some cases, the audit is undertaken by the professional accountants. In fact, the audit of each statutory corporation is conducted as per provisions contained in the applicable Act and such provisions vary from one corporation to another.

The form and the contents of the audit report, as prescribed for different corporations, are similar to those prescribed under the Companies Act, 1956. Besides, the nature of audit and the powers and responsibilities of the auditor in the case of statutory corporations are almost similar to those as in case of company audit.

19.3.3 Audit of Government Companies

A government company is one in which not less than 51% of the paid-up share capital is held by the central government, one or more state governments or jointly by the central government and one or more state governments.

Audit of government companies is governed by Section 619 of the Companies Act, 1956. The important provisions relating to the audit of government companies as contained in Section 619 are given below:

1. Appointment of auditor

The auditor of a government company is appointed or reappointed by the central government on the advice of the C&AG of India [Section 619(2)].

The limits of company audit as specified in Sub-sections (1B) and (1C) of Section 224 also apply in relation to the appointment or reappointment of an auditor of a government company.

2. Remuneration

The Act is silent about the fixation of remuneration of an auditor of a government company. As the central government is the appointing authority, it is natural that the remuneration of the auditor will be fixed by the central government.

3. Audit procedure

C&AG requires that the auditor gives specific answers to questions, which are contained in a questionnaire that the auditor gets from the C&AG. This is in addition to the report to be submitted by the auditor under Section 224 of the Companies Act. In fact, the C&AG has the power to direct the manner in which the accounts of the government companies shall be audited by the auditor and to give such instructions in regard to any matter relating to the performance of his functions as such [Section 619(3)(a)].

The direction of the C&AG as per Section 619(3)(a) in questionnaire form includes specific questions on the following matters:

- System of accounts and book-keeping
- Internal control
- Manufacturing and production accounts
- Profit and loss account
- Balance sheet
- General review
- Accounting policies
- Financial notes

Therefore, the auditor of a government company first of all conducts a full company audit, which concludes in giving a report as per provisions of Section 224 of the Companies Act. In addition to the audit report, the auditor is required to send a special report containing the answers to the questions of the questionnaire of the C&AG only. This is not within the scope of company audit or duties of the company auditor under the Companies Act.

4. Supplementary audit by the C & AG

The C&AG has the power to conduct the supplementary audit of the accounts of the government companies by his authorised person [Section 619 (3)(b)]. The C&AG also conducts another type of audit in government companies on a regular interval on the basis of the power under Section 619 (3)(b). This audit is in the nature of propriety-cum-efficiency audit under which the activities of the company, its performance, various transactions, utilisation of assets and other facilities, managerial effectiveness etc. are examined.

5. Audit report

The statutory auditor of these types of companies has to submit a copy of his audit report to the C&AG who has the right to comment upon the report. Any comments of the C&AG to the audit report are required to be placed before the annual general meeting of the company at the same time and in the same manner as the audit report [Section 619(5)].

19.4 GOVERNMENT AUDIT

Government audit means the audit of accounts of departments and offices of the central government, the state governments and the union territories. Under Article 149 of the constitution of India, the C&AG of India is empowered to conduct complete audit of accounts of governments and of those undertakings, which are directly under a ministry or government department.

Objectives

An introduction to Indian government accounts and audit, a book issued under the authority of the C&AG of India, states that the main objectives of the government audit are to ensure the following:

1. That there is provision of funds for the expenditure duly authorised by a competent authority.
2. That the expenditure is in accordance with a sanction properly accorded and is incurred by an officer competent to incur it.
3. That the payment has, as a fact, been made and has been made to the proper person and that it has been so acknowledged and recorded that a second claim against the government on the same account is impossible.
4. That the charge is correctly classified and that if a charge is debitable to the personal account of a contractor, employee or other individual, or is recoverable from him under any rule or order, it is recorded as such in a prescribed account.
5. That in the case of audit of receipts of sums due are regularly recovered and checked against demand and sums received are duly brought to credit in the accounts.
6. That in the case of audit of stores and stock, where a priced account is maintained, stores are priced with reasonable accuracy and that the rates initially fixed are reviewed from time to time, correlated with market rates and revised when necessary.
7. That the articles are counted periodically and otherwise examined for verification of the accuracy of the quantity balances in the books and that the total of the valued account tallies with the physical numerical balance of stock materials at the rates applicable to the various classes of stores.
8. That expenditure conforms to the following general principles which have, for long, been recognised as standards of financial propriety:
   (a) That the expenditure is not prima facie more than the occasion demands, and that every government servant exercises the same vigilance in respect of expenditure incurred from public money as a person of ordinary prudence would exercise in respect of expenditure of his own money.

(b) That no authority exercises its powers of sanctioning expenditure to pass an order which will be, directly or indirectly, to its own advantage.

(c) That public money is not utilised for the benefit of a particular person or section of the community unless

- the amount of expenditure involved is insignificant, or
- a claim for the amount could be enforced in a court of law, or
- the expenditure is in pursuance of a recognised policy or custom.

(d) That the amount of allowances granted to meet expenditure of a particular type is so regulated that the allowances are not, on the whole, sources of profit to the recipients.

In a nutshell, government audit encompasses two main elements. These are as follows:

(i) Fiscal accountability—audit of provision of funds, sanctions, compliance and propriety

(ii) Managerial accountability—audit of efficiency, economy and effectiveness

19.5 DISTINCTION BETWEEN GOVERNMENT AUDIT AND COMMERCIAL AUDIT

Government audit is not same as commercial audit. Certain special aspects are required to be covered under government audit, which are not required for commercial audit.

The distinction between government audit and commercial audit can be outlined in the following ways, as shown in Table 19.1.

TABLE 19.1 Distinction between government and commercial audit

Points of distinction	*Government audit*	*Commercial audit*
1. Nature of audit	Government audit is conducted almost continuously throughout the year, because the number of transactions is many and involves large sums of money.	Commercial audit is mostly periodical in nature.
2. Auditor	The audit officers of the Indian Audit and Accounts Department do government audit.	Mostly professional chartered accountants conduct commercial audit.
3. Dominating factor	Propriety-cum-efficiency audit is predominant in government audit.	This aspect is not strictly adhered in case of commercial audit.
4. Preparation of accounts	In this case, the indian Audit and Accounts Department and its field offices prepare or compile the major part of government accounts and also audit the accounts.	In commercial audit, the auditor audits the accounts prepared by others. The auditor is not at all responsible for the preparation and/or compilation of accounts.

Contd.

Contd.

5. Method of accounting	In government audit, the auditor has to see whether the accounts have been prepared according to the prescribed rule of government accounts.	In commercial audit, the auditor has to see whether the accounts have been prepared on the basis of double entry system.
6. Objective	Government audit is concerned with examining the propriety of expenditure.	The primary objective of this audit is to see whether the balance sheet prepared gives a true and fair views of the state of affairs of the enterprise and the profit and loss account gives a true and fair view of the profit or loss of the enterprise.
7. Vouching of payment	Government spending is done by the treasury officer or disbursement officer, who makes a detailed scrutiny of the bills before payment. So, government auditor is relieved of detailed checking of payments.	In commercial offices, the cashier does not have to make such a scrutiny before payment. So, payments require proper vouching in commercial audit.

In fact, the government auditor, unlike the independent financial auditor, is concerned with examining the economy, efficiency and effectiveness (i.e. three E's) of various schemes or projects. The government auditor seeks to get the following answers.

- Whether the projects have been completed at the minimum cost, i.e. whether the project cost is economical or not.
- Whether the project has efficiently been completed, i.e. whether the projects are suffering from deficiencies or not.
- Whether the projects have been performed in the most effective way, i.e., whether the projects become successful projects or not.

It can, thus, be seen that the objectives of government audit are much wider than those of independent financial audit. In government audit, there is a greater emphasis on examining compliance with standards of financial propriety, compliance with rules and procedures and the efficiency and performance of various projects or schemes than in an independent financial audit. The difference in objectives of audit generates from the consideration of public interest and the urge to exercise stringent financial controls over public money.

19.6 COMPTROLLER AND AUDITOR GENERAL OF INDIA

Under the Constitution of India the position of the C&AG of India is similar to that of the judge of the Supreme Court of India. He enjoys an independent status under the Constitution of India. The C&AG is appointed as per constitutional provision and his terms and conditions of service, powers and duties, rights and responsibilities are governed by the relevant Act of parliament.

The Constitution of India gives a special status to the C&AG and contains provisions to safeguard his independence. Following are the important provisions with regard to C&AG:

1. Appointment and removal

Article 148 of the Constitution provides that the C&AG shall be appointed by the President of India and can be removed from office only in a like manner and on the like grounds as a Judge of the Supreme Court. Thus, the C&AG can be removed only on the ground of proven misbehaviour or incapacity and only through an order of the President of India after each house of Parliament has recommended the removal by the required majority.

2. Remuneration

The salary and other terms of service of the C&AG are determined by the Parliament. His term of office is six years, unless within this term he reaches the age of 65 years, in which case his term will extend only up to 65 years. However, he can resign from his office at any time by submitting a resignation letter to the President of India.

3. Duties

The Act assigns the C&AG the following duties with regard to audit:

- To audit and report on all expenditures from the consolidated fund of India and the consolidated fund of each state/union territory with a legislative assembly.
- To audit and report on all receipts which are payable into the consolidated fund of India and consolidated fund of each state/union territory with a legislative assembly.
- To audit and report on all transactions of the union and of the states relating to contingency funds and public accounts.
- To audit the accounts of stores and stocks kept in any office or department of the union or of a state.
- To audit and report on all trading, manufacturing and profit and loss accounts, balance sheets and other subsidiary accounts kept in any department of the union or of a state.
- To audit and report on all receipts and expenditures of any body or authority if it is substantially financed by grants or loans from the Consolidated Fund of India or from the Consolidated Fund of any state/union territory that has a legislative assembly, subject to the provisions of any applicable law in force.
- To scrutinise the procedure by which the sanctioning authority satisfies itself regarding the fulfilment of the conditions of any grant or loan given for any specific purpose from the consolidated fund of India or from the consolidated fund of any state/union territory that has a legislative assembly.
- To audit the accounts of government companies and corporations in accordance with the provisions of the Companies Act, 1956 or other relevant legislation.
- To audit the accounts of certain other bodies or authorities at the request of the President of India/governor of any state/administrator of a union territory having a legislative assembly.

- To conduct audit in any body or authority not within his auditing jurisdiction, if he considers that such an audit is necessary in view of substantial government investment or advances. However, it has to be proposed to the President of India or governor of the concerned state or administrator of the concerned union territory in public interest and get the approval before such audit takes place.

4. Powers

To discharge the above duties, the C&AG will be given the following powers:

- He can visit any office of the government, where principal or subsidiary accounts are kept.
- He can require that the books of accounts, supporting papers and documents relating to the transactions under audit are to be sent to a place to be specified by him for the purpose of examination.
- He can call for any information from appropriate persons, which he may require for the performance of his duties.
- He can make any such queries or observations to the persons in charge of affairs in an office, as he may consider necessary.
- In carrying out the audit, the C&AG has the power to dispense with any part of detailed audit of any accounts and class of transactions and to apply such limited checks in relation to such accounts or transactions as he may determine.

5. Audit report

Article 151 of the constitution requires that the audit reports of the C&AG relating to the accounts of the central/state government should be submitted to the President of India/governor of the concerned state who shall cause them to be laid before the parliament/state legislature.

POINTS TO PONDER

- The audit of government accounts and the accounts of public sector undertakings has a special significance and importance in view of the public accountability of government and innumerable transactions involving large sums of public money.
- Government audit is totally different from audit of commercial firms and the audit of public sector undertakings has the features of both commercial audit and government audit.
- Special statutes have been set up for audit of several public sector undertakings. In many such undertakings, the C&AG has to conduct statutory audit. In some of the undertakings though professional accountants conduct the statutory audit, the C&AG is empowered to conduct separate audit.
- Public sector undertakings are of three different types: departmental commercial undertakings, statutory corporations and government companies. Public sector undertakings differ from private sector undertakings in many ways and it is necessary to keep them in mind before actually conducting the audit of such undertaking.

- The audit of a public sector undertaking has to adopt some of the techniques of the government audit and at the same time should follow the standard practices and techniques of a private concern. The auditors of the private sector undertakings are adopting bolder approach as compared to those of private sector undertakings.
- The Comptroller and Auditor General of India is empowered to conduct audit of departmental undertakings. The audit is primarily in the nature of commercial audit, but it is extended to include the examination of the regularity and propriety of transactions, authority of expenditure etc.
- In case of statutory corporations the auditor general is fully empowered to undertake their audit and in some cases, the professional accountants undertake the audit. In fact, the audit of each statutory corporation is conducted as per the provisions contained in the applicable Act and such provisions vary from one corporation to another.
- The provisions of the Companies Act govern audit of government companies. The C&AG has the power to conduct supplementary audit of the accounts of the government companies. The statutory auditor of these types of companies has to submit a copy of his audit report to the C&AG who has the right to comment upon the report.
- Under the Constitution of India the position of the C&AG of India is similar to that of the judge of the Supreme Court of India. His terms and conditions of service, powers and duties, rights and responsibilities are governed by the relevant Act of the Parliament.
- Article 151 of the Constitution requires that the audit reports of the C&AG relating to the accounts of the central/state government should be submitted to the President of India/ governor of the concerned state who shall cause them to be laid before the parliament/ state legislature.

REVIEW QUESTIONS

Short-answer Questions

1. How is the auditor of a government company appointed?
2. What are the basic features of statutory corporation?
3. State the objectives of government audit.
4. Who conducts government audit? How is he appointed?
5. What is a government company?
6. What do you mean by 'supplementary audit' by C&AG?
7. State the main features of departmental undertakings.
8. State the appointment procedure and terms of office of C&AG of India.

Essay-type Questions

1. Describe the procedure of auditing for government accounts and the accounts of public sector undertakings.
2. How does government audit differ from commercial audit? Describe the broad objectives of government audit.

3. Indicate the main features of public sector undertaking. How is it different from private sector undertakings?
4. Define government company. How is the auditor of a government company appointed and removed? What are the powers and duties of the auditor?
5. Describe the manner in which the Comptroller and Auditor General controls the audit of government companies.
6. State the objectives of audit of government accounts and compare them with those of the audit under the Companies Act.
7. Describe the provisions of the Companies Act relating to the audit of government companies.
8. Describe the main features which affect auditing of public sector undertaking.
9. Describe the procedure for audit of (a) departmental undertakings and (b) statutory corporations.

CHAPTER 20

Auditing in an EDP Environment

CHAPTER OUTLINE

20.1 INTRODUCTION

In recent years there has been a rapid development in the use of computers as a means of producing financial information. This development has created certain problems for the auditor in that although general auditing principles have not been affected, it is sometimes necessary to use specialised auditing procedures and techniques.

As a result of this, there has emerged from within the accounting profession a group of electronic data processing (EDP) audit specialists, equipped with sufficient technical expertise to make an intelligent analysis of complex computer audit situations.

The intention of this chapter is to outline the various factors, which need to be taken into consideration in evaluating internal control within EDP systems and to draw attention to the modifications in audit procedures, which may be required in certain circumstances.

20.2 GENERAL APPROACH TO AN EDP-BASED AUDIT

It is normal for the auditor to base his approach to an EDP-based audit upon two completely separate types of review:

20.2.1 Organisational Review

Organisational review is the review of the organisational controls within the computer installation itself. This review seeks to examine the internal control within the computer installation, to ensure the following:

(a) An acceptable standard of discipline and efficiency is maintained.

(b) An adequate division of duties exists, thus preventing any undue concentration of functions.

Serious weaknesses in internal control within the EDP department itself can throw doubt on the validity of all the data it produces.

20.2.2 System Review

System review is a detailed review of the controls operating within each computer-based accounting system. This review seeks to establish that controls operate within each individual system which, inter alia, ensure the following:

(a) All data is completely and accurately processed

(b) Permanent data is adequately protected

(c) A satisfactory 'audit trial' exists

Both types of review are carried out by the use of questionnaires and these questionnaires are based on the 'key question' principle. It is necessary to evaluate both the general and computer questionnaires together to obtain a proper understanding of the system and to access the significance of individual controls.

20.3 COMPUTER INSTALLATION REVIEW

The organisational review seeks to establish that there are no serious internal control weaknesses within the installation, which could throw doubt on the validity of the information produced.

Adopting this approach, the auditor should seek to establish that six key controls operate within the installation. These controls are as follows:

1. Controls by management over the activities of the EDP function

The degree of control which general management should exercise over the EDP department will depend both upon the nature and complexity of the business and the complexity of the computer installation.

The following minimum standards should, however, apply:

(a) The EDP manager should report directly to senior management.

(b) All significant aspects of EDP activity should be regularly reported.

It should therefore be ascertained that the person to whom the EDP Manager reports is a member of the senior management team and has sufficient authority to ensure that the department will receive adequate support and effective management.

The auditor should also enquire into the manner in which the activities of the department are reported to senior management. Ideally, a monthly control report should be prepared, which should include the following information:

(a) An analysis of computer usage, showing productive and non-productive time separately

(b) A manpower allocation report

(c) A report on projects under development

(d) An analysis of expenditure against budget

2. Controls to ensure the continuing existence of EDP facilities

Arrangements should exist within every EDP installation, which attempts either to eliminate or to minimise the possibilities of EDP facilities being completely destroyed by any reason. These arrangements are significant in that the loss of certain vital information could seriously disrupt an organisation's general business and profitability.

The auditor should enquire into the existence of the following controls:

(a) Insurance cover The following risks should be insured:

- Loss of equipment
- Loss of file devices
- Reconstruction of files (i.e. the cost of reconstituting the data from external sources)
- Consequential loss
- Employee fidelity

(b) Emergency precautions The operating area should be fitted with fire-detection equipment and also with fire-fighting equipment. The computer operators should also be fully aware of the emergency procedures to be adopted in the event of fire. Adequate security measures should also exist to ensure that authorised persons could not gain access to key areas within the department.

(c) Stand-by facilities Arrangements should exist whereby data can be processed at another installation in the event of machine failure. These arrangements are particularly important where certain systems are time-critical (e.g. payrolls).

It is unfortunately rather common for these arrangements to be made only on a casual basis, since most machine breakdowns are only of a temporary nature. The auditor should therefore enquire into the stand-by arrangements in some detail. In particular, he should direct his attention to the following points:

- Whether the arrangements are verbal, written or contractual.
- Whether or not the stand-by equipment is fully compatible and whether any recent changes have been made.
- Whether significant running time would be available if prolonged use of the stand-by facility were necessary.

(d) Back-up copies of files, programmes and documentation Processing arrangements should be such that a recent copy of all master files and programmes are available in the event of the current copy being either lost, corrupted or destroyed. Similarly, a copy of all system-flowcharts and programme listings should also be maintained, so that loss of the originals would not destroy all evidence of programme details.

The nature of the back-up arrangements and the frequency to which copies should be made will vary between installations and also different systems within an installation. It is considered, however, that the following minimum standards should apply:

(i) Programmes and systems documentation: A back-up copy of each programme should be maintained and stored under secure conditions in a place remote from the computer room. This will minimise the risk of both original and copy being destroyed. Similarly, a back-up copy of system documentation should also be maintained. Arrangements should also exist to ensure that copy programmes and documentation are regularly updated with amendments.

(ii) Master-files: At least one recent copy of each master file should always be stored under secure conditions off the premises. Security is further strengthened by means of processing files on a generation basis. Under this system, a copy of the file can always be re-created before the live edition of the file is updated with current transaction data.

(e) Equipment maintenance The equipment should be subject to maintenance as recommended by the manufacturer. The auditor should enquire into the maintenance arrangements and ensure that they comply with the manufacturer's recommendations.

3. Safeguarding of the client's records

The division of duties within the EDP department and the general procedural arrangements should be such that the records of the client are not exposed to any undue risk of loss or corruption, either accidental or deliberate.

The auditor should therefore direct his attention to the following aspects of internal control:

(a) Division of duties within the EDP department In common with other departments of the organisation, the extent to which duties can be divided between the staff within the EDP department depends to a very large extent upon the sise of the department.

Ideally, the following duties should be carried out by separate individuals:

- Data initiation (outside the EDP department)
- Data Control (within the EDP department)
- Data preparation (entering and verifying)
- Job scheduling
- Operation of the computer
- Maintenance of programmes and the file library
- Systems development
- Programming of new systems

It should be emphasised that the full division of duties as listed above will only be found in very large institutions. Small installations, for example, rarely employ a file librarian and frequently combine the activities of systems development and programming.

(b) Storage of information, files and programmes Procedural controls should be such that files and input and output data should not be accessible to unauthorised persons. The following matters warrant particular attention:

- Files should always be stored securely, preferably in a separate file library.
- Access to the files should be limited to authorised personnel only.
- Output should not be accessible to visitors to the department.
- Systems and programme documentation should be stored securely.

(c) Processing of files As stated earlier, files should always be processed on a generation basis, thus ensuring that a copy can always be re-created should be the current edition of the file be either lost or destroyed.

The auditor should enquire into the number of generations of master files that are kept and should access the adequacy of the storage arrangements for each generation.

(d) Procedures to prevent accidental overwriting of files Operating procedures should incorporate controls designed to prevent the accidental overwriting of files. The auditor would normally expect to find the following procedures in operation:

(i) Files should be subject to retention period checks on set-up i.e. the file label has a date imprinted on it, before which the file may not be overwritten or erased.

(ii) Files should be written both internally and externally.

(iii) Files should be stored in an orderly fashion to prevent accidental selection of the incorrect file.

(iv) Operators should be given details of file labels before processing, so that operating problems can be resolved.

(e) Amendments to programmes Strict control should be exercised over amendments made to existing programmes. This is not only to safeguard fraudulent manipulation or suppression of data, but also to ensure that costly amendments are not made without first establishing that they are both desirable and necessary.

The auditor should ensure the following

(i) Operators are instructed only to accept amendments, which have been authorised, by either the EDP manager or the operations manager.

(ii) Amended versions of programmes are thoroughly tested before implementation.

(iii) All programme amendments are recorded in the relevant programme documentation, the back-up documentation and also in a central record of all amendments.

4. Control over the data passing through the EDP department

Control over data submitted for processing is of vital concern to the auditor. The controls established within each system, such as control total checks and validation checks should be examined in detail by means of separate audit reviews of each individual system. Additionally, the auditor should examine as part of his installation review the general standard of controls, which are in operation within the EDP department, particularly within the data control section.

There are three main areas of control to which the auditor should direct his attention. These are as follows:

(a) Controls maintained by user departments In all batch-processing installation, it should be regarded as a cardinal rule that all user departments should maintain strict input controls over the data, which they submit for processing.

The type of control maintained will clearly vary according to the nature of the business and the individual requirements of each system. During his installation review the auditor should therefore ascertain whether or not (i) all data is batched before it is submitted for processing, (ii) user departments are required to maintain input/output controls in the form of batch total summaries, and (iii) there are indications that these user controls are effective.

(b) Data control function within the EDP department A data control section invariably exists in all but the smallest of installations. Its functions are to receive data from user departments, assemble it into a state ready for processing and to monitor its progress through the various stages of processing.

Again, the auditor will review the activities of this section in detail during each of his reviews. During his installation review, however, he should seek to establish the following.

- A data control section does exist within the EDP department.
- Staff within the data control section do not have other duties, which give rise to internal control weaknesses.
- Authorisation controls exist which ensures that all authorised data is received form users and that only authorised data is accepted for processing.
- A record is maintained of all data received and of its progress through processing
- Control totals are balanced to output after processing.
- The data control section exercises anticipatory control over the receipt of data from users.

(c) Storage arrangements within the EDP department There should be secure storage arrangements, both during and outside normal working hours, for the following

- Unprocessed data in the data control section
- Data in the record room

- Data in the job assembly area (if any)
- Input documents after processing
- Output documents after processing
- Undistributed output.

5. Controls over the operation of the computer

The procedural controls relating to the operation of the computer should also be reviewed, the object being to ensure that there are no internal control weaknesses, which could give rise to the mis-processing of data.

The points to be considered during this aspect of the review are as follows:

(a) Number of operators present during processing Ideally, there should always be two operators present during processing. This means that collusion would have to exist before data could be deliberately copied, manipulated or destroyed. If two or more operators are employed, the auditor should ensure that adequate cover arrangements exist in the event of holidays, sickness, extended shifts and lunch or tea breaks. In such a situation, the rotation of operators' duties is also of significance.

If it is not the standard practice for at least two operators to be present during processing, the auditor should seek to assess other controls which may exist and which may compensate for the absence of control over operators' activities.

(b) 'Hands-on' testing There should invariably be a rule, within all except the smallest of installations, that system analysts and programmers are not allowed access to the computer operating area, other than for 'hands-on testing'. Hands-on testing is the term used to describe the situation where the programmer tests out, on the computer, programmes which he is writing and developing.

It should also be a rule that during hands-on testing, at least one operator should be present, who operates the computer. If no operator is present, special precautions should exist which ensure that the programmer or the analyst cannot access live files and programmes.

(c) File library From an internal control point of view, it is clearly preferable that files and programmes are stored in a separate file library. Where such library exists, it should be under the control of a file librarian. Operators should not have access to this library.

Where such a library does exist, the auditor should establish that it is a requirement that all files are stored in this library when not in use. He should inspect other areas within the operations suit to confirm that this requirement is being observed.

(d) Review of operators' activities It should be an accepted principle within the installation that operators' activities should be recorded and reviewed. The manner in which this is carried out will vary according to the nature of the installation.

(e) Access to the operating area Clear access to the operating area should be subject to rigid security.

The auditor should therefore ensure the following.

- Unauthorised persons cannot gain access to the operating area either during or outside normal working hours.

- Checks exist which ensure that operators do not bring unauthorised files or work into the operating area.
- It is not possible for operators to remove files or work from the operating area without authorisation.

6. Control over the resources, assets and liabilities of the EDP department

To contribute his review of the computer installation, the auditor should conduct a review of the internal control surrounding the general activities of the EDP department. The points that should be covered within this area of review are as follows:

(a) Protection of confidential information Controls should exist which ensure that confidential information is adequately protected. Such controls will take one or other of the following forms:

- Attendance of users during the processing of sensitive applications
- Security grading of printouts, with a corresponding restriction of distribution
- If machine time is sold, special precautions relating to the protection of files, programmes and data whilst visitors are in the operating area

(b) Development of new systems and applications Procedures within the department should ensure that computer systems are only developed in situations where there is a genuine need for them and that they are developed along practical and commercial lines.

The controls surrounding systems development should therefore ensure the following:

(i) Feasibility studies are always carried out before new applications are authorised and undertaken. Such studies should have regard to all the relevant factors including: obtaining users co-operation proving a need for the application setting realistic time-scales for implementation etc.

(ii) Systems and programmes under development are reviewed at critical stages during their development. It is clearly essential that systems, when developed, are acceptable to all concerned. Reviews should therefore be carried out as follows:

- Users should approve the system before development begins.
- Auditors should be involved before programming begins to ensure that acceptable control standards are incorporated into the system.
- The system analysts should review all programmes before they are compiled.
- The programmer should extensively test the programmes.
- The analyst should review the results of programme testing.
- The user department should formally authorize the system as ready for implementation

(c) Sale of machine time/data conversion facilities If computer time and/or operating facilities are sold on anything more than an occasional basis, controls should exist to ensure that all income is duly received. The auditor should therefore enquire into the following:

(i) The system surrounding the invoicing and collection of revenue.

(ii) The rates charged and the comparison of these rates against commercial bureau charges.

(d) Cost control over the activities of the EDP department The auditor should establish that there is an adequate form of review over the activities of the EDP department. As a corollary to this enquiry, it is appropriate to enquire under this heading into the detailed mechanics of cost control. In particular, the attention should be paid to the following factors:

- Any cost accounts prepared by the EDP department
- The reconciliation of these cost accounts to the main financial accounts
- The comparison of actual costs against budget
- The means by which management review variances

20.4 COMPUTER SYSTEM REVIEW

Having completed his review of the installation and satisfied himself as to the adequacy or otherwise of the design and operation of the various procedural controls, the auditor will be in a position to review in detail the design and operation of each of the individual systems.

His approach to this task will be similar to that employed in any other system based audit, which include the following:

1. Documenting the system

The task of documenting a computer system is not dissimilar from that of documenting any other accounting system. In fact, the auditor is invariably aided in his work in that he will normally find that the system has already been well documented by the analysts who designed the system.

The amount of documentation, which will be available, will clearly vary from installation to installation. In some cases it will be necessary to supplement the documentation with the auditor's own notes and flowcharts, whereas in other cases the notes and flowcharts provided by the client will prove sufficient.

The documentation will need to be assembled in a manner, which will facilitate an evaluation of the system on the 'key question' principle. Clearly, no hard and fast rules can be laid down, but it will normally be convenient to use the outline system flowchart as the principal record of the system and to supplement this flowchart with the following four main schedules:

- Schedule of input types
- Schedule of master files
- Schedule of intermediary files
- Schedule of reports printed

The outline system flowchart, together with the four main supporting schedules, should provide the auditor with the bulk of the information, which he requires for his evaluation of the system.

2. Evaluating the system

Having completed his documentation of the system, the auditor can proceed with his evaluation of the internal controls operating within the system.

He will do this by means of an internal control questionnaire. The questionnaire should seek to establish that the following seven key controls operate:

- That it is possible to trace transactions through each stage of processing, i.e. a satisfactory audit trial exists.
- That there are controls, which prove prima facie that transaction data, is processed correctly.
- That there are adequate controls to protect standing data.
- That controls exist to ensure that all authorised, and only authorised data is processed.
- That adequate control is exercised over rejections and resubmission of corrected data for reprocessing.
- That the system provides adequate management information and that it is broadly suited to its purpose.
- That the system is adequately documented.

3. Designing the audit programme

Having documented the system and having evaluated the controls operating within the system, the auditor will be in a position to design his audit programme.

It should be emphasised that the principles involved are identical to those in any other system-based audit, namely that the auditor is seeking to assess and test the operation of the system, so that he can rely on the information produced by the system.

If he can satisfy himself as to the reliability of the system, this does not of course obviate the necessity for balance sheet verification work. Thus, even though the auditor is satisfied as to the operation of the computer systems, it will still be necessary to verify, for example, purchase ledger balances against circulars and statements and stock ledger balances against physical stock counts.

20.4.1 Transaction and Weakness Test

The principles to be employed in designing computer system audit tests are again similar to those employed in designing audit tests in respect of manual or mechanised systems. If the answer to a key question is positive and the auditor is satisfied that no fundamental internal control weakness exists, and then he imposes a transaction test to establish that the system is operating satisfactorily. If, however, the answer to a key question is negative, he imposes special weakness test to assess the significance of that weakness. If at the conclusion of those tests he is satisfied that no major error could occur, he reports the weakness to the management and continues with normal balance sheet verification work. If he thinks that a major error could occur, he must then impose additional verification tests or perhaps qualify the audit report.

It is not practical to specify a standard audit programme, which can be used in all cases where no major weakness has been identified. It is, however, possible to give an indication of the normal tests, which would be included in a transactions audit programme where there is no loss of audit trial.

20.4.2 Loss of Audit Trial

The tests indicated above deal with the basically simple situation where all information is processed in batch form and where it is possible to link the input directly with output.

However, losses of and changes in traditional audit trials are encountered increasingly in the more advanced computer applications. A typical example would be a large public company with a sales ledger comprising over half a lakh balances. It would be impractical to print out a full list of balances each month, so the control totals are printed, together with certain exception reports, such as overdue balances. There is, therefore, no output report against which the auditor can compare input.

A commonsense attitude should be adapted to losses of audit trial of this nature. The auditor must adapt his technique to suit the situation. A number of choices are open to him including some sophisticated techniques.

Techniques used in these circumstances include the following:

- Arranging for special printouts of additional information for the auditor's use. This often involves an additional suite of programmes, which are activated at the auditor's request.
- Clerical re-creation, i.e. to verify a sales total when no detailed listings have been produced, the copy invoices can be add-listed and the totals compared against the computer reports.
- Testing on a total basis, ignoring individual items.
- Use of a computer audit programme to directly interrogate the magnetic file and printout information specifically selected by the auditor.
- Use of a test pack to test the correct processing of data.
- Relying on alternative tests.

20.5 APPROACHES TO EDP AUDITING

Rapid changes in hardware and software have changed the conceptual approach to auditing in an EDP environment. In earlier times, audit approach consisted of ignoring the existence of computer, was treated it as a black box and audit was conducted around the computer. However, the increasing developments of computers has since led to computers being used in two different ways:

1. As a tool to the auditor in conducting audit such as printing confirmation requests
2. As the target of the audit where data are submitted to the computer and the results are analysed for processing reliability and accuracy of the computer system

The auditor must plan whether to use the computer to assist the audit or whether to audit without using the computer. These two approaches are commonly known as "auditing around the computer" and "auditing through the computer".

20.5.1 Auditing Around the Computer

Auditing around the computer involves arriving at a conclusion through examining the internal control system for computer installation and the input and output only for application systems. On the basis of the quality of the input and output of the application system, the auditors take decision about the quality of the processing carried out. Under this approach, the auditor considers the computer as a black box and as a result the application system processing is not examined directly.

Usually the auditors adopt this approach of auditing around the computer, when any of the following conditions are fulfilled.

- The system itself is very simple.
- The system is batch-oriented.
- The system uses generalised software, which is well tested and used widely by many concerns.

For these well-defined systems, generalised software packages often are available. For example, software vendors have already developed packages for value added tax calculation. If these software packages are provided by a recognised vendor, have received widespread use and appear error-free, the auditor may decide not to test directly the processing aspects of the system. However, the auditor must ensure that the installation has not modified the package in any way and that adequate controls exist to prevent unauthorised modification of the package.

The basic advantage of auditing around the computer is its simplicity. The auditors having little technical knowledge of computers can be trained easily to perform the audit.

However, this approach is also not free from defects. There are two major limitations to this approach. Firstly, the type of computer system where it is applicable is very restricted. It should not be used in those systems having complexity in terms of size or type of processing. Secondly, the auditor cannot assess very well the likelihood of the system degrading if the environment changes. The auditor should be concerned with the ability of the concern to adjust with a changed environment. Systems can be designed and programmes can be written in certain ways so that a change in the environment will not disturb the system to process data incorrectly or for it to degrade quickly.

20.5.2 Auditing through the Computer

The auditor can use the computer to test the logic and controls existing within the system and the records produced by the system. Depending upon the complexity of the application system being audited, the approach may be fairly simple or require extensive technical competence on the part of the auditor.

Following are the situations where auditing through computer must be adapted:

1. The logic of the system is complex and there are large portions that facilitate use of the system or efficient processing.
2. The application system processes large volumes of inputs and produces large volumes of output that makes extensive direct examination of the validity of input and output difficult.
3. Because of cost-benefit considerations, there are substantial gaps in the visible audit trial.
4. Significant parts of the internal control system are embodied in the computer system.

The main advantage of this auditing approach is that the auditor has increased power to effectively test a computer system. The range and capability of tests that can be performed increases and the auditor acquires greater confidence that data processing is correct. By examining the system's processing the auditor can also assess the system's ability to cope with environment change.

The main disadvantage of this approach is the high cost sometimes involved and the need for extensive technical expertise when systems are complex. However, these disadvantages are really spurious if auditing through the computer is the only viable method of carrying out the audit.

20.6 SPECIAL TECHNIQUES FOR AUDITING IN AN EDP ENVIRONMENT

As in the case of manual systems, auditing in an EDP environment is done for the following purposes:

(a) To study and evaluate the system through which the information under audit is generated, including the various internal controls in the system.

(b) To carry out appropriate substantive procedures.

Due to the special characteristics of an EDP environment, auditors often use the computer for performing several compliance procedures as well as substantive procedures. The techniques, which involve the use of the computer for audit purposes, are known as 'Computer assisted audit techniques' (CAATs).

What are CAATs?

Computer assisted audit techniques involve the use of computers in the process of an audit rather than limiting it to an entirely manual approach. CAATs are defined as computer based tools and techniques, which facilitate auditors to increase their personal productivity as well as that of audit function. CAATs are software tools for auditors to access, analyse and interpret data and to draw an opinion for an audit objective.

Need for CAATs

Statement on AAS-16 states that effectiveness and efficiency of audit procedures may be improved through use of CAATs. CAATs may be used in performing various auditing procedures, including the following:

- Tests of details of transactions and balances
- Analytical procedures
- Tests for general controls
- Sampling programmes to extract data for audit testing
- Tests of application controls
- Re-performing calculations performed by the entity's accounting system

Guidance note on CAAT issued by the Institute of Chartered Accountants of India describes CAATs as important tools for the auditor in performing audits. During the course of audit, the auditor has to obtain sufficient, relevant and useful evidence to achieve the audit objectives effectively. Audit findings and conclusions are to be supported by appropriate analysis and interpretation of the evidence.

In auditing a computerised environment where all significant operations are computerised, it may be impractical to perform audit completely and with assurance unless the auditor uses CAATs for collection and evaluation of audit evidence by performing both compliance and substantive tests. By using CAATs, it is possible for the auditor to perform audit more effectively and efficiently and also have greater assurance on the audit process.

Considerations in the use of CAATs

When planning an audit, the auditor may consider an appropriate combination of manual and computer assisted audit techniques. In determining whether to use CAATs, the factors to be considered include the following:

- The IT knowledge, expertise and experience of the audit team
- The availability of CAATs and suitable computer facilities and data
- The impracticability of manual tests
- Effectiveness and efficiency and
- Time constraints

Before using CAATs the auditor considers the controls incorporated in the design of the entity's computer system to which CAAT would be applied in order to determine whether, and if so, CAAT should be used.

Types of CAATs

CAATs can be broadly categorised into the following three types:

1. *Generalised audit software (GAS)* These are also referred as Package Programmes. GAS refers to generalised computer programmes designed to perform data processing functions such as reading data, selecting and analysing information, performing calculations, creating data files and reporting in a format specified by the auditor. GAS is standard off-the-shelf audit software, which can be used across enterprises and platforms.

2. *Specialised audit software (SAS)* These are also referred to as Purpose-Written programmes. They perform audit tasks in specific circumstances. These are specifically written for performing audit tests for specific type of applications. These programmes may be developed by the auditor, the entity being audited or an outside programmer hired by the auditor. In some cases, the auditor may use an entity's existing programmes in their original or modified state because it may be more efficient than developing independent programmes.

3. *Utility software* These are used by an entity to perform common data processing functions, such as sorting, creating and printing files. Utility software also includes utility programmes available in system programmes for performing debugging or analysis of various aspects of usage/access. These programmes are generally not designed for audit purposes but can be used for performing specific tests.

CAATs and more specifically audit software have the potential to enable auditors to recognise computer as a tool to assist them in the audit process. Audit software give auditors access to data in the medium in which it is stored, eliminating the boundaries of how it can be audited. Once the auditors accept and learn how to use audit software, they will be in a better position to create value addition in their audit. The greatest barrier in promoting use of audit software is failure to recognise opportunities to use audit software for audit. Understanding and recognising how CAATs can be used and knowing how to use audit software is most critical to its effective use.

Using audit software enhances the effectiveness of audit and enables the auditor to provide better assurance to their clients. In an increasingly computerised environment, it is critical for the auditor to move from ticks to clicks and learn to harness the power of computers for audit. Using audit software as their tool for auditing digitised data, auditor can shift focus from time consuming manual verification audit procedures to intelligent analysis of data to provide assurance to clients and manage audit risks.

POINTS TO PONDER

- There has been a rapid development in the use of computers in recent years as a means of producing financial information. As a result, there has emerged from within the accounting profession a group of EDP audit specialists equipped with technical expertise to make an intelligent analysis of complex computer audit situations.
- It is normal for the auditor to base his approach to an EDP based audit upon two completely separate types of review, i.e., organisational review and system review.
- Organisational review is the review of the organisational controls within the computer installation itself. This review seeks to examine the internal control within the computer installation. On the other hand, system review is a detailed review of the controls operating within each computer based accounting system. This review seeks to establish that controls operate within each individual system.
- Adopting computer installation review, the auditor seeks to establish that six key controls operate within the installation. These key controls include controls by management over the activities of the EDP function, controls to ensure the continuing existence of EDP facilities, safeguarding of the client's records, controls over the data passing through the EDP department, controls over the operation of the computer and controls over the resources, assets and liabilities of the EDP department.
- Adopting computer system review, the auditor seeks to establish that controls operate within each computer system through documenting the system, evaluating the system, and designing the audit programme.
- The principles to be employed in designing computer system audit tests are similar to those employed in designing audit tests in respect of manual or mechanised system. Basically two types of tests are employed. These are transaction test and weakness test.
- Rapid changes in hardware and software have changed the conceptual approach to auditing in an EDP environment. The auditor must plan whether to use computer to assist the audit or whether to audit without using the computer. These two approaches are commonly known as 'auditing around the computer' and 'auditing through the computer'.
- Auditing around the computer involves arriving at a conclusion through examining the internal control system for computer installation and the input and output only for application systems. Under this approach, the auditor considers the computer as a black box and as a result the application system processing is not examined directly.
- Under auditing through the computer, the auditor can use the computer to test the logic and controls existing within the system and the records produced by the system. By

examining the system's processing the auditor can assess the system's ability to cope with the environment change.

- CAATs involve the use of computers in the process of an audit rather than limiting it to an entirely manual approach. CAATs are defined as computer-based tools and techniques, which facilitates auditors to increase their personal productivity as well that of audit functions. These are software tools for auditors to access, analyse and interpret data and to draw an opinion for an audit objective.
- CAATs can be broadly categorised into three groups, which include Generalised audit software (GAS), Specialised audit software (SAS) and Utility software. Using audit software enhances the effectiveness of audit and enables the auditor to provide better assurance to the clients.

REVIEW QUESTIONS

Short-answer Questions

1. What are the features of an EDP environment that affect the nature, timing or extent of audit procedures?
2. What do you mean by the term 'computer assisted audit techniques'? State the factors to be considered before using these techniques.
3. Describe briefly the common types of computer assisted audit techniques?
4. Write short notes on:
   (a) Batch total
   (b) Test data
   (c) Check digit
5. State the primary purpose of generalised audit software.

Essay-type Questions

1. You have been appointed as the auditor of a company, which maintains its accounts on computers. Write in detail the audit approach that you would follow in the case of the company.
2. Describe the similarities and differences in the approach of an auditor to conduct audit of accounts maintained manually and those maintained on computers.
3. State the controls that can be applied over inputs and processing of data in a computerised accounting environment.
4. Write notes on the following:
   (a) Hands on testing
   (b) Files library
   (c) Auditing around the computer
   (d) Utility software.
5. Describe the steps to be followed in reviewing computer installation.

ANNEXURE A

Important Case Decisions

1. LEEDS ESTATE BUILDING AND INVESTMENT CO. VS SHEPHERD (1887)

Subject

Auditor's liability for not studying the Articles of Association of the company.

Fact

In this case, the auditor had not discovered that certain payments relating to dividends, directors' fees and bonus were irregular. This was because, he had not concerned himself with the company's Articles of Association. He was held liable for damages.

Legal View

This case had established that it is not sufficient for an auditor to concern himself with the arithmetical accuracy of the books and accounts. He has a duty to ensure that the transactions are in order. When an auditor takes over a company audit, one of his first actions is to obtain a copy of the Memorandum and Articles and note important points therein affecting the accounts. So, the auditor was held guilty of negligence for not satisfying himself that certain transactions were ultra vires the Articles of Association of the company.

2. LEE VS NEUCHATEL CO. LTD. (1889)

Subject

Requirement of charging depreciation of wasting assets.

Fact

The Articles of Association of the company provided for the distribution of profit on preference shares and ordinary shares at the rate of 7% and 4% respectively. For that the consent of the shareholders is a must. Moreover, the Articles of Association of the company contained a clause which did not bind the directors to make reserve for replacement on renewal of any property. The directors decided to declare dividend out of profits of the company to the preference shareholders without making good the loss of depreciation of wasting assets, i.e. mines and other assets of the company. One of the ordinary shareholders, Mr. Charles John Lee, brought an action against the directors of the company restraining them to pay dividend without making good the depreciation of assets of the business.

Legal View

It was held that the company may distribute dividend without making good the depreciation on wasting assets if it is authorised by its Articles of Association to do so, In fact, the object of charging depreciation is for the replacement of assets, but when the wasting assets are subject to exhaustion, the company formed is to go into liquidation, the question of replacement does not arise.

However, under the Indian Companies Act, depreciation on all depreciable assets must be provided including the wasting assets before declaration or payment of dividend from profits.

3. BOLTON VS NATAL LAND AND COLONISATION CO. LTD. (1892)

Subject

Payment of dividend out of current profits without writing off capital loss.

Fact

The business of the company comprised buying, selling, letting, cultivating and otherwise dealing with land in South Africa. In the year 1892, the company, under peculiar circumstances, debited to its profit and loss account £ 70,000 as bad debt and credited in the same profit and loss account with an equal amount arising from revaluation in the value of land over and above the cost price. Accordingly, the profit and loss account was balanced. Subsequently, the company earned working profit and declared dividend from the said source in respect of arrear dividend of 1885.

Legal View

An action was brought before the court against the company restraining it to capitalise a part of the reserve that had been created by revaluating the assets of the company. The basic reason behind such action was that the profits of the business were not realised. But it was held that surplus of capital assets resulting from bona fide revaluation of assets, even though it is unrealised, may be available for issuing bonus shares.

However, the application of this decision cannot be made possible in India after the introduction of the Indian Companies Act, 1956.

4. LUBBOCK VS BRITISH BANK OF SOUTH AMERICA (1892)

Subject

Payment of dividend out of capital profit.

Fact

The bank was carrying its business in Brazil and in some other countries. It sold its business in Brazil to a Brazilian company. Subsequently, it repurchased its business from that Brazilian Company and in the process of sale and repurchase gained £ 2,05,000. The directors wanted to credit this sum to profit and loss account and distribute the same as dividend. Thereupon, the plaintiff on behalf of himself and other shareholders brought an action, which was of a friendly character, to restrain the directors from distributing the sum on the ground that it represented accretion of capital assets and thus paying it out as dividend would amount to payment of dividend out of capital.

Legal View

The court gave its verdict in favour of directors stating that the sum was profit on capital and not part of capital itself. This is because, there was surplus on the asset side after assigning capital and external liabilities on one side of the balance sheet and the assets on the other. It was held that the directors were justified in carrying the amount to the profit and loss account for distribution as dividend as the Articles did not prohibit the distribution.

5. LONDON AND GENERAL BANK LTD. (1895)

Subject

Information and means of information are by no means equivalent terms. Auditor's duty is to give correct information to the shareholders and not means of information.

Fact

The company, in this case, had not made adequate provision for bad debts. The auditor had discovered that debts were doubtful and had clearly reported the situation to the directors, but, when the directors failed to make provisions, instead of reporting the fact equally clearly to the shareholders, he simply made the statement that "the values of the assets are dependent upon realisation". It was held that the auditor had failed in his duty to convey information clearly in his report and he was held liable for certain dividends improperly paid.

Legal View

This case is important, because it was stated unequivocally that an auditor has a duty to convey facts clearly to the shareholders. It was held in this case that "a person whose duty is to convey information to others does not discharge that duty by simply giving them so much information as is calculated to induce them or some of them to ask for more."

This case established the fact that an auditor who shrinks from fully and clearly disclosing all the material facts known to him is putting himself at risk. The court also discussed the basic duty of an auditor. It was laid down that he must exercise reasonable care and skill, but that he is in no way an insurer and is not required to guarantee the accounts.

6. WILMER VS MCNAMARA CO. LTD. (1895)

Subject

Payment of dividend without writing off depreciation of fixed assets.

Fact

In the annual general meeting a resolution was passed declaring dividend to the preference shareholders from profit without making any provision for depreciation of fixed assets. Mr. Wilmer, an ordinary shareholder, thereupon moved the court to prevent the company from giving effect to the resolution. The plaintiff contended that the loss of capital must first be made good and particularly because the company had provided for full depreciation on its assets in the earlier years.

Legal View

It was held that a company could not be restrained from declaring a dividend out of current profits merely because, no provision had been made for the depreciation on fixed assets.

However, the decision of this case in no way hold good in India after the introduction of Section 205(l)(b) of the Indian Companies Act, 1956.

7. KINGSTON COTTON MILLS CO. LTD. (1896)

Subject

Auditor's right in accepting stock certificate from the management.

Fact

In this case, the accounts had been manipulated by overvaluation of stock by the managing director, who had certified the stock valuation to the auditor. It was held in the court of appeal that it was not the duty of the auditor to take stock, and that in the absence of suspicious circumstances he was not guilty of negligence in accepting the certificate of a responsible official with regard to the value of stock.

Legal View

As far as the main question is involved, whether the auditor could place total reliance on the stock certificate of a responsible official with regard to the value of stock in the absence of suspicious circumstances, this case is now of historical interest only. At present, the Companies Act requires that auditors should state whether accounts show a true and fair view. The professional accountancy bodies have issued statements regarding detailed audit work to be carried out in relation to stock verification and valuation and attendance by the auditor at stock-taking.

It was held at that time that there was no breach of duty on the part of the auditor. An auditor is not supposed to take stock himself and in the absence of suspicious circumstances, he can accept a stock certificate issued by a trusted official of the company. However, in the present context, it does not seem that the auditor could simply accept a stock certificate from a responsible official where stock was a material item, and then plead this case in justification when defending the inevitable action for misfeasance or negligence.

8. IRISH WOOLEN CO. LTD. VS TYSON AND OTHERS (1900)

Subject

Liability of an auditor for his failure to detect falsification of accounts.

Fact

The auditor was found to have been negligent in that he had failed to discover that the company's liabilities were understated due to the suppression of creditor's invoices. This fraud would have been discovered if the auditor had either checked the ledger balances against the creditor's statements or scrutinised the dates entered in the first few weeks of the next period.

Legal View

This case again shows the courts refusing to accept that the auditor had discharged his duties by checking the arithmetical accuracy of the entries in the books. He must exercise due skill and care in checking the validity of these entries. The auditor was, therefore, liable for damages sustained by the company by reason of his negligence.

9. FOSTER VS NEW TRINIDAD LAKE ASPHALTE CO. LTD. (1901)

Subject

Payment of dividend out of capital profit.

Fact

The company along with the assets of the other company took over a debt of £ 1,00,000 secured by promissory note, at its formation. At that time, the debt was considered valueless. Later on, the debt was paid in full, together with an interest accrued amounting to £ 26,258,16s. The directors proposed to distribute the amount as dividend as the directors treated the said amount as capital profit. But one shareholder brought an action before the court restraining the company to pay dividend on the ground that the decrease in the value of other assets should have been considered.

Legal View

It was held in this case that the question of what profit is available for dividend depends upon the results of the whole account taken fairly for the year, capital as well as profit and loss, and though dividends may be paid out of earned profits in proper cases, not withstanding a depreciation of capital, a realised accretion to the estimate value of one item of capital asset cannot be deemed to profit divisible among the shareholders without reference to the result of the whole account fairly taken. So, the realised appreciation in the value of book debts should not be considered as profit available for dividend.

10. LONDON OIL STORAGE CO. LTD. VS SEEAR, HASLUCK & CO. (1904)

Subject

Auditor's liability for not verifying petty cash.

Fact

This was another case where the auditors had concerned themselves only with the entries in the books and not with the verification procedures. The balance sheet showed cash balance of almost £ 800, which agreed with the books, but the actual balance was only £ 30, the difference having been misappropriated. The auditor was held to have been negligent in not verifying the balance. However, damages of only five guineas were awarded against the auditor, because, the court held that the director responsible for supervising the fraudulent employee was the person primarily responsible for the loss.

Legal View

There are two important aspects to this case. The first is that the court again held that the auditors have a duty to verify assets and not merely to check bookkeeping entries. The second and the very important, is that the auditors are responsible for the loss resulting directly from their negligence and thus are not responsible where the loss has resulted from other causes.

11. SHORT AND COMPTON VS BRACKETT (1904)

Subject

Auditor's negligence in duty for non-detection of fraud during the period of investigation.

Fact

The plaintiff sued for the fees for having investigated the books of the defendant firm in respect of the proposed admission of partner in the firm. It was subsequently revealed that an employee of the firm defrauded the firm by defalcation of wage sheet. The important point to be noted in this case that a part of the fraud was made by an employee during the period of investigation. A counter sue was made by the defendant against the plaintiff to the original case for alleged negligence in failure to discover the fraud.

Legal View

It was proved by the court that when the plaintiff checked the wage sheet, it was correct at that time. Therefore, the counter-claim was dismissed by the court.

12. NEWTON VS BIRMINGHAM SMALL ARMS CO. LTD. (1906)

Subject

Power of the Articles of Association to impose restriction on the statutory duties of an auditor.

Fact

The fact of the case was that the Articles of the company was amended through a special resolution authorising the directors to create secret reserve and use the same in the interest of the company in future. However, the most serious matter was that the amendment also imposed restrictions on the auditor from disclosing the existence and mode of utilisation of secret reserve. The validity of the resolution was challenged by one of the shareholders, A. J. Newton, in the court.

Legal View

It was held that any provision in the Articles of Association, curbing the auditor's statutory duties relating to his report to the shareholders is ultra vires, as being accepted canon of law. Hence, Articles of the company under no circumstances, can restrain the auditor from reporting to share-holders the creation of secret reserve and its utilisation. The auditors are required to report the true and fair state of affairs of the company. So, any regulation precluding the auditors from discharging his duty is inconsistent with the act.

In our country also, the Companies Act requires that the balance sheet should reflect a true and fair view of the state of affairs of the company. The balance sheet will not definitely present a true and fair view if secret reserve exists in the accounts. So, creation of secret reserve is not possible in our country under the existing law subject to certain exceptions.

13. SMITH VS SHEARD (1906)

Subject

Auditor's liability for non-detection of fraud, when he acts only as an accountant.

Fact

The plaintiff had incurred losses owing to the defalcations of an employee. The actual contract with the accountant was in question. The defendant denied that he had ever agreed to audit the books, he was only instructed to check the postings in order to make out a balance. But in sending the bill of charges, his clerk had inadvertently used the word "audit", instead of "auditing of posting". The balance sheet and the accounts sent in did not contain any signature or certificate.

Legal View

It was held that the accountant was held liable for damages. The jury found that there was a contract to audit, though the decision was very much against the opinion of the judge.

14. BOND VS BARROW HAEMATITE STEEL CO. LTD. (1912)

Subject

Transfer of profits to reserves; payment of dividend before making good loss of capital.

Fact

Empowered by the Articles of Association, the directors carried forward the entire credit balance of the profit and loss account of a year to reserves. For certain years no depreciation had been provided in the accounts in respect of building, works, plant and mining leases and subsequently it was discovered after revaluation that the company's capital was considerably reduced. The transfer of profits to reserves without payment of dividend was intended to make good this loss of capital. An application was also made to the court for capital reduction, but this was rejected. After these, some preference shareholders brought actions against the company to compel it to pay dividend out of current profits without transfer of profits to reserves for making good the loss of capital.

Legal View

It was held that when the articles empower the directors to transfer profits to reserves before payment of dividend and the directors do so to the extent it is necessary to make good loss of capital, preference shareholders cannot restrain the directors from such an action in order to get dividend from current profit.

15. COLMER VS MERRETT, SON AND STREET (1914)

Subject

Gross negligence of an auditor to detect falsification of accounts.

Fact

Mr. Colmer, an engineer, claimed damages from the defendant, the auditor, for the losses sustained by him by investing heavy sum of money on the reliance of his report. In fact, the auditor was given only three days time to prepare the annual accounts. Therefore, he did not undertake the complete audit or investigation. The report was based on approximation.

Legal View

It was held that assessment of financial position along with the preparation of annual accounts for the purpose of investigation was not possible within a period of two or three days. The investigating auditor had taken only the ready-made information into consideration. He had not checked the truth and fairness of the accounting records. So, he was held liable for gross negligence in his duty.

16. AMMONIA SODA CO. LTD. VS ARTHUR CHAMBERLIN AND OTHERS (1918)

Subject

Payment of dividend without meeting the deficiency of capital.

Fact

An action was taken by the company against its two former directors, asking them to refund to the company a sum amounting to £ 1268 14s. 4d., which was illegally paid as dividend during the years 1912 to 1915. The company was incorporated as a private limited company in July 1908. Thereafter, by a special resolution, passed in October 1911, it was converted into a public limited company. The company's profit and loss account showed a debit balance amounting to £ 19,028, 5s. 4d.The directors were entrusted to value the land and accordingly it was valued at £ 79,166 and the addition of expenses for the innovation of new bed of rock self amounting to £ 20, 542. 2s. 4d. was added to the value of land. The sum was credited to reserve account and was used to write off the following:

1. The debit balance of the profit and loss account amounting to £ 12,970. 18s. 3d,
2. Goodwill for £ 1,500.
3. Cash bonus for £ 1,980.

And the balance of £ 4,091. 4s. 5d. was transferred to reserve account.

During half year ended 31.01.1912, the company made net profit of £ 7,348. 13s. The value of the land was increased in the balance sheet to the extent of £ 16,450 18s. 3d, thus eliminating the credit balance for £ 4091 4s. 5d., which was left to the credit of the reserve account. In the years 1912 to 1915, dividends amounting to £ 1,268. 14s. 4d. were paid to the preference shareholders.

Legal View

The court decided that the assets of the business may be written up as a result of bona fide revaluation and that the current profits may be divided without making good past losses of the business.

However, the decision of this case in no way hold good in India after the introduction of Section 205 (1) (b) of the Indian Companies Act, 1956.

17. CHAS FOX AND SON VS MORRIS GRAND & CO. (1918)

Subject

Liability of accountants for non-examination of bank passbook.

Fact

The auditors were employed to check the books and prepare accounts. But they did not examine the passbook, for which they could not detect defalcations. Their defense was that they acted as accountants and not as auditors and for the preparation of accounts and checking the arithmetical accuracy of books, examination of passbook was unnecessary.

Legal View

The auditors were held liable for damages. The court held that it was the implied duty of the accountants to see that 'Cash at Bank', which they had inserted in the balance sheet, actually existed.

18. ARTHUR E. GREEN & CO. VS THE CENTRAL ADVANCE & DISCOUNT CORPORATION LTD. (1920)

Subject

Auditor's duty and liability in regard to bad and doubtful debts.

Fact

The case concerned the failure of the company to make adequate provision for bad and doubtful debts. The auditors relied upon the bad debt provisions made by the managers, despite the fact that many debts not provided for were old and some of them were even statute-barred. The auditors were found to have been negligent.

Legal View

The decision indicates that the auditors must exercise proper skill and care in carrying out their own tests to establish the value of material assets. They were not adequately performing their duties by relying on a certificate provided by a responsible official.

19. STEPLEY VS RED BROTHERS (1924)

Subject

Writing off the debit balance of profit and loss account from revaluation profit and payment of dividend out of current profit.

Fact

The company had written off the balance of goodwill account (£ 51,000) out of reserve. In a later year, the profit having being found inadequate for both setting off the debit balance of the profit and loss account and paying dividend on preference shares including arrear dividend, the directors decided to write up goodwill by £ 40,000, being the conservative value of goodwill and credit the sum to reserve account, which could be utilised for writing off the debit balance (£ 25,500) of the profit and loss account and paying the dividend. A shareholder, thereupon, moved the court for an injunction to restrain the directors from writing back £ 40,000, which was previously written off out of reserves created from profit.

Legal View

It was held that a company could write up at a fair value the goodwill, which was written off excessively in the earlier years and utilise the sum for writing off the debit balance of the profit and loss account and distribute the current profit as dividend.

20. THE CITY EQUITABLE FIRE INSURANCE CO. LTD. (1924)

Subject

Window dressing of balance sheet and auditor's inability to detect the manipulation of accounts.

Fact

This case concerned various alleged frauds in relation to the accounts of the company. The most important of these with regard to auditing principles was that securities owned by the company were deposited with its stock brokers. The auditors accepted a certificate from the stock brokers in respect of such securities for a very material amount. Had they insisted on inspecting the securities, these could not have been produced as they had been pledged by the stock brokers. An additional complication was that, the chairman of the company was also a partner in the firm of stock brokers.

The auditors escaped liability because the company had a clause in its articles, which provided that the directors, auditors and officers of the company should be indemnified by the company except in the case of willful default.

Legal View

The importance of this case was that it demonstrated the importance of auditors' actually inspecting documents of title by third parties held. Only where such documents are held by one of the major banks or are not very substantial and are held in the ordinary course of a business by another independent third party should the auditor accept a certificate. Moreover, if the auditor entertains the slightest doubt of the desirability of accepting a certificate, it would always be wise to insist on actual inspection.

21. TRUSTEES OF APFEL VS ANNAN DEXTER AND CO. (1926)

Subject

The difference between the work of an accountant and that of an auditor and the liability of an auditor.

Fact

Mrs. Apfel had a business in which her two sons were managers. Those managers misappropriated the assets of the business gradually. Consequently, she had become insolvent. In order to submit the accounts of the business to the Tax Authority, she appointed M/s. Annan Dexter & Co. Chartered Accountants. After her insolvency, the trustees brought an action against the auditors demanding a compensation of £ 28,600. It was pointed out that the auditor had acted negligently and that is why, they did not trace out the fraud of the managers.

Legal View

The court declared that the auditors were innocent. The auditors proved that they were asked to prepare the accounts and not to audit them. Hence, they were not responsible and no action could be taken against any person who was appointed to work of accountants and not of auditors.

22. ARMITAGE VS BREWER & KNOTT (1932)

Subject

Auditor's negligence in duty for non-detection of fraud.

Fact

A lady book-keeper had embezzled a large sum of money by manipulating the wage sheets. She had complete control over the books, vouchers, wage sheets and other documents. There was no system of internal check in force. The auditors were appointed to conduct a continuous and a detailed audit. The charge against them was that they failed to exercise reasonable care and skill in the course of examination of documents i.e. they failed to vouch and verify book entries. The defense put forth by the auditors was that the frauds could not be possibly detected by exercise of ordinary and reasonable care.

Legal View

The case was decided against the auditors and they were ordered to pay damages amounting to £ 1,259 to the plaintiff. It may be remembered that according to the instructions issued to the auditor, it was clear that there was a suspicion that fraud had been committed and hence, the auditor ought to have been extra careful.

23. WESTMINSTER ROAD CONSTRUCTION AND ENGINEERING CO. LTD. (1932)

Subject

Auditor's liability for failure to detect omission of liabilities from balance sheet and over-valuation of work-in-progress.

Fact

This case concerned misfeasance by the auditor of a company, which had subsequently gone into liquidation. The auditor was held to have been negligent for failing of detect the omission of liabilities from the balance sheet in circumstances where their omission should have been apparent and for failing to detect the overvaluation of work-in-progress in circumstances where there was available evidence to have enabled him to do so.

Legal View

This case again underlined the need for sound verification procedures and with regard to the work-in-progress underlined the need for the auditor to make use of all available records and information.

24. ALLEN CRAIG & CO. (LONDON) LTD. (1934)

Subject

The company auditor's responsibility to submit the audit report of the company to the concerned officials.

Fact

The company made a loss in each year of its existence, and there was a deficiency of assets to meet liabilities of over £ 40,000. In submitting the accounts for the year to 30th June 1924, the auditor sent a letter to the company drawing attention to the serious position of the company, this being quite apart from the normal audit report. In 1927, in submitting the accounts for the years to 30th June 1925 and 1926 respectively, the auditor sent further letters, showing that there was a deficiency as regards creditors of nearly £ 11,000.

The liquidator of the company took out a summon for misfeasance against the former managing director and the auditor asking for a declaration that such parties were liable for the debts of the company incurred after 30th June, 1925.

Legal View

It was held that the duty of the auditors, after having signed the report to be annexed to a balance sheet is confined only to forwarding that report to the secretary of the company. It will be for the secretary or the directors of the company to convene a general meeting and send the balance sheet and report to members entitled to receive it. The auditor, in no way, will be held liable in this situation.

25. LEECH VS STOKES BROS. (1937)

Subject

Auditor's liability for non-detection of frauds, when he acts only as an accountant.

Fact

The defendants had prepared accounts for a number of years for a firm of solicitors for the purpose of submission to the Inspector of Taxes. No balance sheets were ever prepared. The instructions were given by one of the partners, Dublin, and on his death, a new partner employed another accountant to audit the accounts, as a result of which defalcations of the client's money by the cashier were discovered. Action for damages on the ground of negligence was brought against the defendants.

Legal View

The negligence alleged were the following

1. Failure to prepare a balance sheet
2. Failure to vouch or test certain fees brought into the accounts
3. Failure to reconcile the bank account and cash

The defendants were able to prove that they were not employed to audit the accounts, but only to prepare a profit and loss account for income tax.

The courts found that there was no negligence in not preparing a balance sheet or in not refusing to prepare a profit and loss account until the books were written up to enable them to prepare a balance sheet.

26. S. P. CATTERSON AND SONS LTD. (1937)

Subject

Inadequacy of internal check system and the duty of the auditor.

Fact

In this case, the company had a poor system for dealing with sales in that the same invoice book was used for both cash sales and credit sales and this led to defalcations. The auditors had drawn attention of the directors to the shortcomings of the system, but no action had been taken. The auditor was acquitted of negligence on the ground that the primary duty for exercising control vested with the directors.

Legal View

The auditors had reported about the weaknesses in the system rightly to the directors. This should now be done formally in 'Internal Control Letters' (Letters of Weaknesses). So, the auditor was not held liable.

27. SOCKOCHINSKY VS BRIGHT GRAHAM & CO. (1938)

Subject

Right of auditor to retain working papers prepared by him to carry out the assignment.

Fact

In this case, an important and pertinent question was raised, this is regarding the ownership of the working papers. Sockochinsky, the auditor, claimed that he had collected the information for the purpose of discharging his duties, therefore, he was entitled to the possession of these papers. On the other hand, the client claimed that the auditor had acted as agent of the business and he should surrender these papers to the client as every other agent does. The auditor had also argued that in case he is charged of negligence by his client, he could produce these papers as evidence in his defense.

Legal View

It was held that the working papers belonged to the auditor, because they were independent contractors and not agents of the clients in this context. So, an auditor as an independent professional is entitled to the working papers prepared by him.

28. COMMISSIONER OF INCOME TAX, MADRAS VS G. M. DANDEKAR (1952)

Subject

Liability of an auditor to a third party.

Fact

Mr. Dandekar, a chartered accountant, was appointed by A. Mohammed & Co. to prepare the statement of accounts and income tax returns. He examined the books of accounts and signed a few statements including the trading and profit and loss account and the balance sheet. He also forwarded the statements of account of the firm to the income tax department stating that the accounts were verified by him. But the income tax department later discovered that the profits shown in the above statements were incorrect and false. The department, therefore, brought legal action against the auditor for his negligence in duty.

Legal View

The case was decided in favour of the auditor and he was not held guilty for negligence. It was held that the role of an auditor to the assessee is just like a lawyer or an advocate in a court. It is the responsibility of the income tax officer to investigate the accounts. The auditor owed no duty to the income tax department (third party) and as such, no question of negligence in duty could arise.

29. REGINA VS WAKE AND STONE (1954)

Subject

Liability of the directors and the auditors for false statement in the prospectus.

Fact

The prospectus of the defendant company Wake and Stone, contained the figures for stock and work-in-progress which was duly certified by the auditor of the company, was subsequently proved to be false, deceptive and misleading. A case was filed by the plaintiff against the company and its auditors for inflating the stocks and work-in-progress figure. It was pleaded on behalf of the auditor that he relied on the statement given by the managing director.

Legal View

Both the managing director and the auditor were found guilty. But the nature of punishment in the two cases was different. The managing director was sentenced to imprisonment and the auditor was fined £ 200 or in the alternative six months imprisonment for having signed the report for the prospectus recklessly.

30. BASU R. B. VS P. K. MUKHERJEE (1957)

Subject

Professional misconduct of an auditor under Clause 10, Part I of the First Schedule of the Chartered Accountants Act, 1949.

Fact

Mr. P. K. Mukherjee, a chartered accountant, was employed by the complainant for the purpose of income tax appeal before the Income Tax Appellate Tribunal. The remuneration for this purpose to be paid had been fixed on certain percentage of the relief of tax.

The complainant submitted a complaint to the Institute of Chartered Accountants of India on the following grounds:

1. That the respondent failed to appear at the hearing of the appeal before the tribunal inspire of agreement between them.
2. That a large sum of money were wrongfully taken by him by false representation of the case.

Legal View

The court could not establish any of the above charges against the respondent. However, the disciplinary committee of the Institute of Chartered Accountants of India made a charge against Mr. Mukherjee that he had charged his fees at a certain percentage of relief of tax on the ground that no practising chartered accountant can accept fees on percentage basis as per the provision of Clause 10, Part I of the First Schedule of the Chartered Accountants Act, 1949. Hence, he was held guilty of professional misconduct and suspended from practice for a period of three months.

31. THOMAS GARRAND AND SONS LTD. (1967)

Subject

Liability of an auditor for his failure to detect falsification of accounts.

Fact

The accounts of this company had allegedly been manipulated in the following ways:

(i) The stock figures were inflated.
(ii) Purchases relating to the current period were charged in the succeeding period.
(iii) Sales made after the accounting date were credited in the earlier period.

The auditors were found liable for misfeasance in respect of dividends paid by the company, where had the accounts not been manipulated, no profit would have been available. The auditors' negligence arose primarily from their failure to follow up the alterations of the purchase invoices. They had discovered the alterations, but accepted explanations too easily.

Legal View

Two main conclusions can be drawn from this case. Firstly, the need for sound audit tests on the year-end cut-off procedures and secondly, the fact that once the auditors have discovered suspicious circumstances in this case, the alteration of the dates on the invoices, they have a duty to probe the matter thoroughly, and must not be easily satisfied by explanations provided by directors or officials.

ANNEXURE B

Objective Type Questions

1. Auditing refers to
   (a) preparation and checking of accounts
   (b) examination of accounts business units only
   (c) examination of accounts by professional accountants
   (d) checking of vouchers
2. Auditing is a branch of
   (a) natural Science (b) social science
   (c) abstract Science (d) none of them
3. Statutory audit means
   (a) compulsory audit (b) audit as required by law
   (c) external audit (d) all of them
4. Main object of auditing is
   (a) detection of errors
   (b) to find out whether P&L/c a/c and B/S show true and fair state
   (c) detection of frauds
   (d) detection and prevention of frauds and errors
5. Auditing is luxury for a
   (a) joint stock company (b) partnership firm
   (c) small shopkeeper (d) government company
6. Limitation of audit is
   (a) that it does not reveal complete picture
   (b) that it does not guarantee accuracy of accounts
   (c) that auditor may be biased
   (d) all of the above
7. Auditing is compulsory for
   (a) small scale business enterprises (b) all partnership firms
   (c) all joint stock companies (d) all proprietary concerns
8. Propriety audit refers to
   (a) verification of accounts
   (b) examination of accounts of proprietary concerns

(c) enquiry against justification and
(d) audit of government companies
(e) necessity of expenses

9. Property audit is normally undertaken in case of
(a) joint stock company (b) government company
(c) statutory corporation (d) government departments

10. Government may order for special audit under
(a) Section 227 (b) Section 233A
(c) Section 233B (d) Section 224

11. Special audit is necessary for
(a) manufacturing concern (b) processing concern
(c) inefficient concern (d) trading concern

12. Government may order for cost audit under
(a) Section 227 (b) Section 233A
(c) Section233B (d) Section 224

13. Central government may order for cost audit of
(a) trading concerns (b) mining concerns
(c) insurance company (d) non-processing concerns

14. Interim audit refers to
(a) examination of accounts continuously
(b) examination of accounts intermittently
(c) audit work to find out and check interim profits of a company
(d) carrying on audit for bonus purposes at the end of year

15. Final audit implies
(a) audit of accounts at the end of year
(b) finally checking of accounts to reveal frauds
(c) audit for submitting report immediately
(d) audit of banking companies at the end of year

16. A continuous audit is specially needed for
(a) any trading concerns (b) smaller concerns
(c) banking companies (d) any manufacturing concern

17. Alteration of figures after audit is a limitation of
(a) final audit (b) continuous audit
(c) interim audit (d) none of the above

18. Management audit means
(a) audit undertaken on behalf of the management
(b) evaluating performance of various management processes and functions
(c) audit undertaken on behalf of government to punish management
(d) compulsory audit of company management

19. Systems audit implies
    (a) systematic examination to improve accounts
    (b) audit undertaken to auditing systems
    (c) enquiring accounting and control systems
    (d) checking the performance of management
20. Internal audit means
    (a) audit undertaken to ascertain truth and fairness of state of affairs
    (b) audit undertaken internally to evaluate management functions
    (c) audit by independent auditor to improve internal affairs
    (d) audit undertaken by employees of the organisation to check financial irregularitie
21. Internal audit is
    (a) compulsory for a company with paid-up capital of Rs.25 lakh and above
    (b) voluntary for a company
    (c) not necessary for a company
    (d) necessary for a company
22. Internal audit is undertaken
    (a) by independent auditor
    (b) statutorily appointed auditor
    (c) by a person appointed by the management
    (d) by a Government auditor
23. Internal auditor is appointed by the
    (a) management (b) shareholders
    (c) government (d) C&AG
24. The scope of work of internal audit is decided by the
    (a) shareholders (b) management
    (c) government (d) law
25. The scope of work of statutory audit for a company is decided by the
    (a) shareholders (b) management
    (c) government (d) law
26. The object of internal audit is
    (a) to prevent errors and fraud (b) to detect errors and frauds
    (c) to improve financial control (d) all of the above
27. Internal auditor can be removed by the
    (a) government (b) shareholders
    (c) management (d) company Law Board
28. Control and management of audit profession is in the hands of
    (a) government
    (b) C&AG
    (c) Institute of Charted Accountants of India
    (d) Institute of Cost and Work Accountants of India

29. Institute of Chartered Accountants of India was established on
    (a) April 1, 1956
    (b) April 1, 1949
    (c) July 1, 1956
    (d) July 1, 1949
30. Internal check refers to
    (a) checking of record by the cashier
    (b) checking of accounts by the internal auditor
    (c) checking of work of one person by another automatically
    (d) managerial control internally over the subordinates
31. The object of internal check is to
    (a) control wastages of resources
    (b) prevent errors and frauds
    (c) verify the cash receipts and payment
    (d) facilitate quick decision by the management
32. Effective internal check system reduces
    (a) the liability of auditor
    (b) work of auditor
    (c) both work as well as liability of auditor
    (d) responsibilities of an auditor
33. Internal check is a part of
    (a) internal audit
    (b) internal accounting
    (c) external audit
    (d) internal control
34. Internal check is carried on by
    (a) special staff
    (b) internal auditor
    (c) accountant
    (d) none of the above
35. Internal check is suitable for
    (a) large concerns
    (b) small concerns
    (c) petty shopkeepers
    (d) none of the above
36. Internal check involves
    (a) reduction of work of cashier
    (b) division of responsibilities of members of staff
    (c) verification of inventory
    (d) collusion among the members of staff
37. Internal check is carried on by
    (a) staff specially appointed for the purpose
    (b) internal auditor
    (c) the members of the staff among themselves
    (d) supervisor of the staff
38. Internal check is essential for
    (a) petty traders
    (b) cash transactions in a large concern
    (c) a concern using automatic equipments
    (d) none of the above

39. Misappropriation of goods may be checked by
    (a) proper supervision over stock
    (b) punishment of employees
    (c) checking of employees
    (d) none of the above
40. Window dressing implies
    (a) curtailment of expenses
    (b) under-valuation of assets
    (c) checking wastages
    (d) over-valuation of assets
41. Falsification of accounts is undertaken by
    (a) auditors
    (b) clerks
    (c) accountants
    (d) responsible officials
42. Errors of omission are
    (a) technical errors
    (b) errors of principle
    (c) compensating errors
    (d) none of the above
43. Valuation of assets on wrong basis is
    (a) technical error
    (b) clerical errors
    (c) error of principle
    (d) compensating error
44. Test checking refers to
    (a) testing of accounting records
    (b) testing of honesty of employees
    (c) intensive checking of a selected number of transactions
    (d) checking of all transactions recorded
45. Test checking should not be applied to
    (a) purchases book
    (b) sales book
    (c) stock book
    (d) cash book
46. Test checking should not be applied to
    (a) sales book
    (b) purchases book
    (c) bank reconciliation statement
    (d) bills book
47. Cost of removal of business to a more convenient place is a
    (a) capital expenditure
    (b) revenue expenditure
    (c) deferred revenue expenditure
    (d) none of the above
48. Expenses on experiments are
    (a) revenue expenses
    (b) capital expenses
    (c) deferred revenue expenses
    (d) none of the above
49. Vouching implies
    (a) inspection of receipts
    (b) examination of vouchers to check authenticity of records
    (c) surprise checking of accounting records
    (d) examining the various assets
50. Payment for goods purchased should be vouched with the help of
    (a) creditors statement
    (b) correspondence with the suppliers
    (c) cash memos
    (d) ledger accounts

51. Payment for wages should be vouched with the help of
    (a) piece work statement (b) wages sheets
    (c) minute book (d) bank pass book
52. Commission paid should be vouched with the help of
    (a) salary book (b) wages sheet
    (c) creditors statement (d) commission book and related agreements
53. The most reliable voucher is one, which originates
    (a) in the concern
    (b) outside the concern
    (c) outside the concern and sent directly to the auditor
    (d) in the concern and sent directly to the auditor
54. Sales proceeds from machine should be vouched with the help of
    (a) cash book (b) sale contract
    (c) brokers' statement (d) none of the above
55. Payment for building purchased should be vouched with he help of
    (a) title deed (b) correspondence with the brokers
    (c) building account (d) cash book
56. Partner's drawing should be vouched with the help of
    (a) stock book (b) cash book
    (c) memorandum drawing book (d) agreement deed
57. Investment should be vouched with the help of
    (a) commission book (b) brokers' book
    (c) sales deeds (d) minute book
58. Receipts from debtors should be vouched wit the help of
    (a) counterfoil receipts and cash book (b) supplier's statement
    (c) sales deeds (d) general ledger
59. Bad debt recovered should be vouched with the help of
    (a) debtors statement (b) general ledger
    (c) dividends book (d) counterfoils of dividend warrants
60. Receipts from sale of investment should be vouched with the help of
    (a) brokers' budget notes (b) brokers' sold notes
    (c) minute book (d) inventory of investment
61. Purchases returns should be vouched with the help of
    (a) bought notes (b) credit notes
    (c) goods inwards book (d) cash book
62. Payment for bills should be vouched with the help of
    (a) debtors' statement (b) creditors' statement
    (c) bills returned (d) bills with the suppliers

63. Verification refers to
   (a) examination of journal and ledger
   (b) examination of vouchers related to assets
   (c) examining the physical existence and valuation of assets
   (d) calculation of value of assets
64. Object of verification is
   (a) physical verification of assets
   (b) checking value of assets
   (c) examining the authority of their acquisition
   (d) all of the above
65. Which of the following statement is correct ?
   (a) valuation is a part of verification
   (b) verification is a part of valuation
   (c) valuation is a valuer
   (d) valuation has nothing to do with verification
66. Stock should be valued at
   (a) cost
   (b) market value
   (c) cost or market price, whichever is lower
   (d) cost less depreciation
67. Valuation means
   (a) calculating value of assets
   (b) checking the value of assets
   (c) checking the physical existence of assets
   (d) examining the authenticity of assets
68. "Auditor is not a Valuer" was stated in
   (a) Kingston Cotton Mills Case (b) London and General Bank Case
   (c) Lee vs Neuchatel Co. Ltd. Case (d) London Oil Storage Co. Case
69. Fixed assets are valued at
   (a) cost (b) market value
   (c) cost or market price, whichever is less (d) cost less depreciation
70. Plantation products are valued at
   (a) cost
   (b) market
   (c) cost or market price, whichever is lower
   (d) net amount subsequently realised
71. Incomplete contracts should be valued on the basis of
   (a) net profit of the period
   (b) two-thirds of net profit of the period
   (c) two-thirds of estimated profit of the period
   (d) none of the above

72. Joint audit implies
    (a) audit of two concerns together
    (b) audit of joint stock companies
    (b) audit of joint sector companies
    (d) audit by two firms of CA
73. Loans given should be verified with the help of
    (a) statement of loans
    (b) schedule of book debts
    (c) inspection of agreement
    (d) certificate from the bank
74. Book debts should be verified with the help of
    (a) balance sheet
    (b) amount received from debtors
    (c) debtors' schedule
    (d) certificate from the management
75. To verify goodwill, the auditor should check
    (a) sales deed
    (b) purchase agreement
    (c) balance sheet
    (d) certificate from the management
76. Investments in hand should be verified with the help of
    (a) schedule of investments
    (b) balance sheet
    (c) inspection of securities
    (d) certificate from the bank
77. First auditor of a company is appointed by the
    (a) shareholders
    (b) central government
    (c) Company Law Board
    (d) Board of Directors
78. Which of the following persons is qualified to be a company auditor?
    (a) an employee of the company
    (b) a body corporate
    (c) a person who is indebted to the company for Rs.10, 000
    (d) a person who is a member of a private company
79. Which of the following persons is not qualified to be a company auditor?
    (a) a body corporate
    (b) an employee of the company
    (c) a man of unsound mind
    (d) all of the above
80. The first auditor of company will hold office
    (a) for a period of one year
    (b) till holding of statutory meeting
    (c) till the conclusion of first annual general meeting
    (d) till a new auditor is appointed
81. The following cannot be appointed as an auditor of the company
    (a) a chartered accountant
    (b) a firm of CA
    (c) a body corporate
    (d) none of the above
82. Normally, a company auditor is appointed by the
    (a) central government
    (b) shareholders
    (c) Board of Directors
    (d) C&AG
83. An auditor in a casual vacancy is appointed by the
    (a) central government
    (b) shareholders
    (c) Board of directors
    (d) C&AG

84. If an auditor, not appointed at general meeting, he is appointed by the
(a) central government (b) Shareholders
(c) Board of Directors (d) none of them
85. A vacancy caused by resignation of the auditor is filled only
(a) by Board of Directors
(b) At the general meeting of shareholder
(c) by the central government
(d) by the company law board
86. A special auditor is appointed by the
(a) shareholders (b) Board of Directors
(c) central government (d) C&AG
87. A government auditor may be appointed by the
(a) central government on the advice of C&AG
(b) shareholders
(c) Board of Directors
(d) C&AG
88. A company auditor can be removed before expiry of his term by
(a) shareholders (b) Board of Directors
(c) central government (d) state government
89. Remuneration of a company auditor is fixed by the
(a) shareholders (b) Board of Directors
(c) central government (d) appointing authority
90. A company auditor, in general, has to submit his report to
(a) shareholders (b) Board of Directors
(c) central government (d) C&AG
91. An auditor of government company has to submit his report to the
(a) shareholders (b) ministry concerned
(c) central government (d) C&AG
92. Amount of share premium may be utilised for
(a) payment of dividend (b) writing off of preliminary expenses
(c) routine expenses (d) purchase of fixed assets
93. Shares can be issued at Premium under Section
(a) 76 (b) 78
(c) 79 (d) 80
94. Dividend cannot be paid out of
(a) capital profits (b) capital receipts
(c) revenue receipts (d) none of above
95. A chartered accountant sent a circular soliciting his work. He will be liable for
(a) misfeasance (b) negligence
(c) professional misconduct (d) none of the above

96. Civil liability of an auditor implies liability for
    (a) fraud (b) misappropriation of cash
    (c) incorrect reporting (d) misfeasance
97. An auditor, working in honorary capacity is
    (a) liable (b) not liable
    (c) criminally liable (d) none of the above
98. A company auditor should see that the dividend has been paid
    (a) after charging depreciation (b) out of capital profits
    (c) out of accumulated profits (d) none of the above
99. In his audit report, the company auditor should state
    (a) correct state of affairs (b) true state of affairs
    (c) fair state of affairs (d) true and fair state of affairs
100. Companies Auditor's Report Order (CARO) is applicable to
    (a) banking companies (b) trading companies
    (c) insurance companies (d) none of the above
101. Under the Companies Act, 1956 annual audit is compulsory for
    (a) private limited companies (b) public limited companies
    (c) companies listed on a stock exchange (d) all companies
102. The Companies Auditor's Report Order does not cover the following
    (a) an overseas branch of an Indian company
    (b) indian branch of a company incorporated outside India
    (c) the head office of a company incorporated outside India
    (d) all of them
103. The branch auditor of a limited company can be appointed by
    (a) board of directors of the company
    (b) statutory auditor if authorised by the company in general meeting
    (c) company itself in general meeting
    (d) none of the above.
104. Cost audit report is to be furnished to
    (a) the central government with a copy to the company
    (b) the central government only
    (c) the company only
    (d) the shareholders of the company
105. All the books of account and supporting vouchers of a company are seized by the tax authorities. The auditor would most likely to express
    (a) a qualified report (b) an adverse report
    (c) a disclaimer of opinion (d) none of the above
106. A control procedure often used in cases where computer files can be accessed from terminals is the use of
    (a) check digit (b) password
    (c) batch total (d) system analyst

107. An error report, containing erroneous data detected by programmed control procedures, should be reviewed and followed up by
   (a) system analyst
   (b) computer programmer
   (c) check digit control
   (d) EDP internal auditor
108. The values of certain artwork held as investments by the enterprise have been estimated by a qualified valuer engaged by the enterprise. You should
   (a) accept the valuation
   (b) engage another valuer for valuation
   (c) reject the valuation
   (d) disclaim an opinion
109. The most common audit procedure for verification of ownership of land is
   (a) examination of correspondence concerning purchase of land
   (b) examination of title deed of the land
   (c) examination of minutes of the board meeting concerning purchase of land
   (d) physical verification of land
110. To discover unrecorded disposal of fixed assets, the auditor should check
   (a) examination of insurance policies
   (b) review of repair and maintenance expenses
   (c) examination of invoices relating to additions to fixed assets.
   (d) scrutiny of cash book
111. Independent financial audit can best be described as
   (a) a branch of accounting
   (b) a legal requirement
   (c) a tool to protect the shareholders interest
   (d) a function of attestation
112. Following type of audit is not statutorily required for companies in India
   (a) cost audit
   (b) tax audit
   (c) annual financial audit
   (d) internal audit
113. The audit which involves examining the effects of the activities of an enterprise on environment is known as
   (a) system audit
   (b) green audit
   (c) cost audit
   (d) none of them
114. Following audit aims at measuring the efficiency with which an enterprise has used energy
   (a) environmental audit
   (b) management audit
   (c) energy audit
   (d) none of them
115. In case of payments, the most reliable evidence is
   (a) receipts sent by the person to whom payment is made
   (b) entry relating to payment in the bank passbook
   (c) entry relating to payment in the cash book
   (d) none of the above
116. Direct confirmation procedure can be applied to
   (a) debtors only
   (b) creditors only
   (c) both
   (d) none of them

117. An audit engagement letter should preferably be sent
   (a) before the commencement of audit
   (b) immediately after the commencement of audit
   (c) any time before the completion of audit
   (d) after the completion of audit
118. Internal check usually operates
   (a) before the processing of a transaction
   (b) as a part of the processing of a transaction
   (c) after the processing of the transaction
   (d) at all stages of the transaction
119. The scope of internal audit of a company is determined by
   (a) shareholders (b) management
   (c) Provisions of the Companies Act (d) all of them
120. Statistical sampling involves the use of statistical techniques for
   (a) determination of sample size (b) selection of sample
   (c) interpretation of sample results (d) all of them
121. Statistical sampling techniques can be employed by an auditor in carrying out
   (a) compliance procedures (b) substantive procedures
   (c) both the procedures (d) none of them
122. Following document would be considered most reliable in case of receipts from customers
   (a) daily cash receipts statement
   (b) copy of acknowledgement sent to the customers
   (c) bank pay-in-slip
   (d) bank statement
123. The general accepted basis of valuation of fixed assets is
   (a) net realisable value (b) historical cost less depreciation
   (c) replacement cost (d) none of the above
124. An auditor finds that fictitious sales have been recorded to inflate profit. The auditor should
   (a) ignore it (b) allow it
   (c) qualify his audit report (d) none of the above
125. The auditor did not check the adequacy of provision for bad and doubtful debts. He can be
   (a) held liable for it (b) not liable for it
   (c) liable criminally for it (d) none of the above

ANNEXURE C

Model Questions and Answers

A. SHORT AND PRACTICAL QUESTIONS

Q. 1. Define the term 'audit'.

Answer: The word 'audit' is derived from the Latin word 'audire', which means, "to hear". In olden times, whenever the owners of a business suspected fraud, they appointed certain persons to check the accounts. Such persons sent for the accountant and 'heard' what they had to say in connection with the accounts.

The dictionary meaning of audit is official examination of accounts. Obviously, the person who examines the accounts must be a person who knows what to examine, how to examine and to whom his examination report and observations are to be submitted. In brief, it can be said that auditing is the process by which competent independent individuals collect and evaluate evidence to form an opinion and communicate his opinion to the person interested through his audit report.

Montgomery, a leading American accountant, defines auditing as: "Auditing is a systematic examination of the books and records of a business or other organisations, in order to check or verify and to report upon results thereof."

The ICAI has defined auditing in its AAS-1 as:"An audit is the independent examination of financial information of any entity, whether profit oriented or not and irrespective of its size or legal form, when such an examination is conducted with a view to express an opinion thereon."

From the above definitions, it is seen that an auditor has not only to see the arithmetical accuracy of the books of accounts but has to go further and find out whether the transactions entered in the books of original entry are correct or not. It is possible to perform this function by inspecting, comparing, checking, reviewing, scrutinising the vouchers supporting the transactions in the books of accounts and examining the correspondence, minute books of the shareholders' and directors' meeting, Memorandum of Association and Articles of Associations, etc.

Q. 2. State the social objective of auditing.

Answer: Audit is a social science which has certain social objectives. It should make contributions towards the fulfilment of social purposes. Auditing work, to be effectively performed, have to function for the following.

1. Protection of shareholders interest:

Auditors are the representatives of the shareholders. Naturally, it is the duty of an auditor to see whether the interest of the shareholders are protected or not. The shareholders' interest can be protected by ensuring stable solvency, profitability and efficiency position of the company form of organisation.

2. Protection of national interest:

Another vital social objective of an audit is to see that the national interest is protected. The national interest can be protected only when cases of evasions of taxes are prevented. So, tax evasion should be discouraged for national interest as there is no denying the fact that raising revenue through taxation is a must for the development of the country.

3. Safeguarding capital erosion:

Mere examination of the books of accounts will not help to locate those factors, which are responsible for capital erosion. In order to stop capital erosion of the business, different systems of audit should be introduced. Capital erosion is very dangerous, because it tends to liquidate the business. So, the function of an audit from social point of view is to stress and scrutinise those aspects, which are responsible for capital erosion.

4. Measurement of fair wages:

Measurement of fair wages does not come under the purview of general audit. It should be the social objective of an audit to see whether the wages for workers are fair and in conformity with the general price index.

5. Fair prices for consumers:

As a part of the society, the business organisation should charge fair prices from the consumers. It will not only create goodwill of the organisation but also ensure its future growth. An auditor should take care of this social aspect of auditing.

6. Fair return for investors:

If the capital of a company is not utilised efficiently, the company will not be able to earn fair profit. On the other hand, the growth of the business may be withheld. Both high and low turnover of capital stand on the way to fair return. This rate of turnover should be compared with turnover rate of other companies belonging to the same industry. Justice to the investors depends on the solvency and profitability position of the business, which becomes favourable through the earning of fair return.

Q. 3. 'Auditing is a dynamic social science.' Explain.

Answer: In the above statement, two objectives of auditing are used, i.e. 'dynamic' and 'social', to describe the characteristics of the functions of auditing. The first objective is used to describe the changing roles of the professionals involved in the function of auditing and the second objective is used to give an idea about the field of study of auditing.

Auditing is considered dynamic in the sense that the role of auditor changes with the changes of the need of the users. At present, the shareholders of a company are demanding more transparency in accounts in order to take correct decision on the basis of audited accounts. In addition to that, legal obligation of the auditors are increasing to a great extent due to the introduction of new provisions of the Acts governing the accounts and improved version of generally accepted accounting principles. To match with these dynamic needs of the users of accounting information, the auditor has to be dynamic.

On the other hand, auditing belongs to social science group of subjects. Social science deals with the problems of the society and tries to eliminate social injustice. Auditing as a profession has some social obligations also. In order to protect the interest of the society including the shareholders, customers, governments, financers and suppliers, the auditor has to see whether the books of accounts of the organisation gives a true and fair view of the state of affairs of the organisation. In order to ensure reliability on accounts prepared, he has to check the accounts with reasonable care and skill.

So, in the present changing society, the auditing profession has become very dynamic in order to meet the social needs of the time.

Q. 4. State important features of internal audit.

Answer: Internal audit is conducted by specially assigned staff within the organisation. It is an audit through which a thorough examination of the accounting transactions as well as the system according to which these transactions have been recorded is conducted. Internal audit is undertaken to verify the accuracy and authenticity of the financial accounting and statistical records presented to the management. As per SAP-7, the scope and objectives of internal audit vary widely and are dependent upon the size and structure of the entity and the requirements of its management.

(a) The internal audit system is considered to be a part of the management control system and not merely an assistant thereto.
(b) Internal audit often differs in its scope and emphasis; it is more managerial than accounting.
(c) The nature and extent of checking also depends on the size and type of the business organisation.
(d) It embraces not only the operational audit of various operational activities in the organisation but also includes the audit of management itself.
(e) The function of internal audit can be considered as an integral part of the internal control system.
(f) Internal audit is continuous in nature. The work of internal auditor starts after the transactions are completed.
(g) Generally the internal audit is conducted by the permanent staff of the organisation. Sometimes outside agencies may be asked to conduct internal audit.
(h) The existence of internal audit is a help to the external auditor.

Q. 5. What are the ways and means of removing the drawbacks of continuous audit?

Answer: In a large enterprise, continuous audit is a must for proper and timely completion of audit. So, some special measures have to be taken for avoiding the limitations of continuous audit as far as practicable. The following measures can be taken to overcome the shortcomings of continuous audit:

1. Use of audit notebook:

The auditor must record in his notebook the work completed by him and his assistants from time to time, material errors detected and rectified, raised by him and his staff and explanations given by the client. Before starting the work each time, the auditor should have a look over the notebook and books of accounts to know the extent of work completed up to last visit or whether any query remains unanswered or whether any alteration has been made.

2. Use of special ticks in checking:

The auditor may use a different tick for checking the figures altered before audit. Such variation in tick mark should be slight and unnoticeable. This will enable the auditor to identify whether any unauthorised alteration has been made subsequent to audit.

3. No change in audit staff:

The duties of audit staff should not be changed in order to maintain the flow of work undisturbed and to ensure the follow-up of unresolved points. However, to avoid monotony in work, the nature of duty of the audit staff may be changed after completion of annual audit.

4. No change in audited figures:

Clear instruction must be given to client for not changing any audited figure. If any extra-ordinary situation requires such change, it should be done with prior intimation to the auditor and with the help of rectification entry only.

5. Casting in ink:

The casting of periodical total of the various books of accounts should be written in ink as and when they are checked.

6. Incomplete work:

Checking of each part of work, whenever undertaken, should be completed in one visit and should not be left incomplete to be completed for the next visit.

7. Sound audit programme:

There should be well-framed audit programme indicating the extent of work to be completed, allocation of work and time schedule of various works. This will make the continuous audit very effective.

Q. 6. State the advantages and disadvantages of written audit programmes containing details of the work to be performed.

Answer: The principal advantages of a written or prepared audit programme are as follows:

(a) The danger of any essential part of the work being omitted or overlooked is minimised.

(b) Staff engaged on any audit may be changed at any time with the minimum of dislocation.

(c) Audit managers are enabled more effectively to control the progress of several audit simultaneously.

(d) If each auditor is required to initial the programme for the work performed by him, the responsibility may be allocated, should any subsequent query arise.

(e) A permanent record of the actual work performed is maintained and evidence is afforded which may enable the auditor to rebut any possible charge of negligence that may be alleged against him.

The disadvantages of a written audit programme include the following:

(a) The work of audit may tend to become mechanical if the programme is followed too rigidly and as a result, initiative on the part of the staff engaged on the audit may be discouraged.

(b) Excess or insufficient work may be carried out in certain cases.

(c) Unless the programme is reviewed and revised frequently in the light of current experience, it may become outdated and will not give effect to changes which occur in the nature of the client's business or in the system of accounting and internal check employed.

Q. 7. Tabulate six documents or papers, which would normally be retained on the permanent audit file for a limited company.

Answer: The documents or papers, which would normally be retained on the permanent audit file for a limited company, include the following:

(a) Copies of the Memorandum and Articles of Association.
(b) Details of the corporate structure and management organisational plan.
(c) Extracts from the minutes, contracts and any other documents, which have continuing importance to the audit.
(d) Relevant financial information including ratios and trends covering the previous ten years.
(e) Knowledge of the business giving the history of the company and details about its products and the markets in which it operates.

A copy of any bank certificate request letter sent by the client to its bankers asking that the auditors should be supplied with information regarding bank balances, securities held in safe custody, etc.

Q. 8. What are 'check lists' and 'flow charts' and why would you expect to find them in audit working papers?

Answer: 'Check lists' are 'aides-memoire' to the auditor to ensure all important aspects of the accounts have been considered. Check lists can also be used in assessing the internal control systems, when they would list the crucial questions the auditor must ask. Check lists should be completed, signed and placed on the current working papers file to evidence the fact that the matters included have been covered.

'Flow charts' are used as pictorial descriptions of either manual or computer systems. They can either show a simple flow of documents or they can include aspects of control over the documents throughout the system. Flow charts can be a considerably more efficient way of recording a system than a narrative and thus are useful to the auditor and his staff.

Q. 9. How does flow chart differ from an organisational chart? What are the main advantages in using a flow chart during an audit?

Answer: Flow charts are diagrammatic records of the flows of documentation within the organisation. They usually show the checks, authorisation controls and accounting procedural steps through which a document must pass. It usually shows the source of the document, each processing stage it passes through, the departments which act upon it and the stage and phase it is eventually filed.

On the other hand, an organisational chart is the diagrammatic representation of the chain of responsibilities within an organisation, showing the persons who are functionally in charge of individual activities and the persons to whom they must report.

The main advantages in using a flow chart during an audit are:

(a) they ease understanding,
(b) they provide a permanent record of the system at the time it was prepared,
(c) they assure all documents are accounted for and
(d) they assist standardisation of system recording.

Q. 10. What are the two basic types of audit tests? Give examples of each type and explain the purpose of each test.

Answer: The two types of audit tests are as follows:

1. Compliance test: A compliance test is a test which seeks to provide audit evidence that the internal control procedures are being applied as prescribed.

Examples

(i) Checking for authorisation on a credit note: This should confirm that all credit notes are suitably authorised before being issued.

(ii) Checking for the casting stamp on a purchase invoice: This should confirm that all invoices are cast before being paid.

(iii) Checking that copy of goods despatched notes are attached to the copy of sales invoices: This should confirm that invoices would only be posted to the sales ledger after the goods have been despatched.

2. Substantive test: A substantive test is a test of a transaction or balance, which seeks to provide audit evidence as to the completeness, accuracy and validity of the information contained in the accounting records or financial statements.

Examples

(i) Circularisation of debtors to confirm the accuracy of the balance on the sales ledger.

(ii) Checking the posting of day-book totals to the nominal ledger, which should confirm accuracy of posting.

(iii) Matching a purchase invoice with the original order and goods received note to confirm that the purchase is bona fide.

Q. 11. Explain what is meant by the expression 'examination in depth' and illustrate by reference to the verification of a payment made to a creditor for goods supplied.

Answer: 'Examination in depth' involves the tracing of a transaction through the different stages from its initiation to its conclusion. The records and supporting vouchers applicable at each successive stage are examined to an appropriate extent, bearing in mind the quality of internal check operating at that stage.

For example, the verification of a payment made to a trade creditor for goods supplied is frequently carried out by simply examining the paid cheque returned from the bank, ensuring that it is drawn in favour of the creditor and restrictively crossed. Verification of this transaction 'in depth', however, would involve examination of the following further items:

(a) A copy of the original order and the authority thereof

(b) The goods received note and evidence that the goods have been examined to ensure their conformity with the original order, both as to quantity and quality

(c) The supplier's invoice and statement of account

(d) Evidence in the stock records of the inclusion of the goods into stock

Q. 12. State what you understand by the term 'cut-off procedure' and some of the points with which you as auditor would be concerned.

Answer: 'Cut-off procedure' is the procedure operated by a company in relation to stock in trade, which ensures that at the balance sheet date there is complete accord between the physical stock brought into account on the one hand and the related records of purchases and sales on the other.

The auditor would be concerned with such matters as the following:

(a) The procedure for linking sales records with stock records so that goods sold and invoiced to customers are excluded from stock, even though they have not left the premises.

(b) The procedure for linking purchases records with stock records so that all goods purchased are included in the stock, even though not yet received.

(c) The procedure which ensures that goods not belonging to the company, e.g. goods held by the company as agent or on a sale or return basis, etc. are not included in the stock, and that goods belonging to the company and held by other parties on a similar basis are included in the inventory,

(d) Where stock has been taken on a date other than the balance sheet date, the procedure for adjusting the inventory to take into account movements to and from stock, which have taken place between the stock taking date and the balance sheet date.

Q. 13. Design a checklist for your use in considering whether or not the audit report should be qualified.

Answer: A qualification checklist should include the following:

(i) Does the balance sheet show a true and fair view?

(ii) Does the profit and loss account show a true and fair view?

(iii) Have all the requirements of the Companies Act been duly complied with?

(iv) Has the company kept proper accounting records?

(v) Has the company received proper returns from branches not visited by the auditor?

(vi) Are the accounts in agreement with the underlying accounting records?

(vii) Has the auditor received all the information and explanations necessary for the performance of his duties?

(viii) Has sufficient, relevant and reliable evidence been obtained on which to form an opinion?

(ix) Are there any material aspects of the financial statements about which the auditor has reservations?

(x) Are the accounting practices being followed continuously in a consistent way?

Q. 14. What audit tests would you instruct your staff to make to examine the reasons for the delay between cash receipts being recorded in the cash book and appearing on the bank statement?

Answer: The following audit tests should be carried out to determine the reasons for the delay in cash recording:

(a) Ascertain the existing banking procedure from the responsible employee.

(b) Test that the procedures are being followed covering

  (i) movement of cash from counters to central collection point,

  (ii) recording of cash in the company's books of accounts,

  (iii) preparation of a bank paying-in-slip,

  (iv) transfer of cash to the bank,

  (v) checking details on the bank statement to the paying-in-slip. There should be no undue delay at any stage.

(c) Observe the staff at each stage and note any reasons why a delay may occur.

Q. 15. Tabulate and explain the different types of internal control on which the auditor may wish to place reliance.

Answer: Internal control is a system of control that management sets up to enable it to carry out its responsibilities. It extends beyond pure financial and accounting matters and the custody of the company's assets. It could include, for example, functions such as work study, operations research and production quality control.

The different types of internal controls on which the auditor may wish to place reliance include the following:

(a) Organisational controls, e.g. plan of the organisation detailing responsibilities
(b) Segregation of duties and in particular the separation of the function of authorisation, execution, custody and recording
(c) Physical controls, i.e. the controls designed to restrict access to assets to authorised personnel
(d) Authorisation and approval, i.e. the controls that ensure that all transaction is authorised by a responsible official
(e) Arithmetical and accounting controls, e.g. checks over the arithmetical accuracy of the records such as the use of control accounts and reconciliations
(f) Personnel, i.e. the procedures that ensure that personnel have capabilities commensurate with their responsibilities and include selection and training procedures
(g) Supervision, e.g. controls over the day-to-day transactions of the business and their recording
(h) Management controls that cover the overall supervision of the business including the review of management accounts, budgets and internal audit

Q. 16. In a large manufacturing concern, the management suspects inclusion of 'dummy workers' in wage sheets. What would you, as an auditor, suggest to detect such frauds?

Answer: Effective and appropriate internal control system should be adopted in order to detect the inclusion of the names of dummy workers in the wage sheets. The application of suitable internal check system, however, depends on the nature and procedures of wage payment of the factory concerned. However, following outlines of the system can be suggested:

(a) Each worker should be provided with a time card or job card as the case may be. Proper records in detail about each worker must be maintained in such cards. The foreman in charge should initial the entries in the cards. At the end of the week or month, the card should be sent to wage office.
(b) Due care should be given in the preparation of wage sheets. Wage sheets should not be prepared by those employees, who are responsible for recording the attendance of the workers. The work of wage sheet preparation should be assigned to a number of employees in such a way that the work done by one is automatically checked by the other.
(c) Payment of wages should not be made by those employees, who have taken part in the preparation of wage sheet. It should be done by the cashier in the presence of a responsible officer and also the foreman, who can recognise the workers.
(d) Proper records related to overtime authorised and granted to the workers must be maintained. For casual workers, separate records should he maintained.

Q. 17. Mention different types of frauds that are possible in credit sales, and state in what way an auditor should proceed to detect them.

Answer: Different types of frauds are possible in credit sales, which may include (a) misappropriation of goods returned from customers, (b) misappropriation of the payments received, and (c) inclusion of fictitious sales to inflate profits.

In order to detect frauds in credit sales as mentioned above, the auditor should proceed in the following way:

(a) In order to detect misappropriation of goods returned from the customers, the auditor should ascertain first the system of recording the goods returned and find out its weaknesses, if any. He should check the entries in the sales returns book with goods inwards book. He should also refer to the correspondence entered into between the client and the customers returning the goods, and check thoroughly all credit notes to be made along with the correspondence, goods inward book and the gate keeper's records.

(b) In order to detect misappropriation of payments received, the auditor would verify the statement received from the customer. The auditor would see that the balances thereon agree with the aggregate of unpaid invoices and the credit notes in the relevant customers' folder. In case of suspicion, he should write to the customer concerned ascertaining the balance, which remains unpaid, and then compare it with the records.

(c) In order to detect inclusion of fictitious sales with a view to inflate profits, the auditor should check the sales invoices carefully. The auditor should check particularly the sales entered towards the close of the accounting period with a view to find whether sales relating to the next period have been treated as sales for the current period. He should also check the goods outward book and gatekeeper's record exhaustively with the related invoices to see that only real sales have been included in the books.

Q. 18. Your client, proprietor of a big retail store, wants protection against losses of sale proceeds. The client deals mainly in cash sales. Suggest a suitable system of internal check for the same.

Answer: With a view to protect against the misappropriation of cash out of the sale proceeds by the salesmen, the following system of internal check is suggested:

(i) There should be complete segregation of responsibilities of the salesmen, the cashier and the accountant. Nobody should be allowed to do the job of others.

(ii) For each section, counter or department, separate salesman should be appointed.

(iii) As far as possible, mechanical cash register should be maintained.

(iv) The salesman should issue sales bills in triplicate. He should hand over two copies to the customer and retain the other copy.

(v) These two copies of the bill should be presented by the customer to the cashier.

(vi) The cashier should check the bill, receive the payment and stamp the bill as 'Paid'. Original copy of the bill should be handed over to the customer.

(vii) The customer should collect the goods purchased on presentation of the original bill, stamped as paid from another counter near the gate.

(viii) Each salesman should prepare the summary sheet with the help of the copy of the bill that remains with him and submit it to the accountant.

(ix) The cashier should enter the day's total sales in the cash sales sheet with the help of bill retained by him and report it to the accountant.

(x) Any discrepancy found by the accountant should be immediately reported to the general manager.

Q. 19. As an auditor, how would you safeguard your client against payment for the fictitious purchases while verifying the purchases?

Answer: The auditor has to be very cautious while verifying the purchases that no payments have been made for the fictitious purchases. For this purpose, he may have to take the following actions:

- He should examine first the internal control system in connection with purchases and satisfy himself with regard to its effectiveness.
- He should ensure that before passing the invoices for payment, they are checked with the original order, with goods received book and the stock records.
- He should inspect the invoices and see that the authorities responsible for passing them for payment have duly checked them and initialled.
- He should test check the invoices to see that dates given in the invoices are for the period concerned and they have been addressed in the name of the client.
- He should also compare a number of invoices with the records in the goods received book and stock records.
- He can make physical verification of the goods purchased, if a part of it is still in the stock.
- He should also compare the supplier's statement with the supplier's account.
- Postings in the various suppliers' accounts should also be checked and compared with the statement received from them.

Q. 20. The trial balance of a firm does not agree on account of certain errors. You, as an auditor, are called upon to locate errors. How would you proceed?

Answer: It is to be noted in this context that it is not the duty of an auditor to locate errors, if the trial balance does not agree. However, if the auditor is specifically called upon to locate errors to tally trial balance, he should take the following steps:

- He should ensure that all transfer of balances from various accounts have been made. It may happen that some of the balances might have been left from being transferred to trial balance.
- He should check the totals of various subsidiary books and see that they have been duly transferred to the trial balance.
- He should see that the debit and credit items have been shown in their respective sides correctly.
- He should check the balances of various accounts and see in particular whether the opening balances have been brought down in the accounts or not.
- He should also compare various items in the trial balance of the current year with that of the previous year and see that all the usual items have been included therein.
- Find out the difference of both the sides of the trial balance. Check the difference and see if there is any item of this value to find out whether any item of debit side has been written on

the credit side or vice versa. Similarly, double the difference and check with several accounts.

- Check the totalling and if the error is divisible by 9, it may be due to misplacement of or transposition of figures, for instance, 53 for 35.
- Even if the errors are not traceable, transfer the balance to a suspense account and this account should be closed only when the errors are discovered.

Q. 21. How would you, as an auditor, proceed in the following cases?

(a) Receipts of amounts exceeding Rs. 500 without affixing revenue stamps

(b) No vouchers are available against some payments

Answer: The auditor should proceed in the following way:

(a) If this is an exceptional case, the auditor may accept them provided he is satisfied with the genuineness. But, if he has any suspicion about its genuineness, he must draw the attention of his client to this aspect.

But, if these have happened in all cases that no revenue stamps are affixed against the payments exceeding Rs. 500, the auditor should ask the client to immediately affix the required revenue stamps against all these payments.

It may be noted in this context that the vouchers may be perfectly good evidence of the payment and the auditor could not refuse it on the ground only of non-stamping.

(b) If no vouchers are available against such payments, the auditor must demand necessary vouchers. But if the amount is very small or if the expenses are explainable, e.g. tips to the office bearers at the income tax office, expenses for bus fair, etc. the auditor may not pursue the client for the vouchers. In other cases, he must seek proper explanation and if he is not satisfied with the explanations offered, he should seek secondary evidences in that connection.

Q. 22. What is a "letter of representation"? What purpose does it serve?

Answer: A letter of representation is a reminder to the management that they are responsible for the preparation of the accounts and for the truth and fairness of the information contained therein.

It is a formal record of all representations made to the auditor during the course of the audit. It is also a contributory form of audit evidence, but it in no way relieves the auditor from checking any of the information in the accounts.

The purpose of a letter of representation is to provide a formal record of representations made to or relied upon by the auditor. It also ensures that there can be no misunderstanding between the directors and the auditors as to the representations, which were made during the course of the audit.

A letter of representation does not absolve an auditor from his duty to carry out all other audit procedures, which he considers necessary. In order to satisfy himself on each item in the final accounts, an auditor must obtain a sufficient variety of reliable audit evidence, and it is unlikely that he will consider it proper to rely exclusively on the confirmation contained in a letter of representation without other supporting evidence being available for examination.

Q. 23. What factors would influence an auditor in considering the acceptability as evidence of certificates received from third parties?

Answer: The factors, which would influence an auditor when considering the acceptability of any third party certificates as evidence, are as follows:

- It is written.
- It is received in direct response to a request made by the auditor himself.
- The third party is properly qualified for the purpose of the certificate and that his status is credible and has integrity in the opinion of the auditor, e.g. a certificate of 'work done to date' on a contract issued by a qualified architect.
- The third party is independent of the company, e.g. a certificate from a share broker, whose brother is the managing director of the company cannot be said to come from a fully independent source.
- The extent to which additional evidence exists to substantiate the representations made by third parties, e.g. copy of correspondence referring to the delivery of title deeds to the company's bankers for safe keeping.
- The presence of a disclaimer clause.
- The third party's nominal business is to hold the assets in question, e.g. title deeds held by a share broker would not be considered normal business and the auditor would be put on enquiry.

Q. 24. Discuss the right of lien of an auditor of a limited company.

Answer: According to general principles of law, any person having the lawful possession of somebody else's property on which he has worked may retain the property for non-payment of his dues. On similar grounds, auditor can also exercise lien on books and documents placed at his possession by the client, for non-payment of fees for work done on the books and documents.

For this purpose, the following conditions should generally be considered:

- Documents retained must belong to the client who owes the money.
- Documents must have come into the possession of the auditor on the authority of the client.
- The auditor can retain the documents only if he has done work on the documents assigned to him.
- Such documents can be retained which are connected with the work on which fees has not been paid.

Besides, the auditor has uncontestable lien on his working papers as well as all the schedules, computations, etc. made available by the client to him as was held in the case 'Sockochinsky vs Bright Graham & Co. (1938).

It may be noted that the rights of an auditor being statutory rights cannot be restricted or curtailed either by the Articles of Association or resolution of the members. Any provision of this nature by the auditee company is ultra vires and hence, void as was decided in the case Newton vs Birmingham Small Arms Co. Ltd. (1906).

Q. 25. You are the Senior Audit Manager of a company's financial statements for the year ended 31st March, 200x. What evidence would you look for to verify the following amounts appearing in the balance sheet?

(a) Leasehold building stated at Rs. 8,50,000
(b) Rates paid in advance of Rs. 18,750
(c) Salesman's commission of Rs. 20,000
(d) Interest receivable of Rs. 4,150

Answer: Evidence required for the verification of the following:

(a) Leasehold Building Rs. 8,50,000

(i) on existence—physical inspection of the property
(ii) on ownership—inspection of the lease agreement noting down the duration and terms including premium paid
(iii) on valuation—checking of the calculation of the premium paid being written off over the duration of the lease
(iv) on disclosure—depending on the length of lease left to run, the amount should be disclosed as long or short period leasehold building in the fixed assets category

(b) Rates paid in advance Rs. 18,750

(i) The original rates demand notice should be obtained and the period and the amount to be noted.
(ii) The actual payment should be checked from the cash book.
(iii) The calculation of the prepayments should be checked.
(iv) The item should be included in current assets in the balance sheet.

(c) Salesmen's Commission Rs. 20,000

(i) Evidence of the existence of the salesmen from personnel records
(ii) Evidence of the rates by reference to contracts of employment. Calculations should be checked
(iii) Evidence of sales by reference to a sample of sales invoices
(iv) Any amounts due but not paid should be included in creditors and can be checked against invoices and the payroll

(d) Interest receivable Rs. 4,150

(i) The amount of the loan or deposit on which the interest is earned should be established at various periods.
(ii) The loan or deposit certificate or agreement gives the interest rate and the calculation can be checked.
(iii) The date of the last payment can be verified from the cash book and the receipt of the interest after date may also be checked from cash book and the bank statement.
(iv) If the amount is due from a bank, confirmation should be possible via the bank letter.

Q. 26. 'Teeming and lading' method of fraud by employees are sometimes encountered by the auditor. What normal audit procedures would be likely to disclose such irregularity?

Answer: The misappropriation of money received from debtors by the method of 'teeming and lading' should be disclosed by the following procedures:

(i) Examine carefully the make-up of the sales ledger balances, making special inquiry into accounts, which appear to be falling more and more into arrears. Particular attention should be paid to cases where credits have been entered for payments on account where it has hitherto been the debtor's practice to settle their accounts regularly.

(ii) If the auditor's suspicions are aroused, he should obtain the original bank paying-in-slips and compare the detailed items thereon with the entries in the cash book to see if there is evidence of any remittances having been split, part having been credited to one account and part to another.

(iii) If receipts for remittances are issued, check the counterfoils thereof, with the **entries in the cash** book, noting discrepancies in the amount and in the dates of **entry.**

(iv) If possible, arrange with the client that statements of account, prepared by or under the supervision of the auditor's staff, be sent to all debtors, asking for confirmation of the amounts shown to be outstanding.

Q. 27. An auditor of a limited company did not verify the investment; he inserted a note in the balance sheet— "Investments not verified". The shareholders approved and adopted the accounts at the annual general meeting. Subsequently, it transpired that the investments were misappropriated and the company suffered a loss.

Can the auditor be sued for damages for negligence or otherwise in the discharge of his duties?

Answer: In case of audit of a limited company, an auditor has to comply with the statutory duties as prescribed in the Companies Act, 1956. Verification of investments is a very important function of an auditor, since, it is an important asset shown in the balance sheet. The auditor cannot be expected to give a report on the 'truth and fairness' of the financial statements of the company without verifying its investment. If he specifically mentions in his audit report the fact that, he did not verify the investments, he would not be relieved from his statutory duties. Such statutory duties can never be curbed, though they may be extended.

Under Section 543 of the Companies Act, 1956 the auditor may also be held guilty for misfeasance or breach of duty in relation to the company in the event of winding up, provided such misfeasance has directly resulted in damages to the company.

Thus, the auditor will be held liable in this case as the company suffered a loss because of such breach of duty.

Q. 28. While auditing the accounts of a company, you are unable to verify the cash in hand at the date of the balance sheet. How would you satisfy yourself as to its correctness?

Answer: If it is not at all possible to verify the cash in hand at the end of the year, it would be better for the auditor to instruct the client to deposit the whole amount of cash in hand into the bank on that date and withdraw the amount on the next day. But, if the time is over and such instruction cannot be communicated to the client, the cash book of the next period up to the date of the audit should be vouched and cash in hand on that date should be verified. If required, there should be a surprise check of the balance of cash in hand on some other date.

It may be noted in this context that the acceptance of the certificate in connection with the balance of cash in hand from manager or other high officials is not at all safe, specially when the cash balance is exceptionally large. If the certificate is false, the auditor cannot avoid his responsibility.

Q. 29. Discuss the duties of an auditor if he finds that there is a change in the basis of valuation of stock of a trading company.

Answer: If there is any change in the method of valuation of closing stock, it has very significant effect on the final accounts of a business concern, i.e. profit or loss of a particular period as well as the financial position of the business concern. Hence, the auditor should be very careful in this respect. If the auditor finds that some changes have been made, a note should be given in the balance sheet about this fact and if possible, its total effect on the financial result as well as on the financial position.

The auditor should be more cautious if he finds that such changes in amounts switch over from one generally accepted method of valuation to another method of valuation. The auditor should raise objection against this conversion and if the management does not accept this objection, the auditor may also qualify his report. But, in case the change is from a method not commonly accepted or a wrong one to a generally accepted method, the auditor should not raise any objection.

Q. 30. Earlier, in the last century, company law required auditors to report whether in their opinions, the view presented by accounts of companies was 'true and correct' whereas the present requirement is that the view should be 'true or fair'. Explain the reasons for this important change.

Answer: The major criticism of the phrase 'true and correct' was that, in an accounting sense, there was insufficient distinction between the words 'true' and 'correct'. As such, every figure in the accounts could not be justified and substantiated as both true and correct but, at the same time, the figures together could present a view to the reader of the accounts which could be misleading or even totally false when the accounts were read as a whole.

It was for this reason that the word 'fair' was used to replace 'correct' despite the inherent vagueness and absence of precision that the former word implies. The word 'fair' by definition requires a judgement, which can only be determined subjectively. This subjectivity and the related exercising of judgement provides the term with its true strength, at the same time it provides the auditor with his greatest challenge,

An auditor's assessment of whether accounts give a true and fair view, lacking as it does any legal or professional definition, necessitates a consideration of the account as a whole and the forming of an opinion concerning the overall impression conveyed by the accounts to the auditor. It also involves consideration of the substance of the information disclosed in the accounts as well as its form,

Q. 31. Indicate the prescribed circumstances in which an auditor, appointed under the Companies Act, is required to qualify his report.

Answer: The auditor must qualify his report if he is unable to report affirmatively on either of the following:

(a) The accounts show a true and fair view.

(b) The accounts have been prepared in accordance with the Companies Act.

He must qualify his report in the following circumstances:

- Proper accounting records have not been kept.
- The accounts do not agree with the underlying records.
- He has not received adequate returns suitable for audit purposes from branches not visited by him.

- He has not received all explanations and information, which he considers necessary for the purpose of his audit.

Q. 32. List six steps, which an auditor should take to minimise the danger of claims against him for negligent work.

Answer: Negligence, as applied to the auditor, means some act or omission, which occurs because the auditor has failed to exercise that degree of professional care and skill, appropriate to the circumstances of the case, which is expected of him.

The steps, which an auditor should take to minimise the danger of claims against him for negligent work, are as follows:

(a) Issue a letter of engagement in which the scope of work and the extent of the responsibilities undertaken should be clearly set out distinguishing between audit duties and other services.

(b) In the case of audit of non-incorporated enterprises an 'accountants' report should be issued with the financial statements in which the work carried out should be clearly explained.

(c) Ensure that the firm's standards are continuously reviewed and monitored and that they meet the minimum requirements set out in the auditing standards and guidelines issued by the Institute of Chartered Accountants of India.

(d) Prepare well-documented, comprehensive working papers containing audit conclusions as a vital means of defense against possible claims.

(e) Ensure that there is no appropriate training programme for partners and staff to cope with current changes in accounting procedures, legislation and auditing practices.

(f) Seek specialist advice whenever in doubt over complicated issues or recommend to the client that he should seek such advice himself.

Q. 33. Mention four important items in each case where the auditor would refer to each of the following books:
(a) Board's meeting minutes book
(b) Shareholder's meeting minutes books

Answer:

(a) Board's meeting minutes book:

The auditor would refer the Board's meeting minutes book on the following matters as the Board of Directors has the power to take decisions on these matters.

(i) Issue of debentures and borrowing moneys otherwise than on debentures [Section 292(1) (b) and (c)]

(ii) Investing funds of the company and for making loans [Section 292 (1) (d) and (e)]

(iii) Investing in shares or debentures of companies, making inter-company loans within the limits prescribed [Section 372A]

(iv) Giving consent to contracts of company with any director or his relative, firm, private company, etc. [Section 297]

(b) Shareholders meeting minutes book:

The following matters shall be sanctioned by the shareholders at a general meeting.

(i) Appointment of auditors and fixation of their remuneration or the authorisation therefore, other than the appointment made by the Board or by the central government [Section 224]

(ii) Declaration of dividend [Regulation 85]

(iii) Appointment of relatives of directors, etc. to an office or place of profit in the company [Section 314]

(iv) Sale, lease or disposal of the whole of company's undertaking or a substantial part of it and making of donations above certain limits [Section 293]

Q. 34. Briefly explain the importance of the concept of materiality in relation to accounting.

Answer: The importance of the concept of materiality in relation to accounting arises because its presence overrides normal accounting conventions, provided that it is applied in order to serve the prime accounting objective of presenting a true and fair view. Thus, it would not serve this objective, if trivial items of expenditure on assets, which are fixed in nature, are capitalised or insubstantial liabilities are occurred at the year-end simply for the sake of accuracy. Materiality is a recognised and time-honoured convention that insignificant and immaterial items should not be allowed to obscure the significant ones.

An item becomes material from the auditing viewpoint when its non-disclosure, misstatement or omission would be likely to distort the view given by the accounts, or if knowledge of the matter would be likely to influence the user of the financial statements.

Q. 35. Distinguish clearly between 'confirmation' and 'physical verification'.

Answer: The term 'confirmation' implies those techniques adopted by an auditor, which affirms certain facts or balances from certain competent parties. The competent party may be the external third party or the internal management. In conducting audit assignment effectively, there is a need for such confirmation on the part of the auditor. He may get such confirmation from the debtors, bankers, and brokers, etc. regarding certain assets, which may be in their possession. He may also require confirmation from them regarding certain transactions entered into between the company and those third parties.

Following are the examples of certain items, which require confirmation from the third parties:

(a) Bank balances for which the confirmation may be required to be obtained from the bankers

(b) Debtors balances for which the confirmation may be required to be obtained from the customers

On the other hand, the term 'physical verification' is defined as a process involved in the verification of certain assets of the company. It is undertaken with a view to verify the actual physical existence of the assets. Only tangible assets are subjected to physical verification such as stock, investment etc.

Following are the examples of certain items, which require physical verification: (i) closing stock and stores and spare parts of the concern, and (ii) cash balance at the end of the period.

Q. 36. Give your opinion on whether the following persons can be appointed auditors of a limited company or not.

(a) A firm of chartered accountants in practice, a partner of which is a secretary of the company

(b) A chartered accountant in practice owing Rs. 500 to the company

(c) A member of the Institute of Chartered Accountants of India, who is of unsound mind, holding a certificate of practice

Answer:

(a) As one of the partners of the firm is the secretary of the company, the firm cannot be appointed as the auditors of the company. A secretary is an employee of the company and according to Section 226(3b) of the Companies Act, 1956, an employee of the company cannot be appointed its auditor.

(b) He can be appointed as an auditor of the company as he is indebted to the company for an amount of Rs. 500 only, i.e. less than Rs. 1000. According to Section 226(3d) of the Companies Act, 1956, a person who owes to the company an amount exceeding Rs. 1,000 cannot be appointed as an auditor of the company,

(c) A member of the Institute of Chartered Accountants of India, holding a certificate of practice, can be appointed as an auditor of the company even if he is of unsound mind provided he has not been adjudged a man of unsound mind by a competent court. Hence, so long as he has not been adjudged a man of unsound mind, he may be so appointed.

Q. 37. Shareholders of a company passed a resolution in its annual general meeting reappointing A as auditor and B as joint auditor for the current year. They further resolved that if both or either of them declines assignment, the Board might fill up the vacancy. The Board subsequently decided to appoint C in case any of the auditors declines assignment. A and B decline and C joins as the auditor. Is appointment of C legal under the provisions of Companies Act, 1956?

Answer: The appointment of C by the Board is not valid in this case. Section 224 of the Companies Act, 1956 deals with the appointment of an auditor. According to this section, the Board of Directors can appoint an auditor, if there is a casual vacancy or a vacancy caused by resignation. In this case, the vacancy is neither casual nor caused by resignation.

The shareholders, however, can authorise the Board to give an appointment in any circumstance, which does not contravene Section 224, if the Articles of the company do not provide otherwise.

Thus the appointment of C is invalid. It may become valid only if the action of shareholders in authorising the Board to fill the vacancy was not contrary to the provisions of the Articles of the company.

Q. 38. After completing the audit of a limited company for the first half year of its financial year, the auditor expires and in his place another auditor is appointed to fill up the vacancy. State the extent to which the new auditor will rely on the work performed by the late auditor while completing the year's audit.

Answer: The accounts are closed and balanced at the end of the year and the new auditor should check the accounts of the latter half of the financial year exhaustively. But it should be noted that the ultimate responsibility of any discrepancy in accounts even for the first half of the financial year rests on the new auditor. The new auditor cannot claim that such accounts were audited by the late auditor and not by him. Hence, the new auditor should review the work done by the late auditor. The audit programme of the late auditor should be carefully consulted. The new auditor should make a test check of the audit work already completed by the late auditor and if he finds that there is nothing wrong, he may leave the detailed checking of the same. But, if he finds something wrong, he must check exhaustively as to satisfy himself, regarding the accuracy of the accounting records.

Q. 39. Distinguish clearly between contingent liability and future liability.

Answer: A contingent liability is one, which may or may not become an actual liability at a future date depending upon the happening of certain event. Thus, a contingent liability is a future liability, where a future liability need not be a contingent one. For instance, a liability in respect of damages, for which the case is pending before the court of law is a contingent liability and if according to the courts' decision, the liability is settled, it will become a future liability. It would become a future liability only when the court gives the judgement against the company. Otherwise it will not be a liability for the company at all. Such uncertainty regarding liability does not exist in case of a future liability.

A future liability is a real liability. It is an accruing liability, which has to be paid by a company at a future date, and there is no uncertainty in this respect. For example, if a company is under legal obligation to pay gratuity, it is a future liability and has to be paid at a future date.

Q. 40. Can a company pay interest out of capital legally? If so, mention the various conditions under which it can do so?

Answer: In general, a company cannot pay interest out of its capital. It is only when a company has been formed to undertake some construction or other related work and would not be able to earn sufficient profits for some years, can it legally pay interest on the paid-up capital.

According to Sections 208(2) to 208(7) of the Companies Act, 1956 the following conditions must be fulfilled before such payment can be made:

- Payment must be authorised by the Articles or by a special resolution.
- No such payment, even though authorised as mentioned above, shall be made without the previous sanction of the central government.
- The central government may, at the expense of the company, appoint a person to inquire into the circumstances and to report to the central government.
- Payment can be made only for such periods as may be determined by the central government.
- The rate of interest, in no case, exceeds 4% per annum or such other rate as the central government may direct by a notification in the official gazette.
- The payment of interest shall not operate as a reduction of the amount paid-up on the shares in respect of which it is paid.

Q. 41. There is a very large accumulation in the unclaimed dividend account of a company. The Directors want to transfer this to the profit and loss account for redistribution as dividend. Can they do so?

Answer: The unclaimed dividends constitute a debt and legally the company cannot utilise it unless it is statute barred. Under Article 120 of the First Schedule to the Indian Limitations Act, 1908, it does not become statute barred for 6 years. Therefore, the question of utilisation of the unclaimed dividend does not arise at all until it becomes statute barred.

However, power may be obtained to forfeit the unclaimed dividends through the Articles of the company, but this is not conventional and usual practice. If it is done, the recognised stock exchange will not grant an official quotation of the shares, where the company has this power of forfeiture.

From the financial point of view also it will be better if it is not utilised for the distribution of dividends but transferred to the reserves to enhance the financial strength of the concern. It may be utilised for writing off bad debts.

Q. 42. State the provisions of the Companies Act regarding change in the method of depreciation.

Answer: According to Section. 205(2) and 350 of the Companies Act 1956, two methods of charging depreciation, namely straight-line method and reducing balance method have been recognised. However, a company is also allowed to follow any other method of charging depreciation duly approved by the central government. Whatever method of depreciation is followed by a company, it should be followed consistently. Consistency in the method is necessary to ensure comparability of the results of the operations of the enterprise from period to period. It is to be noted that Companies Act 1956 does not restrain a company to change the method of depreciation.

However, AS-6 issued by the Institute of Chartered Accountants of India has suggested the change in the method of depreciation only when:

- the change is required by the statute or for compliance with an accounting standard, or
- the change in the method of depreciation will ensure more appropriate presentation of financial statements.

If the change in the method of depreciation has to be effected due to any of the above reasons, following procedures should be observed:

(a) The change in the method should be implemented with retrospective effect. In other words, depreciation should be recalculated in accordance with the new method from the date of the asset coming into use.

(b) The adjustment for excess or short depreciation should be treated as prior period and extra ordinary item and should be reflected in income statement accordingly.

(c) The change in the method of depreciation should be treated as change in accounting policy and should be disclosed accordingly.

Q. 43. State the applicability of Accounting Standards in the preparation and presentation of accounts of insurance companies.

Answer: The Accounting Standards as issued by the Institute of Chartered Accountants of India are applicable to the preparation of financial statements of the insurer, subject to Para 1 of Part 1 of Schedule A of the IRDA (Preparation of Financial Statements and Auditor's Report of the Insurance Companies) Regulations, 2000.

The applicability of Accounting Standards to the life insurance companies are discussed below:

Accounting Standard-3

According to the IRDA (Preparation of Financial Statements and Auditor's Report of Insurance Companies) Regulations, 2000, the Receipts and Payments Account of an insurer should be prepared using the 'Direct Method' as mentioned in AS-3 on Cash Flow Statements.

Accounting Standard-4

Accounting Standard-4 on 'Contingencies and Events Occurring After the Balance Sheet Date' that deals with accounting treatment of contingent losses and gains and events occurring after the balance sheet date excludes from its applicability the liabilities of companies carrying on life insurance business in view of special considerations applicable to such liabilities. The Standard excludes, from its applicability, the liabilities arising out of policies issued and not other liabilities, which do not arise out of policies issued by the insurance companies such as liabilities arising out of income-tax dispute. Thus, the Standard applies to such other liabilities.

Accounting Standard-9

AS-9 on 'Revenue Recognition' does not apply to revenue of insurance companies arising from insurance contracts, in view of the fact that revenue recognition from insurance contracts requires special considerations. The Standard is applicable to the insurance companies only in respect of income not earned from the insurance contracts such as interest, dividend, rent, etc.

Accounting Standard-13

Under Paragraph 2 (c) of AS-13 on 'Accounting for Investments' it has been provided that the Standard does not deal with the investments of life insurance enterprises.

Accounting Standard-17

So far as the applicability of AS-17 on segment reporting is concerned, the regulations have disregarded the applicability clause contained in the Standard by providing that irrespective of the fact that the securities of the company are traded or not, AS-17 would be applicable to an insurer carrying on life insurance business.

B. ESSAY-TYPE QUESTIONS

Q. 44. State the duties of the auditor of a company regarding depreciation.

Answer: Apart from fixed assets in respect of which depreciation must be provided, it also has to be provided on semi-permanent assets, e.g. patents, trademarks, etc. Since, the auditor is not in a position to estimate the working life of a majority of them, for this he has to rely on the opinion of persons who have a technical knowledge of the assets. He must, however, satisfy himself that an honest attempt has been made to estimate the working life of each asset, that the total provision for depreciation is adequate and the method adopted for determining that amount to be written off is properly disclosed in the profit and loss account and the balance sheet.

In part III of Schedule VI of the Companies Act, it is provided that any amount written off as depreciation is to be regarded as a provision, but that any amount so written off, which is in excess of the amount, to which in the opinion of the Directors is reasonably necessary for the purpose, to be regarded as a 'reserve'. The amount should be shown as a reserve under the head "Reserve and Surplus" on the liabilities side of the balance sheet. It is the duty of the auditor to ensure himself that the above provisions are being followed in maintaining depreciation accounting.

So, the duties of an auditor in connection with depreciation can be stated as follows:

- The auditor will see which method of depreciation, i.e. whether straight-line method or reducing balance method as stipulated in Schedule XIV to the Companies (Amendment) Act 1988, is being followed by the company.

- The auditor will check that depreciation has been provided at the rates not less than the rates specified in schedule XIV to the Companies (Amendment) Act 1988.
- He will see that if any other method of depreciation is in use, it has got the approval of the central government.
- He will also see that the method of depreciation and the rate of depreciation, which are not in accordance with Schedule XIV, have been duly disclosed.
- The auditor will ensure that if an asset is sold, discarded, demolished or destroyed, the excess of written down value over its sale proceeds or its scrap value have been written off in the financial year in which it is sold, discarded, demolished or destroyed.
- The auditor should ensure that the provision for depreciation on additions, deletions, etc. during the accounting year have been made on pro rata basis.
- He will see that extra shift depreciation for double shift or triple shift working has been computed in respect of plant and machineries in proportion of the number of days the company worked double shift or triple shift, as the case may be, bears to the total number of normal working days during the year.
- The auditor should see that dividend has been declared only out of profits arrived at after provision for depreciation.
- He will see that the amount of depreciation written off has been clearly disclosed in the profit and loss account.
- He should see that the accounting policy of the company has clearly stated the method of depreciation in use.
- The auditor should satisfy himself that adequate amount of depreciation has been provided. If he is not satisfied with the adequacy of amount of depreciation, he will persuade the management to make further provision for depreciation.
- He will see the same method of charging depreciation is being followed year after year. If there is any change in the method of depreciation he will enquire into the reason and satisfy himself with its justification.
- He will see that excess depreciation provided so far has been transferred to reserve and shown under the head 'Reserves and Surplus' on the liabilities side of the balance sheet.
- The auditor should check that the following information has been disclosed in the financial statements:
  (a) the historical cost or other amount substituted for historical cost of each class of depreciable assets
  (b) total depreciation for the period for each class of assets
  (c) the related accumulated depreciation.

Q. 45. The chairman of System International Limited, a large trading company with extensive overseas interests, has asked you to accept the nomination to replace the present auditors at the next annual general meeting of the company.

(a) Before acceptance of any new audit assignment, there are a number of reasons for non-acceptance that have to be considered. List the circumstances in which acceptance of the nomination would be inappropriate under the following:

(i) Legal aspect
(ii) Ethical aspect
(iii) Practical aspect

(b) Strict rules are there relating to professional etiquette on change of appointment. List the steps that should occur in the case of the change of auditor of System International Ltd. Explain the purpose of such rule.

Answer: (a) It would be inappropriate for a person to accept a nomination as auditor under the following circumstances:

(i) Legal aspect

Section 226(3) of the Companies Act, 1956 provides the disqualifications. According to it, the following persons are not qualified to be appointed as auditor of a company:

- An officer or employee of the company
- A person who is a partner or who is in employment of an officer or employee of the company
- A person who is indebted to the company for an amount exceeding Rs. 1,000 or who has given any guarantee or provided any security in connection with indebtness of any third person

(ii) Ethical aspect

Following are the circumstances where a person cannot accept a nomination as auditor on ethical ground:

- A potential conflict of interest between the company and an existing client might arise
- The person has a personal relationship with a senior member of the company's staff
- The person is financially involved with the company and wishes to remain so
- The person might not wish to be professionally associated with this firm for some reason arising out of the need to change auditors

(iii) Practical aspect

Following are the circumstances where a person cannot accept a nomination as auditor on practical ground:

- The job might be beyond the capacity of the audit firm, because it requires too many staff or expertise not available within the firm
- The client may have locations, which the audit firm cannot visit or arrange to have audited
- The client may not be willing to pay the fee that the audit firm would need to charge
- The following steps should be taken when a change of auditors takes place:
  (i) The proposed auditor should request permission from the company to contact the previous auditors and if permission is refused, the nomination should be declined.
  (ii) The proposed auditor should contact the previous auditor and ensure that there are no professional reasons why he should not accept the appointment.
  (iii) The existing auditor must obtain the company's permission to discuss its affairs with the proposed auditor. If refused, the proposed auditor should be informed of this and should then decline the nomination.
  (iv) The existing auditor should give the proposed auditor all information relevant to the decision of accepting the appointment.

The purpose of these provisions is to protect both the existing and the proposed auditors. The former by allowing him to express his opinion as to why the change is taking place and the latter by ensuring his decision is made with full knowledge of all circumstances.

Q. 46. You have been approached by the partners of PQR and Co., who carry on a trading business, to audit the accounts of their business in place of XY & Co., Chartered Accountants, who, you are informed, have resigned. You are required to state the following:

(a) The action you would take before accepting the nomination, giving your reasons.

(b) On the assumption that you accept the nomination, the information which you would require before commencing the detailed audit work for the first year.

Answer: (a) The retiring auditors should communicate to ensure that there is no professional reasons why the audit should not be accepted. The auditors should consider if they could accept the nomination in the light of the professional ethics and conduct. They should consider if they could cope with the job, given the technical and staffing requirements, as no audit should be accepted if it is beyond the capabilities of the firm.

(b) Upon accepting nomination, but before commencing any detailed work, the following information should be required:

(i) Confirmation of the validity of the appointment by reference to the minutes of the appropriate meeting

(ii) The precise nature and scope of the duties required of the auditor. To avoid dispute or misunderstanding in the future, written instructions should be obtained

(iii) The provisions of the partnership agreement so far as it concerns the following:

- Capital and whether each partner has contributed a fixed amount or not
- The proportions in which profits and losses are shared
- Salaries
- Interest, if any, to be allowed to the partners on capital account balances, or charged in respect of their drawings
- Interest, if any, to be allowed on the loans by the partners to the firm or to be charged on loans by the firm to the partners
- The restrictions, if any, imposed on the partners' drawings
- Matters which must be taken into account in determining the profits of the business available for division among the partners, e.g. the creation of reserves, provision for depreciation, etc.
- The extent to which the authority of any partner is limited

(iv) If no partnership agreement exists, the course of action of the partners in past years should be ascertained and a written statement signed by all the partners should be obtained as to their agreement on the matters set out in (iii) above

(v) The nature of the business, particularly with regard to technical matters and processes, which will assist the auditor in understanding the transactions

(vi) A list of the principal officers with details of their duties and responsibilities

(vii) Particulars of the system of internal controls and checks in force
(viii) Particulars of the system of accounts in operation and details of the accounting records kept
(ix) Bankers and authorised cheque signatories
(x) Copies of previous years' accounts

Q.47. What is internal control? Why is internal control required to be introduced in an enterprise? What are the different types of internal control system? State the advantages and disadvantages of internal control system.

Answer: Internal control refers to the various methods and procedures adopted for the control of production, distribution and the whole system (financial and non-financial) of the enterprise.

In other words, internal control system i.e. the whole system of controls, financial or otherwise, established by the management in order to carry on the business of the enterprise in an orderly and efficient manner, ensure adherence to management policies, safeguard the assets and secure as far as possible the completeness and accuracy of the records.

The special report on internal control of the American Institute of the Certified Public Accountants and its statements on auditing procedures contain the following definition of internal control: "Internal control comprises the plan of organisation and all the coordinated methods and measures adopted within a business to safeguard its assets, check the accuracy and reliability of its accounting data, promote operations efficiency and encourage employees to prescribed managerial policies."

In the opinion of W. W. Bigg, "Internal control is best regarded as indicating the whole system of controls, financial or otherwise, established by the management in the conduct of a business including internal check, internal audit and other forms of control."

So, on the basis of above definitions, it may be stated that a system of internal control provides a measure for the management to obtain information, protection and control which are quite important for the successful working of a business organisation.

Objectives of Internal Control:

Internal control is of fundamental importance to the auditor, because before he can plan the tests he intends to carry out in his audit programme, he must decide the extent to which he intends to rely on the system of internal control. But before depending upon the internal control system of the organisation, the auditor should ensure that the following objectives of internal control as per AAS-6 are achieved by the organisation:

1. Proper Authorisation: Transactions are executed with management's general and specific authorisation.

2. Prompt recording of transactions: All the transactions are promptly recorded in the correct amount in the appropriate accounts and in the accounting period in which executed so as to permit preparation of financial information within a framework of recognised accounting policies and to maintain accountability of assets.

3. Restricted access to assets: Access to assets is permitted only in accordance with management's authorisation.

4. Actions against deviations: The recorded accountability for assets is compared with the existing assets at reasonable intervals and appropriate action is taken with regard to any differences.

Types of Internal Control:

The types of internal control can be categorised as follows:

(a) Organisation

An enterprise should (i) have a plan of organisation, (ii) define and allocate responsibilities (every function should be in the charge of a specified person who might be called the responsible officials), and (ii) identify lines of reporting.

In all cases, the delegation of authority and responsibility should be clearly specified. An employee should always know the precise powers delegated to him, the extent of his authority and to whom he should report.

(b) Segregation of duties

(i) No one person should be responsible for the recording and processing of a complete transaction.

(ii) The involvement of several people reduces the risk of intentional manipulation or accidental error and increases the element of checking of work.

(iii) Functions which for a given transaction should be separated include initiation, authorisation, execution, custody and recording.

(c) Physical

(i) This concerns physical custody of assets and involves procedures designed to limit access to authorised personnel only.

(ii) Access can be direct or indirect.

(iii) These controls are especially important in case of valuable, portable, exchangeable or desirable assets.

(d) Authorisation and approval

This is a special case of type (a). All transactions should require authorisation or approval by an appropriate person. The limits to these authorisations should be specified. For example, all credit sales must be approved by the credit control department or all overtime must be authorised by the works manager.

(e) Arithmetical and accounting

(i) These are the controls in the recording function which check that the transactions have been authorised, that they are all included and that they are correctly recorded and accurately processed.

(ii) Procedures include checking the arithmetical accuracy of the records, the maintenance and checking of totals, reconciliation, control accounts, trial balances, accounting for documents and preview. Preview means that before an important action involving the company's property is taken, the person concerned should review the documents available to see that all that should have been done has been done.

(f) Personnel

(i) Procedures should be designed to ensure that personnel operating a system are competent and motivated to carry out the tasks assigned to them, as the proper functioning of a system depends upon the competence and integrity of the operating personnel.

(ii) Measures include appropriate remuneration, promotion and career development prospects, selection of people with appropriate personal characteristics and training and assignment to tasks of the right level.

(g) Supervision

All actions by all levels of staff should be supervised. The responsibility for supervision should be clearly laid down and communicated to the person being supervised.

(h) Management

(i) These are controls, exercised by management, which are outside and over and above the day-to-day routine of the system.

(ii) They include overall supervisory controls, review of management accounts, comparison with budgets, internal audit and any other special review procedures.

Advantages

The various advantages that may be derived from internal control system are summarised as follow:

1. Identification of defects: Under internal control system, the total activities are segregated in such a way that the work preformed by one employee is automatically checked by another employee. So, if there is any defect in the system, it is easily detected.

2. Flexibility: In this system, year-wise comparative analysis is done. So, if there is any change in the mode of operation, the changes in the system could easily be accommodated. So, the opportunity for flexibility is available.

3. Savings in time: If the internal control system is in operation in an organisation, there is no need for the preparation of separate audit programmes for each and every audit engagement. Thus it saves time to a great extent.

4. Lesser risk of omission: Under this system, the total work is sub-divided into a number of activities and each employee is assigned with each type of activity. So, there is least chance of oversight or omission of any matter.

5. Provision for training facility: Due to lack of adequate experience, the auditor may face difficulty in establishing a close relationship between audit programme and the internal control system. This system itself provides training facilities to auditors to overcome this difficulty.

Disadvantages: It is also important to appreciate the following inherent limitations of internal control system:

1. Chances of human error: The possibility of human error due to carelessness, mistakes of judgment or the misunderstanding of instructions may make the system ineffective.

2. Costly: Management's usual requirement is that a control procedure should be cost-effective. But in many cases, the cost of internal control procedure is not proportionate to the potential loss due to fraud and error.

3. Ignorance of unusual activity: It is fact that most of the internal control techniques are directed towards anticipated types of transactions and not on unusual transactions.

4. Collusion: There may be the possibility of circumvention of controls through collusion with parties outside the entity or with employees of the entity.

5. Abuses of responsibility: It may happen that a person responsible for exercising control has abused that responsibility.

6. Rigidity: There is the possibility that the system may become inadequate due to changes in the conditions and compliance with procedures may deteriorate.

Q. 48. You have just been appointed as auditor of Hindusthan Engineering Ltd., to fill a casual vacancy created by the death of the previous auditor, Mr. 'Ex', a sole practitioner. He has died after carrying out the audit of the company's accounts, but without having signed the audit report of the members for the accounting period.

Set out the considerations, which apply, and the steps, which you would take in these circumstances.

Answer: In taking over an unfinished audit from the late Mr. Ex, the first consideration to be borne in mind by the new auditor is that he is the one, who is to sign the audit report, and therefore, bears total responsibility for the audit. Mr. Ex's work cannot be accepted without a thorough review. Any opinion will be affected by the capability or otherwise of Mr. Ex. to carry out an efficient audit. It will be important to find out whether he died after a long illness or whether he was in apparently good health before dying suddenly.

The extent of any extra work needed by the new auditor will depend on the results of this review. He cannot sign an audit report based on standards of work lower than his own.

The steps, which should be taken, are as follows:

(a) Request the audit working papers from the executors of Mr. Ex. They are not obliged to release them and if, for any reason, they refuse the request, the audit will have to be started again.

(b) Carry out a full review of the audit work done by Mr. Ex. This will involve the following:
  (i) Obtaining background knowledge of Hindusthan Engineering Limited's business
  (ii) Discovering and assessing the company's systems and internal controls
  (iii) Determining what further audit work, in the new auditor's view, is necessary to arrive at an opinion on the truth and fairness of the view given by the accounts

(c) Carry out, resulting from the review, any further audit work. However, it would be advisable to include a certain amount of test checking as an integral part of the review. If it appears that Mr. Ex's work was in any way negligent or below the standard that the new auditor would set for himself, or departed materially from the principles laid down by the auditing standards and guidelines, the new auditor will have to carry out a complete audit himself.

(d) The overall aim of the new auditor must be to ensure that the duties imposed on an auditor by the Companies Act have been properly carried out and that he has obtained all the evidence required to give his opinion on the accounts.

Q. 49. What is joint audit? Discuss whether the liability of joint auditors is joint or several. Indicate the matters, which ought to be borne in mind when acting as joint auditors.

Answer: Meaning of joint audit

An audit is said to be joint audit when two or more persons or firms of chartered accountants are jointly appointed to conduct the audit of a company. The practice of appointing joint auditors has been adopted by large sized companies, which want to pool the resources of two or more auditors so that the audit work may be undertaken effectively and quickly. The joint auditors stand on equal footing so far as the professional work of audit is undertaken by them.

Liabilities of joint auditors

Section 227 of the Companies Act, 1956 does not contemplate any division of work of audit between two or more persons. Thus, according to the provisions of this section, the joint auditor has an individual responsibility only. Also, it is not quite proper to hold an auditor responsible for the work not done by him. If there are two auditors and both of them are held responsible jointly, that would create many practical problems.

While the Companies Act is silent on this issue, the Institute of Chartered Accountants of India has issued a "Statement on the Responsibility of Joint Auditors". In this statement, it has been made clear that it would not be correct to hold an auditor responsible for the specifically allotted work of another. Each joint auditor will be held responsible only for the work allocated to him. According to the statement, we cannot hold an auditor responsible for the work done by another auditor who is equally qualified and competent to undertake the audit work. This also makes it clear that where the work cannot be clearly divided, the responsibility will be jointly shared between them.

Factors to be borne in mind while acting as joint auditors

The following factors should be borne in mind when acting as joint auditors of a large public limited company:

(a) Responsibility: The auditor's statutory duty and legal responsibility cannot be divided between the two firms. Both the firms must satisfy that the quality of work performed and that the opinion to be expressed is based on the audit evidence obtained.

(b) Allocation of work: The work to be done by each firm should be clearly set out in a written agreement between the firms. This should ensure that no aspect of audit is omitted and also that duplication of work is minimised. It is likely that certain key items in the financial statements, such as stock, will require attention from both the firms and this should be arranged accordingly.

(c) Review of working papers: There will be a full and mutual exchange of information between the two firms. This can be achieved by regular meetings and periodic reviews of working papers. This is necessary so that all problems can be discussed at the earliest opportunity and suitable action agreed upon to confirm that the quality of work performed is acceptable to both firms.

(d) Independence: In this case, one firm is providing other services, including accountancy work for the client and this might lead to problems over the objectivity of their audit work. As far as possible, it should be arranged that the firm does not have the responsibility to audit areas of the financial statements prepared by their own staff.

(e) Fees: The ethical guide states that the fees should be based on time spent and the level of responsibility of the staff involved. The firms should initially agree the method the audit work should be allocated and the audit fee should be split accordingly.

Q. 50. State the steps to be followed in conducting audit of a bank.

As in the cases of any other audit, the audit of banks involves the following stages:

(a) Preliminary work
(b) Evaluation of internal control system
(c) Preparation of audit programme for substantive testing and its execution.
(d) Preparation and submission of audit report.

A. Preliminary Work

AAS-20. Knowledge of the business requires that in performing an audit of financial statements, the auditor should have or obtain knowledge of the business sufficient to enable the auditor to identify and understand the events, transactions and practices that in the auditors judgment, may have a significant effect on the financial statements or on the examination or audit report. The auditor's level of knowledge for an engagement would include a general knowledge of the economy and the industry within which the entity operates, and a more particular knowledge of how the entity operates. Knowledge of the business provides a frame of reference within which the auditor exercises professional judgment and assists him in assessing risks and identifying problems, planning and performing the audit effectively and efficiently, and evaluating the audit evidence.

The auditor should accordingly acquire a knowledge of the regulatory environment in which the bank operates. Thus, the auditor should familiarise himself with the relevant provisions of applicable law(s). He should be well acquainted with the provisions of the Banking Regulation Act 1949, as well as any other applicable law(s) (e.g. Companies Act, 1956 in the case of audit of a banking company) particularly in so far as they relate to preparation and presentation of financial statements and their audit. The auditor should also have an understanding of the various guidelines issued by Reserve Bank of India in so far as such guidelines have a bearing on his work.

The auditor should also acquire knowledge of the economic environment in which the bank operates. Similarly, the auditor needs to acquire good working knowledge of the services offered by the bank. In acquiring such knowledge, the auditor needs to be aware of the many variations in the basic deposit, loans and treasury services that are offered and continue to be developed by banks in response to market conditions. To do so, the auditor needs to understand the nature of services rendered through instruments such as letters of credit, acceptance, forward contracts, and other similar instruments. A bank's loan portfolio may have large concentration of credit to highly specialised industries, for example, hire purchase and leasing, software, infrastructure, etc. Evaluating the nature of these may require knowledge of the business and reporting practices of those industries. Besides, there are a number of risks associated with banking activities, which, though not unique to banking, are sufficiently important in that they serve to shape banking operations. An understanding of the nature of these risks may help the auditor in perceiving the risk inherent in different aspects of a bank's operations and thus assist him in determining the degree of reliance on internal control and the nature, timing and extent of his other audit procedures.

The auditor should also obtain an understanding of the accounting system of the bank and the terminology used by the bank to describe various types of transactions and operations. Most banks have well-designed accounting and procedures manual which can serve as an important source of information on these aspects.

In the case of joint auditors, it would be preferable that each joint auditor also obtains a general understanding of the books and records, etc. relating to the work of other joint auditors.

In addition to the above, the auditor should also undertake the following:

- Review relevant instructions issued by the bank, particularly those relating to closing of annual accounts. These instructions contain standardised accounting procedure required to be followed at head office, at regional offices, zonal offices and branches.
- Review the audit report for the previous year including the long form audit report. In case of branch auditors, the audit report on the financial statements of the branch for the previous year or for the audit last conducted should be reviewed. The purpose of his review is to

understand the nature of observations/comments made on the financial statements and for enquiring into the follow-up action taken on matters contained in such report.

- Review the revenue audit reports, internal audit reports, inspection reports and concurrent audit reports pertaining to the bank/branch, as the case may be.

The above review would help the auditor in gaining an understanding of the nature and volume of operations and the structure of assets and liabilities of the bank/branch as also of the nature of adverse feature observed in the past.

B. Evaluation of internal control system

Internal control evaluation is an important element of audit process. In the case of audit of banks, it assumes even greater importance due to the enormous volume of transactions entered into by banks. Evaluation of design and operation of internal control system enables the bank auditors to perform more effective audits. The auditor should, therefore, study and evaluate the design and operation of internal controls. This would assist him in determining the nature, timing and extent of substantive procedures in various areas, depending upon whether the internal controls are adequate and observed in practice.

C. Preparation of audit program for substantive testing and its execution

Having familiarised himself with the requirements of audit, the auditor should prepare an audit program for substantive testing which should adequately cover the scope of his work. In framing the audit program, due weightage should be given by the auditor to areas where, in his view, there are weaknesses in the internal controls. The audit program for central auditors would be different from that of the branch auditors. At the branch level, basic banking operations are to be covered by the audit. On the other hand, the central auditors have to deal with consolidation of branch returns (both audited and unaudited), investments and items normally dealt with at the head office.

The auditor should ensure that the work is executed in accordance with the audit programme by persons having the requisite skills and competence.

D. Preparation and submission of audit report

The audit report is the end product of the audit. It is through the medium of the audit report that the auditor conveys his observations/comments on the financial statements. The form and content of the audit report should be determined by the auditor taking into account his terms of engagement and applicable statutory, regulatory and professional requirements.

Q. 51. Does Companies (Auditor's Report) Order, 1988 amount to social audit?

Answer: After the issue of the Manufacturing and Other Companies (Auditor's Report) Order, 1988 (revised), there has been a controversy whether this is a social audit or not? It was thought that it had extended the scope of audit considerably and it has now made the auditor more responsive to the needs of the society and as such this has been taken to be social audit. But this is not totally true. In fact, social audit has much wider implications and "encompasses an assessment of what a company contributes to the society and what it takes away from it".

It gave rise to such a controversy on account of the fact that when this order was promulgated it was stated that it was introducing "regulatory social audit". The object of such order was also stated to be "to ensure that the social objective of company audit by chartered accountants is achieved in a great measure, considering the basic fact that under modern conditions, companies have to subserve public interest rather than purely private gain of the investors. Thus, it would help in introducing social audit to some extent but to call it social audit would be a bit exaggeration. It can better be said that it is a step towards social audit.

It is to be noted in this context that some of the obligations of the auditor as introduced in the order, have already been assumed by many firms of auditors. With the passage of time, the auditors have started undertaking more careful examination of the accounts rather than simply undertake what is known as "verificatory audit'. With the growth of large number of central government and state government undertakings in the country, the auditors are becoming conscious of this fact and changing their attitude accordingly.

It has also been pointed out that some of the additional matters on which the auditor has to make a statement in his report under this order represent merely a statutory recognition of what were already recognised as 'standard auditing practices'. It has been further pointed out that the 'auditing procedures' as discussed in the 'Statement of Auditing and Assurance Standards' issued by the ICA1 is more or less similar, regarding stocks and fixed assets, to what is implied in this order.

So, it can be concluded from the above discussion that CARO cannot be considered as a part of social audit.

Q. 52. What is government audit? What are the objectives of government audit? Distinguish between government audit and commercial audit.

Answer: Government audit refers to the audit of accounts of departments and offices of the central government, the state governments and the union territories. Under Article 149 of the Constitution of India, the Comptroller and Auditor General of India is empowered to conduct complete audit of accounts of governments and of those undertakings which are directly under a ministry or government department.

Objectives

An Introduction to Indian Government Accounts and Audit, a book issued under the authority of the Comptroller and Auditor General of India, states that the main objectives of the government audit are to ensure:

- That there is provision of funds for the expenditure duly authorised by a competent authority
- That the expenditure is in accordance with a sanction properly accorded and is incurred by an officer competent to incur it
- That the payment has, as a fact, been made and has been made to the proper person and that it has been so acknowledged and recorded that a second claim against the government on the same account is impossible
- That the charge is correctly classified and that if a charge is debitable to the personal account of a contractor, employee or other individual, or is recoverable from him under any rule or order, it is recorded as such in a prescribed account
- That in the case of audit of receipts sums due are regularly recovered and checked against demand and sums received are duly brought to credit in the accounts
- That in the case of audit of stores and stock, where a priced account is maintained, stores are priced with reasonable accuracy and that the rates initially fixed are reviewed from time to time, correlated with market rates and revised when necessary
- That the articles are counted periodically and otherwise examined for verification of the accuracy of the quantity balances in the books and that the total of the valued account tallies with the physical numerical balance of stock materials at the rates applicable to the various classes of stores

- That expenditure conforms to the following general principles which have, for long, been recognised as standards of financial propriety, namely,
  - (a) That the expenditure is not prima facie more than the occasion demands, and that every government servant exercises the same vigilance in respect of expenditure incurred from public moneys as a person of ordinary prudence would exercise in respect of expenditure of his own money
  - (b) That no authority exercises its powers of sanctioning expenditure to pass an order which will be, directly or indirectly, to its own advantage
  - (c) That public moneys are not utilised for the benefit of a particular person or section of the community unless
    - the amount of expenditure involved is insignificant, or
    - a claim for the amount could be enforced in a court of law, or
    - the expenditure is in pursuance of a recognised policy or custom, and
  - (d) That the amount of allowances granted to meet expenditure of a particular type is so regulated that the allowances are not, on the whole, sources of profit to the recipients.

In a nutshell, government audit encompasses two main elements. These are as follows:

(i) Fiscal accountability—audit of provision of funds, sanctions, compliance and propriety and
(ii) Managerial accountability— audit of efficiency, economy and effectiveness.

Distinction between Government Audit and Commercial Audit

Government audit is not same as commercial audit. Certain special aspects are required to be covered under government audit, which are not at all required for commercial audit.

The distinction between government audit and commercial audit can be outlined in the following way:

Points of distinction	Government audit	Commercial audit
1. Nature of audit	Government audit is conducted almost continuously throughout the year, because the number of transactions is many and involves large sums of money.	Commercial audit is mostly periodical in nature.
2. Auditor	The audit officers of the Indian audit and accounts department do government audit.	Professional chartered accountants mostly conduct commercial audit.
3. Dominating factor	Propriety-cum-efficiency audit is predominant in government audit.	This aspect is not strictly adhered in case of commercial audit.
4. Preparation of accounts	In this case, the Indian Audit and accounts department including its field offices prepares or compiles the major part of government accounts and also audits the accounts.	In commercial audit, the auditor audits the accounts prepared by others. The auditor is not at all responsible for the preparation and/ or compilation of accounts.

Contd.

Contd.

5. Method of accounting	In government audit, the auditor has to see whether the accounts have been prepared according to the prescribed rule of government accounts.	In commercial audit, the auditor has to see whether the accounts have been prepared on the basis of double entry system.
6. Objective	Government audit is concerned with examining the propriety of expenditure.	The primary objective of this audit is to see whether the balance sheet prepared gives a true and fair vies of the state of affairs of the enterprise and the profit and loss account gives a true and fair view of the profit or loss of the enterprise.
7. Vouching of payment	Government spending is done by the treasury officer or disbursement officer, who makes a detailed scrutiny of the bills before payment. So, government auditor is relieved of detailed checking of payments.	In commercial offices, the cashier does not have to make such a scrutiny before payment. So, payments require proper vouching in commercial audit.

In fact, the government auditor, unlike the independent financial auditor, is concerned with examining the economy, efficiency, and effectiveness (i.e. three E's) of various schemes or projects. The government auditor seeks to get the following answers:

(a) Whether the projects have been completed at the minimum cost, i.e. whether the project cost is economical or not.

(b) Whether the project has efficiently been completed, i.e. whether the projects are not suffering from deficiencies.

(c) Whether the projects have been performed in the most effective way, i.e. whether the projects become successful projects or not.

It can, thus, be seen that the objectives of government audit are much wider than those of independent financial audit. In government audit, there is a greater emphasis on examining compliance with standards of financial propriety, compliance with rules and procedures and the efficiency and performance of various projects or schemes than in an independent financial audit. The difference in objectives of audit generates from the consideration of public interest and the urge to exercise stringent financial controls over public money.

Q. 53. What are CAATs? Why CAATs are required? What are the different types of CAATs used in accounting in a computerised environment?

Answer: Computer assisted audit techniques involve the use of computers in the process of an audit rather than limiting it to an entirely manual approach. CAATs are defined as computer based tools and techniques, which facilitate auditors to increase their personal productivity as well as that of audit function. CAATs are software tools for auditors to access, analyse and interpret data and to draw an opinion for an audit objective.

Need for CAATs

Statement on AAS- 16 states that effectiveness and efficiency of audit procedures may be improved through use of CAATs. CAATs may be used in performing various auditing procedures, including the following-

- Tests of details of transactions and balances
- Analytical procedures
- Tests for general controls
- Sampling programmes to extract data for audit testing
- Tests of application controls
- Re-performing calculations performed by the entity's accounting system

Guidance note on CAAT issued by the Institute of Chartered Accountants of India describes CAATs as important tools for the auditor in performing audits. During the course of audit, auditor is to obtain sufficient, relevant and useful evidence to achieve the audit objectives effectively. Audit findings and conclusions are to be supported by appropriate analysis and interpretation of the evidence.

In auditing a computerised environment where all significant operations are computerised, it may be impractical to perform audit completely and with assurance unless the auditor uses CAATs for collection and evaluation of audit evidence by performing both compliance and substantive tests. By using CAATs, it is possible for the auditor to perform audit more effectively and efficiently and also have greater assurance on the audit process.

Types of CAATs

CAATs can be broadly categorised into the following three types:

1. Generalised Audit Software (GAS)

These are also referred as Package Programmes. GAS refers to generalised computer programmes designed to perform data-processing functions such as reading data, selecting and analysing information, performing calculations, creating data files and reporting in a format specified by the auditor. GAS is standard off-the-shelf audit software, which can be used across enterprises and platforms.

2. Specialised Audit Software (SAS)

These are also referred to as purpose-written programmes. They perform audit tasks in specific circumstances. These are specifically written for performing audit tests for specific type of applications. These programmes may be developed by the auditor, the entity being audited or an outside programmer hired by the auditor. In some cases, the auditor may use an entity's existing programmes in their original or modified state because it may be more efficient than developing independent programmes.

3. Utility software

These are used by an entity to perform common data processing functions, such as sorting, creating and printing files. Utility software also includes utility programmes available in system programmes for performing debugging or analysis of various aspects of usage/access. These programmes are generally not designed for audit purposes but can be used for performing specific tests.

CAATs and more specifically audit software have the potential to enable auditors to recognise computer as a tool to assist them in the audit process. Audit software give auditors access to data in the medium in which it is stored, eliminating the boundaries of how it can be audited. Once the auditors accept and learn how to use audit software, they will be in a better position to create value addition in their audit. The greatest barrier in promoting use of audit software is failure to recognise opportunities to use audit software for audit. Understanding and recognising how CAATs can be used and knowing how to use audit software is most critical to its effective use.

Using audit software enhances the effectiveness of audit and enables auditor to provide better assurance to their clients. In an increasingly computerised environment, it is critical for the auditor to move from ticks to clicks and learn to harness the power of computers for audit. Using audit software as their tool for auditing digitised data, auditor can shift focus from time consuming manual verification audit procedures to intelligent analysis of data to provide assurance to clients and manage audit risks.

Q. 54. Distinguish between statutory audit and non-statutory audit.

Answer: Statutory audit is that type of audit, which is required to be conducted to fulfil the prescribed norms of the statute governing a particular organisation. In other words, when an audit is conducted compulsorily as per the provisions of the statute, it is called statutory audit. In our country organisations like joint stock companies, co-operative societies etc. are required to get their accounts audited according to the statutes governing these organisations.

Non-statutory audit is that type of audit, which is not required to be conducted to satisfy any legal requirement. This type of audit is usually undertaken to enjoy the benefits of audited accounts. In our country, there is no legal compulsion in conducting audit of sole-proprietorship business or partnership firms, yet the organisations get their accounts audited to derive certain benefits.

The difference between statutory audit and non-statutory audit can be outlined in the following way:

Points of difference	*Statutory audit*	*Non-statutory audit*
1. Legal requirements	Statutory audit is conducted to fulfill legal requirements.	There is no legal compulsion in conducting this type of audit. Different organisations get their accounts audited to derive certain benefits.
2. Purpose	Statutory audit is mainly conducted to protect the interest of the shareholders or the public in general.	Non-statutory audit is conducted mainly to provide benefits to the owners of the businesses, viz. sole-proprietor, partners, etc.
3. Submission of audit report	The statutory auditor is required to submit his audit report to the shareholders.	Non-statutory auditor is required to submit his audit report to the owners, i.e. proprietor or partners.
4. Qualification of auditor	The auditor should possess the required qualifications as prescribed by the respective governing statute.	There is no hard and fast rule regarding the qualifications of an auditor in case of non-statutory audit.

Contd.

Contd.

5. Appointment of auditor	The appointment procedure of the auditor is given in the respective statute and the auditor should be appointed by following that prescribed procedure.	There is no prescribed procedure for the appointment of auditor in this type of audit. Auditors are appointed as per the agreement with the owners.
6. Rights and duties of auditor	The rights and duties of a statutory auditor is provided in the statute itself. In no situation, these rights and duties are possible to be changed.	The rights and duties of a non-statutory auditor are determined as per the agreement entered into between the auditor and the auditee.
7. Liabilities of auditor	The statutory auditor can be held liable both as per common law of the country and as per the governing statute.	The non-statutory auditor can be held liable only as per common law of the country.
8. Remuneration of auditor	Remuneration of statutory auditors is usually determined by the respective statute or the statute prescribes the procedure of fixation of remuneration of the auditor.	The remuneration of the non-statutory auditor is determined on the basis of agreement between the auditor and the auditee.
9. Area of audit	The statutory auditor must cover all the accounting areas of the organisation. In no case, can it be partial.	Area of audit depends on the requirements of the organisation. There may be complete as well as partial audit.
10. Regularity	Statutory audit is usually conducted on regular basis.	There is no regularity in conducting non-statutory audit. This type of audit is conducted as and when it is required by the organisation.

Q. 55. Comment on the following statements:
(a) 'Accounting is a necessity, but auditing is a luxury.'
(b) 'Auditing is a technique of accounting control.'

Answer:

(a) It is often told that accounting is a necessity, but auditing is a luxury. The first part of the statement is totally correct, but the correctness of the second part of the statement depends on the situation under which auditing is conducted.

Accounting is necessary to ascertain the financial result as well as financial position of an organisation. Whatever may be the nature, type and size of an organisation, each organisation has to adopt accounting to measure its own performance. In case of a business organisation, profit and loss account and balance sheet are prepared to ascertain the financial result as well as financial position of a particular period of time. Similarly, in case of non-profit seeking organisations, though the objective is not to earn profit, these organisations also prepare accounts to know the surplus generated. Without adopting accounting by maintaining books of accounts for recording financial and economic events, no organisation can maintain its scarce fund and it is also not possible to have idea about the incomes and expenses of the organisation. Hence, it is rightly said that accounting is a necessity.

Auditing is not a luxury in most of the cases. In case of company form of organisations, where ownership is totally separated from the management, auditing ensures the proper utilisation of fund provided by the shareholders and other loan providers. That is why, in the Companies Act, auditing has been made compulsory by introducing required provisions with a view to protect the interest of the shareholders and other interested parties. For the same reason, the co-operative societies and other statutory organisations are also required to conduct audit of their accounts. But auditing is not compulsory in case of sole-proprietorship and partnership firms. If the accounts of these types of organisations are maintained properly and if the proprietor or the partners are confident about the accuracy and reliability of the accounts maintained, then auditing may be considered unnecessary and to some extent luxury. However, if the accounts of these organisations are not audited, they will fail to enjoy some of the important benefits of conducting audit. The banks and other financial institutions provide loans on the basis of audited balance sheet and profit and loss account, the insurance companies settle their insurance claims on the basis of audited balance sheet and even if there is any disagreement among the partners regarding their accounts, the court will give decisions on the basis of audited accounts. Hence, it is inappropriate to say that auditing is a luxury. It is better to say that both accounting and auditing are required to know the true and fair view of the financial position and financial performance of an organisation.

(b) The basic functions of accounting is to record the economic events that have the effect in changing the financial position of an organisation and to prepare the financial statements at the end of a particular accounting period. The objectives behind these functions of accounting are to know the financial result and the financial position of that organisation in a particular accounting period and at the end of the accounting period. The users of the financial statements include the management, the shareholders, creditors, investors, loan providing agencies and the public in general.

Auditors are appointed in these organisations to check the authenticity and reliability of the books of accounts maintained by these organisations and the relevant documents preserved in order to support the transactions. After checking the books of accounts and relevant documents, the auditors are required to submit a report to the owners of the organisation. In the report, the auditors have to state as to whether the books of accounts maintained by the organisation give a true and fair view of the state of affairs of the organisation as disclosed in the financial statements. If the books of accounts fail to give a true and fair picture of the financial activities of that organisation, the auditor will report accordingly.

In the light of the above two concepts about the functions of accounting and auditing, it can be said that auditing is a technique of accounting control. In keeping the books of accounts or maintaining records through proper recording of economic events of an organisation, the accountants may make mistakes, i.e. accounting error may be there or they may adopt unfair practices to manipulate accounts to mislead the users. If there are accounting errors or frauds in the records and documents, the books of accounts will not disclose the true and fair view of the financial position of the organisation. In conducting audit, the auditor has to go through the entries recorded in the books of accounts and supporting documents to ensure him about the truth and fairness of the financial statements prepared on the basis of the books of accounts maintained. If he finds any inconsistency and irregularity in the books of accounts, he will raise objections and report accordingly. As a result, the persons involved in maintaining the books of accounts and relevant documents become very cautious in discharging their duties, because they know that if there is any

INDEX

NOTES

NOTES

NOTES

NOTES